EDWARD VI: THE THRESHOLD OF POWER

By the same author

THE DEVELOPMENT OF RELIGIOUS TOLERATION IN ENGLAND

I From the beginning of the English Reformation to the death of Queen Elizabeth I

II From the Accession of James I to the Convention of the Long Parliament, 1603–1640

III From the Convention of the Long Parliament to the Restoration, 1640–1660

IV Attainment of the Theory and Accommodations in Thought and Institutions, 1640–1660

PHILANTHROPY IN ENGLAND, 1480–1660

THE CHARITIES OF LONDON, 1480–1660

THE CHARITIES OF RURAL ENGLAND, 1480–1660

THE CHRONICLE AND POLITICAL PAPERS OF KING EDWARD VI (*editor*)

EDWARD VI: THE YOUNG KING (The Protectorship of the Duke of Somerset)

EDWARD VI:
THE THRESHOLD OF POWER

THE DOMINANCE OF THE DUKE OF NORTHUMBERLAND

BY

W. K. JORDAN

President Emeritus, Radcliffe College
Leroy B. Williams Professor of History and
Political Science, Harvard University

London

GEORGE ALLEN & UNWIN LTD

RUSKIN HOUSE   MUSEUM STREET

FIRST PUBLISHED IN 1970

© *George Allen & Unwin Ltd* 1970

ISBN 0 04 942083 6

71 7774
942.053

PRINTED IN GREAT BRITAIN
in 11 on 12 pt Ehrhardt type
AT THE ABERDEEN UNIVERSITY PRESS

26. JUN. 1971

FOR FRANCES

P. 31-2
P. 36 2-400

PREFACE

This volume concludes a study in which I have endeavoured to treat the history of a short but very important reign. The two volumes are principally concerned with presenting a full narrative history of the period, with, however, rather lengthy essays on certain matters which seem to require monographic treatment. I have dealt with a reign dominated by three great figures: Somerset, who has gained stature in my judgement as I have proceeded; Northumberland, closer knowledge of whose government and inglorious end has tended to persuade me that he was far more than an adventurer with full-blown treason in his heart; and the King himself, emerging into regal competence during his last two years, and at the end forcing an impossible, though understandable, effort to alter the succession to the throne.

In this study I have sought to examine the principal sources, both printed and manuscript, and I have meant to give consideration to the extensive and valuable studies of other scholars who have had a special interest in this period. I have sought, as well, to offer a 'whole view' of the reign, with attention to the thought and aspirations of men—and the classes of men—which gave it historical substance. In this intention I have not been completely successful, for several topics remain scantly noticed since it now seems clear to me that they deserve monographic treatment, and since I have adhered to an early decision to admit no more than two *excurses* to each volume. I shall hope, however, to add several essays in appropriate journals on such topics as the history of English administration of Ireland in this period, the standard of living of the several classes of men in the era, the beginnings of domestic building under Renaissance influences, and the state of local administration during the Edwardian age. These further studies, it might be added, are to a large extent well begun.

In a period when institutional Christianity was yielding to forces of fragmentation, the student finds it difficult indeed to characterize with reasonable accuracy the various groupings which were rapidly forming. A word on my own usage may therefore be appropriate. By 'Conservative (or Orthodox) Catholics' I mean those who remained steady and faithful to the doctrine, the usages, and the administrative structure of the ancient Church. I have ordinarily applied the term 'Henrician Catholics' to those of the clergy and laity who found it possible (or expedient) to follow the full course of that great monarch's pilgrimage of faith. The words 'Anglican' (or 'Centrist') have been used to describe the thought and policy of such men as Somerset, Cranmer, and Ridley, who made great contribution by fixing the guide lines for the future Church of England, and who were characterized by the quality of moderation. By 'Evangelical Protestants' I mean those of the Church of England who pressed eloquently and relentlessly for the further—the complete—reform of the doctrine, the worship, and the preaching in God's true Church, and whose great exemplar was surely Bishop Hooper. These men expressed no nostalgia whatsoever for the ancient Church, and their faces were set towards Zurich and Geneva. By 'Radical Protestantism' I limit my meaning quite strictly to the developing sectarianism in Edwardian England, which was not to assume full form or power for another generation, but which none the less scandalized all the more orthodox groupings which have been mentioned.

It remains for me to express my gratitude to those who have lent me particularly valued assistance. Once more I must say that Madeleine Rowse Gleason (Mrs Sidney Gleason) has given me gently critical and always wise counsel at every stage of this work. Three of my graduate students—Messrs Cary Carson, Alan Kreider, and Paul Needham—have interrupted their own studies in London to check manuscripts for me when I have found myself bewildered by my own notes. Mr Nigel Surry placed at my disposal the manuscript work on the portraiture of Edward VI, on which he and his father, the late Launcelot Surry, have long been engaged. Further acknowledgement has been made in the notes of still other assistance extended to me by scholars who are also students in this field. My working conventions in the preparation of this volume are those employed in the earlier companion work and need not be rehearsed again. Finally, I must in all conscience express my appreciation and my debt to Messrs George Allen and Unwin, who for a full generation have been my publishers and who have always dealt with me with great kindness and with an almost pampering consideration.

July, 1969   W. K. J.
Cambridge, Mass.

CONTENTS

	PAGE
PREFACE	9
TABLE OF ABBREVIATIONS	15

I THE FONT OF POWER: THE EDU-
CATION AND DEVELOPMENT OF
THE KING (1547–1550) 17

II THE TRIUMPH OF REACTION
(1549–1551) 28
  1. The jettisoning of Roman Catholic support 28
  2. Warwick secures dominance (October, 1549–
    early 1550) 32
  3. Reaction in Parliament: the reversal of Somer-
    set's policies (Third session of the first Parlia-
    ment, November 4, 1549–February 1, 1550) 36

III GOVERNMENT BY FEARFUL MEN
(1550–1552) 45
  1. Rule without Parliament (February, 1550–
    January, 1552) 45
  2. The packing of the Privy Council and lesser
    offices of state 48
  3. The fall of Lord Rich (December 1551) 54
  4. The obsessive fear of public disorders (October
    1549–October 1551) 56

IV THE DESTRUCTION OF THE
DUKE OF SOMERSET 70
  1. Somerset's release and re-admission to the
    Privy Council (February-April 1550) 70
  2. Mounting tension between Somerset and War-
    wick (May, 1550-September, 1551) 73
  3. The evidence against Somerset (September-
    November, 1551) 81
  4. The trial of the Duke of Somerset (November-
    December, 1551) 92
  5. The execution of the Duke of Somerset
    (January 22, 1552) 98

PAGE

6. Somerset's character   105
7. The policy of vengeance (1552)   110

V THE PRICE OF WEAKNESS: FOR-
   EIGN AFFAIRS (Late 1549 to the end of the
   reign)   116
   1. The trial of a French entente   116
   2. The deterioration of relations with the Empire
      (1549–1551)   134
   3. Abandonment of the dream of Scottish Union
      (1549–1553)   146
   4. England's withdrawal from European affairs
      (1552–1553)   155
   5. Northumberland in the role of peacemaker
      (1553)   174

VI THE DISMANTLING OF ROMAN
    CATHOLIC FAITH: THE EXPRO-
    PRIATION OF THE CHANTRIES
    [EXCURSUS I]   181

VII RISE OF THE SECULAR CHARIT-
     ABLE IMPULSE (1547–1553)
     [EXCURSUS II]   204
     1. General statement and conclusions   204
     2. Founding of the royal hospitals and the devel-
        opment of the ideal of social rehabilitation 214
     3. The advancement and the secularization of
        education   223
     4. The secularization and strengthening of alms-
        house foundations   235

VIII THE PLANTING OF A PROTESTANT
      POLITY (1550–1553)   240
      1. Pressure for conformity on the Roman Catholic
         bishops and intellectuals   240
      2. Pressure on the lesser clergy and the conserva-
         tive laity   250
      3. The case of Mary Tudor: the later phase (1550–
         1553)   256
      4. Measures for the reform of worship   265
      5. Bishop Ridley's administration of Rochester
         and London (1547–1553)   270

PAGE

6. The thrust of evangelical Protestantism 275
7. Hooper and the vestiarian controversy (1550) 293
8. Hooper as a bishop (1551–1553) 298
9. The refugee community: the link with Continental Protestantism 306
10. The problem of radical sectarianism (1549–1553) 326

IX THE TRIUMPH OF PROTESTANTISM (1551–1553) 335
   1. Parliament in session (First Parliament, fourth session: January 23, 1552–April 15, 1552) 335
   A. The secular measures 335
   B. The ecclesiastical measures: the adoption of the second *Book of Common Prayer* 342
     (1) Lesser parliamentary measures and the *Short Catechism* 352
     (2) The *Articles of Faith* (1553) 354
     (3) Proposals for the codification of ecclesiastical laws (1549–1553) 357

X THE DEFINITION OF A PROTESTANT POLITY (1551–1553) 362
   1. The general thrust of Northumberland's policy 362
   2. The assault on the Church: the bishoprics 375
   3. The assault on the Church: church goods 386

XI THE COMPLETION OF THE KING'S EDUCATION AND THE BEGINNING OF MATURE CONCERNS (1550–1553) 402
   1. The young King (1550–1552) 402
   2. The thought and influence of William Thomas 415
   3. The beginnings of the assumption of power (1551–1552) 419
   4. Royal illness and royal pleasure (1552) 423
   5. The penalties of fear: the problem of public order (October, 1551–1553) 427
   6. The weakening of the military resources of the state (1550–1553) 434

XII THE APPRENTICESHIP OF POWER 440
   1. Concern with the reform of administration 440
   2. The quest for solutions (1551–1553) 444

PAGE

XIII CRISIS IN THE SOCIETY (1550–1553)   456
1. Northumberland's fiscal administration   456
2. The sweating sickness (1551)   466
3. Efforts to control and enhance the economy   471
4. Deterioration of relations with the Hanse (1547–1553)   482
5. Discovery and exploration   489

XIV THE ASSAULT ON THE SUCCESSION (1553)   494
1. Northumberland's dilemma: the bitter fruits of power   494
2. Edward's second Parliament (March 1–March 31, 1553)   504
3. The illness and death of the King (January–July 6, 1553)   510
4. The shattering of the conspiracy   520
5. The character of Edward VI   532

INDEX   536

TABLE OF ABBREVIATIONS

A.P.C.	*Acts of the Privy Council of England.* Ed. by J. R. Dasent. New series, vols. II (1547–1550), III (1550–1552), IV (1552–1554). L., 1890–1892.
Cal. Pat. Rolls, Edw. VI	*Calendar of the patent rolls preserved in the Public Record Office.* [Ed. by R. H. Brodie.] 5 vols. and Index. L., 1924–1929.
Cal. S.P. Dom., Edw. VI	*Calendar of state papers, domestic series, of the reigns of Edward VI, etc.* Vol. I (1547–1580), ed. by Robert Lemon, L., 1856. Vol. VI (Mar. 1601–Mar. 24, 1603, with addenda, 1547–1565), ed. by Mary A. E. Green. L., 1870.
Cal. S.P. For., Edw. VI	*Calendar of state papers, foreign series, of the reign of Edward VI., 1547–1553, etc.* Ed. by William B. Turnbull. L., 1861.
Cal. S.P. Scotland	*Calendar of the state papers relating to Scotland and Mary, Queen of Scots, 1547–1603, etc.* Vol. I (Feb. 1547–1563), ed. by Joseph Bain. Edinburgh, 1898.
Cal. S.P. Span.	*Calendar of letters, despatches, and state papers, relating to the negotiations between England and Spain, etc.* Vol. IX (Jan. 29, 1547–Dec. 1549), ed. by M. A. S. Hume and Royall Tyler, L., 1912. Vols. X (1550–1552) and XI (1553), ed. by Royall Tyler, L., 1914–1916.
Cal. S.P. Ven.	*Calendar of state papers and manuscripts, relating to English affairs, existing in the archives . . . of Venice, etc.* Vol. VI, pt. 3 (Nov. 1557–Dec. 24, 1558, with additions, 1363–1557). Ed. by Rawdon Brown. L., 1873.
C.J.	*Commons Journals.*
DNB	*Dictionary of National Biography.*
Edward VI, *Chronicle*	*The Chronicle and political papers of King Edward VI.* Ed. by W. K. Jordan. L. and Ithaca, 1966.
E.H.R.	*English Historical Review* [first references to articles in learned journals will include the

	name of the author and the title; subsequent citations, the name of the author and the journal reference].
Grey Friars Chronicle	*Chronicle of the Grey Friars of London.* Ed. by J. G. Nichols. Camden Soc., vol. LIII. L., 1852.
Hayward, *Edward VI*	Hayward, John, *The life and reign of King Edward VI.* L., 1630, 1636; used in White Kennett, *A complete history of England, etc.,* II. (L., 1719), 273–328.
HMC	Historical Manuscripts Commission publications.
L.J.	*Journals of the House of Lords.*
Machyn, *Diary*	*The diary of Henry Machyn, citizen and merchant-taylor of London, from A.D. 1550 to A.D. 1563.* Ed. by J. G. Nichols. Camden Soc., vol. XLII. L., 1848.
S.P. Dom., Edw. VI	P.R.O., State Papers Domestic.
Two London Chronicles	*Two London chronicles from the collections of John Stow.* Ed. by C. L. Kingsford. Camden Miscellany, XII. L., 1910.
VCH	Victoria County History publications.
Wriothesley, *Chronicle*	Wriothesley, Charles, *A chronicle of England during the reigns of the Tudors, etc.* 2 vols. Ed. by W. D. Hamilton. Camden Soc., n.s. XI and XX. L., 1875, 1877.

I

THE FONT OF POWER: THE EDUCATION AND DEVELOPMENT OF THE KING

(1547–1550)

Edward VI was not yet ten years of age when he succeeded to the throne, no more than twelve when in late 1549 the brilliantly contrived, and wholly ruthless, *coup d'état* of the Earl of Warwick toppled the Duke of Somerset, Lord Protector and uncle of the King, from the seats of power. He was, then, a child, albeit an amazingly precocious one, during the course of the tumultuous events with which we were concerned in the first volume of this study. And a child he was to remain in his interests and activities during the first months of Northumberland's tenure of power, until the spring of 1550 when his own writings and what we know of his conduct betoken an early maturity of interests, a growing personal concern with governmental problems, and the first faint indications of occasional intervention in the affairs of state. During much of the interval with which we are now concerned he was, of course, still a schoolboy, bringing to an amazing maturity the superb education which Cheke, Cox, Belmain and others had begun when he was very young.[1]

The King's own state diary, which we have entitled the *Chronicle*, does record at some length the stirring days of his succession and coronation, but the evidence is persuasive that this was written some years after the events there related, doubtless as an exercise set by his tutors.[2] Before the coronation service the garrulous and ubiquitous imperial envoy, Van der Delft, had addressed the young King in French, but was told by Seymour that his royal nephew understood Latin better, though the ambassador's judgement was that 'he seemed to me to understand one just as little as the other'.[3] During

---

[1] Jordan, W. K., *Edward VI: the young King* (Allen & Unwin, London, and Harvard University Press, Cambridge, Mass., 1968), 38–45.

[2] Edward VI, *Chronicle*, 4–5.

[3] *Cal. S.P. Span.*, IX, 46–47.

the early months of his reign Edward was never far from the Protector's presence and stern guidance, though for a season his other maternal uncle, Lord Sudeley, had tempted him with pocket money and blandishments which were treasonable in intent if not in fact, and which were an important part of the evidence which brought Sudeley to the block. The King and his court lived principally at Whitehall or Greenwich, but Edward tended to spend his summers at Hampton Court. He was also on occasion resident at St James's Palace, as for example during the whole of the first session of his first Parliament, and not infrequently was lodged at least briefly at Oatlands and at Windsor, particularly when he was proceeding to or from Hampton Court. But wherever he went, he was always accompanied by Somerset, the 'Queen's side' of the various palaces being prepared for the Lord Protector and his wife.[1]

There is abundant evidence in the *Chronicle* that even in his childhood the King was enthralled by feats of arms and joustings, though he was never permitted personally to incur the dangers of these 'contact sports'.[2] He understood, too, the almost obsessive national concern for his health and well-being, remarking in his twelfth year that 'in the mean season, because there was a rumour that I was dead, I passed through London'.[3] He was deeply troubled, too, by the savage risings in the summer of 1549, setting down in considerable detail, and with no evidence of sympathy for the rebels, the bloody annal of the revolts which in Devonshire and Norfolk had to be put down with the use of all available main force.[4] The King also heard many sermons at court, though they were usually arranged on the occasion of the great festivals of the church and particularly in the Lenten season. There was never from the outset any doubt of his stalwart Protestantism, which may well have been deepened by the great Protestant divines chosen to preach before him. We know that Ridley, William Barlow, and Holbeach were amongst those who preached before him in Lent in his first regnal year, while in 1548 there are records of £1 each paid to Ridley, John Taylor, John Redman, Thomas Becon, Giles Eyre, and the famous Latimer for sermons preached at court. In the spring of 1549 Latimer preached his justly renowned series of Friday sermons before the King, and it is pathetic to recall that the cash which Edward accepted secretly from Thomas Seymour was in part to provide a personal reward to

[1] Edward, like all diarists, was preoccupied with his journeyings. Very nearly a complete itinerary can be constructed from his *Chronicle*.
[2] Edward VI, *Chronicle*, 9, 31–32, 33, as early examples.
[3] *Ibid*. 13 (the date can be fixed as July 23, 1549).
[4] *Ibid*. 13–16, 17–18.

this great preacher. But, as we shall later point out in detail, Edward was never deeply concerned with matters of religious doctrine, his interest in ecclesiastical affairs being almost wholly administrative. Nor did he attempt to follow Hooper's stern injunction to 'have before you every Sunday one sermon', and, in a later Lenten sermon, that, 'seeing there is in the year 8,760 hours, it shall not be much for your highness, nor for all your household, to bestow of them 52 in the year to hear the sermon of God'.[1]

The life and activities of the court were inevitably restrained because of the youth of the monarch, whose personal tastes were only beginning to assert themselves, and perhaps as importantly by the somewhat sombre preferences of the Lord Protector. None the less the court was a considerable establishment to which was paid £16,868 12s od in the second regnal year for a wide variety of services and the diet of a large number of officials and servants. The King was allotted £20 monthly for his alms, including his personal gifts which seem in the early months of the reign to have run to about £1 17s 11d weekly.[2] Retainers were paid to three physicians, six surgeons, and two apothecaries in the early months of the reign; this medical staff was shortly enlarged to include quarterly payments ranging from £2 10s od to £12 10s od for the services of four physicians (Dr Thomas Bill, Dr Bentley, Dr Huicke, and Dr Cornelius Zifridus) and as many as eight surgeons, with a similar range of payments. The King was also served by a French cook, a stone engraver, an organ maker, and three court painters (Anthony Toto, Bartholomew Penn, and Levina Teerlinc, who received emoluments ranging from £6 5s to £10 quarterly).[3] Sir Thomas Paston was paid a considerable salary as keeper of the royal gallery at Greenwich, while John Belmain, the King's French tutor, received a far more modest £6 13s 4d quarterly for his services.[4] Five scholars and writers, only one of whom (Stephen Vaughan) attained any considerable repute, had quarterly stipends of from £1 10s 5d to £5, while the running accounts are studded with the payments of £1 to divers divines for their sermons at court. These chamber accounts are most revealing of the taste of the King, suggesting that he shared

[1] *Early writings of John Hooper, etc.*, ed. by Samuel Carr (Parker Soc., Cambridge, 1843), 541, 558.
[2] *Trevelyan papers, etc.*, pts. i and ii ed. by J. P. Collier (Camden Soc. LXVII and LXXXIV, 1857 and 1863): pt. i, 192; pt. ii, 16; S. P. Dom., Edw. VI, VII, 26: May 1549. (We follow the accounts of Sir William Cavendish, Treasurer of the King's Chamber.)
[3] *Trevelyan Papers*, pt. i, 194–197; *ibid.* pt. ii, 25–26.
[4] *Ibid.* pt. i, 194.

the musical ability and interests of all his family. Thus in March 1549 monthly stipends are listed for seventeen instrumentalists, most of whom were foreigners and the largest number of them Italian. There were payments as well to two 'singing men', eight minstrels, and five interlude players.[1] In the summer of 1549, in the dark days of rebellion, these gentle outlays gave way to heavy expenditures for German household troops to guard the court and King: £445 15s 10d to Captain van Bruen for 'certain Almaines', or £1208 6s 0d to Captain Henry Hartford and his 420 German horse, these sums being for monthly service and paid in advance, so seriously shaken was English credit.[2]

With the ascendancy of Northumberland,[3] the court came rather quickly to be considerably enlivened, the King being diverted and enthralled by frequent martial displays, long and elaborate celebrations of the Christmas season, and occasional masques and interludes. Quiet steps were also taken to remove completely the Seymour influence about the person of the King, with a Council order at the time of the Protector's fall that it 'should be requisite to have some noblemen appointed to be ordinarily attendant about his Majesty's person in his privy chamber, to give order for the good government of his most royal person, and for the honourable education of his highness in these his tender years in learning and virtue'. Six such nobles were appointed (Northampton, Arundel, Warwick, St John, Russell, and Wentworth), of whom at least two should at all times be with the King. The Privy Chamber was further reorganized when 'four principal gentlemen' were appointed, with salaries of £100 p.a. each, they being charged with 'the singular care' of the person of the King,[4] while three gentlemen should always be on guard in the King's chamber and five grooms should always be present, 'of which one to watch in the bedchamber'.[5]

While Warwick was immediately and persistently concerned with

---

[1] *Trevelyan Papers, etc.*, pts. i and ii ed. by J. P. Collier (Camden Soc. LXVII and LXXXIV, 1857 and 1863): pt. i, 197, 200; *ibid*. pt. ii, 22–24.

[2] *Ibid*. pt. ii, 32.

[3] We shall tend to refer to John Dudley as Duke of Northumberland throughout this volume, though it will be remembered that he was not elevated to the title until October 11, 1551(*vide post*, 53).

[4] They were Sir Edward Rogers, Sir Thomas Darcy, Sir Andrew Dudley, and Sir Thomas Wroth, to whom were later added Sir Henry Sidney and Sir Henry Neville, all honourable men of considerable military experience.

[5] Edward VI, *Chronicle*, 26; Richardson, W. C., *History of the Court of Augmentations, 1536–1554* (Baton Rouge, 1961), 359; Nichols, J. G., *Literary remains of King Edward the Sixth* (2 vols., Roxburghe Club, L., 1857; repr., N.Y.,[1964]), I, cxxxiv; *A.P.C.*, II, 344–345: Oct. 15, 1549.

the security and control of the King's person, he left quite undisturbed the excellent educational arrangements established by Henry VIII and broadened by Somerset. Richard Cox, a Cambridge humanist known to be Protestant in his sympathies, was first appointed Edward's tutor in 1544. He had enjoyed a brilliant career as a reforming headmaster of Eton and was a friend of Archbishop Cranmer, who very probably recommended him to Henry VIII. An excellent Latinist, a skilful teacher, and a natural administrator, Cox was to lay the foundation for the remarkable education of the young Prince and King, whom he served as tutor until 1550. Closely associated with him in the teaching tasks was Sir John Cheke, who since 1540 had served as the first Regius Professor of Greek at Cambridge and who was the most gifted of the notable, and closely connected, group of humanists in the two universities who were to serve the state with such distinction during the reign of King Edward. Cheke's influence over the young Prince was great and sustained. It was he who grounded him so thoroughly in the Greek and Latin classics, who encouraged him to develop the habit of constant writing as an academic discipline and to cultivate the skills of self-expression. At the same time a French humanist and schoolmaster, Jean Belmain, was engaged to teach Edward the French language and may well have influenced the young King's religious development, since he was a stout Calvinist in persuasion.[1] Other and lesser men taught the boy music, deportment, and riskless sports; but Cheke and Cox remained his masters, shaped his style, and gave to him an extraordinary and humane education. 'Few monarchs in history have been as well equipped for their task as was Edward VI; he stood as a prince who would have delighted the fastidious and demanding taste of Erasmus.'[2]

[1] Belmain wrote several learned tracts, all Calvinist in temper. He probably translated from the Greek into French a letter of St Basil on the eremitic life in *c.* 1550 (Royal MS. 16. E. i), and made a manuscript translation of the *Second Book of Common Prayer* into French (*ibid.* 20. A. xiv). Belmain had some correspondence with Calvin regarding the King. In late May 1552 he wrote from Greenwich, saying that Edward found great pleasure in Calvin's writings and that the reformer might feel free to address the King directly. He had also sent Calvin a copy of Edward's short treatise in French (*A l'encontre les abus du monde*), strongly Protestant in tone, but did not wish it published since this might be regarded as a vainglorious action. Belmain would shortly send Calvin his French version of the second Prayer Book and suggested that the great reformer might also wish to write to Cheke, who had been principally responsible for the education of the King, 'a young plant, whose flowers are pleasant and whose ripe fruits will be great' (*Joannis Calvini Opera . . . Omnia,* XIV (Brunswick, 1875), *Thesaurus Epist. Calv.,* 324–325). Also, *vide* Jordan, *Edward VI,* 42.

[2] Edward VI, *Chronicle,* xii. The treatment of Edward's education is drawn principally from the *Introduction* to this volume.

Cheke and Cox very sensibly arranged that the young King should gain some experience in the art of living with others by sharing his leisure and some aspects of his more formal education with a number of well-born boys of his own age, some fourteen of whom may be identified and most of whom were the sons of English nobles. Of this whole group, however, Edward became the close friend of only one, Barnaby Fitzpatrick, the son of an obscure Irish peer, with whom to the end of his life Edward remained on easy and intimate terms.

Some of the fruits of the educational methods of Cheke and Cox may be assessed by a brief comment on the academic exercises, the set pieces, written by Edward VI, well over a hundred of which survive. There are, first of all, upwards of sixty letters, addressed to members of his own family, to Barnaby Fitzpatrick, and to Cranmer and other bishops. These were rather stilted Latin or French pieces, telling us little about the boy, and so formal in tone, save for a few to Catherine Parr, the Princess Elizabeth, and Barnaby Fitzpatrick, that they evoked equally formal replies.[1] More interesting are the fifty-six Latin and Greek exercises which survive, which seem to have replaced the formal letters in Cheke's teaching method and all of which appear to have been done after Edward ascended the throne, with a particularly heavy concentration in 1551.[2] These are in form declamations on set and conventional subjects, formal in subject matter and in style. But they do display an impressive command of Latin which the King had attained by his fourteenth year and a broadening facility in Greek which, however, he never fully mastered. There are, as well, three exercises in French, set by Belmain on religious topics, which are Calvinistic in temper and straitly, sometimes rather awkwardly, anti-papal in sentiment.[3] But however one may criticize the subject matter, Belmain had undoubtedly instilled in his royal pupil an easy and perceptive knowledge of the French language. Taking in view the *corpus* of these formal exercises, we have the sense that until about May, 1551 they were set and closely criticized by his tutors, while thereafter the King was completing the shaping and polishing of his style and his grasp of the processes of presentation, chiefly on his own initiative and for his own purposes. Already by this date, too, he was displaying keen interest in military engineering and had gained an excellent knowledge of geography,

---

[1] To be found principally in Harl. MS. 5087; Cotton MSS., Nero, C, x; and Add. MS. 5845. Almost the whole *corpus* of these letters has been printed in excellent texts by Nichols (*Remains*, I, 1–92).

[2] Harl. MS. 5087; Add. MS. 4724.

[3] These we have seen in the texts supplied by Nichols, *Remains*, I, 145–205.

knowing in detail the principal ports and havens of the British Isles and a great deal of European geography, especially of the French and Flemish coasts.[1] So too, in his most important composition, the *Chronicle*, this same transition in the nature and purpose of his writing may be observed, though in this document the evidences of the King's precocious intellectual maturity may be dated somewhat earlier.

This state diary extends nominally from the date of Henry VIII's death to its inexplicable and abrupt close on November 28, 1552, a short while before the onset of Edward's fatal illness. But in a detailed and more informal sense it deals with the period after March 24, 1550, and for this interval it is an important source for the history of the reign. The King himself in two places in the manuscript [2] entitled the work as his 'Chronicle', though the word has been carefully lined out in one place (one supposes by its author), while in the other this title is used at the beginning of entries which were contemporaneous rather than reminiscent in nature. Bishop Burnet, who printed the work in a wholly unsatisfactory edition, gave it the title of 'Journal', a word not used in this sense in the sixteenth century and which in any event does not well express either the content or form of the document.[3] Perhaps the most accurate title which could be provided for this formally title-less work would be 'Political Diary', but 'Diary' was a word unknown in the author's generation and conveys as well a sense of personal and intimate writing not to be found in this sternly sober recital of events. Hence we have restored the King's own wavering choice of title for this important and revealing work.

We have spoken of the quality and depth of the young King's education and of the exercises which display such an impressive grasp of languages, liberality of knowledge, and polished control of the arts of presentation. Little of this humanistic quality is to be found in the *Chronicle*, which was in the very nature of the case terse, telegraphic, and reminiscent rather than expository. Entries are brief and were evidently designed to recall the whole of events only noted here. None the less, Edward used language boldly and was a coiner of words, a good many of which survive in modern

[1] Hayward, *Edward VI*, 277.

[2] Cotton MSS., Nero, C, x.

[3] In *The history of the reformation of the Church of England* (3 vols., L., 1679–1719; ed. by Nicholas Pocock, 7 vols., Oxford, 1865). Far more satisfactory was J. G. Nichols's printed text published in 1857–1858 under the title, *Literary remains of King Edward the Sixth*, to which we have paid warranted tribute (Edward VI, *Chronicle*, xv). See the latter work, xiii–xiv, for a history of the manuscript.

usage. The *Chronicle* displays a remarkable facility of expression and a usually perceptive sense of the meaning and trend of events.

The *Chronicle* gains its great interest and importance from the fact that it is an extremely reliable historical source, and because it displays for us the moving record of the maturing of a precocious mind and temperament. We see in it the finally successful struggle of a closely guarded, steadily watched, and too tightly disciplined child, who was also a sovereign, to attain independence of judgement and personality. We see, too, a child who was also a Tudor, in the whole meaning of the word, who was reaching out for the essentials of power, and who could be cold and forbidding as he contemplated the uses and meaning of power. So swiftly did intellectual maturity come to this child that in reading this work one has constantly to remember that it was begun in diary form when he was aged twelve years and five months, and that its last cold and ungenerous entry was made when he was no more than fifteen years and one month. 'The whole weight of the evidence which the text supplies . . . suggests that the young King stood ready to grasp the reins of power just as he was stricken with tuberculosis, a debilitating and shortly a fatal illness.' The evidence of the *Chronicle*, and of his other writings, 'would also suggest that few sovereigns of his years have ever possessed a clearer sense of direction, of tasks to be accomplished, than did this young monarch, or to have been endowed with greater resources wherewith to secure their accomplishment'.[1]

Certainly in English history, and very possibly in European history, there is no source quite of the nature of the *Chronicle*. As has been suggested, the document stands as one of the principal sources for our knowledge of the reign and it is not infrequently our only source for information regarding events of considerable importance. Wherever it may be tested by other official documents the *Chronicle* is reliable, while the whole of it is marked by an almost frightening objectivity as men and events are noted down. It is quite certain that the King from the age of thirteen onwards was watching the course of events with an observing, an independent, and an increasingly critical eye. He was assiduously and certainly intelligently preparing himself for responsibilities which all men assumed lay just ahead for him. Already he was in temperament, in ability, and in his remarkable capacity for noting and mastering detail much like his great sister and his paternal grandfather.

A study of the contents of the *Chronicle* reveals that most of the events and decisions there noted may be found in fuller form in the

[1] Edward VI, *Chronicle*, xvii.

Acts of the Privy Council, the *State Papers Domestic,* and the *State Papers Foreign.* This of course means that from a very young age the King was quite fully informed of the flow of knowledge and data available to his government, as it sought to lay out a course of policy. But it is equally clear that the King's information, especially on foreign affairs and military events abroad, often went well beyond the official documents, or at least those that survive. This knowledge seems to have been derived from his conversations with foreign diplomatists accredited to him; from his frequent meetings with his principal secretaries, Petre and Cecil; from William Thomas, a humanist trying to turn civil servant, whom we believe had a considerable influence on the King after late 1550; and in certain instances from wholly unknown sources.[1]

As one reads the *Chronicle,* which in a true sense is a record of what interested the young King, a decided revision of the traditional assessment of his character and personality emerges. His driving concern, clearly, was with the dull but essential tasks of administration and more particularly with the whole process of conciliar and fiscal administration. On these matters his ideas were his own and we can say with certainty that a general administrative reform was at hand when he was stricken with his last illness. It is equally clear that he was searching for the causes of the ruinous inflationary process then under way, that his economic thinking was conservative and remarkably sophisticated, and that he brought considerable personal influence to bear in ending the successive debasements of the coinage which his father had begun. It is also abundantly evident that after the summer of 1550 Edward VI was becoming ardently interested in the course of European diplomacy, following with an intelligent concern even the day-to-day developments during a period when Warwick's policy was paralysed by an ineptitude mixed with fear. He followed with excited interest, as well, military events in Germany, Italy, France, and Flanders, with the suggestion of a martial ardour which, had the young King lived, might have turned English foreign policy on bold and possibly dangerous courses.[2]

So too, a reading of the *Chronicle* and the remarkable political

---

[1] *Vide post,* 415–418, for our remarks on Thomas and his relations with the King.

[2] The King's deep interest in the progress of the war was continuous after June, 1551, and from that time forward until the *Chronicle* ended in November, 1552, occupied something like half the total space. The King's interest was at once in the larger diplomatic issues and in the exciting details of skirmishes, sieges, and marches. For examples, *vide* Edward VI, *Chronicle,* 65–66, 74, 77, 78, 81–82, 85, 86, 91, 96, 97, 102, 109, 112, 114–115, 117–118, 120–121, 125–128, 131, 132–133, 134, 136–137, 138, 139–141, 142, 145–146, 147, 150, 151, 152–153, 154.

memoranda prepared by the young King suggest his deepening concern with the social and economic dislocations of his generation. Here was a rapidly broadening area of royal concern, which strongly suggests that he had absorbed from Somerset, from Latimer, whose preaching we know moved him, from Hales and from others of the Commonwealth Party an intense moral conviction that reform of the society and its institutions was essential in England. We shall see that he was to intervene with great strength and passion when he committed financial resources of the Crown in the momentous decision to build adequate social institutions for the City of London, thereby, one may believe, providing the needed catalyst for a full century of private charity which was to reshape or to build desperately needed resources for the care of the poor, the curing of the sick, the education of the ignorant, and the social rehabilitation of the derelict.[1]

An examination of the *Chronicle* and the various state papers written by the King enforces a still more important revision of our estimate of him, his interests, and his aspirations for his realm. One finds in these intensely personal documents little evidence of religious warmth, much less of zeal or of concern with religious matters, save as his supremacy and ultimate sovereignty were involved. There can be no doubt that he was an advanced Protestant in his religious convictions and that he was personally a pious youth. But these personal convictions seem to have left his policy almost untouched. The root concern in all his writings is with the maintenance of the structure of royal power. There is in fact in the *Chronicle* almost no interest exhibited in purely religious matters, not more than five per cent of the whole text being so concerned and well over half of that meagre proportion having to do with essentially administrative matters. Here again, his mind and concerns lie much nearer to those of his great and wholly Erastian sister Elizabeth, than to the obsessive personal religious policy which brought ruin to his sister Mary.

The *Chronicle* and the other surviving writings tell us a great deal about the policy, the ability, and the interests of Edward VI, but little about his personality. The *Chronicle* must be described as a cold, harsh, and emotionless document. There are in it only momentary flashes of boyish enthusiasm, there is nothing of the brooding uncertainty of adolescence, little of affection for any human being. The death of his Seymour grandmother (October, 1550) goes unnoticed. The execution of Somerset, his own uncle and his head of

[1] *Vide post, Excursus* II, 214–223.

state, is dismissed with a cold phrase that exhibits no emotion whatsoever. 'The earlier destruction of Thomas Seymour, deserved though it was, is harshly noted, even though that engaging rogue had sought to pervert the boy with pocket money and furtive backstairs plotting.'[1] Only in his letters to Barnaby Fitzpatrick and in his evident attachment to the visiting French envoy, the Marshal St André, are to be found at least glimpses of boyish excitement and enthusiasm. Edward VI was made of stern Tudor stuff, and he had for years been disciplined and rigorously schooled for the great office to which he acceded at so tender an age. He was the font of all power in his realm, but he had seen plot and counterplot launched by those who wished to rule at least for a season in his name. It is clear that he bestowed complete confidence in neither Somerset nor Northumberland. There are no evidences of fear, but the King was alert, always suspicious of men and their motives, and always deeply aware that his own preservation was required for the security of the realm. 'The tutors selected with such shrewd care by Henry VIII had made a king; they had also destroyed a boy.'[2]

[1] Edward VI, *Chronicle*, xxiii.
[2] *Ibid*. xxiv. Edward VI's political and economic papers and the beginnings of his accession to personal power will be discussed in later pages; *vide post*, 441–444, 450–455.

II

THE TRIUMPH OF REACTION (1549-1551)

1. THE JETTISONING OF ROMAN CATHOLIC SUPPORT

We have seen that Warwick, that masterly and almost instinctive conspirator, in gathering all possible force to accomplish the ruin of Somerset, had persuaded seasoned Roman Catholic politicians like Wriothesley, as well as more naive conservatives like the Earl of Arundel, that in return for what may be described as Roman Catholic support the course of the Reformation would be halted, or even reversed, once the Protector was removed from power. We know nothing regarding the precise nature of these commitments, though it is probable that Warwick made many. But at the least it can be said that some measure of assurance had been given to Southampton, Arundel, and Southwell, who at the moment of decision stood high in the deliberations of the Privy Council, to which they had been restored.[1] The violently Protestant Bishop Ponet, describing the circumstances a few years later, charged that in the critical days 'Wriothesley, that before was banished the court, is lodged, with his wife and son, next the King: every man repaireth to Wriothesley, honoureth Wriothesley, sueth unto Wriothesley, as the Assyrians did to Hamen, and all things be done by his advice, and who but Wriothesley?' Arundel, he continued, was 'promised to be next to the King, groom of his stool, or comptroller of his house, at the least. Southwell, for his whisking and double diligence, must be a great counsellor in any wise.'[2] This Catholic circle, for a brief season restored to influence, included also in its lower ranges Sir Thomas and Sir John Arundell, of no relation to the Earl but both connected by marriage with the Howards and with Sir Richard and Sir Robert Southwell.[3]

---

[1] Jordan, *Edward VI*, 502, 507; Pollard, A. F., *England under Protector Somerset* (L., 1900), 260–261.

[2] P[onet], D. I., *A shorte treatise of politike pouuer, etc.* ([Strassburg], 1556), I, iii.

[3] Pollard, A. F., *The history of England . . . (1547–1603)* (L., 1911), 42–43.

The rising influence of this conservative party seemed frightening indeed to those of the reformed faith, as well as to the politiques who had dominated the Privy Council in the days of the Duke of Somerset. Wriothesley and Arundel were among the six peers immediately entrusted with the King's person,[1] while Southwell resumed an active role in the deliberations of the Council. The imperial ambassador was persuaded that both Gardiner and Bonner were about to be released,[2] while the mass was quietly celebrated in certain of the Oxford colleges and there were reports that the Latin service was restored in numerous parishes.[3] Hooper, certainly the most effective as he was the most outspoken of the evangelical party, wrote gloomily to Bullinger on November 7, 1549, that with Somerset now in the Tower there was much fear of a violent alteration in religion. Two weeks earlier silence had been imposed on all preachers and lecturers, and it is evident that Hooper was greatly disturbed.[4] Writing again to the Swiss reformer towards the end of December, he was more hopeful for the safety of Somerset and the stability of the reformed faith in the realm. He had been assured of Cranmer's now clearly held 'right views as to the nature of Christ's presence in the Supper', and was comforted as well by the fact that six or seven of the bishops were firmly and openly committed to the course of the Reformation.[5] Bullinger, who had been gravely alarmed, was likewise assured by Dryander that the foreign divines in England stood in no danger and that Bucer and Ochino continued to feel that they were working under almost ideal conditions.[6]

These rumours and uncertainties, occasioned by Warwick's guile, were troublesome and not easily quieted. On Christmas Day, 1549, however, Warwick revealed his true policy in very explicit terms in a carefully composed statement, issued to the bishops in the King's name, to which both he and Arundel were signatories. All men were reminded that the Book of Common Prayer was the usage of the Church of England as ordained by Parliament and was to be used by all persons in the realm.

'Yet divers evil disposed persons, since the apprehension of the Duke of Somerset, have bruited abroad that they should have again their old Latin services, their conjured bread and water, with such like vain and superstitious ceremonies, as if the setting forth of the said book had only been the Duke's act.'

[1] Edward VI, *Chronicle*, 18. [2] *Cal. S.P. Span.*, IX, 458.
[3] *Ibid.* 455; Robinson, Hastings, ed., *Original letters relative to the English Reformation*, etc. (2 vols., Parker Soc., Cambridge, 1846–1847), II, 464.
[4] *Ibid.* I, 69–70. [5] *Ibid.* 71–72. [6] *Ibid.* 353–354: Dec. 3, 1549.

The King had accordingly declared the Book of Common Prayer to be grounded in law and Holy Scripture and commanded his subjects to put away any thought of the former Latin service, which would be 'preferring ignorance to knowledge, and darkness to light, and a preparation to bring in papistry and superstition again'. The bishops were further commanded to require the clergy to gather up all copies of former uses and services and 'to deface or destroy them', sending to prison any who refused to obey the orders, and likewise to employ excommunication and 'other censures of the church' against those of the laity who refused the legally ordained communion service.[1]

This strong and unequivocal statement of religious policy went far towards quieting rumours and it dashed all hopes which may have been entertained by the Romanist faction. It was clear to Van der Delft even in late November that Warwick was imposing his authority, had tricked the Catholics, and that only Wriothesley was strong enough to raise any effective opposition.[2] But the former Lord Chancellor had already once been ruined and broken in the early months of the reign. He now appears to have attended no Council meeting after October 18, 1549, and was formally dismissed from that body in February, 1550; in June he was permitted to return to his beloved Titchfield where he died a few weeks later.

Arundel, more compliant because he had subscribed to the Declaration on Religion of December 25th, sought desperately to keep his post as Lord Chamberlain and to stay at least within the fringes of power. He was not to be so easily jettisoned as was the Earl of Southampton. His last attendance at the Council was on January 11th, however, and then wild and surely baseless charges, of the bizarre quality which only a Warwick could have invented, were laid against him. The King records that 'The Earl of Arundel [was] committed to his house for certain crimes of suspicion against him, as plucking down of bolts and locks at Westminster, giving of my stuff away, etc.'[3] Arundel was well acquainted with Warwick's ruthlessness against his enemies, for he had lent help in framing the equally improbable allegations against Somerset; he knew too that any formal resistance was as useless as it was dangerous. Hence when he was brought before the Council on February 21st he chose to throw himself on the mercy of the King rather than stand trial. He was accordingly dismissed from office, was fined £12,000,

---

[1] S.P. Dom., Edw. VI, IX, 57; also in Stowe MS. 142, f. 16.
[2] *Cal. S.P. Span.*, IX, 477.
[3] Edward VI, *Chronicle*, 19.

payable at the rate of £1000 p.a., and shortly afterwards was ordered to retire to his estates in Sussex where he should stand ready to serve as Lord Lieutenant.[1] The lesser figures, whose support Warwick had purchased with his promise of favour and his intimations of a more conservative religious policy, were simply brushed aside, save for Sir Richard Southwell who was fined £500 and for a season committed to the Tower on charges of 'certain bills of sedition written with his hand'.[2]

These events were followed with intelligent concern by the imperial envoy whose hopes were aroused for only a few days following the *coup d'état*. He had visited the Princess Mary some days before January 14th and reported that she too was not deceived by Warwick's guile. She expected no assistance from his governance, saying that 'the Earl of Warwick is the most unstable man in England. The conspiracy against the Lord Protector has envy and ambition as its only motives.' Hence she had declined to attend court at the Christmas season because she wished no 'argument with the King, my brother', who was now personally employing his influence against the true faith. Van der Delft had no illusions: Warwick had simply beguiled Southampton, Arundel, and others of the old nobility who favoured Catholicism, in order to gain a firmer basis of power wherewith to overthrow the Protector. And now he had thrown his whole support to the younger nobility who were Protestant in faith and had allied himself with the Protestant faction generally.[3] This judgement the imperial ambassador thought fully confirmed when on January 18th he wrote to the Emperor that the restraints on Somerset in the Tower had been relaxed, that the Duchess and Warwick's wife 'exchange banquets and festivities daily', and that the way was being prepared for the Duke's early release.[4]

The brief flirtation with those who wished a return at least to Henrician Romanism was, then, no more than a skilful and unscrupulous trick of Warwick to gain the temporary support which he required as he marshalled his forces against Somerset. Warwick was moved only by expediency in this action as he was in the policy which marked his course during the remainder of his life. He had no other recourse than to lend his support to the Protestant faction

---

[1] *A.P.C.*, II, 398: Feb. 21, 1550. The fine was remitted, and Arundel later threw his support to Somerset; it was he who at the end of the reign arrested Dudley in Queen Mary's name.

[2] Edward VI, *Chronicle*, 19. Southwell lived to take an active role against Northumberland in 1553 and to receive from Queen Mary in that year an annual pension of £100 (Rymer, Thomas, *Foedera, etc.*, XV (L., 1728), 355).

[3] *Cal. S.P. Span.*, X, 6–7.   [4] *Ibid.* 14.

because, as the Princess Mary well knew, the King was staunchly Protestant and was beginning to make his power felt. He knew as well that the dominant classes in the English society were already at least moderately Protestant in complexion and that the thrust of sentiment was even now in the direction of evangelical Protestantism. Nor could Warwick have found a solid structure of power had he allied himself with half-forgotten peers of conservative habit and sentiment who lay wholly outside the apparatus of power which had for three years governed England. Warwick simply had to embrace Protestantism if he were to govern at all. Why he embraced radical-evangelical Protestantism is more difficult to answer. In large part, surely, the reason was that the initiative and guidance of English thought lay with this party and his whole position would be, or so it seemed, the more secure if in his devotion to Protestantism he outdid the essentially moderate Somerset and Archbishop Cranmer. It may also have occurred to him in early 1550, as it surely did in 1551, that with this policy alone ran the expectation of further ecclesiastical spoil.[1] His policy in this respect is somewhat difficult to fathom because it was rooted in no deeply held conviction of his own. He found it expedient to govern as an ardent Protestant; he thought it expedient to die a Roman Catholic.

2. WARWICK SECURES DOMINANCE (OCTOBER 1549– EARLY 1550)

There was no bath of blood following on Somerset's fall, the negotiations between the London Lords and the Protector at Windsor having achieved a formula by which Somerset yielded power with a commitment that he would be spared and his estate not wholly confiscated. He was, however, a prisoner in the Tower. Though several of his adherents had been imprisoned, a list of prisoners in the Tower which we may date October 22, 1549, suggests that, of those who had been arrested at the time of the *coup d'état*, not more than eleven were being held, Somerset being one. Aside from the personal agents of the Duke, only Sir Michael Stanhope, Sir Thomas Smith, and Sir John Thynne may be regarded as state prisoners of importance. And these men were shortly to be released,

---

[1] For other comments see: Chapman, Hester W., *The last Tudor king. A study of Edward VI* (L., 1958), 185–186; Constant, G., *The Reformation in England*, II (N.Y., 1942), 146; Froude, J. A., *History of England, etc.*, V (L., 1860), 256; Parker, T. M., *The English Reformation to 1558* (L., 1950), 136–137.

as the way was being prepared for the pardon of the Duke himself.[1]
It did not suit Warwick's purposes to undertake severe punishment against Somerset, and it is unlikely that he could at this season
have carried his associates in the Privy Council with him had he
attempted so to do. The role of magnanimity was forced on Dudley
by circumstances, and probably also sprang from his own preference
at this moment when he was moving with considerable skill to ensure
his own position. This easing of tensions was furthered by the release on November 2nd of five of the prisoners still being held for
complicity in the Western Rising,[2] and even by the lifting of the
severe restraints long imposed on the Duke of Norfolk, who was now
to be permitted certain furnishings in his rooms in the Tower, to see
his wife at convenient times, and to have limited freedom to walk in
the garden and gallery in the Tower.[3]

Warwick also moved carefully and with modesty in the advancement of his own position and dignity. He laid no claims on the protectorship, he was content with a formal rank which placed him
fourth amongst the Privy Councillors, and he delayed his claims on
a duchy for many months to come. He was, however, deeply concerned with the substance, if not the trappings, of power. Probably
late in 1549, too, he was troubled by the possible flaws which might
be held to exist in the authority of the Council now that the person
and office of the Lord Protector had been removed from the fabric
of the body in which sovereignty resided. Accordingly, a new form
of commission was drafted in the name of the King for the members
of the Council. The document, which we think was never sealed,
rehearsed the history of the manner in which power had been vested
in the ruling junta by the will of Henry VIII 'as now appears enrolled
in Chancery', as a consequence of 'lack of knowledge and experience, which our young age and few years . . . could not have conceived and gotten' for the administration of the realm. Hence power
had been vested in 'executors and councillors' in whom the King
reposed complete trust for the 'direction of our affairs, private and
public'. Now, knowing how necessary such Councillors were to him,
all their actions, or of a majority of them, were confirmed and ratified
to the present date. Having now reached twelve years of age, but

---

[1] S.P. Dom., Edw. VI, IX, 48 (Oct. 22, 1549), which we have compared with S.P.
Dom., Edw. VI, V, 10, which internal evidence would date between December, 1548
and Whitsun, 1549. Most of the prisoners still held in October, 1549 were well-born
Scots taken in battle and not yet ransomed. A few prisoners accused of serious crimes
and several persons still being held as trouble-makers from the time of the summer
risings were also in the list.

[2] *A.P.C.*, II, 354.   [3] *Ibid*. 400: Feb. 24, 1550.

understanding still 'how much unable yet for a time we are for want of perfect knowledge and experience to take unto our own . . . direction of our affairs', the members of the King's Council were commanded to continue in the government of his person and the ordering of the affairs of the realm. Thus the commission was intended to have the effect of confirming past actions, including the deposition of the Duke of Somerset, and to provide a fully legal basis for the continuance of the sovereign powers of the ruling group who were also in legal fact the Privy Council.[1]

In the early weeks of 1550 a number of adjustments were made and rewards conferred within the ranks of the Council and the household, in part to tighten the structure of Warwick's power and in part to signal the dismissal of the Catholics who had been tricked into a brief participation in the realities of power and policy. William Cecil, who had been inconstant in his support of Somerset, was in late January, with certain lesser adherents of the Duke, released from the Tower under a bond of 1000 marks and some months afterwards restored to office as Secretary of State.[2] Paget, who had been more stalwart in his support but who had played an important role in persuading Somerset to accept terms, was restored to office and favour, being at the same time raised to the peerage as Lord Paget of Beaudesert, and then left London on January 22, 1550, with others, on a special mission to the French king.[3] In February these shifts and adjustments were for the time being completed, having been begun in October when Warwick assumed office as Lord Admiral conjoined with that of President of the Council.[4] St John was created Earl of Wiltshire and Lord Treasurer, Russell was raised to an earldom, and Northampton was appointed to the post of Lord Great Chamberlain. At about the same time Sir Anthony Wingfield, who had served as Captain of the Guard, was made Comptroller of the Household, while Lord Wentworth was made Lord Great Chamberlain of the Household.[5] All these

---

[1] Cotton MSS., Titus, B, ii, 49, f. 104 (renumbered 91–94). This document extends to 7½ pages. It may be dated some time after Oct. 12, 1549, probably very late in that year. We are unable to identify the hand.

[2] A.P.C., II, 372: Jan. 25, 1550. His position had been uncertain as late as Nov. 16, 1549, when the normally incorrigible and wholly courageous Duchess of Suffolk wrote to assure him that she would never fail him. 'For your troubles I cannot but be sorry', and she grieved for his 'burden': 'Good Cecil, mistrust not but that you shall have all that I can do, yea, if there be anything which you think I may do, forbear me not'. (Lansdowne MS. 2, #24, f. 59)

[3] Edward VI, Chronicle, 19–20; Stow, John, The annales, or generall chronicle of England, etc., (L., 1565, 1615), 603.

[4] A.P.C., II, 347: Oct. 19, 1549.   [5] Stow, Annales, 603.

promotions, with the exception of Paget's elevation, were clearly designed to pay Warwick's political debts accumulated during the weeks following the *coup* and to lend further strength and security to the great personal power which he now wielded.

Warwick and the Council were also concerned, during the weeks which followed the crushing of the great risings and the crisis which immediately arose when the Lord Protector was stripped of his office and power, with the necessity of strengthening the defensive strategy which England was now assuming in the formal state of war in which she found herself with both France and Scotland. Soon after the fall of Somerset, substantial stores of armament, but no ordnance, were forwarded to Boulogne and Calais to meet long and detailed lists of needs which had gone untended during the period of domestic turbulence in England.[1] In a series of meetings the Council lent belated attention to the whole military and naval situation, shifting forces which could be spared to satisfy the more desperate needs and surveying the more exposed positions such as the Scilly Isles.[2] Though Warwick, as we shall later see, was prepared to end the war with France on almost any terms, it was recognized that in order to retain any bargaining counters at all Boulogne with its great system of defences must be held against the somewhat desultory siege under which it lay. Hence in early November the Council ordered the large sum of £8000 to be forwarded to Boulogne towards the payment of arrears of soldiers' wages there,[3] while a few days later it unhappily faced the fact that unless re-enforcements were sent thither, the town must inevitably fall. Accordingly, plans, never fully executed, were drafted for the dispatch to Boulogne of a large army under the command of the Earl of Huntingdon, with the field command to be vested in such competent professional officers as Sir James Croft, Sir Edward Hastings, and Edward Chamberlain.[4] At the same time, there was considerable fear of French landings on the south coast which was in so far as possible countered by somewhat feeble naval dispositions and the appointment of a new and, it was hoped, more vigorous commander for the key military and naval base at Portsmouth.[5]

Warwick had, then, handled the translation of power into his own hands with considerable skill and he had comported himself with a persuasive modesty. In November, 1549 Van der Delft reported to his imperial master that Warwick was clearly the leader of the

[1] *A.P.C.*, II, 348–351, 351–355: Oct. 20–22, Oct. 23–Nov. 10, 1549.
[2] S.P. Dom., Edw. VI, IX, 51: Oct. 1549; *ibid.* 49: Oct. 31, 1549; *ibid.* 54: Nov. 5, 1549; *A.P.C.*, II, 354: Nov. 5, 1549.   [3] *Ibid.* 355: Nov. 9, 1549.
[4] *Ibid.* II, 356–357: Nov. 12, 1549.   [5] *Ibid.* 358–359.

Protestant party, that Paget had been restored and was deep in the Earl's counsel, and that he had been able to gain an interview with Warwick only after repeated insistence. In this long meeting the imperial ambassador pleaded the case for a restoration of the Henrician Settlement, to which the Earl replied, 'I am not as opinionated as you think, but we have a law here which was made not by the Duke of Somerset alone but by all the members for the kingdom'. This settlement he meant to maintain.[1] Warwick in turn was sharply critical of the Emperor who had lent England no assistance in the war with France, thereby forcing him to recall troops needed in Scotland in order to strengthen the Boulogne defences.

The Earl carried his power easily and with dignity, and certainly by the spring of 1550 the fact of that power was fully accepted by his colleagues on the Council and by the King. At an unknown date, but probably in September, 1550, he could write to Cecil, now wholly in his service, chiding him gently because an agreed proclamation relating to the supply of grain had not been promulgated by the Council after it had been seen by the Lord Chancellor. He was away from London 'to take a bayne [bath] for the better surety of my health', and did not wish to be further disturbed about the matter. He would sign any document approved by Cecil and others of the Council, for there should be no further delay.[2] Not long afterwards, too, his policy and mien had persuaded the radical reformers that he lent them full support. Ulmis, writing to Bullinger, could say that, save for Suffolk, Warwick alone 'governs the state, and supports and upholds it on his own shoulders'. He was now regarded as the 'terror of the papists'. Much of Somerset's difficulty had sprung from the fact that he 'was of a more gentle and pliant nature in religious matters'.[3] But now England and the reformed faith might repose full confidence in the Hammer of the Lord.

3. REACTION IN PARLIAMENT: THE REVERSAL OF SOMERSET'S POLICIES (THIRD SESSION OF THE FIRST PARLIAMENT, NOVEMBER 4, 1549–FEBRUARY 1, 1550)

The third session of Edward VI's first Parliament had been summoned shortly before the Protector's fall, and the fact that the date was near at hand accounts in part for the speed with which Warwick moved and for the relative leniency with which Somerset and his

---

[1] *Cal. S.P. Span.*, IX, 477.
[2] S.P. Dom., Edw. VI, X, 30 (the probable date is Sept. 15, 1550).
[3] Robinson, *Original letters*, II, 439: Dec. 4, 1551.

adherents were treated. The session was opened on November 4th, a scant three weeks after Somerset had entered the Tower, and it spans the period when Warwick was gathering to himself the full substance of power. We have seen that the classes which completely dominated the early Tudor Parliaments—the nobility and the gentry—had been deeply alienated by the Protector's social and economic policies of reform, with the consequence that the reactionary temper of Warwick and the Council fitted closely, as it reflected, the frightened mood of a strong and vigorous majority in Parliament.[1] This was, accordingly, a Parliament which was conservative in its mood, and one which displayed every disposition to support the government's policy of restoring and maintaining public order—the risings of 1549 had thoroughly alarmed the governing classes of England. Hence Warwick and the House of Commons were agreed in their wish to roll back so far as they dared the whole of Somerset's policy of reform and experimentation. This was to be an important parliament, though the bulk of its not inconsiderable legislation was essentially negative in temper and effect. Yet there remained in the House of Commons a relatively strong, an articulate, and a determined reform party which may be said to reflect the social and economic views of the Commonwealth Party and which was evidently unshaken in its devotion to Somerset and his aspirations for England. On the three points of sheep, enclosures, and the care of the poor, this group was not easily overridden and it introduced and fought for a *corpus* of reform legislation which the government and the dominant groups in Parliament defeated only after considerable exertion. There is also abundant evidence that the mood of reaction in Parliament was tempered and to a degree constrained by the vigorous and courageous efforts of the Commonwealth Men in the House of Commons.

The most reactionary of all the measures passed by this Parliament was 3 and 4 Edward VI, c. 5, an act for 'the punishment of unlawful assemblies and risings of the King's subjects'.[2] This statute had the effect of extending and broadening the law of treason in such wise as to place in the hands of the government and the gentry the means for striking down any overt or threatened turbulence. It was declared high treason for twelve or more persons to assemble for the purpose of killing or taking any of the Privy Council, forcibly to alter laws, or failing to disband when so ordered by any official.

---

[1] Jordan, *Edward VI*, 494 ff.

[2] *C.J.*, I, 12–13; *L.J.*, I, 357 ff.; *The statutes of the realm*, ed. by A. Luders, T. E. Tomlins, *et al.* (11 vols., L., 1810–1828), IV, i, 104–108.

Similarly, it was to be held a felony when any such group assembled for the purpose of breaking any enclosure, enforcing a right of way or right of common over an enclosure, or refused to disband when ordered. Persons calling or inciting such assemblies by whatever means were subject to the pains of felony, while any assembly of forty or more persons which 'in forcible manner, unlawfully and of their own authority' attempted such actions should be deemed guilty of high treason, as should their wives and servants if they lent voluntary aid. It should also be noted that no limit of time was set for bringing charges under the act and that the customary evidence of two witnesses was not required under its language.

This savage measure clearly reflected the terror of the dominant classes of England in the black and frightened days of the summer of 1549. The act itself reveals this fact, for it recited that the recent uproars had their origin when a small number of malcontents assembled and were quickly joined by 'a great number of evil disposed persons' who 'did come and join themselves to the said small number, whereby the same evil disposed persons took upon them such boldness that they could not be reduced to obedience without much blood shedding'.[1] Hence such assemblies must be instantly repressed, and authority was vested in any officer holding the King's commission to order their dispersal, and if need be to gather and employ such force as might be required. Any man, of whatever rank, refusing to serve the King for such purposes, was to forfeit all his lands and copyholds for his lifetime.

We know little about the debate on this Draconian measure, but the complex and protracted proceedings, especially in the Commons, suggest that it was strongly opposed at least in certain of its provisions and that some amendments had to be accepted. Having been introduced in the Lords on November 9th, and at one stage referred to the Attorney General, the measure was ordered engrossed on November 16th on its fourth reading. The House of Commons heard the measure first on November 19th and then on the 29th committed it to the Lord Chancellor, from whom it returned as a new bill, first read on December 5th. At least eight readings were given the bill in the next fortnight, the debate on December 20th being the only business admitted for the day. It finally passed an evidently deeply divided House of Commons on December 23rd and then in its new form was approved by the Lords on December 28th.[2]

---

[1] *Statutes of the realm*, IV, i, 106.

[2] *C.J.*, I, 12–13; *L.J.*, I, 372–373. For other comments on the measure, *vide* Pollard, *Somerset*, 272–274; Burnet, *Reformation*, II, 247.

The deep-seated fear in the governing classes was also revealed in a measure prohibiting 'fond and fantastical prophecy', which may be regarded as bringing to an end the almost complete freedom of expression and publication which Somerset had not only permitted but encouraged. This statute, passed on December 26th, held that the recent rebellion had been stirred by the publication of fantastical prophecies concerning the King and other honourable persons to the disquiet of the realm. Hence any person setting forth such prophecies in writing, printing, singing, or speaking, or who sought to raise rebellions or dissensions and disturbances should be imprisoned for a year and fined for the first offence, for life with forfeiture of all goods for the second.[1]

Symbolically and politically, the most important of the measures repudiating Somerset's social and economic policy was the repeal of the famous sheep and cloth tax (2 Edward VI, c. 36), which sought to translate into law the reform programme of the Commonwealth Party and which may well be regarded as the first serious effort of a government in England to employ the taxing power deliberately for the attainment of social ends.[2] Early in the session a bill protesting the law was presented by certain Devonshire clothiers, probably with governmental consent, if not suggestion, for on the next day (November 18th) it was ordered that a joint deputation from the Commons and Lords should wait on the Council to know the King's pleasure in the matter. It was reported back on the 20th, and again in more formal fashion on the 30th, that the King (Privy Council) had accepted the petition for relief and had given licence to Parliament to treat of the matter. Accordingly, a measure was introduced repealing this section of the subsidy act in question and stating that the tax on sheep 'is to your poor commons, having but few sheep in number, a great charge and also . . . cumbrous for all your commissioners and officers'. The measure, which restored the income lost to the crown by a subsidy of one shilling in the pound, passed the Commons on January 14, 1550, and the Lords, where no opposition was recorded, two days later.[3] Thus, early and easily, the measure which had been designed to be the cornerstone of Somerset's dedicated and persistent effort to restore the balance between arable and pasture farming was swept away.

The measures thus far discussed, though they possessed significant social and economic consequences, were primarily political in

---

[1] 3 and 4 Edward VI, c. 15; *Statutes of the realm*, IV, i, 114-115.
[2] Jordan, *Edward VI*, 434-435, for a full discussion of the measure.
[3] *C.J.*, I, 11-14; *L.J.*, I, 381; *Statutes of the realm*, IV, i, 122-124.

their nature and intent. They were designed to settle political and administrative power securely once more in the dominant classes of England and to re-establish that union of purpose between the crown and the gentry and merchant aristocracy which had for more than two generations afforded to the English society such remarkable order and stability. It was precisely this stability which Somerset had grievously upset by his social and economic policy which sought to widen the area of opportunity and participation in English life. But this session of Parliament was likewise concerned with more specifically social and economic legislation, with political overtones, which would restore the solid elements of power to the landowning classes in which responsibility for the maintenance of order had once more been securely vested.

The most important, and shocking, of these statutes was 3 and 4 Edward VI, c. 3, concerning the improvements of commons and waste grounds, designed to prevent such episodes as one that occurred while the bill was being drafted when five inhabitants of Hertfordshire were bound over and compelled to restore enclosure palings which they had taken down at the lodge at Tittenhanger Park.[1] The statute had the effect of rescinding the whole body of anti-enclosure legislation set on the statute books by both Henry VII and Henry VIII, and of reviving the statutes of Merton (20 Henry III, c. 4) and of Westminster (13 Edward I, c. 46). It accordingly vested arbitrary powers in lords of the manor with respect to the enclosure of commons and wastes, so long as a sufficient common was left for the tenants. It did provide for triple damages when a successful action of novel disseisen was brought against an enclosure, but left little basis for such an action so long as an area of three acres was left around houses already standing in wastes and commons. The statute, which clearly suggested that the lord had powers of enclosure of waste and commons even when he possessed no clear or demonstrable title, was passed in short order in the Lords, though its progress was slow in the Commons where there were at least five readings of the bill.[2] Savagely reactionary in its effect, too, was 3 and 4 Edward VI, c. 17, which revived for a term of three years two statutes of the late Henrician period which made it a felony to hunt unlawfully in any park, chase, or enclosed ground. The act recited that these laws had been repealed by the great omnibus statute of 1 Edward VI which had rescinded all new felonies created after 1 Henry VIII.

---

[1] *A.P.C.*, II, 361: Nov. 24, 1549.

[2] *C.J.*, I, 13–14; *Statutes of the realm*, IV, i, 102–103; for Pollard's comments, *vide* *Somerset*, 271–272.

The consequence, it was argued, had been 'outrageous disorders' so great 'as in some of your grace's parks were slain 500 deer in a day within very few miles of . . . London', with an attendant breeding of boldness and disorder.[1]

There were also important, though in no sense reactionary, statutes passed in this session for amending the economy. A carefully drawn measure sought at least to ensure the quality of English cloth, ordering an elaborate system of inspections and penalties in an effort to restore the reputation of this great export commodity in a rapidly weakening market.[2] Another measure was aimed at regulating the sale and quality of butter and cheese, endeavouring to curtail speculation and the profits of middlemen by the provision that no one buying these commodities should sell them again save in 'open shop, fair or market, and not in gross'. For reasons which one wishes he knew, the bill was opposed in the Lords, though it passed on January 18 despite the negative votes of four of the lay peers, Paget being one, and five of the bishops.[3] Social rather than economic considerations probably prevailed in still another statute, aimed at 'many young folks and servants of sundry occupations' who on the completion of their apprenticeship wandered from place to place as journeymen with no settled employment. The act forbade the employment of such persons for periods of less than three months and specified that employers having three apprentices should employ at least one journeyman, those with more an equal number of journeymen and apprentices.[4]

This measure had as its principal concern, of course, the restraints on freedom of movement and the control of vagabondage, which the whole society feared and which was more specifically set out in 3 and 4 Edward VI, c. 16. This wholly commendable act repealed the harsh statute enacted in the first session of this Parliament (1 Edward VI, c. 3) in 1547, which under certain conditions had declared vagabonds and beggars to be slaves in order to force them to employment,[5] and which dealt harshly and blindly with the whole problem of poverty. The new statute confessed that this measure had been unenforceable and accordingly restored 22 Henry VIII, c. 12,

---

[1] *Statutes of the realm*, IV, i, 117–118; for Somerset's repeal of the whole body of tyrannous Henrician legislation, *vide* Jordan, *Edward VI*, 172–175.

[2] 3 and 4 Edward VI, c. 2; *C.J.*, I, 13–14; *Statutes of the Realm*, IV, i, 101–102.

[3] 3 and 4 Edward VI, c. 21; *C.J.*, I, 13–14; *Statutes of the realm*, IV, i, 120.

[4] 3 and 4 Edward VI, c. 22; *Statutes of the realm*, IV, i, 121–122.

[5] *Vide* Jordan, *Edward VI*, 177–178, for a full discussion of this law, the only one of Somerset's measures which, even in contemporary terms, must be described as brutally reactionary.

the last legislative attempt to deal seriously with the problems of poverty and vagabondage. But it went well beyond the earlier statute by adding administrative provisions which to a limited degree reflected the rapidly maturing interest of the merchant aristocracy and the private conscience generally in the age-old problem of the poor. The new statute defined as vagabondage the 'idle loitering of common labourers of husbandry' who refused to work 'for such reasonable wages as is most commonly given in the parts where such persons shall dwell'. Such persons were forbidden to wander and, if incorrigible, were to be punished, though by measures well short of slavery. At the same time all maimed, aged, and impotent persons were to be cared for in the parish of their birth by private benefactions and alms, and were not to be permitted to beg. Impotent persons who could work were to be provided labour as appointed by their parish or in the service of private persons who would give them employment sufficient for their meat and drink. Monthly surveys were ordered in London and other urban communities, and impotent persons harbouring in such places were to be returned to their native parishes for care there. It was further enacted that the children of such poor persons might be taken from their parents and after a hearing before the justices of the peace put into useful service until the age of fifteen years for girls and eighteen for boys.[1]

It may be observed that this carefully articulated statute was to stand, with only minor amendments, until the passage of the important Elizabethan act of 1571. The measure was quickly adopted by Parliament, having been approved by the Commons less than two weeks after it had come down from the Lords. It possessed the great merit of distinguishing between the incorrigible vagrants and the impotent and unemployed poor, as well as establishing firmly the direct responsibility for the maintenance of the worthy poor and the derelict as a charge on the charity of their home parish. What it did not do was to invoke the power of taxation to give sanction and full effect to the intention of the law. Private charity, as we shall see, was to be generously stimulated by this statute and by the sense of national responsibility which it expressed, but it was not until the great Elizabethan statute was passed at the very close of her reign that the problem of poverty and impotence was met with sufficient resources.[2]

---

[1] 3 and 4 Edward VI, c. 16; *Statutes of the realm*, IV, i, 115–117.

[2] *Vide* Jordan, W. K., *Philanthropy in England, 1480–1660, etc.* (L.,1959), 86–98, and *post*, for a fuller discussion of these matters.

This, it may be suggested, completes the rather short list of important enactments passed by the third session of this Parliament, save for three measures concerned with religious matters which may more suitably be discussed later.[1] The whole content of these measures, the statute on vagabondage and the poor aside, may be regarded as reactionary and as deliberately designed to repudiate and destroy Somerset's bold social and economic policies which had as their intention the lifting up of poorer classes of men to a greater share in the resources of the English society. These measures restored England to the gentry and to the more recent and thrusting nobility.

But the stark recital of the statutes enacted by this session of Parliament—there were twenty-four in all—seriously oversimplifies the structure of parliamentary interests and sentiments. The government, and the frightened members who so solidly represented the gentry, did possess the strength to write into law the reactionary statutes which we have considered in some detail. But, as we have seen, there was at the same time a strong reforming group left in the House of Commons, probably admirers of the Lord Protector, who had on occasion forced amendments on particularly savage bills and who seem to have defeated others favoured by the Privy Council. Nor was that by any means all. The strength of this reforming sentiment is more clearly revealed when one considers the titles— few of the drafts survive—of the fifty-two bills introduced in the session, almost entirely in the House of Commons, which failed of passage. Of this number, about half (25) dealt with social and economic matters, six propounded religious changes, and seven were concerned with borough privileges and benefits. Of these proposed enactments, introduced privately and with no support from the government, eleven enjoyed no more than a first reading, nineteen had a second reading (and were debated), seventeen survived for a third reading and five for a fourth. In all, thirteen of these bills were actually passed by the House of Commons but failed, for a variety of reasons, to become law. It may be added that one certainly reactionary bill, 'for gifts of rebel goods and lands, made by the Lieutenants', was defeated in the Commons on its third reading, while a related measure introduced some days later (January 24th) disappeared after its second reading. Another brutally reactionary bill making it a felony to break dikes in the Isle of Ely was either lost on its second reading (November 13, 1549) or vanished into committee. Still other instances could be cited of measures of a reforming nature which were at least strongly, though unsuccessfully, urged by members

[1] 3 and 4 Edward VI, cs. 10, 11, 12.

still imbued with the general social philosophy of the Commonwealth Party. None the less, the structure of Warwick's power stood impressively complete in the third session of Parliament, because his personal convictions and philosophy of government coincided with the sentiments of men who had been badly frightened by the internecine disturbances of 1549 and the dangerous irresolution of the former Lord Protector in suppressing them. Reaction there undoubtedly was, and it was for a season to run strongly, but there was no cession to the Earl of Warwick of any of the irreparable power of a tyranny.

III

GOVERNMENT BY FEARFUL MEN
(1550–1552)

1. RULE WITHOUT PARLIAMENT (FEBRUARY, 1550–JANUARY, 1552)

The relatively minor difficulties which the government experienced in the third session of Parliament may account in part for Warwick's extreme reluctance to call it into session again. Moreover, in that session there was undoubtedly cautious but staunchly held sentiment which would have welcomed the restoration of the Lord Protector, and this disposition was steadily to increase in the months to come. Even more persuasive, we may be sure, was Warwick's intention of gaining security of position with the King and his colleagues on the Council before exposing his informally vested aggregate of power to parliamentary scrutiny and possible debate. It should also be noted that Warwick was in every meeting awkward in his relations with the House of Commons, nervous and ill at ease when Parliament was in session, and petulantly uncomfortable until the members were packed off home. Hence it was that for almost two years he governed without convening Parliament, even during an interval when English foreign relations were in a state of paralysis and when his government stood in grave need of parliamentary subsidies. The stubborn and insensitive nature of the man is suggested by the reminder that he did not convene the fourth session of Edward's first Parliament until the day after Somerset had been put to death. In this amazing action there is blended in uncertain proportion the brutal arrogance of the man and a desperate insecurity.

Hence there were successive and rather awkward prorogations of Parliament, betraying the government's uncertainty and inducing a general sense of restlessness in the realm at large. The first prorogation was announced in early April, 1550, the new session being set for October of that year.[1] Then on August 14, 1550, about six months

---

[1] Edward VI, *Chronicle*, 23 (under date Apr. 2).

after the adjournment of the last session, the Council informed the Lord Chancellor that Parliament should be further prorogued until January 20, 1551, 'for divers good and urgent considerations'.[1] Rich replied at once, protesting the decision and stating his view that it was 'not convenient' to order a prorogation. But the Council stood firm:[2] the date for the next meeting was set for February 20, 1551[3]. However, on or about October 5, 1550, another prorogation was ordered.[4] Again, successive further prorogations were made, with the result that the fourth session was not summoned, as we have observed, until January, 1552.

This vacillation, with its scarcely concealed suggestion of weakness and apprehension in the ruling junta, excited foreign as well as English comment. Thus Daniel Barbaro, in his formal report on his tenure of eighteen months as Venetian envoy in England, commented that Parliament performed most useful functions in England, since they were 'calculated to allay all tumult and sedition; they are useful and secure, as measures adopted by popular opinion and consent . . . all members of Parliament having full liberty'. It was the recognized capacity of the Council to 'mediate between the people and the Sovereign' and to refer all important matters to Parliament. But at the present time (May, 1551), he shrewdly noted, questions which should be determined in Parliament were in fact settled by the Privy Council. Among such matters was the cession of Boulogne, 'which the country felt bitterly', not to mention the petitions and complaints of the people which have not been submitted to Parliament. The government continued to summon parliaments which it then postponed, and when sessions had been called they were adjourned directly the government's wants were supplied.[5] So too, the imperial ambassador, writing at about the same date, commented on the restlessness and apprehension in the realm because a promised session of Parliament had once more been postponed.[6]

The nervous concern of the government with Parliament was also suggested by a number of rather crude and not very successful efforts to gain a more compliant and sympathetic body. This concern could, indeed, even express itself in occasional interventions in important local choices for governmental posts. Thus in November,

[1] A.P.C., III, 104.
[2] Ibid. 107: Aug. 17, 1550.
[3] Edward VI, Chronicle, 43.
[4] Ibid. 48.
[5] Cal. S.P. Ven., V, 343.
[6] Cal. S.P. Span., X, 226: Mar. 1, 1551; from Jean Scheyfve, who had replaced Van der Delft in May 1550.

1550, when Thomas Hayes (a goldsmith), the chamberlain of London, died, the mayor and aldermen, as custom and law required, promptly nominated two men—Henry Fisher, a grocer, and John Sturgeon, a haberdasher—between whom the Common Council should choose. The Privy Council in the King's name indicated its strong preference for Fisher, this being 'the first suit that the King's Majesty had required of them'. But when the Common Council met, Sturgeon, then in Flanders, was none the less chosen by a 'trying of hands quietly, without noise or disturbance', to the great embarrassment of the Privy Council.[1]

Nor was the government much more successful in its efforts to dictate the choice of nominees to fill vacancies in the ranks of Parliament, while the apprehensions raised by its action in this respect were much more serious than those created by its abortive intervention in London. Parliament had, of course, been elected in 1547, with the inevitable result that there were numerous vacancies when it was at last convened in early 1552. Accordingly, in late October (1551) the Council required the Chancellor to determine how many members had died since the last elections in order 'that grave and wise men might be elected to supply their places, for the avoiding of the disorder that hath been noted in sundry young men and others of small judgement'.[2] One of the vacancies was in Reading, to which John Seymour, Somerset's eldest son by his first marriage, was elected, to the fury of the Council which in peremptory fashion disallowed the choice and ordered that someone else be returned. In another instance of direct intervention, the sheriff of Hertfordshire was instructed to elect a successor to Sir Henry Parker, a knight of the shire, and so 'to use the matter . . . as Mr Sadlier may be elected, for that he seems most fittest of any other person there abouts'. Death had also created a vacancy of a knight of the shire in Surrey, the sheriff there being informed that Sir Thomas Saunders was to be chosen.[3] Warwick likewise took the precaution of making certain that particularly friendly peers should attend the forthcoming session of Parliament, even when it meant withdrawing men from somewhat sensitive military commands.[4] One should not stress too much the significance of such overt interventions—Henry VIII had on occasion done so, and the practice was not unknown to Elizabeth. But these do have a slightly different quality and pattern; they exhibit clearly the anxiety of an insecure ruling faction towards a

[1] Wriothesley, *Chronicle*, II, 44.
[2] *A.P.C.*, III, 400.   [3] *Ibid.* 457, 459, 470–471.
[4] S.P. Dom., Edw. VI, XIV, 1, arranging for the attendance of Lord Conyers.

meeting of Parliament which in January, 1552 could no longer be postponed and for which interventions more sinister in appearance than in reality were made.

2. THE PACKING OF THE PRIVY COUNCIL AND LESSER OFFICES OF STATE

Warwick's somewhat erratic moves to secure his own predominance in the Council were delayed for some months after his accession to power. Thus, Somerset was first released from the Tower and then shortly re-admitted to the Council, though shorn of his power as Lord Protector.[1] It is important to observe that, until July, 1550, Warwick took no part in the business of the Council and was absent from London, being dangerously ill of an uncertainly described sickness.[2] In this interval Somerset's influence was rising rapidly, and the more cautious members of the Council were especially disturbed by his leniency towards Gardiner and by his insistence that the great but radical preacher, Hooper, be appointed to the see of Gloucester, against the decided opposition of most of the bishops.[3] They were generally apprehensive; an admirer of Somerset as personally devoted as Cecil was even greatly alarmed.[4] Somerset's influence was, however, almost wholly eclipsed on the return of Warwick to the Council board in early July, and a symbolic reversal of Somerset's policy of moderation was signalled by the articles laid before Gardiner on July 8, which the Council knew full well he would not sign.

Even before the onset of Warwick's illness, it was evident to the imperial envoy that he was 'absolute master here, and the Lords of the Council are under his orders'. Van der Delft related to the Emperor that Councillors attended daily at the Earl's house to learn his pleasure and that no action was taken save as he commanded. Yet, 'he hardly ever appears in public, but by shamming illness . . . attempts to hide his pride and ambition'. The observant Fleming also related the gossip that Warwick was scheming to bring Somerset within the orbit of his power and that much of the prize money gained from privateering now went straight into Warwick's coffers.[5]

---

[1] *Vide post*, 72 ff.

[2] Robinson, *Original letters*, I, 89: Hooper to Bullinger; *et vide* minutes of the Privy Council for the interval.   [3] Robinson, *Original letters*, II, 410.

[4] Read, Conyers, *Mr. Secretary Cecil and Queen Elizabeth* (L., 1955), 62–63.

[5] *Cal. S.P. Span.*, X, 43–44. A little later (Mar. 17, 1550) the ambassador wrote that Warwick would see no one on the plea of his illness, which Van der Delft still thought feigned (*ibid.* 47–48).

The solid element of power still required was gained when in April, 1550 Warwick was appointed 'general Warden of the North', on the ground that the dominance of France in Scottish affairs made it necessary to name 'a notable ruler' who would exercise a vigorous command.[1] This action lodged in Warwick a dangerous and a sufficient aggregate of private power which all men sensed he would ruthlessly and effectively employ if his authority were brooked. Warwick was now in truth an over-mighty subject and rumours spread which darken any analysis of his intentions. Even as mild and sensible a divine as Bucer, alarmed by Warwick's increasingly radical and irresponsible religious policy, feared that the Reformation was proceeding too rapidly and hinted in a courageous appeal to the King that he doubted even the sincerity of Warwick's policy. The greatest of care, he wrote, must be exercised that 'those are not to be listened to who will that the religion of Christ be thrust upon men only by proclamations and laws', and to view the Church of Christ as a store of wealth which they may seize.[2]

Warwick's persistent and unconcealed effort to aggrandize his position may also be observed in the appointments and replacements made in the Privy Council in which the totality of sovereign power was now vested. Save for the removal of Wriothesley at the outset of the reign—and that for due cause[3]—Somerset had made very few changes in the roster of the original Council, although he possessed the specific power to do so. The Protector had sought at no time, indeed, to build a faction either in the Council or among officials of the second rank and, in part for this reason, was powerless when conspiracy closed around him. But Warwick from the outset was extremely careful in his appointments to the Council, to which he made twelve in the course of two years, of which surely eight, and possibly nine, were his personal followers or adherents.[4] By the time of Somerset's final fall in the autumn of 1551 the Council was

[1] *A.P.C.*, II, 6: Apr. 20, 1550; Edward VI, *Chronicle*, 24. At the same time Warwick's close ally Herbert was made 'President of Wales' with a stipend of 500 marks p.a. *Vide post*, 62, for the particulars.

[2] Bucer, Martin, *De regno Christi* (Basel, 1557), ii (cap. v), 60–61.

[3] *Vide* Jordan, *Edward VI*, 69–72.

[4] Those approved were: the Duke of Suffolk, the Earls of Westmorland and Huntingdon, Viscount Hereford, Lord Clinton, Bishop Goodrich, Lord Cobham, Sir John Mason (who was promptly packed off to France as a protégé of Paget), Sir Philip Hoby, Sir Robert Bowes, Sir Richard Cotton, and Sir John Gates (Edward VI, *Chronicle*, 25; *A.P.C.*, III, 36: May 23, 1550; *ibid.* 363: Sept. 25, 1551; Gammon, Samuel Rhea, *Master of practises. A life of William, Lord Paget of Beaudesert, etc.* (unpubl. Ph.D. thesis, Princeton University, 1953), 266). Lord Derby, who was being courted by Warwick, was also on Aug. 9, 1551, sworn of the Council on the odd condition that he attend only when summoned (*A.P.C.*, IV, 328).

fairly fashioned to fit with John Dudley's concept of power, with his increasingly arrogant demands for loyalty, with his own apprehensions, and possibly his aspirations for the future.[1]

Among those able to extricate themselves from the wreckage of Somerset's fall in late 1549 was Sir William Cecil, who was in fact to become one of the most trusted of Warwick's advisers and to whom was extended more of confidence than was returned by this always cautious civil servant. Cecil's relations with the Princess Elizabeth had been close since 1548, and in July 1550 he was appointed agent for the administration of her estates. Then in early September, 1550 he was sworn of the Council as a principal secretary, sharing this important administrative post with Sir William Petre, also an administrator of uncommon competence.[2] The bulk of the business of state began to flow through Cecil, particularly since Petre was often absent on diplomatic assignments.[3] But the extraordinary ability and dedication of the man, his close friendship with numerous officials and diplomatists in the service of the state, and his clarity of vision all began to tell, with the consequence that before many months he was lending important counsel in foreign affairs and had established himself deeply in Warwick's confidence. Thus in November, 1551, in what was probably a private memorandum, he was reflecting on the perils to which England lay exposed if the Emperor should raise a religious war against her while seeking simultaneously to crush the Reformation on the

---

[1] The full list of membership of the Privy Council as of Nov. 2, 1551, follows, and may be compared with the roster as it stood on Mar. 21, 1547, when Somerset was securely seated in power (*vide* Jordan, *Edward VI*, 80):

Archbishop Cranmer	Sir Thomas Cheyney
Lord Rich (Lord Chancellor)	Sir Anthony Wingfield
Marquis of Winchester (Paulet)	Sir John Gates
Duke of Northumberland (Dudley)	Sir Ralph Sadler
Earl of Bedford (Russell)	Sir William Petre
Duke of Suffolk (Grey)	Sir William Cecil
Lord Darcy	Sir Nicholas Wotton
Earl of Shrewsbury (Talbot)	Sir John Gage
Earl of Westmorland (Neville)	Sir John Mason
Earl of Huntingdon (Hastings)	Sir Philip Hoby
Earl of Pembroke (Herbert)	Sir Robert Bowes
Viscount Hereford (Devereux)	Sir Edward North
Lord Clinton	Sir John Baker
Marquis of Northampton (Parr)	Sir Edward Montague
Thomas Goodrich (Bishop of Ely)	Sir Thomas Bromley
Lord Cobham	Sir Richard Cotton
Lord Paget	

[2] *A.P.C.*, III, 118: Sept. 5, 1550; Lansdowne MS. 2, #42: William Turner to Cecil, Oct. 24, 1550, congratulating him on his escape from danger at court.

[3] Read, *Cecil*, 65.

Continent. Cecil was a stalwart Protestant, but in his view the majority of his nation were still Catholic in sympathy. The government was, so he argued, now fully able to control and guide its people, but only if peace were maintained.[1]

But if Cecil had been able quickly to establish himself in the favour and confidence of the Earl of Warwick, Paget most decidedly had not. Perhaps the ablest member of the Council, certainly the most skilful of English diplomatists in his generation, frank and brutally honest in his counsel, Paget remained a friend to Somerset and in early 1551 outraged Warwick by his opposition to some unstated matter of Council business. Warwick's ominous and angry reaction suggests that as early as January, 1551 a bitter feud divided the Council, possibly respecting the draft of the proposed new commission establishing more securely the legal basis of its authority.[2] Warwick demanded that Paget be vigilant and circumspect 'in the matter which you have in hand', suggesting as well that 'the 1d. chancellor [Rich] and the 1d. treasurer [Winchester]' had stood with Paget in opposition, as well as 'the 1d. Privy Seal [Bedford]'. He would wish 'as well for the King's surety as for the truth of the matter, that men should not be against the perfect reforming of it, especially as it hath been thus far debated, which I reckon a happy thing'.[3] Try as the Earl did to mould the Privy Council to his imperious will, all was evidently not quiet in Zion.

Warwick preferred rough and imprudent soldiers or grasping and conscienceless administrators as his most trusted friends, several of whom he took into his service and plottings. One of them, Sir John Gates (1504?–1553), he brought into the Privy Council. Gates, the scion of an Essex gentle family, had seen military and minor administrative service under Henry VIII, and had profited modestly from such monastic lands as he had been able to purchase. He was created a Knight of the Bath soon after Edward's accession and was respected at least for the skill he displayed in the occasional jousts held at court. In June, 1550 he was made sheriff of Essex, being sent down a few weeks later with thirty men in his train to see that Ridley's injunctions were being enforced and to take steps to prevent the Princess Mary from fleeing the realm.[4] Already much in Warwick's favour, he was in April, 1551 made Vice-Chamberlain and

---

[1] Read, *Cecil*, 68–69, citing S.P. For., Suppl., 70, Bundle 147.   [2] *Vide ante*. 33–34.

[3] Cotton MSS., Titus, B, ii, 28, f. 57 [renumbered f. 38]: Jan. 22, 1551. The difficulty in analysing this document proceeds in part from the fact that Warwick was not a truly literate man. Many of his memoranda, especially when he was angry, are very murky in language.

[4] Edward VI, *Chronicle*, 37.

entrusted with the sensitive post of Captain of the Guard,[1] while a year later he was given twenty-five men-at-arms in his personal retinue.[2] At about the same date he was made a commissioner for the sale of chantry lands and on July 4, 1552, was created Chancellor of the Duchy of Lancaster with an annuity of £200 p.a. for life from the Duchy lands.[3] Gates was known as Warwick's creature in the Council. He was feared because of his ruthlessness and his untruthfulness, and his wealth fattened as Dudley repaid his sheep-like loyalty from the resources of the crown. He had been given lands valued at £50 15s 11d p.a. net for his services to Henry VIII, which Warwick handsomely increased with lands, mostly in Hampshire, to the value of £115 5s 11d p.a. net in September, 1551.[4] From the estate of the attainted Sir Ralph Vane, who died with Somerset, he gained property in Westminster worth £13 6s 8d p.a. in 1552,[5] and on the surrender of his annuity as Chancellor of the Duchy of Lancaster he was given lands, mostly from Somerset's estate, rounding out his property in Hampshire and possessing an annual worth of £150 p.a.[6] In all, therefore, for faithful services rendered to his master, with whom he was to suffer death for treason, Gates was enriched with crown lands with a capital value of almost £6600.[7]

Another of Warwick's confidants and henchmen was Sir Thomas Palmer, also of gentle birth. A professional soldier of some ability, much given to gaming, and intrepid in his personal courage, Palmer served Henry VIII for years in various junior military capacities. Utterly reckless in the field and incompetent for independent command, he had been severely castigated by Somerset for his imprudence in the war with Scotland,[8] for which he should have been court-martialled or cashiered. From this date forward this proud and foolish man conceived an implacable hatred for Somerset whom he betrayed to Warwick on October 7, 1550, by the most suspicious revelations of the Duke's alleged treasons.[9] Palmer was himself pardoned of all treasons, technically incurred by his own

---

[1] Edward VI, *Chronicle*, 58.   [2] *Ibid*. 119.

[3] *Ibid*. 134.

[4] S.P. Dom., Edw. VI, XIX, f. 37; *Cal. Pat. Rolls, Edw. VI*, IV, 154.

[5] S.P. Dom., Edw. VI, XIX, f. 44; *Cal. Pat. Rolls, Edw. VI*, IV, 325.

[6] S.P. Dom., Edw. VI, XIX, f. 50; *Cal. Pat. Rolls, Edw. VI*, V, 143-144; S.P. Dom., Edw. VI, XVIII, 23.

[7] Strype reckoned that the whole capital worth of Gates's estate was upwards of £12,820 (Strype, John, *Ecclesiastical memorials . . . of the Church of England, etc.* (3 vols. in 6 pts., Oxford, 1822), II, i, 479-482).

[8] *Vide* Jordan, *Edward VI*, 285-286.

[9] *Vide post*, 83 ff.

declaration, and during the remainder of the reign profited in office and lands from the generosity of Northumberland who owed him much.[1] Palmer died bravely with Northumberland, making a defiant speech in which he declared himself a sincere Protestant. None the less, few more sinister and despicable figures may be found in Tudor history. But such men as Gates and Palmer were precisely of the character which Northumberland required for his purposes.

The symbol of Warwick's accession to the seats of power, and the token of his dominance in the ruling junta, came when on October 11, 1551, he was elevated to a duchy in the peerage, while at the same ceremony others whom he wished either to bind to himself or to placate were likewise honoured. Among those attending the ceremonies was the Duke of Somerset who, after the letters patent had been read, stood on one side of the King with the newly invested Duke of Northumberland on the other. The formal reason advanced for this elevation was that Grey (Dorset) had indicated to the King his inability to serve as 'General Warden of the Marches towards Scotland', and the King, having in view the appointment of Warwick in his stead, had determined, 'the noble houses of this his realm being of late much decayed, to erect other in their stead by rewarding such as have already well served, and may be thereby the rather encouraged to continue the same', to advance first the Earl of Warwick and then the others that day to be dignified.[2] Accordingly, Warwick was created Duke of Northumberland, the Marquis of Dorset was made Duke of Suffolk, the Earl of Wiltshire became Marquis of Winchester, and Sir William Herbert was created Earl of Pembroke. At the same time lesser honours were conferred on William Cecil, John Cheke, Henry Sidney, and Henry Neville, who were dubbed knights.[3] After the elaborate ceremony, the newly elevated or created peers sat at dinner together with five of their fellows, 'first on the bench . . . the Duke of Suffolk, next to him the Duke of Northumberland . . . and then on the other side a little lower sat the Duke of Somerset' and the others.[4] The bizarre and somewhat sinister nature of the occasion, and the conspiratorial genius of the now Duke of Northumberland are attested by the fact that five days later Somerset was arrested on charges of treason, preparations for this action having been begun well before the occasion of this strange dinner. Now greatly strengthened in prestige

[1] For land grants to Palmer, *vide* S.P. Dom., Edw. VI, XIX, ff. 3, 44, 56; *Cal. Pat. Rolls, Edw. VI*, I, 161; *ibid.* IV, 320; *ibid.* V, 81–82.

[2] Nichols, *Remains*, II, 350–351; *A.P.C.*, III, 379–380: Oct. 4, 1551.

[3] S.P. Dom., Edw. VI, XIII, 56–57; Machyn, *Diary*, 10; Edward VI, *Chronicle*, 86.

[4] Nichols, *Remains*, II, 352.

and in the King's favour, with political debts paid and new obligations created, Dudley was more fully armed for the seizure of the
complete personal power which his dark and possibly twisted mind
required.

3. THE FALL OF LORD RICH (DECEMBER, 1551)

One member of the Privy Council, as constituted at the beginning
of the reign, who seemed secure in posts of high authority and trust
was Lord Rich, who since 1548 had been Lord Chancellor. His
services to the state stretched back to 1533 when he had been
appointed Solicitor-General, and he had at all times and on all
questions shown himself compliant in policy and indifferent in
matters of faith. In the autumn crisis of 1549 he had returned from
Essex, where he had been most effective in repressing quite
serious disorders, to join Warwick and the London Lords in the
conspiracy being formed against the Lord Protector. It was Rich
who was chosen to win the support of the London officials, while his
support of Dudley was of great moment because he used the Great
Seal to lend validity and impressive sanction to all the actions taken
by the London Lords.[1] He was likewise entrusted by the Council,
after the Protector's deprivation, with advancing rapidly and harshly
the proceedings against Gardiner and Bonner, and he was probably
responsible for framing various communications to the Princess
Mary which bore heavily on her conscience.

But there were limits on Rich's compliance, for he was a good
lawyer, a stickler for form, and possibly not a little aghast at the informal and almost contemptuous fashion in which Warwick was
employing the Privy Council for the attainment of his purposes. On
September 30, 1551, the Council, with only eight members present
and signing the order, drafted a commission for the examination of
the Bishop of Worcester (Heath) and the Bishop of Chichester (Day),
both of whom had been moderately but stubbornly conservative in
their religious views. Though there had been no quorum at the
Council meeting, Rich was instructed to seal the commission and
forward it to those named as commissioners, with a letter from
Warwick and the Council giving instruction on certain points.[2]
Rich did seal the commission, but sent it back to the Council as
defective until sufficient additional signatures had been gained to

---

[1] Jordan, *Edward VI*, 446, 461, 511; Coyle, Mary, *Sir Richard Rich Lord Rich, 1496–1567* (unpublished Harvard Ph.D. thesis, 1965), *Pref.*
[2] Edward VI, *Chronicle*, 84: Oct. 1, 1551.

validate it. This action enraged Warwick and evoked from the King an angry personal letter to Rich: 'I wrote a letter that I marvelled that he would refuse to sign that bill or deliver that letter that I had willed anyone about me to write. Also that it should be a great impediment for me to send all my Council and I should seem to be in bondage. But by oversight it chanced and [not] thinking the more the better.' The King insisted that his express direction on the advice of his Council was fully sufficient in this and all similar circumstances.[1]

Almost at once the crisis precipitated by Somerset's second arrest broke, making it indispensable to Northumberland, as he now was, to possess effective control of the Great Seal. Rich, who was frequently ill in this period, had on October 26th declared his illness and with perfect propriety issued a commission to the Master of the Rolls, two common law judges, and three Masters in Chancery to hear causes in his absence.[2] None the less there was a steady flow of instructions from the Council directly to Rich ordering the sealing of important documents and patents, under procedures which the Council sought to justify in a carefully drawn instruction to him on November 10th. It was admitted that it had been the custom for bills and documents prepared for the King's signature to be endorsed by at least six of the Council, though this in fact implied an unintended deprivation of the royal authority. Hence it was now determined that the royal signet alone should constitute a sufficient authority, though it was agreed that a docket of such documents as were sent to the King for signature should be signed and kept by the Council as a witness that these bills had gone to him with their advice. There was added the somewhat snide rebuke to Rich that 'the same docket . . . remain as a warrant with them that shall prefer the said bills to His Majesty's signature'. Three days later the Council wrote directly to Rich outlining the new procedure and requiring, 'if any such thing signed by his Majesty alone do come to his Lordship's hands to pass the seal, that he stay not thereat, but cause it to be passed, as was accustomed in the King's Majesty's time late deceased'.[3]

The continuous pressure brought to bear on Rich in this matter became wholly explicable when a few days later (November 16th) he was ordered to make out the commission for the trial of the Duke of Somerset. Northumberland, always cautious, had taken elaborate

---

[1] Edward VI, *Chronicle*, 84–85: Oct. 2, 1551; S.P. Dom., Edw. VI, XIII, 55: Oct. 1, 1551, for the full text of the King's letter. The two entries cited have been crossed off in the ms. of the *Chronicle*, probably by a later hand.

[2] *Cal. Pat. Rolls, Edw. VI*, IV, 113–114.

[3] *A.P.C.*, III, 411, 416: Nov. 10 and 13, 1551.

pains to make certain that his will would be obeyed and, always harbouring resentments, maintained a steady harassment of Rich which on December 21st secured his resignation from the chancellorship, shortly to be vested in Bishop Goodrich of Ely. In the King's words, 'Richard Lord Rich, Chancellor of England . . . did deliver his seal to the Lord Treasurer, the Lord Great Master, and the Lord Chamberlain, sent to him for that purpose, during the time of his sickness, and chiefly of the Parliament'.[1]

4. THE OBSESSIVE FEAR OF PUBLIC DISORDERS (OCTOBER, 1549–OCTOBER, 1551)

Northumberland's tenure of power and the whole of his policy were enfeebled by a persistent fear of disorder. The great risings of the summer of 1549, towards whose bloody reduction he had personally contributed so much, had not only revealed to the governing classes of England a black hatred endemic in the landless rural population, but after Somerset's overthrow haunted the ruling junta which correctly sensed that the 'good Duke' had somehow captured the fervent loyalty of the poor and the unenfranchised of the realm and had fixed in the thinking of the rulers of England the fear that the commons would rise again in his name. Hence it was that Somerset had been speedily released from prison and brought back with an undefined status into the Privy Council, as part of Northumberland's effort to quiet the turbulence of the realm. As was predictable, this simply did not, could not, achieve its purpose as clusters of power began once more to gather around the former Protector, with the inevitable result that he was again and finally stricken down in late 1551 and brought to trial a few weeks later. We shall survey the evidence of unrest and turbulence during what should have been the period of greatest quiet, stretching from the time after the Protector's first fall when it was clear that his person would not be harmed to the moment when Northumberland, in a desperate decision, so greatly exercised and assaulted English opinion and sentiments by bringing him to what can only be described as a travesty of a trial.

---

[1] Edward VI, *Chronicle*, 101; *et vide ibid.* 102, 107, for the conclusion of the matter; Cotton MSS., Julius, B, ix, f. 2, for the appointment of Goodrich. It was to be almost a year before Rich attended a meeting of the Privy Council. An interesting document in HMC, *Salisbury MSS.*, I, 94, lists the names of several persons evidently discussed as possible successors to Rich, and including, besides Goodrich, Cecil and Petre. There are several marks against Goodrich's name. There is no substance to the apocryphal story (repeated by Burnet, *Reformation*, II, 310) that Rich placed himself in Northumberland's power when a note, addressed 'To the Duke', disclosing to Somerset the plot against him, was by mistake delivered to Northumberland.

During this interval of about two years it is evident that the Council expended more of its time and energy in ferreting out disorders and moving against the threat of treason than on any other subject. The feebleness of Northumberland's foreign policy is fully explained by the fact that he was so completely absorbed in a chronic domestic crisis that he possessed neither energy nor resources to concern himself seriously with foreign affairs. He sought to govern without convening Parliament for the sufficient reason that he dared not face the House of Commons nor arouse public expectation. Each spring this obsessive concern mounted into a kind of governmental hysteria as the dreaded summer months approached. As a professional soldier, who remembered well the great stirs in Devon and Norfolk, Northumberland was paralysed in policy, too, because he knew he could not trust the traditional county levies. The military power available to him lay only in private bands of horse which trusted counsellors and peers were licensed to maintain, and in such mercenary companies as his shattered exchequer could finance. Privy Councillors experienced in military affairs were sent into their home counties every spring; trusted peers were ordered to remain at home with lieutenancy commissions; and every effort was made to move quickly and with brutal force against any symptoms of public disorder. All Tudor governments were sensitive to and concerned with such unquiet, of course, but that which moved Northumberland was different in quality and in degree; he was weak in the true resources of political power and his every action was that of a frightened man who could and did do inexplicably desperate and violent things as a kind of reflex action springing from his own insecurity.

In this analysis of what can only be described as a dangerous and endemic turbulence we shall omit any reference to the northern counties and to Lancashire, Wales, and Cornwall—distant areas which even Henry VIII had never reduced to full discipline and obedience—and shall concentrate on the areas of the realm (mostly the Home Counties) which were settled, prosperous, and populous, the regions from which the crown had long drawn its true resources of power and from which it had come to expect fullness of support in occasions of emergency. It will also be recalled that the savagely reactionary measures passed only weeks after the Risings by the third session of Parliament in 1549, had reflected the frightened mood of the classes in which wealth and power were vested in Tudor England and had armed the government with arbitrary and condign power in dealing with unlawful assemblies, resistance to enclosures, hunting in parks, and spoken or written expressions of opposition to the ruling junta.[1] The weight of repression had been screwed down by statute quite as far as it could go.

In the last weeks of 1549 the government was at least reassured that a 'general plague of rebelling' in the sensitive areas near London, in Kent, Sussex, and Essex, had been brought under control,[2] though it was known that deep resentment remained amongst the commons. In London the freedom of the press which Somerset had permitted had been suspended, a tallow chandler and a yeoman being in serious difficulties with the Privy Council for printing books not formally authorized by the Privy Council, while Petre, Smith, and Cecil were appointed a committee to review works presented for examination.[3] This early attempt to control the expression of opinion, made while violent insurrections were still in progress, was expanded and tightened by proclamations issued in May, 1550 and in April, 1551. Severe measures were likewise announced in late October (1549) against 'lewd and seditious persons', favouring the now imprisoned Somerset, who 'spread abroad and ... in conventicles and assemblies where they think they may speak their pleasure' disseminated false reports that the present good laws in religion were to be repealed and the Roman mass restored.[4]

The early winter months of 1550 were relatively calm, but the continuing apprehension of the Council was evident. Lord Rich, who had been principally responsible for holding Essex quiet during the risings of the preceding summer, was exercised because the working habits and orderly lives of the commoners in his county were being disturbed by the spreading practice of arranging sermons on weekdays in evangelically inclined parishes. After consideration, the Council informed Bishop Ridley of its concern and asked him to halt the practice: 'because at this present it may increase the people's idleness, who of themselves are so much disposed to it, as all the ways that may be devised are little enough to draw them to work'.[5] But, clearly, it was fear of disorder which moved the Lord Chancellor and the government to act. Thus, a Suffolk man named Bell was hanged and quartered at Tyburn, having been convicted on charges of attempting to kindle a new rising in Suffolk and Essex.[6] Weight was

[1] Vide ante, 37–39.

[2] HMC, 12th rpt., App. IV: Rutland papers, I, 42.

[3] A.P.C., II, 312.

[4] Hughes, Paul L., and Larkin, James F., Tudor royal proclamations. Vol. I. The early Tudors (1485–1553) (New Haven and L., 1964), 484: Oct. 30, 1549.

[5] Strype, Memorials, II, i, 341–342.

[6] Stow, Annales, 604; Two London chronicles, 21.

given to the recently passed statute against unlawful assemblies by a proclamation dated February 1, 1550, charging all persons 'being assembled immediately to disperse themselves and peaceably to depart to their habitations or to their lawful business' under the severe pains of the statute.[1] There were other scattered instances of unrest with which the Council dealt promptly in these months when England still lay quiet after the exhaustion of the violent events of 1549. Sir Roger Townshend in Norfolk was instructed to pillory one William Whitered for seditious words and to cut off one of his ears, at the next market day in the nearest market town.[2] Instructions were issued and rewards offered to several Kentish constables for the arrest of Lawrence Atwood of East Malling for his seditious words, though the culprit seems to have escaped.[3] And as highly placed a dignitary as Sir John Gates was ordered to arrest 'certain light fellows' who had come from Suffolk into Essex, 'where they drink all day and look upon books in the night'. Gates was to seize these books and to send the suspected persons up to London for examination.[4] At about the same time the Council forwarded to the mayor of Bristol two seditious bills recently uttered there in manuscript, requiring him to seek to identify the author by handwriting comparisons and to examine the suspected persons if they could be found.[5]

As spring came the nervousness of the government increased, all reports of seditious stirrings being immediately and harshly handled. The apprehensions of the Council centred particularly on Kent, where there was undoubtedly serious malaise complicated by the presence of numerous radical sectaries. The Council believed it had uncovered a serious plot for a rising in the county early in May,[6] while two men, one of Gravesend and the other of Linton, were freed, after investigation, on condition they obey all laws and inform the justices of 'any manner of thing or things that shall be spoken or talked against any of them'.[7] Letters were also dispatched to justices of the peace throughout the realm, instructing them to constitute themselves into quarters and to lend full attention to the execution of all laws, but especially those relating to vagabondage, unlawful games, forestalling, and all instances of unlawful activity.[8] A proclamation was issued in early May ordering all persons in London

[1] *Statutes of the realm*, IV, i, 104–108, as incorporated in 3 and 4 Edward VI, c. 5.
[2] *A.P.C.*, II, 385: Feb. 7, 1550.
[3] *Ibid*. 404: Mar. 1, 1550.
[4] *Ibid*. 407: Mar. 8, 1550.
[5] *Ibid*. 421: Mar. 29, 1550.
[6] Strype, *Memorials*, II, i, 343.
[7] *A.P.C.*, II, 423, 425: Apr. 1 and 8, 1550; Edward VI, *Chronicle*, 28.
[8] *A.P.C.*, II, 431: Apr. 17, 1550.

who had not lived there for as long as three years or who were not gainfully employed to 'get themselves home again . . . into their native counties' in accordance with the provisions of the recently passed statute against vagabondage,[1] while in mid-May the Council complained of continued illegal assemblies in the realm where had been 'conspired divers and sundry evil facts, and enterprises and disorders, tending to rebellion'. Any person learning of such an assembly or plan for insurrection was enjoined to report the fact at once to the nearest Lord Lieutenant and should have as his reward £20 and the King's full pardon.[2]

The Council was gravely concerned when persistent rumours of a projected rising in Kent and Sussex were forwarded by Culpepper, the Sheriff of Kent. The report had it that the occasion of a wedding was to afford the opportunity for a stir which was to begin at Heathfield. Letters were immediately dispatched to the leading gentry of the two counties, and we are told 'the gentlemen of Kent took the party that was the inventor of this; and afterwards he suffered punishment'.[3] During these weeks the Council was also troubled because a certain 'Captain Red Cap', who had been involved in the 1549 risings, was on his release from prison feasted by the commoners in several villages in Middlesex, where there was considerable agrarian restlessness.[4] Probably typical of the tightened security under which England lay was the report of Sir Richard Manners of Nottinghamshire that he had broken up a serious plot there, led by certain constables who had ridden two and two from parish to parish raising the commons in the King's name.[5] The harried Council, trying to sort out facts from wild rumours, was itself confused, as witness the episode when one Thomas Lovett appeared before them with accusations against named persons in several counties who were supposed to be fomenting stirs. On May 20th two men of Oxfordshire so accused were released by the Council after examination and Lovett was himself ordered held under suspicion that he was a stirrer as well as an undoubted liar.[6] So exercised was the Council by these intimations of the black mood of the commons, that Russell and Herbert were ordered back to the western counties, while troops returning from Boulogne were assigned to barracks in Dorset, Hampshire, Sussex, Essex, Kent,

---

[1] Hughes and Larkin, *Tudor proclamations*, I, 489–490: May 7, 1550.

[2] *Ibid.* 491–492: May 17, 1550; *A.P.C.*, III, 38: May 28, 1550.

[3] Edward VI, *Chronicle*, 32; *A.P.C.*, III, 35: May 23, 1550; Strype, *Memorials*, II, i, 343; VCH, *Sussex*, I, 516.

[4] *A.P.C.*, III, 6: Apr. 20, 1550.   [5] *Ibid.* 31: May 15, 1550.

[6] *Ibid.* 31, 34.

and Suffolk, all of which were regarded as potentially explosive.[1] At the same time the Trinity Term of the assizes was postponed until Michaelmas in order to have all gentry free to bring force to bear against unlawful assemblies, while in Kent, on May 14th, three men were executed on charges that they had sought to raise a rebellion there.[2]

This mounting nervousness of the ruling junta reached its height in June and July, the dreaded and apocalyptic months. Writing in mid-June, Traheron reported to Bullinger that though Protestantism was again prospering in England, the whole realm stirred with unquietness.[3] A proclamation issued on June 11th ordered all officers to depart immediately to their commands under severe penalty, and was reconfirmed in July by another which ordered all discharged officers and soldiers to leave the City of London within three days under pain of imprisonment.[4] No disorder was to be brooked, as witness the stern action taken against Lord Stourton who with his retainers had set upon William Hartgill, for which Stourton was clapped into the Fleet and both parties to the fracas placed under heavy bond to keep the peace.[5] Still the countryside stirred ominously in these dreaded weeks. There was a disturbance in and about Rumford, Essex, which was quieted when several of those involved were imprisoned;[6] unquiet in Sussex led to orders that 'a privy search [be] made . . . for all vagabonds, gypsies, conspirators, prophets, ill players, and such like'.[7] The imperial ambassador reported that there was great malaise in the whole realm and a widespread fear that revolts would erupt once the harvest had been gathered. Commoners were forbidden to keep weapons, suspected houses were searched and troops dispatched to the gentry for use in breaking up illegal assemblies. Scheyfve also credited the greatly exaggerated rumour that a large body—he says 10,000—of commoners had massed at Sittingbourne, Kent, but were dispersed by Lord Grey. So grave was the concern regarding Kent that the Lord Warden was at that time scouring the county with 1000 horse to overawe the peasantry. Similar measures, he added, were under way in other parts of England as well, but the commons remained ugly in mood, alleging that promises to them had been betrayed, that their

[1] Pollard, *History of England*, 56.
[2] Stow, *Annales*, 604.
[3] Robinson, *Original letters*, I, 324.
[4] Hughes and Larkin, *Tudor proclamations*, I, 495: June 11, 1550; *ibid.* 498: July 20, 1550.   [5] *A.P.C.*, III, 42: June 5, 1550.
[6] Edward VI, *Chronicle*, 37; Strype, *Memorials*, II, i, 343.
[7] Edward VI, *Chronicle*, 37.

lands had been taken, and that their rents had been doubled.[1] These efforts, taxing so heavily the resources and the energy of the Council, were greatly increased as they were complicated by the rumours and false leads with which the government had to deal. Thus Russell reported that two informers in Buckinghamshire had given him false information in matters of great importance to the King and realm, and the justices were to confer on whether these rogues should be sentenced to death or to jail, while a similar situation presented itself at Rochester.[2]

So serious was the situation thought to be in July that for 'urgent considerations' Northumberland's projected journey north to assume the command along the Scottish Border was cancelled, Bowes remaining as Warden of the East and Middle Marches.[3] At the same time, the magic of Somerset's name was invoked when he was commissioned to keep the peace in Oxfordshire, Sussex, Wiltshire, and Hampshire, while a few days later he appeared at Reading for the same purpose.[4] In London, meanwhile, strict order was maintained, while the Council in successive proclamations sought to ensure an adequate supply of foodstuffs in a year of poor harvests and laid down stringent regulations for the prices of essential foods. Rumours in the metropolis were assiduously tracked down and those who spread them were punished, as for example a miller in Southwark who lost both his ears for having spread the story that Somerset had proclaimed himself king.[5] More serious, and more typical, was the demand of the Council on the Mayor of Southampton to investigate the wife of one Thomas Wells, who they were informed had been told by her nephew that 'a stir should be in this realm before Michaelmas next greater than the stir of the last years'. The mayor was to question the aunt regarding the conversation; when no reply was in hand a few days later, the Council forwarded a second and stern letter requiring the desired information, since the nephew was still in gaol and still denied the report.[6]

There was some surcease from these gnawing apprehensions with the coming of autumn in 1550, but no relaxation of vigilance. Thus, to mention a few instances, in late September the Council wrote to the county authorities in Norfolk that the conspiracy alleged against

[1] *Cal. S.P. Span.*, X, 97, 108, 109, 116: June 6–24, 1550.
[2] *A.P.C.*, III, 50: June 20, 1550.
[3] *Ibid.* 88: July 19, 1550.
[4] Edward VI, *Chronicle*, 41, 42: July 26, Aug. 6, 1550.
[5] Stow, *Annales*, 604.
[6] Anderson, R. C., ed., *Letters of the fifteenth and sixteenth centuries from the archives of Southampton* (Southampton Record Soc., 1921), 78–80.

one Goodrich of Dereham might have been maliciously charged, since he had rendered good service to the crown in the rising of 1549. But they were none the less to sift the whole matter and particularly to question certain persons at Wisbech, mentioned in the accusation.[1] Late in October, Sir John Gates with Thomas Mildmay was sent into Essex to investigate seditious bills which had appeared at Chelmsford and Colchester. Then at the year's end certain of the Oxfordshire justices were commissioned to investigate a riot which had occurred near Banbury when the enclosures around Banbury Castle had been thrown down.[2]

It had been a wearing, a troubled year; a year of unrelieved nervous strain on those who had taken the government of England into their hands. Northumberland and the rest may have derived certain gloomy satisfaction from the analysis of the ills of England written in October, 1550 by an unknown author. The printers publish 'whatever anyone devises, be it never so foolish, seditious or dangerous for the people to know'. Players are abroad mounting sketches filled with 'lewd, seditious devices to the danger of King and Council'. At the same time, most of the people tell lies and delight in spreading rumours about Councillors, talking incessantly of affairs of state, breaking the laws, and hoping to 'be winked at' because they know someone in the Council, while every man is so bold that he expects to gain whatever favour he may ask. The people refuse to pay their tithes, the justices do not attend to their duty, the coinage is debased, and the cloth trade has been ruined by overproduction and scanting of quality. The ills of England, it was concluded, were great and they went without correction.[3] In this dour summary of woes and wrongs there was truth, for England lay in the hands of a government which, while reactionary in every instinct, was in fact too weak and apprehensive to maintain the structure of order and loyalty in the realm.

The winter months, as was usual, offered some measure of relief to a government which had been steadily preoccupied with threats of public disorder. But there was still a flow, though diminished, of cases bespeaking the now chronic turbulence of the commons and their supporters. In January, 1551, one Edmund Ford of Sussex was committed to the Fleet for words spoken against members of the Council, to be released after interrogation under bond of 1000 marks.[4] A clergyman, probably of Kent, was reported by Cranmer

---

[1] *A.P.C.*, III, 131-132: Sept. 27, 1550.   [2] *Ibid.* 181-182: Dec. 24, 1550.
[3] Egerton MS. 2623, f. 9: Oct. 1550.
[4] *A.P.C.*, III, 187, 216: Jan. 7 and Feb. 17, 1551.

to have preached seditiously and, in spite of admonitions, to have gone from 'evil to worse', his case being referred to Cranmer and Goodrich for determination.[1] In March, letters were dispatched to the justices in Berkshire calling on them to investigate a riot which had taken place on certain meadow lands at Morton and commanding them to send up for immediate examination four named persons thought to be ringleaders.[2] The Council must have been sorely perplexed indeed when such turbulence reached into the Court itself, especially in matters relating to enclosures. Thus, in late March, one Greenway, a gentleman usher to the King, was examined by the Council on the allegation of a Buckinghamshire neighbour named Lee that the courtier had thrown down his hedges. It was Greenway's contention that it was Lee who had in fact enclosed common meadowlands to the harm of the community and that he had accordingly set two men on removing the enclosures in order to secure a trial at law. The surely weary Council castigated Greenway for his certainly illegal action, but after taking into account his long service to the King forgave him on condition the hedges should be restored at his expense.[3]

Far more serious, and reaching into the very centre of power, was a violent altercation between Warwick and Sir Ralph Vane, an ardent follower of Somerset, a reckless and fearless soldier, and a man given to choleric rages. Sir Henry Isley deposed that he, with an unspecified number of Warwick's servants at his command, repaired to Posterne Park (Kent) where they were confronted by Vane leading sixty armed men. Vane, who claimed the herbage, commanded them to remove Warwick's cattle from the park and threatened force with his present company plus another forty men already assembled and three hundred more who lay at his command. Vane, when haled before the Council, denied that he had had more than twenty-six or twenty-seven of his servants in his train and that he had mentioned the two or three hundred men in reserve only to frighten Isley. But other witnesses swore that Vane did have forces in hand of from 160 to 180 men, and he was accordingly sent to the Tower with certain of his servants, five of whom were released in May. Vane was himself discharged on June 8th under heavy bond and a promise not to molest Warwick in his possession of Posterne Park.[4] This was, of course, an exceedingly dangerous enmity and a potentially explosive incident which may well be connected with the

[1] A.P.C., III, 217: Feb. 18, 1551.   [2] Ibid. 243: Mar. 26, 1551.
[3] Ibid. 247, 252: Mar. 31 and Apr. 6, 1551.
[4] Ibid. 244, 245-246, 279, 296.

condign vengeance taken against Vane, after a travesty of a trial, when Somerset was done to death.

In April the uneasy government began to prepare itself for disturbances which it correctly assumed would command much of its time, energy, and force during the coming summer. Carefully considered commissions of lieutenancy were issued, imposing on numerous senior members of the Council direct military responsibility which removed them for a season from participation in the central administrative body of the realm. Among these were Sir Thomas Cheyney, assigned to Kent; Bedford to Dorset, Devon, Cornwall, and Somerset; Huntingdon to Leicestershire and Rutland; Somerset to Berkshire and Hampshire; Northampton to Surrey, Northamptonshire, Bedfordshire, Buckinghamshire, Cambridge, and Hertfordshire.[1] To gird them with full authority and to lend them all possible assistance, letters were dispatched to all justices of the peace in the realm commanding them to put strictly into execution all laws against vagabonds, unlawful games, seditious assemblies, and the spreading of incendiary rumours, while in all their actions they were instructed to keep steadily in view the maintenance of quiet in the realm.[2]

In a further effort to damp down turbulence a proclamation was issued a few days later appealing to the whole nation to preserve a 'perfect quietness'. The Privy Council was grieved that so many subjects ignored wholesome laws and 'sow, spread abroad, and tell from man to man, false lies, tales, rumours, and seditious devices' against the King, his Council, and his magistrates. Against such destroyers the King would, if need be, use sufficient force, but first he gently appealed to all men to live within the framework of law so that the government might devote all its efforts to 'reduce again this realm unto that prosperity, estimation, and wealth which by sundry occasions in process of time hath and is decayed'. Hence all magistrates were called upon to enforce the laws, to compel all vagabonds and idle men to return to their homes, to strike down baseless and seditious rumours, and to enforce the laws against unlicensed printing.[3] This effort to control propaganda and to check the numerous libels and scurrilous bills, launched especially against Northumberland, inspired a more detailed proclamation in May against 'slanderous and wicked bills' attacking Councillors and other noble persons. Such bills, it was said, were spread abroad in the

---

[1] *A.P.C.*, III, 258–259: Apr. 14, 1551.

[2] *Ibid.* 260: Apr. 15, 1551.

[3] Hughes and Larkin, *Tudor proclamations*, I, 514–518: Apr. 28, 1551.

streets and posted in 'privy corners', and were admittedly extremely difficult to root out. Hence it was now ordained that any man failing to destroy such bills on sight should lie under the same penalties as he who had uttered it.[1]

This spate of incendiary attacks on the government was centred in London, which was now literate and in which there was deep-rooted sympathy for Somerset. Means of control were not very effective and on April 19th the Recorder of the City, with numerous substantial citizens, had waited on the Privy Council with a sampling of books and bills calculated to stir the City to rebellion.[2] The Council had thought it had evidence that some violent incident might trigger uprisings across the realm, and warned the Lord Mayor and aldermen on April 12th that a conspiracy tending to rebellion existed in London and required them to force out the vagabonds, to halt the inflow of foreigners, and to secure a unity of service amongst the churches of the City.[3] The government was persuaded that the existing unrest might break out in violent riots on May Day and would probably be directed against the large foreign population, which, as we have seen, had settled in the City under Somerset's tolerant policy.[4] The Council thought, as well, that it had evidence of a well devised plan for risings in Kent and Essex, which it at least believed had been broken up by the interrogation of suspects in late April. The imperial ambassador thought the situation extremely explosive, particularly since he was informed that Northumberland believed that Somerset was disaffected and in touch with Derby and Shrewsbury who had failed to obey a summons to attend meetings of the Council held to deal with the situation.[5] Strong defensive forces were posted in or near London, vagrants were driven out, four of the reputed ringleaders were hanged, and the Council sought to gain authority by at least an appearance of unanimity by conspicuously dining together with an elaborate show of amity on several occasions.[6] At the same time, a connected conspiracy in Essex, centring on Chelmsford, in which the ringleaders were 'minded to declare the coming of strangers and so to bring people together in Chelmsford and then to spoil the rich men's houses if they could', was

---

[1] Hughes and Larkin, *Tudor proclamations*, I, 522–523: May 20, 1551.
[2] *A.P.C.*, III, 262.
[3] *Ibid.* 256–257.
[4] Jordan, *Edward VI*, 189–205.
[5] *Cal. S.P. Span.*, X, 278–280: Apr. 21, 1551; Hayward, *Edward VI*, 317; Edward VI, *Chronicle*, 59. It was also rumoured that the Princess Mary would go westward to join Shrewsbury, presumably as part of a plot to overthrow Northumberland (*A.P.C.*, III, 264: Apr. 24, 1551).
[6] *Cal. S.P. Span.*, X, 290–291: May 12, 1551.

suppressed—and its purpose derided by Edward with the contemptuous expletive, 'Woodcock'.[1]

There is little further evidence for the existence of a serious conspiracy or a planned stir in London or Essex in the spring of 1551, and such evidence as we do have seems decidedly circumstantial and somehow implausible. There was discontent; bills and libels there certainly were; and a kind of implacable hostility to Northumberland there most certainly was. But one is disposed to wonder whether this feared rising was not in the main conjured up by the apprehension, the fatigue, and the exaggerated suspicions of the Privy Council, among whom Northumberland was now almost pathological in his fear of plots against both his person and his government.

The fact is that turbulence was kept fairly firmly in check during the summer months of 1551. The elaborate, and expensive, prudential measures taken by the government were vested with sufficient force; prices were more successfully kept under control; and a terrible epidemic of sweating sickness tended to immobilize the population of the realm and to turn men's minds towards prayer rather than to incendiary libels and the laying down of hedges.[2] There were a few evidences of seditious talk or activity, but the Council moved with dispatch to break them up or to fasten on the ringleaders. Thus a landlord of an inn at Woodstock relieved his conscience by reporting a seditious letter of which he knew;[3] men were pilloried and lost their ears in Ipswich and London for seditious mutterings;[4] there were more serious evidences of agrarian discontent in Gloucestershire and Worcestershire which occasioned preparations in the city of Hereford to maintain order if need should arise; and the King somewhat obscurely recorded that the Duke of Somerset in late August broke up a conspiracy at Wokingham (Berks) 'for the destruction of the gentlemen there', putting the ringleaders to death.[5]

Far more serious and numerous evidences of seditious intent and activity are to be found in the autumn of 1551, particularly as the net of Northumberland's second conspiracy began to be gathered around the Duke of Somerset. In early September, Sir John Harrington had written to Clinton, then in Lincolnshire, that he had broken up a serious plot of 'divers evil disposed persons' in Leicestershire, Northamptonshire, and Rutland who sought to raise a stir.

[1] Edward VI, *Chronicle*, 59; Hayward, *Edward VI*, 317.
[2] *Vide post*, 466–471.
[3] *A.P.C.*, III, 272, 273, 452, 460, 461.
[4] *Ibid.* 293, 295: June 4 and 5, 1551.
[5] VCH, *Hereford*, I, 378; Edward VI, *Chronicle*, 78.

Harrington had proceeded at once to Uppingham where one of the ringleaders lived and 'took the same in his house before any creature in town knew'. He then moved at once to Morcott, Rutland, where, with the aid of Sir Thomas Tresham, the sheriff and other of the gentry, three suspected brothers were seized, and still more suspects later arrested. Then, with additional gentry of the region in support, he had ridden post-haste back to Uppingham where it was rumoured a rising was to be launched, but found none assembled. He assured the Council that a close watch was posted in the area and that he had the force of the whole countryside with him, save for certain 'light knaves, horsecorsers, and craftsmen', though he warned Clinton that his interrogations suggested that the disaffection might possibly extend into Lincolnshire and Norfolk. Clinton, in forwarding the letter to Cecil for the Council, indicated that he had warned the justices of the peace in Lincolnshire, but urged that Cecil's father at Stamford should be asked to do the same.[1]

The truly desperate fears of the government, as Northumberland braced himself and his supporters for the final overthrow of Somerset, were savagely displayed in the treatment of a man named Appleyard who lay under suspicion of complicity in fomenting the rumoured rising in Northamptonshire. In one of those rare instances when a Tudor jury flouted the known wishes of the government for securing conviction, Appleyard was twice brought before a jury and twice acquitted. He was thereupon taken to Leicester for trial, the Solicitor-General (Sir Edward Griffin) warning the jury that if they did not convict the accused they would find themselves answering in the Star Chamber. The defendant was accordingly found guilty and was hanged forthwith. But grave damage had been done not only to the dignity of the law but also to the repute of the government. Sir Robert Stafford, one of the most respected and powerful of the gentry of the county, according to four witnesses publicly denounced the action once the hanging was completed. 'But now that the man is dead, who was as tall a yeoman as ever I saw bred in Northamptonshire, I desire you to satisfy my conscience.' Stafford declared that he had been vigilant in teaching the people the heinous nature of the sin of rebellion, but Appleyard had denied the charge and had been convicted of treason on the testimony of only one witness, who had himself been implicated in the threatened stir. Stafford expressed outrage that the Solicitor-General had told the

---

[1] HMC, *Salisbury MSS.*, I, 92, printed *in extenso* in Haynes, Samuel, *A collection of state papers . . . left by William Cecill Lord Burghley, etc.*, vol. I (L., 1740), 114–115; S.P. Dom., Edw. VI, XIII, 37: Sept. 2 and 3, 1551.

jury that if they did not pass sentence, he would himself hang Appleyard. 'I pray God', he was reported to have added, that 'our justices have done well, or else I would wish them expelled and others put in their places.'[1]

The Appleyard case, concluded only a month before Somerset's arrest, was only the most shocking of the great number we have mentioned that occurred in the Home Counties during the period of two years when John Dudley was seeking to establish his authority. It is quite clear that the Council was extremely apprehensive during the entire interval, that it must have been principally preoccupied with matters of security, and that it was in fact moved by hysterical fears during the always troublesome spring and summer months. Northumberland, with only the most slender basis of evidence, found in the person and the persistent popularity of Somerset the explanation for this chronic turbulence and seems to have been persuaded well before September, 1551 that it could be relieved only by the catharsis of Somerset's destruction. As should have been predictable, the trial and execution of Somerset were rather to harden discontent into hatred, to persuade whole classes of men that Northumberland's every move and intention were sinister, and to drive him almost unwittingly to seek safety in a mounting power which was to become irresponsible if not despotic. So driven was he, so fearful was he, that preoccupation with plots and counter-plots, and the very act of clinging to power, were to absorb almost the whole of the energy and resources of his government. There are elements of real tragedy in Northumberland's hopeless and feckless struggle to establish some elements of stability and legitimacy in his regimen.

[1] S.P. Dom., Edw. VI, Addenda III, 78, 79: Sept. 19, 1551; *Cal. S.P. Dom., Edw. VI*, VI, 407–408.

IV

THE DESTRUCTION OF THE DUKE OF SOMERSET

1. SOMERSET'S RELEASE AND RE-ADMISSION TO THE PRIVY COUNCIL (FEBRUARY–APRIL, 1550)

We have already discussed the great political crisis of the autumn of 1549, springing from the fears engendered by the searing insurrection of that summer and coming into focus in the conspiracy with which Warwick secured the ruin of the Duke of Somerset.[1] Somerset's fall was as complete as it was catastrophic, for in the end it was clear that he enjoyed support only from Cranmer, Paget, and Smith among his former colleagues. The gates of the Tower closed on Somerset on October 14, 1549. A few days later a list of the personal items needed by the prisoner of state was presented, requesting no more than a really spartan list of clothing, towels, table napkins, and £10 to pay for his laundry, cleaning, and other necessities.[2] He could hardly have been cheered in the straits in which he found himself by a New Year's gift of verses by William Gray, which assured him that his present adversity would cause him the better to know God's will, teach him liberality of both person and tongue, and persuade him to hear all parties speak and to come to his conclusions with gentleness.[3]

[1] Jordan, *Edward VI*, 494 ff.

[2] Cotton MSS., Titus, B, ii, 53, ff. 47–48 (old nos., ff. 66–67). The Duchess of Somerset, for a short while imprisoned with him, presented a much longer list of clothing, books, silver, tableware, and £20 in money (*ibid*. f. 47b).

[3] Gray, William, *New Year's gift, etc.*, in Furnivall, F. J., *Ballads from manuscripts* (2 vols., L., 1868–1873), I, 417. Gray also indited verses to Somerset a year later, well after the Duke's release. He then urged him to re-assert his authority in the interests of the realm at large and its people, for the Lords of the Council cared not for the pressing needs of the realm:

. . . The lords be not at leisure;
They walk up and down at the Chamber door,
Make room for the rich, and keep back the poor.
(*Ibid*. 421)

The explicit terms on which Somerset had relinquished the threat of force and the person of the King had been that he would not be harmed, that his estate would remain inviolate, and that he would not be stripped of his rank, save, as it was clearly assumed, that he must eschew the title and office of Lord Protector. We have seen, too, that twenty-nine articles of accusation had been laid against him, which fell far short of the wild charges of treason launched by the London Lords at the height of the crisis. These articles, we have observed, were vague and inchoate, being in fact a crude propaganda piece. Only six of them laid bare Somerset's real faults as Lord Protector, accusing him of hotness of temper, arrogance of conduct, and a mulish stubbornness when his policy was questioned by his colleagues. The articles, which were carelessly drafted and seem to be no more than a random gathering of notes compiled by the London Lords in defence of their own conduct,[1] were laid before the Duke for endorsement, four of the Council and as many of the bishops being designated to examine him and to make certain that his signature had been freely given. On January 14th he was formally declared deposed from the office of Lord Protector. Though there is no certain evidence, it seems clear that there must have been an understanding that his release would follow shortly on his submission, which was made on January 27th.[2] Only a few more days were to elapse until the Lieutenant of the Tower was ordered to bring Somerset 'without great guard or business' to Sir John York's house in the City, much frequented by Warwick.[3] After a brief interval Somerset was released from custody on recognizance of £10,000, on condition that he reside with his family at either Syon or Sheen and keep within a radius of four miles from his chosen residence. There was the further stipulation that if the King and Council passed near his house he would not seek access to the sovereign.[4] Not many days later (February 18th) he received the free pardon of the King and his estates were restored, save for certain nibblings which had taken place during the days of his imprisonment.[5]

For about six weeks Somerset was free under what amounted to house arrest, barred from access to the King, and excluded from the seats of power. But the Duke had supporters amongst the nobility

---

[1] Jordan, *Edward VI*, 522–523.

[2] Robinson, *Original letters*, II, 480: Martyr to Bullinger, Jan. 27, 1550; Stow, *Annales*, 602–603, for the submission.   [3] *A.P.C.*, II, 384: Feb. 6, 1550.

[4] *Ibid.* 384–385; Edward VI, *Chronicle*, 23; Robinson, *Original letters*, II, 464, which reports great joy among the good men of the Gospel; *ibid.* 399; *Cal. S.P. Span.*, X, 28: Feb. 10, 1550; Nichols, *Grey Friars Chronicle*, 66.

[5] Rymer, *Foedera*, XV, 205–207; Stow, *Annales*, 604; Pollard, *Somerset*, 282.

and within the Council itself who were urging his restoration to the Council, while prudence must have persuaded Warwick that Somerset could be more easily watched and even controlled within the Council than if he stood alone as a gathering point of faction and as a symbol attracting the loyalty and power which his immense reputation among the lower classes could evoke. The history of these negotiations between the Council and Somerset is obscure, but it seems certain that Cecil had urged the Duchess of Suffolk to use her great influence to secure the Duke's restoration not long before March 25th when she made her courageous reply. She confided that her greatest fear, presumably of Somerset's continued imprisonment or worse, had now been dispelled. She was now sure that God would relieve the 'deep suspects in the Council's heart' against the Duke. She doubted if she should follow Cecil's request that she come to London in order to intervene personally for the Duke, while assuring him that 'if I could be any ways persuaded that I might do my lord any good I would most gladly put myself in any adventure, but alas if I come and am not able to do for him that I would and unable to do what we staked long on', then she would do him harm rather than good. Then, before sealing her letter, the Duchess added overleaf that she had just had reliable news from London that Somerset would shortly be restored to the Council, which left her mind settled in the view that she should not now intervene, but rather let every honest man have his day.[1]

The news from the Duchess of Suffolk's confidant was wholly accurate, for only a few days later (April 8th) Somerset dined amicably with the King and Council at Greenwich and on April 10th was restored to the Council. The earliest meeting of the Council which he certainly attended was that held on May 7th, though it was not until four days later that his restoration of status was completed with the decision that since he had been recalled to the Council he should likewise be freely admitted to the Privy Chamber. In this same season Somerset wrote to Lord Cobham thanking him for courtesies to his son, for his friendship, and, it is more than hinted, for Cobham's support in gaining his return to the Council. That the Duke had settled easily into his customary role of exercising power was suggested by still another letter of the Duchess of Suffolk to Cecil, expressing through him her thanks to the Duke for having intervened to secure a hearing in a legal dispute in which she felt wrong had been done to one of the parties.[2]

[1] S.P. Dom., Edw. VI, X, 2: Mar. 25 [1550]. The letter was written from the Duchess's 'cottage' at Kingston.   [2] See footnote on p. 73.

The Duchess of Suffolk, in fact, expressed to Cecil the hope that a marriage might be arranged between Somerset's daughter, Anne Seymour, who had been given an excellent humanistic education, and one of her own infinitely gifted sons, who were only then entering Cambridge for their education. But, liberally disposed as she always was, the Duchess added that she had no wish to pursue any match not wholly desired by the young people in question.[1] Even as she wrote, however, arrangements were being made for the marriage of Anne with Warwick's eldest son, John Dudley, Lord Lisle, who had also enjoyed an imposing humanistic education. It can hardly be doubted that this marriage compact represented a serious effort on the part of Warwick and Somerset to compose their differences and to restore harmony within the ruling junta. Once the decision was made, there was no delay, the King attending the brilliant ceremony at Sheen, followed by 'a fair dinner made and dancing finished'.[2]

2. MOUNTING TENSION BETWEEN SOMERSET AND WARWICK (MAY, 1550–SEPTEMBER, 1551)

There is every reason for believing that both Somerset and Warwick sought for some weeks to find a common ground and to effect a working rapprochement. But, however sincerely they may have tried, it was quickly evident that the effort had failed. Either man could and did dominate the Council when the other was absent, but they could neither work nor rule together. There was now between them a deep-seated fear and distrust. Far more important, the two peers differed profoundly in their personal attitudes and aspirations on

---

[2] (Page 72.) *A.P.C.*, II, 427: Apr. 10, 1550; *ibid.*, III, 19, 29: Apr. 27, 1550; Stow, *Annales*, 604; Tytler, P. F., *England under the reigns of Edward VI and Mary, etc.* (2 vols. L., 1839), I, 279–280; S.P. Dom., Edw. VI, X, 5: Apr. 27, 1550; *ibid.* 32: Sept. 18, 1550.

[1] *Ibid.* 6: May 9, 1550. Both boys, Henry and Charles, were to die in the next year; *vide post*, 471.

[2] Edward VI, *Chronicle*, 32; Nichols, *Remains*, II, 274; Wriothesley, *Chronicle*, II, 41; *Cal. S.P. Span.*, X, 86: on May 2 the imperial ambassador reported that Warwick and Somerset were in intimate and daily contact; Froude, *History of England*, V, 290. The marriage was ill-fated. Lisle, later Earl of Warwick, was condemned with his father. Though spared by Mary he died a few days after being released from the Tower in 1554. His widow married Edward Unton, a Berkshire gentleman, in the course of the next year, by whom she had seven children, the youngest son, Sir Henry Unton, in due time serving as ambassador to France. Late in life Anne Seymour was adjudged to have been insane since 1566.

It should be added that on the day following the marriage of his brother, Robert Dudley, Warwick's fifth son and the future Earl of Leicester, married Sir John Robsart's daughter, Amy, whose mysterious death in 1560 cast some doubt on the relations of Queen Elizabeth and Robert Dudley (Edward VI, *Chronicle*, 33).

every important policy problem of the age. Somerset had been articulate in his condemnation of Warwick's search for a French alliance and, for that matter, of the whole sweep of his foreign policy. Somerset lent his steady support to the centrist Anglican position represented by Cranmer's thought and the moderate Protestantism enshrined in the first Book of Common Prayer;[1] Warwick was to lend strong and on the whole irresponsible encouragement to the evangelical Protestant wing and was shortly to embark on a coldly secular plundering of the remaining resources of the Church. The tolerant and magnanimous Somerset strongly supported the limited freedom of worship which the Princess Mary now enjoyed and wished to release Bishop Gardiner as soon as a face-saving formula could be found; Warwick desired and enforced a policy of increasing repression against even moderate Roman Catholicism. Somerset was unyielding in his now ineffectual support of radical measures of social and economic reforms; Warwick quite sincerely regarded these as the true cause of the great insurrection of 1549 and enlisted the immensely strong, though frightened, support of the dominant political and economic power of the realm for his policy of social reaction. There were, then, fundamental differences of policy and outlook which were simply irreconcilable, however earnestly the two men, both impetuous and arrogant, sought to restore the affection and mutual admiration which had characterized their youth.

The fact was, too, that Somerset found it quite impossible to move the Privy Council by persuasion, in part because his own credit had fallen so low and in part because, as we have seen, it was now really packed with Warwick's adherents. Surely there must have been friends among Somerset's servants who advised him simply to withdraw from public life until reaction had run its course or until his already considerable strength in Parliament, which Warwick fearfully refrained from calling, had given him some larger measure of support. It may be that he sought to follow this course for a season, for it is evident that in 1550–1551 he was giving far more of his time to the ordering of his estates, improving his properties in Berkshire, calling on Thynne for a detailed inventory of his holdings, and putting in order his lovely house at Wells which the straitened

---

[1] Shortly after his release Somerset ordered the publication of Coverdale's translation of Werdmueller's devotional work, *A spiritual and most precious pearl*, for which he supplied a *Preface*. Somerset acknowledged that the work had greatly comforted him during his 'great trouble', when it 'pleased God for a time to attempt us with his scourge. and to prove if we loved him'. He wished all men who were troubled and afflicted to have the solace of the work. There was a deep strain of quiet piety in Somerset (2nd ed., 1550, in *Writings and translations of Myles Coverdale, etc.*, ed. by George Pearson (Parker Soc., Cambridge, 1844)).

Bishop of Bath so envied him.[1] But the thrust of ambition and the habits of power were too dominant in Somerset's nature, as was the great personal pride of one who was the King's uncle and who, until conspiracy overwhelmed him, had been the Lord Protector of England. There was simply no possible ground for reconciliation, and, unhappily, any overt move of opposition which Somerset or his adherents could make might with some justice be construed as conspiracy against the state.

The appearance of conspiracy was first supplied by the overly eager, and not wholly authorized, actions of one of Somerset's most trusted servants, Richard Whalley, a steward with Thynne of Somerset's properties and since the early days of the reign Crown Receiver for Yorkshire.[2] Whalley was one of the Protector's servants whom the Council had ordered detained in October, 1549, but had regained his freedom, as had Cecil, on January 25, 1550, when he was bound in 1000 marks. Within a month, however, Whalley was again under suspicion for his reckless support of Somerset, while in the next month Sir Ralph Vane, as courageous as he was irrepressible, was questioned for the same offence. Warwick, who could on occasion be as charming as he was persuasive, sought Whalley out for an important and successful interview on June 25, 1550, which Whalley in turn reported fully to Cecil. Warwick expressed his personal affection for the Duke, but spoke freely of Somerset's stubborn forcing of such matters as the release of Gardiner and the Arundells, which 'the whole Council doth much dislike'. Further, Somerset at Council meetings betrayed the same mien and temper with which he had ruled that body as Protector. Nor, Warwick continued, was 'he in that credit and best opinion with the King's majesty, as he believeth and is by some fondly persuaded'. If Somerset would only work through and with the Council, he might have all he reasonably desired, but by 'taking private ways by himself, and attempting such perilous causes . . . he will so far overthrow himself as shall pass the power of his friends to recover'.[3] There was surely honest concern,

---

[1] HMC, *Bath MSS. at Longleat*, App. IV: *Seymour papers*, 113–114; S.P. Dom., Edw. VI, X, 19, 23: Aug. 2 and 16, 1550.

[2] The *DNB* supplies an admirable memoir of this talented but somewhat unscrupulous man. Educated at Cambridge, he ingratiated himself with Henry VIII and was employed by Cromwell on the expropriation of the monasteries. After persistent interrogation he turned state's evidence against Somerset. *Vide post*, 111 for the later disposition of his case.

[3] S.P. Dom., Edw. VI, X, 9: June 26, 1550; see also the comments of Froude (*History of England*, V, 369–370) and Read (*Cecil*, 60–61) on this important document. The letter is printed in large part by Tytler (*England*, II, 21–24). Whalley was seeking contact with Somerset a few days later (July 1st) when he asked Cecil for the Duke's itinerary on his journey westward (S.P. Dom., Edw. VI, X, 11).

as there was a clear and carefully expressed warning to Somerset in this judgement of Warwick, the whole of which was intended to be delivered to the late Protector by Cecil, who now enjoyed the trust of both protagonists.

Warwick's stress in this conversation with Whalley on Somerset's repeated interventions on behalf of Gardiner and the Arundells reflects not only the Earl's almost psychotic mood of reaction during the first year of his tenure of power, but also a completely erroneous suspicion that Somerset was at this season seeking to build a party. He strongly and courageously defended Mary's liberty to hear the mass in her own household,[1] and in May and June, when Warwick was much away from court, was nearly successful in securing the release of Bishop Gardiner. At the same time he persisted in his efforts to free Sir Thomas and Sir John Arundell, who had been held in the Tower for many months, without proofs of complicity, because Lord Russell had regarded them as unreliable during the Western Rising.[2] It was also reported in these difficult weeks that Somerset and his adherents laid their confidence in Parliament where they would represent that 'the people [were] oppressed with fresh taxes, the King poorer than ever', and that 'those in power governed simply after their own caprice, without respecting the laws and customs of the realm.[3]' This fear we know to have been very real with Warwick, who, during Somerset's absence in August, 1550, persuaded the Council that Parliament should not be reconvened until January, 1551. Then during Warwick's absence in October, it was resolved to convene the members at an earlier date, only to have this understanding cancelled on his return. Parliament was not in fact to be convened again until after Somerset's final fall.[4]

The relations between the two peers were so far strained by the late summer of 1550 that they tended to communicate, especially when either was away from the court, through Cecil, whose great ability was beginning to manifest itself in the deliberations of the Council and who was rapidly gaining Warwick's confidence. Thus in mid-September, when the 'revelations' of the wholly unreliable Scot, Ninian Menville, against Bishop Tunstall, long a friend of Somerset, were first laid before Warwick, the lines of communication were through the Principal Secretary. These accusations, which

---

[1] *Vide* Jordan, *Edward VI*, 206–209, and *post*, 256–264, for this much belaboured matter.
[2] Edward VI, *Chronicle*, 19n. Sir Thomas Arundell was released under bond on Oct. 4, 1551 (*A.P.C.*, III, 378–379), Sir John in 1552. It must be said that Sir Thomas as soon as he was released formed a connection with Somerset which in Feb. 1552 cost him his life.   [3] Raumer, Friedrich von, *Briefe aus Paris, etc.*, pt. ii (Leipzig, 1831), 72–73.
[4] *Vide ante*, 45–46; *A.P.C.*, III, 104, 107, 141.

were in time to lead to an attempt to deprive Tunstall and to re-organize the great see that he administered, had been hinted at by Warwick in a conversation with the Bishop, whose 'answer was so cold that I could not tell what to make of it'. He wished Cecil to lay before Somerset the abstract of this conversation, with the gibe that it might lead to the downfall of Tunstall 'and yield to the King as good a rest as the Bishop of Winchester is like to do, if the cards be true'.[1]

The insecurity of Somerset's position and evidence of his relative weakness in the Privy Council was also suggested when in October (1550) his mother (and the King's grandmother) died at an advanced age. She had lived quietly and frugally out of public notice for many years, there being so far as we can determine no reference to her in the sources, even of the most casual sort, after her grandson's accession. Nor is there any reference to her in the King's own *Chronicle*, even at the time of her death, which is only one of many evidences of the essential coldness of her grandson. But Somerset took the occasion to lay before the King and Council a question which he must have regarded as a singularly revealing test of his own status and power: whether there should be a state funeral, with the prescribed elaborate ritual and the wearing of mourning. In his own estimate the former customary usage should be followed in view of her high estate and to prevent the public discussion sure to ensue if there were omissions of usage. But the Council ruled differently, holding that the wearing of mourning profited not the dead and harmed those of little faith; that the practice of public mourning was passing amongst all classes; that among 'many of the wiser sort' there would be criticism because of 'the impertinent charges'; and that all private men should 'reserve their private sorrows to their own houses'. Hence they had referred the matter directly to the King, who had dispensed the Duke from such mourning and who with them expressed the view that such public observances served 'rather to pomp than to any edifying'.[2] Sensible as the decision may have been, it can only be regarded as a deliberate weakening of Somerset's position in the Council and a warning that he no longer possessed the fruits of power. The Council's decision was all the more remarkable, and the warning to the Duke all the clearer, when a few months later Lady Seymour's nephew, Thomas, first Baron Wentworth, since the removal of Arundel the Lord

---

[1] S.P. Dom., Edw. VI, X, 31: Sept. 16, 1550; for the assault on Tunstall and his bishopric, *vide post*, 381–386.

[2] *A.P.C.*, III, 142–143; Harl. MS. 352, f. 130; Nichols, *Remains*, I, cxlviii–cxlix.

Chamberlain of the Household, died, 'leaving behind him sixteen children'.[1] For this impecunious peer an elaborate state funeral was arranged, a large company of mourners attended at the Abbey, and there was even a bread dole, so reminiscent of the usages of an earlier generation.[2]

There is persuasive evidence that Somerset, effectively barred as he was from the exercise of power and embittered by the successive injuries done his pride, was casting about for support, now entrusting far too much responsibility to servants better trained in the arts of war than in political negotiation, and that he moved gradually and, one believes, really insensibly into the morass of conspiracy as it was understood by the sixteenth-century mind. The imperial ambassador, an admirer of the Duke, reported in the autumn that the Council was deeply divided and that Somerset was for the first time actively seeking to gain supporters and to engage the deep loyalty which the commons always reposed in him.[3] An unknown French observer was persuaded that Somerset was privy to rumours being spread about that the social and economic troubles in which England found herself were wholly the responsibility of Warwick. Further, it was reported, preparations were being made to lay the facts before Parliament when it was next convened, proving that the country was poorly governed, that the people were oppressed by needless taxes, and that they were ruled by men who followed their own will rather than the laws and customs of the country.[4]

Far more serious was the fact that the division and tension in the Privy Council was believed to have spread to the peerage at large, there being rumours that both Derby and Shrewsbury had quarrelled with Warwick regarding their lands and territorial possessions. Both, it was reported, had been summoned to court but declined to appear until Parliament was convened. Derby, a quiet but firm conservative in his religious views, who had voted in the Lords against every important religious innovation, was clearly sulking in the north, and then aroused further apprehension by an intransigent claim which he laid on the Isle of Man.[5] Somewhat later, presumably in an effort to sort out and relieve the tension amongst the nobility, Arundel and Derby were both summoned to the Council,

---

[1] Edward VI, *Chronicle*, 54.

[2] Machyn, *Diary*, 4.

[3] *Cal. S.P. Span.*, X, 186: Nov. 4, 1550.

[4] Raumer, *Briefe aus Paris*, ii, 72, citing *Rélation de l'accusation et mort du Duc de Somerset* (formerly in St Germains des Prés archives, vol. 740; now in Bibliothèque Nationale MS. 15888, ff. 205–210).

[5] *Cal. S.P. Span.*, X, 168: Sept. 1, 1550; *Cal. S.P. For.*, *Edw. VI*, #370.

but with the remarkable, indeed the inexplicable, proviso that they be sworn 'to attend only when they or either of them should be called unto' a session of the Council.[1] One has the sense, too, that a list of the peers, Somerset being excluded, which bears no notations save for three different symbols laid against most of the names, suggests that a careful effort was being made sometime before March, 1551 to assess the strength that was believed to prevail against Somerset.[2] More revealing by far was a letter of about the same date (February 17, 1551), almost certainly from Shrewsbury to a friend in London, who was either of the Privy Council or a member of the court. Shrewsbury was troubled because an unnamed person had sought to discover his sentiments towards Somerset and Warwick, even suggesting that by his friendship towards both he had sought to set them at further variance. This he had not done and would not do. He would seek rather to preserve the 'quietness, unity, and concord' of the realm. The King's very trust imposed in him caused him to deplore any dissension which might disturb the state. He had heard rumours of enmity between the two peers, but suggested they were both too wise to quarrel and that they were closely bound by marriage. He trusted that this was the case, for 'I think not a little danger and disquietness to the whole realm would grow thereof' if any real enmity should exist. This interesting and high-minded letter, from one never an admirer or warm supporter of Warwick, suggests a mind troubled by the awareness that he must write with great caution and responsibility at this moment when it seemed that a reckless struggle for power might again fracture the structure of sovereignty in England.[3]

The delicately poised situation was nearly unbalanced by the further and heavy-handed efforts of Richard Whalley to win support for the Duke. So inept were these blundering moves that one wonders whether he was wholly responsible mentally, and one finds it difficult to believe that Somerset knew in detail what his admirer was doing. Whalley was certainly speaking with available members

[1] *A.P.C.*, III, 328–329: Aug. 9, 1551.
[2] The document may be dated before the death of Lord Wentworth on March 3, 1551. No symbols appear against the names of the following: Rutland, Huntingdon, Pembroke, Dacre, Morley, Cobham, Wentworth, Darcy of Chiche, Burgavenny, and Lord Darcy. Somerset possessed considerable support among most of these peers, but so did he among a few whose names carry the same symbol as that against the name of Warwick. (Cotton MSS., Titus, B, ii, 38, f. 73.)
[3] Shrewsbury had in the winter of 1549–1550 returned to the North for another tour of duty as president of the Council of the North. We cannot certainly identify the London correspondent, though it was probably the Earl of Huntingdon (Francis Hastings), to whom Shrewsbury was related in his mother's line. (Cotton MSS., Titus, B, ii, 23, f. 48.)

of the House of Commons and with at least Rutland amongst the peers of the desirability of restoring Somerset as Protector when Parliament should be reconvened. Rutland reported this conversation to the Council which examined them both on February 16, 1551, and, in spite of Whalley's unwavering denial of the words he had used, committed him to the Fleet.[1] The interrogation also suggested that Sir Francis Leek had overheard the conversation, but when examined on February 18th he would admit to no more than that Whalley had been at his house where he had 'prattled very much'. But Leek would not admit that Rutland, immediately after the conversation with Whalley, had said that he 'misliked much' Whalley's talk and that a clear effort was being made to determine whether the Earl was a supporter of Warwick or of Somerset. Nothing could be fully proved against Whalley, who was released under a recognizance of £1,000 on April 2nd, only to resume his inexpert and extremely dangerous efforts in conversations with Shrewsbury during the summer.[2] It need scarcely be said that Whalley was one of those to be arrested when in the autumn Warwick moved to destroy Somerset.

The spring of 1551 was, then, troubled and uneasy. In late March, as we have noted, Somerset's most loyal and reckless partisan, Sir Ralph Vane, was imprisoned after threatening to wage private war on Warwick because of a dispute over pasture rights which both claimed in Posterne Park.[3] In April there were recurrent rumours that Somerset would go north to gather strength. The tension was so great in these weeks, though no overt move was made by either side, that responsible foreign observers thought a political upheaval was at hand. It was Scheyfve's judgement that Somerset had lost much of his strength, save among the many who believed that religious innovations had gone too far and too rapidly.[4] A month later it was his appraisal of the situation that any immediate danger of revolt was past, since the government had taken strict measures against vagrants and suspected persons, while anyone spreading rumours of friction between the Council and Derby and Shrewsbury was to be summarily dealt with.[5] Daniel Barbaro, in reporting to the Doge and Senate, expressed the view that the structure of power established by Henry VIII's will was from the outset unworkable and was now dissolving. Nothing remained save the

---

[1] Edward VI, *Chronicle*, 52–53; *A.P.C.*, III, 215.   [2] *Ibid.*, 248, 391, 398.
[3] *Vide ante*, 75–76; *A.P.C.*, III, 244: Mar. 27, 1551.
[4] *Cal. S.P. Span.*, X, 262: Apr. 9, 1551.
[5] *Ibid.*, 290–291: May 12, 1551.

'reputation of the present King', in whom there was great hope if, Barbaro implied, he could speedily assume the responsibilities of power.[1] And from distant Florence it was reported that a news-sheet was being circulated in Rome with the intelligence that the northern peers in England were disaffected towards Warwick, that the Londoners complained because of the competition of the thousands of religious refugees who had been admitted, while there was constant 'chopping and changing in the Council'. Those deepest in opposition, the report quite inaccurately suggested, were Shrewsbury, Derby, Dacre, and that formidable lawyer turned soldier, Sir Robert Bowes.[2]

Then, though the 'chopping and changing' in the Council did continue, a kind of false calm descended on events through the summer of 1551. There is no evidence of serious or new enmity between Warwick and Somerset in these weeks, when the Earl was much involved in seeking an arrangement for the marriage of his fourth son, Guildford, to Margaret Clifford, daughter of the Earl of Cumberland and distantly related to the King. July was almost wholly occupied by the state visit from France bringing to Edward the Order of St Michael, during which time the Council made a successful effort to appear in harmony and unanimity.[3] Somerset was unusually regular in his attendance on meetings of the Privy Council during these weeks, while in late August he was entrusted with forces for the repression of a conspiracy being raised against the gentry in the neighbourhood of Wokingham.[4] The Duke was almost immediately afterwards stricken with a severe illness, followed by an outbreak of sweating sickness in his household, which kept him from court during the month of September. This was precisely what Warwick required to mobilize his forces, to gather, when he did not evoke, the essential evidence of conspiracy, and with a really masterly skill to prepare for the destruction of the Duke of Somerset.

3. THE EVIDENCE AGAINST SOMERSET
(SEPTEMBER–NOVEMBER, 1551)

These preparations were continued during the course of September. So far had the credit and the power of the Duke of Somerset

[1] *Cal. S.P. Ven.*, V, 339: May, 1551.
[2] *Cal. S.P. For., Edw. VI*, #370i: Francis Peto to Warwick, June 6, 1551.
[3] *Vide post*, 131–134, for a full discussion of the embassy.
[4] Edward VI, *Chronicle*, 78. The incident is obscure. Somerset had been appointed Lord Lieutenant of Berkshire and Buckinghamshire on his return to the Council.

sunk, and so politically naive was he, that he seems to have been almost the last among the governing group to sense that he stood in grave personal danger. Among the Councillors only Paget, who was to be disabled by baseless accusations, lent him his full support, mitigated by the frank strictures which he had always laid against Somerset's social and economic policies. The strongly evangelical group within the Council were estranged by Somerset's leniency towards Gardiner and by his steady opposition to any further limitations on the Princess Mary's private worship. This sentiment may account in part at least for Cecil's abrupt withdrawal of support, though his actions during the weeks of crisis suggest more strongly self-serving mixed with fear of John Dudley. Even as courageous a friend as the Duchess of Suffolk was now estranged, while as warm a former supporter as Morison confessed to Nicholas Throckmorton that he had earlier thought that 'imprisonment and such a throng of faults forgiven him would have made him a new heart if his old had been anything set upon revenging'. Now he conceded that Throckmorton had been correct in his earlier analysis: 'You weighed what men offended are wont to work ... you thought he would not forgive displeasure and I thought he could not forget good turns so lately done to him.'[1]

Somerset's position was also weakened—as events were to prove, fatally so—by the cold hostility which the King had borne for him since the *contretemps* at Hampton Court and Windsor two years earlier. His household had been carefully chosen for him by Warwick; the Earl had gained Edward's personal confidence and even admiration; and there is abundant evidence that the King's version of the events of the crisis of October, 1551, which constitutes our principal source, reflects the skilful and on the whole false colouring which Warwick and his immediate followers supplied to the young monarch. Edward's fourteenth birthday was to occur in the midst of Northumberland's final preparations.

It seems certain that arrangements for proceeding against Somerset had been completed by the end of September when letters were dispatched to important absent members of the Council (Clinton, Bedford, and Huntingdon) requiring them to repair to court with 'convenient speed' for their advice on the King's affairs.[2] On the same date a special letter was dispatched to Somerset, who had

---

[1] Read, *Cecil*, 72, citing P.R.O., S.P. 68–69: Nov. 18, 1551, which we have not found. *Cal. S.P. For., Edw. VI.*, #489, seems to be identical.

[2] *A.P.C.*, III, 374: Sept. 30, 1551. Clinton, then on a special embassy to France, did not in fact return to England until after Somerset's trial.

been away from Court for a month because of a death in his household from sweating sickness, summoning him to attend and 'to make no matter of absence thereof'.[1] Further, and more urgent, letters were dispatched to Somerset, Bedford, and Dorset on October 2nd requiring their presence on the 4th, the implausible reason advanced being the expected arrival of a special French envoy to announce the birth of Henry II's third son.[2]

Then, shortly after Somerset had returned to Court, Warwick reported to the King that Sir Thomas Palmer had come to him on October 7th to confess a treasonable conspiracy directly involving the Duke. The accusation was that on April 23rd Somerset would have gone north to 'raise the people' had he not been assured by Sir William Herbert (who a few days later was created Earl of Pembroke) that his person was in no danger, and also, one infers, after a conversation with Lord Grey of Wilton. Palmer also deposed that at a later date Somerset was at the least privy to a bizarre plan to secure the attendance of Warwick and Northampton at a banquet at which they and 'divers other[s]' would be cut down, while the City and the Tower would be secured by Sir Ralph Vane, Sir Thomas Arundell, Sir Miles Partridge, Alexander Seymour, and one Lawrence Hammond.[3]

This fantastic accusation, made by a completely unreliable adventurer, commonly known since early 1551 as a creature of the Earl of Warwick, who had hated Somerset since 1548 and had long been distrusted by him, was to stand as the prime evidence of conspiracy alleged in securing the orders for Somerset's arrest, though the wilder charges were never pressed.[4] We shall later assess this central 'evidence' in relation to the accusations laid against Somerset, but may here say that it was worthless on the face of it, smelled of collusion, and was later almost certainly repudiated by Palmer himself. But it was quite sufficient for the immediate purpose of setting in train the proceedings against the former Protector. The imperial ambassador as early as October 10th reported that rumours were abroad in London that Warwick and his party were weaving a plot around Somerset, that his arrest was imminent, that his sole

---

[1] *A.P.C.*, III, 374. Somerset was listed as attending Council meetings on Oct. 4, 5, 6, 11, 12, 13, 16; he was arrested on the 16th.

[2] *Ibid.* 379. The envoy (Jarnac) arrived on the 5th, staying in Court only one night (Edward VI, *Chronicle*, 85–86).

[3] *Ibid.* 86–88. The King seems never to have doubted this incredible story. The two entries (Oct. 7th and 11th) are oddly placed in the *Chronicle*, suggesting that Edward was told the story in two instalments.

[4] *Vide* Jordan, *Edward VI*, 285–287, and *ante*, 52–53, for the relations of Somerset and Palmer.

highly placed defender, Paget, was already under house arrest, and that Warwick had secured himself by careful military preparations.[1] On the day following came the royal affirmation of Dudley's status and power when, with Somerset present, he was raised high in the peerage to the Duchy of Northumberland, while others whose support he required were either ennobled or invested with knighthood.[2] And on this same day the ominous order went out to the Court of Augmentations to list the debts owed by Somerset to the crown.

Politically naive and always overly trusting, Somerset seems to have had no sense of personal danger until his cause was in fact in ruins. His suspicions were probably first aroused in the autumn by the examination by the Council, in his absence and with no note in its record, of a Mrs Woodcock of Poole (Dorset) who claimed to have heard a voice warning that 'he whom the King did best trust should deceive him and work treason against him'. The Council must have concluded that she was gently mad, for she was sent home, only to hear the voice again, which this time was reported to her clergyman, Thomas Hancock, who had earlier had personal dealings with the then Lord Protector.[3] Hancock took the whole story directly to Somerset, who expressed surprise and outrage, since 'this is strange, that those things should come before the Council, and I not hear of it. I am of the Council also.' When Hancock further expressed the opinion that it was Paulet who had examined Mrs Woodcock, the Duke concurred that 'it is like to be so'.[4]

Somerset had returned from Syon House to Court on October 4th. Even a week later, despite the hostile activities of Northumberland and his followers, and despite the ominous implications of the advancements in the peerage, Somerset seems to have made no move to set his apprehensions at rest, but finally on the 14th confessed to Cecil, whom he had always trusted, that 'he suspected some ill'. To this enquiry Cecil gave the cold and sharp reply that 'if he were not guilty he might be of good courage; if he were, he had nothing to say but to lament him'. Then Somerset, suspicious of Palmer, if we interpret the King's obscure entry correctly, sought to learn the facts from him, only to be further entrapped by his denial of the accusation which he had in fact already made. On the

[1] *Cal. S.P. Span.*, X, 381.
[2] *Vide ante*, 53.   [3] Jordan, *Edward VI*, 152–153.
[4] Strype, *Cranmer*, I, 379–380; Nichols, J. G. ed., *Narratives of the days of the Reformation, etc.* (Camden Soc. LXXVII, 1859), 79–80.

next day the King and Court removed from Windsor to West-minster to gain the better protection of the gendarmery already defensively disposed and, as it may have been explained to the King, 'because it was thought this matter might easilier [*sic*] and surelier be dispatched there'.[1]

The 'dispatching' occurred on the next day, October 16th, when Somerset was arrested after having dined with the King and just possibly in his presence. Then, according to the King's account, other suspects were apprehended in the course of the afternoon: Palmer, perhaps conveniently, 'on the terrace walking there'; Lawrence Hammond while passing 'Mr. Vice-Chamberlain's door' was taken by a ruse;[2] Francis Newdigate when he appeared to answer, as he thought, a summons from Somerset;[3] John Seymour and Davy Seymour, who were evidently within the palace pre-cincts;[4] and Arundel and Grey as they rode into Westminster from the country.[5] Sir Ralph Vane, more courageous and dangerous than any of those thus far taken, sought to flee, saying that 'if he could get home he cared for none of them all, he was so strong', but before nightfall was found hidden under straw in the stable of his servant in Lambeth and taken captive.[6] Moving swiftly and evidently according to plan, others amongst Somerset's supporters and de-pendents were gathered in during the course of the next two days, the principal ones being Sir Miles Partridge, William Crane, Sir Michael Stanhope, Sir Thomas Arundell, Sir John Thynne, and that famous soldier, Sir Thomas Holcroft.[7]

The Council lost little time in giving to the imperial ambassador a highly coloured and in part quite false account of what had hap-pened. Cecil was its principal spokesman, explaining that Somerset had plotted to seize the Tower and subdue London, to take several unnamed castles in the north, and then to raise the commons. These moves were to be attended by the slaughter of his colleagues of the

[1] Edward VI, *Chronicle*, 88. The Court had removed to Hampton on July 8th to avoid the plague, and then to Windsor on Aug. 13th (Machyn, *Diary*, 7–9).

[2] He was probably a yeoman of the guard, and was shortly released with no punish-ment.   [3] The steward of the Duke's household.

[4] John Seymour was the Duke's eldest son by his first marriage. He died in Dec., 1552 while still in the Tower. David Seymour was a distant relation, who was never held by stricter order than house arrest.

[5] Edward VI, *Chronicle*, 88.   [6] *Ibid.* 88–89.

[7] *Ibid.* 89; *A.P.C.*, III, 389, 391, for the list of those, twelve in all, lodged with Somerset in the Tower. Whalley was arrested on Oct. 18th, with a number of lesser persons (*ibid.* 391; Machyn, *Diary*, 10; *Grey Friars Chronicle*, 71). In addition to those already mentioned, Sir Thomas Stradling and Sir Nicholas Pointz were taken into custody. In all, thirty-nine persons were probably arrested and imprisoned for at least a season, of whom seven were servants.

Council by a hired assassin, which has been averted by the detection of the plot and the arrest of the Duke and his accomplices. When Scheyfve expressed his astonishment, Northumberland intervened to say that he too could not explain it, 'for the Duke had enjoyed the greatest reputation and authority with the Council, and had possessed a huge fortune of 30,000 to 40,000 angels (*i.e.* £15,000 to £20,000)'. But, he continued, 'this evil plot had long been in preparation, and the Council had suspected it, but their great zeal for the repose of the realm had caused them to wink at it for the time'. This bizarre version of the facts was believed by neither Scheyfve nor his imperial master. In the same dispatch Scheyfve added that Northumberland's *coup* had caused great unrest in London and in the country at large. There was a deep resentment fed by 'the hatred borne towards the Duke of Northumberland and his party by many Lords, and, above all, by the commons, who are saying quite openly that the Duke of Somerset is being unjustly accused'.[1]

Almost certainly, too, it was on the day of Somerset's arrest that a circular statement was forwarded to all the justices of the peace of the realm giving the Council's version of the action just taken. The Council had gained knowledge 'of certain heinous and detestable attempts purposed, and almost put in execution' by Somerset 'with a great confederacy of his adherents, against the state of the realm'. Somerset's purpose, it was declared, included harm to the King, the destruction of certain of the nobility, and the establishment of 'his private singular government'. The plot had been effectively thwarted, the Duke had been quickly taken and imprisoned, and now all justices were to be held responsible for the maintenance of good order under the imminent peril of the moment.[2] This immediate propaganda effort was intensified somewhat later when another long and slightly hysterical pronouncement declared Somerset to merit a shameful death for his robberies, crimes, and treasons, further averring the completely false charge that he intended to secure the succession to the throne for himself. This tract was prefaced by a bitter attack as well on the Duchess of Somerset, 'that imperious and insolent woman his wife, whose ambitious wit and mischievous persuasions led him and directed him also in the weighty affairs and government of the realm to the great harm and dishonour of the same'.[3]

---

[1] *Cal. S.P. Span.*, X, 384–386: Oct. 18, 1551.   [2] S.P. Dom., Edw. VI, XIII, 57.
[3] HMC, *7th rept.*, App., 607: *Molyneux MSS.* It will be observed that each recital of the 'conspiracy' alleged new and different offences against Somerset.

The ruling junta likewise took the most careful pains to maintain full control over London and to influence sentiment there by the most outlandish of propaganda. On the day of Somerset's arrest the gendarmery and 'bands of horse' were moved in such wise as to control the approaches to the City, while on the next day the City authorities were commanded to set a night watch. Three days later all London officials and the wardens of the livery companies were convened to hear a letter read from the Privy Council, relating that Somerset had intended to seize the Tower and the Isle of Wight, and then to 'have destroyed the City of London, and the substantial men of the same'.[1] The Council required all householders to look to their families, vagabonds were to be expelled, every gate was to be manned by day and locked and guarded by night, while suspected persons 'in mask' and masterless men were to be taken into custody.[2] These measures were watched closely by the imperial ambassador, who seems to have been fully persuaded that most of the accusations, always shifting and always more incredible, were quite false. The Privy Council, he wrote, had taken great pains to persuade London of Somerset's guilt, but had quite failed to do so, since the people, including some of rank, 'believe him to be a good man wrongly accused of this conspiracy' and credit the responsibility to Northumberland's fear and jealousy. Northumberland, he believed, had resented and feared Somerset's growing strength among all classes of men. Moved by ruthless ambition, Northumberland had felt obliged to strike, and to protect himself had seen to it that the King had been so completely deceived by 'evil accounts . . . that he shows no feeling' for his own uncle.[3] Scheyfve's analysis was shrewd and his conclusions not far from the mark.

The credibility of Palmer's revelations of treason was further strained when on October 19th he made yet another confession. He now alleged that Vane, presumably on April 23rd, had stood ready to assail the household troops with 2000 footmen and Somerset's 100 horse, 'besides his friends which stood by, and the idle people which took part'. If the rising failed, the plan was to call out the apprentices of the City by the cry of 'Liberty, liberty', and then Somerset was to make his way to the Isle of Wight or to Poole to

---

[1] Wriothesley, *Chronicle*, II, 57; Machyn, *Diary*, 10–11 (Machyn dates this meeting Oct. 22nd); *Grey Friars Chronicle*, 71.

[2] Wriothesley, *Chronicle*, II, 57–58; *A.P.C.*, III, 390. Some weeks later, on Nov. 30th, the Council ordered the City to set a double watch and to fix a rigorous curfew (Wriothesley, *Chronicle*, II, 62).

[3] *Cal. S.P. Span.*, X, 388–390: Oct. 26, 1551.

gather fresh forces.[1] A few days later the accusations thus far brought against Somerset were discussed by the Council with the intention of preparing a declaration to be issued 'to stay the minds of the people'. This was necessary because Palmer's fresh lot of allegations had altered the structure of the charges which a week earlier had been circulated to all foreign rulers, English ambassadors abroad, and the 'chief men' in the counties.[2] The most important question facing the Council was of course the reaction of France, with which England now enjoyed a close and an almost subservient diplomatic relation. Pickering, in Paris, wrote that he had reported English developments to Henry II in person, stressing that the 'perilous conspiracy lately purposed in England, very dangerous to the King's Majesty', had been exposed and broken. He had said too that Somerset had sought to gather sole power into his hands by 'certain heinous and detestable attempts' against the government of the realm and the King's own person. He had to add that the King 'paused a great while', and then made no more than a polite and conventional reply. But in a later conversation with Montmorency, Pickering gained the assurance which he wanted: that 'there is good store [of troops] in France', which were pledged in the event of need—the Constable adding that the English government should be vigilant lest the Emperor use the occasion for the advancement of the interests of 'some that are nearer of kindred unto the King than the Duke'.[3]

Now greatly distracted by the state visit of the Dowager Queen of Scotland, who had arrived in England on October 22nd,[4] the Council none the less felt it necessary to begin the close interrogation of the prisoners already in the Tower in the hope of gaining some measure of corroboration for Palmer's wild charges. Twelve of those being held were selected, ranging downwards in status from Lord Grey to certain of the servants.[5] One of the latter, William

---

[1] Edward VI, *Chronicle*, 89. The King's account, which is the principal source, is not clear on the date of this intended rising. I am almost inclined to believe that Edward refers to a muster of the gendarmery which had on Oct. 8th been set for Nov. 8th (*ibid.* 86). Somewhat later it was deposed that the intended rising was planned for August (*vide post*, 92), but see also the indictment which sets the date of the plot as Apr. 20th (*vide post*, 93).

[2] Edward VI, *Chronicle*, 90, 91: Oct. 24th and 17th.

[3] Pickering to Council, Oct. 27, 1551: *Cal. S.P. For.*, *Edw. VI*, #468; Tytler, *England*, II, 86–94. The sagacious Regent of the Netherlands was evidently coolly sceptical when, on Oct. 23rd, Chamberlain informed her of his sovereign's escape from 'this present peril'. She expressed surprise and then questioned the English ambassador minutely on the circumstances of the conspiracy (*Cal. S.P. For.*, *Edw. VI*, #163).

[4] *Vide post*, 150, 153–154.

[5] *A.P.C.*, III, 397: Oct. 25, 1551.

Crane, who seems to have served Somerset in some capacity, confessed that the 'feast of assassination' was to take place at Paget's house, that the Earl of Arundel and Stanhope were fully privy to the plot, and that he had himself sought to enlist the aid of friends of Somerset in London during August for the intended *coup*.[1] Others were also named by Crane as having had close connections with Somerset during the summer, including John Brende[2] and the Earl of Derby's son, Lord Strange, who deposed then and at the trial that Somerset had asked him to seek to persuade the King to consider marriage with the Duke's third daughter, Jane, then about ten years of age.[3]

The statements of Crane opened another line of enquiry which the Council on November 5th resolved to exploit as rigorously as might be required, notifying Darcy, the Lieutenant of the Tower, that its examiners were to have free access to the prisoners and that he was to assist them by 'putting the prisoners, or any of them, to such tortures as they shall think expedient'.[4] All the prisoners were also to be more closely guarded, with no communication, liberties, or writing materials permitted them, save by the written consent of at least six of the Council.[5] Crane seems to have supplied more details, probably under torture, which, combined with depositions also gained from Arundel, Palmer, and John Seymour, were synthesized into what Northumberland and Northampton, the prime movers in the proceedings, must have realized was a flimsy charge indeed. Crane deposed that Somerset and the Earl of Arundel had indeed discussed the arrest of the Lords of the Council, among them Pembroke. At this, the Earl had protested that Pembroke was an honest man. Somerset and Arundel had further agreed that the religion of the realm would remain unaltered. They had met on several occasions, their talk being of the reform of the estate of the realm, and they had further agreed that Northumberland and Northampton would be imprisoned as Somerset had earlier been. Arundel had also maintained that Parliament must be called to provide a legal basis for government, 'lest, peradventure, of one

---

[1] Edward VI, *Chronicle*, 92–93.

[2] Brende was a highly competent officer who had served with distinction in the Scottish war and who had since been employed in minor diplomatic capacities in Scotland and the Baltic. He was likewise a translator from the Latin of considerable gifts (Davis, Harold, 'John Brende: soldier and translator', in *Huntington Library Quarterly*, I (1938), 421–426).

[3] There may well have been truth in Strange's story. Derby had been called in discreetly to send his son up for examination (*A.P.C.*, III, 398).

[4] *Ibid*. 407. We do not know how many of the prisoners were put to torture; it seems quite certain that Somerset was not so abused.

[5] *Ibid*. 401–403: Oct. 31, 1551.

evil might happen a worse'. Following this conversation, Crane had been sent by Somerset to his wife to say that he would not 'further meddle with the apprehension of any of the Council', and commanding her to tell her brother (Stanhope) to talk no more with Arundel about the matter.

Arundel was an honourable and trustworthy man and the strong probability is that his deposition lays out fully the extent and nature of the 'conspiracy' to which he and possibly Grey were privy with Somerset. One further attempt was made to find more substantial grounds of complicity which would give some credibility to Palmer's hysterical accusations. When in early November Northumberland, Northampton, and Bedford personally examined the Earl, Arundel would admit no more than that he had talked with Somerset of the possible arrest of Northumberland and Northampton, apparently at a Council meeting, though he had at no time intended harm to their persons. He at first testified that there had been but one conversation, though later he admitted that there were several, and added that he had warned Somerset that rumours of a plot were abroad.[1]

In assembling and assessing the flimsy evidence which the Council had in hand, there must be weighed certain implications in the questions put to Somerset in the Tower, to which his replies, unfortunately, do not survive. The Council was seeking further proof that he had intended to arrest Northumberland, there being now no further reference to a projected—and wholesale—assassination. It also sought more information regarding a rumoured attempt by Vane to discredit Northumberland with the Princess Elizabeth, Pembroke, and others of the Council. It pressed hard too to determine the number of meetings Somerset had had with Arundel on the 'misliking of the state and government; and what you did conclude to the reformation thereof'. There was the suggestion, too, that Paget might have been privy to these plans and the implied belief that Somerset intended to convene Parliament in conjunction with his overthrow of Northumberland.[2] A few days later Arundel was placed in close custody after a final and unsuccessful attempt by the Council to browbeat him into more incriminating admissions. He pointed out that he had been dismissed from the Council for his

---

[1] S.P. Dom., Edw. VI, XIII, 65, 66, 67.

[2] Ellis, *Original letters*, ser. 2, II, 214. I have not found the manuscript. Ellis notes that it was among the Cotton MSS., being then so 'decayed, torn, and discoloured' that he was printing it to preserve the text. He also indicated that it was endorsed in Cecil's hand, as a 'Writing of the Duke of Somerset in the Tower of London'.

earlier refusal to vote for Somerset's release from his first imprisonment. When Northumberland gravely suggested that the evidence
indicated that he was of Somerset's faction, the completely courageous Earl rejoined that neither he nor any of his line had ever been
traitors, but that all knew who had. This vicious reply was said to
have so infuriated Northumberland that Arundel was at once
arrested.

Promises of reward, threats, and torture had failed to bring to
light any substantial evidence against the Duke of Somerset. This
was also the conclusion of London, where the 'principal merchants
. . . are particularly dissatisfied with this manner of procedure,
calling the Duke of Northumberland a tyrant, hating him, saying
that his one object is to lord it over all', and remaining convinced
that the charges were contrived. The persuasion was widespread
that the extent of Somerset's plotting was to secure the arrest of
Northumberland and his principal followers, and then to lay the
problem of the structure of the government before Parliament.[1]
This assessment may be regarded as almost certainly correct.

This, then, represents the extent of the evidence accumulated
against Somerset, much of which was so incredible on the face of it
that it was never introduced in the trial. The alleged plot to assassinate Northumberland, Northampton, and Pembroke was so clearly
an invention that it was not pursued during the interrogation, much
less at the trial. Nor was Pembroke asked to testify on the alleged,
and crucial, point that Somerset would have gone north to recruit
power had it not been for the assurances given him in conversation.
Nor was Palmer's allegation that Grey was privy to the plot ever
investigated, much less the story that the planned assassination was
to take place in Paget's house. Palmer bore deep resentment against
Somerset, was known to be unreliable, and was high in the favour
of Northumberland until they together made their expiation of
treason in 1553. Crane was an adventurer, a man who had lost his
lands, and his garbled testimony was at least in part extracted by
torture. All the other principals, Arundel, Vane, Partridge, and
Stanhope, swore that they were innocent of the charges on which
they were convicted. No less a judge than Sir Edward Coke found
the indictment against Somerset at once faulty and insufficient, 'for
it pursueth not the words or matter of the said branch of the said
Act [3 and 4 Edward VI, c. 5]' on which it was founded.[2] Simon

[1] *Cal. S.P. Span.*, X, 392–393: Nov. 16, 1551.
[2] Coke, Edward, *The third part of the Institutes of the laws of England, etc.* (L., 1797),
13.

Renard, who enjoyed Queen Mary's complete confidence and who was the most reliable of ambassadors, reported categorically to Charles V immediately after the execution of Northumberland and Palmer that both men had confessed that the really damaging charges against Somerset had been contrived, according to Palmer, with the full knowledge of Northumberland.[1] This testimony, so impeccable in its authority, must be full credited. Moreover, it is corroborated by an unknown contemporary who wrote that Palmer before his execution repudiated his share in a ghastly crime, though he claimed never to have alleged that Somerset was plotting expressly against Northumberland.[2] Somerset, to put it exactly, was brilliantly and successfully framed.

What, then, remains of solid, or at least credible, evidence against Somerset? It seems fairly certain that in April, 1551 he had contemplated the arrest of Northumberland and Northampton, and, for a moment, of Pembroke, with the intention of taking power into his own hands until his actions could be validated by Parliament. This plan he had certainly discussed in the abstract with Arundel and just possibly with Paget. To have given substance to this undertaking would have required power which Somerset did not possess and far more support in the Council than he in fact enjoyed. There is further evidence that Somerset himself quickly abandoned the plan, probably because it was wholly quixotic, but that he could not control the enthusiasm of Vane, Whalley, and Partridge, who did make blundering efforts to gain support for what would have been a treasonable undertaking had it been launched. Though there is no certain evidence, it is at least probable that Palmer may have gained fragmentary information concerning these discussions; his febrile imagination and the counsel of Northumberland supplied the rest.

4. THE TRIAL OF THE DUKE OF SOMERSET (NOVEMBER–DECEMBER, 1551)

Northumberland had, however, enough in hand to risk the trial of his adversary. He knew that no more credible evidence could be gained, and he was desperately anxious to complete the destruction

---

[1] *Cal. S. P. Span.*, XI, 185, 187: Aug. 27, 1553.

[2] Raumer, *Briefe aus Paris*, pt. ii, 73, citing *Rélation de l'accusation et mort du Duc de Somerset*. The manuscript from which von Raumer made his translation is in the Bibliothèque Nationale, MS. 15888, ff. 205–210. Froude apparently saw it, while Pollard was unable to find it, using Froude's reference to the Fonds St Germains des Prés, vol. 740. The author is unknown. The chief value of the document lies in lending independent, though evidently rather remote, support to Renard's conclusive evidence.

of Somerset before Parliament, so often prorogued, should come into session in January. The security measures in the Tower were accordingly tightened in early November.[1] Paget, who had been warned to absent himself from Council during the course of the summer, was committed to the Fleet on October 21st on baseless charges of conspiring against Northumberland's life, and was on November 8th removed to the Tower, where a few days later he was required to surrender the seal of the Duchy of Lancaster.[2] That the ruling junta was ready to move was signalled on November 16th, when the sheriffs of Middlesex, Surrey, and Kent were ordered to return 'good and substantial full juries of knights and esquires of the best sort' in the course of the following week.[3] A few days later Somerset was removed to a safer lodging in the Tower, while the Council ordered the watch in the City to be doubled and required the magistrates to make two thorough searches of London for suspicious persons in the interval remaining before Christmas.[4] On November 23rd the King records that the Marquis of Winchester had been appointed to serve as High Steward for the arraignment of the Duke of Somerset, which was at hand.[5]

A special commission of judges, including Bromley and Portman, was appointed on November 16th for taking indictments by the grand jury assembled by them at Westminster five days later. The indictment handed down was almost completely fictitious or muddled in its allegations, such as that on April 20th at Somerset House the Duke, with other persons, had conspired to 'deprive the King of his royal dignity; and to seize the King's person; and, at his, the Duke's will and pleasure to exercise royal authority'. To further these treasonable designs Somerset, with Partridge, Stanhope, Holcroft, Newdigate, and others, had assembled with the intention of seizing and imprisoning Northumberland, then to take the Tower and its treasure into their hands. It was also alleged that on the same day the Duke had incited the citizens of London to rebellion by calling them out with drums and trumpets and with the cry of 'Liberty, liberty', a statement which every citizen of London knew to be wholly untrue. Then for added measure the indictment recited that on May 20th Somerset, with the lesser persons before named, sought once more to raise rebellion and to take and imprison

[1] *A.P.C.*, III, 411, 413.
[2] Gammon, *Master of practises*, 258; *A.P.C.*, III, 419. Paget was never tried on this charge, his ruin being accomplished on other grounds (*vide post*, 113–115).
[3] *A.P.C.*, III, 419: Nov. 19, 1551.
[4] *Ibid.* 423–424, 425.
[5] Edward VI, *Chronicle*, 96.

Northumberland, Northampton, and Pembroke. The lesser associates, with the addition of Vane, Sir Thomas Arundell, and John
Seymour, were brought within the scope of the indictments, which
were returned to Chancery on November 23rd.[1] On the next day
the King directed the Lord Chancellor to make out a commission
under the Great Seal for the trial of Somerset and the others named
on charges of high treason.[2]

Northumberland and the Council were now moving with great
speed towards the trial and were exhibiting extreme nervousness as
they reflected on sentiment in London. On November 30th Hoby,
as Lieutenant of the Tower, was commanded to take the Order of
the Garter from Somerset and to inform him that his trial was at
hand, though in a final examination the Duke 'would confess
nothing'.[3] Stow, who followed these events closely, tells us that in
preparation for the trial the Council on November 30th ordered
every householder to 'see to his family and keep his house', while
those with armed harness were to stay within until called.[4]

Meanwhile, the peers who were to try Somerset had been summoned, those on hand on November 30th having heard Palmer,
Hammond, Crane, and Newdigate swear, just before the trial commenced, that their confessions had been true and given without
'any kind of compulsion, force, envy, or displeasure'.[5] On the day of
the trial the number of the peers present had increased to twenty-
eight.[6] Those present numbered exactly half the peerage of England,
but the charges which have been levelled that the trial was packed
seem unsustained when the list of those not there is analysed.[7]

Somerset was taken from the Tower by water at 5 a.m. on December 1st, 'shooting London Bridge' and thence to Westminster

[1] *Fourth report*, Dep. Keeper of Public Records (1843), App. II, 228–229: 'Baga de secretis', pouch xix.

[2] There is a tentative, as well as a hurried, quality about the document. Phrases were stricken out and the name of Miles Partridge was added to the list of those to be tried under the indictments. The Chancellor was required to 'make a sufficient commission, sealed with the great seal of England' for the trial before the Marquis of Winchester as 'our seneschal for determining and hearing these treasons and felonies'. Winchester was to proceed 'in such sort and manner as in the like causes of the last Duke of Bucking- ham and the Marquess of Exeter . . . and no otherwise', the last phrase being deleted. (S.P. Dom., Edw. VI, XIII, 64.)

[3] Harl. MS. 523, #15, f. 26: Council to Hoby.

[4] Stow, *Annales*, 606.

[5] Edward VI, *Chronicle*, 97: Nov. 30, 1551.

[6] The King gives the number as twenty-six, but he names twenty-eight (*ibid.* 97–98), if, as we have done, Winchester be counted.

[7] Fifteen of the absences are immediately explicable. Four of the peers (Norfolk, Arundel, Grey of Wilton, and Paget) were in the Tower; the peerages of Grey of Ruthen and Courtenay were in abeyance; six of the peers were disqualified as minors; Clinton

Hall where the court of his peers was assembled.[1] We are told by an anonymous source that Winchester sat as High Steward under a cloth of state raised three steps above the floor, while the peers sat on benches, one step lower.[2] The indictments against Somerset were read at once, with five particulars of treason and felony to which the Duke pleaded not guilty and left himself to the judgement of his peers. The statements of Palmer, Crane, and Whalley were then read. Somerset angrily rejoined that he had never intended to raise a force in the North and 'declared all ill he could devise against Palmer' and that 'the worse Palmer was, the more he served his purpose'. He denied categorically that he had ever planned a banquet at which Northumberland and others would be assassinated and rejected the absurdity that he with a force of 100 could contemplate an assault either on London or on a gendarmery of 900. He denied as well Lord Strange's deposition, which Strange however reiterated under oath, and assailed the testimony of others of his accusers as unreliable or false. At this point 'the lawyers rehearsed' and the peers 'went together', it being wondered at that 'a mean action' should be expanded into a charge of treason.[3]

---

was abroad in France on a diplomatic mission, and Willoughby may well have been instructed to stay with his command at Calais. And, finally, Rich, who as Lord Chancellor would in normal course have presided at the trial, was in process of resigning the Great Seal because of illness and his clashes with Northumberland. He had shut himself up in his London house and had written to Northampton that he was stricken with a mortal complaint. The formalities of his resignation were not completed until Dec. 21st.

There remain thirteen peers whose absence is not immediately explicable. Shrewsbury, who, as we have seen, sought to remain neutral, may well have been instructed to stay with his important command in the North. The Earls of Cumberland and Westmorland were distant, but they had taken no active interest in politics throughout the reign, and remain shadowy figures. So too, John de Vere, 16th Earl of Oxford, had remained aloof from politics, though he was a moderate Protestant and had been regarded as friendly to Somerset. There remain nine barons not in attendance (Dacre of the North, de la Warr, Conyers, Darcy of Aston, Mordaunt, Morley, Mounteagle, Sandys, Vaux), most of whom had lived quietly on their estates throughout the reign, but three of whom (de la Warr, Conyers, and Sandys) had at least on earlier occasions been friendly to Somerset. Though we believe the evidence against Somerset to have been largely contrived and the trial itself to have been a travesty of justice, it most assuredly cannot be said that the court of his peers was packed. (Vide Edward VI, Chronicle, 97–98, for the list of the peers in attendance. The list of peers returned by the Serjeant-at-Arms on November 30th differs slightly from what we believe to be the final accurate count by the King (Fourth rpt., Dep. Keeper of Public Records, App. II, 230). The former counts Mounteagle and Sandys as present, while not mentioning Latimer and Cromwell, present according to the King's list.)   [1] Stow, Annales, 607; A.P.C., III, 432.

[2] Harl. MS. 2194, #10, ff. 19–20. This volume is entitled Lords Stewards of England and trials before them. The larger part of the document was composed temp. Charles I, but this portion clearly dates from the Elizabethan period.

[3] We are drawing from two accounts: the King's, to be found in the Chronicle, 98–99, and Harl. MS. 2194, # 10, ff. 19–20. They differ little save in particulars.

There was evidently sharp questioning from the peers and decided disagreement on the charges of treason, upon which Northumberland 'seemingly sad . . . denied that he would ever consider any practice against himself as treason'.[1] In the discussion that followed, Northampton was 'contentious with many', while other peers belatedly raised the question of whether Northumberland, Northampton, and Pembroke should take part in the trial in which most of the charges so directly concerned them. The answer was given that a peer in such an instance stood above challenge. After further differences of judgement Somerset was acquitted of the charge of high treason, and then by a divided vote was 'by voices most favouring' convicted of felony under the terms of 3 and 4 Edward VI, c. 5. The Duke apparently made no rejoinder, but 'gave thanks to the Lords for their open trial and cried mercy' of Northumberland, Northampton, and Pembroke 'for his ill meaning against them, and made suit for his . . . [life], wife and children, servants and debts, and so departed without the ax of the Tower'. Thereupon, the King tells us, the great concourse of people awaiting the verdict 'shouted half a dozen times so loud that from the hall . . . door it was heard at Charing Cross plainly, and rumours went that he was quit of all'.[2] The imperial ambassador, reporting on the trial a few days after its conclusion, had formed the judgement that Somerset had 'talked with some of his familiars and friends' regarding ways to overthrow Northumberland, but had never planned to kill him. He tells us, too, that several of the peers were ill content with the verdict as found, feeling that the Duke should have been acquitted even of the charge of felony.[3]

We have observed that most of the evidence adduced against

---

[1] There is in the King's account of the trial a not very clear suggestion that Somerset, while maintaining he had no intention of killing Northumberland, Northampton, and Pembroke, had spoken of it and then changed his mind, 'and yet seemed to confess he went about their death' (Edward VI, *Chronicle*, 99). But it must be remembered that the King's version reflects what Northumberland told him of the trial. Harl. MS. 2194 makes no mention of any such admission and, more significantly, Paulet, in writing to Clinton on the day after the trial to lay all the evidence against Somerset before him, makes no mention of the matter (Tytler, *England*, II, 97).

[2] Seeing the axe turned away from the prisoner, the people outside thought the Duke stood free of the charges (Edward VI, *Chronicle*, 99–100; Harl. MS. 2194, #10, ff. 19–20). Stow (*Annales*, 607) tells us that the people 'made such a shriek, casting up of caps . . . that their cry was heard to the Long Acre beyond Charing Cross, which made the Lords astonished'; *et vide* Machyn, *Diary*, 12.

[3] *Cal. S.P. Span.*, X, 407: Dec. 10, 1551. Hoby, too, thought that Somerset had 'acquitted himself very wisely of whatsoever could be laid at his charge', and that the sentence of felony was gained wholly by Northumberland's means. (*The travaile and life of Sir Thomas Hoby, etc.*, ed. by Edgar Powell (Camden Misc. X, L., 1902), 75).

Somerset was so clearly contrived that little of it could in the end be introduced against him. Northumberland in effect withdrew the charge of treason when anxious questions were raised amongst the peers, but there remained the equally capital indictment of felony. The governing statute (3 and 4 Edward VI, c. 5) had been passed in part for the protection of the magnates of the Council, and it was a felony to call together or to incite an unlawful assembly by any means. There remains the possibility that Somerset had contemplated a stir in London, just as he had certainly contemplated the seizure of his principal enemies amongst the Councillors. But there is no evidence available to us, as there was none which Northumberland could develop, that there was a serious disturbance in London on the days in question. Even the presumption of a planned conspiracy, never assembled, rests on the worthless testimony of Palmer and of Crane (under torture) and was indignantly denied by Vane, Stanhope, and Partridge, who were held to have been privy to it. The evidence, to use Coke's careful phrase, was 'altogether insufficient'. What the peers were really determining at Westminster Hall was that Somerset was too articulate, too stubborn, and potentially too dangerous to leave alive. The sixteenth century knew no other way to remove a discredited minister of state than to destroy him.

But the Lords of the Council, quite as much as the King, had been astonished at the ebullient vigour of London sentiment when the hundreds who had waited outside Westminster Hall expressed themselves when they mistakenly thought that the Duke stood free. Arundel and Paget were privately examined in the Star Chamber; they may well have owed their lives to the fear of further exciting public opinion.[1] To show their solidarity and to over-awe the City, the Councillors, as peers with their bands of horse, a few days later (December 7) assembled in a muster boasting upwards of 700 horse, 180 of the gentleman 'pensioners and their bands, with the old men of arms, all well-armed men', with the 'horses all fair and great', and with their pennons preceding them 'passed twice about St James's Field and compassed it [a]round and so departed'.[2] The excited young King was there to review his troops, 'each band fully harnessed, and each with trumpets and standard, all of whom' passed twice before him 'five in a rank'.[3] The City was forewarned as it was over-awed, though the more experienced imperial ambassador reported

---

[1] Froude, History of England, V, 383-384.

[2] Edward VI, Chronicle, 100; Machyn, Diary, 12-13; Two London Chronicles (Camden Misc. XII), 25.   [3] Stow, Annales, 607.

that in truth the muster was confused and the troops evidently unseasoned.[1] Over-awed the City might be, but the Duke of Northumberland's great fear was of articulate and powerful support for Somerset in Parliament which, often prorogued, was appointed to convene only a few weeks hence. Somerset he knew must be destroyed before that date or his own overweening authority might vanish. Evil actions done carry the seeds of evil actions to come.

5. THE EXECUTION OF THE DUKE OF SOMERSET (JANUARY 22, 1552)

Not only did Northumberland stand in nervous fear of the unpredictable sentiments of Parliament, but it seems probable that he remained uncertain and apprehensive lest the King intervene with a pardon for his uncle. Considerable public business was laid before Edward during December,[2] while Northumberland and the Council gave sustained attention to planning unusually elaborate entertainments to distract the young monarch during the holiday season extending from December 24th until January 6th. Thus Northumberland personally instructed Sir Thomas Cawarden to appoint George Ferrers as 'Lord of Misrule' and to proceed with lavish planning, even though the time available was unfortunately short. The 'Lord of Misrule' was to be in the royal household for the full Twelve Days, and was to be given all assistance that he might require.[3] The Duke and the Council were deeply involved in the most unusual tasks of planning the entertainment, down to the details of the fancy dress of those attending, including a 'jerkyn for the tumbler, strait to his body', and twenty-four liveries for servants.[4] So elaborate were the entertainments, in fact, that the Master of Revels records a very heavy outlay for the King's diversion.[5]

Even contemporary observers had no doubt that Edward's distraction was the concern of Northumberland, though Holinshed perhaps correctly thought the holiday festivities were also planned to divert the City where 'the minds and ears of murmerers were meetly well appeased'.[6] Scheyfve, who paid his respects to the King on New Year's Day, had no doubt that the plan had been to divert

---

[1] *Cal. S.P. Span.*, X, 408.

[2] Edward VI, *Chronicle*, 100–102.

[3] Kempe, A. J., ed., *The Loseley manuscripts, etc.* (L., 1836), 23–25.

[4] *Ibid.* 27.   [5] *Ibid.* 54.

[6] Holinshed, Raphael, *Chronicles, etc.* (2 vols., L., 1577), ed. by Henry Ellis (6 vols., L., 1807–1808), III, 1032–1033.

the King, though he added that Northumberland also hoped to win the favour of the gentry by the elaborate presentation. He noted, too, that there had been no 'Lord of Misrule' appointed for the holiday season for some years past, and that at least 100 persons had roles in the festivities. He quite correctly deduced, too, that Northumberland had for some time past accorded the King greater participation in the tasks of government in order to dispel hostility to his own great power and more recently to 'cause the King to forget the Duke of Somerset as quickly as possible'.[1]

The King was enthralled by the entertainments so carefully planned for his pleasure and distraction. On December 23rd he removed to Greenwich where the arrrangements had been made, noting on the following day that he 'began to keep holy this Christmas and continued till Twelfth Night'.[2] He was particularly delighted with a tilting held on January 3rd in which eighteen sons of peers and courtiers ran six courses, all accomplishing 'their courses right well, and so departed again'. Three days later these participants, with two additions, 'came in to the tourney, and fought right well' before him. That same evening came the climax of the holiday activities when a play in which *Riches* and *Youth*, with 'pretty reasoning', each claimed that he was the better.[3] There followed an elaborate masque which deeply shocked the imperial, French, and Venetian ambassadors, all of whom were present. Scheyfve explained that though several of the scenes were witty and harmless, one represented 'a religious procession of priests and bishops', who paraded through the court, bearing 'under an infamous tabernacle' a sacrilegious representation of the Holy Sacrament in its monstrance, which was greeted with great ridicule by the Court.[4] Then came an undescribed masque by women participants, with a banquet of '120 dishes', and, the King rather plaintively concludes, 'this was the end of Christmas'.[5] But this was not quite the end of the period surely designed to secure the distraction of the King. On January 17th, only a few days before the execution of Edward's uncle, another elaborate tilting was arranged for his entertainment.[6] Then on the 21st, the King noted that he returned to his palace in Westminster to await the grim event of the morrow.

[1] *Cal. S.P. Span.*, X, 437–438, 444: Jan. 14 and 18, 1552.
[2] Edward VI, *Chronicle*, 102.
[3] *Ibid.* 104–105. The interlude may have been written by Sir Thomas Chaloner.
[4] *Cal. S.P. Span.*, X, 444: Jan. 18, 1552.
[5] Edward VI, *Chronicle*, 105.
[6] *Ibid.* 106.

Meanwhile, and almost certainly with the King's full knowledge and consent, the Council under Northumberland's guidance had determined that Somerset's execution must be carried out before Parliament convened on the 23rd. On January 19th the decision was made in Council, with sixteen members present, when an instrument in the King's own hand was laid before it ordering that 'The Duke of Somerset and his confederates . . . be considered, as appertaineth to our surety and the quietness of our realm that by their punishment [and execution according to the laws] example may be showed to others'.[1] The instrument had been drafted by or for the King on the 18th, the pregnant interpolation possibly having been added, in an unknown hand, before Cecil laid it before the Council. This has been construed as meaning that the Council acted without the King's full knowledge and consent, but this can hardly be true since the interpolation adds little of command and would surely have been questioned in Council had it been a sinister and dangerously fraudulent change in the royal instruction.[2] The interpolation, we would conclude, was probably added after the event.

It seems likely that Somerset had sensed from the moment of his conviction that Northumberland intended no mercy, and so poisoned was the mind of the King towards him that there would be no royal intervention. He had composed his mind by reading the Bible and by private devotions, one of which, composed the day before his death, was scribbled on the pocket calendar which he had brought to the Tower:

> Fear of the Lord is the b[e]ginning of wisdom.
> Put thy trust in the Lord with all thy heart.
> Be not wise in thine own conceit, but fear the
>   Lord and flee from evil.

> From the Tower, the day before my death.[3]

On this same day the warrant for his execution was drawn.[4]

The Council had straitly ordered the constables of London to warn every householder to remain in his house until 10 a.m. on January 22nd, thereby limiting the number who would seek to witness the

---

[1] Cotton MSS., Vespasian, F, xiii, 171.

[2] Pollard, *Somerset*, 307–308; Chapman, *The last Tudor king*, 236–237; Tytler, *England*, II, 68–70.

[3] Stowe MS. 1066. Interestingly, at the end is written the name of his first wife, long since repudiated and dead: 'Katerine Hartford, Caterine Seamour.' The devotions found in Harl. MS. 2342, # 31–35, ff. 137–143, were, we think, those of Lady Jane Grey, and not Somerset's.

[4] Rymer, *Foedera*, XV, 295–296.

execution. None the less, long before daylight people from the City and its suburbs were streaming to Tower Hill, where by 7 a.m. a great multitude had assembled. Stow, who was an eye-witness, tells us that before 8 a.m. the Duke was brought out to the block by the Warden of the Tower and the sheriff's officers, stiffened by a contingent of the royal guard.[1] Somerset immediately knelt in private prayer, and then rose to make the customary address to those assembled.[2] Somerset declared that though he had 'never offended against the King either by word or deed', and had been as faithful to the realm as any man, he must none the less die as an act of obedience to law. He must also remind his auditors that so long as he wielded authority he had set forth and furthered religion in the realm. He rejoiced that 'now the state of Christian religion cometh most near unto the form and order of the primitive church', which he exhorted his auditors to accept and embrace as a great benefit bestowed by God on England.

At this point in the tense proceedings all authorities note that there was a great stir in the packed crowd, the people being 'driven into a great fear, few or none knowing the cause: wherefore', Stow wrote, 'I think it good to write what I saw concerning that matter.' The cause of the confusion was the arrival from outlying hamlets of armed horsemen who had been ordered to assume guard duty at 7 a.m. Finding themselves late, this contingent pressed shouting to the scaffold, which caused the crowd to think that an attempt was being made to rescue Somerset. The frightened spectators thereupon scattered 'some one way some another, many fell into the Tower Ditch, and they which tarried thought some pardon had been

---

[1] Stow, *Annales*, 607.

[2] We follow Foxe's text of the speech from the scaffold, the account of which he says he had from 'a certain noble personage, who not only was there present . . . but also, in a manner, next unto him upon the scaffold' (*Acts and monuments*, VI, 293–295). Stow, be it noted, gives only a very condensed account. Grafton followed Foxe. There is still another eye-witness account in Cotton Charters, IV, 17. The hand is contemporaneous. The narrative is clearly not derived from Foxe, from which it differs in a number of particulars. This version has been printed by Ellis (*Original letters*, ser. 2, II, 215–216) in a fairly accurate rendering, save for the fact that two lines were dropped. To compli-cate matters further Francis Bourgoyne, a French minister at Corbigny, in the see of Autun, who had fled from persecution in 1547, also provides an account. Bourgoyne had come to England recently and now forwarded to Calvin on the day of the execution an account of the speech given to him—'for certain reasons [I] was not present at the sight'—by two most reliable informants, Richard Vauville and Utenhove. This version differs quite radically from the texts we have cited, as does a brief account of Somerset's remarks to be found in Harl. MS. 2194, #10, ff. 19–20. As was usual on such occasions, everyone present heard what he wished to hear. Stow is undoubtedly the impeccable authority for the account of the execution; Foxe, as is so often the case with mid-six-teenth-century sources, probably provides the most reliable text of the speech.

brought, some said it thundered, some that a great rumbling was in the earth under them, some that the ground moved, but there was no such matter', that excellent historian, Stow, concluded, 'more than the trampling of their feet, which made some noise'.[1] And then the evidently dangerously exercised crowd, which was becoming a mob, was further stirred when Sir Anthony Browne, on duty with the guard, was observed riding towards the scaffold. The crowd instantly concluded that Browne had arrived with the royal pardon and cast up their caps and cried 'Pardon, pardon is come; God save the King'. It was Somerset himself who quieted the assembly and then continued with his speech. He told them that there would be no pardon and that he was contented with his death as he had been with his services to the King, for 'I have always been most diligent about his majesty in his affairs, both at home and abroad, and no less diligent in seeking the common commodity of the whole realm'. He declared that he wished all the Council the grace and favour of God. If any men had been offended by him, he asked their forgiveness just as he gave his own. Now, he concluded, 'I once again require . . . that you will keep yourselves quiet and still, lest, through your tumult, you might trouble me. For albeit the spirit be willing and ready, the flesh is frail and wavering.'[2] His words at an end, the Duke knelt with Richard Cox, long his nephew's tutor, for his last devotions. Then, the ritual of courtesies to the Lieutenant of the Tower, the sheriffs, and the executioner completed, he knelt and when the words 'Lord Jesus, save me' were on his lips, the axe fell, ending the life of this strange yet great man.

Somerset had borne himself with great dignity and magnanimity

[1] Stow, *Annales*, 607. Foxe says that the noise sounded like a great storm or like an explosion of powder (*Acts and monuments*, VI, 294); Grafton follows Stow in attributing the stir to the arrival of the tardy troops (Grafton, Richard, *A chronicle at large, and meere history of the affayres of England, etc.* (L., 1568); ed. by Henry Ellis as *Grafton's Chronicle, or History of England, etc.* (2 vols., L., 1809), II, 527-528); the Cotton Charters account records that the 'great sound' seemed to many present to be 'above in the eleme(nt) as [if] it had been the sound of gunpowder set on fire in a close house bursting out, and by another sound upon the ground as [if] it had been the sight of a great number of great horses running on the people to over-run them'. Many present fell down, others ran to and fro, shouting and praying, 'while I looked when one or other should strike me on the head, so was I stunned' (Ellis, *Original letters*, ser. 2, II, 215-216). Holinshed follows Stow's account (*Chronicles*, III, 1034) with minor variations. Machyn thought the noise sounded like gunfire or horsemen riding in the distance, and added that the troops on guard also panicked momentarily (*Diary*, 14). Wriothesley remained mystified after the event: 'there was such a fear and disturbance among the people suddenly . . . that some tumbled down the ditch, and some ran towards the houses thereby and fell, that it was marvel to see and hear, but how the cause was, God knoweth' (*Chronicle*, II, 65).

[2] Foxe, *Acts and monuments*, VI, 293-295.

in these last dreadful moments of his life. Once more he had categorically denied that he meant injury to the King or the realm and there was no admission of any measure of guilt under the terms of the statute under which he had been tried. Both Northumberland and Palmer under similar circumstances were later to admit that the Duke was done to death under false and partially contrived charges. But the King, too, must bear some measure of responsibility. He was now in his fifteenth year, was frequently at the Council board, was beginning the slow process of assuming the realities of regimen, and was, as his *Chronicle* displays, extraordinarily astute and well-informed. Yet his sole observation on the tragedy that had occurred was the cold and brutal entry in his journal, 'The Duke of Somerset had his head cut off upon Tower Hill between eight and nine o'clock in the morning'[1]. This is all and that was all there ever was to be. It is true that the King had been deliberately and systematically misled with respect to the facts, that he had been skilfully and happily diverted during the days when the decision was being taken, and that he had borne evident dislike for his uncle since the days in 1549 when Somerset had used him as a pawn when for a brief moment he had contemplated raising the country to retain his power. But when all these things are said, there remains unexplained the young King's incredible coldness and the fact that at no time did he require a sifting or a fair appraisal of the evidence being gathered to destroy Somerset.[2]

There was deep resentment and foreboding amongst all classes of men in England after the deed was done and all understood that it had been accomplished by Northumberland's ruthlessness and power. But so naked did that power now stand that most men sought to make such adjustments as they might to the political realities. But none, surely, more quickly and skilfully than the faithless Richard Morison, greatly advanced by Somerset and now ambassador at the Emperor's court. When the news of Somerset's arrest reached him in Innsbruck he wrote at once to Cecil that 'the Duke hath years but too many, as it appeareth; a God's blessing, let

---

[1] Edward VI, *Chronicle*, 107.

[2] There have, of course, been many efforts to explain Edward's failure to intervene, all of which centre on his youth and his personal admiration for Northumberland. They are all based on sentimental conjectures. One of these argued that the King gave no open sign of his feelings because to do so was unbecoming to a monarch. None the less, so it is said, he would often sigh and weep when Somerset's name was mentioned, saying that the Duke had done nothing wrong, and enquiring, 'Did ever before a King's uncle, a Lord Protector, lose his head for felony, a felony not clear in law and weakly proved.' (Harl. MS. 2194, #10, ff. 19–20.)

him bear his burden, or cast it off where he can'.[1] On the same day he explained to Sir Nicholas Throckmorton his reasons for having hoped the Duke's first imprisonment would lend him a new character. But now it was clear that he stood undone by an over-reaching ambition.[2] And to Northampton, who had cause for hating Somerset, he explained that his grounds for pleading for mercy after the Duke's first imprisonment had been that only Somerset could control the ruthless and intriguing ambitions of Wriothesley. But 'for Somerset's falling or standing, what had I to do more than others', Morison enquired.[3] In all this special pleading of a completely egocentric man there is evidence of great fear, a perhaps very human wish to shrink back as far as possible from the great peer now in mortal danger, and to make peace at any price with the new nexus of power.

Scheyfve, on the contrary, never moved from his conviction that Somerset had been innocent and had been destroyed by Northumberland, who would now advance his ambitions without serious opposition. About a month after the execution he reported that Somerset was mourned by the people and that it was well known that Northumberland had been resolved to accomplish his death before Parliament should assemble. He thought, too, that Cranmer stood in peril because of his efforts to secure Somerset's pardon, that Paget, Rich, and even Paulet were in some danger if Northumberland should attempt to clear the ground for his power.[4] Foreign interest in this dramatic and inexplicable event was intense. Calvin, for example, pressed all his correspondents in England for news and explanation. Francis Bourgoyne, in writing to him, praised the wisdom and the great achievements of the Duke, but suggested that he had never been quite the same after consenting to his brother's destruction.[5] But perhaps the most sensible and human of all the comments on what had transpired was made by Anne of Cleves, then living comfortably at Dartford, who informed her brother of Somerset's execution, adding, 'God knows what will happen next; and everything is so costly here in this country that I don't know how I can run my house'.[6]

Northumberland had little to fear from the self-abasement of

[1] Cal. S.P. For., Edw. VI, #488: Nov. 18, 1551.
[2] Ibid. #489: Nov. 18, 1551.
[3] Ibid. #491: Nov. 18, 1551.
[4] Cal. S.P. Span., X, 452–453: Feb. 12, 1552.
[5] Robinson, Original letters, II, 735: Bourgoyne to Calvin.
[6] Bouterwek, K. W., 'Anna von Cleve, Gemahlin Heinrichs viij. Königs von England', in Zeitschrift des Bergischen Geschichtsvereins, VI (1869), 140.

careerists like Morison, or for that matter from the conviction of the Emperor that Somerset had been guilty of no high crime against the state. But he stood in real terror of the turbulent discontent of the commons of England who had found in Somerset a symbol of hope and who bore against Northumberland a deadly, though sometimes impish, detestation. This could not be brought fully under control; it imparted to Northumberland's policy and actions a kind of evident terror, and it began at once. Thus on January 24th the Council considered evidence that Matthew Colthurst had caused bonfires to be made at Bath on December 3rd when the first, and false, news of Somerset's acquittal arrived. He had also caused the bells to be rung for hours, had dispensed bread and drink to all comers at the bonfires, and on the following day had sent his servant through the streets giving 2d each to the poor, 'where he never gave 1d. in his life before'. The complainant from Bath alleged also that one Thomas Holland had returned from London shortly before Christmas (1551) and had displayed a shilling which he falsely contended bore Northumberland's emblem of the ragged staff on one side. When he protested that it was only the Lion, Holland upbraided him, saying, 'Tush, tush, hold thy peace, fool! Thou shalt see another world ere Candlemas; the Duke of Somerset shall come forth of the Tower, and the Duke of Northumberland shall go in.'[1] The Council lent its grave attention too to a libellous and seditious ditty recently sung by William Tomson in Northampton. The mayor there was ordered to determine whether the song was of Tomson's composition, and if so to pillory him and cut off both ears; if not, the culprit was to be sent up to London for examination.[2] There had been much of festering and ugly discontent since the days when Somerset had been expelled from the seats of power; there was to be much more in the frightened days to come.

6. SOMERSET'S CHARACTER

The Duke of Somerset was one of the most complex figures in sixteenth-century history; indeed, in many ways he scarcely seems to belong in the century in which birth placed him. We have elsewhere traced out the frictions and causes which in their totality occasioned his first fall from power almost immediately after the great insurrections were brought under control in the autumn of

[1] *A.P.C.*, III, 462: Jan. 24, 1552.
[2] *Ibid.* 465: Jan. 25, 1552.

1549.[1] He had then been restored in status and wealth, had been readmitted to the ruling junta which was the Council, and his house had been joined with that of John Dudley's in a marriage alliance which must have meant that these two overweening personalities were resolved to live in amity. Though it is certain that Northumberland had been moved principally because he knew that there was powerful sympathy for Somerset in Parliament and the realm at large, his first actions none the less displayed a considerable magnanimity. It is also clear that restoration to the Council was not accompanied by any substantial restoration of confidence in Somerset's political wisdom and that in the whole of the Council there was no one who had not by October 1549 been at least partially alienated. These realities the Duke of Somerset never accepted or even fully understood. There can be no doubt that he was seeking a full restoration of power, though not by the fanciful or treasonable means which Northumberland and his hirelings thought it necessary to allege.

Somerset had many serious faults as a political leader. Though surely a great statesman in the sense that he possessed a noble vision of what England might be, he was at once naive and inept in the political leadership which he sought to supply. Always imperious in nature, he had likewise grown arrogant in his exercise of power; he handled men too roughly and inflicted on them wounds which would not heal. Northumberland could never forget the Protector's brusqueness in refusing small favours and in rebuking him for his enclosures; Russell had been verbally castigated like a schoolboy for his military blunderings in Devon; Herbert had been alienated by Somerset's overt sympathy for his tenants; Northampton had been publicly shamed for his marital woes and for his shortcomings as a field commander; and Wharton and Lord Grey had been harshly rebuked for their failures in the North. Somerset enjoyed an amazing capacity for wounding other men and an almost complete insensitivity or incredulity when it was pointed out that he had done so. His understanding of other men was dangerously faulty, while he was almost completely naive in estimating their true sentiments and convictions. He was given to sharpness of speech, haughtiness of manner, and to an aloofness which made it extremely difficult to work with him or for him. While lending great and punctilious formal respect to the King, he had failed utterly to win either the affection or the confidence of a sensitive and precocious boy, who never forgave his uncle for the humiliations and probably fright to

[1] Jordan, *Edward VI*, 494–505.

which he was exposed during those frantic hours when Somerset was considering and rejecting the waging of civil war in order to regain his power.

All these failings aroused widespread and often bitter resentments amongst men who sought to share power with Somerset, and who became exceedingly nervous and uncertain as he adopted a mien which could only be described as regal. Their personal relations with the Duke were also exacerbated by the arrogance and vanity of his Duchess, who was at once fierce and proud in her deep devotion to her husband, and who was all too prone to meddle in minor affairs of state. Heavy strictures were also laid on him for his plundering of the wealth of the state, though it must here be said that his fortune came to him principally from inheritance and from the grants made to him earlier by Henry VIII. But even more disliked and exploited were his buildings and renovations for his own uses, which were conspicuous by their very nature and on the scale more nearly of a sovereign than of a subject.

Somerset had failed, too, because he refused even to contemplate raising faction in the Privy Council by exercising as Protector his undoubted power to dismiss and appoint members at will. There is the suggestion, in fact, that his credit amongst his colleagues on the Council had been lost—and that irretrievably—before he fully sensed that his power, in the first crisis, and his life, in the second, were in grave danger. So too, by a strange irony, one of the most eminent and skilful generals of his age stripped himself of all military power when he bestowed the two high commands required to repress the risings of 1549 on Russell, whom he alienated by his harsh—and just—criticism, and on Warwick, whom he had long since embittered. Somerset stood helpless and alone when Russell's forces were added to those of Warwick in 1549; care was taken after his restoration to the Council that this great soldier should be without resources when the trap of Warwick's conspiracy was once more closed around him in the autumn of 1551.

Subsuming and to a degree explaining all these tragic weaknesses and failures was the essential failure of Somerset's political and social policy. The reform measures which he had driven through a reluctant Parliament alienated and seriously frightened the landowning classes of England, so completely and perfectly represented by the ruling junta. Somerset was determined to secure and to enforce far-reaching and extremely radical reforms which would right the wrongs and grievances of the commoners of England; the costs were to be laid against the fortunes of the dominant political and economic classes of the realm. As the first punitive measures to secure these reforms began to have their effect and to confirm the stubborn intentions of the Protector, a mood of embittered reaction amongst the gentry and the nobility came swiftly to pervade the realm. Then rebellion swept the land as those who had been lifted up to a vision of what England might become sensed that the Protector did not enjoy the power or the support required for implementing his own announced policies. In a sense these risings had been provoked by the political naiveté and the blundering idealism of the Duke of Somerset; in another sense they may be said to have been triggered by a blind and hopeless effort of the commons to lend strength to his hand. But Somerset was a responsible governor of the realm; he had no other choice than to crush rebellion against the King and his estate. In so doing he destroyed the sources of his own support and hence at the moment of crisis found himself literally alone.

Despite the many flaws in his nature, there remains much of greatness in Somerset's policy and character. He had made himself a well-educated man, becoming a competent Latinist, speaking and writing French with ease, and knowing some German. He admired, as he understood, intellectuals and, as we have seen, had brought a considerable number of them into his government and the court circle, especially in the second rank of responsibility and power. We have observed that he had lent direct encouragement to the Commonwealth Party, deeply imbued as it was in Christian humanism, and had adopted much of the social and economic aspirations of the group. Somerset had moved with great vigour to reform the English society and to alleviate the economic condition of the commons of England. The costs of the programme of reform which he supported with such tenacity were to be borne by the gentry and the nobility of England and they would have been high. He had sought to lead the way by reconstituting the tenures on his own great estates by Act of Parliament, but there were to be no followers amongst the landed classes of the realm. His policy was firmly and punitively set against the enclosers, the rack-renters, and the covetous men of England. These policies quickly alienated the landowning classes who undoubtedly lent their support to his deeply frightened colleagues in the Council, who twice at the moment of crisis were to throw their overweening strength to Dudley. We have seen, too, that Somerset by pressing for reforms which he could not carry into effect had so raised the hopes and expectations of the commons that they rose in a dangerous insurrection which destroyed his credit as it did his power. The Duke of Somerset was in a true sense a victim of his own idealism.

From the pervading gentleness and idealism of his nature there also sprang the deep devotion of the Lord Protector to a policy of religious toleration which, perhaps in part unconsciously, he sought to apply in a period of singular difficulty. It must be remembered that during a term of power of almost three years no man in England was put to death for heretical beliefs. Protestantism was allowed to plant itself by the vigour and persuasiveness of its own resources, rather than by a brutal assault of persecution or repression on men's faith. His personal tolerance was evidently almost unbounded and his personal relations were civilized, whether he was dealing with intransigent Catholics like Mary and Gardiner or with 'hot gospellers' like Ponet and Hancock. His own Protestantism was firm, dating back to the days of Henry VIII, and it was to sustain him in the last hours of his life. His was a moderate, an essentially non-sectarian religious faith, that was to contribute greatly to the centrist tradition in the development of Anglican thought. It seems certain that the essential compromises inherent in the first Book of Common Prayer expressed his own religious convictions quite perfectly, and this explains why those who pressed so zealously for further reformation came to doubt the evangelical warmth of Somerset's piety. But his contribution to religious peace, to the moderate tendencies of Anglicanism, and to the ultimate triumph of religious toleration in English life had been great indeed.

There was, in fact, nothing of the zealot, nothing of the fanatic, in Somerset's nature. His temper was short and he could and did wound by the lash of his words, but there remained no silent grudge or festering animosity towards men, even towards those who in the end betrayed him. Somerset was, then, a magnanimous man, which in some respects may mean a defenceless man in a world that was rough, dangerous, and sinister. The capacity for conspiracy, for double-dealing, and for the ruthless thrust for power was simply not in him. It is this fact which destroyed him. None the less he had given to English life a certain tone and temper which were not to be wholly lost. In some respects he surely ruled badly or at the least unwisely. But he also ruled with greatness of style, magnanimity of spirit, and an enduring tenderness for the great mass of the poor and the unregarded. Surely, he remains on balance a great man and a great spirit. All this, interestingly enough, the historians and chroniclers of the age seem somehow to have sensed. Perhaps among them all Holinshed put it best: 'For all men did see in the decay of this Duke, the public ruin of all England, except such as indeed perceived nothing.'[1]

7. THE POLICY OF VENGEANCE (1552)

Somerset's destruction was followed almost immediately by the trial and execution of four of his party, men who were alleged to have shared in his conspiratorial plans against Northumberland and his principal supporters in the Council. Sir Ralph Vane, Sir Thomas Arundell, Sir Miles Partridge, and Sir Michael Stanhope were executed on February 26th, all stoutly denying their guilt under the charges brought against them.[2] It is interesting to observe that most of the property of these attainted men was almost immediately granted to court officials of the second rank who had lent support to Northumberland and who were known as men who did his bidding. Thus Vane's estate in Middlesex, valued at £13 6s 8d p.a., was vested in Sir John Gates, while his far more valuable manor of Enfield and other manors in Kent were given to Sir William Sidney of the Privy Chamber. Stanhope's household goods at Beddington (Surrey) were granted to Thomas, Lord Darcy, while Partridge's considerable estate at Kew was disposed to Sir Henry Gates, a brother to Sir John. Arundell's lands in the West went mostly to Lord Clinton. These were by no means great estates, but they were disposed with an almost indecent haste in order to buttress the political dominance of Northumberland.[3]

It is quite impossible to speak with certainty regarding the degree of guilt of these men, for the records are thin and fragile, but one can at least say that the case against them could have been no stronger than that against Somerset himself. Vane was a fearless, fiery, and probably dangerous man, who, as we have noted, on an earlier occasion had deliberately stood his ground against Northumberland.[4] He was indicted on charges of having incited Somerset to treasonable conspiracy and, 'answering like a ruffian' to the charges, was on January 27th sentenced to death by hanging. Dr Bill was appointed to give him spiritual solace and he met his death bravely and with an absolute denial of his guilt.[5] Stanhope, a soldier

---

[1] Holinshed, *Chronicles*, III, 1035.

[2] *Grey Friars Chronicle*, 73–74.

[3] Strype, *Memorials*, II, i, 541–542; Nichols, *Remains*, II, 431; S.P. Dom., Edw. VI, XIX, ff. 6, 29, 13, 22, 14, 51.

[4] *Vide ante*, 64–65.

[5] *Fourth rpt.*, Dep. Keeper of Public Records (1843), App. II, 231–232: 'Baga de secretis'; Edward VI, *Chronicle*, 108; *A.P.C.*, III, 466.

of some distinction, and a man of moderate judgement, was during his whole career a known supporter of Somerset and—probably quite as damaging—was a half-brother of the Duchess of Somerset.[1] Partridge, known as a reckless gambler, a valiant and honoured soldier in the Scottish campaign, and a man of occasionally turbulent conduct, lies under greater suspicion than the rest, though it remains scarcely credible that Somerset would, as alleged by Palmer, have entrusted him with planning the raising of London.[2] Far greater doubt remains regarding the guilt of Sir Thomas Arundell, against whom Northumberland's suspicion had been aroused at an earlier date because of Somerset's efforts to secure his release from prison where he was held on dubious charges of unreliability during the Western Rising. These doubts were evidently shared by the trial jury which had to be bludgeoned into finding a verdict of guilty; in the King's words:

'Sir Thomas Arundel was likewise cast [i.e., convicted] of felony in treason, after long controversy; for the matter was brought in trial by seven of the clock in the morning [of the] 28th day; at noon the quest went together; they sat shut up together in a house, without meat or drink, because they could not agree, all that day and all night; this 29th day in the morning they did cast him.'[3]

Few indeed in Tudor England are the instances in a treason case where a jury manfully tried to stand its ground against the verdict which it knew the government required.

The rest of those held under suspicion were never brought to formal trial and escaped with their lives, if not their fortunes. Richard Whalley, whom Rutland had accused of 'evil words . . . very seditious and of great import', had been closely examined and had in effect turned state's evidence against the Duke, his benefactor. He was held a close prisoner until June, 1552 when he was freed after resigning as Receiver for Yorkshire and paying a heavy fine. But three months later he was back in prison on charges of peculation as Receiver, to be held in strait confinement until Mary's accession. He was released a ruined and stripped man, heavily in debt, and forced to sell Welbeck Abbey and Wimbledon.[4] So too,

---

[1] *Fourth rpt.*, Dep. Keeper of Public Records (1843), App. II, 231–232.

[2] Edward VI, *Chronicle*, 109; *Fourth rpt.*, Dep. Keeper of Public Records (1843), App. II, 231–232; *DNB*.

[3] *Ibid.* 108; *Fourth rpt.*, Dep. Keeper of Public Records (1843), App. II, 231–232.

[4] *A.P.C.*, III, 215; HMC, *Salisbury MSS.*, I, 96; Turberville, A. S., *A history of Welbeck Abbey, etc.*, I (L., [1938]), 8–10.

John Thynne, whose fortunes had been bound since boyhood with those of Somerset, escaped trial and was released in June, 1552 upon paying a heavy fine and relinquishing a minor governmental office.[1] Sir Thomas Holcroft, a brave and honourable soldier, who had been held on the flimsiest of charges, was also granted his freedom in June, after relinquishing his offices and supplying bonds. Northumberland himself ordered the release of two lesser men, Fisher and Brende, being persuaded that they had been sufficiently punished.[2] And then, almost completing the release of the lesser adherents of the Duke of Somerset, Bannister and Crane, 'the one for his large confession, the other because little matter appeared against him', were delivered out of the Tower.[3]

There remain only the few of the great and powerful of the realm who had been held in prison because of the closeness of their ties with Somerset. Lord Grey of Wilton, a redoubtable and completely reliable soldier, who had won a deserved reputation in the Scottish campaign and in repressing the Western Rising, was granted his full pardon on June 10, 1552, and three months later was entrusted with the important command of Deputy of Calais, shortly thereafter being named commander at Guînes.[4] In harder case was the Earl of Arundel, a Catholic in sentiment, who had found himself badgered and buffeted through much of the reign. He had been courted by Northumberland when the first conspiracy against Somerset had been formed, only to find himself ejected from the seats of power on fantastic charges directly Dudley's position was secure.[5] He had, as we have seen, been skilful and humane in maintaining order in Sussex during the insurrection of 1549. There can be no doubt that he had held conversations with Somerset looking forward to a change in the structure of the government, though the only hard evidence that could be gained against him was the unreliable testimony of Crane.[6] Committed to the Tower on November 8, 1551,[7] Arundel was never brought to trial and resisted all efforts to wring further and more damaging testimony from him in repeated examinations. But he was made to understand that his freedom could not be gained or his lands recovered until he had signed a submission and confession, which be it said he later repudiated. The ritual of submission was exacted

---

[1] Lodge, Edmund, *Illustrations of British history, etc.* (3 vols., L., 1838), I, 170; HMC, *Salisbury MSS.*, I, 96; *DNB*.

[2] *A.P.C.*, III, 405, 476–477; S.P. Dom., Edw. VI, XIV, 33: May 31, 1552.

[3] Edward VI, *Chronicle*, 131: June 13, 1552.

[4] *Ibid.* 130.

[5] *Ibid.* 19.

[6] Jordan, *Edward VI*, 452.

[7] Edward VI, *Chronicle*, 94–95.

on December 3, 1552, when he acknowledged having been a confederate of Somerset's, confessed that he was 'privy and of knowledge of the said dangerous conspiracy', and further admitted that he had not revealed all he should regarding the plot against Northumberland. Then, having been fined 6000 marks payable over the term of six years, and having given bonds of 10,000 marks, he was set free.[1] Arundel was to have no further influence until shortly before the King's death when Northumberland restored him to the Council and remitted his crushing fine. But he had not forgotten Northumberland's earlier perfidy; it must have given him the greatest satisfaction to betray the Duke at the first possible opportunity and to lead the force to Cambridge which brought Northumberland back to the Tower under charges of undoubted high treason.

Of all those who suffered unfairly as a consequence of Northumberland's venom mixed with fear, the calculated brutality with which Paget was treated was in all respects the most undeserved and pointless. He had been high in Henry VIII's favour and trust in that monarch's later years, he had lent great service in uniting the ruling junta in 1547, and, though deeply loyal to Somerset, had been the frankest of the Protector's critics in and out of the Council. He was undoubtedly the most able of the Edwardian Councillors, and was the steadiest and most competent of the diplomatists of his generation. But Northumberland never forgave him his honourable support of Somerset and was always irritably displeased when Paget was at the Council board. Hence, long before conspiracy was charged against Somerset, Paget had been warned to absent himself from court in the early summer of 1551 and thereafter was only once recorded as present at a Council meeting. Then early in October he was ordered to keep to his house on the ridiculous charge that he had given offence to the Emperor by maintaining that he had not in 1549 promised freedom of worship in her household to the Princess Mary.[2] Without further charges, and despite the fact that there could have been no conversation with Somerset or Arundel, Paget was sent to the Fleet on October 21st and then to the Tower.[3] All his possessions were sequestrated, while his books and papers were held sealed in his London house.[4] Paget was subjected to further humiliation when the seals of the Duchy of Lancaster were taken from him and handed over to one of the most devoted of

---

[1] *A.P.C.*, IV, 185–186.
[2] Jordan, *Edward VI*, 208–209, for this episode.
[3] *Vide ante*, 84, 89.   [4] *A.P.C.*, IV, 27–28: Apr. 26, 1552.

Northumberland's henchmen, Sir John Gates. Every effort was employed to ruin him, including Palmer's preposterous charge that the 'banquet of assassination' was to have been held in Paget's house. But there was simply no evidence of conspiracy that could be adduced even by Northumberland's fertile mind, though Paget continued to be held in strait imprisonment in the Tower.

Paget, of lower middle class London origin, had lifted himself in status by his own great abilities and dedicated service to the state over a period of many years. He was now a baron, albeit of recent creation, had won the Garter, and possessed considerable estates, though his fortune was relatively modest when compared with those of most of his colleagues on the Council. Hence what may well have been his greatest humiliation came when in April, 1552 he was ordered degraded 'from the Order of the Garter for divers his offenses, and chiefly because he was no gentleman of blood, neither of father's side nor mother's side', the Garter and the George being vested on the Earl of Warwick, Northumberland's heir.[1]

The offence finally and formally alleged against Paget was corruption in his administration as Chancellor of the Duchy of Lancaster, it being made clear to him that he would remain in prison unless he signed a submission and confession suitable to Northumberland. At least two drafts of the submission did not meet the Duke's requirements, and Paget was once more before the Council before a confession was signed that met the full requirements of vengeance.[2] He admitted the sale of lands without full authority, taking fines of lands for his own profit, and making leases in reversion for a term of more than twenty-one years.[3] Though it remains impossible to determine all the facts in the case, considerable doubt remains regarding the extent of Paget's corrupt practices, beyond the accepted norm of the age, since only a year earlier Northumberland had surveyed the Duchy revenues and found no fault. More persuasively, the Duchy income in 1551 was only £1000 p.a. less than in 1543 despite the sales and grants made of its properties by both Henry VIII and Edward VI.[4] But the dominating fact is that in the Tudor age a prisoner of state signed whatever confession of minor offences was placed before him under promise of freedom; otherwise capital charges were likely to follow.

Paget was released from the Tower to his London house, but a

[1] Edward VI, *Chronicle*, 119; Stow, *Annales*, 608; Wriothesley, *Chronicle*, II, 69.
[2] S.P. Dom., Edw. VI, XIV, 33, 34: May 30 and 31, 1552.
[3] Edward VI, *Chronicle*, 129, 131.
[4] Gammon, *Master of practises*, 276.

few days later was again called before the Council to be informed that his fine was £8000 and that he was to forfeit all his steward-ships and keeperships. Furthermore, he and his household were to remove to his Staffordshire estate within six weeks and there to remain in rural isolation.[1] At this point Paget rebelled at the indig-nities being heaped upon him. His estate was small and his debts heavy, and he was unable to pay the fine laid on him unless there should be a merciful reduction. He protested as well, 'with the effusion of many tears', the order to remove to Staffordshire. His wife suffered from a stitch in her side and a liver complaint that required the services of her London physician, while he confessed to a fistula 'which so much troubles him that . . . he rots as he goes'. Further he had only two country houses: Barton which could not accommodate his household and Beaudesert which, 'though it be pretty is yet so small as after one month it will wax unsavory for him to continue in . . . and then he shall have no place to remove unto but to some inn'.[2] The plea of comfort had its effect on his former con-freres, for 'the Lord Paget was licensed to tarry at London and thereabouts till Michaelmas, because he had no provision in his country',[3] while in September 1552 the Council fully relieved him of the rustication order.[4] Meanwhile, Paget was negotiating for some reduction of the great fine laid against him, the last entry in the King's *Chronicle* recording the first stage of remission when £2000 was forgiven.[5] He was seeking desperately to save his lands by paying as much as possible in cash, the first instalment of £1000 being paid in December, for he knew that Northumberland prized Beaudesert and the Staffordshire estate.[6] In April, 1553 when the Duke was casting about for all possible support, the remainder of Paget's fine was remitted. But during the last tense and dangerous weeks of the reign Paget sought to keep clear of Northumberland and his inducements. When the moment of crisis came Paget re-joined his old colleagues in London to share in the proclamation of Mary as Queen and, it is somewhat satisfying to note, it was Paget and Arundel who were dispatched by the London Lords to inform her of the proclamation by which she had been declared Queen of England.

[1] HMC, *Salisbury MSS.*, I, 96: June 20, 1552.
[2] Lodge, *Illustrations*, I, 171–172; HMC, *Salisbury MSS.*, I, 96.
[3] Edward VI, *Chronicle*, 133.
[4] *A.P.C.* IV, 131: Sept. 27, 1552; Lansdowne MS. 2, f. 78.
[5] Edward VI, *Chronicle*, 156: Nov. 28, 1552.
[6] *A.P.C.*, IV, 176–177: Nov. 23, 1552; S.P. Dom., Edw. VI, XV, 58: Nov.?, 1552.

V

THE PRICE OF WEAKNESS: FOREIGN
AFFAIRS (Late 1549 to the end of the reign)

1. THE TRIAL OF A FRENCH ENTENTE

The disasters of the black summer of 1549 were completed for
England by the formal declaration of war by Henry II on August 8th.
Though this action was by no means unexpected, it came at a time
when England, her naval forces aside, could deploy literally no
further military resources to meet the new emergency. The bitter
rising in Norfolk was not brought in hand until late in August,
while the even more serious insurrection in the west of England was
not finally quelled until early September. All available and trustworthy military power had been sent against the risings, including
troops drawn down from the Border and men brought home from
Calais and Boulogne, even though it was well known to English
intelligence that Henry II was massing large forces against the
Boulogne enclave. These grave circumstances were greatly worsened when in September Warwick launched against Somerset the
conspiracy which was to topple the Protector from power and in
mid-October to lodge him in prison. But these courses had required
troops, and had also occupied the whole of English attention during
weeks when she was formally at war with a major power.[1] Moreover, once he had attained ascendancy in the Council, Warwick's
preoccupation, as we have seen, was to consolidate his position and
to keep order in a realm which was turbulent and, in his judgement,
for two years on the verge of rebellion. The fact is that he dared not
wage vigorous war against France; from the beginning his policy
was to secure peace at any possible price. Nor was that by any
means all; Warwick was wholly prepared to undertake a complete
reversal of Somerset's foreign policy by aligning England closely
with France, thereby gravely prejudicing her relations with the
Emperor.

[1] *Vide* Jordan, *Edward VI*, 453 ff., for a full discussion of these matters.

Montmorency had instilled in Henry II from the day of his accession (1547) the determination to re-take Boulogne by force as a matter of honour, even though the treaty terms exacted by Henry VIII from Francis I called for its restoration, upon payment of a stipulated sum, in 1554. De Selve, in London, had been able to secure accurate maps of the Boulogne defences, and numerous probing attacks had been made, even before the declaration of war, to feel out these defences.[1] Privateering operations against England had likewise been loosed, while heavy concentrations of troops and siege supplies were accumulated at Ardres and Montreuil-sur-Mer.[2] However, the first act of war against England was a sortie of a fleet of heavy galleys against English naval vessels anchored off Jersey, which failed completely and in which the French were said to have lost a thousand men, with the English left in full control of the Channel.[3] On land the French were far more successful, the outworks of Boulogne at Blackness and 'the Almain camp' being won by treason, which in turn uncovered the defences of the strong fortifications at Newhaven.[4] Henry II assumed personal command of his army on August 17th, the French after a sharp field engagement taking the remaining outfort at Bolemberg.[5] But there remained heavily fortified and well commanded main defences of Boulogne proper. Henry II had no taste for the dull routines of siege warfare, or for the plague which had now broken out in both armies, and retired to other pursuits, leaving his army in the capable hands of Châtillon (Gaspard de Coligny).[6]

At the outset of the French attack on the Boulogne outforts, the Emperor had sent forward a herald who solemnly warned Henry II of his own treaty obligations to intervene in the event the 'Old Conquest' (Calais) should be assaulted. The French were accordingly scrupulous in avoiding clashes on the Calais borders, only a few miles distant, but were none the less in the early days of the

---

[1] Bibl. Nat., Fonds du Bethune: Mem. du regne de Henry II, 1 F.3117, ff. 42–44, describes each fort in detail, with an intimate critique of each English commander, down to the rank of captain (Haigneré, D., 'Boulogne sous l'occupation anglaise en 1549', in *Bull. de la soc. acad. de . . . Boulogne-sur-Mer*, I (1864–1872), 432–445); *et vide* Haigneré, D., 'Rapport d'un espion français en 1549', in *ibid.* IV (1885–1890), 277.

[2] Decrue, Francis, *Anne Duc de Montmorency, etc.* (Paris, 1889), 79–82, 83.

[3] Edward VI, *Chronicle*, 13; Hayward, *Edward VI*, 298; Stow, *Annales*, 597.

[4] The name used by the English for the fortifications at Ambleteuse.

[5] Edward VI, *Chronicle*, 13; Stow, *Annales*, 597; Decrue, *Montmorency*, 85.

[6] Gerrebout, J., 'Monographie d'Ambleteuse', in *Mémoires de la soc. acad. de . . . Boulogne-sur-Mer*, XXVIII (1917), 117–122; Lefebvre, M., *Histoire générale . . . de Calais, etc.* (2 vols., Paris, 1766), II, 269–270; *Cal. S.P. Span.*, IX, 426–428: Renard to Emperor, Aug. 8, 1549.

operation able to sever communications between the two English enclaves, thereby making it extremely difficult to supply Boulogne.[1] Châtillon accordingly pressed his attack on the pier in Boulogne harbour, against which he was said to have fired 20,000 shot before an assault was undertaken, though it must be noted that at no time was he able to sever English sea communication with Boulogne. After the first month of hostilities the principal French gains had been made by surprise or treachery, and it was the judgement of the imperial ambassador in Paris (Renard) that the campaign was going badly for France.[2]

None the less, Boulogne stood in need of heavy reinforcements and staffing with more experienced officers, which the Council confessed to Hoby, then with the Emperor, it simply could not supply, even though the domestic turmoils were at last in hand.[3] Hence renewed petitions for direct assistance were to be laid before the Emperor. The convulsion of Somerset's fall followed, with the result that it was late October before any significant measures could be taken for strengthening the Boulogne garrison. A circular memorandum reciting Somerset's wickedness was sent to all English ambassadors abroad on October 11th.[4] Then, a few days later, the Council instructed the Lords Lieutenant in the several counties to make levies of troops to be assembled at Dover, first drafting idle men who would not labour and those who were 'the greatest doers and ringleaders in the late commotion'.[5]

In our earlier discussion of events preliminary to the formal war with France, we observed that Paget had failed in his effort in June, 1549 to secure from the Emperor the inclusion of Boulogne under the treaty terms which governed Calais, the 'Old Conquest'.[6] It was only after his diplomatists had assured him of this failure that Henry II had dared launch avowed war on the English in the Boulogne enclave. The Emperor had informed Renard fully of this dreary and hopeless negotiation, suggesting that the whole intent of Paget's special mission had been to gain greater strength for England in negotiations that she would probably have to undertake with France for the cession of Boulogne.[7] But Warwick and the

---

[1] Lennel, F., *Histoire de Calais, etc.* (2 vols., Calais, 1910), II, 243.
[2] *Cal. S.P. Span.*, IX, 434–435, 436, 439; Hayward, *Edward VI*, 298.
[3] *Cal. S.P. For., Edw. VI*, #196: Sept 7, 1549.
[4] *Ibid.* #201.
[5] S.P. Dom., Edw. VI, IX: Oct. 16, 1549; *ibid.* 54. It is clear that these new levies had not been dispatched as late as Nov. 27, 1549 (*ibid.* 56).
[6] Jordan, *Edward VI*, 301, 304.
[7] *Cal. S.P. Span.*, IX, 422–423: Aug. 2, 1549.

Council determined to try once more for imperial support, instructing the experienced diplomatist, Sir Thomas Cheyney, as well as the persuasive Hoby, to proceed to the Emperor in order to give the now official version of Somerset's overthrow and to lodge a strong appeal for the loan of forces to be employed for the defence of Boulogne.[1] On the same day, Van der Delft wrote unhappily that the Privy Council had not informed him of the purposes of the special mission and that the Emperor was not confiding in him, though he would 'gladly take a more prominent part in these doings'.[2] Cheyney laid before Charles a flat request for permission to recruit 4000 foot and 2000 horse in the imperial domains for immediate service in recapturing the Boulogne outforts, for otherwise the city could not be long defended. He gained little but sympathy from the Emperor who did however reluctantly give permission for recruiting 600 German horse and 4000–5000 foot in Friesland, provided they were transported by sea and that England gave satisfaction regarding certain of the Boulogne fortifications which Charles held were on imperial territory. But he made it clear that he would not involve himself in possible war with Henry by lending any overt aid. At the same time, he correctly suggested to Cheyney that France was in no position to undertake aggressive siege operations on the strong central fortifications still held by England.[3]

A surprise assault having failed, Warwick, now firmly seated in power in England and the insurrections there at an end, and the attitude of the Emperor uncertain, Henry II was disposed to treat, while Warwick was desperately anxious for peace on almost any bearable terms. As early as November 7 Van der Delft correctly reported that Anthony Guidotti, a Florentine merchant long settled in London and much trusted by the Council, had been sent to Paris with instructions to feel out conditions of peace, though meanwhile Boulogne was receiving reinforcements.[4] The Privy Council informed Cobham and his commanders at Calais that Châtillon would be sending a representative through the lines for preliminary discussions, 'whether his purposes be real, or only to espy upon the English' defences there.[5] Already, the heartened

---

[1] Cal. S.P. For., Edw. VI, #202: Oct. 22, 1549.   [2] Cal. S.P. Span., IX, 463.
[3] Ibid. 478: Nov. 27, 1549; Strype, Memorials, II, i, 296–297.
[4] Cal. S.P. Span., IX, 469. The King noted that Guidotti 'made divers errands from the Constable of France [Montmorency] to make peace with us (Edward VI, Chronicle, 20). Guidotti was rewarded by a knighthood and a yearly pension of £250 on Apr. 17, 1550, a further pension being given to his son John.
[5] Harl. MS. 284, #38, f. 56: Nov. 25, 1549.

English were taking a stronger stand on Boulogne, counting heavily on the promised imperial mercenaries and calling for the restoration of the outforts.[1] The French, for their part, were troubled by desertions and low morale among their own mercenary troops and were seriously concerned as the first trickle of English reinforcements for Calais were arriving.[2] Guidotti was in Paris in late December with definite orders to treat and, it was rumoured, with proposals for a marriage treaty between Edward and the French Princess Elizabeth.[3] By mid-January the peripatetic Guidotti was back in London with assurances that the French monarch also desired to treat.[4] Accordingly, commissioners for negotiation were appointed: Lord Russell, Paget, Sir William Petre, and Sir John Mason for England, and an equally formidable group of soldier-diplomatists headed by Châtillon and Rochepot (François de Montmorency), for the French.

The English commissioners were instructed by the Council to hold the discussions at Calais or Guînes if possible, and were authorized to cede Boulogne on condition that the marriage treaty with Scotland be recognized by France, the key fortifications at Boulogne be razed and the full ransom for its return paid. Finally, they were to promise if need be that all save two of the English strong-points in Scotland would be abandoned.[5] The English instructions, delivered in stages, were so loosely drawn as to be unrestricted, and there is evidence that the commissioners were told privately to haggle for all they could get and then await instructions from the Council. There were no meetings until February 19, 1550, some days having been spent in rather acrid discussion of the formal meeting place, the Privy Council in the end instructing its representatives to accede to French insistence that the conversations be held in the Boulogne area.[6]

The French, negotiating from strength, from the outset refused to be concerned with any substantial topic other than the 'leaving of Bulloin'. They were thus unwilling even to discuss support for the English marriage treaty with Scotland, countering rather with the demand that the English withdraw entirely from the northern

[1] Cal. S.P. Span., IX, 481.   [2] Ibid. 481–482, 488.
[3] Ibid. 490: Dec. 20, 1549; Mémoires de la vie de François de Scepeaux, Sire de Vieilleville (vol. XXVI of Collection complète des mémoires relatifs à l'histoire de France, etc. (Paris, 1822)), 324.   [4] Harl. MS. 523, #44, f. 56.
[5] Cotton MSS., Caligula, E, iv, f. 272; Harl. MS. 36, #12, f. 69; Sloane MS. 4149, #5: Jan. 10, 1549.
[6] Ibid. ff. 203–210b. The instructions to the French commissioners may be found in Bibl. Nat. MSS., 3125, ff. 20–27.

realm. Paget reported to Warwick that they refused to recognize any debts or pensions formerly paid to England, since they had been obliged to expend such large sums in protecting their shipping from English privateers.[1] Paget warned that the French were fully aware of English weakness and 'the evil condition of our estate at home', and he advised Warwick that the Council must consider whether it would be better to cede Boulogne for what could be got, or 'for want and insufficiency' to lose it in a continuing war.[2]

Paget, though recently under suspicion as an adherent of the Duke of Somerset, was clearly in charge of the negotiations on the English side, and his dispatches to Warwick were perceptive, brutally frank, and forceful. In a private letter to Warwick, he emphasized that the French correctly had a low estimate of English strength, and that they intended to have Boulogne. He therefore urged that England conclude the war on the best terms possible, for the nation must have peace in order to settle her estate and regain her accustomed strength.[3] This advice was fully accepted by the Council, and the commissioners, now limiting their discussion to the Boulogne issue, moved with dispatch to conclude an agreement on March 24th for a treaty of peace, conditional on the restitution of Boulogne on payment of 400,000 crowns in two instalments. The English artillery and military stores were to be retained.[4] Almost immediately £30,000 was forwarded by the Council to Boulogne for payment of arrearages to the garrison and labourers, while numerous peers were asked to permit appointment of their sons as honorary hostages in the traditional exchange.[5] The peace was formally proclaimed in England on March 28th,[6] and was, so we are told, received 'with great bonfires with great cheer at every constable's door in every parish'.[7]

The formalities for the surrender of Boulogne and the conclusion of the ratification were speedily concluded. The French hostages, who were to be sumptuously entertained, began arriving in mid-April,[8] while Lord Clinton, appointed to make the surrender,

---

[1] Cotton MSS., Caligula, E, iv, 203–210b.
[2] *Ibid.* ff. 214–216b; *ibid.* 55, f. 275 (now 284–286); the latter document is badly scorched.
[3] Lansdowne MS. 2, f. 33; Froude, *History of England*, V, 265–267; Cotton MSS., Caligula, E, iv, ff. 237, 276–279.
[4] Rymer, *Foedera*, XV, 212–215; Hayward, *Edward VI*, 312. Renard had accurately set out the terms as early as March 15 (*Cal. S.P. Span.*, X, 45); *et vide ibid.* 53.
[5] *A.P.C.*, II, 418, 420: Mar. 26 and 28, 1550.
[6] Hughes and Larkin, *Tudor proclamations*, I, 486–487; Add. MS. 5485, f. 43; Harl. MS. 288, #59, f. 103.
[7] *Grey Friars Chronicle*, 66.   [8] Edward VI, *Chronicle*, 26, 27.

handed over the city to Châtillon on April 25th and marched away to Calais with an already much reduced garrison force to be employed for strengthening the border defences there.[1] The first of the two instalments of the French ransom payments was made at Calais, after which Clinton returned to London where, 'after thanks, he was made Admiral of England . . . taken into the Privy Council and promised further reward'.[2] In part, the justly famous Boulogne light horse was dispersed in the Calais enclave, though the larger part was transported to England for service in London, on the northern border, and in Ireland.[3]

The details for sealing the treaty of peace were concluded by special diplomatic missions in May. On May 18th, Henry II made a triumphal entrance into Boulogne in order formally to retake possession there. We are told that the royal party was amazed at the strength of the central fortifications and that the remaining English officers were bitter, saying the Privy Council would come to rue the surrender.[4] Somewhat earlier Lord Cobham, Petre, and Mason, who was to stay on in France as ambassador, had been received at Amiens where Henry II was sworn to the treaty in a ceremony of great pomp and dignity.[5] On May 23rd Châtillon landed at Woolwich with the French mission and was met by 'three-score gentlemen . . . and also saluted with great peals both at Woolwich, Deptford, and the Tower'.[6] On the day following they had an audience with the King, and on the next day 'the ambassadors came to the court, where they saw me take the oath for the acceptance of the treaty, and afterwards dined with me', with martial pastimes afforded after the state dinner.[7] On the 29th the French party was entertained by Somerset, now partially restored in favour, the dinner being followed by elaborate entertainments on the Thames. Just before the departure of the mission, the only known substantial discussion of diplomatic matters was held, when the French met with the full Council for a review of such remaining unresolved matters as the exchange of prisoners, the restoration of ships, and English relations with Scotland.[8]

The superb spectacle of the entertainment of the French mission

---

[1] Edward VI, *Chronicle*, 27; Wriothesley, *Chronicle*, II, 37; *Two London chronicles* (Camden Misc. XII), 21; Stow, *Annales*, 604.

[2] *Ibid.* 29; *A.P.C.*, III, 24: May 4, 1550.

[3] *Ibid.* 30; *Cal. S.P. Span.*, X, 86–87; *A.P.C.*, III, 30: May 11, 1550.

[4] *Cal. S.P. Span.*, X, 92–93; Edward VI, *Chronicle*, 31.

[5] Harl. MS. 284, #51, f. 76; *Cal. S.P. Span.*, X, 87–88; Edward VI, *Chronicle*, 31.

[6] *Cal. S.P. For.*, *Edw. VI*, #215; Edward VI, *Chronicle*, 31.   [7] *Ibid.* 31–32.

[8] *Ibid.* #215: June 2, 1550; Edward VI, *Chronicle*, 31–32; Wriothesley, *Chronicle*, II, 39–40, for a full and exciting narrative of the mission.

could hardly conceal the harsh realities of the treaty. Boulogne was in truth worthless to England, but it had been wrested from France by Henry VIII as a symbol of his power, at immense cost in men and treasure. Warwick could not dedicate the power and the economic resources required for its successful defence in a long siege. But the fact remained that the city, with its strong inner fortifications, had not been really defended at all. England was exhausted after a period of turbulence and intractable risings and had likewise just suffered the convulsion of a change in government which was at once unpopular and untried. Warwick simply had to gain peace at almost any price; this had been the advice of that experienced realist, Paget, and this governing consideration the English negotiators could not conceal. The mantle of the Emperor's protection—and little more—still held Calais secure for England. But Charles could not be induced to add Boulogne to his burdens. All this is quite clear and is fully defensible in terms of English foreign policy. But Warwick's weakness in policy was exhibited not by the cession of Boulogne, not much before the treaty date for its return, but rather by his continuous later yieldings to French diplomacy while pursuing a policy, both foreign and domestic, which brought him to the brink of war with the Emperor. His foreign policy—if indeed he had one—was as weak as it was feckless.

The surrender of Boulogne also had the effect of weakening the defences of Calais, which occupied a very different place indeed in English sentiment and policy. This last remnant of the great English medieval holdings in France was considered part of the realm, was a rich and bustling commercial centre for trade with Europe, and had for generations past been heavily, and expensively, defended. The boundaries of the Pale, regarding which there were chronic frictions with France, enclosed an area of approximately 120 square miles. The town of Calais lay within great walls, rectangular in shape and something like 1200 yards in length and 400 yards in width. The whole system of fortifications was surrounded by a moat, its inner defences including not only the famous castle, but the tower on Risebank, an island dominating the approaches to the harbour. Under the English occupation numerous sea-walls and canals had been constructed, greatly increasing the agricultural resources of the Pale, which was in time of peace nearly self-sufficient. A number of lightly held strong-points lay along the border, useful principally for observation and reconnaissance. But there were also very strong outforts, covering the central fortifications, the principal of which were Newnhambridge [Neuillet],

Hammes Castle, and Guînes. Newnhambridge had its own commander, and this square fort, supplied with fifty-five pieces of light
artillery, was protected by marshes and deep watercourses. Hammes
Castle, built on a large mound and pentagonal in shape, and in
1547 possessing thirteen brass pieces and seventy-one iron cannon,
dominated much of the marsh area of the Pale. By far the strongest
of the outforts was Guînes Castle, nearly square in shape and surrounded by earthen walls and a formidable moat. Guînes, which
had always taken the first shock of any major French incursion, was
heavily garrisoned and armed with fifty-six modern brass pieces
and an incredibly large array of 230 iron pieces, several of large bore.
The whole of the Pale was, then, very heavily armed, with 563
artillery pieces in the outworks and 478 in the fortified precincts of
Calais, but these elaborate and extensive fortifications were difficult
to maintain and required a large, and experienced, garrison.[1]

English apprehensions regarding Calais were in no way relieved
following the cession of Boulogne, despite the treaty of amity with
France. The French pressed hard and aggressively against the ill-
defined frontier, almost immediately after peace was concluded.
The English sent Armagil Wade [Waad], Clerk of the Calais
Council, to France to set out the English position on border and
trade dispositions and with authority to suggest a standing commission of local commanders to resolve such contentions.[2] With
this proposal the French agreed after a decorous interval, England
appointing its four commissioners for the delineation of the boundaries and the settlement of local disputes on July 21, 1550.[3] But
meanwhile the expensive decision had been taken to victual Calais
for four months and to entrust to the best of English military
engineers, Thomas Petitt, the strengthening of the fortifications at
Risebank, Newnhambridge, Guînes, and certain lesser strong
points. The first instalment of the ransom for Boulogne, amounting

[1] This discussion owes much to Sandeman, G. A. C., *Calais under English rule*
(Oxford, 1908), 27–39, 114–115, and to Dillon, H. A., 'Calais and the Pale', in *Archaeologia*, LIII (1893), 290–303; and, most particularly, to the great survey of the Pale made
in 1556 (nos. 371, 372, Misc. Books formerly in Augmentation Office, P.R.O.). Also
consulted were Cotton MSS., Augustus, I, ii, 75, entitled 'Country of Guynes and
Bolenois', temp. Henry VIII; *ibid*. f. 71, a coloured map of Calais and the Pale, also
temp. Henry VIII; the beautiful maps of uncertain provenance, printed by Lennel, F.,
Calais par l'image. Notices historiques (Calais, 1904), from his album of Calais maps and
drawings, 67, 68, 69; Lefebvre (*Histoire de Calais*, II, frontispiece) also provides a most
useful map.

[2] *A.P.C.*, III, 82–83: June 17, 1550. Wade was later appointed Clerk of the Privy
Council.

[3] The English commission was headed by Sir John Wallop, the commander at Guînes
(Edward VI, *Chronicle*, 41; *Cal. S.P. For.*, *Edw. VI*, #223: July 17, 1550).

because of the 'great decay of our money' to £70,000, was almost immediately hypothecated for the payment of arrears in garrison wages to military units in Calais, Ireland, and along the Scottish Border.[1] Vigorous direction was given to these fairly extensive defensive preparations by the appointment of Lord Willoughby as governor of Calais, who oversaw the reparations under way, re-organized the garrison, and extended the area which could be flooded in the event of an emergency. The Council transmitted to Willoughby in September intelligence reports on the increase of French troops on his border, while in mid-October he was ordered to complete his victualling and was informed that 600 additional troops would be forwarded to him in small groups, in order not to arouse French suspicions. This tension was further heightened when French foraging parties crossed the boundaries into Fiennes Wood to gather fuel claimed by the English. Though the joint commission was designed to solve such frictions, the Council none the less thought it prudent on October 24, 1550, to dispatch a force of 1000 exper-ienced troops for the further strengthening of the enclave.[2]

Neither country wanted these frictions to get out of hand and the French government, it must be said, was sensible in its under-standing that the corollary to the cession of Boulogne must be the rather capricious and belligerent strengthening of Calais. Sir John Mason saw the French king on November 1st, when he indicated the English willingness to renew negotiations on the boundary only if the French foray party were withdrawn. A more formal request for resumption of the work of the joint commission was then made by the French ambassador in London, asking also that Sir Thomas Wyatt, much trusted by both sides, be added to that body. Accord-ingly, on November 29th the commission was reconstituted and began its tedious work, though Wyatt was unable to serve because of illness.[3] The work of the commission was enhanced a few weeks later when an effort was made to check the plague of piracy which was endemic in both countries.[4] Mason reported in early February that he had talked at length with Henry II and the Constable who had assured him of French amity and that military preparations visibly under way in France were for protection against the Emperor.

[1] Edward VI, *Chronicle*, 34–35; *A.P.C.*, III, 93–94: July 27, 1550; Edward VI, *Chronicle*, 41 (Edward's estimate for these expenses works out to £37,000).

[2] *A.P.C.*, III, 125–126: Sept. 18, 1550; *ibid.* 144, 147: Oct. 19 and 25, 1550; Lefebvre, *Histoire de Calais*, II, 271–272; Edward VI, *Chronicle*, 47, 49.

[3] *A.P.C.*, III, 156: Nov. 11, 1550; Lennel, *Histoire de Calais*, II, 244; *Cal. S.P. For., Edw. VI*, #255, 258, 262.

[4] Cotton MSS., Caligula, E, iv, 50, f. 245.

He reported too that the religious services according to the English rites held in his house remained unquestioned, even though a number of Scots and French ordinarily attended on Sunday. But a little earlier, the equally experienced Nicholas Wotton had warned the Council that France would never be content so long as she had not gained Calais, that her 'king is young and lusty, and of mind to do great acts', and that England's best assurance was in the Emperor. Such reflection also tempered Mason's enthusiasm for the new French mood, when he reported in a dispatch to the Council that the Guise faction was at once powerful and implacable in its hatred of a reformed England, being restrained only by the moderate courses of the Constable.[1]

Mason, who had served with high credit in France, now ill and badly paid, had been petitioning for his recall, and in this relatively tranquil interval was informed that Sir William Pickering would shortly arrive to relieve him.[2] Mason prepared to leave in a mood of restrained optimism, feeling that unless the French were 'devils and no men', a friendlier tone was now evident in French relations and that England might fully trust Montmorency, who had proposed that state visits by the two sovereigns would be useful and who wished that England would compete with France in proofs of friendship.[3] Mason's comparative equanimity may well have been in part sustained by the knowledge, as the King reported in excited detail, that the renovation of the Calais perimeter was now completed and that even more ambitious defensive plans were under discussion.[4] But the course of diplomacy was leisurely in sixteenth-century Europe, with the result that it was April before Pickering arrived with his credentials to relieve Mason, who in one of his last dispatches warned that the English position was being weakened by persistent rumours of discord in the Privy Council and who significantly complained that in the past ten weeks he had had little of news and almost no instruction from that governing body.[5]

That this appearance of amity was now securely part of French policy in rebuilding its defences against the Habsburgs, is attested by a long and important letter of Henry II to Charles de Marillac, a

[1] *Cal. S.P. For., Edw. VI*, #289: Feb. 7, 1551; HMC, *Salisbury MSS.*, I, 82: Jan. 2, 1551; *Cal. S.P. For., Edw. VI*, #295: Feb. 23, 1551.

[2] *Ibid.* #292: Feb. 17, 1551; *ibid.* #297, 298, 300: Feb. 27, 1551.

[3] *Ibid.* #304, 305: Mar. 17 and 18, 1551.

[4] Edward VI, *Chronicle*, 55: Mar. 10, 1551.

[5] *Cal. S.P. For., Edw. VI*, #332: Apr. 29, 1551; HMC, *Salisbury MSS.*, I, 85, 86; Harl. MS. 353, #35, f. 113b: June 30, 1551, for the formal instructions. Mason refers, of course, to the mounting tension between Somerset and Warwick.

skilled professional diplomatist who had served France as ambassador in England from 1539 to 1543, but who was now accredited to the Emperor. He had assured England of his peaceful intentions and friendship, he had employed every occasion to implement the new policy and asked Marillac to stress before the Emperor the close friendship which now bound the two countries.[1] To these overtures Warwick responded by hastening the settlement of the war with Scotland through the mediating efforts of the French diplomatist, Lansac, while in April the King noted that his French brother had been chosen to the Order of the Garter.[2] The imperial ambassador had watched these developments with concern, correctly concluding that a marriage treaty between Edward and the Princess Elizabeth, then aged six, the eldest daughter of Henry II, must be under preliminary discussion. He added, again correctly, the rumour that Warwick and his followers strongly supported the proposed union, while it was as strongly condemned by Somerset and his adherents.[3] So too, in Paris, the imperial envoy, Renard, surely the most skilful diplomatist of his generation, heard similar reports, though he at first thought that France had agreed to support a revived marriage treaty with Mary of Scotland. The outstanding commercial and Scottish problems were, he believed, mostly resolved and he astutely pointed out that England was in fact so weak that she possessed little room for diplomatic manoeuvres. He suggested to the Emperor that Anglo-French discussions had relieved Pickering of any fear of a French attack on Calais and that preliminary conversations on a marriage treaty with France had proceeded far enough for formal negotiations to begin.[4]

The formal reason for the diplomatic mission now to be appointed was to confer the Order of the Garter on Henry II. The embassy was headed by the Marquis of Northampton and Bishop Goodrich, with a professional stiffening of experienced diplomatists and lawyers among whom were Sir William Pickering, Sir John Mason, Sir Philip Hoby, Sir Thomas Smith, and Dr John Oliver, a Master of Requests. On May 1st a Council warrant was issued for the payment of 1000 marks to Northampton for his expenses, and a few days later an appropriation of £1680 was made towards the charges of those accompanying him, with payments to be scheduled at

---

[1] Druffel, August von, ed., *Beiträge zur Reichsgeschichte, 1546–1551* (*Briefe und Akten zur Geschichte des sechzehnten Jahrhunderts*, etc., vol. I, Munich, 1873), 581: Feb. 23, 1551.

[2] Edward VI, *Chronicle*, 59.

[3] *Cal. S.P. Span.*, X, 227: Mar. 1, 1551.

[4] *Ibid.* 243–244, 249: Mar. 9 and 21, 1551.

£200 for an earl, lesser lords from £100 to 200 marks, 100 marks each for gentlemen of the Privy Chamber, knights £50 each, and others at £40 each.[1] This done, as many as thirty largely decorative members, including three earls, five barons, and a goodly concourse of knights and gentlemen, were named to the embassy. When the inevitable servants and groms were added to this ponderous, but richly accoutred array, the whole party numbered well over two hundred persons.[2] Meanwhile, on May 10th Montmorency had informed the English ambassador of his master's delight in the projected mission, and indicated that he would send a similar mission to England, to be led by no less a dignitary than Jacques d'Albon, Seigneur de St André and Marshal of France, with the delicate suggestion that he would delay the French departure until Northampton had crossed the Channel.[3] But the informal indication was clear that St André would bring with him the Order of St Michael with which Edward was to be invested.[4]

Northampton and his party were formally instructed on May 20th to treat on all outstanding differences with France and to press for a marriage treaty, first with Mary Stuart, and that, as was certainly assumed, being refused, to negotiate for the hand of the Princess Elizabeth of France. The envoys were to insist on a dowry of at least 800,000 crowns and a dot of 12,000 marks a year, with a forfeiture penalty of 100,000 crowns 'at the most'.[5] This unwieldy mission began its stately journey on May 22nd when Northampton took leave of Edward. The Marquis was met at Nantes by Châtillon, who welcomed the English at an elaborate dinner and then escorted them to Chateaubriand where the King lay and where elaborate preparations had been made for their reception. Henry II received them warmly, embracing each envoy, and the whole English concourse was lodged comfortably in the town. Northampton reported that, having bestowed the Order of the Garter on the King in a solemn ceremony, they had been given entertainment in shooting,

---

[1] *Cal. S.P. For.*, *Edw. VI*, #335, #336 (May 1, 1551), #344 (May 14), #349 (May 20); Edward VI, *Chronicle*, 60.

[2] Edward VI, *Chronicle*, 61; *Cal. S.P. For.*, *Edw. VI*, #375; Sir Philip Hoby, a member of the mission, related that the whole embassy numbered 260 persons (*The travaile and life of Sir Thomas Hoby . . .*, etc. (Camden Misc. X, L., 1902), 67).

[3] *Cal. S.P. For.*, *Edw. VI*, ##341, 347: May 10 and 19, 1551.

[4] As early as May 10 the excited Edward was summoning divers lords and gentlemen 'for to furnish the court' against the French arrival (Edward VI, *Chronicle*, 62).

[5] *Cal. S.P. For.*, *Edw. VI*, ##349, 351: May 20, 1551; Edward VI, *Chronicle*, 63; Sloane MS. 4149, #6, and cf. *ibid.* 2442, f. 75. Northampton was, of course, principally a decorative figurehead for the mission; Mason, Smith, and Pickering seem to have been the principal negotiators.

tennis, dancing, and singing. But no diplomatic negotiation had as yet begun, save for Henry II's expressed hope that the two kingdoms might, as near neighbours should, live in perpetual amity.[1] Meanwhile, imperial diplomatists were watching this set piece of what can perhaps be best described as late medieval diplomacy by pageantry, with careful attention. Renard, as late as May 21st, was still convinced that a marriage treaty with Mary Stuart was the intention of the negotiation, while Scheyfve in London, in describing Northampton's departure, noted that 'not a few Englishmen of rank say that this friendship is too sudden and vehement to last, and that no Frenchmen have ever been welcomed in this manner in England'.[2]

We are told by Edward VI, who followed Northampton's mission with close attention, that after the vesting with the Order of the Garter had been completed, Northampton raised at once with Henry II the preliminary request that French agreement and assistance be lent to the long buried marriage compact between England and Scotland.[3] Northampton adduced the full legal, historical, and moral arguments for the union of the two kingdoms by marriage. But to this Henry gave no reply save that he would appoint commissioners to treat. He accordingly designated Montmorency, the Cardinal of Lorraine (Charles de Guise), the Cardinal of Châtillon (Odet de Coligny), and the Duke of Guise with full authority to negotiate. Northampton then laid the same arguments before them, offering to submit the sealed Treaty of Greenwich and other historical documentation, to which the Constable rather harshly, but certainly unequivocally, replied: 'To be plain and frank with you, seeing you require us so to be, the matter hath cost us both much riches and no little blood, and so much doth the honour of France hang hereupon as we cannot tell how to talk with you therein, the marriage being already concluded between her [Mary Stuart] and the Dauphin; and, therefore, we would be glad to hear no more thereof.'[4]

The raising of this question was, of course, no more than a diplomatic reflex action, so long had England been obsessed with the marriage. Northampton dropped the proposal immediately and then

[1] Northampton was in Paris on June 4, but was waiting for the reception at Nantes, since preparations were not complete at the French court. (*Cal. S.P. For.*, *Edw. VI*, ##357, 360, 365, 368, 375 (June 8, 1551); *Briefwechsel des Herzogs Christoph von Wirtemberg*, ed. by Viktor Ernst, vol. I: 1550–1552 (Stuttgart, 1899), 213: June 20, 1551; Stow, *Annales*, 605; Harl. MS. 295, #65, f. 153b; Cotton MSS., Julius, C, ix, 9, f. 79; Edward VI, *Chronicle*, 67–68.

[2] *Cal. S.P. Span.*, X, 298, 299.

[3] Edward VI, *Chronicle*, 67–68: June 20, 1551.

[4] *Cal. S.P. For.*, *Edw. VI*, ##375, 387; Edward VI, *Chronicle*, 68.

stated that he was commanded to treat for the hand of Elizabeth, to which Montmorency replied that the suit found favour and that he too was empowered to treat. The sticking-point, it was immediately clear, was the amount of the dowry, the English having first suggested the huge total of 1,500,000 crowns, at which the French 'made a mock'.[1] In not even delicately pitched haggling the English envoys dropped their requirements to 800,000 crowns, while the French worked their way up by slow stages from an initial offering of 100,000 to 200,000 crowns. At this point Northampton adjourned the discussions, sending William Thomas to London for further instructions and asking for a quick reply since Henry II was leaving shortly for Nantes and since the burden of the English mission's horse bore heavily on the resources of Chateaubriand.[2] The amended instructions were promptly returned, stating that no less than 600,000 crowns would be acceptable, that no commitment was to be made for an offensive-defensive treaty, and that no alteration of religion in England was even to be discussed.[3]

Further and rather indecisive haggling followed in France, with 'reasonings and showings of precedent' on both sides, it at last being agreed that the princess should be brought to England 'at her father's charge three months before she was twelve, sufficiently jeweled and stuffed'.[4] Again at the beginning of July the English envoys asked for further instructions and were told to try for a dowry of 400,000 and, that failing, to settle on 200,000 crowns, provided the charge for setting the princess down in England be paid by France.[5] The negotiators met again on July 17th, the French indicating that they must ask for a quick conclusion since the Queen was about to be confined. It was apparent that the French would not be bludgeoned or wheedled beyond 200,000 crowns, to which they had agreed.[6] On this same day Mason wrote to Herbert in some satisfaction, feeling that an honest bargain had been reached and expressing great satisfaction with Northampton's share in the negotiations. This dignitary could report on July 20th that the treaty had been signed and sealed on the previous day and that he was leaving at once for home.[7] At the leave-taking the usual gifts

[1] Edward VI, *Chronicle*, 68–69; *Cal. S.P. For.*, *Edw. VI*, #375.

[2] *Ibid.* #389: June 26; Edward VI, *Chronicle*, 68–69.

[3] *Cal. S.P. For.*, *Edw. VI*, #397; Harl. MS. 353, #33, f. 110; Sloane MS. 2442, ff. 78, 79.

[4] Edward VI, *Chronicle*, 69.

[5] *Cal. S.P. For.*, *Edw. VI*, #399: July 2, 1551; Harl. MS. 353, #34, f. 112.

[6] *Ibid.* #406; Edward VI, *Chronicle*, 74.

[7] *Ibid.* #411: July 20, 1551; Rymer, *Foedera*, XV, 273–281, and Bibl. Nat. MS. 3111, ff. 27–48, for treaty terms.

were bestowed, that for Northampton being valued at £500, a handsome £200 for the Bishop of Ely, £150 for Hoby, and, as Edward somewhat indignantly noted, 'the rest all about one scantling'.[1]

The treaty was extravagantly praised in semi-official propaganda pieces, but there were many who regretted the abandonment of Somerset's policy of peace with the Empire and the maintenance of a free hand in Scotland and with France.[2] John Abell, writing from Strassburg to Cecil, warned of the wiles of French diplomacy and evidently believed that Montmorency had no other purpose than to neutralize England while he undertook further adventures against the Emperor. So too, the shrewd English diplomatist, Nicholas Wotton, writing from Augsburg, warned Cecil that French diplomacy was not to be trusted.[3] This analysis was, indeed, not far from the mark, for Henry II was arming himself for another in the series of sharp, bloody, and expensive wars wherewith the Valois had long probed for the weak points in the Habsburg encirclement of France. An honourable marriage treaty had, it is true, been subscribed, but it was not the treaty which English sentiment and policy most desired. England had, in fact, been compelled to come to terms with Scotland by French prescription. Northumberland had preserved the appearances of dignity, but the negotiations had been completely dominated by French policy and self-interest. Dudley did not deceive himself, as he certainly did not delude the French; his uncertainty and his obsessive fears of further risings in England had left him impotent in foreign affairs. Actually—and herein we discover the weakness of his foreign policy—he was throughout his brief tenure of power to be fully protected by rapidly worsening relations between France and the Empire. 'Northumberland had bought time when he might have had it free and he had bought it in such a way that he could not use it to any good purpose.'[4]

The most effective French diplomatic effort in the elaborate negotiation of the treaty of amity and marriage with England was the brilliant success of the carefully chosen special embassy which brought to Edward the Order of St Michael. Led, as we have noted, by the vivacious and equable St André, it included numerous high nobility and a carefully ordered stiffening of highly competent

---

[1] I.e, a small portion or amount. Edward VI, *Chronicle*, 76.
[2] *Vide Petri Bellopoeli de pace*, etc. (L., 1552), *passim*, a long and grandiloquent treatise in praise of Northumberland's diplomacy.
[3] HMC, *Salisbury MSS.*, I, 87–88: June 23, 1551; *ibid*. 88: July 14, 1551.
[4] Wernham, R. B., *Before the Armada*, etc. (L. and N.Y., 1966), 200.

professional diplomatists, including the Seigneur de Boisdauphin (René de Laval) who was to stay on in London as ambassador for the remainder of the reign.[1] St André left the French court on June 11th with sixteen accredited members of his party, moving slowly in order to exchange greetings with Northampton (at Saumur) before passing on to Boulogne from whence he would sail when he had a fair wind and assurances that the Channel was free of imperial marauders.[2] Meanwhile the young King had been notified formally of his election to the Order by the resident French ambassador. The Privy Council requested Mason to express to Henry II the special gratification of their sovereign: 'The King's Majesty's young nature being of such modesty that in his most gladness hath not much outward show thereof, and besides that His Majesty's French speech being not natural to him, cannot so abundantly express the joy of his heart as if he should have answered in his natural speech.'[3] French diplomacy was at its most impressive in the planning and execution of this mission, Renard rather dourly reporting that the English were to be courted assiduously and that St André and Boisdauphin were prepared to extend the most elaborate and lavish of entertainment.[4]

The French party, numbering in all about four hundred, in the end sailed from Calais and Dieppe, an English naval escort beating out to sea to meet them. Preparations had been made for Clinton and Cobham to welcome the flotilla at Gravesend, but the French made a surprise landing at Rye, 'as some thought for fear of the Flemings lying at the land's end [*i.e.*, off South Foreland], chiefly because they saw our ships were let by the wind [so] that they could not come out'.[5] The English plans for reception and escort were at once hastily reorganized, Sir Peter Meutas and Alexander Culpepper sheriff for Kent, hastening to Rye where gentlemen to the number of one thousand brought the French party in easy stages through Kent to Gravesend, where it once more boarded ship for the formal arrival as originally planned. The Marshal St André was 'saluted with all my ships being in the Thames, fifty and odd, all with shot well furnished and so with the ordnance of the Tower', and thence to

[1] *Thirty-seventh rpt.*, Dep. Keeper of Public Records, App. I, no. 3, 183–184.

[2] *Cal. S.P. For.*, *Edw. VI*, ##380, 382; Edward VI, *Chronicle*, 64–65.

[3] *Ibid.* #381: June 16, 1551.

[4] *Cal. S.P. Span.*, X, 307: June 13, 1551; Decrue, *Montmorency*, 86–87, 89.

[5] Edward VI, *Chronicle*, 70; Romier, Lucien, *La carrière d'un favori, Jacques d'Albon de Saint-André, etc.* (Paris, 1909), 67–68. As the *Grey Friars Chronicle*, 69–70 rather sourly puts it under date of July 4, 'divers Lords of France with a Cardinal' arrived in England.

Durham Place on the evening of July 11th, where the French delegation were to be lodged.[1]

The evidently excited Edward received St André in his first meeting on July 14th and it was immediately apparent that the charm and warmth of the Marshal's personality had done their work. At no other point in the *Chronicle* does the tight self-discipline of the young King give way quite so completely to loquacious enthusiasm and pleasure, when the boy seems somehow to be precisely his true age. It was Somerset who brought and introduced St André, who remained for dinner and who was then taken to the King's 'inner chamber' for a private conversation with him. St André stressed the great friendship which his master bore for England and stated that it was the wish of France that all future frictions be resolved by diplomacy rather than war. 'I answered him that I thanked him for his Order and also his love, etc., and I would show like love in all points.'[2]

The Order of St Michael was conferred on July 16th at Hampton Court. The three French envoys, preceded by French gentlemen bearing the robes of the Order, entered the presence chamber to find the English nobility assembled and Edward 'an angel in human form'—it being impossible to imagine 'a more beautiful face and figure', so a French observer reported. The state robes and jewels being arranged, Edward then led the assembly to his chapel where he took the communion in English form, and with his hand on the Bible swore the oath of the Order, and was invested by St André. Afterwards, the King relates, 'they dined with me and talked after dinner and saw some pastime and so went home [*i.e.*, to Richmond] again'.[3]

The delighted King pressed St André to stay on and lavished warm and generous hospitality on him. The French diplomatist was shown the private royal apartments and pictures, and on the 19th was once more entertained at supper. On the next day he visited privately with the King, and then hunted and watched the royal guard at martial exercises. The full day was devoted to St André, for in the afternoon he 'dined with me, heard me play on the lute, ride

[1] Edward VI, *Chronicle*, 70–71; Romier, *St André*, 69–70. Since a virulent epidemic of sweating sickness was then raging in London, the King removed from Greenwich to Hampton Court on that day; St André was moved to Richmond on the 13th. Edward presented St André with a portrait of himself, whose history is noted, *post*, 409–410.

[2] Edward VI, *Chronicle*, 72. This conversation is recorded in one of the longest entries in the *Chronicle*.

[3] *Ibid.* 72–73; *Mémoires de Vieilleville* (Petitot, *Collection*, XXVI), 339–344; 'Papiers des Pot de Rhodes', *Mémoires de la commission historique du Cher*, II (Bourges and Paris, 1864), 146–148; Add. MS. 6297, f. 7; *ibid.* 25,247, f. 203b.

[rode?], came to me in my study, supped with me, and so departed to Richmond'.[1] Then on the 23rd in a private audience St André expressed his master's gratification that the negotiations for the marriage treaty were proceeding so satisfactorily, before retiring to a formal diplomatic reception at which the new resident ambassador, Boisdauphin, was presented and at which the King conversed as the occasion arose, in French, Latin, Italian, and Spanish. There was still more hunting; St André spent one night as the guest of Northumberland at Sheen, and was entertained in a banqueting house built for the occasion in Hyde Park at a cost of £450 9s 7d.[2] And then, as this diplomatic idyll came towards its close, the King made his gifts, with a shocking prodigality when compared with those bestowed by the frugal Henry II,[3] of £3000 for St André, £1000 for de Gyé, as much for Chemault, and £500 each to three other members of the embassy. His work for his royal master completed, and the King of England enthralled by his great charm, St André sailed for Boulogne on August 3rd, with an English naval squadron lending cover.[4]

Northumberland had by the sealing of the marriage treaty in effect given France a free hand in Scotland. More than this, he had assured France of English neutrality in the renewal of the Habsburg–Valois war which Montmorency believed to be near at hand. Montmorency's estimates were correct and his sense of timing was impeccable. The English marriage treaty was signed in July and ratified in December. English policy had been immobilized and so it was to remain during the rest of Dudley's tenure of power. English neutrality had been purchased very cheaply indeed.

2. THE DETERIORATION OF RELATIONS WITH THE EMPIRE (1549–1551)

We have already observed that Charles V had lent his friendship and a considerable measure of protection to the government of the Lord Protector. But when the crisis of Somerset's rule came in the summer of 1549, when rebellion was spreading and out of hand, and when the government knew full well that a declaration of war

---

[1] Edward VI, *Chronicle*, 73.
[2] *Ibid.* 75. The Banqueting House was very large, measuring 62 feet by 21 feet, and with 'three ranges of brick for roasting, and furnaces for boiling' (HMC, *Salisbury MSS.*, I, 92–93).
[3] *Vide ante*, 131.
[4] Edward VI, *Chronicle*, 75, 76; Romier, *St André*, 72–73; *Cal. S.P. Span.*, X, 332–333.

by Henry II, and possibly even an invasion, must be faced, the Emperor made it clear to Paget, who had been sent over to ask for active assistance at almost any price, that he would not accept responsibility for the defence of Boulogne and that he would take no military action which would give France cause for war. When Paget returned from the Continent empty-handed and discouraged, the government was so completely occupied with quelling insurrection that for a period of almost six weeks normal diplomatic correspondence simply withered. England possessed no foreign policy, in fact, during the weeks that stretched from late July, 1549 to the unseating of Somerset in the autumn.[1]

The *coup d'état* engineered and led by Warwick in October was watched closely by Charles V and his astute sister Mary, Regent in the Netherlands. But they were without accurate or detailed information since the imperial envoy regarded it principally as a Roman Catholic reaction which he thought might be successful. Charles did, however, quickly sense that Warwick's chief preoccupation would be to rid himself of the drain of resources imposed by Boulogne, that England would of necessity treat for terms with France, and that it would be as pointless as it was hazardous to intervene. The Emperor was, however, quite unprepared for the aggressive and unyielding support which Warwick lent to evangelical Protestantism, particularly since his personal pride and honour were deeply involved in the rapidly worsening position of his cousin, the Princess Mary. Somerset had treated the Princess mildly and, while unwilling to make any formal commitments respecting the toleration of her private worship, had in fact allowed her much liberty and had contented the Emperor with private diplomatic assurances that the exercise of her faith would be protected so long as it was quietly conducted in her own household.

The further and governing fact was that Charles V had no need for an English alliance during a period of almost two years from the time of Warwick's accession to power. He stood at the summit of his career. By the exercise of patience and restraint he had won over the principal German princes and had damped down the religious divisions of Germany. The Schmalkaldic League had thereby been gravely weakened and was soon in ruins when it sustained a decisive defeat at Mühlberg (1547) after the defection of the brilliant but mercurial Maurice of Saxony. Bringing pressure to bear on the papacy for the re-convention of the Council of Trent and on German Protestantism by the promulgation of the *Interim* settlement of

[1] Jordan, *Edward VI*, 295-304; *vide ante*, 116.

religion (May, 1548), the Emperor now wielded great power and was able to turn his attention to his dynastic plans for securing the ultimate succession to the imperial title for his son, Philip. He was able to exert pressure as well on the reassembled Council of Trent (September, 1551–April, 1552), though his own moderate inclinations were to be confounded by its stubborn doctrinal conservatism and by Henry II's refusal to acknowledge the Council or to permit the French bishops even to attend it. France once more felt herself encircled by the immensity and ubiquity of Habsburg power and, having concluded the treaty of amity with England, began once more to stir troubles in northern Italy in the summer of 1551. Henry was fishing as well in the troubled waters of German politics, exploiting Protestant discontent with the severity of the *Interim*, and encouraging the ambitions of Maurice, who in the autumn of 1551 associated himself with the Protestant princes in an offensive alliance (Treaty of Friedwald, January, 1552). In consequence a war on a large scale broke out in March, 1552 when Maurice attacked the Emperor while Henry II simultaneously invaded Lorraine.

The Emperor, thus preoccupied, had been unwilling to involve himself in what he regarded as a petty, but on the whole useful little war between England and France, since it possessed for him the virtue of a steady drain on the martial ardour of Henry II. Nor had the Emperor's steady policy of neutrality been shaken by the dramatic events of the *coup d'état*, which, as we have noted, Van der Delft misinterpreted to mean that Roman Catholic reaction was about to prevail in England.[1] In a brief and almost peremptory dispatch to his envoy, Charles ordered him categorically not to meddle directly in English events, and at the most to advise, if there should be opportunity, that religion be restored as it was at the end of Henry VIII's reign in order to unite the country, strengthen its defensive resources, and in time to hand over an undamaged sovereignty to the King when he came of age.[2]

For a period of weeks, in fact, the chronic commercial difficulties in the Netherlands aside, there was almost no diplomatic correspondence with the Empire while the treaty of peace and the cession of Boulogne were being negotiated. Official protests were lodged because of English fortifications raised at Gravelines without imperial permission and Charles did demand the return of Sebastian Cabot to his service.[3] The Emperor also protested formally that the

---

[1] *Cal. S.P. Span.*, IX, 454–455, 456–459, 459–460: Van der Delft to Emperor, Sept. 23, 1549–Oct. 14, 1549.   [2] *Ibid.* 460–461.
[3] *A.P.C.*, II, 374–375: Jan. 29, 1550.

peace concluded with France in some particulars included Scotland, with which he was technically still at war as an ally of England, but both Wotton and Paget were convincing in explaining that the negotiations had been only with France, that only a few strongpoints of no great use had been abandoned in Scotland, and that the English treaty with the Emperor remained quite unimpaired.[1] At the same time, the Emperor intervened directly in the German states to bring an end to the recruiting for the English service, which he had permitted during the period of Somerset's aggressive policy in Scotland and, under more severe limitations, during the brief interval when Boulogne was under siege.[2]

In May, 1550 the Emperor recalled Van der Delft on the probably correct grounds of ill health, for he died shortly afterwards in Antwerp where he had retired.[3] Van der Delft had served with some distinction in his post for six years and until Paget's fall from power possessed reasonably accurate sources of information. But, as we have observed, he had seriously misinterpreted the significance of Warwick's *coup d'état*, and was thereafter chiefly concerned with the freedom of worship and the personal safety of the Princess Mary. In part at least his recall may have been occasioned by the fact that he was not privy to the details of a plan being discussed in Brussels for spiriting Mary out of the realm, about which his successor, Jean Scheyfve, came to London fully informed. Scheyfve, a dull and rather lazy man who neither knew nor learned any English, was without adequate contacts and disliked the post in which he was held for the remainder of the reign. The always well-informed Queen Regent thought him incompetent and urged his replacement by the brilliant Simon Renard in Paris, who in fact was even then a better and more perceptive commentator on English affairs. Renard possessed an amazing ability to keep in view the whole complex structure of European diplomacy with a cool understanding of events, of men, and of policies.

The diplomatic crisis which dominated much of the period of Northumberland's rule was in part the consequence of the steadily increasing pressure which the government, inspired by the King, brought to bear on the Princess Mary to secure her conformity in religion. This important, measured, and rather ugly, development of policy we shall treat as an aspect of the domestic history of the

[1] Edward VI, *Chronicle*, 26; *Cal. S.P. Span.*, X, 60–61, 71: Apr. 12 and 22, 1550. The Emperor concluded a formal treaty of peace with Scotland in late 1550 (Edward VI, *Chronicle*, 50).

[2] Druffel, *Briefe und Akten*, I, 350, 362, 363–364, 389–390, 398.

[3] *Cal. S.P. Span.*, X, 89–90, 91: May 13 and 23, 1550.

reign,[1] but it may be briefly sketched here. When it became clear that the Council was prepared to force compliance from Mary, when her household officers were imprisoned, and when she herself became hysterically concerned regarding her own safety, the Emperor gave his reluctant consent to a plan to carry her out of the country. The plot failed, exposing Mary to even sterner pressure for conformity, to which the Council was now deeply committed. The outraged Emperor made it clear that any harm to Mary or any proscription of her personal faith would touch his honour and lead to his direct intervention.

When steps were taken to break up Mary's household and to deprive her of her chaplains, Scheyfve presented himself in April 1551 'with [a] short message from his master of [threatened] war', and demanded to know at once whether the Princess was in fact to be deprived of the mass.[2] The Council temporized, but renewed pressure on Mary resulted in a violent imperial protest at her ill-treatment, lodged with the Council on September 4th, which gained no more than the Council's declaration that it was the King's will that her violation of the law of the realm no longer be tolerated, though no compulsion would be used to secure her acceptance of the new service. Both Charles and his sister seriously considered an invasion of England in the autumn of 1551, but by this time the Emperor's fortunes were again at a low ebb and his distractions many. In consequence a working compromise was reached under which Mary's elaborate household services were halted, but the Princess was permitted for the remainder of the reign to retain a chaplain in her house and to worship according to the ancient rite in her private quarters. Charles was no bigot, and he well knew that his cousin was, but his honour and pride had been outraged and his attitude towards England embittered for the remainder of Edward's reign.

Nor were matters helped in the course of this needless but mounting crisis when in the summer of 1550 arrangements were made to recall, on his own request, the highly skilled and amiable Hoby, who had been at the Emperor's court for two years, and to replace him with the brilliant humanist, Richard Morison, who possessed no qualifications whatsoever for this sensitive post. Vain, arrogant, and intemperately Protestant, Morison succeeded in doing no more than outrage the Emperor, while his rambling and conceited dispatches added nothing to the Council's knowledge of the Emperor or of

---

[1] Vide post, 256–264.
[2] Edward VI, Chronicle, 56.

his policy.[1] At the same time, however, Sir Thomas Chamberlain, a sober and competent diplomatist, was appointed representative to the Regent in Flanders in order to deal with a crisis there springing from an abrasive commercial dispute which was severely damaging both economies.[2]

The commercial relations of England with Flanders, indispensable for both countries, were regulated by the treaty of 1495 which had established close and reasonably unrestricted conditions of trade. But by a kind of reflex consequence, when political relations between England and the empire were tense or unfriendly, commercial relations with the Low Countries became abraded. One of Scheyfve's instructions, which he sought to implement directly after assuming his post in London, was to represent to the Privy Council the need for a general study of commercial frictions, and particularly to point out that trade was hindered by unauthorized tolls, charges, and dues unknown to the underlying and now old commercial treaty. While the Council vehemently denied that new or unauthorized tolls had been laid on trade, it agreed with evident enthusiasm to enter into direct negotiations for a better commercial understanding.[3] Scheyfve, who had his spies in the port-towns, also complained that numerous Scottish ships, manned partly by English seamen, were harboured in English ports whence they carried on a deliberate and piratical warfare against Flemish shipping.[4] This the Council indignantly denied, angrily pointing to a recent and severe proclamation against piracy, and demanding a formal list of the imperial subjects who had suffered, with an authenticated memorandum of their claims.[5] Scheyfve, who thought these dull commercial cases beneath his diplomatic dignity, was pressed hard by the Regent, who had an earthy interest in such matters. He complained in September, 1550 that his files on the seizures of shipping and cargoes disappeared into the maw of the Admiralty Court, to which they were referred by the Council, and there they proceeded with no more than glacial slowness.[6] Again,

---

[1] *A.P.C.*, III, 45: June 11, 1550; *Cal. S.P. Span.*, X, 167: Aug. 22, 1550; Harl. MS. 523, #14, f. 25, for the Council's instructions to Hoby prior to his return; *Cal. S.P. Span.*, X, 176, for Scheyfve's report that Morison had sailed: 'he is a learned and lettered man, and well thought of for his proficiency in the new theology'.

[2] Chamberlain was for some time president of the guild of English merchants trading to Flanders, a post resembling that of a modern consul (*ibid.* IX, 246). He had also served in 1548, with Sir Thomas Smith, in an earlier effort to smooth out Anglo-Flemish relations. [3] *Cal. S.P. Span.*, X, 100–104, 110, 111: June 6–24, 1550.

[4] *Ibid.* 114–115: June 24, 1550.

[5] *Ibid.* 119, 141: July 3 and 26, 1550.

[6] *Ibid.* 178–179: Sept. 24, 1550.

having been prodded by the Regent, Scheyfve lodged (on January 8, 1551) a formal complaint protesting continuing seizures of goods, failure to control piracy, and outrageous searches of vessels, without, however, securing any helpful support or action from the Council.[1]

The Regent was threatening retaliatory action in Flanders which could scarcely be seriously pursued, however, without ruinous injury to the Antwerp market. She likewise continued to press the reluctant Scheyfve, who went so far as to lay before the Council a charge that Clinton, as Lord Admiral, was condoning piracy, and with ugly (and undocumented) implications that he was profiting from it. At the same time, he somewhat inconsistently reported that seventy-five English and Scottish pirates had been taken, of which number forty had been condemned to death.[2] There was, in fact, considerable sustained vitality in Clinton's efforts to rid the North Sea of English and Scottish privateers in this period, and the Privy Council noted in June, 1551 that the Regent was dealing with a gentler hand with English merchants and their cargoes in the Low Countries.[3]

When war broke out with France, the Emperor and his sister were anxious to secure at least English naval neutrality. Scheyfve expressed his concern to Northumberland regarding rumours that England would offer asylum to French privateers bringing Flemish prizes into its ports and asked for assurance that French warships would not be received in English harbours. Dudley heatedly enquired, 'Do you want the King to keep up a fleet especially to drive off the French men of war', but none the less gave informal pledges to abide by the treaty commitments to the Empire.[4] But the Regent remained troubled regarding the English position, stressing to the Emperor the need for more accurate information; 'in order to do this it would be necessary to have an intelligent ambassador there, such as Renard'. She also toyed with the idea of an invasion of England in order to rescue Edward from his advisers or to put Mary on the throne, though what she really wanted was 'a fine commodious port' which could be employed to set a flanking naval wedge against France.[5]

Continuous and troublesome as these frictions were in the relations of England with the Empire, they were as nothing compared

---

[1] *Cal. S.P. Span.*, X, 200–201: Jan. 21, 1551.
[2] *Ibid.* 266–269: Apr. 9, 1551.
[3] *Cal. S.P. For., Edw. VI*, #398: June 30, 1551.
[4] *Cal. S.P. Span.*, X, 373: Sept. 26, 1551.
[5] *Ibid.* 378–379: Oct. 5, 1551.

with the very real fears and intense emotions of English merchants trading to the Low Countries when the Emperor permitted the publication of an edict in April, 1550 confirming all previous actions against unlicensed printing and intimating that the Inquisition stood free to proceed against heretics in all parts of the Netherlands, notwithstanding any former pledges and immunities. The edict provoked serious and violent opposition in the Netherlands, and had twice to be modified (September and November, 1550). St Mauris warned the Regent that English merchants were as incensed as they were frightened by the action, which might result in the ruin of Antwerp unless, at the very least, foreign merchants should be exempted.[1] Scheyfve wrote in alarm from London that English sentiment was outraged by the edict, that English merchants were already fleeing from Antwerp, and that numerous vessels loaded for Antwerp had returned with their cargoes.[2] All this was confirmed by Renard, writing from Paris, who warned the Emperor that such severe actions served only to drive the English into the arms of France and to spur on the discussion of a possible marriage treaty already informally under way.[3] These measures were also stubbornly opposed by Charles's sensible and politique sister, who was herself suspected of once having had some measure of Lutheran sympathy. This strong-minded woman saw to it that the prescriptive force of the edicts was somewhat relieved. But great harm had been done to Antwerp; the English now added a religious reason to others as they considered a complete withdrawal from that great banking and trading *entrepôt*. As importantly, ever-increasing numbers of highly articulate, well-to-do, and stalwartly Protestant refugees from the Netherlands sought asylum in England as the way was prepared in the Low Countries for the trial of the full force of the Inquisition against Protestantism.[4]

Even more seriously affecting Anglo-imperial relations was the unresolved question of the extent of diplomatic immunity in the exercise of an heretical faith permissible in a country which had now invoked the full powers of the Inquisition. The first evidences of the hardening lines of nationally ordained faiths, intolerantly enforced, with all their sad portents for the future relations of nation with

[1] *Cal. S.P. Span.*, X, 139–140: July 24, 1550.   [2] *Ibid.* 152–153: Aug. 3, 1550.
[3] *Ibid.* 167, 171: Aug. 17 and Sept. 1, 1550.
[4] We have purposely limited our attention to imperial sources in the discussion of mounting commercial frictions between England and the Low Countries in the period under review. The rising English discontent with Antwerp, through which a very large proportion of English commerce flowed, will be discussed in a later and somewhat different connection.

nation, suddenly appear in the difficulties of Charles V with England. Chamberlain in Brussels and Antwerp found the English service of worship in his own household proscribed by law in late 1550 and reported the facts to the Council. The Council determined immediately to complain to the imperial ambassador and to indicate clearly that unless the English ambassador in Flanders was granted freedom of worship in his household, the similar privilege of the imperial ambassador in London would be revoked.[1] Scheyfve reported a few few days later that Goodrich and Petre had presented the English position to him and that they were both unyielding in their stand on the matter.[2] Charles realized full well the sensitive issues raised by the case and temporized as long as was possible. But the Council re-stated the English position with even more vehemence a few weeks later and in this meeting with Scheyfve formally requested that the matter be laid before the imperial government.[3]

At precisely this juncture, unfortunately, the heady and self-assured Morison, without considerable diplomatic experience, raised the whole question with the Emperor in a highly offensive manner. The discussion was forced on Charles by Morison, who, according to the Emperor's angry report of the meeting, was 'in the habit of proclaiming his religion stoutly on every occasion, and according to his custom, he launched forth into persuasive arguments', claiming that the English religion was the one true faith and generally speaking in an unbecoming manner. Thus goaded, the Emperor flatly refused any concessions and hinted that if the issue were pressed further it could only lead to a mutual recall of ambassadors. Morison persisted in his effort to engage in a doctrinal controversy with the Emperor, alleging that the reformed faith in England was founded squarely on both the Old and New Testaments and even proposing that a disputation be held in England on the question of the verity of the two churches. Charles was very properly incensed with this demagoguery and 'finally ordered him to be silent, and to withdraw at once from our presence'. He required his ambassador in London to complain immediately to the Council of grave diplomatic misconduct and to state that 'we believe him to have been sent to us as an ambassador, and not as a preacher'.[4]

By his incredible boorishness Morison had, of course, accomplished nothing more than hopelessly to obscure the very real and

---

[1] *A.P.C.*, III, 190–191: Jan. 13, 1551.   [2] *Cal. S.P. Span.*, X, 204: Jan. 27, 1551.
[3] *Ibid.* 225: Mar. 1, 1551.
[4] *Ibid.* 238–241: Mar. 7, 1551.

critical diplomatic questions which the English government had raised and now sought to press. In interviews with Scheyfve, both Somerset and Warwick disavowed Morison's presentation of the issue, saying he had gone far beyond his instructions. In a later meeting the Council expressed formal regret for the episode, and informed the imperial envoy that they had determined to recall Morison and to send out the suave Nicholas Wotton, who had at one earlier time served well on his embassy to the Emperor.[1]

Morison, in an apologetic dispatch, sent on the same date as Wotton's, stood his ground. His letter was filled with his usual inconsequential gossip, but towards its close moved to an angry self-defence. He was not in good favour with the Emperor, but 'I trust your Lordships do perceive the fault was in the matter and not in me, that I sped no better. Mr Wotton hath a more mannerly nay then I had, but even as flat a nay as mine was, the Emperor's choler spent upon me, hath taught him to use others with the more gentleness.[2]' To Wotton, in his first interview, Charles spent most of his wrath in complaining of the ill-treatment of Mary, who was being badgered to forsake her religion, 'in which her mother, her grandmother, and all our family lived and died'. To this Wotton quietly and effectively replied only that at the date of his departure from England she was in fact honourably and comfortably maintained, but that in England there was one king and but one law, and 'the Lady Mary being no king, must content herself to be a subject'. Then they moved to the immediate and ticklish subject of diplomatic immunity, on which Charles was intransigent. No religious service other than his own would be tolerated in the Netherlands, and if this resulted in restraints on the worship of his ambassador in London, Scheyfve would at once be recalled.[3]

But Wotton was under firm instruction to persist in the matter at issue, and persist he did, quietly but tenaciously.[4] After apologizing for Morison's conduct, Wotton none the less pressed firmly for reciprocity in the matter of religious observances, pointing out that even the Turks took this view and extended such liberties. Charles, who could be utterly charming, admitted that he had been angry, excusing his choler as occasioned by illness and lengthening years. But in the matter of reciprocity he could not yield because his faith was old and he was sure in it. Wotton, for his part, tried to point

---

[1] *Cal. S.P. Span.*, X, 255: Apr. 6, 1551. The Emperor, his anger cooled, soon relented and Morison was not immediately recalled.

[2] *Cal. S.P. For., Edw. VI*, #392: June 30, 1551.   [3] *Ibid.* #393: June 30, 1551.

[4] *Ibid.* #429: Aug. 15, 1551; Edward VI, *Chronicle*, 58; *Cal. S.P. For., Edw. VI*, #317.

out that the two faiths differed only on such matters as the reform of ceremonies, to which the Emperor warily replied that 'those who undertook religious innovations were better armed with arguments, by means of which they presumed to uphold their actions, than those who abided by the main trunk of the Church's prescription, the latter being content to believe, and continue in their faith, observing it without contention'.[1]

In a later conference with the Emperor on the question, it was Charles himself who drew the conversation to the verity of the Roman and the reformed faiths. Charles charged that England had been seduced by heretics like Bucer and Ochino, to which Wotton quickly replied that though they were accounted great and wise men in his realm, a hundred like them could not have secured the settlement of religion in England unless its truth had been self-evident to all.[2] This amiable conversation was fully reported by the Emperor to Scheyfve, with an indication that on the unsettled question of diplomatic immunity in matters of worship, he had felt obliged to give a categorical *no*.[3] But the English position was equally firm, the Council having a short while earlier re-stated its position that freedom of worship must be reciprocally permitted as a condition of diplomatic relations.[4] This position had long been fully accepted in the relations of England and France, but it was not to be completely or happily resolved between England and the Habsburg dominions for many years to come. What happened instead was a winking at the realities, a probably wise decision to engage in no more Morisonian polemics, while a slow adjustment to the circumstances of the modern world came gradually to be made, with the result that by about 1600 the question had been tacitly settled on the side of diplomatic toleration.[5]

It may well be that the last opportunity to preserve the Anglo-imperial entente, which Somerset had fostered, passed in November 1550. We have noted that in the months immediately following the cession of Boulogne, which cost Warwick dearly in the coin of prestige, there were justified fears in England of an assault in force on the great fortified works in the Calais enclave. The most serious incident occurred when a French force of about 400 penetrated two miles into the perimeter, from which they were turned back only after much negotiation. Both Hoby, who was returning to his

[1] *Cal. S.P. Span.*, X, 311–315: June 29, 1551.
[2] *Cal. S.P. For.*, *Edw. VI*, #436: Sept. 1, 1551.
[3] *Cal. S.P. Span.*, X, 349–350.   [4] *A.P.C.*, III, 330: Aug. 9, 1551.
[5] Mattingley, Garrett, *Renaissance diplomacy* (Boston, 1955), 281.

post with the Emperor, and Morison laid before Charles the Council's opinion that the French interventions were manifestly warlike and enquired whether Charles would now honour his treaty obligations with respect to the 'Old Conquest' in the event of an assault in force on Calais. The Emperor's reply was, to say the least, equivocal, for he pointed out that the French raid had been small, was confined to a region still in dispute, and that a state of war, which would invoke the treaty, did not exist.[1] This somewhat brusque refusal to lend aid, or to define clearly the conditions under which it would be extended, added momentum and possibly finality to Warwick's policy of coming to terms with France under any conditions short of ceding Calais and undoubtedly opened the way for the conclusion of the marriage treaty.

Yet, as the negotiations for the marriage treaty proceeded and when the splendour of the joint diplomatic missions was observed, imperial diplomacy began to exhibit a nervous sense of isolation and no little concern. Thus Scheyfve expressed his fear that England was being drawn into an offensive alliance with France and described with awe the elaborate preparations being made for the visit of the special French embassy shortly expected in London.[2] This concern was shared by the far more perceptive Renard in Paris, who in mid-July was relieved when Mason, Hoby, and Pickering all called on him to state categorically that the treaty being concluded with France would in no way impair relations with the Emperor. 'They assured me', Renard concluded, 'that they were not blinded, nor were their eyes so dazzled that they could not see the disposition of affairs in France, or know the temper of the French and the aims they had in view.' Then, only a few days later, he was reassured when Mason and Hoby called again to apprise him of the general terms of the marriage treaty then being concluded.[3] In London, too, the Council took steps to inform the imperial envoy that the treaty contained no provision prejudicial to the Emperor, though Scheyfve could not secure the precise details of the marriage covenants.[4] And, finally, the Council instructed Wotton to lend further and personal assurance to the Emperor on this point, while once more stating categorically the government's intention to require the Princess Mary to respect the religious services by law established.[5]

[1] *Cal. S.P. Span.*, X, 188–190: Nov. 11, 1550.
[2] *Ibid.* 324: July 6, 1551.
[3] *Ibid.* 328–329: July 11/13, 1551.   [4] *Ibid.* 341–342: Aug. 5, 1551.
[5] *Cal. S.P. For.*, *Edw. VI*, #429: Aug. 15, 1551.

A fortnight later France declared war on the Empire, as we have seen, principally because of festering frictions in northern Italy. On account of the lateness of the year there was little military action, but Charles knew that in the coming spring he would surely be attacked in Flanders and he knew as well that the faithless Maurice was preparing to revolt. The Emperor was sick, ageing, and choleric, dreading the campaign which he must now lead, and he was disturbed by the closeness of the ties recently forged between France and England. At the very least English policy had been immobilized. The Bishop of Arras reported to the Regent that his master threatened to return his Orders from both France and England, while his brother, Ferdinand, bewailed the fate of the Princess Mary who could not now be protected.[1] The spreading and deepening war, which in its initial phases went badly for the Emperor and nearly occasioned a decisive military defeat, was to continue during the remainder of Edward's reign and was to gain for Northumberland almost complete liberty of action in the domestic concerns which now engaged his whole attention. He had gained an inglorious peace for England, and that peace he was disposed to exploit to his own advantage.

3. ABANDONMENT OF THE DREAM OF SCOTTISH UNION (1549–1553)

The calamities which overwhelmed England in the summer and autumn of 1549 likewise account for the abandonment of a policy towards Scotland which may be said to have run unbroken from the battle of Solway Moss to the abandonment of Haddington in September, 1549. England was seeking during these seven years far more than a marriage treaty binding Edward and Mary Stuart; the goal was nothing less than a union of the two crowns, the exorcising of French influence in the North, and the extension of political order over the whole of Britain. Commendable and far-sighted as this policy was, it was doomed because it came too early, because both Henry and Somerset sought to impose it by brute force, and because it could not be anticipated that in time a common and highly evangelical thrust of reformation would be the principal unifying force.[2]

---

[1] Druffel, *Briefe und Akten*, I, 761, 773; Henne, Alexandre, *Histoire du règne de Charles-Quint en Belgique*, IX (Brussels and Leipzig, 1859), 156.

[2] Jordan, *Edward VI*, 241–304, for a full discussion of Scottish relations to the evacuation of Haddington.

With serious and still unrepressed rebellion raging in two quarters of the realm, with an already massive French intervention under way in Scotland which would predictably lead to a declaration of war on England, Somerset found himself in August, 1549 unable to spare the resources required to hold a series of interlocking strong-points which had for many months given him effective control of Scotland. Rutland was sent in with 6000 troops to bring out the Haddington garrison and then the Border forces were rapidly drawn down for service against the insurrections, for duty in Boulogne, or to be employed in the event of a French invasion of England. But Somerset stubbornly, perhaps quixotically, still held such fortified places as Broughty, Lauder, Home, Dunglass, Roxburgh, and Eyemouth at the moment of his own fall, the Scots being too weak and discouraged to mount an autumn offensive to force the English out. Thus the war which Somerset had so brilliantly begun came to a desultory and inglorious end as Warwick, insecure in his position and desperately anxious to come to terms with France, completed the withdrawal of English forces from Scotland and then found himself driven inexorably towards a settlement which conceded to France an overweening influence in Scottish affairs.

Rutland, young and inexperienced and without adequate troops or stores, was left in the North at Berwick with no clear understanding of policy and for a number of weeks without precise orders. By his raiding and re-enforcement of the strong-points, he felt in November that he had kept the Scots and French off balance until the season for field operations was past.[1] He expressed considerable relief when his best troops, the mercenary companies, were ordered south, for they had been terrorizing the countryside and were, in his view, unreliable.[2] But he was now left without re-enforcements for the remaining strong-points which were held by men who had been on garrison duty for a year and who were now 'so naked that they run away, sicken, and die daily'.[3] Later in the month he wrote in a mood of hopeless discouragement, for he possessed neither power nor orders for the relief of the forts which, at half strength, could not hold longer unless they could supply themselves from the countryside.[4] His gloomy predictions were confirmed when Home Castle, ill-supplied and ill-defended, fell on December 16th and Broughty Castle, so brilliantly defended for

---

[1] HMC, *12th rpt.*, App. IV: *Rutland papers*, I, 46–47: Nov. 1, 1549.
[2] *Ibid.* I, 48, 49–50: Nov. 4–11, 1549.
[3] *Ibid.* 50: Nov. 22, 1549.   [4] *Ibid.* 51–52.

more than two years, surrendered on February 6, 1550, when it was charged the garrison and their wives and children were brutally slaughtered.[1] Rutland's own urgent requests for relief from an impossible command went unheeded by the Council which was 'in that unquietness and trouble among themselves', as a consequence of Somerset's fall.[2] There was, to put it bluntly, a period of near paralysis in governance and policy until Warwick had established his power.

The final abandonment of the English position in Scotland came when in the negotiations leading to the Treaty of Boulogne Warwick agreed on a cessation of hostilities in Scotland, where the French were in fact in control, and conceded that the Scots should be included in the treaty.[3] Formal effect was given to this undertaking when on April 18, 1550, Mary Stuart, with the consent of the Queen Mother and the governor, ratified the treaty, sending Thomas Erskine to England as her negotiator for the settlement of outstanding issues.[4] Warwick's commitment required the English withdrawal from the remaining strong-points, outlawed further Border raids by both nations, and left to negotiation the thorny question of delineating the precise frontier between the two countries.[5] Lauder, already under siege, was thereupon surrendered,[6] while a few days later Dunglass was given up,[7] to be followed by the rapid withdrawal of the remaining garrisons. Erskine passed through London on his way to France, where, it must have been humiliatingly clear to Warwick, the course of the boundary negotiations was in fact to be determined.[8]

But, perhaps predictably, once martial pressure from England was lifted, festering resentment in Scotland against French military and diplomatic control became dangerously evident. The untamed Scottish nobles and the strongly Protestant Lowlands declared that Mary of Lorraine and her Guise brothers were intent on converting the realm into a French province. Arran had vehemently opposed the comprehension of Scotland, as a helpless satellite, in the Anglo-French treaty and was successful in baulking the Queen

---

[1] *A diurnal of remarkable occurrents, etc.* (Bannatyne Club Publ. #43, Edinburgh, 1833), 49–50; *A.P.C.*, II, 407.

[2] HMC, *12th rpt.*, App. IV: *Rutland papers*, I, 55.

[3] *Vide ante*, 120, 127.

[4] *Cal. S.P. Scotland*, I, 182; *The register of the Privy Council of Scotland*, vol. I: 1545–1569, ed. by J. H. Burton (Edinburgh, 1877), 85–93: Apr. 20, 1550.

[5] Cotton MSS., Caligula, B, vii, 185, f. 417.

[6] Edward VI, *Chronicle*, 26.

[7] *Ibid.* 28: Apr. 30, 1550.

[8] *Ibid.* 29–30, 31, 38.

Mother's schemes for securing her own appointment as regent. So sensitive were the issues that Mary of Lorraine felt obliged to ask for a reduction of the French garrison forces and in September to journey into France to make more secure the support of French policy for her own position.[1] Under these circumstances considerable delay, fostered also by English policy, was to occur before the difficult task of finding an agreed boundary was even begun.

A complete re-ordering of Border policy was intended when in April Warwick was made 'General Warden of the North', on the grounds that the defence of the region required 'a notable ruler', who, incidentally, was to receive the huge stipend of £1000 p.a. in addition to a private band of one hundred horse maintained at governmental expense.[2] We find no evidence that Warwick intended personally to exercise command in the North, the action probably being part of his steady building of his own power and resources in this interval. This was to a degree confirmed by the King's notation that the Council on July 18th agreed that 'the Lord Bowes should tarry in his wardenship still, and the Earl of Warwick should tarry here and be recompensed'.[3] The appointment of Warwick may also well have a direct connection with the fact that most of the northern magnates still supported Somerset, save for the irascible and not particularly competent Wharton, who had been dismissed when he refused to obey the orders of Lord Grey.[4] Wharton hated Somerset in consequence, and had ever since been an outspoken adherent of Warwick and his principal supporter in the North. It seems certain that Wharton was receiving his due reward when at Warwick's request he was named the Earl's deputy there with half the great stipend allotted by the Council.[5]

With the thorny question of the frontier not yet even under discussion, what can only be described as a semi-peace prevailed. On complaints by both Flemish and English merchants of Scottish piracy off the English coasts, all vessels of Scottish ownership were declared barred from English ports.[6] Sir Richard Lee and Sir Thomas Palmer were sent north to inspect and strengthen such

---

[1] Vide post, 150, 153–154.

[2] Edward VI, Chronicle, 24: Apr. 8, 1550; A.P.C., III, 6: Apr. 20, 1550. It may here be noted that the King's entries often ante-dated a formal action of the Council, reflecting the date of the decision rather than of the action.

[3] Edward VI, Chronicle, 40.

[4] Jordan, Edward VI, 296.

[5] Edward VI, Chronicle, 138: July 31, 1552; James, M. E., Change and continuity in the Tudor North. The rise of . . . Lord Wharton (York, 1965), 38–39.

[6] Hughes and Larkin, Tudor proclamations, I, 497: July 15, 1550.

important bases for Border defence as Berwick and Carlisle against the raids expected in the coming winter.[1] In August England found herself in the humiliating position of appealing to France to check anticipated Border raids, which did in fact take place when Maxwell with 2000 Scots and a stiffening of French troops assailed the Grahams along the frontier, being thrown back across the border only when Lord Dacre intervened with his force.[2]

While these harassments were being dealt with by England, elaborate and friendly arrangements were being made for Mary of Lorraine to pass through England on her projected visit to France.[3] Safe-conduct was proffered to the Queen Mother and a party of 140 men and 200 horses who were to accompany her, as well as for the fifteen French galleys which were to carry her overseas. The plan for the journey was in fact reversed, Mary crossing directly to France from Scotland in September and returning about a year later by way of England. In her train were many of the Scottish nobility who were to be purchased by French gold, titles, and persuasion. From France a delegation was dispatched to extract from Arran an agreement to resign the regency when Mary Stuart should attain the age of twelve, he being compensated with the sop of the Duchy of Châtelherault.[4]

Meanwhile, the promised negotiations for the delimiting of the frontier remained in a kind of diplomatic limbo, though Erskine had rather urgently raised the subject as Mary of Lorraine was crossing to France.[5] Pressure of a more formidable sort was applied when a Franco-Scottish force began the construction of a fort far too near the great staging-point of Berwick, which was, however, abandoned when English troops appeared in strength.[6] Lord Dacre, the most vigorous and competent of all the commanders left along the Border in these months, ordered his subordinates to report on the general state of the Western Marches and the measures that must be taken if peace and tranquillity were to be preserved.[7] This mounting pressure was confirmed by as careful an observer as Mason, in France, who in late 1550 reported French naval and

---

[1] *A.P.C.*, III, 90–91: July 22, 1550.

[2] *Cal. S.P. For.*, *Edw. VI*, ##230, 231: Aug. 18 and 21, 1550; Edward VI, *Chronicle*, 44. This marauding force was led by Sir John Maxwell, brother of the then Earl of Maxwell. Sir John was appointed Warden of the Western Marches in March 1552, but expended most of his considerable energy in clan·feuds.

[3] *Vide ante*, 148–149.

[4] *A.P.C.*, III, 95, 101: Aug. 3 and 10, 1550; *Cal. S.P. Scotland*, I, 183; Brown, P. Hume, *History of Scotland* (3 vols., Cambridge, 1899–1909), II, 36–37.

[5] *A.P.C.*, III, 132: Sept. 28, 1550.   [6] *Cal. S.P. Span.*, X, 186: Nov. 4, 1550.

[7] Harl. MS. 36, #14, f. 69: Nov. 21, 1550.

military preparations under way and who was certain that they
would be employed in war on England unless the Scottish treaty
were concluded.[1] Against this rising threat, the Council could
think of no more formidable measures than to appoint the totally
incompetent Dorset, shortly to be advanced to a duchy, as Warden
of the Northern Marches, with however three experienced soldiers
as his sub-wardens, and to prepare for the humiliating task of
drawing a frontier line which—so the English had contended for
almost a decade—no longer existed.[2] That the time had come to
yield was made clear when in February, 1551 news reached London
that a great French fleet of 160 sail had landed stores of grain,
powder, ordnance, and men in Scotland, which betokened the
complete dominance which France enjoyed and intended to exercise
there.[3]

The English government had, however, at least armed itself with
an excellent survey of frontier conditions, prepared, probably in
late 1550, by Sir Robert Bowes, a soldier and lawyer who had made
himself the leading expert on Scottish and Border affairs. Bowes
declared that the English 'debatable ground' measured about 8
miles long and 4 miles wide, the Scottish about 7 miles in length
and 4 in width. He felt that no frontier settlement could succeed
unless provision was made for careful annual inspections in order
to prevent encroachments and to cure local troubles. The retention
and strengthening of Norham Castle, standing on the 'utter frontier'
he also regarded as indispensable for England. So devastated was
the frontier that new towns needed to be built and the region re-
populated in order to provide an economic base for the entire area.
So far out of discipline was the Middle March that blood feuds and
senseless marauding were endemic, making any concerted defence
quite impossible. The Warden must be given summary powers to
bring the region back under the rule of law and order, which
Bowes regarded as important also for the whole of Northumberland, which was turbulent and out of hand. The inhabitants owed
military service, when called upon by the Warden, for not more than
two or three times a year and then subject to the understanding
that they would remain in Scotland for no more than one day and
two nights. This remarkable critique must have impressed on the
Council the view that almost any reasonable frontier line might well
be accepted; the problem was not so much the tenure of a wasted

---

[1] *Cal. S.P. For., Edw. VI*, #270: Dec. 30, 1550; *ibid.* #285: Jan. 29, 1551.
[2] *A.P.C.*, III, 223: Feb. 25, 1551; Edward VI, *Chronicle*, 53.
[3] *Ibid.* 54–55.

countryside as the building of a civilized community south of the line now to be defined.[1]

The calculated increase of French pressure on England served to secure the appointment of commissioners, so long promised for the settlement of the frontier boundaries. Edward records that, on April 3rd, Lansac (Louis de Saint Gelais) arrived from France with the list of the Franco-Scottish members, they being Villeparisis (Henri Clutin d'Oysel), the French ambassador in Scotland, the Bishops of Ross and Orkney, and the Master of Ruthven and Erskine.[2] A few days later the English commission, consisting of Thirlby (Norwich), Bowes, Sir Leonard Beckwith, and Sir Thomas Chaloner, was named by the Privy Council, with instructions to settle outstanding frictions, and particularly the Border disputes. The commissioners were further enjoined to inform themselves of the true boundaries from old treaties, even though on the grounds of conquest England might claim an enlargement. The King was prepared to yield the remaining strong-points and fisheries known to be in Scotland, while the debatable grounds were to be neutralized.[3] The joint commission, whose meetings were held at Norham Castle in May, quickly agreed on a restoration of the frontier line to that which preceded the Scottish wars of Henry VIII, while delaying the implementation of the declaration until an accurate map could be drawn and accepted. Meanwhile, Chaloner complained to Cecil that the English members were without more than vague preliminary instructions, having in the course of eleven days had no reply from the Council to their questions, whereas their Scottish counterparts were in daily communication with Arran.[4] None the less, in about a month treaty terms were concluded restoring the *status quo ante*, leaving until a later date the actual Border delimitation.[5]

[1] Cotton MSS., Titus, F, xiii, ff. 160–214; printed in Hodgson, John, *A history of Northumberland*, pt. III, vol. II (Newcastle-upon-Tyne, 1828), 171 ff., in a not wholly satisfactory text. Bowes was appointed one of the English commissioners on the boundary. His judgement on the turbulence of Northumberland was confirmed by another source. The unknown author of *Articles concerning Northumberland* (1552?) stated that the inhabitants would not keep watches, man the forts, or fortify the towns, nor would they render forage and victuals at reasonable prices or respond as they should to muster calls (*Cal. S.P. Dom.*, *Edw. VI*, VI, 422).

[2] Edward VI, *Chronicle*, 57; Teulet, Alexandre, *Rélations politiques de la France . . . avec l'Ecosse au XVIᵉ siècle*, I (Paris, 1862), 258.

[3] *A.P.C.*, III, 252–253: Apr. 6, 1551; Edward VI, *Chronicle*, 57–58; Sloane MSS., 2442, ff. 222, 223b; *Cal. S.P. Scotland*, I, 185–186.

[4] *Ibid.* 185: Norham, May 14, 1551.

[5] Edward VI, *Chronicle*, 65, 73–74: June 13 and July 19, 1551; Rymer, *Foedera*, XV, 265–271.

In the mean season, the King was greatly impressed, and his *Chronicle* suggests, entertained by the passage of the formidable Mary of Lorraine through his realm. We have seen that her state visit to France, and to her daughter being educated there against the day of her marriage to the Dauphin, had extended for more than a year and had greatly strengthened the structure of her power in Scotland. In late September, 1551, the English government extended the date of her passport until Christmas and assured her that she might pass overland to Scotland. Not sailing until October, the Dowager Queen was driven by a storm into Portsmouth, whence she wrote to the King that she would proceed overland and would take the occasion to visit him.[1] After an appropriate English escort had been assembled, she moved from great house to great house on her journey to Hampton Court, the progress requiring a full five days.[2] A short way from Hampton Court Mary was met by a resplendent escort of the nobility and gentry, to the number of 120, and so was brought to court where some sixty wives of the peers and the court gentry welcomed her and took her 'to her lodging on the Queen's side, which was all hanged with arras, and so was the hall and all the other lodgings of mine in the house very finely dressed. And for this night and the next day all was spent in dancing and pastime, as though it were a court, and great presence of gentlemen resorted thither'.[3] After 'perusing' Hampton Court on the next day, Mary was escorted to London where on November 4th a great state reception and dinner was held for her by the King at Westminster. 'We were served by two services: two sewers, cup bearers, carvers, and gentlemen. Her maître d'hôtel came before her service, and mine officers before mine. There were two cupboards, one of gold four stages [in] height, another of massy silver six stages. . . . After dinner, when she had heard some music, I brought her to the hall and so she went away.'[4] On November 6th, Mary set out, escorted by Northumberland with his band of one hundred, Pembroke, Wiltshire, and other of the nobility and gentry, 'whereof 40 gentlemen apparelled in black velvet, guarded with white', led her party as far as Shoreditch Church where one hundred of the gentlemen of Middlesex took her on the first stage of the long journey.[5] Elaborate arrangements had been made by Cecil for seventeen stages on the trip north, with from ten to twenty escorts

---

[1] *A.P.C.*, III, 397: Oct. 25, 1551; Edward VI, *Chronicle*, 89; *Cal. S.P. For.*, *Edw. VI*, #477: Nov. 5, 1551, for a full account of the visit.
[2] Edward VI, *Chronicle*, 90–91.   [3] *Ibid.* 92: Oct. 31, 1551.
[4] *Ibid.* 93–94.   [5] Stow, *Annales*, 606.

drawn from the countryside until Norham Castle was reached, where the Queen passed into Scotland to find problems in her relations with England not yet fully resolved by the joint commission.[1]

The initiative for the precise delimiting of the Border frontier and its neutralization had now passed to England which did not wish to continue to commit substantial forces for checking the persistent marauding raids. An official protest was lodged by the King with Arran and his Council late in December, 1551, charging that the Scottish commissioners failed to keep appointments with their English opposite numbers and that four English subjects had recently been slain by a party raiding into the West March.[2] In January the French ambassador intervened with specific proposals for the neutralization of the Border area,[3] which were amended after further discussion in London. It was agreed that the disputed lands should be equally shared, that a more vigorous commission should be appointed by both sides to secure the implementation of the treaty terms, that a meeting should take place in the area as soon as a map could be prepared, and that 'the less privy the border-ers be made to the division hereof, the more likely it is the thing shall take place'. Almost immediately the new English commission, consisting of Westmorland, Wharton, Sir Thomas Palmer, and Sir Thomas Chaloner, was appointed to carry forward the agreed division.[4] At once, however, there were difficulties in drawing the definitive map, the Council reporting to its commissioners that earlier treaties revealed no helpful information and suggesting that a search be made in the records of former wardens for 'old writings' and that ancient men in the area who might be of assistance be examined.[5]

This weary—and dreary—business was at last brought to a con-clusion, it is clear because France insisted that this remaining defect in the treaty of peace be cured and her prestige in Scotland further enhanced. Helpful instructions were forwarded to the Scottish commissioners in late March, 1552, ordering them to take testi-mony in the boundary area from responsible persons on both sides and to agree to an equal division when there was conflicting testi-mony. English subjects who found themselves on the Scottish side were to be permitted to make their allegiance, and matters which could not be equitably determined by negotiation were to be decided

---

[1] Harl. MS. 290, #2, f. 7; *ibid.* #3, f. 8.
[2] *Cal. S.P. Scotland*, I, 189: Dec. 21, 1551.   [3] Edward VI, *Chronicle*, 106–107.
[4] *Ibid.* 114; *A.P.C.*, III, 492–493: Feb. 28, 1552.
[5] *Ibid.* IV, 17: Apr. 10, 1552; Harl. MS. 289, #25, f. 34, #26, f. 36, #27, f. 41.

by lot.[1] But so thorny were the detailed questions of boundary and so constant were the disorders on the Scottish side of the frontier that the Duke of Northumberland felt it necessary to inspect the Border in person, 'a pay of £10,000 to go before him'.[2] Then, following his personal inspection, the map setting out the frontier in detail was agreed upon by the Council and the French ambassador, the boundary to be clearly marked by pillars set at intervals.[3]

Thus was this unhappy episode in the long and tragic relations of the two countries brought to its squabbling close. Somerset's dream of a united kingdom had been thwarted and destroyed, in part by his own ruthless determination to impose good by ill means, and in larger part by Northumberland's complete capitulation to French diplomacy. It will have been observed that France was directly concerned in the negotiations and that it was France that specified the terms of the peace which Northumberland so desperately required. Scotland had been delivered up and stood in 1553 as a province of France, bound by ties of a projected marriage, and with no foreign policy save as it was defined and manipulated from Paris. What English weakness and Northumberland's misguided policy had accomplished was to lay the groundwork for the dangerous situation in which Queen Elizabeth found herself at the time of her accession, and from which she was able to extricate herself only by a brilliant but hazardous diplomacy. Yet the pillars marking a neutralized frontier did not in 1553 really sever the two nations, or rather the two peoples. It was the leaven of Calvinism, of a Reformation in which both peoples were fully involved, which carried the assurance of a common faith, a common culture, and, for that matter, of an ultimate union.

4. ENGLAND'S WITHDRAWAL FROM EUROPEAN AFFAIRS
(1552–1553)

We have seen that war broke out between France and the Empire in September, 1551, Henry II having been emboldened by Maurice's preparations for treason and the restless efforts of the

---

[1] *Register of the Privy Council of Scotland*, I, 120–121: Mar. 20, 1552.

[2] Northumberland did not leave for the North until mid-June, having been delayed by a death in his household. He returned to London at the end of August.

[3] *A.P.C.*, IV, 113, 118: Aug. 16 and 29, 1552; *Cal. S.P. Scotland*, I, 190–191. The agreement was formally signed by the joint commission on Sept. 24, 1552. The boundary line was carefully defined on a line running from 'the water of Sark' to the River Esk. The governing decision had been made by Northumberland in late June 1552 (HMC, *Salisbury MSS.*, I, 96–97).

German Protestant states to escape from the imperial hegemony. French policy likewise gained greater strength and security from the fact that England lay immobilized by her own internal weakness and from the brilliant diplomatic success which had won for France not only Boulogne but a marriage treaty with Edward VI. England had abandoned her claims—and her policy—in Scotland; the Emperor had been alienated by the harsh treatment of the Princess Mary; commercial harassment against Flanders and unseemly quarrels respecting diplomatic immunity continued to abrade relations between the two powers. France was to placate England and bedazzle her young sovereign in small matters, but remained hostile on larger questions, while the possibility of an assault on Calais or a French-stiffened invasion from Scotland was never out of Northumberland's apprehensive mind. Nor did his capitulation to France enjoy full support in the Privy Council where Somerset expressed steady doubt, if not opposition, and where his influence still lent some protection to the Princess Mary. But Northumberland had gathered the reins of power firmly in his own hands and quickly made clear to his associates his determination not to become directly involved in a war which by the spring of 1552 had already engulfed half of Europe.

None the less, the astute Regent in Flanders, whose advice Charles was always inclined to follow, was in October, 1551 certain that England would join France in war; it was in this month that she had proposed a quick thrust into England in order to seat Mary on the throne, and, as importantly in her view, to gain a strong and defensible port. Gradually, however, it became evident that neither insult nor incidents would draw England in, though as we shall see the very fact of war, as well as continued English privateering, raised a host of admiralty claims from both combatants which Northumberland wearily sought to resolve.

For their part, the French had eloquently and skilfully stated their position to Edward and the Council at the outbreak of hostilities. The Emperor had harassed their shipping and their naval vessels, had once more intervened with great forces in Italy, and planned to intercept the Dowager Queen of Scotland on her return journey.[1] Hence it was as to a friendly, if neutral power, that was formally proclaimed in London on September 11.[2] England speedily announced her neutrality, but the Emperor was with cause outraged by the presence in Henry II's forces in the Flemish and

---

[1] Edward VI, *Chronicle*, 79–80.   [2] *Ibid.* 81.

Lorraine campaign of about 400 seasoned English light horse, employed as mercenaries, who gave a good account of themselves under the direct command of the Duc d'Aumale.[1] England's close friendship with France was also noted by several of the dissident Protestant princes of Germany, who appealed to England for direct military intervention on the grounds of faith or, if that were not possible, for financial aid in their 'war of liberation' from the trammels of the *Interim*.[2] To these rather murky proposals, a carefully worded reply was made on November 14, 1551, suggesting deep sympathy with their religious problems and enquiring whether 'they could get unto them any such strength of other princes as were able to maintain the war and to do the reciproque to me again if need so requires'. More specifically, the grant of a war subsidy could be considered only if Maurice, the Duke of Mecklenburg, and John of Brandenburg secured the firm alliance of the Duke of Prussia and the support of the great Baltic trading towns. This cautious reply was carried back by John Füss, Maurice's diplomatic agent, and seems to have been regarded as so vague as to be without value.[3]

These negotiations were, of course, handled in London directly by the Privy Council, since they were highly secret and since they involved states with which England did not maintain full diplomatic relations. But in this period of war, in which diplomatic contacts with the major states were of the utmost importance, there is abundant evidence that Northumberland was so preoccupied with domestic problems or so beguiled with the prospects of neutrality, that the standards of diplomatic relations, steadily improving in the second half of the reign of Henry VIII and through the whole of Somerset's tenure of power, were now in process of rapid deterioration. From mid-1551 to the end of the reign the number of diplomatic communications from resident ambassadors abroad is considerably less than half that prevailing in the time of the Lord Protector. Ambassadors were poorly paid,

---

[1] Rabutin, François de, *Commentaires des guerres en la Gaule Belgique (1551–1559)*, ed. by C. G. de Taurines (2 vols., Paris, 1932), I, 52.

[2] The principal were Maurice, Elector of Saxony, the Marquis of Brandenburg, the Duke of Mecklenburg, the Landgrave of Hesse, and the recently liberated John Frederick, Duke of Saxony (Edward VI, *Chronicle*, 90; Barthold, F. W., 'Philipp Franz und Johann Philipp, Wild- und Rheingrafen zu Dhaun, etc.', in *Historisches Taschenbuch*, n.s. IX (1848), 373, 382; Lisch, G. C. F., *Urkundensammlung zur Geschichte des Geschlechts von Maltzan* (5 vols., Schwerin, 1853), V, 244–246, 251, 255–256; *Twenty-seventh rpt.*, Dep. Keeper of Public Records (1866), App., 134, #LXI).

[3] Edward VI, *Chronicle*, 95–96; and see *ibid.* 96n. 174, for a fuller documentation of this rather hazy negotiation.

and even these insufficient stipends were often months in arrears. Pickering's responsible protests that his allowance did not meet half his costs was brusquely brushed aside.[1] A year later he was reduced to begging for his payment, for he had 'not twenty crowns left'.[2] It seems indeed that the foreign service was rapidly disintegrating, for just as the number (and quality) of dispatches declined, so did the complaints of long delays in reply from London or a complete want of information increase. Thus Vannes in Venice asserted that there were wild rumours abroad of a serious crisis in England which he was able to dispel only because he had private letters from home.[3] At this very moment Morison, Chamberlain, and Pickering were all pleading for their recall, Morison writing in November that he 'learns nothing out of England' and would be relieved to know whether his own letters even 'come to the Council'.[4]

The whole of the diplomatic service from early 1551 forward seems, then, to have lost the rather high standards of professionalism so carefully built up over the preceding generation. Bonner, Morison, and Paget did not know French sufficiently well to negotiate in the language, and both Paget and Thirlby would resort to Latin when precision of discussion was required. Morison's vain and pretentious dispatches were in the main worthless, when not misleading, while his flow of coy and irrelevant letters to Cecil do neither man credit.[5] For this deterioration Northumberland was principally to blame, since he was without serious and intelligent interest in foreign affairs, yet would not relinquish responsibility to any member of the junta. Shortly after Somerset's second arrest the ambassadors abroad sought to adjust their procedures to the changed circumstances, frequently addressing their dispatches to Northumberland directly, rather than to the Council; but most of these reports simply went unanswered. Then, at about the beginning of 1552 the ambassadors came customarily to address their dispatches and enquiries to Cecil, in whom Northumberland now reposed great confidence and who did seek to bring their questions before the Duke or the Council. Hence it was to Cecil that the proud Chamberlain wrote, saying that it was rumoured that the King and court were about to go on progress. If so, he begged for payment of his diets in advance, since he was without funds, possessed no resources other than a pension of about 100 marks a

---

[1] *Cal. S.P. For.*, *Edw. VI*, #449: Sept. 20, 1551.   [2] *Ibid.* #570: Oct. 12, 1552.
[3] *Ibid.* #571: Oct. 15, 1552.   [4] *Ibid.* #578: Nov. 9, 1552.
[5] *Twenty-seventh rpt.*, Dep. Keeper Public Records (1866), App., 134, #LVIII, as an example.

year, and could borrow in Brussels on no better terms than 25 per cent *per annum*.[1] The *Chronicle* makes quite clear, in many passages, that even the King, whose avid interest in the war then in progress was rapidly maturing, depended heavily on news conveyed to him by foreign ambassadors resident in London, so desultory and fragmentary was the flow of information from his own ambassadors abroad.

While seeking desperately to arm himself against the assault which he knew that Maurice and the German princes would levy against him in the spring, the Emperor was filled with foreboding, particularly since he regarded English policy as at once irresponsible and unpredictable. Only Paget remained to lend credence and some support to his contention that Mary had been extended guarantees with respect to her faith, but in October, 1551 news came that this once formidable and experienced diplomatist had been excluded from the Council.[2] The economy of the Netherlands, Charles's indispensable resource in time of war, was severely threatened by a discriminatory imposition laid by England on Flemish imports, while a new levy was being laid on cloth exports to Flanders. And there was talk of removing the mart for cloth from Antwerp to Calais, which would mean the ruin of Flanders.[3] This development, which Scheyfve had in fact exaggerated, may account in part for the discouraged tone of the Emperor's letter to his sister, in which he asked her whether the economy of the Low Countries could bear an assault on England, which, as we know, she had earlier recommended, for Charles confessed that he was without the resources necessary to carry out his policy or to wage war.[4] The English harassment of trade deepened when a temporary embargo was laid on the shipment of cloth to Flanders, a move actually planned in order to place shipments under governmental control for purposes of paying down England's external debt in Flanders. This, Northumberland vigorously maintained, was not in violation of the old commercial treaty since, as he put it, reasons of state were involved.[5]

During these same months, before the war erupted on a wide front in the spring of 1552, French diplomacy was engaged in a skilful effort to cajole England, to enlist the sympathy and interest of the King, and to neutralize English policy. Thus the slow pageantry of

[1] *Cal. S.P. For., Edw. VI*, #532: Feb. 11, 1552.
[2] *Ibid.* #461: Oct. 16, 1551.
[3] *Cal. S.P. Span.*, X, 445–446.   [4] *Ibid.* 447–448: Jan. 28, 1552.
[5] *Ibid.* 464, 467: Mar. 1 and 6, 1552; *vide post*, 464–466.

the unfolding of the marriage treaty—formally agreed to in all its terms in July 1551—proceeded. Edward sealed the treaty on December 2, 1551, thereupon dispatching Lord Clinton to the French court to secure Henry II's formal ratification, to christen a new prince of France, rather pointedly named 'Edward Henry', and to present handsome and expensive tokens, valued at 3400 crowns, to the royal family.[1] Unhappily, Clinton fell seriously ill after the christening, but Pickering, as ambassador, took his place at a festival of 'music, dancing and playing, with triumph in the Court', where he also delivered to the Princess Elizabeth the English King's token, 'a diamond in a ring'.[2] Clinton, not entirely recovered, returned to England on December 30th with the fully ratified treaty in hand for delivery to the Treasurer.[3]

The play by France on Edward's sentiments and interests was continued with a far more perceptive understanding of youth, surely, than either Somerset or Northumberland ever displayed. A request for the young King's portrait was met; his only close friend, Barnaby Fitzpatrick, was cordially received at the French court for a lengthy stay, and was often in the King's own presence; and in late January, 1552 the English King recorded with some excitement that a handsome gift from Henry II had arrived, consisting of ten horses, two jennets, and two little mules.[4]

But as spring approached the French were far less successful in their effort to involve England directly in the war which was on the point of bursting out in full intensity. Thus on March 8th the French ambassador revealed in great secrecy to Northumberland, and then to the King, the details of the alliance between France and the Protestant princes of Germany, including the brilliant but faithless Maurice, in the hope that England might be induced to enter the alliance.[5] This proposal was more formally laid before the English government on March 20th, when Edward noted that the proposed 'articles I have ... in my study'.[6] It is clear that the young King was now directly involving himself in diplomatic decisions, for a few days later he wrote that 'I did deny after a sort the request to enter into war, as appeareth by the copy of my

---

[1] Edward VI, *Chronicle*, 100; *Twenty-seventh rpt.*, Dep. Keeper Public Records (1866), App., 132, #LIII.

[2] Edward VI, *Chronicle*, 101–102; *Twenty-seventh rpt.*, Dep. Keeper Public Records (1866), App., 133, #LIV; *Cal. S.P. For., Edw. VI*, #511: Dec. 8, 1551.

[3] *A.P.C.*, III, 453: Dec. 30, 1551.

[4] Edward VI, *Chronicle*, 108; Rawlinson MSS., B 1087, #33, f. 54b (copy).

[5] *Ibid.* 114–115.

[6] *Ibid.* 116.

answer in the study'.[1] The English decision to preserve her neutrality was probably transmitted orally to the French ambassador on March 29th when Hoby and Mason called upon him. The French had, of course, expected no other decision, and in truth the whole weight of their diplomacy had as its object the neutralization of England. They did, however, try once more to secure the limited involvement of England when they asked permission to supply a considerable armed force based on Ardres by passage through the Calais enclave (rather than overland from Boulogne), which was flatly denied, the King noting 'that I could not accomplish [the] desire, because it was against my league with the Emperor'.[2] The truth was that England knew full well in these months of weakness that her now feeble grasp on the 'Old Conquest' depended principally on the treaty—and policy—guarantees of Charles V for its defence.

In the meantime, imperial diplomacy was also addressed to the necessity of keeping England neutral and in maintaining the normal trade flow between England and Flanders, for on this Charles believed his ability to finance the war depended. We have seen that these commercial relations were already abraded by festering disputes, by a domestic depression in England occasioned by the overproduction of cloth, and by Northumberland's desperate efforts to restore England's external credit. Chamberlain, with long experience in the Flemish trade, complained from Brussels to the Council in November, 1551 that English merchants throughout Flanders were suffering from severe war restrictions laid on commerce and that he could gain no audience with the Regent to state his complaints. It was, indeed, his flat advice that England retaliate by an embargo on shipments to Flanders unless satisfaction could be gained.[3]

This rich and lucrative traffic, essential to both England and the Emperor, was also preyed on by French warships and Scottish privateers. So important was its protection that Corneille Scepperus (M. d'Eecke), in command of the imperial fleet in the Low Countries, was called upon for a careful survey of the naval problems involved. Most of the vessels being taken were Dutch, which, being well-sailed and fast, could escape on the high seas but were vulnerable in coastal waters. Trade, he thought, could be maintained so long as the coast was kept free of hostile ships, while he

---

[1] Edward VI, *Chronicle*, 116–117. No copy of the document here mentioned has been found.   [2] *Ibid.* 119–120.
[3] *Cal. S.P. For., Edw. VI*, #473: Nov. 1, 1551.

would recommend an embargo against England if imperial ships were impounded or taken there. It was likewise his view that considerable naval construction must be undertaken, especially of medium-sized craft for coastal defence and for employment on convoy duty to England.[1]

The festering difficulties between England and Flanders, which neither side had sought fully to heal, were in part reflected in the instructions set out by the Council for Sir Philip Hoby, who was to be sent to Bruges on a special embassy. We are told, however, by the King that this was a 'pretence', his principal duty being to take £63,000 in French crowns for the payment of pressing debts falling due in Antwerp and then to wait upon the Regent 'to declare to her the griefs [of] my subjects'.[2] Hoby was a most amiable and engaging man and a skilful negotiator. The Regent, in reporting her conversations with him, wrote that Hoby had stressed the great importance for England of good relations with the Empire and strongly suggested that commercial frictions had weakened them. So great was the harassment, he held, that English merchants were disposed to withdraw entirely from Flanders, though this his King would not countenance. While he disclaimed authority to negotiate, Hoby suggested that the principal grievances were damage to cargo in searches for contraband, frequent detention of English vessels with no cause given, refusal to permit the export of herring to England without special licence, the withholding of stores of gunpowder already purchased, and the chronic complaints regarding searches and seizures by licensed privateers.[3] He may well have added that a vice-admiral (Henry Dudley) had just been appointed to command a flotilla based on the Thames estuary, whose assignment would be the protection of coastal waters and the approaches to the Thames, as had earlier been urged by the Regent.

Hoby's conversations had done much to relieve tensions and were almost immediately followed by a special diplomatic mission, led by de Courrières (Jean de Montmorency), which had as its ostensible purpose a request for courtesy to a great imperial fleet which would shortly appear in the Channel with a convoy from Spain, and for hospitality if any of the vessels found it necessary to

---

[1] *Niederländische Akten und Urkunden zur Geschichte der Hanse, etc.*, vol. I: 1531–1557, ed. by Rudolf Häpke (Munich and Leipzig, 1913), 498–499.

[2] Harl. MS. 353, #36, f. 116; HMC, *Salisbury MSS.*, I, 94; Edward VI, *Chronicle*, 109, 111. This was the first substantial payment against foreign debts which a few months earlier had totalled £250,000. Gresham was at this time engaged in arranging for staggered short-term loans to bring the large English floating debt under control.

[3] *Cal. S.P. Span.*, X, 476–481: Mar. 24, 1552.

put in at an English port. To this request the King replied that orders for the sanctuary of Flemish ships were already in force and would so remain, though he 'thought it not convenient to have more ships to come into my havens than I could well rule and govern'.[1] These reasonable assurances having been given, de Courrières turned to the principal matter in his instructions, the relief of commercial tensions. A detailed discussion of specific grievances on both sides was held, while a point-by-point replication of all the complaints which Hoby had lodged was given by de Courrières and Scheyfve.[2] While few formal concessions were made by either side, the two missions had in fact cleared the air and from June, 1552 forward far more restraint and far less commercial harassment may be observed. The slow, but persistent, swing of English policy towards a better understanding with the Emperor was under way.

But the rapprochement with England had not proceeded so far as the Emperor had hoped. Charles V was at the crisis of his career. Maurice had marched to the south against him on March 18th, being joined at Bischofsheim by William of Hesse. Simultaneously, Henry II had invaded Lorraine and had thrown strong harassing parties against the Flemish frontier. Charles, securing no more than the promise of neutrality from his estranged brother, was at war on several fronts, and his communications were all but disrupted. Then, while at Innsbruck, Maurice secured Ehrenberg castle, commanding the pass, forcing the Emperor, stricken with gout and too ill to ride, to escape by litter across the Brenner Pass to Villach. In the north the campaign had been quite as disastrous. Henry and Montmorency had moved on Strassburg, which however refused to yield and against which the French were in no position to mount a siege. They were also greatly disturbed by reports that the Regent of the Netherlands was moving heavy forces into Luxemburg which could easily cut their supply lines and block a possible retreat. They therefore fell back through Verdun, which was taken, and invaded Luxemburg in order to ward off the expected attack from the north. English fears were aroused when news reached London that heavily fortified Damvillers and Montmédy were taken and that Yvoix had capitulated.[3] Flanders, only lightly held, might well have been in danger had not mutinies broken out among the mercenary regiments in Henry II's army, resulting in pitched battles with French troops, which caused the French king to fall

---

[1] Edward VI, *Chronicle*, 120, 121: Apr. 26 and May 4, 1552.
[2] *Cal. S.P. Span.*, X, 516–517, 531–534: May 8 and June 12, 1552.
[3] Edward VI, *Chronicle*, 131; HMC, *Salisbury MSS.*, I, 95–96.

back towards his own frontiers. But the great foray had served its principal purpose of providing a strong diversion for Maurice and the rebellious German princes. And Metz remained in French hands.[1]

These overt assaults upon Charles V, and more specifically the harassing attacks on the Flemish borders, raised at once the question of England's responsibilities under the Treaty of Utrecht (1542), which, as we have noted, afforded England shelter, since the terms associated the Emperor in the defence of the Calais perimeter. Accordingly, the Queen Regent in a letter to Edward VI pointed out that her frontier had been violated at several places in areas specified by the treaty and hence asked for immediate aid and a declaration of war according to the treaty terms.[2] The formal demand, delivered on July 5th, called for the immediate assistance of 5000 foot, or 700 crowns a day, and entrance into the war as an ally within the period of a month.[3] Scheyfve reported on July 9th that he had experienced difficulty in gaining an audience because so many members of the Council were absent from court, but that he had handed the letter to the King, who had promised early consideration, though Northumberland and Pembroke were both far from London.[4] The Regent's letter was followed by a more formal invocation of the treaty by Charles V, who reminded Edward 'how we informed the French, when they made war on you, that if they invaded your countries included in the treaty', he would at once intervene as he was bound under the treaty terms.[5]

This embarrassing request came at a most difficult time, since the King was leaving immediately on his first progress and the Council not attending him were either in London or widely scattered. None the less, the King tells us that a long and careful preliminary review of the treaty was undertaken at Oatlands on July 10th, while Thirlby and Wotton were instructed to examine the provisions, both Latin and English, in order to extricate England from any obligation that she might have. It was further agreed that Scheyfve was to be told, when he applied again, that the King was on progress and could not act until his Council advised him. If the ambassador still pressed, the reply was to be that in view of his 'young years' and the 'amity sworn with the French king', Edward could not honour the

---

[1] The King followed these events with breathless interest; *vide Chronicle*, 125 ff.
[2] *Cal. S.P. Span.*, X, 537–541 *passim*: June 23, 1552.
[3] Edward VI, *Chronicle*, 134. The treaty had been informally but explicitly confirmed by Paget in a long interview with the Emperor in Brussels in 1549 (*Cal. S.P. Span.*, IX, 410–419).
[4] *Ibid.* X, 548.   [5] *Ibid.* 549: July 1552.

treaty terms but would instead use his influence in mediation. Further, in the event the Emperor was still not content, the ultimate answer was to be that he was not bound by his father's treaty and wished another to be negotiated, and for good measure he would remind the Emperor that he had lent no assistance on the occasion of the recent French incursions into the Calais enclave.[1] Scheyfve could report no more on July 24th than that the King was on his progress, that such senior Councillors as Northumberland, Suffolk, Pembroke, and Shrewsbury were scattered, and that no decision could be reached until the study of the treaty was completed and the Council re-convened.[2] Then on July 31st, while the King was at Halnaker (Sussex), came what must have been the expected reply, that the King must excuse himself on the grounds of his 'tender youth' and because he had been obliged to fight a war alone against France, which had cost him heavily.[3] Slender as his hopes must have been, England's flat refusal to honour its undoubted treaty obligations must have added something to the profound discouragement and ennui which afflicted the Emperor in this crisis of his long and great reign. What he did not know was that no more than a fortnight later the Council dispatched re-enforcements, drawn from the King's own guards, to Guînes with instructions giving the commanders full discretion if the French should press nearer.[4] The bloom of the entente with France was rapidly withering.

English foreign policy was beginning to shift, almost imperceptibly at first, in part also because the King was coming to an early and an impressive maturity and had now to be consulted. Continuous and convincing evidences of an effective and ranging concern with social, financial, administrative, and diplomatic interests on Edward's part are reflected with particular clarity in his *Chronicle*, beginning about September, 1551, just short of his fourteenth birthday. It should be noted that almost exactly half the total bulk of the *Chronicle* is devoted to comment on events from September, 1551 to the abrupt conclusion of the document on November 30, 1552, while the qualitative change may be suggested when it is said that the *Chronicle* becomes a major historical document in the autumn of 1551. The King had begun occasionally to attend Council meetings even before Somerset's fall; but from late 1551 forward his attendance was not uncommon and the evidence

---

[1] Edward VI, *Chronicle*, 135–136; HMC, *Salisbury MSS.*, I, 97.

[2] *Cal. S.P. Span.*, X, 553–554.

[3] *Ibid.* 558: Aug. 3, 1552; Edward VI, *Chronicle*, 137. The Council's reply was delivered by Wotton and Hoby.

[4] *A.P.C.*, IV, 111: Aug. 12, 1552; Edward VI, *Chronicle*, 139.

is clear that he was following the debates and decisions of his Council with a close and critical attention. The imperial ambassador stated that as early as March, 1552 Edward was usually in attendance at Council meetings, especially if important state matters were under discussion, and suggests that his personal authority now lay behind most of its decisions.[1]

The King's direct concern with diplomatic policy is fully demonstrated in an important memorandum, largely in Cecil's hand, but with careful and modifying comments by the King, which may be dated September 23, 1552. The chief question posed in this policy paper was whether England should enter into a more active and binding alliance with the Emperor, and this a scant two months after England's failure to meet her own treaty obligations. The arguments for the French alliance were first briefly sketched by Cecil, but the counter-arguments clearly prevailed. England was already bound to the Emperor by an old treaty, and if she lent no assistance Burgundy was likely to be lost to Charles, to England's great peril, while the Turks would be loosed in Europe. Further, since aid had been refused to Charles he might be driven to seek terms with the French, which would leave England alone and in double jeopardy. Nor had the recent amity with France brought true peace, for her harassment of English shipping and trade remained intolerable. And there was the constant danger of an assault on Calais. The conclusion, drawn in the King's own hand, was that a treaty was to be sought with the Emperor, and by the Emperor with other powers, in order to immobilize French aggression in the affairs of Europe.[2] This shrewd and cautious analysis of the English position, though never fully implemented, betokened not only the active participation of the King in foreign affairs but a gathering shift in English policy.

This gradual movement of English policy was quickened by a bizarre diplomatic episode which we may describe as *l'affaire* Stuckley. Thomas Stuckley, an engaging and irrepressible rogue, first appears in the Berwick garrison in 1546; he fought at Pinkie and was a petty officer at Boulogne with pay set at 6s 8d *per diem*. He was befriended by Somerset, and on the Duke's second arrest fled abroad to France where he served in the Lorraine campaign in 1551–1552.[3] In mid-September Stuckley returned to England with

[1] *Cal. S.P. Span.*, X, 493: Mar. 30, 1552.

[2] Cotton MSS., Nero, C, x, f. 69; Nichols, *Remains*, II, 539–543.

[3] Strype, *Memorials*, II, i, 570–571; Nichols, *Remains*, II, 455; Izon, John, *Sir Thomas Stucley, etc.* (L., 1956), for a popular account of this remarkable career.

a safe-conduct, probably drawn by Lord Clinton, and with a letter of recommendation from Henry II to Edward, stating that Stuckley had served him gallantly and now wished to return home.[1] Stuckley immediately reported to the Council that he had been 'entertained by the French King very gently'. Henry had, indeed, made him a familiar, to whom he had confided his intention to over-run Calais and launch an invasion of England. When Stuckley remonstrated that this was impossible, Henry was said to have replied 'that he meant to land in England in an angle thereof about Falmouth, and said the bulwarks might easily be won, and [that] the people were papistical; also that Mons. de Guise at the same time should enter into England by Scotland side, with the aid of the Scots'.[2] Stuckley signed this incredible deposition on September 19th, the Council at once sending full information to Pickering in Paris with instructions to investigate the story, which the frightened Council was at first inclined to vest with some credence.[3] Moreover, as a precautionary measure in the event there was substance to the story, the King's close friend, Barnaby Fitzpatrick, was summoned home.[4]

From the outset Northumberland doubted the tale, though Cecil and others of the Council were by no means certain that beneath Stuckley's obvious lies there might not be some measure of truth. It was, however, wisely determined to relay the whole story to Henry II, with every appearance of complete innocence. This decision was fortified by Pickering's advice that Stuckley had never consulted him and 'never heard the French King speak no such word, nor never was [Stuckley] in credit with him or the Constable'. Accordingly, Stuckley was thrown into the Tower, where he remained until Mary's accession, while the whole story was revealed to the French ambassador with apologies that his royal master had thus been slandered, 'as other such renegades do daily the same'.[5] Henry II rose gracefully to the high moral tone thus taken, denouncing Stuckley for his lies and 'thanked us much for this so gentle an uttering of the matter, that we would not be led with false bruits and tales'.[6] But, none the less, these 'revelations' had shaken the English government because it knew there was little

[1] *Cal. S.P. For.*, *Edw. VI*, #555: Aug. 3, 1552; Rawlinson MSS., D 1087, #17, f. 25.   [2] Edward VI, *Chronicle*, 143.

[3] *Cal. S.P. For.*, *Edw. VI*, #563; Strype, *Memorials*, II, i, 571–572; S.P. Dom., Edw. VI, XV, 6.

[4] Edward VI, *Chronicle*, 144.

[5] *Ibid.* 148: Oct. 7, 1552; S.P. Dom., Edw. VI, XV, 38.

[6] Edward VI, *Chronicle*, 150.

substance in the French amity for which Northumberland had striven. Just to be certain, the formidable Lord Grey of Wilton was sent over to assume the Calais command and imperial forces were in fact permitted to pass through the Calais perimeter when a few weeks later Charles V attacked Ambleteuse.[1]

As the rumours of the Stuckley 'revelations' were magnified to suggest that a crisis in the diplomatic relations of France and England was at hand, Charles wrote post-haste to his sister for any 'hard news' that she might have.[2] Scheyfve could report only that French seizure of English shipping was engendering friction and that a French commission had arrived to negotiate a settlement. Cloth was once more moving to Flanders without governmental restraint, while a heavy trade with Spain was being developed by ships sailing in protected convoys.[3] Northumberland, in discussing England's failure to carry out its treaty obligations, suggested to Scheyfve that imperial policy had been negligent since no one had paid a state visit to the King since his accession; indeed, even the invocation of the treaty had been transmitted by the Regent of the Netherlands rather than by a special embassy. And for good measure, Northumberland pointed out that had Charles honoured the earlier English appeal for aid, Boulogne might never have been relinquished and the present war avoided. The Duke was courteous and reminiscent in his converse and Scheyfve correctly detected a much friendlier tone. This was fully confirmed by the frank and now highly placed Sir Thomas Gresham, who on this same occasion told the imperial envoy that English merchants had sustained losses of the order of £160,000, while the second instalment of the Boulogne ransom (200,000 crowns) remained unpaid. It would, Gresham confided, have been more honourable and well-advised had England entered the alliance against France, at least in the view of the merchant fraternity, and this conviction would be urged on the King and Council. So high was Gresham in Northumberland's favour that Scheyfve correctly believed that these most indiscreet revelations in fact enjoyed the Duke's approval.[4]

It seems quite certain that an important, though bumbling and murky, effort was undertaken at about this date to indicate to the Emperor that England was considering a reversal of policy and the

---

[1] Lefebvre, *Histoire de Calais*, II, 274–275; Edward VI, *Chronicle*, 144, 147.
[2] *Cal. S.P. Span.*, X, 575.   [3] *Ibid.* 565–566: Sept. 23, 1552.
[4] *Ibid.* 568–569: Oct. 10, 1552; Northumberland condoned Gresham's indiscretion and believed that it had occasioned 'more good will than of long time he [had] seen on that side' (HMC, *Salisbury MSS.*, I, 103).

cultivation of at least a limited entente with him. Incredibly enough, the diplomatist employed was Morison, who in late August had confided to Cecil that if he could he would lend aid to the Emperor, 'being no jot more affectionated to France than . . . to the great Turk'.[1] His instructions were indefinite and tentative. He was to indicate England's regret at the continuing depredations of the Turks and to offer assistance against them if other princes would join, though he was not to discuss Henry II's responsibility for having loosed them against Christian Europe. And if French aggression against the Low Countries should be mentioned, he was not to treat the subject but was to suggest that the Emperor send 'some special man hither' for formal discussion of it. The Council wished above all to know the Emperor's mind and sentiments, to gain a sense of the whole sweep of his policy *vis-à-vis* England.[2] These vague overtures seem never to have resulted in significant conversations but were, so to say, absorbed in the even more quixotic English effort to negotiate a general peace a few months later.[3] None the less, so eroded and hostile were Anglo-French relations by October, 1552 that one wonders whether France might not have levied war on England had not the Emperor with an angry pertinacity begun the siege of Metz. If this had transpired, the English government could have mounted only limited defences, for a process of substantial demobilization had been under way since the cession of Boulogne, made necessary by the financial straits in which England lay. A grim summing up was made for the Council, which revealed that in the decade extending from September, 1542 to September, 1552 the military outlays, including the costs of suppressing insurrection, had been very nearly £3,500,000.[4] A debris of external and internal debt was the inheritance from the Henrician era when England had played the role of a first-rate power. This role the Duke of Northumberland was too weak to support, too uncertain of his own policy even to contemplate.

At the same time, Northumberland was yielding to the strong anti-French sentiments of the realm at large and found himself impelled by October, 1552 to embrace what may broadly be described as Somerset's own foreign policy. The strength of this

[1] *Cal. S.P. For., Edw. VI*, #558: Augsburg, Aug. 22, 1552.

[2] Cotton MSS., Galba, B, xii, 230–233; *Cal. S.P. For., Edw. VI*, #564; Mackie, J. D., *The earlier Tudors, etc.* (Oxford, 1952), 486–487.

[3] *Vide post*, 178–180. The Council's instructions to Morison should have resulted in additional documents relating to this overture, which, however, we have not been able to find.

[4] S.P. Dom., Edw. VI, XV, 11.

sentiment, already in part described, may be further demonstrated
by a most interesting proposal of Thomas Burnaby for 'Distressing
the French'.[1] His views were vehemently anti-French as the result,
he says, of an intimate knowledge of France gained in twenty-eight
journeys there as a diplomatic courier and in other capacities. Hence
he could aver that no credence should be placed in Montmorency,
'for there is no more assurance of his word than to hold an eel by
the tail', and he was 'as popish as I am English'. It was his proposal that France be steadily weakened by building up England's
commercial fleet, by an embargo laid against imports from France,
and, above all else, by an absolute prohibition on the export of coal
to France, which, he contended, was vital to the French economy.
Further, French shipping could be paralysed if the West country-
men were permitted to seize and hold Alderney. The French are as
arrogant as they are confident, but 'if we will know our own strength,
their courage shall be bated well enough'. Keep them from fishing,
give them no safe-conducts, and 'keep them from Newcastle coal
and they cannot live'. Such were the sentiments, which incidentally
Burnaby says he had laid before Somerset, of the articulate classes of
England, and such too was the persuasion of the inarticulate,
inspired by two centuries of history. To these sentiments the policy
of Northumberland was being bent by events and by domestic
pressure.

The drift towards a rapprochement with the Emperor gathered
force during the course of the autumn, while hostility towards
France led to a modest further effort to strengthen the defences of
Calais and Guînes and caused Northumberland to fish in the waters
of espionage by considering a not very hopeful scheme for gaining
Cherbourg by treasonable courses.[2] The vital cloth trade with
Flanders was resumed without let or hindrance on either side,
Scheyfve gleefully reporting in late October that a cloth fleet of
sixty sail was preparing to make the crossing under the protection
of a naval escort.[3] Then in November there came a diplomatic
break for the Empire of considerable moment when a diplomatic
courier's pouch, being carried from Scotland to France, was seized

---

[1] Burnaby was probably a groom of the Privy Chamber, who leased a London dwelling comprising former chantry property, and served on a commission for the peace in
Worcestershire. (*A.P.C.*, II, 215, 223; *Cal. Pat. Rolls, Edw. VI*, I, 91, 325). This document (Lansdowne MS. 2, #85, ff. 187–191) may almost certainly be dated Oct. 1, 1552.
It may well have been addressed to Cecil, as the Lansdowne catalogue suggests, though
evidence is wanting.

[2] S.P. Dom., Edw. VI, XIV, 51: Hoby to Cecil; *ibid*. XV, 26, 26(i): Oct. 18, 1552.

[3] *Cal. S.P. Span.*, X, 579, 581.

at Gravelines by the Flemish authorities. Among the papers were letters from the Queen Dowager of Scotland, communications from several highly placed Frenchmen on duty in Scotland, and dispatches as well from the French ambassador in London. These documents made it abundantly clear that the Guise interest was implacably hostile to England and was intent on perpetuating itself in Scotland, and that the French had prevented the release from jail in Scotland of one George Paris, a renegade Irish rebel, who had once been in favour in the French court and was now being employed by England as a counter-agent.[1] These dispatches the Regent showed informally to Gresham, who promptly forwarded news of them to London. There was little in them not already known to the English government, but the episode deepened as it hardened English suspicions of French intentions and somewhat undeservedly, and immediately, advanced the understanding which was now being sought with the Emperor.[2]

So far had the shift in policy proceeded that in late November the Regent's Treasurer Longin could speak informally to Gresham of a possible marriage alliance for Edward with a Habsburg princess to seal the new amity, while in London Northumberland was pretending illness to avoid a meeting with the French ambassador. At the same time he confided to Cecil and Petre that though many thought him friendly to France, he sought only to exploit its favour, 'which he never desired in all his life but for the service of his master'.[3] It seemed for some weeks in the late autumn that England was moving swiftly towards a close alliance with the Emperor, until Chamberlain in Brussels, certainly by reason of instructions which are missing, denied his own earlier statement, when he had indicated formally that his government regarded the existing treaty of friendship as sufficient.[4] One supposes that the decision to draw back, or more accurately to temper the mood of rapprochement, came from Northumberland, who understood, as many of his colleagues did not, that England was simply in no position to risk war with France.

The steady drift of English policy towards a closer understanding with the Empire was followed with some anxiety by France, which by a probably calculated admixture of arrogance and cajolery sought to dampen, if not to cure, the inevitable frictions and grievances

---

[1] Edward VI, *Chronicle*, 108 n. 23; *Cal. S.P. For., Edw. VI*, pp. 48, 63, 89, 92; *Cal. S.P. Span.*, X, 587–588; *A.P.C.*, III, 471; *ibid.*, IV, 12, 138, 202, 244–245.
[2] Edward VI, *Chronicle*, 152, 155; HMC, *Salisbury MSS.*, I, 100–101, 102.
[3] *Ibid.* 102: Nov. 23, 1552; *Cal. S.P. For., Edw. VI*, #584: Nov. 27, 1552.
[4] *Cal. S.P. Span.*, X, 605–606.

resulting from the war then in progress. Thus, in August, 1552 the French ambassador informed the King that his master was sending over a commission, well trained in civil law, to 'declare which of our merchants' matters have [been] adjudged on their side, and which against them, and for what consideration'.[1] The news evoked from Hoby the unequivocal advice to Cecil not to trust the usual 'fair words' and promises of French diplomacy; instead the Council should insist that merchants who had been plundered be fully compensated.[2] Shortly afterwards two civil lawyers did arrive, with instructions from the French Council, who somewhat presumptuously attempted to prescribe unilaterally the adjudication made on a long list of English claims. They were, however, referred to a commission composed of Wotton, Thomas Smith, and Petre, all lawyers by training, and at least two of them anti-French in their views on foreign affairs. The English commission promptly submitted a list of claims totalling upwards of £50,000, to which the French lawyers could only say that they possessed no authority to bind their government and that the claims would have to be referred back to Paris.[3]

Relations between the two powers had, if anything, been exacerbated by these haggling discussions and nothing had been settled. English sentiments were particularly offended by the case of William Winter and his brother, George, whose ships and goods had been seized, and the grievance of another merchant named Sidney, who had also lost his ship and cargo to French privateers. Northumberland had been outraged by both cases,[4] and after strong specific complaints a special envoy, the Seigneur de Villandry, was dispatched from Paris with more precise instructions.[5] But Villandry worsened matters by somewhat haughtily contending that both Winter's and Sidney's ships and goods had been justly taken, but would be returned *gratuito* in order to meet the English demand in these instances. This offer was instantly and angrily refused as was a suggestion from Villandry that the admiralty law of England be somewhat revised to make it more consonant with French law. Nor

---

[1] Edward VI, *Chronicle*, 139.

[2] HMC, *Salisbury MSS.*, I, 98–99: Aug. 21, 1552.

[3] Edward VI, *Chronicle*, 145: Sept. 29, 1552.

[4] S.P. Dom., Edw. VI, XIV, 29: May 1552. The Winters were merchants trading principally to the Levant (*Cal. S.P. For.*, *Edw. VI*, p. 254). William Winter was also a royal servant, being a surveyor of ships to the King (Edward VI, *Chronicle*, 36, 148). Sidney has not been certainly identified.

[5] Claude de Breton, Seigneur de Villandry (d. 1556) had been finance minister to Francis I.

was the cause of diplomatic conciliation advanced by his demand
that certain Frenchmen be released who were, so the English
claimed, nothing more than pirates.[1]

Villandry returned to Paris to report that some plan of adjudi-
cating the mounting claims was urgently advisable, returning shortly
with Aubespine, with new proposals.[2] It was now suggested that
Henry II was prepared immediately to return four ships on which
legal judgement of seizure had been given, that a board of responsible men be established in Paris to hear English merchants' complaints, and that the King meant forthwith to make minor amendments in the French admiralty law.[3] No substantial concessions
were, however, made; no satisfactory plan of adjudication had been
offered. The English Council with undiplomatic heat replied a
week later that the return of the four ships was not acceptable, for
'so few [would] prejudice the rest', that adjudicature by a French
'inferior council' would possess no powers of remedy, that the
amendments in French admiralty law were 'as ill as their old', and
that in any event they desired 'no more words, but deeds'.[4] Thus the
negotiations had accomplished nothing more than a considerable
worsening in the relations of the two states, neither side being
willing to make any concessions, even of a minor nature. Pickering,
in Paris, meanwhile had conversed with the King, the Constable,
and others of high estate, and was persuaded that the French
intended to offer nothing more than 'fair words'.[5]

But France was now greatly concerned, not only by English
inflexibility in the matter of commercial grievances, but even more
by the entente with the Emperor which it was feared might
shortly ripen into an offensive alliance. Hence in December the
French commissioners were instructed to negotiate and agree to a
modus for the settlement of some still unresolved claims and of
future ones which quite predictably would arise. The hard-bitten
Pickering was at the beginning sceptical that France would yield
more than promises, but a few weeks later wrote from Paris to his
government that in his view a just settlement had in fact been
made.[6] It is possible that a declaration of war had been averted by

[1] Edward VI, *Chronicle*, 148–149: Oct. 8, 1552; HMC, *Salisbury MSS.*, I, 100: Oct.
10, 1552.
[2] Claude de l'Aubespine, Baron de Châteauneuf, Secretary of State to Henry II; *Cal.
S.P. Span.*, X, 578, 590.
[3] Edward VI, *Chronicle*, 153: Nov. 5, 1552.   [4] *Ibid.* 153–154.
[5] *Cal. S.P. For., Edw. VI*, #592: Dec. 9, 1552.
[6] HMC, *Salisbury MSS.*, I, 105: Dec. 22, 1552; *Cal. S.P. Span.*, X, 616: Dec. 28,
1552; *Cal. S.P. For., Edw. VI*, #614: Feb. 4, 1553.

this sudden and humiliating decision of France to yield in matters which were in truth not essential in the conduct of her policy. At almost this precise date too, as we have noted, England suddenly drew back in the quickening pace of her rapprochement with the Empire, for reasons which were probably essentially domestic in their nature.[1]

5. NORTHUMBERLAND IN THE ROLE OF PEACEMAKER
(1553)

It was at this juncture that Northumberland intervened personally and strongly in foreign affairs in a strange effort to negotiate a general peace in Europe. His plan was all the more bizarre since the King was evidently seriously ill before his efforts were concluded and the possible death of the sovereign raised the spectre of probable imperial intervention against which he could safeguard himself only by French amity. We can only conclude that it was not until May or June, 1553 that he was himself persuaded that the King was probably mortally ill and that his great conspiracy against the legal succession did not ripen until very late indeed and then not wholly of his own free will. At the very least one must conclude that his extraordinary diplomatic efforts in 1553 ran counter to the best interests of England which were most certainly best served by the continuation of the Habsburg-Valois war.

It was possibly a rather cloudy dispatch from Chamberlain, in Brussels, which bore most responsibility for the Duke's heady resolution. The ambassador urged the necessity of amity between England and the Netherlands and expressed the conviction that the Emperor was in fact about to make a strong claim for an English alliance.[2] Whatever the occasion, Northumberland determined, without consultation with the Council, to send special ambassadors to the Emperor and to France with instructions to offer England's service in mediating what can only be described as a general European war.[3] For this task, requiring the most sophisticated of diplomatic competence, he passed over diplomatists of great ability and experience—men like Wotton, Paget, and Mason—and even competent, and decorative, nobles in his own Council, to charge his totally inexperienced brother, Sir Andrew, and his son-in-law, Sir

---

[1] *Vide ante*, 171.
[2] HMC, *Salisbury MSS.*, I, 105: Dec. 13, 1552.
[3] S.P. Dom., Edw. VI, XV, 74: Dec. 28, 1552.

Henry Sidney, then barely twenty-four years of age, with these sensitive discussions.[1]

One must say that Northumberland, his mind once decided, moved with undiplomatic dispatch. On January 1st, Andrew Dudley waited on Scheyfve to announce his mission, indicating that he would call on the Regent before proceeding to the Emperor for more definitive consultations.[2] The startled Regent received him on January 8th, strongly urging him to wait in Brussels for the Emperor's expected arrival, and warning that Charles's route to Flanders was uncertain and that he was severely ill. But the importunate Dudley was determined to press on as soon as horses and passports were available. On the 9th he set out despite Chamberlain's remonstrations, ignoring his suggestion that the Emperor disliked giving audiences while travelling.[3] Morison, who had been in the Emperor's train and who was uninformed regarding Dudley's mission, met him first at Trèves and then accompanied him to Luxemburg where with great difficulty an audience was arranged for January 25th. The surely bewildered Emperor declared himself not indisposed to peace, but first he must know his enemy's mind, and he made it abundantly clear that he was unprepared for further discussions until he reached Brussels.[4] There Dudley was obliged to wait for a fortnight before another audience could be gained, only to be told that though he would welcome an end to the war, Charles had no confidence that France would respect a peace once concluded and that he would not discuss the matter until he knew Henry II's terms and sentiments. His bootless mission concluded, Dudley left at once for home, where the Council had just learned

---

[1] *Cal. S.P. For.*, *Edw. VI*, #599: Dec. 27, 1552; Harl. MS. 353, #42, f. 127; Sloane MSS., 2402, f. 81 (for Sidney's instructions).

Sidney had been a member of the King's intimate boyhood circle and had been made one of the four principal gentlemen of Edward's privy chamber. He had married Northumberland's daughter, Mary, in March, 1551. Attractive and gifted as he was, Sidney possessed no experience that would have made him competent to discharge this delicate mission.

Andrew Dudley, as we have seen, was a gifted and courageous soldier, who had served England well at Broughty Craig (Jordan, *Edward VI*, 261, 265–267). More recently he had been in command at Guînes, but had been recalled in 1552 after a bitter quarrel with Willoughby, the Deputy of Calais. Thorny in personality, blunt in speech, he possessed no abilities fitting him for this assignment.

[2] *Cal. S.P. Span.*, XI, 1: Jan. 4, 1553.

[3] *Cal. S.P. For.*, *Edw. VI*, ##603, 606: Jan. 8 and 9, 1553.

[4] *Ibid.* #611: Jan. 25, 1553; *Venetianische Depeschen vom Kaiserhofe*, vol. II, ed. by G. Turba (Historische Commission der kaiserlichen Akademie der Wissenschaften, Vienna, 1892), 590; Katterfeld, Alfred, *Roger Ascham, etc.* (Strassburg and L., 1879), 196 ff.

that the French king had imposed the same hopeless terms, that the initiative should come from Charles.[1]

This feckless preliminary sounding having been made, Northumberland placed his grandiose plan in more carefully chosen and professional diplomatic hands after a lapse of some weeks. But there had been at least one great gain, for from the time of the onset of Edward's severe illness the status of the Princess Mary had been restored and she was now being treated with all due respect. Thus on February 17th Scheyfve could report that she had recently been kindly entertained at Court, that Northumberland had treated her with great consideration, and that the subject of her faith had not been raised.[2] So it continued until the end of the reign, raising again substantial doubt that Northumberland embraced treasonable designs until the last days of Edward's life. Just a month after his amazed report on Mary's restoration to favour, Scheyfve had a long and intimate conversation with Northumberland which was of considerable importance in disclosing the Duke's mind. He was troubled by fears of the dissolution of European politics when the Emperor should die, and his health in this year was known to be very poor indeed. He expressed great sympathy for the imperial policy and none at all for that of France, though he hoped by his diplomacy to find some way for a peaceful solution of the war then in progress. Scheyfve none the less drew from the audience the sense that the Duke fully understood that England's interests were well served by the war and that he intended to pursue a policy of strict neutrality. Northumberland's position he thought insecure, since he was hated by a large Roman Catholic party and was generally so apprehensive that he now sought to rule without consultation with the Privy Council.[3]

The English soundings had inevitably precipitated rumours of secret and important negotiations under way. Chamberlain and Morison from Brussels reported such rumours as being current there, though both envoys doubted their substance.[4] The always prudent Pickering in France conferred with the King and the Constable on these reports and learned that the papacy had also made an offer to mediate, though the French terms were so absurdly high as to cause him to believe that Henry was not ready to treat in good faith.[5] Morison pressed hard for another interview with the Emperor,

[1] *Cal. S.P. For., Edw. VI*, ##616, 619.
[2] *Cal. S.P. Span.*, XI, 8–9: Feb. 17, 1553.
[3] *Ibid.* 17–19: Mar. 17, 1553.
[4] *Cal. S.P. For., Edw. VI*, #631: Mar. 5, 1553.   [5] *Ibid.* #638: Mar. 22, 1553.

who however chose to speak through his sister. The Regent expressed the Emperor's gratitude for the English interest, but since his enemies showed no disposition to negotiate, Charles had no other reply to give to Edward than that which he had conveyed to Dudley. At the same time, he welcomed the interest of the young King in the cause of peace and hoped that he would continue with his efforts.[1]

This discouraging report was certainly in the Council's hands when a final decision was made to send extraordinary diplomatic missions to both of the warring powers in the hope of concluding a successful mediation. Northumberland's decision is all the more inexplicable since by late March it was evident to all who saw him that the King was desperately, probably fatally, ill, while rumours regarding his sore state, and even of his death, were already circulating in England and abroad. Had even a thought of possible conspiracy against the ordained succession crossed Northumberland's mind by April 2nd, when the instructions were delivered, it seems certain that he would have withdrawn from all efforts to mediate. This he could gracefully have done because of the diplomatic rebuffs he had sustained and he could have then employed every effort to strengthen his alliance with France, which for just cause feared even the prospect of the succession of Mary Tudor. Instead, Northumberland pressed hard on his quixotic undertaking even until the time when the Council knew full well that the King's life was measured in weeks.

Instructions and credentials for this strange mission were handed to Dr Wotton, Pickering, and Sir Thomas Chaloner[2] to negotiate with Henry II, it being understood that Chaloner would shortly replace Pickering, who had asked to be recalled, as resident ambassador in France. At the same time, an equally strong embassy was constituted of Thirlby, Sir Philip Hoby, and Morison to carry on simultaneous negotiations with the Emperor in an effort to find a basis for the negotiation of a general peace.[3]

The negotiations in France, though friendly and, for the sake of form, protracted, were from the beginning clearly as feckless as

---

[1] HMC, *Salisbury MSS.*, I, 112–113: Mar. 24, 1553.

[2] Sir Thomas Chaloner had, though very young, been made Clerk of the Council in the late years of Henry VIII. He had gained some diplomatic experience as a commissioner in the negotiations with Scotland. He was a humanist and a close friend of both Haddon and Cheke.

[3] *Cal. S.P. For., Edw. VI*, ##643, 644, 645; Scheyfve's not wholly accurate report in *Cal. S.P. Span.*, XI, 20–21: Mar. 31, 1553; *A.P.C.*, IV, 244, 246: Mar. 27 and Apr. 1, 1553; Shirley, T. G., *Thomas Thirlby, Tudor Bishop* (L., 1964), 119–120.

they were bizarre. France would require as a condition of discussion the surrender of most of the imperial holdings in Italy as well as impossible concessions of strong-points on the Flemish frontier. It was clear too that Henry II had no wish to employ English good offices in a war which had thus far been eminently successful for him, which provoked Chaloner's complaint that the French dealt neither frankly nor courteously with him.[1] The special mission was, then, a manifest failure in its announced purposes. France, in fact, had no wish whatsoever to consider negotiations on reasonable terms until a few weeks later, when the brilliant and increasingly powerful Maurice died of wounds received in the victory he had gained at Sievershausen; wounds sustained, it might be added, just a day before the death of Edward VI.

The imperial negotiations were more protracted and significant, in large part because they carried forward to a limited degree the rapprochement already well under way before this strange diplomatic adventure had been undertaken. The Emperor was informed at the outset that Hoby was to stay on as resident ambassador, relieving Morison who had been ill and who was also uneasy about his wife's health.[2] The embassy reported itself to the Council as fully constituted on April 19th and expressed their hope for an early audience with the Emperor, though they were concerned because of the rumours flying in Brussels regarding King Edward's health.[3] A few days later, however, they were informed of the Emperor's own severe illness and of his wish that they treat for the time being with the Regent. The envoys referred the suggestion back to London, where the somewhat discomfited Council could only acquiesce, forwarding instructions so hazy in content as to make it unclear whether they were to treat for a general mediation or for a league with the Emperor and the Netherlands.[4] Almost immediately these instructions were confounded by the amazing counter-suggestion that the embassy should also bear in mind the possibility of an alliance with the German Protestant princes who were, of course, at war with Charles.[5] The envoys were to proceed no further—thus far their activity had been limited to an informal call on the Regent—until they had consulted with Christopher Mont, long

---

[1] HMC, *Salisbury MSS.*, I, 121: May 16, 1553.

[2] *Ibid.* 120; Lodge, *Illustrations*, I, 212–214; *Cal. S.P. For.*, *Edw. VI*, #650: Apr. 11, 1553.

[3] *Ibid.* ##652, 659: Apr. 11 and 29, 1553.

[4] *Venetianische Depeschen*, II, 601, 606; *Cal. S.P. For.*, *Edw. VI*, ##662, 667, 668–669: Apr. 23–28, 1553; HMC, *Salisbury MSS.*, I, 120: Apr. 30, 1553.

[5] *A.P.C.*, IV: May 5, 1553; Harl. MS. 523, #6, f. 14b.

the government's expert in German diplomacy, regarding such a league.[1]

The ambassadors at least had ample time to spin out the hare-brained instructions and counter-instructions, for the Emperor remained too ill and uncomfortable to receive them for weeks. On May 21st Mont arrived for consultation, the embassy a few days later sending off a discreetly phrased but highly critical estimate of the Council's suggestion of a league comprising the Emperor, England, and the German princes. It was pointed out that this would again free Lutheranism, would engender even further disorder amongst the German princes, and would weaken the Empire's vital interests in the Netherlands. It was their considered estimate that no English ties with the German Protestant princes were possible without the explicit agreement of both Charles and Ferdinand.[2] All this finely spun diplomatic dialectic was of course utterly naive, considering the weakness of England, the now evidently morbid illness of her sovereign, and the Emperor's steady policy of mastering German factionalism.

These grandiose plans fell of their own burden of illogicality and were, so far as we can determine, never submitted in any part to the Regent, the Council on May 31st returning to the original offer of mediation, while urging that the Emperor be seen as soon as possible, since further conversations in Paris were not possible until his mind was known.[3] Thirlby and his brethren were on this very date uncertain that the Emperor was more than barely alive,[4] while the wildest of rumours circulated in Brussels of the death or near-death of Edward VI. The *coup de grace* for this amazing—this almost comic—diplomatic venture came when on or about June 4th Wotton and his colleagues reported that Henry II would undertake no negotiations until the Emperor made a formal proposal, and that the French terms would be large territorial cessions in Italy and a commanding position in Flanders and Artois.[5] The bootless and humiliating enterprise was almost over. On June 8th the envoys gained an audience with the Regent, who thanked them for Edward's intervention but almost gently indicated that there was no possible basis for mediation. Then she had them in to see the Emperor, whom they found sitting up, lean and feeble, but with his

[1] *Cal. S.P. For., Edw. VI,,* #689.

[2] *Ibid.* ##686–687: May 26, 1553.

[3] *Ibid.* #689.

[4] *Twenty-seventh rpt.*, Dep. Keeper Public Records (1866), App., 135, #LXVIII.

[5] Harl. MS. 523, #65, f. 100b; *Cal. S.P. For., Edw. VI*, #693: June 4, 1553; Harl. MS. 523, #99.

wonted bright eyes and with speech unimpaired.[1] But matters did not go so well in England, as the ambassadors knew from the rumours crossing the Channel with every cargo vessel. Morison asked Cecil, in a letter expressing great affection as well as pity for the young monarch whose subject he was, to be assured by his own hand that the King still lived: 'In the mean season, like mariners that have lost their masts, let fall their anchors, and know not where they shall be come, they stand upon the shore and behold the ship, which still maketh proffer to go under the waves.'[2] So it was in England at that very moment.

[1] *Cal. S.P. For.*, *Edw. VI*, #696: June 9, 1553; Hoby, *Travels* (Camden Misc., X), 94.
[2] *Ibid.* #700: June 25, 1553.

VI

THE DISMANTLING OF ROMAN CATHOLIC FAITH: THE EXPROPRIATION OF THE CHANTRIES
[*EXCURSUS* I]

It seems probable that the most shattering and irreversible action of reformation in England was the proscription of prayers for the repose of the souls of the dead. Intimately connected as such prayers were with the teaching of purgatory, bound as they were with the whole elaborate apparatus of chantries, engrained and traditional as such prayers were in deep human sentiment, one may safely conclude that their abolition came as an immense shock to sensitive and pious men who were accustomed to arranging such final propitiatory rites for the souls of their own kin and who themselves were solaced by the reflection that their children or their widows might in due season ensure as much for them against the prospect of eternity.

None the less it must be recalled that such institutionalized prayers were of fairly recent origin in England and in Europe generally. If a chantry may be defined as a service of prayer founded and endowed by one or more benefactors at an altar of a church or chapel for the repose of the souls of specified persons, with a sop for the generality of Christian men, this usage is hardly to be found in England before the thirteenth century. The practice gained considerable momentum following Edward I's richly endowed prayers for his queen, Eleanor of Castile, with an arrangement for masses in numerous communities, and especially in Westminster Abbey. The founding of chantries spread rapidly in the fourteenth century, at least amongst the well-to-do classes who could finance such relatively expensive and formally endowed services. Elaborate legal safeguards surrounded these endowments, which created a freehold for the incumbent, who normally received a fixed amount for his services. As the movement developed, arrangements were made for such foundations by guilds and fraternities, as well as by more modest benefactors. These last usually provided for the maintenance of a light, a trental of masses, an anniversary mass, or an obit once a year, at very modest prices.

To serve this spiritual function a numerous class of unbeneficed clergy developed, men not normally highly educated. Such priests, who were to serve the specific instructions of the donor, were in most cases relieved of the cure of souls, save as they might be expected to assist the parish priest in the saying of divine offices and especially in the celebration of the mass. These stipendiary priests had never been a well-disciplined or a well-regarded clerical group, protected as they normally were even from episcopal visitations by the explicit definition of duty laid down by the founders. In numerous places, and with only partial success, attempts had been made to gather such priests into loosely organized collegiate foundations attached to a parish church, with the incumbent usually as its head.[1]

This intricate system of endowed prayers, so intimately enmeshed in English religious life, was vulnerable from the onset of the English Reformation, since if there was any point on which Protestantism was united it was in the flat and vehement denunciation of the doctrine of purgatory. The assault on the monasteries may be regarded as the first stage in the dismantling of the Catholic faith, for as Latimer put it, 'the founding of monasteries argued purgatory to be; so the pulling of them down argueth it not to be. What uncharitableness and cruelness seemeth it to be to destroy monasteries if purgatory be'.

The whole structure of monastic prayers for the dead had expanded rapidly in England, as indicated in a sampling of ten counties, believed to have accounted for about half of all charitable benefactions in the realm, where a total of £29,225, almost all of which was capital, had been vested in monasteries for prayers in the interval 1480 to 1540. It may be further remarked that this sum represented about half (51.55 per cent) of the amount given during these two generations to all monastic uses. All this capital, fairly recently vested for the endowment of prayers for the dead, and amounting for the realm at large to perhaps as much as £60,000, had been swept away in the monastic expropriations.[2] Interestingly

[1] Wood-Legh, K. L., *Perpetual chantries in Britain* (Cambridge, 1965), 5, 268–269; Cook, G. H., *Medieval chantries and chantry chapels* (L., 1947), 6–9, 47; Thompson, A. Hamilton, *The English clergy and their organization in the later Middle Ages* (Oxford, 1947), 133–145.

[2] Jordan, *Philanthropy in England*, 304.

enough these seizures seem to have aroused relatively little contemporary opposition. What is perhaps more to the point, they had
set a wedge of policy into the whole structure of the chantries.

Henry VIII proceeded slowly and somewhat nervously in the
whole matter, understanding as he did how inextricably interwoven
prayers for the dead were in both thought and sentiment. But a too
little noticed step was taken towards renouncing the doctrine in the
King's Book (1543) which prescribed that only the generality of men
were to be prayed for under the infinite mercy of God. None the
less, the famous statute of 1545 (37 Henry VIII, c. 4) placed in his
hands the chantries of England on the specific ground that they
wanted reformation rather than complete abolition, though the
pressing need for revenue for waging war against Scotland and
France was frankly and brutally put as his principal moving persuasion in the matter. The act was also designed to recover to the
king chantry and collegiate endowemnts already illegally dissolved
since February 4, 1536, while existing chantries not functioning in
accordance with the deeds of gift of the donors might also be confiscated at will by the King. It was likewise provided that the power
thus conferred lay in the King alone and that warrants for confiscation were valid only when signed by him. Henry VIII died less than a
year after the first commissions were issued under the act. But a
number of chantries and colleges were in fact swept into the Court
of Augmentations before the close of 1546. Whether he was moved
by spiritual conviction or by prudence, it is to be remembered that
Henry by will left generous sums for masses for the repose of his
own soul. But it seems predictable that with the process once fully
in motion the chantries would shortly have been swept away had
Henry lived.

Though the Edwardian statute 'whereby certain chantries,
colleges, free chapels, and the possessions of the same be given to the
king's majesty', was passed by Parliament at the close of 1547, we
have reserved discussion of this important and revolutionary
measure until the era of Northumberland's dominance because its
full effects were not immediately felt and because the re-distribu-
tion of the great chantry properties was not fully advanced until the
closing years of the reign. Moreover, the settlement of numerous
chantry endowments for charitable uses was not finally determined
until after Somerset's first fall from power.

The first draft of the bill seems to have been introduced in the
Lords, where it was passed despite the opposition of Cranmer and
five of his conservative colleagues, possibly because the craft guilds

and corporations also seemed threatened under the language of the bill. There was likewise very strong opposition in the Commons, in part at least for the same reason, which occasioned a hurried re-drafting of the measure by the government.[1] The new draft, elim-inating direct reference to the guilds and corporations, found more favour in the Lords, where it was first read on December 10, 1547, and approved on December 15th, though there remained most vehement opposition in the Commons, led by the members sitting for Coventry (Christopher Warenne and Henry Porter) and King's Lynn (Thomas Gawdy and William Overend) who sought to protect the guild and brotherhood lands in their towns, which had in fact, as in so many other communities, been diverted to municipal and other charitable purposes. Their forthright opposition spread, 'divers then being of the Lower House' not only arguing against the expropriation of such guild lands, 'but also incensed many others to hold with them'.[2] The burgesses from Lynn maintained that the guild lands there were used for the maintenance of the pier and sea-walls, which if left untended would spoil the low country stretching around that port town, while those speaking for Coventry pleaded that the guild lands in that large market town were in truth used for the support of one of its churches, and that it would be disastrous if maintenance were withdrawn.

It is quite certain that the bill before Parliament had been drawn with the full knowledge and support of the Lord Protector and that it was his hand that was seeking to guide it through a doubtful Parliament: doubtful in the Lords for spiritual reasons and in the Commons for principally secular considerations. Those of the Council who were responsible for the bill in the Commons thought it unlikely that the article prescribing the expropriation of guild and fraternity lands could be passed and feared 'that the whole body of that act might either sustain peril or hindrance, being already engrossed, and the time of the Parliament prorogation hard at hand'. In discussions with the Protector it was accordingly agreed that in order to save the measure the guild lands of Coventry and Lynn must be specifically exempted and their opposition quieted. Hence in consultation with the four burgesses concerned it was agreed, and letters patent to this effect ordered, that if they would offer no

---

[1] It is probable that Sir James Hales, who had been created a Knight of the Bath at Edward's coronation, was principally responsible for the drafting of the statute. Hales was shortly afterwards appointed a Judge of the Common Pleas. My graduate student, Mr Alan Kreider, who has undertaken a detailed study of the expropriation of the chantries, will deal fully with the history of this important legislation.

[2] *A.P.C.*, II, 193.

further opposition to the proposed legislation, the guild lands would be conveyed back to the two towns by royal grant.[1] Doubts having been relieved and pressures accommodated, the final measure was enacted into law just as Parliament was prorogued for Christmas.

It should be observed that the preamble of the act recited a purely religious reason for the abolition and expropriation of the chantries. Much of the error and superstition afflicting the Christian church had resulted from ignorance of the 'very true and perfect salvation through the death of Jesus Christ', and consequently by the 'devising and phantasing vain opinions of purgatory and masses satisfactory to be done for them which be departed'. This superstitious opinion had been perpetuated by chantries, trentals, and other devices fostering blindness and ignorance. Parliament, the preamble declared, was further moved by the persuasion that these resources should better be converted to such godly uses as the founding of grammar schools, the strengthening of the universities, and 'better provision for the poor and needy', which could only be effected if they were 'committed' to the King for his disposal. Hence all free chapels, colleges, chantries, lands endowing masses for a term of years or supporting perpetual obits, and chantry uses sustained by corporations, guilds, and fraternities, were declared to be vested in the Crown.

The act further provided that commissioners should be empowered under the Great Seal to survey and take over such properties, and instructed to continue existing grammar schools, to assign revenues for the support of needed parish priests, to continue the support of the poor who had been aided by such endowments, and to set aside revenues for the maintenance of piers, jetties, and banks 'against the rages of the sea, havens and creeks'. Authority was also vested in them to fix pensions for dispossessed stipendiary priests and to safeguard parochial chapels of ease for people 'dwelling distant from the parish church' which were supported solely by former chantry revenues. The act further and specifically exempted the Oxford and Cambridge colleges, St George's Chapel at Windsor, Eton, and Winchester, as well as a few other colleges of royal or unusual foundation, while carefully providing that the terms of the law should not be prejudicial 'to the general corporation of any city, borough, or town' or to any lands belonging to them.[2]

Two observations should at once be made respecting this important and revolutionary measure. There was no commitment, though

---

[1] *A.P.C.*, II, 193–195: May 6, 1548.
[2] *Statutes of the realm*, IV, i, 24–33 (1 Edward VI, c. 14).

Cranmer would probably have wished it so, to employ the whole of the capital to be gained from the expropriation for charitable and municipal uses; rather it was the clear intent of the act to retain all such secular uses when they had been ordained by the founding deed of gift or when an earlier erosion of the donor's intention had in fact diverted the foundation to such uses. There was one exception. Though the language of the act is ambiguous, it seems probable that Parliament meant the commissioners to have power to appoint and support parish priests where there was need 'in every great town or parish' with chantry endowments, just as chapels of ease were to be protected and continued. This was not the gloss which was to be laid on the statute by eloquent evangelical critics in the Edwardian period, nor for that matter by more recent critics of the administration of the measure, who would wish that the whole of this great capital could have been used for charitable purposes and for the maintenance of the church. This misunderstanding arose quickly and it was persistent, the Council feeling obliged to state as early as April 17, 1548, that despite the government's interest in the founding of schools and other charitable uses, the bulk of the resources must be employed for the defence of the realm and other state needs, thereby reducing the 'continual charge of taxes, contributions, loans and subsidies'.[1]

It must also be observed that the underlying purpose of the expropriation of the chantries was religious and that in this prime intention it was wholly successful. The act did not specifically abolish propitiatory masses so long as they were not endowed perpetually or for a term of years; this was to await the abolition of the mass itself in England. What it did do was to strike down the whole apparatus of the perpetual mass, which even many conservative churchmen had come to condemn as sterile, of dubious doctrinal soundness, and as linking salvation to wealth far beyond the resources of the generality of men. In this connection even as conservative a bishop as Stephen Gardiner could say in June, 1548, 'ye would say unto me, "There be fewer masses by putting away the chantries". So were there when abbeys were dissolved: . . . But this is no injury . . . to the mass. It consisteth not in the number, nor in the multitude, but in the thing itself.'[2] The pervading institutional system of propitiatory masses stood, then, as a doctrinal affront to Protestantism which simply had to be destroyed before the Church could be reformed. The doctrinal necessity was clear; what was to be done

[1] *A.P.C.*, II, 184–185.
[2] Foxe, VI, *Acts and monuments*, 89–90.

with the assets—and this was what concerned Cranmer and others—was quite another matter.

As directed by the statute, the survey of the chantry properties over the whole realm, Wales included, was conducted by royal commissioners with very large powers. In all, we have counted twenty-five such commissions for the several counties, ranging in number from five to thirteen members. Quite typically, a commission comprised one or more of the officials of the Court of Augmentations, who evidently did most of the detailed work and who lent a remarkable uniformity of procedure to all the surveys. They were joined by from eight to thirteen of the local gentry, in almost all cases the upper gentry, of the county under scrutiny, they being men vested at once with great local prestige and considerable knowledge of their counties, since most of them were also Justices of the Peace. It should also be noted that there were no bishops appointed to the Edwardian commissions. In most counties the work was carefully, honestly, and systematically done, under the direction of the Court of Augmentations, the returns to a series of carefully drawn questions being gathered from the incumbents and the churchwardens of each parish and then drafted by the commissioners into a fairly detailed report for submission to Augmentations or to the Duchy of Lancaster. This administrative structure was completed in June, 1548, when a commission of two—Walter Mildmay, a man of great probity and the general surveyor for the Court of Augmentations, and Robert Keilway [Kellaway], the surveyor of liveries in the Court of Wards—was appointed to arrive at final decisions as the county returns flowed in in a voluminous stream. Both were honest and experienced servants of the crown, being 'most meet thereunto for their tried wisdoms' and 'faithful discretion in such matters'.[1] In their hands, too, was lodged the decision regarding which properties should be expropriated, the allocation of pensions for the dispossessed clergy, the sale of lands at prices determined by the surveyors and auditors of the Court into which the proceeds were paid, and the recommendation to the Council of the continuation or foundation of schools and alms-houses, or of other charitable uses. Regrettably the commissioners kept no separate or really complete record of this last aspect of their work, though we think it is possible to piece together most of their actions from various sources. Also in 1548, a separate commission was appointed, including Keilway, the Chancellor of the Court of Augmentations, the Master of Requests, and the Clerk of the

[1] *A.P.C.*, II, 186.

Hanaper, with power to order the distribution of alms, the repair of roads, and other public works regarded as a proper charge on former chantry lands.[1]

As one studies the chantry returns from the several counties the impression is steadily strengthened that the local commissions, made up as they were principally of well-rooted and locally responsible gentry, employed every effort to find some measure of charitable use either in the deed of gift, if it could be located, or more commonly in the already established diversion of all or a portion of chantry revenues to charitable uses, and especially to schools and almshouses. There are scores of instances where the commissioners strained the facts sufficiently to find a school where there was none or an almshouse which Leland had reported derelict a generation earlier. There are as well many instances where a chantry priest who had taught children quite informally was judged to have kept a school, and it was recommended that he be continued. Nor were the central authorities in any way hostile to this local disposition, perhaps in part because it was not much more expensive, at least during the life of the priest, to continue him as a pensioner. Thus in the county of Essex, though hardly typical, the ten commissioners were lenient indeed in their judgements on the capabilities of the chantry priests, discovered schools where there had been no more than a little informal teaching, and in general evidently inflated the charitable uses which chantry endowments had borne in the past in a valiant, and on the whole successful, effort to save all possible foundations in order that they might be converted to socially useful purposes. This gentle conspiracy was shared in by Mildmay, a native of Chelmsford, who knew every inch of the county and who knew as well that the commissioners were seeking means wherewith the lot of the youth and the poor of the county might be well served. The work of the chantry commissioners was at once far more capably conducted and more generously administered than had been the monastic expropriations not many years earlier.

We may now move to a rather detailed examination of the chantry returns and to an analysis of the disposition made of the considerable properties which fell in to the crown in 1548 and 1549. Whenever available we have employed the returns of the Edwardian Commissioners,[2] collating them with the Henrician returns when they are incomplete, and substituting the Henrician reports for the

---

[1] *Cal. Pat. Rolls, Edw. VI*, I, 232; *ibid.* V, 403.
[2] The Edwardian returns are to be found in the P.R.O., *Certificates of Colleges and Chantries*, E 301, in 121 consecutively numbered rolls.

Edwardian in a few instances when the latter are missing. We have translated the income figures into capital sums throughout by employing a multiplier of 20 in order to establish the more useful capital values.[1] Our statistical analysis has been somewhat complicated by the possibly mistaken decision to credit to a county all endowments vested in it, save for those legally held in London for the benefit of other counties. In reckoning and in listing amounts we have rounded off to the nearest shilling, while in our tables we have further rounded off to the nearest pound, unless otherwise indicated. The weight of the plate confiscated by the commissioners is in some instances meticulously recorded, though there are few indications of the degree of fineness or value. Accordingly, all plate has been arbitrarily valued at 6s the ounce, which is close to the worth of plate of average purity in our period. It should also be emphasized that though the returns were supposed to be uniformly presented, obits and lights are frequently not individually listed, while goods and moveables are in fact not always clearly categorized under our heads of: (1) *stocks, sheep, cattle, etc.*; (2) *goods, ornaments, etc.*; (3) *plate and money*. These heads are occasionally lumped into a single category by the commissioners, and their practice we have in these instances necessarily followed. In most counties the commissioners essayed a trial total, so to speak, but these, like all Tudor exercises in addition, tend to be only roughly correct, our totals compiled by individual entry additions varying in a range of ±10 per cent from those so provided.

Certain other difficulties and frailties of method must also be mentioned at the outset. The returns for some of the counties are incomplete, disordered, or altogether missing, thereby weakening the validity of our conclusions, though it is believed within a fairly narrow range of error.[2] It is also certain that the most serious flaw

---

[1] The reasons supporting the multiplier used are set out in Jordan, *Philanthropy in England*, 37–39, and in Jordan, *Edward VI*, 104, though the fact is that the indicated interest rate gained for Edwardian chantry parcels was 5·16 per cent rather than 5 per cent.

[2] The principal difficulties should perhaps be set out, county by county: The *Berkshire* totals exclude St George's, Windsor, exempted under the act but none the less surveyed by the commissioners. The *Bristol* figures are drawn out from the Gloucestershire return, but the value of ornaments, plate, *etc.*, is carried in the Gloucestershire entry. The *Cambridgeshire* return is missing, save for minor Du/ hy of Lancaster holdings, which have not been listed. For *Cheshire* both the Henrici.. and the Edwardian returns are incomplete and otherwise defective, the commissioners reporting 'divers great numbers of the said chantries, chapels and other the premises . . . as yet concealed, omitted, and kept back from us'. In *Devonshire* goods and plate have been combined in a single total for moveables. The obit count in *Dorset* is incomplete and is in part estimated. The Edwardian survey for *Hampshire* being defective, the Henrician return

in our conclusions arises from the fact that we have found it quite impossible to reckon, or even to estimate with much assurance, the proportion of chantry wealth which before the expropriation had been actually and helpfully devoted to the cure of souls or to assistance, especially in more populous parishes, in the ministration of divine services. It is our sense, based mostly on the 'feel of the materials', that we have somewhat exaggerated these services. Nor is it possible to state precisely how much of chantry wealth was dedicated by the Commissioners to the strengthening and maintenance of the parochial clergy by the appointment of dispossessed chantry priests to normal parish duties. Here too it is our sense that we have probably over-stated the proportion of chantry wealth so disposed. It should also be mentioned that in crediting chantry wealth assigned by the government for the endowment or support of

---

has been used. In *Hertfordshire* both the chantry and obit counts are incomplete and possibly otherwise defective. The return for *Huntingdonshire* is missing, save for those chantries reported as from the Duchy of Lancaster. The computations for *Leicestershire* are certainly imprecise and we have excluded the Great Wigston Hospital as exempt under the statute. The *Lincolnshire* total is much swollen by the great wealth of Thornton College (£11,098 of capital value). The *London (Middlesex)* totals suffer from some exaggeration, since certain of them were stated only as *gross* revenues. The chantry *cum* obit wealth may be further divided: City £82,620; Middlesex £27,480; City Companies £19,204 6s; uncertain, £856 8s. A surprisingly low proportion of London chantry wealth was devoted to social uses because a very large proportion represented 'pure chantry' endowments from various sovereigns and because for many years past London donors had preferred secular trustees for their charitable wealth. It is interesting that of the great total of £130,160 14s. of London chantry wealth, well over half (£69,353 18s) had been vested in the period 1480–1540 (Jordan, W. K., *The charities of London, 1480–1660, etc.* (L., 1960), 273). The absurdly low figure for plate (£577 16s) arises from the fact that London trustees and churchwardens had been rapidly selling plate in anticipation of an expropriation. The *Norfolk* return is missing, save for the Duchy of Lancaster holdings. In *Nottinghamshire* well over half the total reported is accounted for by the great endowments of Southwell College; obits for the county are caught up in the chantry count. There are several difficulties in *Shropshire*: our reckoning of its chantry wealth includes several estimates of the capital value of lands granted for a term of years; the commissioners here were unusually lax in their recording of charitable uses established by deeds of gift; my totals are considerably less than those of the commissioners who seem to have included a number of Henrician surrenders. The *Staffordshire* reckoning is based on E 315.123, E 301.54, and E 301.43 in order to record certain heretofore concealed assets. *North Wales*, for statistical purposes regarded as a single county, also offers difficulties, since full returns have not been found, E 301.76 being incomplete. *South Wales* is also regarded as a single county. The net capital worth (£5883 6s) for *Warwickshire* is very low in relation to the gross worth of £18,126 5s, in large part because of the exemption of the Coventry guilds from the act. Hence the social uses laid against chantry capital in the county seems high, the proportion being a fairly normal 12·17 per cent of gross income, but an extremely high 37·47 per cent of net worth. Neither the Henrician nor the Edwardian return for *Yorkshire* is quite complete. I have drawn from both in my reckonings. Even so, my computations of the value of chantry and obit endowments run about 10 per cent less than the totals given by the commissioners.

schools and almshouses we have included such grants through the year 1559. This has introduced some slight statistical distortion, though in point of fact it might have been better to have carried these allocations from chantry lands to about 1570, since the government remained disposed to yield to soundly based and persistent local petitions for such charitable foundations.

We should also point out that in recording social uses supported by chantry endowments at the moment of expropriation we have inevitably exaggerated both the quantity and the quality of the social responsibility borne by the chantries. Thus, when a chantry priest received say £6 p.a. for the performance of his chantry duties and was also required, or by his generosity volunteered, to offer educational instruction to children of his community, we have regarded this as a school (as the Commissioners almost invariably did) and have so credited the endowment. But the fact almost certainly is that in many, if not most, cases only a small proportion of the priest's time before the expropriation was actually devoted to the tasks of instruction, whereas when the Commissioners ordered a school continued and assigned the whole of the revenues to its needs, there had in truth been a large gain for the educational assets of the community. What had been a vague, an undefined, and a partial commitment to education had been institutionalized, placed under lay control, and settled in a form calculated to attract further and private support.

It is our reckoning that 2502 chantries, colleges, fraternities, and guilds with endowments supporting stipendiary priests were expropriated under the terms of the Edwardian statute in thirty-eight of the forty-two counties comprising England and Wales.[1] To this number should be added 169 'free chapels', separately mentioned in only fourteen counties and presumably fully caught up in the chantry listings in the remaining counties. There were, then, a total of 2671 chantry foundations within the meaning of the act, a number not far off that set down by Camden on the basis of not clearly stated sourced.[2]

We have counted in addition 4587 endowments for obits and

---

[1] We have regarded Bristol as a county, and have grouped the Welsh counties. It will be recalled that there are no satisfactory returns for Cambridgeshire, Huntingdonshire, Norfolk, and North Wales.

[2] Camden's total was 2574, being comprised of 90 colleges, 2374 chantries, and 110 hospitals (Camden, William, *Britannia, etc.* (1753 ed.), I, ccxxx). This estimate was accepted by Giuseppi (*A guide to the manuscripts preserved in the Public Record Office* (2 vols., L., 1923-1924), I, 141) and by Cook (*Medieval chantries*, 60). Professor Dickens is inclined towards a slightly higher estimate, believing that there were 'probably over 3000

lights, though we mention this total with great diffidence since such funds were separately reported in a convincingly systematic fashion by the Commissioners in only twenty-nine counties, being either lumped into the chantry capital total or ignored because of their relative financial insignificance in the remaining counties. These endowments for occasional prayers, for the support of a lamp before an altar, or similar acts of piety were usually very small, and were far more common in rural than in urban parishes. Small though the income was, it must have been a welcome addition to the usually inadequate income of the parish priests who were in almost all instances charged with the performance of the trusts. They were normally endowed with a tiny plot of land, a few sheep, or small village premises, bringing us closer to the life and aspirations of humble men and women than do the far more elaborate arrangements for prayers provided by the perpetually endowed foundations. There is also the pathetic reminder that most of them were ill-founded and poorly administered, since the Commissioners could often not find the property establishing the endowment and many of them had to be reported as lost or without income. They exhibit the frailty of man; but they also exhibit, far more impressively than do the chantries, the lively strength of faith.

The net capital value of the chantry endowments of England and Wales, as reported by the Commissioners in thirty-eight counties, was the large total of £610,255 3s, or not far off from a quarter (22·38 per cent) of the huge sum expropriated by the King's father almost a generation earlier when the monasteries were dissolved. To this must be added the considerable sum of £26,280 4s which represented the total capital worth of the obit and light endowments in those counties where these amounts were differentiated from the chantry totals. At the same time, we believe that relatively little of these obit endowments ever reached the Court of Augmentations because of the difficulty in locating the property and finding a market for these usually small and awkward plots, or because the sheep and cattle had often vanished before expropriation could be effected. In addition, the Commissioners listed various types of movable property, with a probably not much more than nominal worth of £8087 10s, which we have listed under the following heads:

---

chantries' in England (*Thomas Cromwell and the English Reformation* (L., 1959), 139). If there is any virtue in our own estimate that there were something like 198 chantry foundations in the four missing counties, our own total would rise to 2869 (*vide post*, 193).

Stocks of sheep, cattle, *etc.*	£1826 18s
Capital value goods and ornaments	2368 1s
Plate (@ 6s the ounce) and money	3892 11s

In all, then, the net capital value of the endowments supporting prayers for the repose of the souls of the usually well-born and necessarily well-to-do faithful of the past amounted to £644,622 17s, or 23·64 per cent of the wealth which had once supported the monastic orders of the realm.[1]

It is instructive to observe that a considerable proportion of chantry capital had been bestowed relatively recently, even though the vogue for the establishment of these endowments had attained its climax in the fourteenth century. In ten counties which constituted a sample for another study, gifts and bequests for the endowment of prayers in the interval 1480–1560 reached the surprisingly large total of £149,656 11s, Norfolk being included.[2] Yet the total reported by the Commissioners for these same counties was no more than £318,624 12s (Norfolk's total being supplied by estimate), with the result that the comparatively recent foundations constituted 46·97 per cent of the whole. This confirms our view, gained also from the Commissioners' reports themselves, that most chantry foundations were in fact historically rather short-lived unless they were of royal or noble foundation. The casual structure of the trusteeships, the pressing needs of communities, and the

[1] Again, the total ignores the four counties from which we have at best only fragmentary information. For Norfolk, however, we believe we can derive by extrapolation from other sources a reasonably accurate estimate of the total of chantry and obit capital worth. As indicated above, Norfolk was one of ten counties in which 46·97 per cent of the chantry wealth reported to the commissioners had been given or bequeathed in the interval, 1480–1560. In all, £11,328 14s was given or bequeathed for chantries in Norfolk during this same interval, which would yield by estimate £24,119 as the total of chantry and obit wealth at the time of the expropriation, comparing closely with Lincolnshire where we know the total of these endowments was £30,002 13s.

From such sources as are available we would conclude that Cambridgeshire and Huntingdonshire were both relatively weak in chantry endowments, and would guess that they might have amounted to something like £8000 for the former and £5000 for the latter. North Wales was in this era poor and thinly populated as compared with South Wales and we can hardly believe that the chantry *cum* obit endowments could have exceeded £4000. If these most fragile estimates are accepted, £41,119 would be added to the total of chantry and obit endowments for the realm, yielding a grand total of £677,654 7s. But it seems more prudent in all our following discussion to employ the more soundly based total of £610,255 3s for chantry endowments and £26,280 4s for obit funds.

[2] The total of gifts and benefactions for chantries in the ten counties was £140,864 3s through 1540. But the nature of the present analysis suggests that the additions made in the period of the Reformation (1540–1560) should be added. It might be stated that small bequests for this purpose are to be found even in the Elizabethan period, long after they ceased to be legal.

7

erosion occasioned by self-serving administrators were simply too great for these essentially fragile corporate organisms. In all too many cases, even for chantries still surviving, the individuals giving evidence knew neither the name of the original donor nor the date of the foundation, probably the usual prelude to the diversion or disappearance of funds. These institutions were designed for too narrow and much too personal a purpose to serve for many generations and tended therefore to disappear once the name and repute of the donor (one can hardly say benefactor) had withered away in the community in which he, his sins, and his virtues had once waxed green.

The 2671 chantry foundations, so regarded within the meaning of the act, were supposed to be served by 2777 stipendiary priests, the greater number of priests being accounted for by the fact that a few chantries were endowed for two priests and that the colleges were served by several clergy. But this total was in truth sharply reduced by the fact that we have counted 265 chantry posts (or very close to a tenth of the whole number) which were evidently chronically or permanently vacant for a variety of reasons, but usually because the income provided was simply too small to attract even the humblest priest. Employing eleven counties as our sample[1]—counties in which the evidence is particularly full—we may say that the average chantry priest received an income of only £6 6s 8d p.a., an amount which scarcely raised him above the pay of a semi-skilled agricultural labourer in 1550, save for the fact that shelter and a garden plot were usually included. The average stipendiary payment ranged from the incredibly low figure of £4 1s 9d p.a. in Shropshire to £9 p.a. in Bristol. Further, since a fair number of these priests did have comfortable stipends, the median salary of £6 1s 1d p.a. was somewhat below the average. It seems clear that for a long time something like £6 p.a. had been regarded as a reasonable chantry stipend, even the more recent foundations vested in the interval 1480–1540 striking an average of not more than £6 3s 9d p.a.[2] Further—and this of course explains the great number of persisting vacancies—nearly a fifth of all the chantry foundations examined paid a miserable stipend of £3 p.a. or less to the incumbent.

In theory many of these stipends should have been higher than they were, but the attrition of time had done its work. Even after

---

[1] The counties are: Bedfordshire, Berkshire, Bristol, Buckinghamshire, Cornwall, Cumberland, Kent, Oxfordshire, Shropshire, Somerset, and Sussex.

[2] Jordan, *Philanthropy in England*, 307.

the charitable uses imposed on certain of the endowments have been deducted, there remained for the thirty-eight counties regarding which we have reasonably full information a total of £541,562 of net capital directly charged with the payment of clerical stipends. At the prevailing return on land this should have yielded an annual income of about £27,078 and have provided an average stipend of £9 15s for the 2777 chantry priests supposed to be serving in these counties. The erosion of stipend is to be accounted for in several ways, the principal of which were administrative costs, repairs required by buildings, uncollectable rents, and a wide variety of diversions for municipal uses, to lay persons, and plain theft. In even more cases the chantry function in hundreds of parishes had with the passage of time been improperly but quite inevitably conjoined with the cure of souls by the incumbent. Even so, in many poor parishes, the combined emoluments from tithes and a chantry endowment were insufficient for the proper maintenance of the priest.

Discounting the chronic vacancies, then, there were presumably 2512 chantry clergy who were dispossessed and who were eligible for the fairly generous pensions awarded directly from the Court of Augmentations. The act of expropriation provided that pensions should be so settled that those who had received stipends of £5 p.a. or less should have for their support the whole of their former income; those who had enjoyed incomes of from £6 13s 4d p.a. to £10 were assured a settled pension of £6 p.a.; and the relatively few with stipends of £10 p.a. or more were given £6 13s 4d p.a. for life. It was of course further provided that any pensioner receiving an appointment or living equalling his former emolument should be stricken from the pension rolls. Many of the chantry pensioners did in fact receive appointments as schoolmasters, as chaplains in almshouses, and in the parochial clergy, thereby reducing the considerable call on the capital which had been gathered into Augmentations. An interesting analysis of the pension rolls in the great diocese of Lincoln suggests that pensioners there, including surviving regular clergy as well as chantry priests, were so grouped that about 70 per cent of the whole number were receiving pensions which gave them an annual income of £5 p.a. or more,[1] while approximately 84 per cent of the whole number enjoyed such incomes, if emoluments, usually very small, from other sources be taken into account. Hence it is fair to say that most chantry priests did not find their incomes drastically reduced and that they were

[1] Hodgett, G. A. J., *The state of the ex-religious . . . priests in . . . Lincoln, 1547–1574* (Lincoln Rec. Soc. Publ. LIII, 1959), xvi-xviii.

not economically further degraded since, as we have observed, the average chantry stipend had in fact been no more than £6 6s 8d p.a.

It seems clear that slightly more than 2000 former stipendiaries were taken into the pension rolls in the first year after the expropriation, since the Court of Augmentations recorded a total of £11,147 14s 1d paid out for such grants.[1] Arrangements for recording of pension obligations had been carefully provided as early as May, 1548, when it was announced that commissioners were being sent into every shire to admit to the pension rolls, with a warning that such pensioners not flock into London with their claims.[2] This commitment was presumably added to the substantial total still being paid to former regular clergy at the close of Henry VIII's reign, though the load of clerical pensions formed a relatively small proportion of the great total of £63,288 8s, composed principally of secular annuities for various purposes, with which the government was saddled in 1551.[3] In the compelling fiscal crisis of 1551–1552 payment of all pensions fell behind, the government not being able fully to clear its accounts until March, 1554. But this one interval aside, the obligations to the dispossessed chantry priests were promptly and fully honoured.[4]

We have observed that the 'effective', the fully collectable, capital expropriated in the chantries dissolution was the very large total of £610,255 3s in the thirty-eight counties where we possess fairly detailed knowledge of the facts.[5] Against this wealth was laid by the original deeds of gift or by diversions of such uses no more than £68,692 11s of capital which was at the moment of expropriation being demonstrably employed for charitable and other socially useful purposes. This amount, according to our reckoning, was dedicated to the following purposes:

Poor (mostly as periodically distributed alms)	£11,903	16s
Almshouses	23,761	0s
Schools	20,778	13s
Municipal uses of sundry sorts	3,196	17s
Various church purposes	8,082	15s
Other	969	10s
	£68,692	11s

[1] HMC, *Salisbury MSS.*, I, 75: Sept. 17, 1549.

[2] Hughes and Larkin, *Tudor proclamations*, I, 425.

[3] Richardson, *Court of Augmentations*, 178.

[4] It has been noted (Jordan, *Edward VI*, 110) that a capital of £139,381 would have been required properly to have funded the chantry pension obligations.

[5] *Vide ante*, 192. The total, if the presumed value of obit endowments and moveables be added, was £644,622 17s.

In other words, the charitable contribution heretofore made by the chantries to the social needs of the realm did not amount to more than 11·26 per cent of the capital sum with which they had been endowed. To put it bluntly, but accurately, they were in fact not institutions making any significant charitable contribution. To measure their social importance in another way, private and secular donors in ten selected counties gave in the interval 1540–1560 alone the considerable total of £227,032 1s for the various social needs of England, most of the sum being capital and most of it vested in secular trustees who over the years were to administer it with extra-ordinary skill and dedication.[1] Since there is strong reason for believing that in this period the total for these counties constituted about 60 per cent of the whole of private benefactions in England, we may safely assume that approximately £378,387 for the whole of the realm was given or bequeathed by private donors in this period for a wide variety of important social uses. Hence, we may further suggest that the total chantry endowments devoted to charitable causes did not amount to more than about 18 per cent of the whole sum provided by Englishmen expressly for charitable uses in these two decades alone. It seems fair to say that the importance of the chantries as charitable institutions has been grossly exaggerated. The social importance of the chantries, as they stood in 1547, may, indeed, be regarded as a myth—a myth implanted principally by the great Edwardian preachers who wished so fervently that the whole of this great wealth might be dedicated to quite new social and religious causes.

Another myth, even more persistent and bedevilling, is dispelled by an analysis of the charitable dispositions which the government ordered retained or itself established from the chantry wealth being swept into Augmentations. The fact is, to state it categorically at the outset, that the Edwardian government slightly increased the total of chantry capital dedicated to social purposes, the whole of the capital amount so settled in perpetuity being £71,196 2s, this constituting 11·67 per cent of the whole of the effective chantry capital being expropriated. At the same time there was a conscious and certainly fruitful shifting of emphasis by the commissioners

[1] Jordan, *Philanthropy in England*, 246, *et passim*. It was with considerable hesitation that in that study we decided to regard chantry gifts as charitable benefactions (*ibid.* 51). It now seems clear that we should not have done so, for before the present study was undertaken we greatly overestimated the proportion of chantry endowments which was in fact employed for charitable causes. One can, in fact, argue with considerable force that a chantry endowment was by definition the most narrowly selfish of all possible outlays.

among former charitable uses, with a particularly notable concentration of designated funds in the two most important categories of almshouses and schools, the former of which was lifted from £23,761 to £27,702 6s and the latter from £20,778 13s to £27,697 4s. Probably as a consequence of at least a loosely defined policy, the amount dedicated for rather random and desultory poor relief by outright gifts, already out of favour amongst private donors, was sharply reduced from £11,903 16s to £7338 17s. At the same time the capital value for various church uses, and especially for church repair, was somewhat punitively lowered, while the amounts dedicated to a variety of municipal uses were nearly doubled.[1]

It seems possible, too, though the evidence is not clear, that the government was following conscious policy in quite sharply reducing the amount of capital formerly dedicated by the chantries to social uses in a group of six counties (Berkshire, Essex, London, Suffolk, South Wales, and Yorkshire), where in total such capital resources were lowered from £25,609 8s to £18,837 10s. At the same time, however, there are indications of a deliberate policy in the considerable strengthening of such resources in nine counties (Cornwall, Dorset, Gloucestershire, Hereford, Northumberland, Nottinghamshire, Somerset, Warwickshire, and Worcestershire), of which at least seven may be regarded as marginal in terms of wealth and effective social institutions.

We may say generally, then, that there was on balance little if any hurt done to the charitable institutions of England. The great need of the age was for more and better schools and for adequately endowed almshouses, and both these great charitable causes were, as we have seen, somewhat strengthened as a consequence of the settlement of the expropriated lands. These matters we shall

---

[1] The amounts (partly estimated) designated for charitable purposes by the Commissioners or by the Crown before 1560 follow:

Poor relief	£ 7,338 17s
Almshouses	27,702 6s
Schools	27,697 4s
Municipal uses	6,030 5s
Various church purposes	2,329 10s
Other	98 0s

This was by no means the extent of governmental generosity in the founding or endowing of various useful charitable schemes. Most of the total just stated never passed through the Court of Augmentations, but was vested immediately from the chantry resources. It should be mentioned that the government gave as well crown lands to the value of £79,441, a considerable portion of which was derived from chantry lands, for various social needs, including £11,396 for the founding or notable strengthening of twenty-two strategically situated grammar schools and £12,097 for various schemes of social rehabilitation (Jordan, *Edward VI*, 114-115).

shortly treat independently and at some length.[1] But it should be observed here that these institutions were further strengthened, far beyond the slight capital additions which both received, since the whole of former chantry income, rather than the margins of a priest's time and resources, was now dedicated to their use. As importantly, the newly constituted institutions were given knowledgeable and responsible civic or private direction, and were vested for purposes which would in most cases attract later support from private donors.

As we have suggested, the evidence for the injury which may have been done by the dissolution of the chantries to the normal ministrations of the church is much more difficult to gather and assess. It was rare indeed that a chantry priest was permitted by the deed of gift to assume the cure of souls, but in many larger parishes these priests had frequently assisted the incumbent in the saying of divine offices, often reading the gospel and epistle at mass and helping with the singing.[2] Far more important had been the religious services afforded by the numerous free chapels which were for the most part distant from the mother church and which in thinly populated areas served an exceedingly valuable spiritual use. The evidence is strong that the Commissioners usually lent the mantle of their protection to such chapels, either retaining the buildings for religious uses or making it possible for the communities affected to buy them at modest appraisals.[3] But we none the less have the sense, which we cannot satisfactorily document, that over the realm as a whole substantial injury may have been done to the cure of souls in some scores of communities.

We have seen that the Crown gained from the chantry expropriation lands and goods with a capital value of £610,255 3s, setting aside as we have the obit endowments (£26,280 4s) and miscellaneous receipts (£8087 10s) which, plate excepted (£3892 11s), were extremely difficult to garner or to sell. Not many weeks after the chantries act had been passed, and before the surveys were completed, the first wave of sales was set in motion. On April 17, 1548,

---

[1] *Vide post*, 223-239.   [2] Wood-Legh, *Perpetual chantries*, 276.

[3] To take some examples:—in Suffolk the Commissioners seem to have been carefully protective of the free chapels (VCH, *Suffolk*, II, 30) and of large communities where it was thought assistants were needed (*ibid*. 28–29); after a long legal action the inhabitants of Pamber (Hants) regained by a chancery decision the use of their chapel of ease, their church in effect being constituted a parish independent of Monk Sherborne (VCH, *Hants*, IV, 238, 435); it is not true that in Lancashire, with many chapels of ease, none was seized and sold (VCH, *Lancs*, II, 46), but it is fair to say that all such chapels regarded as legally chantries were either exempted or, more commonly, seized and then sold back to the inhabitants at nominal charges ranging from 6s 8d to £2 6s 8d.

the Council resolved that in view of the heavy costs of the war with Scotland, the defensive preparations that must be made against France, the defences that must be raised in Ireland, and the burdensome weight of the King's debts, the Court of Augmentations should proceed, by authority vested in named commissioners, to sell chantry lands to the value of £5,000 p.a. It was further argued that Parliament had in part been disposed to grant these lands into the hands of the King rather than to subject the realm to a 'continual charge of taxes', such as those which Henry VIII had imposed for the prosecution of his wars.[1] This was but the first of successive authorizations under which sales were made through the remainder of the reign, with a particularly heavy concentration in the last regnal year.[2]

We have observed that some portions of the wealth swept into the Court of Augmentations by the expropriation had been dedicated or hypothecated for other uses and could not be sold. We have reckoned that £71,196 2s of these resources had been assigned for charitable uses, while a probably conservative reckoning suggests that the government *should* have regarded at least £139,381 of the wealth as necessary for funding the generous pension awards totalling £11,147 14s p.a. at the outset.[3] In other words, something like £399,678 1s of capital was freely in hand to meet whatever use the ruling junta might determine. As we have already seen, in the course of Edward's reign £272,858 8s was derived by the government from the sale of these lands, while lands with a capital worth of £47,317 were given to favoured persons. The consequence was that by the close of the reign the chantry wealth remaining (if we apply strict auditing principles) possessed a capital worth of about £79,502 13s, much of it scattered land in small tracts or in awkwardly shaped and located urban parcels. Not much more was left at the time of Edward's death than the debris of the chantry lands.[4]

The chantry resources were, then, rapidly disposed of, principally by sale to meet the urgent needs of a financially straitened government, with the climax of sales coming in the last eighteen months of the reign. Great care had been taken to protect, indeed slightly to enlarge, those assets which had in the past sustained socially useful

[1] *A.P.C.*, II, 185-186.

[2] *Ibid.* 184-185; *Cal. Pat. Rolls, Edw. VI*, I, 135, 417-418; *ibid.* II, 51, 57-58, 183; *ibid.* III, 347-348; *ibid.* IV, 354-355, 390-391, 393, 397-398; *ibid.* V, 184, 277, 411; Edward VI, *Chronicle*, 121-122; Strype, *Memorials*, II, ii, 402-409, for a helpful analysis of sales made in the second regnal year.

[3] *Vide* the computations in Jordan, *Edward VI*, 105, 110-111.

[4] *Ibid.* 110-121 *passim*.

causes, and there were no scandals connected with the survey, the gathering of the assets, or their sale and gift. But there was none the less a degree of moral betrayal by the government which had lent its support to the parliamentary declaration that these capital resources should be more largely used for educational, social, and religious purposes; it is not too much to say that this commitment was probably necessary to secure the consent of the House of Commons to the dissolution of chantry endowments. And then, within a few months, it became all too clear that these assets were principally to be used to lend financial strength to a hard-pressed government which had strayed into a dangerous and extremely expensive foreign policy.

This betrayal of the idealism of men like Latimer, Lever, and Hooper was seriously to weaken the moral strength of Somerset's government and it was to suit all too snugly the reckless and cynical policy of his successor. So too, the moral indignation of the reformers and of the Commonwealth Men was aroused by the unseemly scramble of thrusting men for some share in bundles of property so shortly assembled for sale by the Commissioners. Even as the act was being debated the imperial ambassador had reported that 'all the gentry, large and small, are . . . on the look out to receive rewards and benefits from the king'.[1] Thomas Fuller, writing a century later, thought the crowding in of brokers and direct purchasers was even less restrained than for the monastic lands, since many men had some scruple about acquiring them.[2] Just a few days before the first instalment of sales was authorized by the Council a servant of the Earl of Shrewsbury reported to his master that the Commissioners were meeting daily in Mildmay's house and that already prospective London buyers were bidding up the value of metropolitan properties that might be for sale: 'such importunate heaving for houses in London has not the like been seen; twenty years' and thirty years' purchase is nothing, almost, [and] such a stir is among the citizens in purchasing one another's house over his head that well is he that pricks highest. Undoubtedly the sale will be as great thing as hath been heard of'.[3] And the excitement and prospect of quick gain extended to the shires as well, from whence John Johnson, a partner in a family merchant firm centred on Northamptonshire and London, wrote to his brother,

[1] *Cal. S.P. Span.*, IX, 222: Dec. 5, 1547.
[2] Fuller, Thomas, *The church history of Britain, etc.*, ed. by J. S. Brewer (6 vols., Oxford, 1845), III, 478–479.
[3] Lodge, *Illustrations*, I, 149–150, citing Talbot MSS., B 35.

Otwell, in London, proposing that he move at once to buy up the expropriated chantry moveables in the home shire as rapidly as possible. But Otwell, after enquiries, replied in a discouraging tone that 'to compass to get all your chantries stuff in your shire at the price it is praised for, passeth my capacity to attain to, not knowing to whom I may resort to speed therefor'. He feared too that men on the scene would immediately 'snatch up things' and reported that in any case the appraisal values on plate were being set so close to the prevailing London price that little profit would be in prospect.[1]

This scramble for quick profit was in point of fact skilfully contained by the Commissioners, who saw to it that prices were carefully set at the economic value prevailing and who assembled the properties for sale in sizeable lots. But the wrath of the reformers and of the Commonwealth Men was provoked at once by the unseemly haste and what they considered a repudiation of its commitment on the part of the government. By far the most effective of these critics was Lever, who in his great series of London sermons lashed out bitterly against what he regarded as a betrayal of the Reformation. The suppression of the chantries, he tells us, was as necessary as it was godly. And it was wholly right that 'such abundance of goods as was superstitiously spent upon vain ceremonies, or voluptuously upon idle bellies, might come to the king's hands to bear his great charges'. But there was a commitment that some of this wealth would be used for charitable causes; the intention of the legislation was godly, 'but now the use or rather the abuse and misorder of these things is worldly, is wicked, is devilish'.[2] The chantry wealth had fed and fattened landowners who had already ground down their tenants into a hopeless poverty from which actual rebellion had sprung.[3] The specific commitments made in the act for the nurturing of the poor, the education of youth, and the strengthening of the universities had been forgotten and betrayed. He warned his auditors—and this sermon was preached before the King—that the government could not, dared not, condone such evils, for thereby the commonwealth was troubled and men brought to shame and confusion. To put it bluntly, the very statute intended for the advancement of learning and the relief of the poor had been used 'as a most fit instrument to rob learning and to spoil

---

[1] Winchester, Barbara, *Tudor family portrait* (L., [1955]), 194.
[2] Lever, Thomas, *A fruitfull sermon in . . . the Shrouds, etc.* (1550; STC 15543, 15543a), in *Sermons, 1550*, ed. by Edward Arber (Arber English Reprints, no. 25, L., 1871), 32.
[3] *Ibid.* 37.

the poor'.[1] This magnificent rhetoric, this moving plea for healing and constructive charity, did little to stay the course of governmental policy, but it had much to contribute towards the rise of the secular charitable impulse which marks the Edwardian era and to which we shall now lend our consideration. Lever, and the other preachers and moralists who lashed out at the failure of the government immediately and with great resources to endow the social institutions of England, must have known full well that the sovereign power had in fact preserved much and had strengthened even more.

[1] Lever, Thomas, *A sermon preached the third Sunday in Lent before the King's Majesty*, etc., in *Sermons* (Arber Reprints, no. 25), 81–82.

VII

RISE OF THE SECULAR CHARITABLE IMPULSE (1547–1553) [*EXCURSUS* II]

I. GENERAL STATEMENT AND CONCLUSIONS

It is probable that the re-shaping of men's aspirations for their society and its future was the most important historical development in the short but revolutionary Edwardian era. This suggestion may be impressively supported by a study of the sharp and sustained increase in charitable giving during this period and even more significantly by an analysis of the dramatic and, as time was to prove, permanent change in the structure of those aspirations, new and old, which served and sustained them.

In another study we have sought on a larger scale to examine the rapid development of charitable giving and the process of the change of men's aspirations from a predominantly religious concern to an overwhelmingly secular dedication over a long period of time (1480–1660). This was done by an analysis of all gifts and bequests found in a sampling of ten counties which represented roughly a third of the land area of England and Wales, about a third of the population of the realm, and probably not far off from 60 per cent of the huge aggregate of charitable wealth given during this interval of almost two centuries.[1] These benefactions may usefully be set out by decade totals, at least for the interval 1480–1600 in order to afford a statistical background for a study of the Edwardian period, itself comprehended within the two decades, 1541–1550 and 1551–1560.[2]

---

[1] For the particulars, *vide* Jordan, *Philanthropy in England*, 21–29, 240–242, *et passim*.
[2] Table I (derived from *ibid*. 246)

1480–1490	£49,383 19s
1491–1500	75,472 19s
1501–1510	131,220 5s
1511–1520	81,868 12s
1521–1530	107,405 17s
1531–1540	80,243 9s

£525,595 1s [total of charitable giving in the pre-Reformation era]

In the course of the Edwardian era, which for this purpose we have necessarily defined as encompassing the whole of the seven years 1547–1553, a total of £105,758 5s was given in our sample of ten counties for various charitable uses. This sum represented a remarkably disproportionate fraction (46.58 per cent) of the whole amount given for such purposes during the two decades which we have described as the Era of the Reformation. The presentation of a yearly analysis of charitable giving for the Edwardian era would be at once too cumbersome and wanting in perspective, but it may use-fully be said that the flow of philanthropic giving was heavily concentrated in the second half of this short reign, when very nearly three fourths of the whole amount was provided, mostly, be it observed, for intensely secular purposes. For the whole span of the reign, necessarily so defined as to include the early months of Queen Mary's reign, the *per annum* rate of giving was £15,108 7s, an annual flow of charitable funds much greater than that for any decade interval before the Reformation, save only for the years 1501–1510 when the average annual rate works out as £13,122 2s. This earlier decade was, then, the high-water mark for pre-Reformation charitable giving, being very heavily concentrated on the £24,075 7s provided for university foundations and including the huge total of £74,719 13s for various religious uses, of which more than half was for prayers. It should also be observed that a heavy proportion of the gifts and bequests in the earlier decade was derived from the large charitable benefactions of Henry VII and numerous rich bishops who happened to die within this span of years.

The great outpouring of charitable giving in the Edwardian era reveals radically different aspirations and concerns, while it is note-worthy that the great bulk of the whole sum was derived from the generosity of quite different classes of men. The Edwardian gifts were on balance overwhelmingly secular in their purposes. It should also be observed that the philanthropic achievement of the

1541–1550	£71,388 15s	
1551–1560	155,643 6s	
	£227,032 1s	[total of charitable giving in the Reformation era]
1561–1570	92,926 4s	
1571–1580	105,980 2s	
1581–1590	120,550 11s	
1591–1600	126,216 2s	
	£445,672 19s	[total of charitable giving in the Elizabethan period]

Edwardian era was to stand unmatched, in the ultimately important terms of the annual rate of giving, when compared with any other decade in the second half of the sixteenth century, even including the last interval of Elizabeth's reign (1591–1600), and was not to be greatly over-matched by the £21,006 p.a. given in the first decade of the seventeenth century when the great outpouring of charitable wealth may be said to have begun on a vast and infinitely fruitful scale.

Before presenting a detailed analysis of Edwardian charitable giving, it should once more be stated that our totals are derived from a sampling of ten counties which we believe provided about 60 per cent of the charitable wealth for the whole of the realm. If so, we may conclude that something like £176,263 15s may well have been provided by men of the Edwardian age for generously conceived social needs across the whole of England. At the same time, it should be made clear that these totals do not include the considerable sum of £71,196 2s of landed wealth assigned by the crown for charitable causes from the expropriated chantry lands, usually on the recommendation of the Chantry Commissioners.[1]

[1] Table II: Analysis of Edwardian charitable giving, 1547–1553 incl.

Care of the poor

Outright relief	£12,606	0s
Almshouses	9,264	3s
Charity general	821	7s
Total	£22,691	10s (21·46 %)

Social rehabilitation

Prisons	362	1s
Loan funds	1,243	2s
Workhouses and stocks of goods	100	0s
Apprenticeship schemes	3	0s
Sick and hospitals	52,167	3s
Marriage portions	407	1s
Total	£54,282	7s (51.33 %)

Municipal uses

General	1,216	4s
Companies for public uses	871	6s
Public works, roads, streets, *etc.*	3,041	6s
Total	£5,128	16s (4.85 %)

Education

Schools	£15,350	10s
Colleges and universities	1,871	3s
Scholarships and fellowships	1,371	6s
Total	£18,592	19s (17·58 %)

Religion

Church general	£1,016	3s
Prayers	1,074	3s
Church repairs	1,024	1s
Maintenance of clergy	674	3s
Church building (est.)	1,274	3s
Total	£5,062	13s (4·79 %)
Grand Total	£105,758	5s

It is immediately evident that these charitable dispositions were overwhelmingly secular in their intent, with a heavy proportion devoted to bold and on the whole new measures for social rehabilitation, excited principally by the reorganization and then the refounding of the London hospitals under secular control and for secular purposes. Such valuable and experimental efforts to cure poverty and disease had commanded no more than 2·04 per cent of all pre-Reformation charities and 14·83 per cent in the Elizabethan period which followed. There was also a strong interest in the care of the poor in their own parishes and homes or, if they were wholly impotent, in almshouses, such outlays commanding more than a fifth of all charitable wealth. These funds were usually provided in capital amounts under the control of parochial or other lay trustees in order to ensure careful and selective relief rather than the erratic largesse which had marked (and marred) medieval alms-giving. The needs of education likewise commanded widespread and generous support, with slightly more than 14 per cent of the whole of charitable wealth being devoted to the founding of grammar schools or to the revivification of older and often derelict foundations. But the profoundly important—indeed, the almost shocking—reality is that the pattern of giving in the Edwardian era was so overwhelmingly and almost militantly secular. It is almost incredible that no more than 4·79 per cent of all benefactions was dedicated to religious uses in this period when England was embracing Protestantism, when a powerful evangelical movement was under way, and when all men were to a degree stirred by the powerful forces of religious change. This slender proportion must be contrasted with the vast total provided by pre-Reformation benefactors, whose concern with religious aspirations was so great as to command well over half (53·49 per cent) of all the charitable wealth provided from 1480 to 1540. It is equally astonishing that the Edwardian era was even more secular in its interests and aspirations than was the Elizabethan age, when a niggardly 7·17 per cent of charitable giving was dedicated to the various religious causes. And, finally, it should be noted that the Edwardian period was more radically secular in its aspirations than the 'Age of Reformation' of which it was a part, not much more than 15 per cent of the whole amount given in these twenty years for religious causes having been provided by Edwardian donors, though this interval represents 35 per cent of the whole stretch of time from 1541 to 1560. It seems clear, then, that England ventured into a new world during this brief and tumultuous reign, a world possessing a quite different conception of the society, of its needs, and of its·future.

The powerful forces which account for this radical change in the aspirations of Englishmen in the Edwardian era—changes which are so clearly mirrored in the structure of charitable giving, which in its very nature marks accurately the social and moral aspirations of the donor—are at once complex and extremely elusive. But some comment and estimate must be ventured. The precipitate decline in giving for religious uses undoubtedly reflects the uncertainty and the confusion of thought and aspirations in Henry's later years when Protestantism was finding firm root in England despite the wishes of an imperious sovereign, who, however, towards the very end of his reign undoubtedly understood that his realm must become Protestant the better to secure the succession of his young son. In 1547 it was impossible to bequeath one's substance to a monastery; it would have been manifest folly to endow a chantry. The structure and the teachings of faith and saving doctrine were all far too uncertainly defined during most of Edward's reign to elicit that generosity from which institutions are built or strengthened. Then, too, the realm, in so far as it was articulate at all, was deeply divided by an acrid controversy over the nature and definition of Christian faith, of which many rich and self-confident laymen were tiring. Further, it seems safe to say, in the second half of Edward's reign, in which charitable giving was most heavily concentrated, England had become Protestant, if we may measure faith by the wealth, the education, and the zeal of its adherents. And Protestantism anchors itself ultimately in the simple faith of the believer, not in the whole institutionalized apparatus of worship exhibited by Catholicism, which lays such a heavy and continuous burden on the generosity of its believers.

There were other and possibly even more powerful forces of social change which must also be considered not only in estimating the astonishing generosity of Edwardian benefactors, but in explaining the starkly secular nature of their social concerns. For one thing, it would be difficult to over-emphasize the social shock of the expropriation of the chantries and the resolution, to be observed amongst all classes of men, that the social uses which they had supported, frail and small though this support was, must not be lost. England for the first time appraised its social and cultural resources and found them sadly wanting. The efforts, in scores of market towns and hundreds of rural parishes, of substantial and responsible men to save a school, or to continue the support of an almshouse from former chantry income, taught such men that institutions which they were now convinced must be fostered and preserved laid a direct claim, so to say, on their own generosity. Hence the schools that were saved were in a large measure within a few years far more adequately endowed by private generosity. The alms-houses that were needed, but which were derelict when the Com-missioners reported on the social resources of the nation, were now built and endowed in scores of parishes by private effort. And, be it remembered, both schools and almshouses were now with few exceptions placed under the authority and responsibility of lay trustees. The government, both of Somerset and of Northumber-land, was deeply involved in this great effort to make at least a beginning in providing for the realm the institutions and the resources wherewith civilized life could be preserved and nur-tured. The chantries, as we have seen, had lent relatively little support to the social and cultural needs of the nation; but their dissolution was infinitely productive in the sense that it moved men to preserve what they could from the past and to build more fruit-fully with their own resources for the future.

Men in England, too, were reluctantly arriving at the really revolutionary persuasion that extreme poverty and impotence occasioned by age, sickness, or frailty of mind or body must some-how be assumed as a burden of the whole society. We have seen that two generations of fumbling and wrestling with this great social problem were to pass before, at the very end of the century, the decision was made in law to lay a floor of support under the society at the level of subsistence and to meet what had come to be assumed as a direct social responsibility with the resources afforded by the taxing power.[1] One last effort was made in the Edwardian period to proscribe poverty, so to speak, by inhuman penalties laid against vagrancy and idleness, but this measure was speedily re-pealed as being unenforceable and as not dealing directly with the clear separation which had to be made between idleness and vag-rancy tinged with criminality, and true impotence and unemploy-ment.[2] All over England local efforts were being made to effect this separation and to arrange mechanisms and resources for the care of poor and impotent persons.[3] This in turn occasioned the be-ginning of the settling of well constituted and administered endow-ments for the home relief of the poor, almost always in specified

[1] Jordan, *Philanthropy in England*, 77–103.
[2] Jordan, *Edward VI*, 177–178.
[3] As in King's Lynn where in Oct., 1547 it was ordered that badges be prepared for impotent residents of the town, who alone were to be permitted to beg (HMC, *Eleventh rpt.*, App. III: *Southampton and King's Lynn MSS.*, 174).

parishes, which were in time to serve significantly the needs of the society. But even as early as 1547 it was coming to be recognized that private charity was not sufficient, that the taxing power must also be invoked. An historic resolution was marked by the decision of the London Common Council in 1547 that even with the funded resources available and the weekly gifts to the poor boxes in the several parishes of the City, the inhabitants of the capital must pay for the relief of the poor over the next year a half of one whole fifteenth, while weekly voluntary collections should be discontinued.[1] This action, an experimental preliminary to the great Elizabethan Poor Law provisions a half-century later, must be regarded as one of the most revolutionary social actions of all time, for in a very real and direct sense it opened the way for the ever-increasing assumption of responsibility for the well-being of the whole society which has over the past century made of us all citizens of the welfare state.

The quick and generous outpouring of charitable wealth in the Edwardian age also owed much to the naive but strong hope shared by Somerset and the Commonwealth Party that social wrongs might be ameliorated and the plight of the poor relieved by the combined action of the state and private charity. Somerset had little other support for his policies, which seemed to endanger the wealth and privileges of the classes which controlled the resources of power and administration in the mid-sixteenth century. There can be no doubt that his stubborn and high-minded devotion to a programme of revolutionary reform was the prime cause for the gathering of a successful conspiracy against him. But none the less he had moved and he had touched the social conscience of England, with the result, ironically enough, that the flow of private giving, pledged so to speak to the funding of the Duke's social aspirations, quickened and deepened during the tenure of his successor. England stirred restlessly and mightily during these years, and the shock and fright

---

[1] Tawney, R. H., and Eileen Power, *Tudor economic documents, etc.* (3 vols., L., 1924), II, 305–306, citing *Guildhall journal*, xv, 325. Norwich was only a little behind London in invoking taxation for the relief of the poor, a compulsory rate being levied in 1549. Bristol and York were also in the vanguard of this experimentation, with several other provincial cities in their train (Jordan, *Philanthropy in England*, 87). Among these others was Coventry, where the city officials in 1547 ordered a census of the inhabitants to determine 'whether there be more people . . . of the poorest sort that must be set on work'. At the same time a survey of employment possibilities was prepared, in the hope of finding work for at least some of the poor, while the city stock would supply employment for those of the poor not absorbed by private means. (Harris, Mary Dormer, ed., *The Coventry Leet Book: or Mayor's Register, etc.*, pt. III (EETS, O.S. 138, L., 1909), 783–785.)

following on the bloody purging of serious insurrection in two regions of England in the summer of 1549 powerfully stimulated charitable giving for a variety of useful and sorely needed purposes. The schools, the almshouses, and the hospitals, so generously and so widely founded in the later years of the reign, stand, in a sense at least, as the enduring monument to the Duke of Somerset and the Commonwealth Party.

Nor, in our effort to analyse the forces for social change which were permanently altering the aspirations of men in this era, should we fail to emphasize the personal involvement of the young King. From the beginning of the reign, his personal charities had been considerable, almost all devoted to the care of the deserving poor.[1] Somerset kept his nephew under strait rein in his personal finances and outlays, and it is significant that a boy of about twelve years involved himself in a humiliating fashion in Sudeley's treasonable machinations in order to secure additional amounts principally to be used as gifts which were in their nature charitable.[2] As Edward gained a larger measure of control over his personal finances and began to formulate policy, the bent of his own charitable aspirations became clearer as his gifts for the relief of poverty were increased and as he intervened personally to secure the founding and the endowment of the great royal hospitals of London at the close of his tragically short life.

It should also be suggested that the steep increase in charitable giving during Edward's reign, mostly devoted to secular purposes, was a direct consequence of the coming of age and the assumption of heavy social responsibilities by the merchant aristocracy of London. We have dealt at length elsewhere with the immense charitable accomplishment of London's merchant wealth.[3] It is not too much to say that the great flow of these charitable funds, intensely secular in their purposes, had its dramatic beginning in the brief period with which we are now concerned. The crowning achievement of the London merchant aristocracy was the founding and then for a full century the incredibly generous support of the royal hospitals of London. This was, it may be held, the triggering social action from which the famous achievements of London merchant wealth over the next full century were to spring. And this sudden and infinitely fruitful social involvement of the merchant

---

[1] *A.P.C.*, II, 62: Mar. 10, 1547, setting out the details of £408 12s 8d for distribution in the course of a year.

[2] Jordan, *Edward VI*, 374–377.

[3] Jordan, *Charities of London*.

aristocracy was in turn derived from its intervention to save the chantry wealth of the City Companies, already chiefly devoted to social purposes. More than thirty of the City Companies were trustees of chantry endowments, clearly subject to expropriation under the law, ranging downwards in value from nearly £197 p.a. for the mercers and £104 p.a. for the goldsmiths to very modest endowments for several of the lesser companies. The City Companies, acting in concert, dealt directly with the Council in assessing the total net worth of their properties, which at twenty years' purchase (5 per cent) seems to work out at £18,714 11s 2d.[1] But there were other small properties involved which brought the total capital worth to £20,000, a huge sum for this generation, which the City Companies agreed to purchase at this price on eight days' demand notice from the Privy Council.[2] At about the same time, and doubtless as part of this great transaction, the City of London also purchased from the crown for 1000 marks the Liberties of Southwark, save only for Southwark Palace, and the King's two prisons within the borough, shortly afterwards ordering 'the avoiding of vagabonds out of the City of London and the Borough of Southwark'.[3]

It can hardly be doubted that implicit in this great transaction was an undertaking on the part of the City Companies to lay all these properties under charitable uses according to an agreed formula. In a detailed (and later) document the value of the properties purchased was set out, together with the covenanted charitable uses to which they were almost invariably dedicated: pensions for decayed brethren of the company, educational purposes, and the relief of poverty. The Haberdashers Company will perhaps suffice as an example. It had purchased chantry properties with a value of £40 12s 2d p.a., wherewith it had undertaken to pay £23 6s 8d p.a. for pensions, £16 13s 4d p.a. for scholarships, and £20 p.a. for free alms to poor but deserving men and women.[4] Though in our statistical analysis we have not regarded this large capital outlay as a charitable benefaction,[5] it should be noted that it does in fact amount to almost a fifth of the sum given for charitable uses during the course of this remarkable reign. It established as well the pattern of

---

[1] Lansdowne MS. 55, #28, f. 86.
[2] Stow, *Annales*, 604. The purchase was completed in late March 1550.
[3] Wriothesley, *Chronicle*, II, 36–38.
[4] Lansdowne MS. 55, #30, ff. 89–92 (this survey dates from 1587).
[5] Since these funds technically should be regarded as a secularization of existing charitable funds heretofore dedicated to religious uses. Our decision is, of course, arguable.

London merchant giving for many decades to come, taught this rich and increasingly responsible commercial community to think and plan in large terms, and prepared it for the next, and immediate, task, of founding and endowing the royal hospitals.

Finally, and subsuming much that we have said, the powerful thrust for social change and reformation undoubtedly owed much to the immensely powerful and beautifully articulate ethic of evangelical Protestantism in the Edwardian era. We shall not at this point discuss the great preaching of men like Latimer, Lever, Hooper, and Ridley—and they are but the foremost. But it may here be said that they were developing a new doctrine of works and that they insisted on a moral and social as well as a doctrinal reformation in England. The whole evangelical wing of the Protestant movement in England, solidifying a generation later into Puritanism, was to a degree naive in its aspirations, but it was bold and deeply persuasive in what it expected of government, of wealth, and of those imbued with faith in Christ. These men wanted social wrongs righted and they wished to see the Church of God in all its glory planted within their own generation.

Even the lesser of them, to take a small sampling quite at random, spoke with great conviction and moral power. The Christian commonwealth cannot escape its direct and religious responsibility for its poor, so Gerrard maintained. Yet, 'who doeth not see how pitifully the poor be despised in every place, be not most men more ready to devour them than to help them, be they not hastiest to make them stark beggars, than to succour and relieve them in their necessity'. No state, he continued, can long prosper or endure where the poor are unjustly pressed down, nor will they when God's Word is clearly understood and well preached.[1] A drumfire of exhortation was maintained by evangelical Protestantism during these critical years, denouncing covetousness and dwelling with eloquent emphasis on the fact that we are designated by Christ as no more than stewards of our wealth. Hence Christian Englishmen will so order their affairs as to spare as much as they can 'to those good deeds of charity that God's Word requireth . . . as to give meat to the hungry, drink to the thirsty, to clothe the naked, to comfort and help the sick . . . to redeem and succour poor prisoners, to amend high ways, to marry poor maidens, and to bring up poor fatherless children'.[2] The only virtue to be found in wealth is what it may accomplish for the society—for Christ's Kingdom—when

---

[1] Gerrard, Philip, *A godly invective, etc.* (L., 1547), B6.
[2] *A new boke, conteyninge an exhortation to the sycke, etc.* ([Ipswich], 1548), A6–A6ᵛ.

we employ it as faithful stewards. Money was caused to say in its defence in a somewhat hackneyed dialogue in better sentiment than verse:

> The poor have my succour in hunger, frost, and snow,
> I feed both horse and man in holy pilgrimages,
> For fair young maidens I purchase marriages;
> When churches and chapels be falling in decay,
> I must make reparation . . .[1]

These were, then, the complex of forces which principally account for the upsurge of charitable giving, on a really large scale, during this brief interval which was the Edwardian era. But far more important historically than the absolute (and dramatic) rise in the amounts given for charitable causes was, as we have observed, the radically different structure of men's aspirations for their society as mirrored in their benefactions. These momentous changes were first clearly manifest amongst the London merchant aristocracy, and the precipitating cause may well have been the necessary purchase and then the re-orientation of a large *corpus* of chantry endowments, followed almost immediately by the opportunity, with direct assistance from the crown, to establish in London a complex, a secular, and an amazingly ambitious system of hospitals which, when taken with other benefactions, provided the City with the most advanced and effective social institutions then afforded by any city in the western world. To these remarkable events we now turn.

2. FOUNDING OF THE ROYAL HOSPITALS AND THE DEVELOPMENT OF THE IDEAL OF SOCIAL REHABILITATION

The merchant aristocracy of London, to some degree even in the fifteenth century, but more distinctly since the first decade of Henry VIII's reign, was not only becoming increasingly secular in its charitable concerns but was likewise coming to view dourly the medieval practice of casual alms for the poor. These convictions were well settled by the mid-sixteenth century when merchant giving had come to be principally dedicated to education, to the institutionalized care of the derelict poor in almshouses or in their parishes, and, most hopefully, for various experimental measures for the social rehabilitation of the poor. Such purposes as loans for the

---

[1] Bieston, Roger, *The bayte and snare of fortune, etc.* (L., 1550?), B ii.

honest poor, apprenticeship schemes, setting up stocks of raw materials on which the poor might be employed, marriage allotments for deserving young people, the care of the sick and the rehabilitation of the indolent, and the safe-guarding of orphans and the children of the derelict, engaged the merchant mind and conscience to a degree not to be observed in the philanthropic aspirations of any other class in the society, save for the tradesmen. The charitable concerns of the London merchant aristocracy were old, and their contribution to the needs and the institutions of the City had been generous long before 1547.[1] But they were to be immensely enlarged and deepened during the Edwardian era. In 1549 the Common Council, having condemned the pouring in to London of the unemployed and of beggars who found sleeping room because citizens were turning their houses into crowded tenements, decreed that henceforward any owner so converting his premises should pay to the almshouse in West Smithfield 'the whole annual value of every such room'.[2]

The Council was also much exercised by the great number of homeless children, many of whom were orphans under no supervision or protection and who contributed to the 'sore decay' of the City.[3] During the mayoralty of the great Sir Andrew Judd, they carefully reviewed the plight of London's orphans and sought to establish rigorous legal safeguards against the early marriages of such children who now 'bestow themselves upon simple and light persons having neither cunning, knowledge, substance, nor good or honest conditions'. Detailed regulations were accordingly set out requiring the consent of the Lord Mayor and Aldermen for the marriage of any orphan girl with an inheritable portion before the age of twenty-one and more generally imposing severe penalties on the unauthorized marriage of all orphan children during their minority.[4]

The City authorities were also deeply concerned because of the visible increase in the number of rootless beggars who haunted the metropolis, augmented after 1550 by considerable numbers of genuinely unemployed as an acute depression in the cloth trade set in. The problem was further complicated by the decay in the fifteenth century of such institutions as London possessed for the

---

[1] Jordan, *Philanthropy in England*, Tables, pp. 384–387, and numerous comments in text; Jordan, *Charities of London*, 63–78, 86 ff.

[2] Hargrave MS. 134, f. 29.

[3] *Ibid.* f. 30.

[4] *Orders taken and enacted, for orphans, etc.* ([L.], 1551; STC #16705+/18843a).

care of the poor and the sick, compounded by the fact that the dissolution of the monasteries effectively destroyed the remaining shell of medieval institutions without immediately providing new or revivified agencies to take their place.[1] So serious was the situation that even before the Dissolution the City authorities had petitioned the King to transfer to the municipal government all the rents and perquisites of the Hospitals of St Bartholomew, St Thomas, and two other small foundations in order that reforms could be effected to secure the care of 'miserable people lying in the street, offending every clean person passing by the way with their filthy and nasty savours . . . and for the avoiding of the great infection and other inconveniences that be like to happen to your citizens'.[2] There is no recorded reply to this petition, but decorous pressure was maintained until Henry VIII, shortly before his departure for France in 1544, re-founded St Bartholomew's as a quasi-religious institution, which by no means met the expectations of the London authorities. Negotiations with the King were accordingly continued until shortly before his death, when an agreement was reached by the terms of which St Bartholomew's and Bethlehem were conveyed by letters patent to the City, which guaranteed to underwrite the considerable sum of 500 marks for their support as hospitals, with any surplus revenues to be dedicated to the relief of the poor.[3]

This action established a pattern of corporate responsibility among the burgher aristocracy of London which speedily led to the foundation and endowment of the five inter-related royal hospitals. Modest contributions had been made by Londoners in every decade since 1480 for the care of the sick, but it was not until the great Edwardian foundations were made that the imagination and aspirations of London were deeply stirred, with the result that the huge total of £52,167 3s was given or bequeathed in the interval 1547–1553 towards the financing of what can only be described as a great system of social institutions. This almost obsessive charitable concern was furthered in the Elizabethan era, when the substantial total of £20,024 was provided, and further increased in the early Stuart period (1601–1640), when additions totalling £40,137 were made to the capital funds supporting the royal hospitals. From 1551 to the outbreak of the Civil War, it may be said, almost every

[1] Gale, Barry G., 'The dissolution and the revolution in London hospital facilities', *Medical History*, XI, (Jan. 1967), 92–93.

[2] *Memoranda, references, and documents relating to the royal hospitals of . . . London* (L., 1836), App., I, 2–3; *et vide ibid.* App., VII–IX.

[3] David, E. J., 'The transformation of London', in *Tudor Studies*, ed. by R. W. Seton-Watson (L., 1924), 301–303.

London merchant and most tradesmen as a matter of course made some testamentary provision for the hospitals of the City, while there were many who made large and well-considered bequests to one or another of the royal hospitals.[1]

St Bartholomew's Hospital, the oldest of these foundations, was of twelfth-century origin and for several generations was well regarded for the care it gave to the poor and sick, as well as to orphan children whose mothers had died there. The Priory, with which it was connected, and the Hospital together possessed net revenues of £304 16s 5d p.a. at the time of the Dissolution, though most of the income was devoted to essentially religious or administrative uses, the secular services of the Hospital having long since been sorely decayed. But immediately after the institution and its assets had been conveyed to the City, ambitious efforts were begun to fund the annual subsidy of 500 marks which the City had undertaken, the considerable total of £1897 12s being given for this purpose within a decade. Even more importantly, the functions of the Hospital were completely reorganized to ensure the proper care of the sick, while the premises were entirely renovated. In 1549 three surgeons were appointed to its staff and in 1568 a physician, while by the close of the century four surgeons and as many physicians lent their services to the work of this great urban hospital. Most of the credit for the founding of this, the first modern hospital, is due to Thomas Vicary, surgeon to four successive Tudor sovereigns, who was appointed a governor in 1548, who lived in the Hospital, and who carried on much of his practice there.[2]

Bethlehem, likewise conveyed by the Crown to the City, was also of medieval origin, having been founded as a convent, but by 1330 was generally regarded as a hospital (almshouse). Before the early fifteenth century the institution began to receive insane patients, an inspection of 1403–1404 suggesting that it then offered shelter to six insane persons and three other sick patients. But its always fragile resources had so withered that by the close of the fifteenth century it possessed little more than its name and its site. Following the secularization of the hospital, however, slow progress was begun towards endowing it, capital gifts of about £860 having been gathered by 1557, most of which was given in the Edwardian era. The hospital was dedicated by the City authorities to the care of an unstated number of insane patients, and in 1557 was given its own

---

[1] Jordan, *Charities of London*, 186–187.
[2] *Ibid.* 188; Dainton, Courtney, *The story of England's hospitals* (L., 1961), 38–43; Gale, in *Medical History*, XI (1967), 95.

board of governors. Important and pioneering as its work was, the hospital failed to attract any really large single capital gift in the course of the century, being principally supported by gifts and small bequests from many of the merchants and tradesmen of the City.[1]

St Thomas's Hospital in Southwark was likewise of medieval origin, Stow telling us that it was founded as an almshouse in 1213 by the then Prior of Bermondsey. The hospital was confiscated as a monastic foundation, at that time evidently being decayed and rendering little of service as either a hospital or an almshouse. The premises were bought from the Crown by the City and it was in 1552 rebuilt as a hospital for the care of poor, lame, and diseased persons, at a cost (with Christ's Hospital) of £2479.[2] The refurbished institution was chartered by the Crown on August 12, 1551, for the 'curing and sustentation of the . . . poor, sick, and weak people', and received as a free gift from the King rents for its support with a capital value of £3097.[3] In 1553 a careful report on the operation of St Thomas's and of Christ's Hospital was prepared for the further consideration of the King, there then being 260 patients in St Thomas's, while the joint charitable foundation also paid subsistence to 500 poor and decayed householders in London, persons still living in their houses. Five surgeons were listed as staffing St Thomas's, with salaries of £15 p.a. each, while the total operating budget of the then conjoined institutions was stated as £3291 5s 4d p.a. Interestingly, in addition to the large capital sums given or bequeathed, outright gifts totalling £3043 15s 7d had been received for the support of the two hospitals in the course of the year, while the governors had met the operating deficit from their own purses.[4]

These great annual charges could not, of course, be independently met even by the excited generosity of London merchants. The needs were hence once more laid before the King with a petition for relief from mortmain for the great capital sum that must be raised. The way had been prepared by a review of the state of Henry VII's rich foundation of the Savoy, instituted as a great almshouse but never functioning properly or usefully because of a kind of paralysis of administration and an uncertainty of purpose.[5] Two years earlier

---

[1] Jordan, *Charities of London*, 189–190.   [2] Harl. MS. 604, #63, ff. 147–148.
[3] Stow, *Annales*, 608; VCH, *Surrey*, IV, 159; Manning, Owen, and William Bray, *History and antiquities of the county of Surrey* (3 vols., L., 1804–1814), III, 616; Jordan, *Charities of London*, 190.   [4] Harl. MS. 604, #63, ff. 147–148.
[5] *Ibid.* #11, ff. 22–23 (renumbered f. 26) for the overly elaborate and expensive administrative arrangements. Other versions of the document are in Cotton MSS., Cleopatra, C, v, and in Harvard University Law School Library, MS. 11.

both Petre and Cecil had been wholly dissatisfied with its administration, for it did not serve the true and pressing needs of the poor.[1]
Its great assets, amounting to £600 p.a., were in 1553 accordingly
conveyed by Edward VI as a major contribution towards the endowment of the royal hospitals, and particularly the pressing needs of
St Thomas's and Christ's Hospital. It was the chronicler Grafton
who related that Edward, perusing the licence for relief from
mortmain and 'looking on the void place [for the amount], called for
pen and ink, and with his own hand wrote this sum, . . . and then
said in the hearing of his Council, Lord God I yield thee most
hearty thanks that thou hast given me life thus long, to finish this
work to the glory of thy name'.[2] But even this great gift and the
large private benefactions pouring in to finance the hospital were
insufficient, the General Court for the four royal hospitals in 1557
in effect deciding that the whole of the endowments in hand should
be employed for the needs of St Thomas's, while Christ's Hospital
should for the time being be financed by monthly collections and
from the profits of Blackwell Hall, subject only to the annual payment of £333 6s 7d for the needs of St Bartholomew's.[3]

We have seen that Christ's Hospital, in which the King was
especially interested, was in the beginning closely linked with St
Thomas's. Though it was built in part on the site of the Friars
Minor, Christ's Hospital was a wholly new foundation made by
Edward VI shortly before his death. Edward's consuming interest
in this foundation, as well as in the royal hospitals generally,
appears on reasonably good authority to have owed much to Bishop
Ridley's famous sermon on charity preached before the King at
Whitehall in January, 1552. Edward, we are told, was deeply
moved and called Ridley to consult with him privately after the
sermon to determine how he might proceed, since he felt a sense of
direct responsibility for the care of London's poor. Ridley, quite
unprepared for the King's quick reaction, had no considered plan
in mind, but advised him to consult with Sir Richard Dobbs, the
then Lord Mayor, with whom the Bishop spoke in the course of the
week. Shortly afterwards Ridley spoke before the aldermen on
possible steps to be taken, while a committee of thirty leading
citizens prepared a careful memorandum defining three classes of

[1] S. P. Dom., Edw. VI, XIII, 43: Sept. 14, 1551.
[2] *Grafton's Chronicle*, II, 531; for the surrender of the Savoy by the Crown, *vide* HMC,
Salisbury MSS., I, 123: June 10, 1553.
[3] Jordan, *Charities of London*, 190. The gifts from the Crown to St Thomas's may be
reckoned at about £15,000 of capital value. London support for the hospital was continuous, with the result that by 1630 the endowments stood at £30,890.

the poor: the impotent, those poor by casualty, and the thriftless. The hospitals already functioning served many within these groupings, but there remained need for a school and a refuge for the children of the poor, as well as a place (Bridewell) where the rogues and thriftless could be set at work and reformed. But above all they were agreed that first they should 'take out of the streets all the fatherless children and other poor men's children that were not able to keep them' and give them food, clothing, lodging, and some means of education.[1]

The projected orphanage-school attracted much attention and elicited wide support, as Christ's Hospital was planned and built. The initial canvass yielded £748, the sponsors then moving from parish to parish to secure the support of the clergy who were provided with 'very fine, witty and learned' propaganda pieces for their use. Collection boxes were then set up in the inns and other public places, while printed bills were drawn for the churchwardens with the name and amount of the contribution left blank for each householder in the City. It will be recalled that £2479 was subscribed for the building of Christ's Hospital and the renovation of St Thomas's, the former being opened on November 23, 1552, for the reception of 380 homeless and helpless children. Christ's Hospital was at first meant to serve principally as a home and hospital for orphan and foundling children, but within a generation the clear outlines of a great grammar school were already beginning to emerge. Serving a complex group of purposes, excellently administered, and flexible in its work, the Hospital gained wide and continuous support from the burghers of London over the next two generations. In 1610 the gifts and bequests for its endowment had reached the great total of £45,999 6s, and the Hospital was then sheltering and educating 630 children as well as supporting 54 who had been put forth on apprenticeships. Few institutions have served mankind so well and so generously.[2]

The fifth and last of the great hospital foundations to be made, or re-established, in this remarkable upsurge of generosity and urban planning was Bridewell. It was hardly a hospital in our sense, the

---

[1] Our account in this paragraph and the next follows principally: *Grafton's Chronicle*, II, 529–530 (Grafton became in 1553 the first Treasurer of Christ's Hospital); *The Christ's Hospital book* (L., 1953), 6–7 (the account is by Howes, who served as Grafton's secretary); Egerton MS. 2877, ff. 14b–15 (this quite full account is anonymous; it probably dates from the late sixteenth century); Holinshed, *Chronicles*, III, 1061; Stow, *Annales*, 608; Wriothesley, *Chronicle*, II, 79–80.

[2] Jordan, *Charities of London*, 191–193; Harl. MS. 604, #63, ff. 147–148, for the first audit and review of the Hospital's financing, dated 1553.

institution serving over the next century as a workhouse, an apprenticeship foundation on a large scale, and as a house of correction for vagrant persons.[1] The need for such an institution to complete the pattern of London's hospitals had for some months been under discussion, when Ridley and a group of the merchant élite of the City proffered to the King the thanks of London for having 'provided help for all maladies and diseases and the virtuous education and bringing up of our miserable and poor children' in hospitals already set up by royal aid and encouragement. And now to complete the grand design, and to attack the problems of vagrancy and idleness, it was petitioned that the disused palace of Bridewell be conveyed to the City for the cure of this 'old sore'. The King having expressed his interest, a committee of civic leaders was appointed to sketch out a plan and recommendations for the consideration of the Privy Council.

The statement thereupon drawn for presentation reviewed the whole structure of poverty and want in the City and the institutions which had so recently been established for the social rehabilitation of the needy. The committee had given much thought to the root cause of beggary and thievery—to social dereliction—and had concluded that it was idleness. And idleness, they submitted, could only be cured by providing useful work. Further, there were many beggars who, having 'fallen into misery by lewd and evil service, by wars, by sickness, or other adverse fortune', had so utterly lost their credit that they simply could not find employment because they were feared and distrusted. All other weak and impotent classes were now provided for in the hospitals already founded, but there remained need for 'an house of occupations to be erected' where the young 'unapt to learning' who could find no employment, the sturdy and the idle, prisoners recently discharged, and others who simply would not labour might be rehabilitated. So successful had been the appeals for the other hospitals, that they were confident that funds could be gained for providing raw material and tools for such occupations as the making of caps, bed-ticking, wool-carding, drawing wire, spinning, knitting, and for the 'fouler sort' the making of nails and other ironware. The committee proposed that the governors number thirty, of whom two should be former mayors and four aldermen. The financing of the undertaking caused them no apprehension, for surely 'the same God who so opened the hearts of a great number of good men to impart liberally of their substance' in the other great undertakings so recently

[1] Jordan, *Charities of London*, 193-194.

launched, 'will open the hearts of godly men' once more for this manifest need. For this purpose they would request the gift of Bridewell, though if that be 'so princely an house . . . to be converted to the harbouring of so evil and miserable a sort of people', then they would pray for the grant of the Savoy.[1]

This eloquent and persuasive petition was warmly endorsed by Ridley in a letter to Cecil, while Barnes, who had succeeded Dobbs as Lord Mayor, also lent active and enthusiastic assistance.[2] But surely Ridley's beautiful plea must have been enough: 'I must be a suitor unto you in our good master, Christ's cause.' The poor of London embody the person of Christ, who, alas, had been abroad in the streets, without lodging, 'hungry, naked and cold'. Now the citizens are willing to refresh Him, to give Him meat, drink, and clothing. For this purpose there stands the great, empty house of the King called Bridewell, if only it may be gained for this holy purpose. 'I have promised my brethren, the citizens, [in this matter] to move you because I do take you for one that feareth God and would that Christ should lie no more abroad in the streets.' Hence he admonished Cecil, 'speak you in our master's cause'.[3] In April, 1553 Bridewell was formally conveyed to the City 'as a workhouse for the poor and idle persons', with the further provision that it was to be supported by rentals to the value of 700 marks p.a. from the Savoy endowments and to be furnished as well with all the beds, bedding, and other furniture remaining in the Savoy.[4] This grant was reluctantly confirmed and completed by Queen Mary, but, as we have seen, the Savoy endowments were in fact almost wholly absorbed by the pressing needs of St Thomas's Hospital, with the result that from the outset Bridewell remained a direct charge on the generosity and the tax rolls of the City. All the City Companies charged themselves with subscriptions totalling £1540 for the equipment of the house, the gift books were once more opened in every parish, and taxes were levied to maintain the work of an institution which in 1570 was spending an estimated £2000 p.a. to carry forward its share in the social rehabilitation of the London

---

[1] *Petition of citizens of London for Bridewell* (1552), in Tawney and Power, *Tudor economic documents*, II, 306–311.

[2] Ridley, Nicholas, *The works of Nicholas Ridley*, ed. by Henry Christmas (Parker Soc., Cambridge, 1841), 535. The letter may probably be dated May 29, 1552.

[3] Lansdowne MS. 3, #28, f. 56. Ridley also indicated that he had solicited the help of Sir John G ates in the matter. Ridley thought that the urging of the Lord Mayor (Sir George Barnes) was decisive, writing to him after the grant: 'And to have brought this to pass, thou obtainedst (not without great diligence and labour both of thee and thy brethren)'. (Ridley, *Works*, 411–412.)

[4] Stow, *Annales*, 609; Wriothesley, *Chronicle*, II, 83.

poor and vagrant. Harsh and inadequate as Bridewell must seem to us, it was none the less a notable landmark along the road of man's humanity to man.[1]

This, in rather sparse detail, recites a magnificent accomplishment by men who were feeling their way towards a nobler and a more humane society.[2] Working in close collaboration with a sympathetic and generous government, these men of London, imbued with a clear and intensely secular understanding of what they wanted England to be, had founded an articulated and nearly complete system of hospitals and related institutions which were to serve the social needs of London for many generations to come. It was the merchant aristocracy that took the lead, sketched out the ambitious design, and then with generosity on a quite bold and grand scale dedicated their fortunes to the building of a new and a better society. The short reign of Edward VI was troubled and it was turbulent, its foreign policy was at once weak and inept, but it was none the less an age of magnificent cultural and social experimentation and of accomplishments which with an amazing prescience sensed the thrusts and needs of the world to come. These men of the mid-sixteenth century moved out with great courage and no little wisdom as they sought to meet the needs of the society which was England.

3. THE ADVANCEMENT AND THE SECULARIZATION OF EDUCATION

The great London achievement of founding and beginning the endowment of a system for social rehabilitation could not be fully imitated in any other region of the realm; in truth it need not have been, because London was at mid-century the single truly urban complex in the whole of England. London philanthropic wealth did, however, flow out in generous and often decisive fashion to found a great variety of desperately needed social institutions across the realm, endowing almshouses, parochial assistance for the poor, or various local schemes of social rehabilitation to which local benefactors were in time to lend their own more modest aid.[3]

---

[1] Jordan, *Charities of London*, 195.

[2] We have mentioned no more than the larger gifts towards the founding of the royal hospitals. More particulars regarding gifts and bequests made to them may be found in Jordan, *Charities of London*, 186–196, and in Jordan, *Philanthropy in England*, 272–274.

[3] *Vide* Jordan, *Charities of London*, 308–318, for a full discussion of these matters. The evidence is that almost one quarter (23.55 per cent) of the whole of London's enormous charitable giving was dedicated to national needs.

But to no segment of the needs of the society was London wealth more generously or firmly dedicated than to the founding and endowing of grammar schools, first in the City itself and then in communities all over England and Wales, usually in parishes where the donor or some near relative had been born. This great philanthropic achievement in the founding of much-needed schools clearly had its substantial beginning in the decade 1511–1520, and then rose precipitously in the era of the Reformation to an early climax, well before the great outpouring of school endowments came in the late Elizabethan era and in the early Stuart period (1601–1640).[1]

There were numerous and complex forces which explain not only the motives which led benefactors to undertake the ambitious and fairly expensive responsibility for planting schools, but also the almost universal interest to be observed in many communities, often not very populous, in enlisting the aid of the crown, of a wealthy local or London donor, or, in some scores of instances, in the combined local efforts of men and women of relatively humble circumstances. These motives were complex and do not lend themselves to ordered categorization, even though we have available a considerable body of evidence, including scores of deeds of gift, in which benefactors try at least to set out their own aspirations for the school they were founding.

The spreading interest in affording a thorough education which would prepare students for entrance to the university owed much, especially in our period, to the powerful thrust of evangelical Protestantism. All the great preachers, of whom Latimer and Lever are only the most famous, lent the movement a fanatical and powerful support, in the deep conviction that an educated and reformed clergy must be provided and that the godly laity must be literate if the Word were to be read and understood. The triumph of Protestantism and the founding of the true Church, in their view, depended ultimately on literacy, with which alone the errors of Rome could be dispelled and then destroyed. Their confidence in the fruits of literacy was of course naive, but it none the less did much to achieve that remarkable, that revolutionary, gain which broadly speaking made England a literate nation in the course of about a half century.

---

[1] Throughout this discussion we shall be using the terms 'school' and 'grammar school' synonymously, though technically incorrectly. Numerous schools pretended or aspired to be grammar schools which were almost certainly not. We are reasonably sure, however, that we have not included elementary schools in our reckonings, save as there were a fair number of schools which by the founder's prescription (or local necessity) undertook to offer both types of education in the same institution.

Closely, perhaps organically, connected with this powerful sentiment was the conviction of the Henrician and Edwardian humanists
that a broad base of literacy and learning must be achieved in order
to serve the state more adequately and effectively. This conviction
was completely shared by the Protector Somerset, who had in fact
established a government, or more accurately an administration,
which drew heavily from the intellectuals in the universities. This
view quite correctly held that the needs of the state now demanded
more highly educated civil servants, that diplomacy could not be
effectively conducted without the aid of skilled and learned men,
and that a new kind of aristocracy, one founded on sophisticated
competence, must replace the old ordering of power vested in semi-
literate nobles and not wholly trustworthy clerics. This humanistic
conception of the nature and ends of education lent subtle and
powerful momentum to the movement only now begun for the
founding of a national system of free, endowed, and secular grammar
schools.

Quite as strong and doubtless even more effective amongst
those who possessed the means required for founding a school was
the deep conviction that poverty could be mastered and routed only
by literacy and the skills and flexibility of mind and abilities which
flow from it. This sentiment was fully set out in scores of deeds of
gift, and it was to become a national conviction by the close of the
sixteenth century; a sentiment which in more sophisticated form
has really animated our culture in the West to our own generation.
The founders expressed the persuasion, as did the literature of the
era, that every boy endowed with native ability and intelligence
must somehow be afforded the opportunity to master the rudiments
of knowledge. Only then would the full resources of the realm be
exploited and only then would poverty, rooted always either in
ignorance or in sheer incompetence, be subdued. Mankind possesses
few resources for dealing with incompetence; it possesses full and
effective resources for dispelling ignorance. It was the merchant
élite of London which was first wholly persuaded of this premise
and which gave so lavishly of its resources over a period of a full
century (1550–1650) in an effort to found a national system of
endowed secondary education. This conviction was tenaciously held
and surely accounts for the fact that from the Edwardian period
onwards merchant benefactors, with only a few notable exceptions,
were interested in the founding of new schools rather than in the
support of the universities.

Less noble, but surely quite as effective, was another powerful force accounting for the founding of schools across the realm. We speak of local pride and the strongly rooted desire for immortality of deed which to a degree at least animates all mankind. To put it another way, beginning about 1540, and for the reasons we have been examining, it became decidedly fashionable and meritorious to found and endow schools, just as a half century earlier it had been favourably regarded by the society when a chantry chapel was built, a monastic roof replaced, or £50 or so disposed in alms to the poor on the occasion of the funeral of a great noble or prelate. Such moods change and, as we have observed, essentially religious aspirations were rapidly giving way to secular motives and concerns. Hence from about 1540 onwards a rich and generous London merchant, putting his affairs in order and contemplating the day of his death, was likely to remember the parish of his birth, the rural kin still there, and his own struggle to gain a necessary literacy. Such men, with increasing frequency, founded grammar schools bearing their own names or linking themselves in the glory of the name of their sovereign. Hence it was that some rich foundations were unwisely made in rural areas too sparsely populated for the resources provided to be used effectively. So it was, too, that beginning with the Edwardian period the possession of a school had become a matter of intense local pride. Fruitful change was sweeping across the realm. In the Middle Ages the size of the village church, the height of its spire as measured against the church in the adjoining parish, were matters of local concern and deep pride, often evoking a local generosity that could scarcely be afforded. All this was gone by the era of Edward VI, but now the existence of a local endowed grammar school possessed quite as much symbolic meaning and perhaps served the community quite as fruitfully. At least it had happened, and the values of the new world in which men now lived were almost wholly secular in form and intent.

In concluding our brief discussion of the complex forces which together account for the surge of giving for grammar school foundations in the Edwardian period, it must once more be observed that the Chantries Act not only touched local pride and fears but likewise triggered the intervention of private giving on a very considerable scale. The government had found it necessary, in meeting highly vocal criticism of the bill, specifically to exempt a fairly wide spectrum of charitable uses to which chantry funds were on occasion dedicated,[1] and the final measure was particularly clear in its implication that schools and educational uses more generally would not

[1] *Vide ante*, 184-185.

be affected. None the less a bill was in fact introduced in the Commons on January 23, 1549, 'for making of schools and giving lands thereto', and was read there for the third time on February 9th. The measure was first read in the Lords on February 18th, where it was evidently permitted to languish in committee, probably because of further assurances given by the government that existing chantry schools were not to be touched. It was this fear of cultural loss in the realm which inspired Lever's bitter and eloquent warning to those in authority. There was danger, he said before the King, that the chantry wealth would be distributed as irresponsibly as was the monastic land. The act itself reiterated the intention to erect schools and aid the universities, yet, he maintained quite incorrectly, even now 'many grammar schools and much charitable provision for the poor be taken, sold, and made away' to the slander of the King's laws and 'the most miserable drowning of youth in ignorance'. The government dare not condone such evils, which trouble the commonwealth and pervert an act intended to advance learning into a 'most fit instrument to rob learning and to spoil the poor'.[1] The great danger, he urged, lies in powerful men who seek this wealth for their own covetous use, and 'so craftily [convey] much from the King, from learning, from poverty, and form all the commonwealth, unto their own private advantage'.[2]

Lever, Latimer, Hooper, and all the other great Protestant evangels, and most of the Commonwealth Party as well, were quite mistaken in their facts and needlessly apprehensive, though they could hardly know that the Chantry Commissioners with the support of the government were to be scrupulous in their efforts to protect and conserve all the charitable uses to which chantry wealth had been dedicated by founding deed or even by improper diversion. These Commissioners comprised the most responsible of the gentry of the several counties, men who were inclined in truth to find dedication of use where none really existed and to describe as a school to be preserved the most tenuous and erratic teaching effort of an ill-prepared and often incompetent stipendiary priest. The government was carefully following a policy springing at once from sensitivity to local pressure and its own intention to adhere strictly to the language of the law. What it could not afford to do was to draw deeply on the chantry wealth now in hand for the substantial enlargement and support of local charities, and particularly for the

---

[1] Lever, *Sermon preached the third Sunday in Lent*, in Arber, *Reprints*, no. 25, 81–82.
[2] *Ibid.* 72–73.

founding of many wholly new grammar schools. For this failure, too, it was brought under bitter attack by Lever and others, and it is from this almost abusive condemnation that the myth of the spoliation of the existing chantry schools has sprung and persisted. What happened, rather, was that on balance the chantry schools were preserved and strengthened, while private charity, suddenly aroused and now sensitive to the needs of the nation, moved in with impressive strength and sureness of purpose to begin the founding of new schools and the strengthening of old on a very large scale.

Harrison, in looking back a generation later on the achievements of the Edwardian and early Elizabethan years, could say with some accuracy as well as pride that grammar schools in *ca.* 1577 were distributed generously throughout the realm, 'so that there are not many corporate towns now under the Queen's dominion that have not one grammar school at the least', with a sufficient living for a master and usher appointed to the same.[1] Harrison was broadly correct in his statement, but what he does not say is that the tradition of private foundation had gathered its first great momentum in the Edwardian era.

We have suggested that a fair beginning had been made in the founding and support of grammar schools in the interval 1480–1540 when the total of £36,292 13s was bestowed for the purpose.[2] In the Reformation decades (1541–1560) a total of £29,399 10s was dedicated for this purpose, the *per annum* rate of giving of £604 17s in the earlier era being steeply increased to £1470 p.a. But even more significantly, giving for the founding and endowment of schools was heavily concentrated in the Edwardian years (again regarded as extending from 1547 to 1553 inclusive), when the large sum of £15,350 10s was provided, which in turn works out to £2192 19s p.a., a total not again surpassed until the decade 1571–1580—that

---

[1] Harrison, William, *An historical description of the iland of Britaine, etc.* (L., 1577; ed. by F. J. Furnivall, Bk. II (L., 1877)), 83.

[2] The particulars follow, by decades:

1480–1490	£3,894	0s
1491–1500	1,200	0s
1501–1510	4,230	0s
1511–1520	10,062	4s
1521–1530	9,526	17s
1531–1540	7,379	12s

£36,292 13s   (Jordan, *Philanthropy in England*, 373)

This total we believe to have been almost equal to the capital resources of all schools in our sampling of ten counties which were functioning in 1480.

in which Harrison wrote—when the *per annum* rate of giving for this purpose reached the average of £2264, or only slightly more than in the Edwardian era.[1]

Turning from the analysis derived from a sampling of ten counties, though the inclusion of grammar school foundations made by London wealth in all parts of the realm makes it particularly useful, we shall now essay a comparison of the school resources of the nation at large at the time of Edward's accession and at the close of 1553, a few months after his death.[2] In order to lessen confusion and to determine the impact of the pervading secular interest in education, we shall separate the chantry schools functioning, or supposed to be functioning, at both dates, before attempting a qualitative estimate of all the schools of the realm as they stood at the beginning and at the end of Edward's reign.

We reckon that there were at the moment of Edward's accession 109 chantry schools offering some measure of instruction which together possessed endowments with a capital worth of £17,554 and which were continued, sometimes after a lapse of a few years, with a settled capital of £17,178 from chantry sources. These schools, after capital additions of various sorts, possessed by 1553 an income suggesting a capital value of £18,877 6s. This represented a considerable educational gain for the realm, since the teaching function of many, indeed most, of these chantries had been wholly incidental to the prescribed duties of the priest before the expropriation, but was made complete and central by the settlements now concluded. There were as well ten chantry foundations with resources totalling £1610, certainly or at least probably functioning in 1547 as educational institutions which for various reasons were expropriated by the Commissioners and never revived. For a somewhat larger number (17) of chantry schools, either certainly or probably functioning in 1547, all modest foundations with a total capital worth of £1614 13s, the action of the Commissioners is unknown. These data might well be recapitulated in tabular form:

---

[1] It should once more be noted that these figures relate to benefactions in a sampling of ten counties, London being one, in which we believe that something like 60 per cent of the charitable wealth of the realm was provided.

[2] Our principal sources, which cannot be cited in detail within the compass of this treatment, are the Edwardian chantry returns: E 301 (121 rolls); the Henrician returns, which have been useful as a supplement; the Patent Rolls; the particulars on educational foundations as set out by Leach, A. F., *English schools at the Reformation, 1546–1548* (Westminster, 1896); the *Victoria County History*; and the detailed consideration, based principally on wills, to be found in our *Philanthropy in England, The charities of London,* and *The charities of rural England.*

% *of resources*

(1)	109	schools functioning and continued	£17,554 0s	84.48
(2)	10	schools functioning or probably functioning (and expropriated)	1,610 0s	7.75
(3)	17	schools, functioning or probably functioning (action unknown)	1,614 13s	7.77
	136	schools	£20,778 13s	

At the most, therefore, there were 136 chantry endowments supporting schools or at least some sort of instruction by stipendiary priests at the time of Edward's accession, though the more reliable and fully documented number is 109. The Commissioners were careful in their survey and, as we have noted, were inclined to save any endowment which could by any reasoning be described as a school. Further, the government was favourably disposed towards any strongly put and sustained petition for the re-founding of any former chantry school or even for the employment of chantry resources for founding new schools in such communities. Hence it is that the process of assignment and re-founding was not completed until the mid-Elizabethan era. The immediate disposition ordered by the Commissioners, when combined with subsequent actions of the government, yield the following results:

Capital value

109 chantry schools functioning and continued (plus capital additions)	£18,877 6s
14 moribund, but revived	1,621 18s
31 newly founded, or re-founded, with chantry assets	7,198 0s
154	£27,697 4s[1]

It must therefore be concluded that chantry wealth was so applied as to increase by almost exactly a third (33.30 per cent) the endowments supporting the schools, while at the least the number of functioning schools had been increased by 13.24 per cent. But the greater gains had accrued from the secularization of these institutions, from the fact that they were now wholly devoted to the tasks of education, and, most importantly, that they were now in a

---

[1] Miss Simon by a somewhat different method arrives at closely comparable figures. Her reckoning is that 165 existing schools fell under the terms of the act and that 131 were continued with royal or other help (Simon, Joan, 'A. F. Leach on the Reformation', *British Journal of Educational Studies*, IV (1955), no. 1, 47).

position, and that very rapidly, to attract capital gifts from within the community or even great bequests from native sons who had made their fortunes in London.

It should also be remarked that these 154 schools, hewn from the resources of chantry wealth, were not well distributed geographically, since the number depended wholly on the vagaries of the founders' interests and the educational zeal of the Commissioners in certain of the counties. Almost a third of the whole number were concentrated in Essex,[1] Hereford, Lancashire, and Yorkshire (with twenty-four schools), while eight counties had never had and did not now gain any schools as the result of the settlements following on the expropriation of the chantries.

Alongside—but wholly separate from—these 154 schools derived from chantry resources and secularized and greatly strengthened after the expropriation, there was a smaller but far more securely endowed group of schools which were in the main secular in their foundation and administration and which already engaged the rapidly growing interest of the crown and lay donors in the extension of educational opportunity. There were at the outset of the Edwardian period eighty-one of these schools, and they were on balance much stronger, better known, and more advanced in the curriculum offered than were their chantry school counterparts; and they were certainly much more adequately endowed. There were seventy-eight of this group with a total of £31,899 of endowments, or an average of £409 for the whole number. The remaining three—Eton, Winchester, and King's School (Canterbury)—together had very rich endowments totalling £33,547, with the result that the resources of schools which were non-chantry in structure amounted to £65,446, or almost two-and-a-half times the total assets undergirding the schools of chantry origin or to be established with former chantry resources.[2] It should also be noted that fifteen of these schools had been founded in very recent years (1540–1546), reflecting the rapidly spreading concern of both laity and crown with the needs of education. These schools reflect as well the founding of cathedral schools in certain of the bishoprics and the reorganization and reorientation of other cathedral foundations that had languished.[3]

___

[1] We are suspicious of our totals for Essex which show nine chantries declared to have possessed educational functions and hence ordered continued. The number, one suspects, reflects the educational zeal of the Mildmays, Sir William Petre, and Lord Rich, all of whom were fanatically loyal to the county.

[2] It will be remembered that Eton and Winchester were specifically exempted from the Chantries Act.   [3] See footnote on p. 232.

More significant is the fact that in the Edwardian interval £15,350 10s was given, almost wholly by donors drawn from the merchant aristocracy of London or from the gentry, for strengthening the grammar school resources of the realm, or nearly three-fourths (73·88 per cent) of the whole of the endowments dedicated to educational purposes by all the chantry foundations before the expropriation. Of this impressive total £3163 10s was designated for the further strengthening of existing grammar schools, and the remainder (£12,187) for the founding of the amazing total of thirty-seven new schools across the length and breadth of England.[1] These new, and almost wholly secular, foundations when added to the eighty-one non-chantry institutions functioning in 1547 yield a total of 118 schools, mostly well endowed, serving the educational needs of the realm. To these we may add the 154 schools, now considerably strengthened, which were of chantry origin. In all, then, it appears that the structure of secondary education in England had in the course of only seven years been immensely strengthened and broadened, principally because lay donors had determined that the youth of England were to be armed with the resources of literacy and that the control of the educational system was to be lodged in secular hands. Though these schools were not well or evenly distributed geographically, though many of them were very weak in resources, it must none the less be pointed out that there was in 1553 a school available for each 214 square miles of England and Wales and in average terms for perhaps each 11,000 of the then population. A fair beginning had been made towards providing the instrumentalities wherewith in due season England was to be made a literate nation.

These 272 schools functioning in 1553 were, as has been said, not evenly spread in relation to either population or area. It is probably fair to say that at least twenty English counties were sufficiently served with six or more schools each, while the largest

[3] 31 Henry VIII, c. 9; Frere, W. H. ,*Visitation articles and injunctions of the period of the Reformation*, II (L., 1910), 138–139; Wood, Norman, *The Reformation and English education, etc.* (L., 1931), 20–21; Simon, Joan, 'The Reformation and English education', *Past and Present*, XI (1957), 57. Old cathedral schools at Canterbury, Carlisle, Ely, Norwich, Rochester, and Worcester were to be re-founded and strengthened; at Bristol, Chester, Gloucester, Peterborough, and Westminster new schools were to be founded or languishing schools revived. It is clear that these foundations were not yet completed in 1547. We have counted the net gain in schools flowing from this legislation as six in number.

[1] The founding date for certain of these schools cannot be precisely stated. Included are Bolingbroke *c*. 1553; Thame *c*. 1552–1570; Taunton 1553–1554; and Skipton 1548–1555.

county, Yorkshire, had by this date an amazing concentration of forty schools, of which number sixteen were of quite recent foundation. But there were other counties which must have been ill-served indeed, some poor and some prosperous, some large and some small. Among these (Wales being counted as a single county) there were eight with two or fewer schools, though it should be added that half of these were greatly strengthened in resources in the course of the next half-century.[1]

The effects of the chantry expropriation on English education and

[1] Schools of chantry and non-chantry origin functioning in 1553:

Bedford	3	Lincolnshire	9
Berkshire	9	London (Middlesex)	5
Bristol	1	Norfolk	5
Buckinghamshire	6	Northamptonshire	12
Cambridge	2	Northumberland	3
Cheshire	6	Nottinghamshire	4
Cornwall	7	Oxfordshire	6
Cumberland	2	Rutland	0
Derbyshire	0	Shropshire	5
Devonshire	9	Somerset	7
Dorset	6	Staffordshire	8
Durham	2	Suffolk	4
Essex	12	Surrey	1
Gloucestershire	10	Sussex	4
Hampshire	6	Warwickshire	9
Herefordshire	12	Westmorland	3
Hertfordshire	4	Wiltshire	5
Huntingdon	1	Worcestershire	10
Kent	10	Yorkshire	40
Lancashire	18		
Leicestershire	4	Wales	2

Total 272

The proportions of this work make it improper to deal in greater detail with these schools. But in order to arrive at the conclusions it has been necessary to accumulate a large mass of material dealing with each of the schools functioning (or founded) in 1553. We hope at a later date to deal at length with these particulars. But perhaps we should at least comment on the two counties which seem to have had no schools in 1553. In Derbyshire there seems to have been a medieval school at Chesterfield, which had, however, disappeared before the chantry survey was made. It was re-established in 1598 by letters patent. Leach found thin and conjectural evidence for a medieval school in Derby, but it seems to have come to an end with the dissolution of Darley Abbey. It was re-founded just after 1553, though the arrangements were probably well advanced before the death of Edward VI. In 1554, in return for a payment of about £260 by the burgesses, former monastic and chantry lands were conveyed for founding a free school with a master and usher with £13 6s 8d p.a. of the income, the remainder to be employed for the support of the clergy in two Derby parishes.

In Rutland there had been a school connected with the chantry (Lady Chapel) in the parish church of Whitwell, which was noted in two chantry certificates (nos. 39, 98). The annual value of the chantry was £5 3s 9d. The local need was stated by the summary of the Commissioners, 'school, preachers, or poverty there relieved and maintained, other than by the chantry priest . . . none'. But for uncertain reasons, the chantry was expropriated, possibly because the then incumbent was incapable of teaching.

the powerful and now dominant consequences of private and governmental foundations may be measured, perhaps more usefully, in another fashion, namely by estimating the financial and institutional strength of the 272 schools which were certainly functioning in the realm at the close of the year of Edward's death. We have endeavoured to group these foundations, whether of chantry or non-chantry origin, according to their relative strength as of this date and over the two generations immediately following.[1]

A large proportion of the Edwardian chantry schools which were continued were weak from the beginning, even though the whole of the chantry income was applied for their support. In all, sixty-five of these foundations, or 42·21 per cent of the whole number, must be so described, and the casualty rate amongst this group was high, simply because they failed to attract local or private support. In decided contrast, only thirteen (11·02 per cent) of the non-chantry foundations were weak or failed to gain further charitable support, in the main—the inference is clear—because most of them were eccentric private foundations in villages or rural areas with too small a population base for them to function usefully. More important were the foundations originally marginal in strength which did attract later private benefactions—not a few being in time richly endowed, because they possessed inherent resources for survival. In this group we would place seventy-eight of the former chantry schools, almost exactly half of the whole number, and sixty-three of the secular foundations, or slightly more than half (53·39 per cent) of the total of these schools. This means, of course, that of all the schools derived from chantry sources about 93 per cent were from the beginning either weak or marginal in their resources. There remained, for all of England, fifty-three schools which were from the beginning strongly and securely endowed, and

---

[1] The categories which we have established are as follows: (1) *weak*, by which is meant an institution with capital of £120 or less, with no evidences of local support before 1600, including a number which disappear and several where the Commissioners' report suggests that the foundations were little more than a form of pension for the incumbent; (2) *marginal*, being institutions with resources of £120 to £180, certainly then functioning as a grammar school, some evidence of local support in the next half-century, able to pay the master at least £6 p.a.; (3) *strong*, meaning the possession of endowments of £180 or more, strong later support by the community or by London donors, established by letters patent (as twenty-three were in Edward's reign) or by Act of Parliament, and control well established in lay governors. It may here be added that in average terms a master received an annual stipend of £8 9s 6d in the Edwardian period and an usher £5 9s. In most cases, too, both the master and usher were provided with lodgings. (See Stowe, A. M., *English grammar schools in the reign of Queen Elizabeth* (N.Y., 1908), for an interesting presentation of such salaries in the next generation (1558–1603), when the average pay for the master works out to £16 11s and for ushers to a little short of £9 p.a.).

of these forty-two were of private foundation and only eleven were derived from chantry wealth. The merchants and the gentry were over the course of the next century to build a superb and a widely spread system of secondary education with their own generosity. But the future secular *Grundlagen* had already been well and securely laid, and the dominance of the role of the private benefactor well established, before the brief reign of Edward VI was done.

4. THE SECULARIZATION AND STRENGTHENING OF ALMSHOUSE FOUNDATIONS

Schools are relatively easy to count and to follow as institutions because they were in almost all cases endowed, in the very nature of their functioning have left historical records, and, at least in our period, tended to attract a steady stream of benefactions which were likely to become matters of record. Even so, as we have seen, schools, particularly of medieval origin, were prone to vanish or, more often, to lapse for long periods of time before they reappear, actually as new foundations. We do believe, however, that our data respecting the founding and endowment of sixteenth-century schools are at once reasonably accurate and relatively complete. Not so with the almshouses. There are several reasons why they are historically elusive, especially if they were of medieval origin. Many of them were never endowed and hence had no corporate history; others were maintained during the lifetime of a benefactor and then withered; a great many—perhaps most medieval foundations of this sort—were so badly administered that the bulk, or the whole, of a fixed income was consumed by the administrative outlays legally laid as a first charge against resources. To illustrate the peculiar mortality of these institutions, we may cite data from a sampling of ten counties in which fairly intensive research has been done relating to almshouses, and in this instance we believe that those counties include about half of all the almshouses in England and Wales.[1] We know that at least 262 'hospitals', usually unendowed, were established in these counties during the Middle Ages, of which it seems probable that 140–150 had at some time fulfilled functions which we—and the sixteenth century—associate with almshouses. But in 1480, so great had been the erosion of time against these fragile institutions that no more than seventy-four of

[1] Jordan, *Philanthropy in England*, 258–259.

them survived in any form, of which nearly half (thiry-five) were either derelict, irrelevant in function, or so wasted in resources that administrative and maintenance charges consumed all or nearly all of the available income. There were, then, in these ten counties only thirty-nine houses surviving in 1480 to attend to pressing social needs and to provide the foundation on which the modern world could begin to build its social resources.

In these same ten counties this process of building an important and humane system of institutionalized care for the aged and the derelict got rapidly under way in the Tudor period with the result that £28,153 15s was given for almshouse endowments in the interval 1480–1540, substantially more, it should be stressed, than the whole of chantry capital dedicated to this pious use at the time of the expropriation. The rate of giving, mostly now in capital sums, was greatly increased in the era of the Reformation (1541– 1560) when £22,432 18s was dedicated, and especially during the Edwardian interval when £9264 3s has been recorded in the ten counties for this worthy purpose, or an annual rate of giving of £1323 9s. If we may assume that these totals do, as we believe, represent about half the sum of almshouse giving for all of England, then it may be suggested that England possessed almshouse resources in 1540 of something like £56,307 10s of capital, a proportion of which was vested in conjunction with chantries. But statistics which we shall present later suggest—and abundant detailed evidence confirms—that there had been considerable attrition of these resources over the preceding sixty years, though much less pronounced than had been the case with the medieval foundations. Many of the almshouses were too small and too modestly endowed; trusteeships were almost casually settled; and too many of the houses were organically connected with chantries. But the great London merchants were now beginning to intervene with considerable generosity in the advancement of this noble work, with their carefully drawn deeds of gift, their letters patent and private acts of parliament, and the strictly secular and highly competent administration which they secured from self-perpetuating boards of governors or from the great City Companies.

As was the case with the schools, the chantry expropriation had little effect on the almshouse resources of the nation, save slightly to increase their capital and numbers. More importantly, the action taken by the Commissioners had the effect of lodging them more securely in lay hands, often in the legal charge of the town officials, and of freeing them from a named chantry endowment, thereby placing them in a position in which they might, and usually did, attract quick and generous lay support in the years to come. The Commissioners were undoubtedly scrupulous in protecting and continuing all functioning almshouses, while in about half the counties there is evidence that they were also seeking to enlarge the number by ferreting out derelict or moribund almshouse obligations which could be revived with chantry funds. The Commissioners clearly sought, so to say, to rob King Edward, not the poor.

The chantry records suggest that there were in 1547 a total of seventy-eight functioning almshouses in the realm supported by chantry funds with endowments totalling £22,399—a reasonably adequate support, granted the whole of the resources were really employed for almshouse purposes—or £287 3s of capital for each in average terms. These institutions were declared to be almshouses and were to be continued, the Commissioners assigning the slightly larger total of £23,740 of capital for their support. There were also seven moribund almshouses, directly and legally a charge on chantry endowments, for which no more than £109 in available funds could be discovered. These were all revived by the Commissioners and other chantry funds were added, with the result that the settled capital for this group was £2856. Another group of eight chantries were charged by their deeds of gift with the support of almshouses, but all these were to a degree derelict. These foundations were supported (as chantries) with capital to the worth of £1253, but were expropriated and the almshouses not revived. Another large group of fifty former chantry almshouses were hopelessly derelict and regarded as beyond the possibility of revival. Our data are all too thin for this entire group, but it seems fairly certain that twenty-four of this number had at one time been charges on chantry endowments to the value of £4109. And, finally, the Commissioners established six new almshouse foundations, employing chantry funds from their communities to the value of £1106 6s for this quite new purpose. On balance, then, we may say that chantry funds totalling £23,761 had been dedicated in part to the maintenance of almshouses, though only £22,399 of the amount was actually and fruitfully being so employed at the time of the expropriation.[1]

The actions of the Commissioners had, then, the effect of increasing modestly to £27,702 6s the total of former chantry wealth now devoted to the support of almshouses and of raising the number sustained by that capital from seventy-eight to ninety-one. Far

[1] *Vide ante*, 196,198, for the governing tables.

more important, as we have said, these institutions were now brought under direct local and secular control and were so re-organized and re-oriented that many of them at once began to attract the support of the communities which they served. A large proportion of these new foundations were to survive at least into the nineteenth century, lending more of dignity and decency to the care of the impotent and the aged. These institutions were not, of course, sensibly or conveniently arranged geographically, fourteen counties possessing no more than one (or none) of these chantry-derived almshouses, while no more than seven of the English counties seem fairly adequately served with five or more. But this defect was to a degree remedied by the founding during the early Tudor period of what we may fairly describe as secular almshouses, which was to reach a climax in the Edwardian era.

Existing alongside and complementing the chantry-derived almshouses there were at the moment of Edward's accession about eighty more securely endowed and administered almshouses, a large proportion of which had from the beginning been secular in their control, and most of which may be so designated after the monastic expropriation. These houses were also more adequately endowed than their chantry counterparts, having as we reckon it £30,817 of capital in 1547, or a really considerable average wealth of £385 4s. Further, and this must be remembered, this wealth, administrative costs aside, was wholly devoted to the succour of the hopelessly poor, whereas the primary dedication of all chantry wealth was for the saying of prayers for the repose of souls.

These secular resources for a worthy and pious purpose were dramatically enlarged during the Edwardian period by the founding of twenty-one new institutions, towards which gifts totalling £7127 were dedicated.[1] In all, therefore, there were, by 1553, 101 almshouses which may be described as secular in foundation or control, disposing a total of £37,944 of capital resources. To this may by the end of the reign be conjoined the ninety-one institutions hewn out of chantry resources by the sympathetic support of the government, the dedicated efforts of the Commissioners, and the tenacious resolution of affected communities to preserve and then to strengthen the almshouse resources of the realm. In total, the 192 endowed institutions which we believe to be functioning as alms-houses in 1553 were supported by £65,646 6s of capital funds,

---

[1] It will be recalled that the total given to almshouses in the Edwardian era was £9264 3s. Of this sum £2137 3s was for the enhancement of the resources of earlier foundations.

thiry-four of which, be it noted, had been established or reconstituted in the course of the young King's reign. It would be wrong indeed to suggest that the pressing, and increasing, need for such institutions of refuge had been adequately met by 1553. But a fair beginning had surely been made, a social course had been well charted, and the charitable resources in hand for the care of derelict men and women were now more clearly and surely dedicated to noble and humane uses. The expropriation of the chantries, then, did no injury either to schools or to almshouses; rather it assisted, as it improved, the marshalling of resources, new and old, for a great assault on the twin evils of ignorance and destitution.

VIII

THE PLANTING OF A PROTESTANT POLITY (1550–1553)

I. PRESSURE FOR CONFORMITY ON THE ROMAN CATHOLIC BISHOPS AND INTELLECTUALS

We have dealt at some length in the earlier volume of this study with the planting of the Reformation in England during Somerset's tenure of power. This interval of about three years was notable for a remarkable trial of a policy of nearly unrestrained discussion and an earnest effort to extend to the realm what was surely the first experiment in religious toleration on a national scale in a Christian nation. These years were accordingly characterized by patience with the bishops, almost half of whom were conservative in their views and Catholic in their doctrinal sympathies, though all, trained as they were in the reign of Henry VIII, lent complete support to the Act of Supremacy in all its constitutional and political implications. These bishops were free to speak and to vote in Parliament against governmental measures moving the Church closer to a Protestant profession of faith and order of worship, so long as they did not oppose the express and implied meaning of the royal supremacy. We have also seen that the lesser clergy and the laity were with few exceptions under no considerable pressure to conform, even after the passage of the act establishing the first Book of Common Prayer as the law of the land. Two notable bishops, however—the somewhat literal-minded Bonner (London) and the famous and extremely able Gardiner (Winchester)—did offer outspoken opposition to the planting of the Protestant order of worship and found themselves in immediate difficulties with the sovereign power. Bonner was tried and convicted of contumacy in the autumn of 1549, though the sentence of deprivation was not confirmed until February, 1550. Gardiner, far more subtle and dangerous, was held in prison by a direct order of the Council on charges of contumacy when Northumberland came to power, but had been to a degree protected by a friendship with Somerset which reached back many years.

Somerset's religious policy had been moderate and in all its important respects cautious. He was a devout and an undoubted Protestant in his own convictions, but had declined, with Cranmer's full agreement, to impose religion by overly rigorous courses or to move England more rapidly towards the Protestant faith than the convictions of the articulate and dominant classes of men would accept. This policy had, in fact, been brilliantly successful, for there is every reason to believe that by the time of his fall from power England was lost to Rome and that amongst the classes in which power, wealth, and deep conviction resided, the realm was now moderately Protestant. But in religion as in political and social policy, Northumberland's accession to power marked a radical shift towards harsher courses, an abandonment of the Protector's experiment of toleration and moderation, and a steady pressure towards an evangelical Protestantism for which the realm was unprepared.

We have seen that for a brief moment Northumberland, in his marshalling of overwhelming power to be employed against Somerset, had given some measure of hope, if not assurance, to the Roman Catholics. It is clear that both Bonner and Gardiner expected to be restored to favour, while Southampton for a brief season enjoyed considerable power. Many astute observers thought the Reformation was in great danger. The great Protestant evangelist, Hooper, wrote disconsolately on November 7, 1549, that 'the Papists are hoping and earnestly struggling for their kingdom' and declared that if Bonner were released to his see he (Hooper) would be 'restored to my country and my Father which is in heaven'.[1] But within a few weeks, with his power fully established, Northumberland's policy veered towards the overt support of evangelical Protestantism, from which to the end of the reign it never deviated, while the Roman Catholic bishops and their more articulate supporters amongst the clergy found themselves under a tightening repression which, however, never passed the threshold of true persecution.

The most notable by far of the conservative bishops was Gardiner, whose deepening difficulties with the government led to his imprisonment even under the Duke of Somerset.[2] One has great sympathy for this exceedingly able and earthy man who had for many years

---

[1] Robinson, *Original letters*, I, 69–70.
[2] *Vide* Jordan, *Edward VI*, 155–158, 209–214, for the earlier phases of this case.

been one of the most effective of Henry VIII's civil servants. Gardiner remained a firm believer in the royal supremacy; he asked only that the essentials of the ancient faith be taught and that religious order be maintained; and he made it clear that he would compromise on any matter save the Catholic doctrine of the mass. But in the end Gardiner, worldly and pliant as he had always been, found himself in a position in which he must take his stand on conscience alone. But this remained for the future, since, as we have suggested, Gardiner hoped for his own release, if not his restoration to power in the Council. Thus he wrote immediately to Warwick to congratulate him on having delivered the realm from the 'thraldom' imposed by Somerset and pointed out that his own imprisonment without cause was part and parcel of that thraldom.[1] Some days later he addressed his petition directly to the whole Council, pointing out that for more than a year he had lain in the Tower 'with want of air to relieve my body, want of books to relieve my mind, want of good company, the only solace of this world, and finally, want of a just cause, why I should have come hither at all'.[2] Then, as the configuration of Warwick's policy became clearer, he again grew bitter and legalistic, protesting the illegality of his own exclusion from the Parliament which had been convened in November, 1549.[3]

Gardiner gained no measure of either support or sympathy from Warwick, who feared the Bishop's brilliant intransigence. But shortly after Somerset, who had retained his personal friendship with Gardiner, was readmitted to the Council in April, a reluctant agreement was reached in that body to attempt a reconciliation with the Bishop. It was accordingly determined on June 8, 1550, to offer Gardiner his pardon on condition of his formal acceptance of the Prayer Book, a committee consisting of Somerset, Parr, Paulet, Russell, and Petre being delegated to wait on him in the Tower.[4] Gardiner, argumentative and perverse as always, took the position that he should not give a judgement while in prison, but none the less declared himself a loyal subject and stated that 'having deliberately seen the Book of Common Prayer, although I would not have made it so myself, yet I find such things in it as satisfy my conscience and therefore both I will execute it myself and also see other

---

[1] Gardiner, Stephen, *The letters of Stephen Gardiner*, ed. by J. A. Muller (N.Y. and Cambridge, 1933), 440–441.

[2] Stow, *Annales*, 600.

[3] *Ibid.* 601.

[4] *A.P.C.*, III, 43; Edward VI, *Chronicle*, 34; Harl. MS. 352, f. 99; Foxe, *Acts and monuments*, VI, 79.

my parishioners to do it'.[1] The Bishop further declared, under interrogation, that on the central question of the eucharist the Book was sound, since doctrine had not been touched but only some ceremonies removed.[2]

After this friendly interview, Gardiner seems to have been certain that his release was near at hand, for he gave a farewell dinner for the officials at the Tower and ordered his house at Southwark to be made ready. But neither the Bishop nor the committee of the Council had reckoned with Warwick's unalterable opposition to his release on the basis of the grudging and measured conformity which had been promised. It was accordingly agreed that formal articles of subscription be drafted which would remind the Bishop of his 'notorious and apparent contempt' and which would rehearse his earlier contumacy.[3] These articles added little to the substantial doctrinal declarations which Gardiner had already made. The new, and deliberately degrading, document was laid before him on July 8th by a quite different committee of the Council, composed of Warwick, Paulet, Herbert, and Petre. The Bishop at once declared that he could not subscribe to the preface, but did lend formal assent to the articles respecting faith and the church. With this Warwick was by no means content, for in his view the abject confession of guilt contained in the preface was of the utmost importance, though in still another conference with a Privy Council committee on July 12th Gardiner made it clear that this he could never do.

The impatient Warwick, now evidently determined on Gardiner's deprivation, thereupon insisted on the drafting of a new document for subscription, containing an even more degrading confession of guilt and contumacy, followed by an elaborate and searching set of twenty articles of faith, instead of the earlier six, which, as was predictable, Gardiner refused to sign. Hence on July 19th he was brought formally before the whole Council, where the articles were read to him and he was ordered to sign in full within three months under pain of sequestration to be followed by deprivation proceedings. Gardiner pointed out that certain of the articles dealt with matters prescribed by law and these he would sign and obey, while others were matters of conscience and opinion to which he

[1] Edward VI, *Chronicle*, 35–36.
[2] Foxe, *Acts and monuments*, VI, 113–115. Foxe, who used sources since lost, remains our principal authority on the case of Bishop Gardiner. At all points where Foxe may be checked by other sources, he is, save for chronological confusion on a few matters, wholly reliable.
[3] Tytler, *England*, II, 21–25: June 26, 1550. The articles were drafted by Cecil.

could not give his full assent. Accordingly, he was sent back to the Tower under orders of strait imprisonment, was immediately sequestrated, and preparations were made for his trial which began on December 15, 1550. The issue was now implacably drawn, for Gardiner had taken his final refuge in conscience and had told the Council that rather than express regret for his opposition to the changes in the rites of religion, 'I should sooner by commandment, I think, if ye would bid me, tumble myself desperately into the Thames'.[1]

A formidable commission was appointed by the Crown to hear the charges against Gardiner, including four bishops (Cranmer, Ridley, Goodrich, and Holbeach), Petre from the Council, and four eminent lawyers, one of whom was Sir James Hales. The procedure was slow and deliberate, the trial of the case requiring twenty-two sessions over a period of two months. Gardiner formally declined to acknowledge the competence of the trial body, but none the less lodged written replies under oath to the allegations laid before the commission by the more than eighty witnesses introduced by the state. The government's case was derived from Gardiner's overt opposition to the course of the Reformation in the first year of the reign and his deliberately contumacious sermon delivered on St Peter's Day in June, 1548 contrary to the express instructions of the Council,[2] it being further maintained that this contumacy had persisted. Gardiner based his defence on a long and extremely able statement, running to eighty-five articles, which reviewed the whole history of the case and laid great stress on his share in framing the structure of the Henrician Reformation.[3] Under Somerset he had laboured to stay innovations, but had addressed his advice only to the Protector and the Archbishop, and when it was evident that his counsel was to be ignored, sought to carry out his duty as a loyal subject. He flatly denied that he had been contumacious, for he had preached that the will of the magistrate might not be resisted and had himself obeyed injunctions with which he did not agree. He had given satisfaction to the Council on doctrinal matters, had accepted the Book of Common Prayer, which, he wrote, bespoke 'the truth of the very presence of Christ's most precious body and blood in the sacrament'. He had formally

---

[1] Edward VI, *Chronicle*, 39–40; Harl. MS. 352, ff. 105–108, 113, 115–117; *A.P.C.*, III, 65–66, 67–69, 70, 73–77, 78, 85–87; S.P. Dom., Edw. VI, X, 14: July 19, 1550; Foxe, *Acts and monuments*, VI, 80–85; by far the best secondary account is that by J. A. Muller, *Stephen Gardiner and the Tudor reaction* (L. and N.Y., 1926), 195–203.

[2] *Vide* Jordan, *Edward VI*, 213.

[3] Printed in full by Foxe, *Acts and monuments*, VI, 105–119.

accepted the articles of faith required of him by the Council, but when almost immediately the much longer list of articles was laid before him, he 'was loth to meddle with any more articles' and had no recourse but to petition for his trial.

The testimony introduced by the government was detailed, repetitive, and in part irrelevant to the case in hand, since the witnesses were bent on establishing Henry VIII's distrust of Gardiner and the reasons for his exclusion from the executors named by the royal will. When it was at last concluded, Gardiner filed a general exception and protested vehemently against the malice of Paget whom he had befriended in the days of Henry VIII and launched on his diplomatic career. But on the next day, despite Gardiner's appeal to the King and Council, the sentence definitive was pronounced against him as a 'person most grudging, speaking and repugning against the godly reformation of abuses in religion' as set forth in the reign of Edward VI.[1] At the same time, on Council order, Gardiner was returned to the Tower with vindictive instructions that, since he had spoken bitterly of his judges as 'heretics and sacramentarians', he was to be placed in meaner lodgings and deprived of his servants, as well as books, paper, and pen.[2] At the same time a detailed *apologia* was drafted for English ambassadors abroad, for the Council well knew of the high esteem with which Gardiner was regarded on the Continent. It was stressed that the Bishop had been fairly tried and had been permitted counsel in both the common and the civil law. But his contumacious behaviour made it impossible that he remain a bishop, for even in his trial he had 'railed upon his judges, sought to defame the whole estate of the realm, and in the whole showed himself a subject utterly given to disquiet'.[3]

All this was true, and the wonder is that the government had moved so slowly against the Bishop. All his overt offences had occurred in the early months of the reign and had been to a degree borne with by Somerset because of his personal affection for Gardiner and his own aversion to any repression of faith. Gardiner had been subject to mild imprisonment, but no move was made

[1] We have followed as our principal source the account of Foxe (*Acts and monuments*, VI, 93–266) who printed the *verbatim* record; *vide* also Inner Temple MSS., 538, #45, f. 394, for the commission of trial. Among the bishops, only Thirlby testified in effective defence of Gardiner. He stressed the Bishop's loyalty and services to the state, the forthright anti-papal views which he had steadily expressed in speech and writing, and suggested that so far as his knowledge extended the Bishop had sought to obey the injunctions and orders of the Council.

[2] *A.P.C.*, III, 213–214: Feb. 15, 1551.

[3] *Cal. S.P. For.*, *Edw. VI*, #294: Feb. 22, 1551.

under Somerset to strip him of either his revenues or his high ecclesiastical office. Northumberland, after the one slight and tentative trial of compromise, had moved swiftly and with a steady determination to deprive Gardiner and subject him to strait imprisonment. But even he was restrained from the terrible course which may well have crossed his mind. Gardiner remained in prison, protected one may believe by the moderation which Somerset had planted in English religious life, only to emerge at Mary's accession to the exercise of that fullness of power which he had always craved. But even in that grim and baleful reign Gardiner, as best he could, offered some measure of moderation.

Bishop Bonner, as we have seen, had at an earlier date been imprisoned and then deprived for his much stiffer and more aggressive contumacy, though the sentence of deprivation had not been promulgated by Somerset. There was evidence of increasingly harsh treatment of the Bishop shortly after Northumberland came to power. Thus his bed in the Marshalsea was removed on his refusal to pay a fee of £10 to the knight marshal and he was reduced to lying on straw in his room, with nothing more than a coverlet.[1] Bonner shortly afterwards lodged an appeal with the Council against the still unpronounced sentence of deprivation, the King appointing a committee of eight Council members, four common lawyers and four civilians, to review the findings. After 'long and mature debating' it was determined not to entertain the Bishop's petition and the King instructed the reviewing body thereupon to declare the sentence of deprivation.[2] There was, indeed, sufficient cause for the action, not only because of Bonner's intransigent opposition to the religious policy of the state but because it was of the utmost importance that a reforming bishop replace him in the most populous and sensitive diocese in the realm. Shortly afterwards Ridley was translated from Rochester to London.[3]

Far more difficult—and inexcusable—was the case of Nicholas Heath, Bishop of Worcester since 1544 and 'a most wise and learned man of great policy and of as great integrity'.[4] Heath had been one of a committee of twelve who drafted the new Ordinal of 1550,[5] which on its completion, however, he refused to sign. On March 4, 1550, he was committed to the Fleet for his offence, though he explained to the Council that as with earlier innovations in the

---

[1] *Grey Friars Chronicle*, 65: Jan. 8, 1550.
[2] *A.P.C.*, III, 385–386: Feb. 7, 1550.
[3] *Vide post*, 271 ff.
[4] VCH, *Worcester*, II, 45.   [5] *Vide post*, 293 ff.

service of the church he would obey and administer the Ordinal within his diocese. The sticking-point for him was that the new Ordinal defined the function of the clergy as a mediating rather than as a sacrificing priesthood and that it went too far in stripping the clergy of the miraculous authority and competence with which they were endowed in the ancient service.[1] The Council proceeded cautiously and probably with considerable reluctance against Heath, for he was not brought to judgement until September, 1551 when the King formally appointed a commission of trial.[2] The generally respected Bishop appeared once more before the Council where he expressed thanks for his gentle treatment in the Fleet but would not compromise his doubts regarding the Ordinal, though he would not disobey it. He explained again that this had been his position in other matters as well, such as the taking down of altars in his diocese when legally ordered to do so.[3] When warned that refusal to compromise would surely mean deprivation, Heath expressed himself as content. The order was issued for the commission to proceed, the King a few days later chiding the Chancellor for the long delay in the proceedings against Heath, to which was now conjoined the case of Bishop Day.[4] The cases were thereupon speedily carried forward, both bishops being deprived and their temporalities ordered taken into the King's hands.[5]

The case of George Day, thus disposed with that of his brother of Worcester, had a somewhat different history. Bishop of Chichester since 1543, Day had served on the committee which drafted the first Book of Common Prayer, whose acceptance he none the less opposed in Parliament. At the same time he seems to have preached against the doctrine of transubstantiation in a sermon at Westminster in April, 1550,[6] though it was known that in his cathedral church he had refused to remove the stone altars, the slabs of two of which are still preserved at Chichester.[7] Day was before the Council later in 1550 on charges of improper preaching, which he categorically denied, though he remained intransigently opposed to the taking down of altars as now legally prescribed.[8] The Council, determined to bring the matter to a decision, in late November

[1] *A.P.C.*, II, 403, 405; Burnet, *Reformation*, II, 251.
[2] Edward VI, *Chronicle*, 82–83; S.P. Dom., Edw. VI, XIII, 49.
[3] *A.P.C.*, III, 361: Sept. 22, 1551.
[4] *Ibid.* 369: Sept. 27, 1551; S.P. Dom., Edw. VI, XIII, 55: Oct. 1, 1551.
[5] *A.P.C.*, III, 396; Edward VI, *Chronicle*, 86; *Grey Friars Chronicle*, 71.
[6] Edward VI, *Chronicle*, 23.
[7] VCH, *Sussex*, III, 112.
[8] *A.P.C.*, III, 154: Nov. 8, 1550.

required him to remove all remaining altars in his diocese and to explain in sermons in Chichester and the market-towns the reasons for so doing. When summoned before the Council a few days later, Day refused to yield, pleading his own conscience and mustering his defences from the Scriptures and the Fathers. The Council, evidently moving with reluctance and great caution, ordered him to take advice from Cranmer and other bishops before appearing again. On three later occasions the Council sought to secure Day's conformity in the matter of the altars but found him absolutely unyielding, for 'he would never obey to do this thing' which his conscience could not bear.[1] Bishop Day was thereupon committed to the Fleet and, after a considerable delay, deprived, simultaneously with Nicholas Heath. The Council had moved reluctantly and patiently with Day, and as late as June, 1552 he was all but offered his pardon if he would conform in this one particular. But Day, like Bonner, Gardiner and Heath, had been driven to a sticking-point of principle on which he simply could not yield. He wrote to Cecil that he had not refused to change the form of the altar, for whether it were of wood or of stone was a wholly indifferent matter. But when he was ordered to remove all altars and to substitute tables, 'implying in itself (as I take it) a plain abolishment of the altar (both the name and the thing) from the use and ministration of the Holy Communion', he had no other recourse than to follow the dictates of his conscience.[2]

These are the four cases in which conservative and heretofore compliant bishops found themselves driven back step by step by the aggressive and mounting thrust of evangelical Protestantism to the point where they found they must stand on conscience. Among the conservative bishops were also Rugg of Norwich, whose resignation from his see was occasioned by financial irregularities rather than by matters of faith, and Veysey of Exeter, who was far too old to exercise his spiritual office and who was persuaded to resign after his cupidity had been satisfied. There remains the exceptional case of Cuthbert Tunstall of Durham, also very old, whose imprisonment in 1551 and deprivation a year later flowed from the personal animus of Northumberland and from political and administrative decisions rather than from matters relating to faith.[3] This is not a great number and it must be remembered that those in power moved with care and a considerable measure of humanity as these

[1] *A.P.C.* III, 168–173 *passim.*
[2] Lansdowne MS. 2, #53, f. 121.
[3] *Vide post,* 381–386, for our discussion of the Tunstall case.

intransigent opponents of the Protestant settlement of religion were removed from the high spiritual estates with which they were vested. Never, it is prudent to say, has a major transformation of faith in any nation been accomplished with less of suffering and violence among the important and conspicuous defenders of the orthodoxy being disowned. And, be it remembered, there was no blood shed.

All the bishops who had been imprisoned and then deprived had learned their theology late in their careers—at the moment of personal crisis and decision. Of all of them only Gardiner could be called a scholar, for these men, as servants of Henry VIII, had in their training and activities in the full tide of their careers been administrators, lawyers, and diplomatists. It was the tragedy of the Catholic faith in England in the Edwardian period that it possessed no scholars or teachers of the first rank, for Protestantism had long since captured the loyalty and imagination of the intellectuals of the realm. We have observed that under Somerset not more than about twenty of the Catholic intellectuals, in the university or lower clergy, were deprived of their posts, briefly imprisoned, or fled abroad to await a turn of fortune.[1] Among all these men only Richard Smith possessed the potential capability of speaking boldly and with persuasive learning in defence of the ancient faith, but he was faulted in character and was himself confused. These men had fled the realm or had been deprived under the Duke of Somerset. There were but few more of sufficient prominence or ability to engage the harsher attention of the government of the Duke of Northumberland.

One of these who found himself in considerable difficulty was William Seth, who had served Bonner in a secretarial capacity until the irascible bishop had beaten him with his staff. Seth was examined in March, 1551 on charges of having imported a large number of Smith's polemical works together with books and letters from Ralph Baynes, then in exile in Paris. Seth, by his own admission, had been in Paris where he was in close touch with both Smith and Baynes and had constituted the principal link of Bonner and Day with the exilic group in France. Seth revealed the whole story in detail, confessing that he feared torture, and pleaded successfully for mercy from the Council.[2] At about the same time William Chedsey, a fellow of Corpus Christi College, Oxford, who had disputed with the reformers at Oxford and who had served Bonner as a

---

[1] Jordan, *Edward VI*, 130, 219–224.
[2] HMC, *Salisbury MSS.*, I, 83–85.

chaplain, was haled before the Council for seditious preaching and Romanist views. These charges he in part denied, though they were sustained before the Council by the testimony of several reputable witnesses. Chedsey was consigned to the Marshalsea for several months, being then released to the custody of the Bishop of Ely and surviving to enjoy rich preferments under Queen Mary.[1] So too Owen Oglethorpe, since 1535 president of Magdalen College, Oxford, where he was properly regarded as a pillar of the orthodox party, was examined in 1551 on charges of Roman Catholic sympathies. Always resilient and skilful, Oglethorpe denied that he had preached or taught openly anything contrary to the faith by law ordained. He confessed as well that he regarded the Church as now established as near the primitive church and lent it full support save for reservations and uncertainty regarding the eucharist.[2] In the year following, Oglethorpe, under continuous pressure, was forced to resign his presidency, to which he was reappointed by Queen Mary.

2. PRESSURE ON THE LESSER CLERGY AND THE CONSERVATIVE LAITY

If there was little harassment of the intellectuals amongst the conservative clergy, there was no consistent or sustained effort under Northumberland—nor had there been under the Protector—to force the faith of the lower clergy of the realm. We have found not more than twenty cases in which the clergy discovered themselves in difficulties with the Council—almost all of them under suspicion of seditious utterances. As we have earlier noted, the English parochial clergy, in large part intellectually inert, found no problem in conscience in accepting the established services and had neither the wish nor the opportunity for martyrdom. The policy of moderation and patience towards the parish clergy flowed too from Cranmer's own conviction that change must come only gradually and moderately. Burnet is wholly correct when he tells us that the Archbishop 'considered that men who had grown old in some errors could not easily lay them down, and so were by degrees to be worn out of them'.[3] A random mention of a few of the cases when members of the lower clergy found themselves in serious trouble will suffice. In February, 1550 George Rowe was called before the Council on charges of singing the mass twice at Sudeley during the

---

[1] *A.P.C.*, III, 237, 412: Mar. 16 and Nov. 11, 1551.
[2] Burnet, *Reformation*, V, 312.   [3] *Ibid.* II, 281.

Christmas season, but after being held in London for a short while was released under bond of £40 and his promise to obey the laws.[1] So too the vicar of Sopley (Hampshire) found himself in the Marshalsea in 1551, where none was to 'speak with him' but by order of the Council,[2] while towards the end of the reign there was considerable excitement in London when a Benedictine monk and a suspected Jesuit were under investigation.[3]

One must search in even more fugitive sources for evidences of reasoned and articulate lay opposition to the course of the Reformation in England. Since we know that change had come slowly, almost insensibly, over much of the realm amongst clergy and laity alike, and that the religious sentiments in many rural areas remained stolidly conservative, it is on first thought amazing that there are so few manifestations of articulate Roman Catholic views springing from the laity. The evidence is clear that in the great Western Rising of 1549 there was very strong religious sentiment, which under clerical guidance supplied the principal animating force for the insurrection. Yet even there the surviving literary evidences are few indeed and the formal demands of the rebels seem to reflect rural clerical sentiment rather than to disclose lay thought.[4] The fact is, of course, that conservative religious thought in England was largely inert, inarticulate, and ill-defined. It is also important to observe that the process of religious change in England had been very cautious and moderate, and that the government, particularly under the Protector, forswore the use of repressive measures to secure uniformity. We sometimes forget that while the Act of Uniformity established the first Book of Common Prayer as the only legal service of worship in the realm, it laid only moderate penalties against the clergy refusing to use it and ordered no penalties whatsoever on laymen absenting themselves from the authorized service. These tolerant courses had the effect of confusing, or rather blunting, the whole issue and of permitting the slow accretion of strength and loyalty which was in time to make of England a Protestant nation. This policy, which Queen Elizabeth was to exploit with such masterly skill, had its genesis and initial success in the brief tenure of power of the Duke of Somerset. And this policy Northumberland, wrathful and impatient as he was in his governance of England, continued.

[1] *A.P.C.*, II, 401, 413: Feb. 25 and Mar. 18, 1550.
[2] VCH, *Hants*, V, 132.
[3] S.P. Dom., Edw. VI, XVIII, 20: May 7, 1553.
[4] Jordan, *Edward VI*, 456–459.

Though the difficulties of the vicar of Tathwell in Lincolnshire were not fully set out, it seems probable that he was being vexed by an articulate and Romanist parishioner, 'a busy naughty man', who was declared to be irreformable. The intervention of the Privy Council was requested, an earlier local attempt to still the brawling having failed.[1] There were complaints, also addressed to the Council, that numerous London Catholics were in the summer of 1549 hearing mass at Christchurch where services were conducted for the French embassy, resulting in the first of several desultory efforts to prohibit the attendance of English subjects.[2] It also appears that as late as the autumn of 1550 the communion service at St Paul's, probably in former private chapels, was so conducted as to seem 'a very mass'.[3] Complaints were also lodged against Henry Moore, a former abbot of St Mary de Grace (London) and since 1544 the priest at Stepney, for 'causing the bells to be rung when they were at the sermon, and some times begin to sing in the choir before the sermons were half done, and some times challenged the preacher in the pulpit, for he was a strong, stout popish prelate, whom the godly men of the parish were weary of'. This case was carried to Cranmer, who characteristically declined to do more than administer a gentle rebuke to a priest of undoubted Romanist sympathies.[4]

Though the particulars are hazy, it seems quite certain that public sentiment in the conservative town of Carlisle ran strongly against a married clergyman there, George Greames, for two efforts by the Council were required to secure the restoration of his property and his office as master of choristers.[5] So too, it seems that conservative sentiment in Winchester was supported by John White, since 1541 warden of Winchester College, who confessed that he had been importing and distributing books and letters which opposed the 'King's proceedings' in religion.[6] In the midst of the crisis occasioned by the Princess Mary's insistence on maintaining her private chapel, the Council resolved to punish men of high station for having over a period of months attended these services as devout, though wholly trustworthy, Roman Catholics. They committed to the Fleet for a few weeks, as an example to others, Sir

---

[1] HMC, *Salisbury MSS.*, I, 80–81: Aug. 22, 1550.
[2] *Grey Friars Chronicle*, 61: July 28–29, 1549.
[3] *A.P.C.*, III, 138: Oct. 11, 1550.
[4] Nichols, *Narratives of the Reformation*, 157.
[5] *A.P.C.*, III, 192–193, 278: Jan. 15 and May 20, 1551.
[6] Strype, *Cranmer*, I, 334. White was imprisoned for a short season. He was appointed Bishop of Winchester by Queen Mary in 1556.

Anthony Browne, Sir Richard Morgan, and Sir Clement Smith, all of whom, having made their submission, were released without incurring further penalty.[1] This was, indeed, the singular case of the sharp punishment of known conservatives in religion, who in all other respects were completely loyal. It was evidently precipitated by the festering and still unresolved problem of Mary's own intransigence and the determination to eliminate the Catholic influence surrounding her. There were many such men among the gentry of the realm, whose status remained unimpaired and who were subjected to no official pressure whatsoever.[2]

More interesting are the occasional evidences that survive of the efforts of deeply persuaded and often only semi-literate rural clergy to maintain the traditional services and doctrines. In most dioceses it is clear that the bishops dealt gently with such cases, if indeed they knew in detail what was taught and permitted in the more remote parishes of their sees. But a truly reforming bishop like Hooper at Gloucester could by carefully conducted visitations find much which he could not brook. Thus the incumbent at Bledington was found faulty in doctrine and commanded to cease his superstitious practices,[3] while the rector of Condicote, who also held Batsford, was enjoined to give up his Romish practices and to preach more frequently at Condicote.[4] In this same year (1551) the clergyman at Bourton-on-the-Hill was required to abandon his popish superstitions, and then, ironically enough, found himself deprived by Queen Mary as a married priest.[5] Similarly, the rector of Todenham was censured for his Romanism in 1551 and was deprived, for uncertain causes, three years later.[6]

Much, then, was borne with, much winked at, by a government which was proceeding with the tasks of reformation with extreme care and with a moderation born at once of policy and of political uncertainty. More difficult to control and to counter were the numerous Catholic libels, often scandalous and frequently incendiary,

[1] Edward VI, *Chronicle*, 56; *A.P.C.*, III, 239, 270: Mar. 19 and May 4, 1551. Browne was the son of the Henrician favourite of the same name and was later created Viscount Montague. Morgan, later a Chief Justice of the Common Pleas, was serjeant-at-law. Smith was an uncle by marriage to the King, having married Dorothy Seymour.

[2] One further exception may be mentioned. Sir Francis Englefield was also briefly imprisoned for having heard mass in Mary's chapel. But he remained Sheriff of Berkshire, held posts in the royal household, and was absolutely trusted (VCH, *Berks*, III, 407; *DNB*).

[3] HMC, *Var. Coll.*, VII, 57.

[4] *Ibid.* 54, 57.

[5] VCH, *Gloucestershire*, VI, 205.

[6] *Ibid.* 257.

which were posted or circulated, particularly in London. One such was set on the pulpit of a prominent London church, possibly St Paul's, which declared:

> This pulpit was not here set,
> For knaves to prate in and rail.
> But if no man may them let,
> Mischief will come of them, no fail.

God has given the reformers time in which to babble and tell their lies, but their fall is near:

> Two of the knaves already we had,
> The third is coming as I understand,
> In all the earth there is none so bad,
> I pray God soon rid them out of this land.[1]

Considerably more sophisticated, and enjoying a wider circulation, was the 'Ballad of Little John Nobody', which protested the whole course of the Reformation and the grave discussion of questions of divinity by persons more fit 'to milk kine at a flake'. Every man has his own views and interprets 'the glorious gospel ghostly' as his sect would have it. None the less, bribery, whoredom, and the repression of the poor are rife in England, ignored by those who prate of the Gospel. The author submitted that

> Prayer with them is but prating: therefore they it forbear,
> But alms deeds and holiness they hate it in their thought,
> Therefore pray we to that Prince, that with his blood us bought,
> That he will mend that is amiss. For many a man full freak
> Is sorry for these sects, though they say little or nought.[2]

This libel provoked a furious rejoinder from some unknown Protestant stalwart, who with more of vigour than of metrical gifts declared:

> The pulpits are now replenished with them that preach the truth,
> And popish traitors, banished, which seemed to you great ruth,
> But if you and the friars were clean out of this land,
> This realm to the last years, full firm and sure should stand.

---

[1] Strype, *Cranmer*, II, 874–875. The libel is undated, but the context suggests a time shortly after Somerset's first fall.
[2] Harl. MS. 372, #16, f. 114. The libel is undated.

Just as in the last year (1549) the traitorous Papists were found in the field with weapons in hand, now they seek to sow treason with 'traitorous bills and railing words'. The writer warned them that:

> Some of their carcasses standeth on the gates
> And their heads most fitly on London Bridge

and, 'if ye be found, the same way must ye tridge [trudge]'.[1]

To conclude this sampling of deeply held conservative convictions, posted on churches and passed in the streets in hastily printed libels, we should mention one of high quality, indeed imbued with a haunting beauty. It was addressed to 'Sweet Jesus, with thy mother mild' and regretted the passing of the time when

> ... we have one faith
> And all trod right one ancient path.
> The time is now that each man may
> See new religions coined each day.

Once in England the shepherd safely led the sheep, but now 'each sheep will preach', while the clergy content themselves with their wives and finery.

And even worse,

> The time hath been men did believe
> God's sacraments God's grace did give
> The time is now men say they are
> Uncertain signs and tokens bare.
>
> The time hath been to fast and pray
> And do alms deeds was thought the way.
> The time is now they say indeed
> Such stuff with God hath little need.[2]

So it was that men of deep convictions, and sometimes of deep perception as well, sought in lay language and with lay sentiments to express their sorrow and fear when they sensed that a religious revolution was in progress in England. The thrust and the power lay with the forces of that revolution, and simple men, the inarticulate, and the old-fashioned could do little more than express their apprehension in this semi-literate but poignant form.

[1] Strype, *Cranmer*, II, 875–876.
[2] Add. MS. 5832, ff. 208b–209. The libel is undated.

3. THE CASE OF MARY TUDOR: THE LATER PHASE
(1550–1553)

One is almost tempted to say that as much must be said for Mary Tudor, the appointed heir to the throne. Living in comparative isolation, surrounded by a household of servants rather than advisers, driven by instinct as well as circumstance to make the imperial ambassador her closest confidant, stubbornly and fanatically devoted to the ancient faith, Mary was in process of time to become almost wholly detached from the English scene and was completely to misunderstand the nature of the forces which, to her horror, were making of England a Protestant nation. Mary's loneliness and her almost hysterical Catholicism were understood by Somerset who had lent her kindly treatment and whose Duchess was evidently on intimate terms with this strange daughter of Henry VIII. During the Protector's tenure of power, as we have seen, no suspicion of political conspiracy or, for that matter, even of political interest on Mary's part was to be found, while Somerset was quite willing to extend to her the precious privilege of freedom of worship in her own household, where she might 'do as she pleases quietly and without scandal'.[1]

The Princess Mary had been informed of the plot being raised by Warwick against the Protector in September, 1549, when at least tentative approaches were made seeking her sympathy, if not her direct support. Her own views on the *coup d'état* are unknown, but she had stood completely clear of any involvement, as Charles V had forcefully advised her to do. The wisdom of this course became almost immediately apparent as Warwick violently disowned or destroyed the Catholic support he had gained for his great conspiracy. It became quickly evident that he intended to link his government and policy with evangelical Protestantism. As early as mid-January (1550) Mary was fearful for her religious privileges and for her personal safety, confiding to the imperial envoy that 'Warwick is the most unstable man in England' and that the successful conspiracy against the Protector 'had envy and ambition as its only motives'.[2] These mounting apprehensions were forcefully conveyed to the Emperor by Van der Delft, who at the end of March was

---

[1] Jordan, *Edward VI*, 206–209. And see *ante* 135–138 for the diplomatic aspects of the 'Marian problem' for the period now under consideration. We shall deal briefly with the narrative of Mary's relations with Northumberland's government, since Miss Prescott (*Mary Tudor*, N.Y., 1953) has provided an extended account, to which we owe much.
[2] *Cal. S.P. Span.*, X, 6.

instructed to express to the King and Council in the strongest terms Charles's determination to lend his protection to Mary in the exercise of her faith.[1] The Emperor pressed, indeed, for assurances in this all-important matter under formal letters patent. This demand was rejected in London in sharp language,[2] though Hoby, then at Charles's court, was advised by the Council that Mary had been privately urged 'to hear mass only in her closet', and not to keep in her chapel what amounted to a public church for all her household and her neighbours.[3]

Mary sensed the hostility and the ruthlessness of Warwick, and her courage broke as she found herself frontally facing his resolution. She accordingly asked the Emperor to help her secure refuge abroad, either by assisting in bringing to a conclusion a long-discussed marriage with Don Luiz, brother to the King of Portugal, or by spiriting her out of the country. Charles was aghast at these now frantic requests, realizing that the English government would be implacably opposed to any plan for sanctuary on the Continent and that an attempt to flee would almost certainly be detected. But both Mary and Van der Delft were now convinced that her personal safety was in danger. When the staid and cautious diplomatist pointed out that to flee would almost surely mean the renunciation of the throne and any further possibility of restoring Catholicism, Mary appears to have become hysterical and to have persuaded him of her desperation. These views he set before the Emperor who, himself now deeply exercised, reluctantly agreed to a bizarre scheme under which Van der Delft would be recalled, leaving England by a ship which would take the Princess on board off Maldon from a small craft rowed out from the Essex inlet.[4]

Van der Delft was recalled on May 13, 1550, but the whole elaborate plan collapsed when fears of a spring rising in Essex resulted in local watches being set, one of which was near Mary's house.[5] The now deeply engaged Van der Delft thereupon proposed another plan under which he and his secretary (Jehan Dubois) should coast up the Blackwater to Maldon with a load of grain, fetching Mary out to a Spanish naval vessel which would be cruising off the coast. Van der Delft retired before the scheme, grudgingly approved by the Emperor, could be carried forward. Dubois,

---

[1] *Cal. S.P. Span.*, X, 56–57: Mar. 31, 1550.
[2] Edward VI, *Chronicle*, 25–26: Apr. 10, 1550.
[3] Harl. MS. 523, #2, f. 6: Apr. 21, 1550.
[4] *Cal. S.P. Span.*, X, 47, 94–96; Prescott, *Mary Tudor*, 153–157.
[5] *Ibid. Intro.*, xiv.

having arrived off Harwich on June 30th, was then able to establish contact with Mary's household, only to have the scheme collapse when Sir Robert Rochester, Mary's comptroller, raised objections which should surely have been considered at the outset of this rash undertaking. Mary appears to have been completely confused and uncertain, Dubois holding his 'grain' vessel in readiness for hours at great personal hazard, until Rochester—one wonders how truthfully—reported that the Spanish warship lying off the coast had been sighted and that a local coastal alarm had been sounded.[1] It was agreed that it would be utterly reckless to carry forward a plan which, had it been executed at once after Dubois's arrival, would probably have been successful, with incalculable consequences for the history of England. Though the strictest secrecy had been maintained, information regarding the mad venture leaked out, first as a rumour that Mary was already in Flanders. Immediate steps were taken to prevent such an undertaking during the remainder of the reign, though the Council observed all the amenities by never mentioning the matter to Scheyfve, Van der Delft's successor in London.[2]

For a time, indeed, there was a relief of tension as it became evident that the Emperor was not minded to create a diplomatic crisis if matters were left to drift, though a stricter concern was shown as the always restless Mary shifted her places of residence as dictated by whim or plague.[3] At the same time, the Council made it clear that it was bound by no commitment of religious immunity to the Princess. Mary, as had been her custom, attended court during the Christmas season, only to be humiliated and outraged when the King upbraided her because of the reports that she still habitually heard mass in her chapel. The censorious remarks were made in the presence of a company, whereupon Mary burst into tears, which Paulet sought to placate by confirming that what could be construed as pledges of immunity had in fact been given by Edward who assured her that he intended no harm.[4] It seems evident that at this time it was the King's own stubborn resolution to force Mary to comply that was increasing the pressure from a somewhat hesitant Council. In his own hand Edward had written to her: 'Truly, sister, I will not say more and worse things, because my duty would compel me to use harsher and angrier words. But this I will say

---

[1] *Cal. S.P. Span.*, X, 124–135.
[2] *Ibid.* 146, 156; Prescott, *Mary Tudor*, 168–171.
[3] S.P. Dom., Edw. VI, XI, 12: Nov. 23, 1550?
[4] *Cal. S.P. Span.*, X, 410–411; Edward VI, *Chronicle*, 50.

with certain intention, that I will see my laws strictly obeyed, and those who break them shall be watched and denounced.'[1] The King further explained that her private worship was in no sense assured, being no more than a toleration inspired by the expectation that she would come to obey his laws, 'seeing the love and indulgence we displayed towards you'.[2]

This typically Tudor ukase was opposed and denied by Mary as flatly as she, and her imperial advisers, dared. She insisted, in a letter to the King, that her freedom of worship was ensured by both King and Council and that these assurances had been reported to the Emperor who demanded that they be made formal by letters patent. Further, at Christmas Edward himself had told her that she had nothing to fear. Hence, though she professed obedience to the King, she found it 'not suitable that he should be robbed of freedom by laws and statutes on spiritual matters passed during his minority' and would therefore urge him to make no further changes in religion. As for herself, she could do nothing more than follow the dictates of her conscience.[3]

Meanwhile, the Emperor was following the mounting controversy with personal interest and a sense of outrage. Scheyfve transmitted his blunt demand that the promises, which he declared had been made by Paget and others, that Mary should be permitted to enjoy the mass 'and other rites of religion' as left by Henry VIII, be respected,[4] while the Council explained to its ambassadors abroad that no more than a revocable and private assurance of indulgence had been granted.[5] The festering crisis was brought to a head when on March 15th Mary reluctantly came to court again, accompanied by fifty knights and gentlemen preceding her and eighty gentlemen and ladies in her train, every one, we are told, bearing beads in plain view.[6] The imperial ambassador related to his master that no one in court did Mary the customary courtesy of coming out to meet her, though the 'people ran five or six miles out of town and were marvellously overjoyed to see her, showing clearly how much they love her'.[7]

[1] Cal. S.P. Span., X, 202–212.   [2] Ibid. 209: Jan. 28, 1551.
[3] Ibid. 205–209.   [4] A.P.C., III, 215: Feb. 16, 1551.
[5] Cal. S.P. For., Edw. VI, #294: Feb. 22, 1551. The precise matter in dispute was the Emperor's contention that in June 1549 Paget had told him that the laws regarding religion were now to be enforced on all in the realm, save for the Princess Mary. This Paget categorically denied under oath. The Council's contention was evidently technically correct, that no more than informal assurances had at any time been given to the Princess (Harl. MS. 353, f. 130, for Morison's recapitulation of the controversy).
[6] Machyn, Diary, 4–5: Mar. 15, 1551.
[7] Cal. S.P. Span., X, 264: Apr. 9, 1551; Prescott, Mary Tudor, 178.

Mary, 'after salutations', was almost immediately called alone before the King and Council, where 'was declared how long I had suffered her mass . . . in hope of her reconciliation and how now, being no hope, which I perceived by her letters, except I saw some short amendment, I could not bear it'. The courageous, but tearful, Mary flatly stated that she would not yield her faith, nor would she dissemble her religious views. To this the King rejoined that he had no wish to constrain her faith, but that as a subject she must obey the laws of the realm lest her example 'breed too much inconvenience'.[1] Mary's categorical refusal to yield her worship had evidently been prepared on the Emperor's instruction, for on the next day the King recorded that Scheyfve had called with a short message threatening a declaration of war 'if I would not suffer his cousin the Princess to use her mass'. To this imperial communication, the King significantly added, 'no answer [was] given at this time'.[2]

This threat was taken seriously by the Council, which was especially concerned because the alliance with France was not yet complete and because it fully realized that England dared not risk even a limited war with the Emperor. Though the records of the Council reflect no discussion of the issue, it seems certain that the question was referred to Cranmer, Ridley, and Ponet, who advised that 'to give licence to sin was sin: to suffer and wink at it for a time might be borne'.[3] Morison, in a later account of this surely painful meeting, held that it was now Northumberland who urged that Mary's worship be tolerated, for he 'had such a head that he seldom went about any thing, but he conceived first three or four purposes before hand'.[4] We are further told by Morison that in the debate the King remained stubbornly opposed to any yielding of principle, until Cranmer and Ridley persuaded him that there were abundant scriptural examples of sovereigns who yielded, at least for a season, because of considerations of policy.[5]

There can be no doubt that Edward was persuaded only most reluctantly to abandon a position which he held in principle but which Northumberland and most of his colleagues had assumed as a matter of policy. But Edward, Tudor that he was, was on reflection

[1] Edward VI, *Chronicle*, 55: Mar. 18, 1551.
[2] *Ibid.* 56; *Cal. S.P. Span.*, X, 251–261, for Scheyfve's account of his audience and the later negotiations.
[3] *Ibid.* 56; Egerton MS. 2877, ff. 14b–15.
[4] Harl. MS. 353, f. 130.
[5] Egerton MS. 2877, ff. 14b–15, which records that the King was in tears when he was finally persuaded to yield.

not unmoved by policy as well, the moral grounds having been laid out by the two prelates he trusted most. By April 23rd the King had adopted the view that war with the Emperor would bring ruin to the woollen industry, would find England unprepared, and might put the realm in jeopardy because of Roman Catholic sympathy for Mary. Hence it was agreed that Wotton should be dispatched to the Emperor to explain more fully the Council's position with respect to Mary's worship and to gain time.[1] Meanwhile no cause for war was to be given the Emperor by the proscription of Mary's worship, while at the same time the laws respecting religion were to be enforced against her household.

The Council was extremely cautious in its efforts to break the stalemate with Mary, waiting in fact until August, 1551, when it was evident that France was about to wage war on the Emperor, before making any overt move in its policy of harassment. On August 14th the principal officers of Mary's entourage were summoned to appear before the Privy Council,[2] and were commanded to see to it that no illegal services were held in Mary's household and to convey these instructions to the Princess.[3] With great reluctance, these officers informed Mary of the Council's order on August 16th. Mary immediately forbade them to speak with her chaplains or household and required them to return to London with a personal letter to the King. In this letter Mary used every artifice of persuasion. She had assumed that her brother would allow her the mass which their father had had and freedom in that faith 'wherein also I have been brought up from my youth, and thereunto my conscience doth not only bind me' but which was ensured by the promise made to the Emperor. So gentle had the King always been with her in private that she could not believe the letter signed by him was really drafted by him, but rather by those who wish 'those things to take place' which are agreeable to their private purposes.[4] Mary's household officers were again before the Council on August 23rd when they declined to issue orders to the household, including the chaplains, to cease the singing of the mass in the Princess's establishment.[5] Accordingly, the Council appointed a commission

[1] Edward VI, *Chronicle*, 56, 57.
[2] They were Sir Robert Rochester, Sir Francis Englefield, and Sir Edward Waldegrave.
[3] *A.P.C.*, III, 329, 330, 333; Edward VI, *Chronicle*, 76; HMC, *Twelfth rpt.*, App. I: *Cowper MSS.*, I, 1–2. There were 23 members present at this meeting of the Council, of whom 19 seem to have signed the order. Somerset was present but, significantly, did not sign. [4] *A.P.C.*, III, 338–339.
[5] *Ibid.* 341; Edward VI, *Chronicle*, 78. They were shortly sent to the Tower for a brief imprisonment for contempt.

consisting of Lord Rich, Petre, and Wingfield to wait upon Mary with a letter from the King deploring her obstinacy and instructing her respecting the order to be observed in her household.

It was a bruised and unhappy committee which on August 29th reported on its meeting with Mary on the preceding day. She had knelt while taking the King's letter, and would kiss it, 'not for the matter contained . . . for the matter (said she) I take to proceed not from His Majesty, but from you of the Council'. Then, upon reading the letter, she exclaimed, 'Ah, good master Cecil took much pains here', and asked Rich to be as brief as possible in making his statement for the Council. When informed of the commands they were to issue to her chaplains and household, Mary declared that she would hear no other service than that left by her father, though when the King came of age and maturity of judgement he would find her conformable to his laws. Her chaplains might do as they would, but if they read the new service she would leave her own house. She once more claimed that her faith had been guaranteed to the Emperor and then imperiously rebuked the Council for not lending more of favour to her for her father's sake, 'who made the most part of you almost of nothing'.[1] And at the Council's suggestion that Rochester be replaced by another comptroller to ensure the functioning of her household, she lost her temper completely, exclaiming 'I am sickly, and yet I will not die willingly, but will do the best I can to preserve my life; but if I shall chance to die I will protest openly that you of the Council be the causes of my death'. Then, after the visitors had enjoined her chaplains and household and were beating their retreat, the now hysterical Mary leaned out her window to demand the return of Rochester (on August 24th committed to the Tower), for since his leaving 'I take the account myself of my expenses, and learn how many loaves of bread be made of a bushel of wheat, and iwis my father and my mother never brought me up with baking and brewing'.[2]

The indignities which Mary suffered during the weeks of crisis in the summer of 1551 are inexplicable in view of the fact that, as we have seen, the Council had determined not to press her in matters

[1] This point Mary also made in a letter to an unidentified member of the Council, probably at about the same date. She was grieved that those her father 'made in this world of nothing in respect of that they be come to now' and in whom he had imposed his trust, now break his will and usurp power to themselves against God's law. Though the Council may have forgotten her father, she had not and she intended 'to remain an obedient child to his laws as he left them' until her brother had reached the age of discretion (Lansdowne MS. 1236, #17, f. 28).

[2] *A.P.C.*, III, 348–352: Aug. 29, 1551; S.P. Dom., Edw. VI, XIII, 35, 36, for the full report of Rich and his colleagues; Edward VI, *Chronicle*, 76, 78.

of faith so far that the Emperor would as a matter of personal honour be obliged to intervene. It is as if the Council, thwarted and weak in its foreign policy, were resolved to move strongly and somewhat sadistically against Mary as a person. It is also probable that the Council, under Northumberland's dominance, acted with such conspicuous vigour because Somerset had urged moderate courses in dealing with her and had with considerable vehemence opposed the French entente which gave to England some freedom of action. The principal, and tragic, consequence of the steady badgering of the Princess Mary, whose principal English advisers were in the Tower, was to drive her to complete dependence on the counsels of the imperial ambassador and to self-identification with imperial policy. During these months the Council was, so to speak, settling the guide-lines for Marian policy against the day of her succession.

The imperial ambassador lodged a strong protest with the King and Council in early September (1551), quite improperly demanding that Mary's household officers be released and that her freedom of the mass be assured. The answer was returned that the King had done nothing save to enforce his own laws and evaded the direct demands by explaining that Wotton was to go to the Emperor to discuss the whole range of problems between the two powers.[1] A few days later the crisis was relieved for England by the outbreak of war between France and the Empire.

But the fact was that by her courage and intransigence Mary had won at least a tolerable position for herself and her faith. During the remainder of the reign, though the services of her religion were not held for her household, she enjoyed the comfort of the mass in her private quarters. A working compromise was thus discreetly arranged, while her household was restored by the release of Rochester, Englefield, and Waldegrave in the spring of 1552 'for the better recovery of their health' and without restrictions of movement or bonds.[2] So too, better personal relations with the King were restored when Mary made a brief visit to him in June, entering London on June 11th, and then on the 13th proceeding to the Court at Greenwich.[3] The Council also now treated her with more of gentleness and magnanimity, eliciting a friendly letter from the

---

[1] Edward VI, *Chronicle*, 80; for Scheyfve's report to the Emperor on these conversations, *vide Cal. S.P. Span.*, X, 356–364: Sept. 12, 1551.

[2] *A.P.C.*, III, 508: Mar. 18, 1552; *ibid.* IV, 20: Apr. 14, 1552.

[3] Machyn, *Diary*, 20–21. It is interesting that Edward makes no mention of this short visit in the *Chronicle*.

Princess in which she asked that thanks be given the King for helping her with the cost of reparations on certain of her properties, and also for keeping her informed on developments in foreign policy.[1] The clear evidence of the King's serious illness further lifted the pressure on the Princess and somewhat relieved the isolation in which she had lived, at least until Northumberland began to mire himself in treason. Mary paid her last visit to Edward in early February, 1553, being received, we are told, with more honour and pageantry than on any earlier visit. Lord William Howard and Lord Warwick, Northumberland's son, with a hundred horse in their train, rode out of town to meet Mary and her train of two hundred. But there was grim foreboding in the fact that the King, suffering from chills and a high fever, was so ill that he could not receive her until the 10th when Mary and Edward held their last conversation. We know nothing regarding their discourse, save for Scheyfve's probably correct report that Edward treated his sister with kindness, that he entertained her with small talk, and that religion went unmentioned.[2]

There is pathos as well as an implacable concentration on great issues in this unhappy recital of the relations of Edward's government with the heir to the throne of England. The Reformation was not fully or securely settled in the realm and it was clear from the outset that Mary, should she succeed, would at any cost attempt a complete reversal of religious policy. This was fully understood by the Council, itself overwhelmingly Protestant or politique in persuasion. The Council's religious policy was hardened and then became strongly and somewhat vehemently Protestant as the King's personal religious views took full form and as he began to intervene directly and decisively in the attempted coercion of Mary Tudor and to lend his support to the now strong and superbly led evangelical movement within the body of English Protestantism. Mary was the single—and stubborn—impediment to all that the King wished for his realm in matters of faith. It can hence scarcely be wondered that he and his Council employed every artifice of graduated pressure to break her will and to compel her to conform. But Edward's span of life was too short, with the consequence that on his death the realm was delivered up to the zealous and possibly mad determination of a lonely and embittered woman to restore by quick and dreadful means a faith which the nation would not accept on the sovereign's terms.

[1] S.P. Dom., Edw. VI, XV, 65: Dec. 4, 1552.
[2] *Cal. S.P. Span.*, XI, 8-9: Feb. 17, 1553; Machyn, *Diary*, 30-31.

4. MEASURES FOR THE REFORM OF WORSHIP

In our discussion of religious policy in the period of Northumberland's primacy we have thus far been concerned with the measure of restraint laid upon the exercise of the Roman Catholic faith in the realm. More important in securing the planting and the ultimate triumph of Protestantism were the courses followed in the reformation of faith and worship. Dudley's policy in religion was at the beginning not fully understood since, in order to accomplish the ruin of Somerset, he had formed a momentary coalition with conservative nobles and former Councillors which he quickly and ruthlessly dissolved once he had gained power. His favour and power, it quickly became clear, were to be disposed in the support of evangelical Protestantism, and the progress of the reformed faith was to be assisted, and hurried, in every possible way.

The first certain indication of Northumberland's personal policy was to be found in a proclamation, dated December 25, 1549, which was in form addressed to the bishops and which preceded legislation to be introduced in Parliament just a few days later. The proclamation pointed out that the Book of Common Prayer had been authorized by act of Parliament and so stood, though evil persons had since the Protector's arrest 'noised and bruited abroad that they should have again their old Latin service, their conjured bread and water', and similar superstitious ceremonies, as if the 'setting forth of the said book had been the only act of the said Duke'. The King considered the Book to be his own act and the act of the whole state in Parliament assembled, and to be grounded upon Holy Scripture. Hence, to remove the possibility of further superstition in worship, he now ordered the bishops to require the parish clergy of the realm to deliver to them all books of service after the former Uses of Sarum, Lincoln, York, Bangor, Hereford, or for any private use, and so to deface them that they might not be used again.[1]

This proclamation was issued under the sufficient powers granted by the Act of Supremacy while the third session of Edward's first Parliament was in session. But then, possibly to give it more solemn sanction, it was confirmed by a bill introduced in the Commons on January 2, 1550, as an 'act for the abolishing and putting away of divers books and images'. Save for a less eloquent and revealing

---

[1] Hughes and Larkin, *Tudor proclamations*, I, 485; Cardwell, Edward, *Documentary annals of the reformed Church of England, etc.* (2 vols., Oxford, 1844), I, 85–87; Dugmore, C. W., *The mass and the English reformers* (L., 1958), 142; Foxe, *Acts and monuments*, VI, 3–4.

preamble, the act, concluded on January 25th, added little to the content of the proclamation, excepting that conjoined with it was a flat instruction to destroy all images heretofore removed or still remaining in all churches or chapels. The act also imposed fines for those failing to deliver up old service books, though exempting the English and Latin primers of Henry VIII provided all invocations or prayers to the saints were carefully blotted out. So far as we know the measure met no opposition in the House of Commons, though in the Lords five of the peers (Derby, Morley, Stourton, Windsor, and Wharton) voted against it, as did six of the conservative bishops (Tunstall, Aldrich, Thirlby, Heath, Day, and Sampson).[1]

Of greater religious significance, and also hurried by governmental pressure, was the authorization of a new form of ordination of clergy, with all its doctrinal and ceremonial significance, particularly in the consecration of the upper clergy. An enabling act, in effect approving the service in advance of the text, was driven through Parliament in the final weeks of the session. The statute simply provided that a commission of six bishops and six other men 'of this realm learned in God's law' be constituted by the King to frame a form of consecration for bishops and priests, which, when completed, the King should set forth by proclamation.[2] In the final vote on this measure on February 1st nine of the bishops lent their support, while five of the conservatives voted in the negative as they had on an earlier reading of the bill.

The reasons for this haste are not wholly clear nor is the composition of the commission, appointed a few days after the passage of the act, certainly known. We do know that Cranmer and Ridley had in hand a draft of the *Ordinal*, which was laid before the commission and approved, with Heath dissenting, and that Heath was brought before the Council and imprisoned because 'he would not assent to the book made by the rest of the bishops and clergy appointed'.[3] Cranmer had given the matter close personal attention during the summer of 1549, probably with the assistance of Bucer, then his house guest, whose *De ordinatione legitima* may have been prepared for the Archbishop's use. The *Ordinal* as approved

[1] *Statutes of the realm*, IV, i, 110–111: 3 and 4 Edward VI, c. 10; Wilkins, David, *Concilia* (4 vols., L., 1737), IV, 37; Add. MSS., 5151, f. 298, for a draft of the measure.

[2] *Statutes of the realm*, IV, i, 112: 3 and 4 Edward VI, c. 12; Edward VI, *Chronicle*, 19.

[3] *Vide ante*, 246–247. Messenger suggests, quite tentatively, that the bishops may have been Cranmer, Ridley, Holbeach, Goodrich, Heath, and Skip. Robertson and Redman, who were almost certainly members, in the role of 'other learned divines', were Roman Catholic in sympathy. (Messenger, E. C., *The Reformation, the mass and the priesthood, etc.* (2 vols., L. [1936–1937]), I, 450–451.)

follows closely Bucer's rendering of the Lutheran rite, but with numerous simplifications. The ritual retained the laying on of hands and the prayer of consecration, but omitted these important words when the priest received the eucharistic vessels, symbolic of his sacrificial capacity: 'Receive power to offer sacrifice to God and celebrate the mass for the living and the dead.' In the consecration of bishops, around which such hot controversy was soon to swirl, the swearing of obedience to the Oath of Supremacy 'by God, all saints, and the holy Evangelists' was retained, while after the Gospel and Credo, 'the elected Bishop having upon him a surplice and a cope' was to be presented by two bishops, in the same garb.[1]

The new *Ordinal* had evoked at least formal opposition from the conservative bishops and clergy, but the bitter and sustained criticism was to come from John Hooper and the evangelical party of which he was the spiritual leader, now warmly supported by Northumberland. Full of courage and anger Hooper brought the *Ordinal* under scathing attack in his Lenten sermon before the Court in February, 1550. He denounced the oath by the saints as popish and was aghast 'that he that will be admitted to the ministry of God's Word or His sacraments must come in white vestments', which he declared to be unknown in Holy Scripture. Nor could scriptural authority be found for the popish requirement that the candidate must hold the bread and chalice in one hand and the book in the other.[2] Writing shortly afterwards to Bullinger, Hooper expressed his discouragement at the progress of the Reformation and at the survival of the accretions of popery, particularly in the *Ordinal*, to which he was utterly opposed and regarding which he had already been haled before the Council and admonished.[3] Thus the groundwork had been laid for the violent controversy which broke out, and which could not be quieted, when Hooper was himself appointed to a bishopric.[4] The clear and widening fracture in the body of the Anglican communion—to persist for generations—was already exhibiting its divisive presence.

No such division in Protestant thought and aspirations is apparent in the decision in November, 1550 to continue a systmatic dean fairly thorough effort to remove the altars in cathedral and parish

---

[1] *The form and manner of making Archbishops, etc.* (STC #16462, [L.], 1549), *Pref.*, iii; Bucer, *De ordinatione*, in his *Scripta anglicana, etc.* (Basel, 1577), 238–259; Add. MSS., 8849, for a slightly variant text; Powicke, F. M., *The Reformation in England* (L., 1941), 93.

[2] Hooper, *Early writings*, 479; Ridley, Jasper, *Thomas Cranmer* (Oxford, 1962), 309.

[3] Robinson, *Original letters*, I, 81.

[4] *Vide post*, 293 ff.

churches, with all of their silent reminders of the mass and the sacrifice, and to substitute the communion board in the ritual of worship prescribed by the Book of Common Prayer. We have already observed that altars had been removed from many churches well before Somerset's fall from power, though in most instances this dramatic and deeply symbolic step had not been taken unless there was pressure from within the parish itself.[1] As early as the autumn of 1548 the not always accurate ab Ulmis reported to Bullinger that altars were being removed in 'a great part of England' by the common consent 'of the higher classes'.[2] Hooper expressed his own satisfaction in March, 1550 when he wrote to Bullinger that many altars had been over-turned in London since his return to England, while in his famous Lenten sermons he had exhorted the magistrate to turn the remaining popish altars into communion tables, since as long as the altar remains, 'both the ignorant people, and the ignorant and evil-persuaded priest, will dream always of [the] sacrifice'.[3]

But these piece-meal measures contented neither the Council nor Cranmer and Ridley, who wished to proceed to a general effort to replace altars, especially in the thousands of country parishes where few indeed had been removed by local initiative. Bucer was consulted, probably by Ridley, and moderately suggested that though he could find no scriptural injunction for the destruction of altars, the table was more consonant with our Lord's own example. Even more important to him was the fact that the use of a table for communion clearly separated the administration of the Lord's Supper from the popish rite and so ordered it that the people could both see and hear. Consequently, it was his advice that the reform be carried out, as well as others, such as the care of the clergy, the support of education, and the sustenance of the poor, which he delicately suggested were of far greater import.[4]

Accordingly, the Council, over the signatures of Cranmer and Goodrich (as Lord Chancellor), addressed letters to the bishops commanding that all altars be removed and replaced by tables in order to avoid further contention and strife in the realm. The letter claimed that most altars in England had in fact already been overthrown, but stressed that the Council wished all simple men to be

[1] Jordan, *Edward VI*, 182–187.
[2] Robinson, *Original letters*, II, 384.
[3] *Ibid.* I, 79: Mar. 27, 1550; Hooper, *Early writings*, 488.
[4] Gorham, G. C., *Gleanings of a few scattered ears, during the ...Reformation in England, etc.* (L., 1857), 209–212, citing Parker MSS., Camb. C.C.C. MS. 113, f. 41. Bucer's letter was addressed either to Parker or, more probably, to Ridley.

relieved of confusion and misapprehension. The use of an altar 'is to make sacrifice upon it; the use of a table is to serve for men to eat upon'. Hence 'a table [was] to be set up in some convenient part of the chancel' for the ministration of communion, while the reasons for the change were to be set forward 'by some discreet preachers' before the altar was removed.[1] It was to this order that Bishop Day found himself so deeply opposed in conscience that he declined to enforce it in his diocese, for which he was shortly deprived.[2]

Stringent and clear as was the order for the overthrow of altars, the means, and perhaps the will, for strict enforcement were simply not at hand, and abundant evidence might be adduced to suggest how slowly and erratically it was given effect, particularly in conservative rural parishes. In London, under Ridley's stern leadership, the remaining altars were removed and the communion rites as prescribed by the Prayer Book carefully observed. At St Paul's grates were set and veils drawn around the high altar, while at Easter the communion table was employed when Dean May led the service.[3] All altars still standing in London were now removed, save at St Nicholas Willows, though in various parishes in the City and elsewhere in the realm they 'had been pulled down long afore'.[4] But the pace of reform was slower in conservative and rural parishes, for one of which the particulars may be cited. The large parish of Prescot (Lancs), with the living in the gift of King's College, Cambridge, was within the relatively new see of Chester, administered by John Bird, a politique and a minor Henrician diplomatist who managed to avoid all controversy and to neglect his diocese almost completely. The vicar, Robert Brassey, was cautiously Romanist in sympathy, while the conservative Earl of Derby, who had voted against the Prayer Book, lived nearby and exercised considerable direct influence in parochial matters. The churchwardens' accounts reveal almost no change in the services or the traditional furnishings of the church until 1547–1548 when unspecified brass and pewter objects, together with two candlesticks, were sold for £2. Nor do the outlays for 1549–1550 suggest significant changes in the worship of this church. The accounts for the more critical years 1550–1552, however, begin to reflect a grudging yielding to the service by law provided and now enforced with a harsher vigour. A *Prayer Book* was at last purchased, the altar was taken down and safely

---

[1] Cardwell, *Documentary annals*, I, 101; Messenger, *Reformation*, I, 508–509.
[2] *Vide ante*, 247–248.
[3] *Grey Friars Chronicle*, 68, 69; Stow, *Annales*, 604.
[4] *Two London chronicles*, 22.

stored, and a communion table was purchased, while it seems likely that two more prayer books were acquired for parochial use.[1] Thus slowly and by an almost imperceptible erosion was the worship and, doubtless even more slowly, the belief, of a conservative, a remote, and a somewhat insulated rural parish changed. And so it must have been in the thousands of rural parishes all over England.

5. BISHOP RIDLEY'S ADMINISTRATION OF ROCHESTER AND LONDON (1547–1553)

Much of the vigour and planning of the reform measures carried into effect in the Church of England in the years 1549–1551 must be credited to Nicholas Ridley, Bishop first of Rochester and then of London. Ridley was a thoughtful and moderate man, closely linked with Cranmer by ties of long personal friendship, and may be regarded in terms of his theology and his conception of the Church as squarely and immovably in the centrist tradition of the Church of England. About a decade younger than Cranmer, he had known him intimately in their Cambridge days and in 1537 became the Archbishop's chaplain.[2] Ridley's spiritual development, like Cranmer's, was slow and the drift of his thinking towards Protestantism was gradual and in some respects very cautious. None the less, as early as 1540 he had grave doubts regarding many of the ceremonies of the traditional worship and confessed that he could find no support in Scripture for auricular confession. In the same year he was chosen master of his Cambridge College and was appointed a royal chaplain, which suggests that his theological position was still regarded as conservative. We do know, however, from Cranmer's testimony in 1555 that it was Ridley who converted him to the doctrine of the spiritual presence, probably in 1546. This notwithstanding, it had been Henry's intention in the last year of his life to elevate him to the bishopric of Rochester, though the consecration was delayed until some months after Edward's accession. During the early months of the Protectorship Ridley

[1] Bailey, F. A., 'The churchwardens' accounts of Prescot, 1523–1607', in *Transactions of the historic society of Lancashire and Cheshire*, XCII (Liverpool, 1941), 133–194, and XCV (Liverpool, 1943), 1–30. *Vide post*, 388 ff, for a wider range of comment on church-wardens' accounts suggesting change in the service of various churches.

[2] Our brief biographical account rests principally on the admirable life of Ridley by J. G. Ridley (*Nicholas Ridley, etc.* (L., 1957), 35–119), and on the still valuable biographical sketch, written by Sidney Lee, in the *DNB*.

shared with Cranmer a deep abhorrence of the libellous attacks being levelled on the mass, particularly in London, and preached strongly against what he regarded as rapidly spreading Zwinglian views in an important sermon at Paul's Cross in late 1547. Even in his replies to Cranmer's private interrogations regarding the bishops' views of the mass (January ?, 1548), Ridley was far more cautious and conservative than the Archbishop himself.[1] There is, indeed, persuasive evidence that in the course of the year 1548 Cranmer's theological views far outran those of the Bishop of Rochester, who was in part at least deterred by his fear of the highly articulate and rapidly spreading Protestant extremism in London and other urban centres. Ridley was one of a commission appointed to deal with radical sectarianism, while in his own diocese he was proving himself an excellent administrator, a superb preacher, and a stalwart defender of the rites laid down by the Book of Common Prayer.

The decision to translate Ridley to London, the great see then including as well Essex with its centres of stoutly planted Protestant radicalism, was made simultaneously with Bonner's summary deprivation, though because of the appeal lodged by Bonner with the King, which was treated with meticulous legal care, Ridley was not installed until April, 1550, about two months after his appointment.[2] He at once began planning a particularly thorough visitation of his great diocese to see to it that the rites as prescribed by the Book of Common Prayer and the series of sternly Protestant measures of reform ordered by the Privy Council were in fact being carried forward. His policy should have quieted any fear held by Hooper, who in a sermon at court in early 1550 called for a general removal of altars and expressed the hope that Ridley would take the lead in London as he had in Rochester, 'if only his new dignity do not change his conduct'.[3]

In this visitation, which was particularly significant because it gave a considerable degree of stability to religious services and rites in a region where they had been as fluid as they were chaotic, Ridley proceeded with the aid of deputies in Essex; but in London he visited every parish in person, calling the incumbent, the curates,

---

[1] Jordan, *Edward VI*, 312.
[2] The date of his installation is in fact uncertain. The King sets the date as Apr. 3rd (*Chronicle*, 23); Rymer's rendering of the text of the translation states the date as April 11 (*Foedera*, XIV, 222-227); while the *Grey Friars Chronicle* (p. 66) gives Apr. 12th as the date of his installation.
[3] Robinson, *Original letters*, I, 79; Wriothesley, *Chronicle*, II, 38; Burnet, *Reformation*, II, 274-275.

and six leading parishioners before him with the flat injunction that the clergy strictly obey the prescriptions of law or face deprivation. Then towards the conclusion of the visitation all the clergy were summoned to St Paul's where the Bishop again presented his injunctions and required written subscription within four days.

The *Articles and Injunctions* on the basis of which Ridley proceeded were printed, receiving a wide circulation, and deserve some comment since they sketch out fully the state of moderate reformed thought in mid-1550 and specify the symbols of reform which both the Council and a highly respected and powerful bishop believed must be accepted by the clergy. The *Articles* enquired into the morals and general state of the clergy, with detailed questions to determine whether those licensed to preach did so regularly and effectively. Ridley also wished to be satisfied that his clergy vigorously denounced the papacy and its pretensions, while strictly ordering questions to make certain that the services required by the Prayer Book were so carried forward. He enquired, as well, whether there was in any parish knowledge of interludes, plays, or songs, which depraved the Prayer Book, or whether there were parishioners who sought to persuade or compel the clergy to use services not legally ordained. He wished also to be certain that every minister possessed both a Latin and an English New Testament, as well as Erasmus' *Paraphrases*. There were carefully devised questions also enquiring whether there were Anabaptists in any of the parishes, separating themselves from the prescribed service, or intransigent Catholics who received the mass in private houses, as well as whether there remained in any of the churches prohibited paraphernalia of the Roman worship.

Conjoined with the *Articles* were Ridley's carefully phrased *Injunctions*, which he clearly intended to govern worship in every parish in his diocese. The priest must follow the order set out by the Prayer Book in the whole ritual of worship, and most particularly in the administration of the eucharist. Hence no clergyman was permitted to imitate the mass by kissing the 'Lord's board', waving his hands or fingers, shifting the Book from place to place, licking the chalice, setting any light on the communion table, or elevating the sacrament in any manner. Since it was known that altars were still employed in some churches, 'an honest table decently covered' was forthwith to be provided and remaining altars immediately taken down. So explicit was this injunction and so painstaking its enforcement that at the close of the year no altar remained in the great diocese. Ridley also ordered that the *Homilies* be regularly read without omissions, that the churchwardens prohibit all trading, gaming, or unseemly conduct in churches and churchyards during services, and that no clergyman, under pain, maintain or advance such superstitious practices as purgatory, invocation of the saints, or the use of palms, holy bread, or creeping to the cross.[1]

These carefully framed and strict injunctions went far towards ordering divine services in London as laid down by the Prayer Book and in closing the chinks of evasion. The immediate intention was to prohibit further simulation of the mass and to complete the overthrow of altars, necessary, at least as a symbol, for Roman Catholic worship. Ridley drove hard, sometimes impetuously, on the reforming task he had set for himself, and by late 1550 divine services as said throughout his diocese were indubitably, though moderately, Protestant. The Romanist pamphleteers, in and out of England, attacked him bitterly for violation of canon law and even of the Act of Uniformity establishing the Prayer Book, but the stalwart and deeply committed Bishop explained to the Council that, though the first Book of Common Prayer used the words *altar* and *table* interchangeably, the altar had inextricable associations with the mass and that the mass could be held only at an altar.[2]

In his visitation articles Ridley had also laid considerable stress on the duty of those properly licensed to preach to proceed with their indispensable task of exhortation and instruction. Early in the reign restraints had been imposed on complete freedom of preaching because of disorders and violent contentions aroused by the discussion of controversial doctrinal matters, and particularly regarding the as yet unsettled question of the mass. All preachers thereafter were obliged to secure a licence from the Archbishop, who in late 1549 was requiring a subscription to articles of faith which set out a Zwinglian view of the eucharist acceptable even to Hooper.[3] Observers in the period, and especially Bucer and Martyr, were in agreement that the progress of the Reformation in the realm was delayed and to a degree thwarted by the inertness of the clergy and the sheer incapacity of most of them to preach at all. Hence the number of preachers was increased as rapidly as possible by licences

[1] *Articles and injunctions* (L., 1550; STC #10247), no pagin.; Frere, *Visitation articles*, II, 230-240, 241-245.
[2] Ridley, *Works*, 321-324.
[3] Robinson, *Original letters*, I, 71-72, 76; Jordan, *Edward VI*, 187-189.

which were in fact issued by the primate, the bishops, or the Privy Council itself.[1] The specially licensed preachers were through the whole course of the reign extremely effective in advancing the Reformation,[2] though it is doubtful that more than about one hundred were ever so designated by a cautious government fearful at once of intemperate zeal and Romanist opposition. Ridley regarded Latimer, Lever, Bradford, and Knox as the greatest and most effective of the preachers of his time, conspicuously omitting Hooper, surely the most powerful, with whom he had frontally collided.[3]

In the first regnal year Ridley himself, with Ferrar, had moved across the realm as preacher in the train of the royal visitors. In the dark days of the insurrections Coverdale had preached in the West, Hooper in London, Kent, and Essex, and Parker in Norwich. Parker, Edmund Grindal, and Cardmaker were all actively engaged in preaching in Ridley's diocese, while the Bishop was himself a most effective and stimulating preacher. Then there were Robert Horne, created Dean of Durham in 1551, and the saintly John Bradford who preached with great effectiveness and enduring results in numerous places in Lancashire and Cheshire.

So successful had been the evangelistic work of these dedicated and often brilliant men that in December, 1551 further support was accorded it by the appointment of six chaplains to the King, of whom two would at any given time be at court, while their four colleagues would be on circuit in more backward regions of the realm where the Reformation was not yet well rooted—in Wales, Lancashire, Derbyshire, the Scottish Marches, Devonshire, and Hampshire, as well as Norfolk, Suffolk, Essex, Kent, and Sussex in which there were pockets of radical sectarianism. Four of the designated preachers—William Bill, later Dean of Westminster, John Harley, later Bishop of Hereford, Andrew Perne, later Dean of Ely, and Grindal, later Archbishop of Canterbury—were appointed, though the patents for their salaries of £40 p.a. each were not issued until March, 1552. The two remaining special chaplains, Estcourt

---

[1] *A.P.C.*, III, 137: Oct. 7, 1550, licensing Cox, the King's tutor, to repair into Sussex where he was to bring the people to good doctrine; S.P. Dom., Edw. VI, Docquet: June 4, 1552, licensing Bishop Scory to preach himself and to license (or forbid) others to preach in the diocese of Chichester; VCH, *Hants*, V, 277, for the licensing of Hugh Goodacre, vicar of Shalfleet, Hants, by the Lord Protector on the application of the Princess Elizabeth. Goodacre was in 1552 created Primate of Ireland.

[2] Dixon, R. W., *History of the Church of England, etc.* (6 vols., L., 1878–1902), III, 324.

[3] Ridley, *Works*, 59.

and John Bradford, it seems almost certain, were never formally appointed, their names being scored out in the *Chronicle*.[1]

6. THE THRUST OF EVANGELICAL PROTESTANTISM

It seems clear that the driving force by which Protestantism was well and ineradicably established in this short reign resided in a group of something like one hundred licensed preachers (and preaching bishops), almost all of whom were moved by an intense missionary fervour and who were in their doctrinal and ecclesiastical views far more evangelical and harshly Protestant than were the Archbishop and his colleagues. These were resolute and deeply inspired men who not only planted English Protestantism securely but who also were visibly and rapidly moving it in the direction of Zurich rather than Wittenberg. About twenty of these preachers had long been strongly Protestant and had in the reactionary Henrician days found refuge and spiritual sustenance abroad. All of them seem to have been at least for a season in attendance at the universities—and a fair number were formidably learned—and all of them lay under the urgent call to see God's Word truly and widely preached. Standing in the most decided contrast to the overwhelming number of English clergy who were as mute as they were unlettered, these evangelists restored the dignity, the prestige, and the immense power of a preaching clergy with effective and dramatic consequences for the history of English Protestantism. The initiative, the thrust, and the sense of historical direction were vested squarely in these men, and their mission was largely accomplished before the dreadful destruction wrought on them by Mary Tudor. Mary's slaughter, in fact, forever confirmed and validated their ministry, for from her fires great men were to emerge as martyrs.

Among these preachers, some of whom have already been briefly noted, an elite group of about thirty may be regarded as immensely powerful and effective, and of these at least ten were among the greatest preachers England has ever known. We should comment in some detail on the ministry of at least a few of these men whose thought and whose preaching were to lay firmly the foundations of English Protestantism in this reign. In so doing our concern will be with the practical effect of their preaching in moving the realm

---

[1] Edward VI, *Chronicle*, 101: Dec. 18, 1551; Strype, *Memorials*, II, i, 521–522, 524–545; Strype, John, *The history of the life . . . of Edmund Grindal, etc.* (Oxford, 1821), 8–10; Dixon, *Church of England*, III, 326. There was also at least an intention to appoint Knox.

towards evangelical Protestantism, leaving to a later consideration their doctrinal evolution[1] as well as the amazingly radical social and economic thought which characterized the sentiments of almost all these great preachers.[2]

The highly skilled and perceptive Venetian ambassador, Daniel Barbaro, in his formal report to his government in May, 1551, thought there was still much religious disaffection and Romanism in the provinces, but sensed that as a consequence of constant evangelical preaching and propaganda all groups in England were agreed on a 'destestation of the Pope'. Further, he felt certain that Protestantism was making rapid strides under the leadership of steady and skilful preachers, hastened and fortified by the many Protestant refugees who had found their place in the English society.[3] So far had this movement towards Protestantism proceeded, that Giacomo Soranzo, Barbaro's successor, writing a full year after Mary Tudor's accession, judged that the majority of the population were opposed to the restoration of the Roman Catholic service, though he hoped that loyalty to the Queen would dampen opposition.[4] John Coke, writing in c. 1550, also spoke with great pride of the learning and effectiveness of the evangelical clergy, noting too the remarkable phenomenon of 'divers gentle women in England which be not only well studied in holy Scriptures, but also in the Greek and Latin tongues'.[5] To the list of these women which Coke had provided, Hooper added with reverent pride the Princess Elizabeth, who 'not only knows what the true religion is, but has acquired such proficiency in Greek and Latin, that she is able to defend it by the most just arguments and the most happy talent'.[6]

This work of reformation and conversion was carried on in all parts of the realm, though it is clear that only in London and the southern and south-eastern counties had the balance of articulate sentiment swung heavily towards Protestantism by late 1550. Among those who laboured in the distant and still heavily Catholic reaches of the realm, we should mention, in addition to Bradford's mission in Lancashire,[7] the achievements of Bernard Gilpin, a saintly and dedicated preacher whose spiritual charge was at Houghton in Northumberland. Once a year Gilpin made a circuit of

[1] *Vide post*, 278 ff.
[2] *Vide post*, 290–292, *et vide* Jordan, *Edward VI*, 334–335, 396, 416–418.
[3] *Cal. S.P. Ven.*, V, 345–349.   [4] *Ibid.* 556: Aug. 18, 1554.
[5] Coke, John, *The debate between the heraldes of Englande and Fraunce, etc.* (L., 1550), K 1.
[6] Robinson, *Original letters*, I, 76: Hooper to Bullinger.
[7] *Vide ante*, 274.

the whole county, usually in mid-winter when the people were least absorbed with farming tasks, preaching to great assemblies and giving largely from his own funds to the poor and distressed.[1] Infusing the preaching of all these men was a deep and burning evangelical passion, an increasingly radical Protestantism, running well ahead of the official doctrinal position of the Church of England, an intense and usually bitter anti-papalism, and a scarcely concealed suspicion of the Edwardian prelates. These sentiments were deeply rooted in men like Hooper, Bale, Knox, and, a little later, Foxe, and were to wax into full flower in Elizabethan Puritanism.[2] In the great preachers of the Edwardian period, in truth, English Protestantism was to find not only its spiritual and intellectual origins but its almost frightening evangelical ardour.

The most effective pulpit in England was of course that of the royal court, where preaching had been heard only rarely before the reign of Edward VI. Most of the sermons preached before the King and the court were Lenten series, though the number of such services was gradually increased as the reign progressed. Hooper, in fact, in his sixth sermon on Jonah, preached before Edward, bluntly urged that weekly sermons be arranged, 'seeing there is in the year 8,730 hours, it shall not be much for your highness, nor for all your household, to bestow of them 52 in the year to hear' the service of God.[3] Mercifully, this rather peremptory spiritual advice was not to be followed, but even so there were many of these sermons, and—what is more significant—of the twenty-two known court preachers, twenty were either reforming bishops or evangelical preachers of national reputation, such as Latimer, Hooper, Becon, John Taylor, Richard Cox, Matthew Parker, Ponet, and Lever.[4] A fair proportion of these sermons were later published, enjoying a wide distribution and exercising a considerable effect in the moulding of Protestant sentiment in the realm.

Almost as important, and certainly even more immediately effective, were the sermons preached at Paul's Cross, usually to large audiences, the limit of attendance being the range of the preacher's voice. The preachers for these 'command sermons' were

[1] Haweis, J. O. W., *Sketches of the Reformation . . . from the contemporary pulpit* (L., 1844), 92.

[2] White, Helen C., *Tudor books of saints and martyrs* (Madison, Wisc., 1963), 144 ff., for helpful and wise comments on this matter.

[3] Hooper, *Early writings*, 541, 558.

[4] Redman, who preached in 1548, was at that date uncertainly Protestant, and George Day, who had recently renounced transubstantiation, was, as we have seen, shortly to be deprived at Chichester.

carefully chosen by Cranmer or Ridley, often after the intervention of the Privy Council. Thus Matthew Parker, who had already preached at Paul's on at least two occasions, begged Ridley to excuse him when he was again invited in July, 1551. Ridley refused in rather abrupt fashion, saying that of the preachers then available, 'in some, alas, I desire more learning, in some a better judgement, in some more virtue and godly conversation, in some more soberness and discretion'. Hence he found himself unable to excuse Parker, who preached once more in late 1551.[1] In all, there were thirty-three known sermons preached at Paul's in the course of the reign, almost all of them violently anti-Catholic and most of them imbued with evangelical Protestant teachings. The roster of these famous preachers is similar to that of the divines who spoke before the King, with the addition of men like Barlow, Richard Ferrar, and Coverdale, all of whom were advanced Protestants.[2]

The most famous of all the great preachers of this generation—one could in fact argue, of all time—was Hugh Latimer, for whom no biographical comment can possibly be required. Venerable in years in the Edwardian period, Latimer's memory stretched back to the reign of Henry VII and hence embraced an adult recollection of the whole era of the Reformation. At Cambridge he was a contemporary of the early group of reformers, but had yielded his Catholicism only slowly, until in 1524 he was converted to the reformed persuasion by Bilney. His amiable nature and engaging informality made him almost immune against repeated conservative attacks in the Henrician period; he was in fact appointed Bishop of Worcester in 1535, shortly after an accusation of heresy had been lodged against him. Latimer resigned his bishopric into the King's hands soon after the passage of the Six Articles Act, and for the remainder of the reign lived quietly and obscurely save for involvement in the heresy charges brought against Edward Crome in 1546, which may have resulted in Latimer's detention in the Tower during the last months of Henry's life.

Latimer was literally catapulted into a position of great moral authority at the outset of the new reign, living with Cranmer for a season and almost immediately beginning his great career as a preacher. His first sermon under governmental auspices was in defence of the royal injunctions, while in January, 1548 he preached a series of famous sermons at Paul's Cross in which he demanded

---

[1] Ridley to Parker, July 25, 1551 (Parker MSS., Camb. C.C.C. MSS., CXIV, #133).

[2] We have been greatly assisted in the compilation of these sermons by the valuable study of Miller MacLure, *The Paul's Cross sermons, 1534-1642* (Toronto, 1958).

the cleansing of the church of popish superstitions and practices.[1] These were followed by his memorable series of four sermons on *The Plough*, and then in the Lenten season the group of sermons preached before the Court. Thus was launched, at a decisive moment, his extraordinary and powerfully persuasive ministry at large, so to speak, for London and for the nation.

These, as well as many of his other sermons, were quickly gathered by his admirers into editions of his 'collected sermons', and in successive editions were to have an immense circulation during and after his lifetime.[2] It is important to note that Latimer seemed to have no interest in preparing his sermons for publication, for he often spoke either extemporaneously or from no more than rough notes. The texts available to us were those prepared by a Swiss admirer in England, Augustine Bernher, 'not so fully and perfectly as they were uttered',[3] who likewise confessed that the published version was 'not so exactly done as he did speak it: for in very deed I am not able so to do, to write word for word as he did speak'.[4] Bernher, writing in 1562, also reminds us that Latimer preached constantly in Edward's time, 'for the most part every Sunday two sermons', despite his great age and infirmities, and besides this 'ordinarily, winter and summer, about two of the clock in the morning, he was at his book most diligently'.[5] This energetic and busy man was deeply dedicated to winning the realm for Protestantism; he possessed no time or patience for preparing his texts for posterity.

It is also important to observe that Latimer, deeply though he joined his emotions and his mind to the reformed faith, was almost child-like in his want of understanding of or concern with the subtleties of doctrinal controversy which so troubled his generation. In the disputation at Oxford, to which he was most unwillingly forced in 1554, he was obliged to request that the examination be held in English since 'I have not these twenty years much used the Latin tongue', while later he said, 'I understand no Greek'.[6] His thought is suffused by a deep moral instinct and commitment which rests on no clear theological structure, so that, as has been well said, 'not only a papist, but a Pelagian, or even a good pagan could read [him] . . . without a qualm'.[7] He was certainly the last of the

---

[1] *Injunctions given by the most excellent Prince Edward the VI* (L., 1547; STC #10088); Stow, *Annales*, 595.
[2] The principal of these collections were published in 1549, 1562, 1571, 1572, 1584, and 1607, to proceed no farther than the Jacobean period.
[3] Latimer, *Works*, I, xvi.   [4] *Ibid.* 82.   [5] *Ibid.* 320.   [6] *Ibid.* II, 251, 263.
[7] Lewis, C. S., *English literature in the sixteenth century* (Oxford, 1954), 193.

principal reformers to abandon the doctrine of transubstantiation, which Traheron thought he did not fully understand. The truth almost certainly is that Latimer simply did not think in these terms, and hence could not 'without much difficulty and even timidity renounce an opinion which he has once imbibed'.[1] Latimer's concern was with men, with the social wrongs of his age, with the moral reformation of the realm, and with the erection of God's kingdom on this earth. He did not think in theological terms at all.[2]

Taking in view the whole *corpus* of Latimer's sermons that survives, it must be said that they were immensely effective, that they still move the sentiments, and that they lent to early English Protestantism a considerable moral force. When he scathingly denounced corruption at court, we know that courtiers salved their consciences by the return of moneys improperly gained; the dramatic and telling blasts of Latimer and other preachers against public corruption may well be organically connected with the successive commissions on reform that mark the late Edwardian years; and surely it was Latimer who lent the principal moral strength to the thought and policy of the Commonwealth Party, which so completely engaged the aspirations of the Lord Protector.[3] The greatness of Latimer's contribution to the founding of English Protestantism is not only that he was its most eloquent and persuasive defender but that he infused it with a moral and social conscience.

Yet the style and form of the great sermons are curiously faulted. They seem always to be extemporaneous, yet one suspects that they were consciously so devised in order to hold attention and to persuade.[4] The sermons on *The Plough* can only be described as classic, though the famous series of seven preached before the King are most uneven in literary quality and interest—they ramble, are weighted with repetitions, and are at times not well composed or organized. All Latimer's sermons are marked by long digressions and parenthetical material and they are sometimes marred by an over-straining for dramatic effect. He tended to wander from his text and his scriptural elucidation, and then, abruptly, to resume his argument. But in all his sermons Latimer manages to engage our interest, as he certainly did that of his contemporaries, because he is really a great story-teller. It seems evident that his stories occurred to him on the spur of the moment—once, indeed, he says

[1] Robinson, *Original letters*, I, 320.
[2] Dickens, A. G., *The English Reformation* (L., [1964]), 224.
[3] This is the general estimate of Professor Dickens (*English Reformation*, 224); *et vide* Richardson, *Court of Augmentations*, 167.   [4] Lewis, *English literature*, 194.

that an anecdote has just crossed his mind and he will relate it before he forgets—and they usually contrived to lead him away from the thrust of his logic. He possessed an unerring ability to draw a topical reference from the stream of his argument and this surely contributed greatly to his marvellous power as a preacher. Thus in discussing most movingly Mary's want of provision for her Baby, he suggests that she must have used her own kerchief, 'or such like gear', as swaddling clothes. He then digressed for a few lines to a telling and passionate comment on the addiction of women to finery in his own day, and then abruptly returned to his argument.[1]

In an extraordinary action the House of Commons resolved on January 8, 1549, to request 'my Lord's grace, that Mr. Latimer shall be restored to the Bishopric of Worcester' forthwith.[2] The offer seems to have been made by the Protector, but was wisely declined by Latimer who sensed that his vocation—his 'painful travails'—lay in preaching to the nation at large.[3] Fuller, who had a wonderful instinctive sense regarding sixteenth-century matters, also suggests that Latimer would have been most unwilling to have resumed the see on the ruin of Heath's career.[4] Whatever the reason, the refusal was fortunate for the Reformation in England, for Latimer possessed no administrative capabilities or interests whatsoever. So he remained a great and an extraordinarily powerful preacher, a legendary figure in his own time, and just possibly the most important of all the apostles of English Protestantism.

We should also at least mention the thought and evangelical accomplishments of Thomas Lever, a full generation younger than Latimer and much influenced by the deep piety and moral wrath of the older divine. Lever also preached with great eloquence, with a strong call for further and immediate reformation, and with a most effective demand that the society be reformed according to Christian principles.[5]

Also a generation younger than Latimer was still another Cambridge divine, Thomas Becon (1512–1567), who must be regarded as one of the most effective of all the galaxy of famous preachers in the critical period with which we are concerned. Becon, whose ministry has perhaps been underestimated, was a native of Norfolk and was educated at St John's College where he proceeded B.A. in 1530. In several places in his writings he tells us that he was won over to reformed views at Cambridge by Latimer, though he was

[1] Latimer, *Works*, II, 108.   [2] *C.J.*, I, 6.
[3] Latimer, *Works*, I, 320.   [4] Fuller, *Church history*, IV, 69–70.
[5] For further comment on Lever's career, see the wholly adequate *DNB* essay.

not ordained until *c.* 1538 when he was presented to the living at Brenzett in Kent. His rich flow of writings and published sermons began in this period and, though he was cautious, caught him in the net of the Six Articles Act. Becon was obliged to make a formal recantation at Paul's Cross, probably in 1542, for his views on images and clerical marriages, as he later reminded Gardiner and Bonner.[1] Becon thought it prudent to withdraw from the vicinity of London, retiring to Alsop-en-le-Dale (Derbyshire) where he was for a time the guest of the lord of the manor who possessed a fine library of Protestant literature, including the works which Becon had written under the pseudonym of Theodore Basil. He later removed to Staffordshire, attracted by the presence there of Robert Wisdom, with whom he was sheltered by John Old, a clergyman of advanced Protestant sentiments. During his years of retirement Becon supported himself as a tutor and teacher, finding time to complete his own system of thought and to carry forward his writing, his published works being included in the list of heretical books denounced by proclamation on July 8, 1546.

With the accession of Edward VI Becon was quickly appointed to the London living of St Stephen Walbrook, in the gift of the Grocers' Company. He was a friend of Cranmer, and also served as a chaplain to Somerset, residing for some time in the Protector's household. In addition to his preaching, Becon wrote steadily and effectively during the Edwardian period,[2] addressing all his writings consciously and skilfully to the needs and interests of the com-moners and the middle class with whom his life-long concern lay. As he himself expressed it, 'in all my sermons and writings, I have not attempted matters of high knowledge and far removed from the common sense and capacity of the people. . . . To teach the people to know themselves and their salvation . . . I have directed all my studies and travails both in preaching and in writing.' In this aim Becon was eminently successful. His works, many of which were frequently re-issued, enjoyed a wide distribution and they intro-duce a new and tolerant tone into religious discussion in this era of embattled faiths. Though completely and unswervingly a Pro-testant, Becon in his devotional writings spoke for all Christian men, while even in his more polemical works he laid steady stress on the moral and religious obligations of Protestantism rather than on the evils of the Roman church. He summoned men to embrace a moral

---

[1] Becon, Thomas, *The early works of Thomas Becon, etc.*, ed. by John Ayre (Parker Soc., Cambridge, 1843), viii.

[2] His works published between 1541 and 1567 numbered approximately seventy.

reformation whose first task was to found Christ's true Church in England.[1]

The fourth of the great evangelical preachers whom we should consider is John Hooper, nearer to Latimer in age and probably a Cistercian monk in the first years of his career. Hooper was an early convert to Protestantism and an outspoken one, falling into a dispute with Gardiner which in 1539 made it advisable for him to seek refuge abroad. Hooper was in exile for most of ten years, at Zurich gaining the complete confidence and admiration of Bullinger and in 1549 returning to England as the English reformer best known and most highly respected by the leaders of continental Protestantism. Thus there was real excitement in Lasky's letter to Utenhove announcing Hooper's arrival, setting out plans for the Englishman's meeting with the leaders of the Dutch and Walloon congregations in London, and expressing his anticipation of the opportunity to converse with Hooper on theological matters.[2] Hooper immediately undertook, with Cranmer's encouragement, a ministry of preaching in the City of London, for a season lecturing daily, and on occasion two or three times a day, to huge audiences.[3] Then in 1550 he delivered his famous Lenten sermons before the King, in which his demand for a thorough reformation and a complete cleansing of Romanist survivals in the English ritual reveals the uncompromising nature of the man as well as his superb preaching. Micronius, in describing the sermons to Bullinger, tells us that they were preached with full freedom and with great courage, 'only he stirred up some lazy noblemen and bishops against himself, especially because he exhorted the king and Council to a more complete reformation of the church'.[4]

It seems quite certain that Hooper was, after Latimer, the most powerful and persuasive preacher of his generation. His doctrinal views were advanced, being in all important respects Zwinglian, and his preaching made him the darling, as he was the intellectual and spiritual leader, of the articulate classes of London.[5] His reputation

---

[1] An excellent wood-cut of Becon—even the beard is silky and luminous—is to be found as the frontispiece of his *A comfortable epistle* (1554).

[2] Hessels, J. H., *Epistolae et tractatus cum Reformationis tum ecclesiae Londino-Batavae historiam illustrantes, etc.*, II (Cambridge, 1889), 30–31.

[3] Robinson, *Original letters*, II, 557: Sept. 30, 1549.

[4] *Ibid.* 559: May 20, 1550.

[5] Fuller, with his usual apt phrase, says, 'yea, he seemed to some to have brought Switzerland back with him' (*Church history*, IV, 62). Blaurer indicates that Hooper was preparing to leave for England in September 1548 (*Briefwechsel der Brüder Ambrosius und Thomas Blaurer*, ed. by Traugott Schiess, vol. II (Freiburg i. Br., 1910), 724, 730, 740), where he probably arrived in the early spring of the following year.

speedily became European in its breadth. Quite steadily Bullinger and other continental reformers tended to enquire regarding Hooper's views in measuring the progress of the English Reformation. Now in the fullness of his almost prodigal powers, 'he was a man of strong body and perfect health, of strong but unimaginative mind; by no means incapable of humility, but extremely self-sufficient; learned; of tireless patience, absolute sincerity, and considerable benevolence'.[1] His courage was complete, his sermon on Jonah going far beyond even Latimer in its denunciation of social and spiritual evils and in its condemnation of men in high places who were evil because they condoned if they did not foster social wrongs. He was radical in his sentiments and in the bitter harshness of his tone, yet as Dixon has well said, he remained a churchman, differing from his brethren only in his insistent demand that the ritual and practice of the church should forthwith be completely cleansed.[2]

Taking the whole body of his writings in view, one is most struck by the immense power and the subtly persuasive quality of his works. They are marked by an excellent organization, by economy of expression, and by an impressive ability to select a few salient points and then to make them clearly, succinctly, and convincingly. There was no rambling, no waste, none of the anecdotal quality of Latimer's sermons. Suffusing all that he wrote and said is a steady and unchanging evangelical quality of faith and a complete and unyielding Protestantism. In Hooper there is no nostalgia whatsoever for the ancient church, its teachings, or its traditional ritual. There was also much more of solid learning in Hooper's sermons and writings than might be supposed, a random sampling of twenty pages of his *Declaration of Christ* (1548), bearing, Scriptures aside, nine learned references, among them Gregory the Great, Athanasius, Tertullian, Aristotle, Cicero, and Erasmus.[3] Cranmer and Ridley may well have thought that elevation to a bishopric would modify his zeal and temper his intensely evangelical preaching. But, not so. Rather, a crisis of serious nature was immediately created and his diocese was to feel the lash of his impetuous haste for thorough reformation. Hooper was forthright, and all his sermons and writings are somehow contrived to address themselves to men as individuals. Suffusing his writings, too, was a troubled uncertainty because he trusted only few amongst the nobility and held

---

[1] Dixon, *Church of England*, III, 181.   [2] *Ibid.* 185–186.
[3] Hooper was proficient in Latin, Greek, and Hebrew, at a time when 'a little of the last would go far' in England (Fuller, *Church history*, IV, 62).

most of his episcopal colleagues in a scarcely concealed contempt. The mood of haste possessed him—haste for the founding of a true Church—because of his brooding sense that the Church might easily be betrayed by those in power late in Edward's reign. In his tenure of the bishopric of Gloucester Hooper was fashioning the evidences of his own martyrdom.

However much these exemplars of evangelical preaching, of a hastened reformation, might differ in age, in status, and in vigour, they were in almost complete agreement in their aspirations for the Church of England. All of them were possessed of a sense of urgency and by the naive, but powerful, conviction that if there was sound preaching of God's Word across the realm all men must speedily yield to the manifest truth, now preached without restraints. All agreed with Lever that the great danger—the almost insoluble problem—lay in the weakness of the parochial clergy, on whom in the end all rested. Many were unlettered, while among those competent to preach, there were many who were either papists or carnal men.[1] Hence Latimer hailed the presence in England of men like Martyr and Ochino, wishing only that their stipends of 100 marks p.a. could be set at £1000.[2] The building of a learned and a preaching clergy in England must be regarded as the most pressing of the tasks of reformation, all of which was rendered the more difficult because the universities were now filled with the sons of great men and gentry, who 'send their sons thither, and put out poor scholars that should be divines' competent for the task at hand.[3] These men flayed the inert and timorous amongst the clergy, and the caution of the civil authorities, at a time when boldness in preaching the truth and the Reformation were so urgently required.[4] So great was the need, and so few were the qualified preachers, that almost in desperation Hooper set out for his untutored clergy a simple commentary on *Romans* XIII which they were required to read to their parishes, while both he and Becon saw no other solution than to require the teaching of the commandments to adults and to supply simple catechisms for the purpose.[5]

[1] Lever, Thomas, *A sermon preached ye fourth Su[n]daye in Lent, etc.* ([L., 1550]; STC ##15549, 15550).
[2] Latimer, *Third sermon* (1549), in *Works*, I, 141.
[3] Latimer, *The sixth sermon* (1549), in *Works*, I, 203.
[4] Latimer, *A most faithful sermon* (1550), in *Works*, I, 240-241.
[5] Hooper, John, *Godly and most necessary annotations, etc.* (1551), in *Later writings of Bishop Hooper*, ed. by Charles Nevinson (Parker Soc., Cambridge, 1852), 96; Becon, Thomas, *The principles of christen religion, etc.*, in *The catechism of Thomas Becon . . . with other pieces written by him in the reign of Edward the Sixth*, ed. by John Ayre (Parker Soc., Cambridge, 1844), 480-481.

The great gains already made by what the evangelical Protestants regarded as an incomplete and hesitant reformation would be lost and the manifest truth of God obscured unless the Reformation were so advanced that all surviving superstitions and popery should be rooted out. Hence Hooper lent strong support to Ridley's efforts to overthrow the remaining altars, for 'it were well that it might please the magistrate to turn the altars into tables, according to the first institution of Christ: [since] so long as the altars remain, the ignorant people and the ignorant and evil persuaded priests will dream always of sacrifice'.

England stood, all these zealous reformers would agree, poised delicately between God's full grace and His awful wrath. All depended on the progress made in reformation. The King and Council had laid out a godly design for Christ's kingdom in England, which, however, remained unfulfilled because of the covert opposition of the Papists and the enthusiasm of the 'carnal gospellers'. And, at the same time, social wrongs remained unrighted by the great of the realm.[1] Hence they called on the magistrate to complete the holy work so well begun, 'As ye have taken away the mass from the people, so take from them her feathers also, the altar, the vestments, and such like as apparelled her; and let the holy communion be decked with the holy ceremonies' appointed by Christ.[2] The indispensable symbol of the further cleansing which must be accomplished, so Hooper urged, was that the Lord's Supper be administered in complete simplicity, in the most decided contrast to the superstition of the popish rites.[3] So too, in this final work of reformation, the pluralists and the great clergy must be chastened and set at their true tasks of ministry.[4] Even more important, Latimer urged, was bringing the secret Papists under the full weight of the Reformation. These are men who counsel gravely against the correction of 'little abuses' which 'should not be taken in hand at the first for fear of trouble or further inconveniences', who hold that the people must not be subjected to 'sudden alterations' in ritual, and who then subtly delay and thwart the attainment of God's will for England. The realm lies ready for the cleansing required, for the complete and godly reformation which must at once be achieved.[5]

---

[1] Lever, *Sermon preached the fourth Sunday*.

[2] Hooper, John, *An oversight and deliberacion upon the prophete Jonas* (1550), in *Early writings*, 440.   [3] Hooper, *Oversight and deliberacion*, in *Early writings*, 482.

[4] Lever, *A fruitful sermon*, in Arber *Reprints*, #25, 30–32; Hooper, *Oversight and deliberacion*, in *Early writings*, 482.

[5] Latimer, *Sermon . . . preached in the Shrouds* (1548), in *Works*, I, 76–78.

The thought of these men was also characterized by a bitter and uncompromising denunciation of the whole Roman system of worship and belief which was declared to be completely superstitious and beyond the possibility of reform. They fastened their beliefs and their sternly sparse ritual of worship to what they regarded as the clear commandment of Scripture and the practice of the Apostolic Church. Their anti-papalism and their anti-Romanism were harsh and complete; there was no yearning for compromise and no nostalgia for the ancient church.[1] And with profoundly significant portents for the future, there is to be discovered in all of them, and especially in Latimer, a deep-seated anti-prelatism which was pitched quite as much against the institution of episcopacy as against the particular bishops who were at the moment charged with ecclesiastical power.[2]

All these reformers, with the one exception of Latimer, were united in such a violent detestation of the doctrines and usages of the Roman mass that they were catapulted, so to say, into a fervent support of teachings on the Lord's Supper which were very close to Zwinglianism. They taught that here lay the central error of Catholicism, which had built on the foundation of the mass a system of doctrine and of priestly power which bore no relation whatsoever to the Church as founded by Christ. All this must be stripped away and disowned by the true Church of Christ which teaches that the celebration of the eucharist is 'only a commemoration or remembrance of that sacrifice which could not but once be offered, and a certain confirmation or zeal for the infirm and weaklings, that they be redeemed by Christ'. None of the evangelical preachers, accordingly, fully accepted the teachings of the First Book of Common Prayer on this central doctrine of the Christian Church, but were to find themselves intellectually and spiritually far more content with the Second Book which reflected more nearly their advanced and restless sentiments.[3]

[1] Latimer, The fifth sermon, in Works, I, 173–174; Latimer, The fourth sermon (in Lincs), in Works, I, 521; Becon, Thomas, The jewel of joye, etc., in Catechism, 413–414; Hooper, Declaration of Christ, in Early writings, 36; Hooper, Brief and clean confession (1550), in Later writings, 31, 32; Hooper, Comfortable exposition, in Later writings, 268.

[2] Latimer, Sermon . . . made to the Convocation (1537), in Works, I, 45, 47, 50–51; Latimer, Sermon in the Shrouds, in Works, I, 66, 67; Latimer, The second sermon, in Works, I, 122; Latimer, The fourth sermon, in Works, I, 154–155.

[3] Becon, Jewel of Joye, in Catechism, 448–449, 451–453; Becon, Thomas, The gouernance of virtue, etc. (L., 1549), in Early works, 418, 421–426, 426 ff.; Hooper, John, An answer unto my lord of wynchesters booke (1547), in Early writings, 164–165, 205; Hooper, Declaration of Christ, in Early writings, 60–64; Hooper, A declaration of the ten holy comaundementes (1548), in Early writings, 403; Articles concerning Christian religion, in

The thought of these men, and its singular persuasiveness, was also steeped in the passion and sacrifice of Christ. Once given, once achieved, this sacrifice was valid for all time and for all men, and it was the task of the English Reformation to found the true Church directly and solely on the goodness and mercy of Christ. This body of thought was, then, Christo-centric and was unconsciously, especially with Becon, devotional writing of a very high order. This is true even of the earthy and usually somewhat prickly Latimer, who in his seventh sermon before the King (1549) gave us what can only be described as a masterpiece on Christ's passion. This work is eloquent, it is tightly knit, and it is very moving. The language and the sentiment possess cumulative power, and the great preacher's deep personal sense of Christ as the Saviour pervades the whole of the sermon. So too Hooper could be direct, simple, and persuasive when he spoke in these Christo-centric terms. 'I had rather follow the shadow of Christ', he wrote, 'than the body of all the general councils or doctors since the death of Christ.'[1] The Church of Christ knows no other master and possesses no other guide than the transcendent authority of Christ as revealed in the Apostolic Church. God alone absolves us from sin, Becon urged, by the sacrifice of Christ for all those who 'with unfeigned faith and hearty repentance convert, turn, and flee unto his mercy'.[2] The infinite mercy of Christ must be recovered for all men, while the link which binds us to Him must be immediate, personal, and anchored in our faith in His saving sacrifice. Though the theology of these great preachers was relatively unsophisticated and unsystematic, they had none the less founded a Protestant church in England.

These great divines also dealt, at least in passing, with a central aspect of sixteenth-century political theory in their comments on the duty of the subject to the magistrate. This was a most pressing question for the Protestant mind in England, particularly after the great insurrections of 1549 had raised the spectre of anarchy and had offered to Roman Catholic polemicists the persuasive charge that civil dissolution had followed spiritual dissolution in the realm. Hooper found twin dangers to godly order in England: the anarchical

---

Frere, *Visitation articles*, II, 269–270, 277; Hooper, *Brief and clear confession*, in *Later writings*, 32. Latimer stated in his examination in 1554 that his conversion from the Roman view of the mass had not occurred until about 1547, and then principally as a result of Cranmer's writings. He had never accepted the Lutheran teaching, but had moved at that time from the Catholic to the reformed doctrine (Latimer, Hugh, *The disputations held at Oxford* (1554), in *Works*, II, 265).

[1] Hooper, *Declaration of Christ*, in *Early writings*, 26, 27.
[2] Becon, Thomas, *The castel of comfort, etc.*, in *Catechism*, 557.

rages and confusions loosed by the Anabaptists and the obedience lent by the Papists to an alien and hostile power.[1] But reason, fortified by God's own clear mandate, informs us that rulers, even though they be evil, must be obeyed. 'No man, of what degree, state, or authority soever he be, being a private man (as all men be in a monarchy) . . . should meddle' with the state of the realm.[2] Hence the tumults of his generation were godless and befitted the state of beasts rather than of Christian men. Our duty to the magistrate is absolute, for his power stands appointed by God, with the consequence that rebellion raised against a King is rebellion against God Himself.[3] This conviction Hooper amply demonstrated in his own conduct. When on the death of Edward VI there were both commandments and commissions against Mary Tudor, 'I rode myself from place to place . . . to win and stay the people for her party . . . and to help her as much as I could when her highness was in trouble . . . I sent horses out of both shires.'[4] In so doing, Hooper must have known that his faith, his bishopric, and probably his life were all endangered.

Conventional and conservative as this political thought is, there was in it more than a hint of danger for the state, a conviction of righteousness which might imperil the ungodly or the faithless magistrate. Becon tells us that the magistrate likewise has his obligations. He should be learned in God's law 'to maintain pure and Christian religion, to nourish and defend the preachers and students of God's Word, to banish all false religion and idolatry, to punish, yea, and if they will not turn, to kill the preachers and maintainers of false doctrine'.[5] This range of duties, ordained by God, Latimer extended by insisting that the magistrate must keep the commonwealth in order, see that the schools and universities were well nourished, and that justice was faithfully executed.[6] Nor were he and his colleagues, moved as they were by essentially theocratic convictions, at all averse to denouncing corruption and iniquities in high places of state, as when before the King and Court he flayed those who heard his thundering rhetoric: 'Ye all know well enough, what ye were before ye came to your office, and what lands ye had then, and what ye have purchased since, and what buildings ye make daily.'[7] When the power and burning conviction

---

[1] Hooper, *Later writings*, 79–80 (*A godly confession*).   [2] *Ibid.* 84.

[3] *Ibid.* 105 (*Godly and most necessary annotations*); Latimer, *Sermon . . . at Grimsthorpe*, in *Works*, I, 496.

[4] *I.e.*, Worcestershire and Gloucestershire. Hooper, *An apology* (1554), in *Later writings*, 557.   [5] Becon, *Principles of christen religion*, in *Catechism*, 511.

[6] Latimer, *Works*, I, 496–497.   [7] *Ibid.* 261 (*A most faithful sermon*).

of these sermons began to evoke restorations, measured by hundreds of pounds, Latimer declared that a full restitution by those in high office would be more nearly on the scale of £100,000.[1]

These preachers wanted purity of doctrine and of worship above all else, and as a corollary they demanded purity in governance and a large measure of social responsibility in a godly nation. Men must learn, Lever declared, their place in the hierarchy of classes which, however, unites them in one body politic. Resistance to authority is no cure for social and moral ills, 'but as there be divers members in divers places, having divers duties', so there must be 'divers provision in feeding and clothing'; not on a basis of equality, but most certainly on the basis of what is requisite to a man's estate.[2] Christian men owe a complete and unquestioning loyalty to the command of the magistrate. But the godly state, in which these men declared they now lived, was equally charged with large areas of social and moral responsibility to its people. There was, as well, an important further understanding implicit in the relations of magistrate and subject. The civil power may make what laws it will concerning the bodies and the estates of its subjects so long as the laws of nature be not contravened, but touching the Church of Christ—now well and truly founded in England—only the law of God must in all circumstances be obeyed, and hence that Church must be further cleansed of its remaining vestiges of popery.[3] The magistrate also possesses a wide range of godly duties, and must ever recall that he is strictly responsible to God for His rule, for His justice, and for His mercy. We may say, in truth, that the magistrate is ordained for the wealth of his people; he must take heed of the end whereunto he is appointed, and be, indeed, as God would have him to be.[4]

These great preachers likewise shared a common view of the social and moral problems of their age which closely connects them with the Commonwealth Party, of which Latimer may fairly be viewed as the spiritual head in the Edwardian period.[5] They were as vehement as they were inaccurate in denouncing all enclosures for grazing and in flaying the rapacity of the landowning class in its relations with the commons. They lent full and eloquent sympathy to the poor who were caught in a sharp and spiralling inflation. They laid heavy stress on the duty of the governing classes to assume

---

[1] Latimer, *Works*, I, 262.
[2] Lever, *A fruitful sermon* (Arber *Reprints*, #25), 47.
[3] Hooper, *Declaration of Christ*, in *Early writings*, 85.
[4] Hooper, *Godly and most necessary annotations*, in *Later writings*, 107–111.
[5] The social thought of the Commonwealth Party is described in Jordan, *Edward VI*, 416–438.

direct responsibility for the care of poor and helpless men. They declared that there was no assured justice in England, for all favour ran with men of property and influence. These preachers demanded, in fact, that the government itself intervene directly to cure social ills, to restrain the extravagance and conspicuous waste of the rich, and to compel the whole society to care for all members of the commonwealth.[1] Their economic thought was naive; many of the ills which they denounced with such godly vehemence were either past or in process of correction; but they none the less visibly affected social thought in England and evoked what can only be described as a crisis in conscience.

Typical of the magnificent rhetoric and persuasive power of these men—and they are but exemplars of the whole body of the evangelical clergy—was Becon's denunciation of the English gentry of his age, quite as powerful and moving as the more famous passages which could be cited from Latimer's writings. So inexorable has been the pressure of rich and greedy men, those who own the land of England, that the poor have grown desperate. 'The poor mutter in corners and grudge against the rich, the poor break the bond of peace, the poor run headlong into all kinds of mischief, which thing we of late have seen unto our great sorrow, trouble, and disquietness.' England must search its conscience in reflecting on the great risings of 1549. For there was only one root cause: hopeless and desperate poverty. The gentry, long responsible for the care of their poor, have in fact degraded and destroyed them. These men 'are no gentlemen indeed, but pollers and pillers, rakers, and catchers, bribers and extortioners, yea, and very caterpillars of the common weal'. It is they who rend the society, for these are men who despoil and do not lead. 'They labour to possess much, but they distribute nothing. Their hand is stretched out to receive, but shut when they should give. If they once creep into a town or village, they for the most part never cease, till they have devoured and eaten up the whole town.' All that is pleasant and profitable they must have. They have defiled the moral stature of their class by the rapacity which has characterized them. For 'it is justice, mercy, liberality, kindness, gentleness, hospitality for the poor, and such other godly gifts of the mind, and not the multitude of riches,

---

[1] Latimer, *Works*, I, 196-197 (*The sixth sermon*); *ibid.* 243-247 (*A most faithful sermon*, 1550); *ibid.* II, 26-27 (*Seventh sermon, in Lincs*, 1552); *ibid.* 112-113 (*Sermon at Grimsthorpe*); Lever, *Sermon in the Shrouds* (Arber ed.), 34-37, 39; Becon, *Catechism*, 424-434, 436, 438-439 (*Jewel of Joy*); *ibid.* 586-587, 599-600 (*Fortress of the faithful*); Hooper, *Early writings*, 460-461 (*Oversight and deliberation*).

that declare who is a gentlemen and who a churl, who is noble, who unnoble'. These are men who have betrayed as they have all but destroyed a Christian commonwealth.[1]

In the writings of the great evangelical preachers of the Edwardian period there emerged and rapidly matured the principal outlines of the Protestant ethic. Those who possessed wealth and power were denounced for the dreadful sin of covetousness and the whole society was condemned for its coldness and want of concern for the poorer members of Christ's family. We have elsewhere discussed in some detail the formulation, to which these famous preachers made a considerable and early contribution, of a doctrine of the trusteeship of wealth for the service of the whole society and the development, as well, of what can only be described as a Protestant doctrine of good works, which was to lay immense leverage against wealth as it unlocked the sources for the rapidly changing stream of charitable giving for largely secular causes. These

'preachers and their lay colleagues . . . were angry, high-minded, and courageous men who not only denounced the social evils of the age but forged the essential elements of the Protestant ethic by linking it organically with social reformation. In spite of the exaggerations, the economic naiveté, and the godly wrath of these men, of whom Latimer was the greatest, they laid forever on the English conscience a sense of the shame of poverty and a moral responsibility for the enlargement of the ambit of opportunity'.[2]

Most of the impetus and most of the power for this profoundly important development in English life—its consequences were to be revolutionary—had their origin in the inspired and deeply persuasive preaching and writing of the evangelical clergy of the Edwardian period, to be absorbed by that steady and widening strain in English life which in the next generation we so loosely describe as Puritanism. The English conscience had been deeply stirred, as it had been convinced, by such preachers as the four whose thought we have discussed. Great and fruitful consequences to English life and the English character have, in all the generations that have followed, been its fruit.[3]

---

[1] Becon, *Fortress of the faithful* (1550), in *Catechism*, 590–600.

[2] *Vide* Jordan, *Philanthropy in England*, 156–165.

[3] *Vide ante*, 204 ff., for a fuller discussion of the rise of the secular charitable impulse in the Edwardian period. For more specific references to the thought of the preachers under consideration, *vide* Latimer, *Fifth sermon* (on the Lord's Prayer) (*Works*, I, 399, 409–410); Becon, *Fortress of the faithful* (*Catechism*, 590–593); Lever, *Sermon in the Shrouds* (Arber ed., 26–29).

7. HOOPER AND THE VESTIARIAN CONTROVERSY (1550)

It can safely be conjectured that so brilliantly successful had Hooper's preaching been that most English Protestants in 1550 would have ranked him only after Latimer among those who were laying the foundations of the reformed faith in the realm. Until about that date, too, the significant differences in the convictions of men like Hooper and the sentiments of possibly more responsible leaders like Cranmer and Ridley were not fully apparent. Until then all the reformers had been preoccupied in banishing the essential Roman Catholic rites and observances from the legally prescribed service. But minor and presumably indifferent matters remained, often reminiscent of the popish past, which the evangelical reformers now wished to abolish, but which those vested with responsibility were content to bear with lest the worship of the realm be further dislocated and civil quiet endangered. Cranmer, particularly, held moderate views and, with the still fresh memory of the Western Rising in his mind, had no wish to rend popular opinion by proceeding to a thorough and final cleansing of the Church of all traditional rites. So too, younger leaders amongst the bishops, and especially Ridley, resented the implication in the attacks by Hooper and other evangelical leaders that their stand on such matters as the *Ordinal* and the prescriptions regarding vestments made their own Protestantism suspect. Hooper was particularly belligerent in forcing his views, in part surely because he was deeply persuaded that the sufferings of the German Protestants under the *Interim* had been caused by the disposition of the German princes to compromise on rites which were 'indifferent matters'.[1] There were in his opinion too many leaders like Cox who in May, 1550 had written to Bullinger, stating his own preference for complete simplicity in the rites of the church, 'but in this our church, what can I do in so low a station? I can only endeavour to persuade our bishops to be of the same mind with myself.'[2] Hooper was afflicted with no such humility and, as we have seen, pressed hard for the immediate completion of the Reformation, even in matters which he had himself described as 'tolerable things' to be 'borne with for the weak's sake awhile'.[3] The result was an unseemly and a damaging theological brawl when the Council, under Dudley's influence, determined to appoint Hooper Bishop of Gloucester.[4]

[1] Burnet, *Reformation*, III, 348.   [2] *Ibid.* 352.
[3] Hooper, *Oversight and deliberation*, in *Early writings*, 479.
[4] *A.P.C.*, III, 31: May 15, 1550. The actual appointment was made in July, 1550 (Edward VI, *Chronicle*, 40).

It appears that in his first discussion of the matter, probably with the Council, Hooper declined the appointment on the grounds of his opposition to the *Ordinal*,[1] 'both by reason of the shameful and impious form of the oath' and 'those Aaronic habits' which he would be required to wear.[2] Both the King, who was sympathetic to the reformed group and who greatly admired Hooper, and Northumberland seem to have intervened at this juncture, assuring Hooper that his conscience would be respected in all 'reasonable things' at which he might scruple in the consecration, and that he would be relieved of a form of oath 'burdensome to his conscience'.[3] Shortly afterwards (August 5, 1550) the King wrote personally to Cranmer requesting that Hooper be relieved of 'certain rites and ceremonies offensive to his conscience', and expressly relieving the Archbishop of any fear of *praemunire* if he did so dispense.

Hooper accordingly assumed an intransigent position with what he thought was the full support of the civil power, with the consequence that an unseemly and abrasive ecclesiastical dispute ensued. The Council was divided, while Ridley stubbornly maintained that there was no merit in Hooper's position since he had admitted that the matters against which he protested were in fact indifferent. The long and bitter controversy which followed drew the lines and 'first solidly propounded and solemnly set down on both sides' the dispute which was in time to rend English Protestantism.[4] In late May it was reported that Hooper had found other matters at which he scrupled, while a few weeks later Hilles informed Bullinger that Hooper stood steadfast in the controversy and 'perseveres, by the grace of God, to be a most constant asserter of the Gospel' which he 'preaches every where with the greatest freedom agreeably to your orthodox doctrine. . . . He exhorts, yea, he persuades all.'[5] The less reliable Ulmis, writing from Oxford in late May, had been informed that it was Somerset who urged in the Council that concessions be made to Hooper's scruples in the matter of the vestments, while he later reported that the King lent strong support to Hooper, angrily protesting that the subscription to the oath of supremacy should not be taken in the names of the saints and exclaiming, 'what wickedness is here. . . . Are these offices ordained in the name of the saints, or of God.'[6]

[1] *Vide ante*, 266–267.
[2] Robinson, *Original letters*, I, 87: Hooper to Bullinger, June 29, 1550.
[3] *Ibid*. 87; Fuller, *Church history*, IV, 65.
[4] *Ibid*. 67.
[5] Robinson, *Original letters*, I, 270.
[6] *Ibid*. II, 415–416: Aug. 22, 1550.

It is clear that in the course of the summer Hooper's own position changed, his contention now being that the scruples he had advanced were not indifferent matters at all but sprang from conscience. He accordingly sought to state his case for the obdurate stand he had taken in a memorandum handed to the Council on October 3, 1550. This long and overly intricate argument infuriated Ridley, who felt that his own Protestantism was impugned and who laid against Hooper's strictures on the form of the proposed consecration a competent and learned reply.[1] Ridley admitted in his rejoinder that he in fact regarded the prescribed vestments as inessential to the consecration, wearily confessing that he was prepared to see Hooper elevated 'although he come, as he useth, to ride, in a merchant's cloak, having the King's dispensation for the act, and my Lord Archbishop's commission orderly to do the thing'.[2] Hooper appealed to the Bible and to the individual conscience in his stand against Ridley, but there was neither gentleness nor credibility in his charge that the leadership of the Church of England was vested in 'children of the world, superstitious and blind papists'. This provoked from Ridley a direct and savage attack, maintaining that there was implicit Anabaptism in Hooper's sole reliance on the Bible and that an extension of his claim of unassailable conscience would destroy the Church as an institution, which is also 'the very root and well spring of much stubbornness and obstinacy, sedition, and disobedience of the younger sort against their elders'.[3] In this position Ridley enjoyed the full support of Cranmer, for both bishops were frightened by the widespread support which the radical Hooper enjoyed. Both feared the precedent if Hooper should be consecrated as a non-conformist, and by his own prescription. Hence after Hooper had persuaded the King and Council to change the form of the oath required of him, they had no other recourse than to fall back on the much less defensible insistence on the use of the vestments, already gravely weakened since both had declared them to be indifferent matters. What Ridley and Cranmer really feared was Hooper's power as a bishop and his elevation on his own terms.[4]

Hooper had, in fact, gone too far in his somewhat tiresome

---

[1] New College MSS. (Bodl.), 343, ff. 16–17, as cited by C. Hopf, 'Bishop Hooper's notes to the King's Council, etc.', *Journal of Theological Studies*, XLIV (1943), 194–199.

[2] Bradford, John, *The writings of John Bradford, etc.*, ed. by Aubrey Townsend (2 vols., Parker Soc., Cambridge, 1848–1853), II, 390.

[3] *Ibid.* 392, 408; *Vadianische Briefsammlung*, VII (*Mitteilungen zur vaterländischen Geschichte*, XXXa, St Gallen, 1913), 135–136, for Bullinger's comments.

[4] Ridley, *Cranmer*, 309–310.

intransigence. The weary Council on October 6th informed Ridley that it wished no 'stirring up of controversies betwixt men of one profession' and summoned Hooper before them to enjoin him to refrain from further discussion of the *Ordinal*. They had granted his request for permission to put in writing his reasons for dissent, with the provision that he present his views on the following Sunday.[1] Hooper, refusing to yield, now found himself without support in the Council, even Northumberland warning him that the King must be obeyed in all indifferent matters, while a few days later Micronius wrote in some alarm to Bullinger that so exercised was the Council that even the Foreign Church in London might be required to conform to the English usage in ceremonies.[2] The Council sought to quiet the embittered and damaging dispute by commanding Hooper to stop his preaching and to remain quietly in his house.

Hooper, surely wilfully violating the terms of the Council's clear instructions in the matter, laid his case before both Bucer and Martyr, hoping to strengthen his position with truly formidable support. Bucer drafted two important memoranda, the first being a letter to Lasky, who lent Hooper his full support, in which he made it clear that his sympathies lay somewhat reluctantly with the Establishment. He personally would have preferred a thorough reformation of clerical vestments, but the matter was one in which the Church enjoyed a perfect freedom, so long as superstition was not encouraged. The Church of England was harassed by far more important questions and by a strong papistical opposition which should be its principal concern, without adding another division over matters indifferent.[3] This view Bucer enlarged in an unhappy letter to Martyr, deploring the controversy as distracting men from the true problems of the Church, among which he listed the spoiling of its wealth, the want of godly preaching, and the secret service of the mass. A false issue had been raised which could only weaken the resources which should be fully applied to the completion of a glorious Reformation.[4] Then, in a letter to Cranmer, who had asked for his judgement on the controversy 'in the fewest words possible', the great reformer indicated his view that the clergy, including bishops, might wear the prescribed vestments without offence to

---

[1] *A.P.C.*, III, 136.

[2] Robinson, *Original letters*, II, 571, 573, and *ibid.* 426, for Ulmis's later report (Dec. 31, 1550) that only the tolerant protection of Cranmer and Dorset saved Hooper from prison.

[3] Strype, *Memorials*, II, ii, 452.

[4] Bucer, *Scripta anglicana*, 705.

God, since therein they did no more than follow the commandment of the magistrate in an indifferent matter. These vestments
were used in the days of the early fathers and were acceptable also
in that they 'may have some signification and suggestion'. Hence for
any one to hold that it was unlawful or reprehensible to wear such
garments, he found simply indefensible. None the less, since
clearly the use of the ancient vestments had occasioned superstition in some and contention in others, they should in due
season be abolished when the time came for more important reformations such as the abolition of simony, the restoration of schools,
and the better care of the poor.[1]

Nor did Hooper find either support or sympathy from Martyr,
who admitted that though he shared Hooper's wish that the 'simple
and pure way' of Strassburg could be employed for the garb of the
clergy, the matter undoubtedly remained indifferent. The task in
England was first to preach the Gospel and to secure a rooting for
Protestantism, and only then to cure the minor frailties of worship.
Hence now, 'when a change is brought in of the necessary heads of
religion, and that with so great difficulty, if we should make those
things that are indifferent to be impious, so we might alienate the
minds of all'. Nor could he evade his plain duty to warn Hooper of
the dangers of being overly censorious and of exercising the Church
by really needless controversy.[2]

The pugnacious and irrepressible Hooper was not stayed in his
opposition by the counsels of the greatly respected Bucer and
Martyr. Nor was he minded to obey the order of the Privy Council
which had really placed him under house arrest and enjoined him to
remain quiet. He appealed directly to members of the Council,
was abroad at will on the streets of London, and infuriated all by
choosing this moment to publish his *Confession of Faith*, which, incidentally, was to go through many editions.[3] The indignant
Council remanded him to Cranmer for instruction on January 13th,
with the clear indication that he would suffer further punishment if
his contumacy continued. When Cranmer reported a fortnight
later that he could not be brought to conformity, the Council,
noting that he persevered 'in his obstinacy [and] coveteth to prescribe
orders and necessary laws of his head', committed him to the Fleet
until he should lend due obedience.[4]

[1] Bucer, *Scripta anglicana*, 681; free translation in Gorham, *Gleanings*, 214–220.
[2] *Petri Martyris epist. theol.* (1583), p. 1085, text in Gorham, *Gleanings*, 187–196.
[3] *A.P.C.*, III, 191: Jan. 13, 1551.
[4] *Ibid.* 199–200: Jan. 27, 1551.

Less than three weeks in the Fleet sufficed to work the cure which the Council, the primate, and the great Continental reformers had striven in vain to procure, though in a later letter to Bullinger the then Bishop Hooper suggests that it was long conversations with Ridley that at last persuaded him to accept the ordained episcopal habits for his consecration.[1] Whatever the persuasion may have been, Hooper on February 15 (1551) made his submission to Cranmer in measured terms of humility. He expressed regret that his statement had not satisfied the Council. He acknowledged 'the liberty of the sons of God in all external things', with respect as well to the particular question of 'the vestments and rites of episcopal inauguration'. Though his own views remained unaltered, he was persuaded that his 'duty of reverence and obedience' was to yield to authority as it reposed in the Archbishop.[2] The struggle of conscience of this amazing man was over; the Church of England had gained one of its finest and most effective bishops for the short term of years spared to him. In March Hooper was consecrated Bishop of Gloucester wearing the prescribed vestments, with the understanding that he might thereafter wear what he chose save when he appeared to preach or to ordain.

8. HOOPER AS A BISHOP (1551–1553)

Almost the whole of Gloucestershire lay within the diocese of Worcester until 1541 when Henry VIII constituted the new and independent bishopric. From 1497 until Latimer's appointment as bishop in 1535, the see had been the preserve of successive absentee Italian prelates with the consequence that it was out of order, characterized by corruption in the cathedral chapter and by a notoriously ignorant parochial clergy. During his brief tenure as bishop (1535–1539) Latimer had done little to reform the diocese, being in fact without the slightest administrative talent. John Wakeman, formerly abbot of Tewkesbury, who remained cautiously conservative in his religious views, was in 1541 appointed first bishop of the newly constituted see of Gloucester, serving until his death in December, 1549 without distinction either as a spiritual leader or as an administrator. Wakeman had also yielded to strong local pressures by letting out many of the lands of the diocese on very long leases, with the result that the see was rela-

---

[1] Robinson, *Original letters*, I, 91–92: Aug. 1, 1551.
[2] Hooper, *Later writings*, xv–xvi; Gorham, *Gleanings*, 233–235.

tively poor, possessing an income of no more than £300 p.a. in the early Elizabethan period.[1]

Hooper cared little for the temporalities of his see, but moved with characteristic energy to the disciplining and improvement of his clergy and the lifting of the spiritual tone of the diocese. He was, in fact, a remarkable bishop. Foxe, who knew him well, scarcely exaggerated when he wrote that

'No father in his household, no gardener in his garden, nor husbandman in his vineyard, was more or better occupied, than he in his diocese amongst his flock, going about his towns and villages in teaching and preaching to the people there.

That time that he had to spare from preaching, he bestowed either in hearing public causes, or else in private study, prayer, and visiting of schools.'[2]

He was, so Foxe concludes, 'a spectacle to all bishops who shall ever hereafter succeed him', working tirelessly with his clergy, attempting to lay a strict moral discipline on his people, and concerning himself with their physical as well as spiritual welfare. Foxe, who visited him twice, was told by Hooper's servants that every day four servingmen were required to feed the poor who, after instruction in the Creed, the Lord's Prayer, and the Ten Commandments, shared his table. The Bishop's outlays for his household, not surprisingly, ran well beyond his income, but this detail apparently never concerned him. Foxe, whose characters are always shrewdly and critically drawn, was censorious only in his observation that Hooper's deep charitable concern was to a degree masked by a severe and austere manner.[3] But above all else the diocese required strict discipline if it were to be reformed in the manner which he and the other great evangelical preachers had declared to be requisite for the founding of Christ's Church in England.

Within a month after his consecration, Hooper made clear the outlines of his policy and began the work of reforming the spiritual and social state of his see, though to Cecil he bewailed the fact that he lacked effective preachers amongst his clergy. He asked that no further pluralities be granted in his diocese, which he said had already wrought spiritual destruction. Hooper's sympathy with the

---

[1] Price, F. D., 'Gloucester diocese under Bishop Hooper, 1551–1553', *Bristol and Glos. Archaeol. Soc. Trans.*, LX (1938), 63; S.P. Dom., Eliz., XX, 54.

[2] Foxe, *Acts and monuments*, VI, 643–644.

[3] *Ibid*. 639–640.

economic and social idealism of the Commonwealth Party was suggested by his hot complaint of the scarcity of food and the high prices for necessaries in Gloucestershire, where 'all pastures and breeding of cattle is turned into sheep's meat, and they be not kept to be brought to market, but to bear wool, and profit only the master'. Any society stands in peril when wealth has been wrested into a few men's hands. Though Hooper said he followed his bounden duty in teaching obedience to the magistrate, he reminded the Secretary that 'it is the magistrates, and their own doings, that shall most commend them, and win love of the people'. Hunger makes unruly men, and hunger was widespread among the 'little cottages and poor livings' of his county. He could only pray God that the Council would sense the evil that was abroad and then move to destroy it.[1]

Hooper moved immediately towards reform in an important parish, when William Phelps, a Romanist priest of Cirencester, 'upon good advisement and deliberately, after better knowledge' subscribed to a carefully drawn and lengthy statement of the doctrine of the eucharist which bears all the marks of the Bishop's own Zwinglian views. We know nothing of the pressure that may have been applied to Phelps, but his confession, set forth before his parishioners, stated in conclusion that 'I am sorry for my opinion and forsake it from the bottom of my heart, hoping for God's forgiveness for me and those who have erred through my teaching', while promising that 'I will now henceforth study and labour to set forth the true faith'.[2]

Nor did the vigilant Bishop fail to act promptly and with full authority against cases of heresy amongst the laity, however well placed they might be in the community. Thus a 'froward man' of Gloucester, Thomas Penne, who had evidently held some post of responsibility in the city, was haled before Hooper for his expressed conviction that Christ when on earth had not possessed all the attributes of humanity and was now 'everywhere' rather than in heaven. Penne was required to subscribe to a detailed and orthodox statement of faith, in the presence of ten leading citizens, as well as to appear before 'a wise and learned' alderman of Gloucester, who was sent to London to lay Penne's confession and subscription before the Council.[3] So too, the formidable Hooper feared not at all

---

[1] S.P. Dom., Edw. VI, XIII, 13: Apr. 17, 1551.
[2] Harl. MS. 425, #15, ff. 71–72. There is a close similarity to an item printed in Strype, *Cranmer*, II, 902–904 (Foxe MSS.).
[3] S.P. Dom., Edw. VI, XIII, 24, 24i: May 25, 1551.

to reach far into the upper gentry in his determination that the men and women of his bishopric be brought to a godly discipline. Thus he cited Sir Anthony Kingston, one of the Council for the Marches of Wales and a holder of several advowsons, into his court for notorious adultery. Kingston declined to appear, but sought to placate the Bishop by calling on him privately. So outraged was Kingston by the severe castigation laid on him that he was moved to strike the Bishop, whereupon he found himself in really deep trouble, being summoned before the Privy Council, fined £200, and then handed back to Hooper, who required penance of him.[1]

We have cited numerous instances of Hooper's great care with his diocese and have observed his disposition to intervene directly in any cause involving its spiritual or moral health. But these episodic efforts were to be subsumed in the famous visitation of his see in 1551, surely the most searching and efficient of any ever conducted in the history of the Church of England. In April Martyr had reported to Bullinger that Hooper was preaching steadily to 'a numerous and attentive and earnest congregation', which was his whole diocese, as he endeavoured to estimate the spiritual estate which now lay in his charge. In the autumn Martyr wrote again of the noble work of reformation being wrought in Gloucestershire, while gloomily predicting that the great Bishop's work would be hampered until Parliament swept away the remaining superstitions that beclouded the true faith in the Church of England.[2] Meanwhile, Hooper was drawing up the interrogatories and examinations which were shortly to anatomize the capabilities, the intelligence, and the extent of reformed conviction to be found in the clergy of his diocese—clergy thus far probably expecting no more than a routine visitation by the deputies of their new bishop.[3] No clergy, certainly, could ever have been more staggered by what was to occur.

Hooper, in preparation, had carefully set down articles of faith, to which his clergy were to subscribe, which bear a close resemblance to the Edwardian articles establishing the doctrines of the Church of England—not, however, to be promulgated for the realm for another two years. They were sternly Protestant in their doctrinal content, particularly in that they categorically repudiated the teaching of transubstantiation and asserted that Christ was present

---

[1] Robinson, *Original letters*, II, 442: Dec. 4, 1551. I fail to find any reference to the matter in the *Acts of the Privy Council*.
[2] Robinson, *Original letters*, II, 494, 500.
[3] Harl. MS. 419, #49, f. 142.

only 'spiritually by faith'.[1] No other language might be used in the services of the church than that native to its worshippers, while the service must be distinctly spoken. The statement regarding cere-monies is interesting, especially in view of Hooper's own recent intransigence, for he now held that they had not always been everywhere the same and hence might lawfully be changed so long as they were not contrary to the clear Word of God. Consequently those who violated lawfully ordained ceremonies defied the 'com-mon order of the church' and the magistrate, wounded the con-science of the weak, stirred up tumults and sedition, and were worthy of punishment.[2]

The *Injunctions* proper present a clear, powerful, and certainly a detailed formulation of faith and worship. The clergy must 'exhort by word and provoke by example', the minister speaking distinctly so that the 'Scripture of God should heal, help, succour and com-fort as well the poorest as the richest, the unlearned as the learned, him that sitteth next the church door, or nearest the belfry, as him that sitteth in the chancel'.[3] The clergy were also required to study the Bible in a prescribed fashion, and to appear each quarter before Hooper or his deputies for the consideration of doubtful matters, which they might not dispute before the unlearned, preaching only those matters of faith that were clearly set forth in the Bible. Prior to the communion the people were to be carefully instructed in the Ten Commandments, the Articles of Faith, and the confession of sins as set out in the Prayer Book. The clergy were further enjoined to remove from the churches and from their ritual every trace of Romish survivals, as stated in a detailed list of forbidden objects and practices.[4] When windows were installed or repaired, no repre-sentation of a saint was to be employed, and 'if they will have any-thing painted, that it be either branches, flowers, or posies [mottoes] taken out of Holy Scripture', while any images remaining on the walls were to be defaced.[5] No detail escaped the Bishop's vigilant mind, for there were careful instructions on a variety of parochial matters, such as times for the proper ringing of church bells, the control of taverns, and buying and selling on Sunday. Hooper also instructed his clergy to exhort the people four times each year to make their wills while they were in good health, so they might dis-

[1] Hooper, John, *Articles concerning Christian religion . . . within the diocese of Gloucester*, etc., as cited by Frere, *Visitation articles*, II, 269–270.   [2] *Ibid.* 271.
[3] Hooper, John, *Injunctions given . . . within the diocese of Gloucester, 1551–1552*, as cited by Frere, *Visitation articles*, II, 280.
[4] Hooper, *Injunctions*, in Frere, *Visitation articles*, II, 284–285.   [5] *Ibid.* 289.

pose their goods properly and thus 'be an occasion of great quietness
and peace between such as many times fall at strife and contention
about the goods of the dead, for lack of a good and perfect will'.[1]

Completing these elaborate preparations for his visitation,
Hooper set down a long and probing list of questions to be addressed
to both laity and clergy. In all there were twenty-eight principally
concerned with the laity which betray preoccupation with good
morals, quiet conduct, and conformity to the Protestant Establishment. Those who took communion should be able to recite the
Commandments, the Creed, and the Lord's Prayer, while enquiry
should be made whether there were those diligent in their worship
in the time of the mass who were now 'slow comers' to the communion and common prayer.[2] The much longer list of questions—
they number sixty-one—to be addressed to the clergy reveals an
insistence that the service of the Prayer Book be faithfully followed,
that all traces of the Romish worship must have been removed, and
prayers for the dead, in all possible forms, exorcised from the
worship of the church.[3] And, finally, all the clergy were to be carefully examined regarding the Ten Commandments, the Articles of
Faith, and the Lord's Prayer, this representing the floor of literacy
and theological knowledge which Hooper was determined to
establish for the clergy of his diocese—beyond that he doubtless
already sensed he could not quickly aspire.

The revelations of this painstaking visitation were by any standard
appalling and must have filled even the usually sanguine Hooper
with dismay. In all, 311 clergy were examined, 62 more being
absent, in most cases because they were pluralists residing in other
dioceses. Incredible though it seems, we are told that 171—more
than half—were unable to repeat the Decalogue, though all but
33 could at least tell where it was to be found.[4] There were 10 who
could not recite the Lord's Prayer, 27 who were unable to say who
was its author, and 30 who could not specify where it might be
found. It was by no means untypical of the quality of these clergy
that at Haresfield the clergyman 'repeated and knows it to be the
Lord's Prayer, because Christ at His passion delivered it to his
disciples, saying, watch and pray'; at Harescombe the minister
could repeat it, but did not know whether it was the Lord's Prayer

[1] Hooper, *Injunctions*, in Frere, *Visitation articles*, II, 288. This was first urged briefly
in a rubric in the *Office for visitation of the sick* (1549).

[2] Hooper, John, *Interrogatories*, in Frere, *Visitation articles*, II, 292.

[3] *Ibid*. 296–302.

[4] Gairdner, James, 'Bishop Hooper's visitation of Gloucester', *E.H.R.*, XIX (1904),
99.

or not; and at North Cerney the incumbent could repeat the Articles of Faith, 'but not prove from Scripture *quia satis erit sibi credere propterea quod traditus* [*sic*] *authoritate Regia*'.[1]

The shocking ignorance of the clergy of the diocese in part explains why the parochial clergy over the whole realm were intellectually and spiritually inert. Gloucester was in this respect by no means exceptional, save that for generations before the Reformation an unusually large proportion of the livings of the county had been impropriated to the monasteries, which had filled pulpits just as cheaply as possible, with the inevitable consequence that religious life and growth in the parishes had been stunted and backward. Nor had this evil situation been substantially improved by the expropriation of monastic properties by the crown, since these advowsons rapidly passed into lay hands as entities of capital to be exploited so far as the law permitted. Hence Hooper, and all reforming bishops, found themselves with little hope of improving either the economic status of their clergy or their educational qualifications.

This situation is strongly suggested by an analysis of the 286 livings in the see of Gloucester in 1551–1552 in terms of the then owners of the rights of presentation.[2] A rather high proportion, about a third, of the livings were still in the disposition of the crown, and in these 91 parishes an energetic and resolute bishop like Hooper might hope gradually to build a more literate and forceful clergy. In all, 56 of the livings of the see were within the gift of bishops and cathedral chapters, but little influence could in fact be brought to bear save in the 24 parishes where presentation rights belonged either to the Bishop or to the Dean and Chapter of Gloucester. Almost as many advowsons (23) belonged to divers of the nobility, and about half this number to recently ennobled men who possessed some connection with the ruling junta. There was not much hope for a reforming bishop in this quarter, and even less in the 43 parishes now owned by the upper gentry, among whom, incidentally, was Sir Anthony Kingston, patron of no fewer than 4 parishes, who, as we have seen, had been subjected to severe censure by Hooper.[3] An even larger number, 50 in all, were in the hands of members of the lower gentry, few of whom were prepared to impair their property rights or to be easily persuaded to follow the advice of

---

[1] Hooper, *Interrogatories*, in Frere, *Visitation articles*, II, 309.

[2] The count is of parish churches only. In the case of 25 dependent chapels in the diocese the patron was, of course, in fact identical with that of the parish.

[3] *Vide ante*, 301.

their bishop in presentations. Seven of the parishes of the diocese were held by Oxford colleges, 3 by Londoners with no known connection with the county, while in the remaining 13 instances the patron is not named or we are uncertain regarding the status of the impropriator.[1]

Hooper was also seriously handicapped because he had to work through diocesan officials who were not so much corrupt as cautious and inefficient men, conservative in all their instincts, and intensely jealous of their power as they began to sense the thrust and energy of their new bishop. His chancellor was John Williams, who had held his post from the time of the formation of the diocese and who managed to retain it under successive sovereigns and bishops until his death in 1555. The registrar and chief proctors were also cautious and slow time-servers, who remained unmoved by Hooper's reforming zeal.[2] Hooper, having at once taken the measure of his officials and the Chapter, gained power and imposed his authority by taking most of the work of the diocese directly into his own hands. Thus he gave life to the Consistory Court, normally presided over by the Chancellor, by personally presiding over 65 of the 88 sessions held in a single year and by requiring the presence of persons cited with such insistence that in 509 cases only 54 persons failed to lend their attendance—and almost certainly rued their absence.

The already heavy load borne by Hooper was greatly increased when on May 20, 1552, he was, legally speaking, translated to the see of Worcester, on the annexation to it of the bishopric of Gloucester.[3] It was his intention to divide his time evenly between the two counties, but causes were heard in whichever see proved the more convenient. His method in dealing with cases brought before him was direct and forceful and he was renowned for having ruthlessly swept away the system of adjournments and delays so notorious in all the ecclesiastical courts.[4] Under Hooper's leadership, it has been well said,

'the personal touch of the Bishop . . . shines through the dull, formal records of the diocesan administration, bringing together

---

[1] This analysis is drawn from data supplied by Gairdner, in *E.H.R.*, XIX (1904), 101–121.

[2] Price, in *Trans. Bristol and Glos. Archaeol. Soc.*, LX (1938), 68–70. In this paragraph we principally follow this excellent article. Nor were Hooper's officials at Worcester to be any more helpful after his translation to that see. He lamented the incurable weakness of his cathedral clergy, for 'the realm wanteth light in such churches, where as of right it ought most to be' (Strype, *Cranmer*, II, 873).   [3] S.P. Dom., Edw. VI, XIV, 28.

[4] Price, in *Trans. Bristol and Glos. Archaeol. Soc.*, LX (1938), 70–73, 80–81.

unhappy husbands and wives, restoring concord among families divided . . . over disputed wills, pointing out their follies to gossiping and quarrelling women, and giving good advice to all and sundry'.[1]

But he could be severe, and it is noteworthy that he retained the medieval custom of imposing penances, now strengthened by requiring public confession of sin in the church or a market-place. The great Bishop did the best he could with the time and the resources allotted to him. Several of his rural deans were almost illiterate and at least two were corrupt, though he could not, or would not, remove them. In their stead the Bishop went in person, though this was scarcely remarkable since he sought to know at first hand the true state of the cure of souls with which he was charged.[2] He despaired of his clergy, but for his people he expressed great confidence, believing that the Gospel was beginning to shine amongst them. To Cecil, towards the end of the reign, he could write, on completing 'my long and full circuit from church to church in Worcester and Warwickshire: "Doubtless it is a great flock that Christ will save in England. . . . There lacketh nothing among the people but sober, learned, and wise men." '[3] Faithful, laborious, and deeply filled with a sense of his vocation, Hooper set out some days after his sovereign's death on yet another visitation of his diocese,[4] to be ended by his own arrest and the awful death before the magnificent façade of his own cathedral church of Gloucester. There he gave full testimony to the nobility of spirit and the strength of character with which men on occasion may be endued. Nor was that all, for on this dreadful day evangelical Protestantism was to gain one of the greatest of its martyrs.

9. THE REFUGEE COMMUNITY: THE LINK WITH CONTINENTAL PROTESTANTISM

In our earlier consideration of the refugee clergy and scholars who were invited to England after the promulgation of the *Interim*, we observed that upwards of forty came, with invigorating consequences for the English Reformation and for English culture.[5] Most of these men had arrived well before the fall of Somerset.

---

[1] Price, in *Trans. Bristol and Glos. Archaeol. Soc.*, LX (1938), 82–83.
[2] Hooper, *Later writings*, xvii–xix.
[3] HMC, *Salisbury MSS.*, I, 107.
[4] *Ibid.* 125.
[5] Jordan, *Edward VI*, 189–205.

Their leaders were so well and highly placed that their views on spiritual matters were not without influence, as witness the intervention of Martyr and Bucer in the violent controversy raised by Hooper over his consecration oath and the required vestments. Three of these refugee divines—Bucer, Martyr, and Ochino—enjoyed a European reputation, and to their number John Lasky must be added after his somewhat belated arrival in 1550. Another twelve of the group were preachers and theologians of lesser eminence, who lent valuable service to the course of the Reformation and were in the main supported by appointments in the church or in the universities. A considerably larger group, numbering twenty-five to thirty, were lesser men in reputation, often younger in years, but were none the less vigorous and experienced divines of considerable ability and reputation.

It is also important to observe that most of these foreign divines were Zwinglian or Calvinist in their personal religious convictions, while those few who were nominally Lutheran had been intellectually more touched by Melanchthon than by Luther in his later years. Their support, consequently, was on the whole lent to the rapidly increasing strength of the evangelical party within the new establishment, of which such men as Hooper, Latimer, Becon, and Bale were the intellectual and moral leaders, and towards which the thought of such essentially centrist leaders as Cranmer and Ridley was slowly and almost insensibly inclining. The temptation is, in fact, to credit to the foreign divines far more influence than they actually exercised in the development of the thought of the Church of England, neglecting the immensely powerful indigenous forces which were moving the Church towards a closer communion with reformed thought and practice abroad. Almost the whole weight of governmental policy supported this development, and Cranmer's irenic concern lent it steady and powerful favour.

Bucer, the most illustrious of the foreign divines, was, as we have previously observed, well and congenially seated at Cambridge as Regius Professor of Divinity and enjoyed the steady friendship and support of the primate.[1] In January, 1550 he began his famous lectures in the university on the *Ephesians*, while with Cranmer's knowledge he was working on his suggested revisions of the first Book of Common Prayer.[2] He was gently critical of Martyr, who he thought had in the heat of the Oxford disputations proceeded too far towards Zwingli in his definition of the eucharist, particularly

[1] Jordan, *Edward VI*, 193–196.
[2] *Vide post*, 342–346.

since 'the Zurich people have here many and great followers', who he feared would exploit Martyr's position. Bucer was, however, comforted by the fact that the first Book of Common Prayer set forth the 'true exhibition of the body and blood of Christ . . . expressed in words exceedingly clear and weighty'.[1]

Bucer in his turn found himself engaged in a bitter controversy with entrenched conservatives in the university, led by John Young and Thomas Sedgwick, who had attacked his teaching on the doctrine of justification in public lectures. Bucer unhappily denied the charges made against him, stating his full acceptance of the doctrine as rendered in the King's *Homilies* and seeking unsuccessfully to secure a copy of the manuscript of Young's particularly venomous attack.[2] He appealed to Ridley, a visitor to the university, and to Cheke, for their intervention, calling as well on Martyr, who armed him with a complex and highly technical review of patristic writings which lent full support to Bucer's position.[3]

But Bucer remained in high favour, receiving special gifts from the young King and being enjoined to guard his delicate health and to take more lightly the burden of lecturing. He turned at once to completing, as a New Year's gift for Edward, that remarkable work—so full of sanity and tolerance—entitled *De Regno Christi*, which was in its turn to evoke from the King a substantial treatise on the nature of the Christian polity.[4] Bucer attempted as well to continue with his lectures on the *Epistle to the Ephesians*, but his health gave way completely and on February 28 (1551) he died, attended at his bedside by the leading reformers in the university. His death came as a great shock and loss to the newly planted Church of England, whose intellectual and spiritual tone he had helped to set. His funeral, we are told, was attended by upwards of 3000 mourners, while letters, epitaphs, and memoirs flowed in to testify to the veneration in which this gentle and moderate man was held.[5]

Peter Martyr, less forceful and less inclined to reach for leadership, was left on Bucer's death the most important of the foreign scholars

---

[1] Bucer, *Scripta anglicana*, 862: Bucer to Theobold Niger, Apr. 15, 1550.

[2] *Ibid.* 803: Bucer to Edmund Grindal, Aug. 31, 1550.

[3] Parker MS. 102, ff. 91–94, cited in Gorham, *Gleanings*, 168–175.

[4] *Discourse on the reform of abuses in church and state* (April?, 1551); *vide* Edward VI, *Chronicle*, xxiv–xxv, 159–167; and *vide post*, 411.

[5] S.P. Dom., Edw. VI, XIII, 6; Add. MSS., 5873, f. 10; Cheke, Sir John, *De obitu doctissimi . . . doctoris M. Buceri, etc.* (L., 1551), for letters on the event from Cheke, Carr, Martyr, and others, as well as the funeral orations of Haddon and Matthew Parker; most of these materials are also found in Bucer, *Scripta anglicana*, 867–876.

in the realm. He had been drawn into a particularly bitter controversy at Oxford in the spring of 1549 in which he maintained a moderate position on the Lord's Supper against several intransigent Roman Catholics amongst the fellows, who for months afterwards sought to prolong the disputation in order to gain a forum for their views.[1] Martyr's life at Oxford was troubled because of the prevalent conservatism of the colleges and by occasional acts of rowdyism, such as the stoning of his windows at night. He gently advised Bucer to avoid any public controversy—advice, he added, 'perhaps little needed by you who are far more prudent than myself'. He had concluded that it was much better to advance truth and refute errors by lectures or sermons, for 'otherwise . . . they will scatter abroad such reports as they please, and will brag that they have disputed with you'.[2] He was troubled too that among the twenty who had recently been vested with the B.D., a good many were known to be papistical. So complete was the conservative control at Oxford, that for the theological disputations of those proceeding B.D., over which Martyr was to preside, the subject was not given to him in time either to prepare or protest, a particularly unfortunate confrontation being averted when the vicechancellor (Haddon) intervened to prohibit the exercise.[3]

Martyr's judgement and learning were much valued by Cranmer and Ridley and he lent support to them in the steady movement of their policy and thought towards a more clearly enunciated Protestantism for the Church of England. His share in the revision of the Book of Common Prayer was principally indirect, for he found in Bucer's *Censura* a wholly acceptable platform of amendments, which they had in fact agreed on before Bucer's death. He was, however, directly consulted by Cranmer on the reform of ecclesiastical laws, residing for some time with the Archbishop at Lambeth while the work of the commission proceeded.[4] Deeply grieved by the death of his wife in early 1553, Martyr seems to have lived quietly at Oxford for the remaining months of the reign. On Gardiner's intercession, he was permitted to leave England shortly after Mary's accession, returning first to Strassburg and then in 1556 succeeding Pellican in the chair of Hebrew at Zurich.

[1] Bucer was correct in his view that Martyr was really forced into the disputation, wholly against his wishes (*Anecdota Brentiana. Ungedrückte Briefe . . . von Johannes Brenz*, ed. by Th. Pressel (Tübingen, 1868), 304, 305).
[2] Camb. C.C.C. MSS., 119, ff. 105–107, as cited by Gorham, *Gleanings*, 176–177: Sept. 6, 1550.
[3] Strype, *Cranmer*, II, 898–901 (for Latin text); Gorham, *Gleanings*, 181–182: Sept. 10, 1550.   [4] *Vide post*, 357–361.

During the later Edwardian period the flow of refugee preachers, scholars, and young and aspiring intellectuals into England continued unabated, now with a heavier concentration from the Low Countries and from France, where repressive measures were being undertaken. Thus, to note no more than a random sampling of such men, Jerome Colas, who dedicated dull tracts to both Cranmer and Mary, after publishing a French grammar found employment in 1551 as a French tutor to the children of the Countess of Southampton.[1] Elaborate arrangements were made in March, 1550 for the departure of the son of Alexander Schmutz, formerly preacher at Leutmerken, to the land ruled by 'an angelic king' who sought only to expand the Kingdom of God.[2] The always sanguine, and occasionally devious, John Ulmis, then at Oxford, was in May, 1550 urging Ambrose Blaurer to send his nephews, Albert Blaurer and Walter Ulmis, to England, assuring him that nothing more would be needed than a recommendation from Bullinger to Cox, the tutor of the King 'and rector of our academy'.[3] From Lausanne, Agnace d'Albiac presented the King with his recently published book on *Job* and a glowing compliment on his great work of reformation, while commending the bearer, a poor student who wished to complete his divinity studies in England.[4] So too, Jerome Julien, a French refugee from Normandy, in the evident hope of finding godly employment in England, presented Edward in January, 1553 with a New Year's gift of verses of some merit.[5] At about the same time Pierre du Ploiche, another Frenchman, subscribing himself as a teacher dwelling in Trinity Lane, did an interesting and well-turned translation of the Latin version of the *Catechism* and *Litany* into French and English, one supposes for the use of the French Congregation in London. Conjoined with the translation was an exceedingly well done English-French phrase book, secular in tone and nicely fitted to the interests and capacities of young children.[6]

The refugees now streaming into England from several quarters of Europe, doubtless in many cases moved quite as much by economic considerations as by religious convictions, were drawn from various classes of men. Most of these families settled in London, where many had long had trade connections and where there were

---

[1] Royal MSS., 8. A. xvi; 12. D. v; 16. E. xxvii.

[2] *Blaurer Briefwechsel*, III (Freiburg i. Br., 1912), 69, 71, 74.

[3] *Ibid.* 74–76.

[4] *Twenty-seventh rpt.*, Dep. Keeper of Public Records (1866), App., 134, #LXII.

[5] Julien, Jerome, *Les estrenes du conforte d'espoir* (Jan. 6, 1553), Royal MSS., 16. E. iv.

[6] Du Ploiche, Peter, *A treatise in English and French, etc.* (L., 1553).

already clusters of foreigners to which the new arrivals tended to attach themselves. Any estimate of the number of Edwardian refugees is highly conjectural because of the incompleteness of official records. So too, any attempt to categorize the immigration by nations is frustrated by the fact that the terms *German*, *Flemish*, and *Dutch* were used quite inexactly, if not interchangeably.

We can, however, dismiss as greatly exaggerated Scheyfve's advice to his government in early 1551 that a heavy flow of religious 'sectaries' was coming from the Continent, most of them artisans, who were being added to the 10,000 refugees already living in or near London.[1] This considerable migratory movement was still under way as late as May, 1553 when the ambassador reported that a stream of French Protestants was then arriving in London, some of whom were of the gentry or from the professional classes.[2] The subsidy records for 1552 suggest that there were then residing in London about 600 strangers subject to taxation, most of whom were listed as servants, but with a fair number, 40 in all, who already owned taxable property worth £10 or more.[3] This might mean that as many as 3000 aliens were members of households already subject to taxation. An equally reliable contemporary source suggests that in a single year (1550) 483 foreigners were granted denization, at fees ranging from 6s 8d to £1. These were all males, principally heads of families, thus suggesting that as many as 1500 persons were in effect naturalized in this year.[4] An examination of the names informs us that about a fourth of the whole number were either Dutch or German, another fourth were French or Flemish, an eighth Italian, another eighth Scottish, and the remainder of uncertain origin. Somewhat later (1567) evidence gives us a total of 4851 foreigners then residing in London or its suburbs, of which almost two thirds were described as Dutch or Flemish, though including numerous Germans, approximately 14 per cent as French, and about 4 per cent as Italian.[5] This remarkable change in the pattern of place of origin reflects, of course, the heightening of

[1] *Cal. S.P. Span.*, X, 218–219: Jan. 1, 1551.

[2] *Ibid.* XI, 43: May 13, 1553.

[3] Kirk, R. E. G., and Ernest F. Kirk, *Returns of aliens . . . of London*, etc. (Huguenot Soc. Publ. X, pt. I, Aberdeen, 1900), 234–267.

[4] *Cal. Pat. Rolls, Edw. VI*, III, 248–252. Place of residence was not stated, but was London in most cases. This was the peak year, but letters of denization were liberally granted throughout the reign.

[5] Haynes, *State papers*, I, 455–462. This estimate of numbers corresponds closely with Schaible's persuasion that there were as many as 5000 'Germans' alone in and about London in the Edwardian period (Schaible, K. H., *Geschichte der Deutschen in England*, etc. (Strassburg, 1885), 130).

religious repression in the Low Countries and the considerable absorption of earlier refugee families into the English society.

We have no detailed data regarding the occupations of the Edwardian refugees, though it is probable that they were not greatly dissimilar in their skills from the London refugee group in the early Elizabethan period, when about a third were engaged in some aspect of the textile trade, 18 per cent in trade and transport, 11 per cent in the leather trades, 8 per cent in the metals industries, and about as many in woodworking and in food and victuals. Not more than a tenth of the refugees were engaged in non-manual occupations, and in this group the intellectuals were to be found. The remainder were engaged in sundry occupations.[1] It is quite clear from this and other scattered evidence that the refugee colony was at any given moment largely composed of relatively simple people, among whom, however, an extraordinary proportion were skilled artisans, with as well a relatively high proportion of intellectuals and clergy who immediately established a religious and cultural leadership among the group and supplied the links—and impressive they were—with the English government and the Established Church. Anyone working in the London wills of this period must also be impressed by the amazing proportion of the refugee colony who died a decade or so later as well-to-do or even rich burghers and whose children had by that time been almost wholly assimilated by the English society. This refugee stream, self-selected and highly principled as it was, contributed greatly to the economy, the culture, and the religion of the country that had afforded it asylum and a substantial freedom of worship.

The rapidly growing refugee community of Protestants of divers persuasions had for some time been a matter of concern to the government, since it was clear from the outset that they could not be fitted into the parochial structure of the City, for one thing because few of them spoke English. There is a suggestion of an informally organized French group which as early as 1548 was served by the preaching of Richard Vauville, but the principal concern was with the much larger body of Flemings, Dutch, and Germans. Ochino sought in 1548 to persuade Musculus to come to England as the pastor of these German-speaking families, stating with heroic exaggeration that there were more than 5000 'Germans' in London awaiting his pastorate. About a year later (1549) a deputation of the Flemings set forth their crying spiritual needs to

---

[1] Norwood, F. A., *The Reformation refugees as an economic force* (Chicago, 1942), 45, for the figures.

Bucer, who estimated that there were '600 to 800 Germans here, godly men and very anxious for the Word of God'.[1] As early as 1547 the Dutch and Flemings had been holding private services in various parish churches and were by 1549 recognized as a separate congregation numbering perhaps as many as 800.[2] The congregation had no more than informal organization, for as late as June, 1550 Micronius, himself a Fleming, was preaching to them 'inter privatos parietes', though at about the same date he did assume the pastorate.[3]

A number of informed English leaders were also deeply concerned with the spiritual plight of the principal refugee groups, including Hooper, Cranmer, the Duchess of Suffolk, Cheke, and Armagil Wade, clerk of the Privy Council. The King was likewise favourably disposed, on June 29, 1550, recording his intention to surrender Austin Friars to the Germans as their own church, 'for avoiding of all sects of Anabaptists and such like'.[4] The founding charter recited that the King was mindful of the duty of a Christian prince to make certain that the 'pure and undefiled religion may be spread throughout the body of the commonwealth and that a church founded and brought to maturity in truly Christian and apostolic doctrines and rites may be served by holy ministers'. Consequently it was his purpose in establishing the church to secure 'an incorrupt interpretation of the Word of God and apostolic observance'. Hence he incorporated the superintendent and ministers into a 'corpus corporatum et politicum', commanding the civil and ecclesiastical authorities to permit the clergy of the new body 'freely and quietly to practice, enjoy, use, and exercise their own rites and ceremonies without limitation', even when they did not conform to the rites and ceremonies elsewhere employed in the realm.[5]

The first superintendent named to lead the 'German' church was John Lasky, who had administered all the churches in East Friesland for the Countess Anna until in 1548 she felt constrained to accept

[1] Robinson, *Original letters*, II, 539: Bucer to Hardenberg, Aug. 14, 1549.
[2] Pijper, F., *Jan Utenhove, his life and works* (Leyden, 1909), 59–64.
[3] Robinson, *Original letters*, II, 565: Micronius to Bullinger.
[4] Edward VI, *Chronicle*, 37; S.P. Dom., Edw. VI, X, 15: July 24, for an attested copy (Latin) of the letters patent. The hope here expressed by the King was in vain, for a year, later Micronius confessed to Bullinger that the church was troubled by papists, Arians, and sectaries (Robinson, *Original letters*, II, 574: Aug. 14, 1551).
[5] Hessels, J. H., *Epistvlae et tractatus, etc.*, III, i (Cambridge, 1897), 5–7; Burnet, *Reformation*, V, 305–308; Rymer, *Foedera*, XV, 242–244; Harboe, Ludwig, *Zuverlässige Nachrichten von dem Schicksale des Johann von Lasco, etc.* (Copenhagen and Leipzig, 1758), 11–12.

the terms of the *Interim*.[1] A member of a famous Polish noble family, Lasky was reared in the household of his uncle, John, the Primate of Poland, who in 1512–1514 took him as an attendant to the Lateran Council and matriculated him at Bologna. Lasky spent a year in Erasmus' household at Basel (1524–1525), receiving from him numerous marks of favour and the completion of his humanistic education. Appointed Bishop of Vesprian in 1529, Lasky declined higher preferment in the Polish church because he had by 1538 adopted reformed judgements which became increasingly radical. He then settled in Emden (East Friesland) in 1540. He became favourably known to the English reformers, particularly Hooper, and when he left Friesland was invited by Cranmer in August, 1548 to attend an irenic conference which the Archbishop hoped to convene. When he returned to London in the spring of 1550, after a final visit to Emden, he was almost immediately appointed to administer the affairs of the German church, which incidentally included not a few Frisians. Appointed to serve as ministers of the church under Lasky's charge were four refugee clergy of considerable preahcing ability, but of no particular scholarly distinction. Two were German-speaking, one being Walter Deleen, a native of Brabant, who had fled to England as early as 1539, had in recent years held a post in the royal library ('Biblioscopus Regis'), and in January, 1550 dedicated to the King a manuscript New Year's gift consisting of three Latin sermons on the first three chapters of *Genesis*.[2] The second was Micronius (Martin Flandrus), an excellent preacher and pastor, who in 1552 translated into English the order of service in the German church and who betrays a distinct Calvinist sympathy in his doctrinal sentiments.[3] Micronius was a Fleming from Ghent, where he had been trained as a physician. He had fled from Germany because of his advanced religious views and, after meeting Hooper and Utenhove, followed Hooper to England in 1549. Two French-speaking clergy were also appointed to the formidable ministry of the new church, Francis Rivière and Richard Gallus (Vauville), who, as we have noted, had served the French refugees in London informally since 1548.

Among those who had arranged for this remarkable experiment

[1] Lindeboom, J., *Austin Friars. History of the Dutch Reformed Church in London, 1550–1950* (The Hague, 1950), 4.

[2] Royal MSS., 7.D.xx; Hessels, *Epistolae*, II, 51–52.

[3] Micronius, *A short and faythful instruction*, etc. (L., 1552), printed by Pocock, Nicholas, ed., *Troubles connected with the Prayer Book of 1549*, etc. (Camden Soc.. n.s. XXXVII, L., 1884), xxx–xlvi.

in founding a model Protestant church in London was John Utenhove, a member of a rich burgher family who had been educated in
his native Ghent. His family was obliged to flee from the Low
Countries in 1544 because of their pronounced Protestantism,
settling in Aachen where there was already a small Flemish refugee
group. In 1548 Utenhove was in London, favourably impressing
Cranmer and acquainting himself with the Walloon community and
its needs. Utenhove returned to the Continent where he held conferences with Bullinger and Calvin and met with Lasky in Strassburg.
Returning to England in the autumn of 1549, he was active in the
planning of the refugee church, of which he was at the outset made
an elder and over which he exerted a powerful and sustained Calvinistic influence.[1] Utenhove expressed himself as more than
content with the liberality of the King's patent and with his generosity in making available to the congregation the former church
of the Austin Friars, which Edward had also undertaken to renovate
and which he described as the 'temple of Jesus'. Further, the
church had purposely been exempted from episcopal control, despite
the serious doubts of Ridley and other bishops, and was to set forth
the pure Word of God and to establish a worship uncontaminated
by popish survivals.[2]

From the outset the whole undertaking was viewed not only with
apprehension by Ridley, but with disfavour by Paulet and Rich in
the Council, both of whom had been granted property rights in the
great complex of buildings which formerly comprised the Austin
Friars precincts. The work of repair was accordingly delayed until
December (1550), the division of the property being legally effected
in 1551. In consequence the refugee congregation used only the
nave and aisles of the great church, which could not seat the large
congregation when preaching was begun in September, 1550.
Ridley was also reluctant to permit the celebration of the Lord's
Supper according to an alien rite, and in 1552, after the adoption of
the second Book of Common Prayer, he pointed out that by law all
members of the congregation were required to attend their re-
spective parish churches. The Council, irritated by his conservative
obstruction, ordered him to find a common ground of policy with
Lasky, while the King intervened personally and decisively to settle
the legal quibbling in favour of the foreign congregation.[3]

[1] Lindeboom, *Austin Friars*, 7.
[2] Calvin, *Opera* (*Corpus reformatorum*, XLI, Brunswick, 1875), 626–630: Utenhove to
Calvin; Robinson, *Original letters*, II, 568: Micronius to Bullinger, Aug. 28, 1550.
[3] *A.P.C.*, IV, 160–161: Nov. 4, 1552; Strype, *Memorials*, II, i, 376.

Most of what we know regarding the worship and functioning of the German church must be drawn from the elaborate, and ideal, formulary set forth by Lasky in 1551,[1] and the resrospective account which he and Micronius wrote in 1555 after they had fled the Marian persecutions.[2] There was evidently no formally articulated creed, but a lengthy confession of faith did set out a full definition of belief and declared the true Church to be a congregation of believers gathered by God from the multitude of men. To this statement all entering the church were required to subscribe. The whole temper of Lasky's thought in this period was Calvinistic, the organization and the disciplining of the congregation being established on the models of Geneva and Strassburg.[3] The service was similar to that of Strassburg, with particular emphasis on the systematic reading of the Bible, carefully prepared and clearly delivered sermons, and on a tightly maintained discipline over the faith and morals of the congregation.[4] A Swiss traveller and student, Josua Maler, who attended at least one service of the church, with Micronius as the preacher, was greatly impressed by a collation of the Scriptures, in the 'German-Dutch language', held by leading members of the congregation. He also observed that recent arrivals from 'the German nation' were publicly presented, 'under the eye of the Christian community' and well 'commended to the blessing and protection of God'.[5]

The attendance at the German church was so heavy and the linguistic problem so great that almost immediately arrangements were made for separate services for the French and Walloon members, the large chapel of St Anthony in Threadneedle Street, together with its disused school and almshouse, being granted for their worship.[6] There was, however, some dissension within the congregation, probably precipitated by the increasingly radical doctrinal views of its clergyman, Walter Deleen, who was in time

[1] Lasco, John à, *Compendium doctrinae de vera unicaque Dei et Christi ecclesiae, etc.*, in Joannis a Lasco, *Opera, etc.*, ed. by A. Kuyper (2 vols., Amsterdam and The Hague, 1866), II, 285–339.

[2] *Ibid.* 1 ff.: *Forma ac ratio, etc.*; Van Schelven, A. A., *De nederduitsche vluchtelingen-kerken der XVI⁰ eeuw in Engeland en Duitschland, etc.* (The Hague, 1909), 82–87.

[3] Norwood, F. A., 'The Strangers' "model churches" in sixteenth-century England', in *Reformation studies*, ed. by F. H. Littell (Richmond, Va., 1962), 188–189.

[4] Van Schelven, *De nederduitsche vluchtelingenkerken*, 76–77, 88–89.

[5] Müller, Johann Georg, *Bekenntnisse merkwürdiger Männer von sich selbst*, VI (Winterthur, 1822), 241. A native of Zurich, Maler travelled widely in England in 1551, also attending Oxford for a short season.

[6] Beeman, G. B., 'The early history of the Stranger's church, 1550–1561', in *Huguenot Soc. of London Proceedings*, XV (1933–1937), 271–272; Lasky to Bullinger, London, Jan. 7, 1551, in Gorham, *Gleanings*, 225–226; *Cal. S.P. Span.*, X, 261: Apr. 9, 1551.

obliged to recant teachings such as denouncing the custom of god-parents, demanding a wholly stark communion rite, condemning all genuflexions, and denying the doctrine of Christ's descent into hell.[1] These controversies were reported to Calvin himself, who admonished the congregation to live in concord, rebuked the clergyman, and expressed his grief for the scandal which had arisen. This congregation grew rapidly during the later months of the Edwardian period and was lively in its intellectual life.

Then in 1551 still another congregation was formed for worship in the Italian language under the direct oversight of the mother refuge church. Lasky assured Bullinger that he had appointed for its ministry 'a pious and learned man, endowed with a singular gift of speaking'.[2] This preacher was Michael Angelo Florio, kinsman of Simon Florio, an eminent Continental divine. Florio, who already enjoyed a royal pension of £20 p.a., was, however, quickly at logger-heads with his congregation, probably because of his too great zeal and censorious nature. Then, real scandal overcame the Italian church when its minister was suspended from office, and from salary, until he made open confession of admitted fornication. He complained to the Council that many of his congregation had forsaken their church and still spoke 'very slanderously against him and his ministry, and the Gospel which he preached'. On Cecil's request, moreover, Florio provided the Council with a list of four-teen Italians who were daily attending mass and who merited condign punishment. Shortly afterwards this turbulent man was in difficulties for having denounced another refugee clergyman for straying too far from Calvin's doctrine of predestination, which Calvin promptly and sensibly cured by warning the congregation against making 'an idol of me, and a Jerusalem of Geneva'.[3]

The flow of refugees to England was principally a direct and often an immediate response to Continental religious policy. From 1548 onwards active (or feared) persecution of Protestantism in the Low Countries was forcing out a steady stream of refugees, which was greatly augmented when severe repression began in 1550. The death of Francis II (1547) left French Protestantism exposed to sporadic and localized repressions, but because of the disturbed political relations of England and France refugees from that country

[1] Vide ante, 314.
[2] Gerdes, Daniel, Serinium antiquarium (8 vols., Groningen, 1749–1765), IV, i, 467 as cited by Gorham, Gleanings, 226.
[3] Strype, Cranmer, II, 881–885; Strype, Memorials, II, i, 377–378; Smyth, C. I Cranmer and the Reformation under Edward VI (Cambridge, 1926), 222.

ordinarily went first to Switzerland or Germany. But in 1550 some scores of French Protestants arrived in England. At about the same time active persecution at Naples resulted in the flight of numerous Protestants, joined by a fair number of Genoese, some few of whom arrived in England, usually after a journey of several stages.[1]

We have observed that a large proportion of these refugees, of whatever national origin, settled in London, which had long possessed foreign enclaves and which after the founding of the foreign churches provided protective institutions at once spiritual and social in their nature. But other, and much smaller, aggregations of refugee Protestants were gathering in various towns and cities, normally those with long-standing commercial ties with the Continent. In Norwich a substantial number of Dutch and Flemish weavers were admitted, who with a considerably larger group who joined them in the Elizabethan period were to contribute significantly to the revival of the cloth industry in Norfolk.[2] So too, Colchester received in the Edwardian period a number of Dutch and Flemish settlers, perhaps as many as fifty families, who were in time to be gathered into the Dutch church there.[3] There was likewise at Southampton a considerable settlement of refugees from both the Low Countries and Italy, for whom a disused church was provided, which was also to serve the spiritual needs of Channel Islanders resident in the city.[4] We have observed elsewhere that as early as 1548–1549 Utenhove was concerned with the formation of a small French and Walloon church at Canterbury, comprised mainly of weavers, for which Rivière was the first pastor.[5] Other, and smaller, dispersions of refugees to the market and cloth towns were occurring, but the numbers of these families were so small that they seem speedily to have been absorbed into the communities in which they had settled. There was one interesting exception: the deliberate effort to found a foreign community and church at Glastonbury, springing as it did principally from Somerset's deep interest in social experimentation.

The settlement of this community seems to have been made on

---

[1] Here we follow principally William Page, 'Denizations and naturalizations of aliens in England', Huguenot Soc. of London, *Publications*, VIII (1893), xxvii–xxix.

[2] Jordan, *Charities of rural England*, 90 *et passim*.

[3] Moens, W. J. C., ed., *Register of baptisms in the Dutch church at Colchester, etc.* (Huguenot Soc. of London, *Publications*, XII, 1905), 110.

[4] Smyth, *Cranmer*, 223.

[5] Jordan, *Edward VI*, 197–198; VCH, *Kent*, II, 79; Pijper, *Utenhove*, App., Letter #3; Burn, J. S., *The history of the French, Walloon, Dutch and other foreign Protestant refugees settled in England, etc.* (L., 1846), 38–39.

the personal and direct authority of Somerset, with the administrative assistance of Cecil, probably on the representations of
Valérand Poulain. Poulain, a native of Lille and educated at Louvain,
became a Protestant shortly after his ordination in 1540[1] and had
served a Walloon-French congregation for some time settled in
Strassburg. On the promulgation of the *Interim*, not long after his
arrival in England as a refugee with Bucer and Fagius, a considerable portion of his congregation followed their minister across the
Channel. Poulain was responsible for arranging for this mass migration and during its English stay was skilful in holding it intact, in
establishing its worship, and in his dealings with the governmental
authorities.[2] The plan accepted by Somerset was for the founding
of a somewhat isolated colony of weavers in the numerous remaining
buildings of the former abbey of Glastonbury. An English overseer,
Henry Cornish, was appointed to supervise the business affairs of
the community to which the Duke had advanced £484 14s as a loan,
as well as houses, lands, and the promise of support until the group
could become self-sufficient. Thus in June, 1550, he exchanged lands
in Lincolnshire with the King for the remaining lands and tenements
at Glastonbury. He also entered into an agreement with the community which would provide each household with five acres of land
for the maintenance of two cows, and underwrote the manufacture of
cloth with tools and materials initially to be supplied by him.[3]

At this juncture, and almost coincident with Somerset's arrest
and trial, thirty-four families and ten widows arrived in Glastonbury with the news that an additional ten families were following,
or a total number of persons perhaps in excess of two hundred. It
was at once evident that the administration of this considerable
undertaking had not been well or thoroughly organized, for workrooms were not immediately available, only six houses were ready,
though another twenty-two could be made habitable, leaving another
ten houses which must be made ready as vacancies occurred.[4]

---

[1] Cowell, J. H., 'The French-Walloon church at Glastonbury, 1550-1553', Huguenot
Soc. of London *Proceedings*, XIII (1923-1929), 507-508; *vide* Jordan, *Edward VI*, 197,
for an earlier reference to Poulain.

[2] Schickler, Fernand de, *Les églises du refuge en Angleterre* (3 vols., Paris, 1892), I,
59-63; Poulain, V., *Ordre des prières . . . en l'église de Glastonbury* (L., 1552), for the
established service which clearly followed that of the Strassburg church.

[3] Strype, *Cranmer*, I, 347-348; Green, Emanuel, 'On some Flemish weavers settled
at Glastonbury, A.D. 1551', Somersetshire Archaeol. and Nat. Hist. Soc. *Proceedings*,
XXVI (1880), pt. ii, 17-18.

[4] Cowell, in *Huguenot Soc. Proc.*, XIII, 486-492; Norwood, *Reformation refugees*,
30-31; Strype, *Memorials*, II, i, 378; Burn, *Protestant refugees*, 91; Green, in *Som.
Archaeol. and Nat. Hist. Soc. Proc.*, XXVI, ii, 17-19.

Somerset's fall, it must have seemed, would complete the wrecking of this interesting and bold enterprise. But Poulain, though possessing none save spiritual authority, proved himself an able administrator, and immediately, and persuasively, laid the problems of his congregation before the Privy Council, praying that all of the assurances and commitments of the Duke be ratified and carried forward.[1] At about the same time Poulain petitioned specifically, and successfully, that debts contracted in England by the community to a total of £131 0s 9d be paid, and sought the support of Petre in making certain that his petition should be speedily laid before the Council.[2] The Council did recognize its full responsibilities for the plight of the Glastonbury community, having in fact less than a fortnight after Somerset's arrest instructed the auditor to see that the allowances assured by the Duke were continued and that the refugees be gently dealt with.[3] Not quite a month later Poulain was informed that Cornish would remain responsible to the government and that he had been instructed to make the promised properties available, to pay the workmen, and to carry out the commitments which Somerset had made.[4]

The Privy Council, in fact, lent careful and sympathetic attention to the affairs of the community, appointing a committee presided over by William Barlow, Bishop of Bath, to attend to its needs, and deciding immediately to advance £340 for the purchase of wool and other necessaries for the refugees.[5] The Council also prevailed on two greatly respected Glastonbury residents (Powis and Hyatt) to assess the requirements of the settlement and to make their own recommendations for its care. The debts of the congregation were then discharged; available land was taken over in order to provide more pasturage; and repairs were at once begun on thirty additional houses. On the settlement's petition, it was also granted power to choose from its own number five persons who would oversee its affairs, to import needed commodities free of duty, and to enjoy all privileges granted to other clothworkers and dyers in the realm. They were also empowered to employ their own order of worship and discipline, Poulain's liturgy thereby attaining a formal appro-

---

[1] S.P. Dom., Edw. VI, XIII, 70, 71: Dec. 11, 1551. Poulain, while deeply shocked by Somerset's execution, none the less urged Calvin not to publish anything which would excite passions in England and further divide the godly (Robinson, *Original letters*, II, 737–738: Mar. 7, 1552).

[2] S.P. Dom., Edw. VI, XIII, 72, 73: Dec. 18, 1551.

[3] *A.P.C.*, III, 400: Oct. 28, 1551.

[4] *Ibid.* 415: Nov. 14, 1551.

[5] S.P. Dom., Edw. VI, XIII, 74, 75, 76, 77: Dec. 18, 1551.

val.[1] It may be said that by mid-1552 the affairs of the community were in order; the worship of the group under the skilled and highly effective leadership of Poulain was well established; relations with the local English community had been greatly improved; and the increasing cloth production gave promise that this boldly experimental undertaking might even be economically successful. But there was little time left for this effort to found a new Zion in the west of England. Shortly after the accession of Mary Tudor, Poulain, sensing the implacable hostility of the new sovereign, carried the whole community to further exile in Frankfort.[2]

It is not too much to say that the close and organic connections between England and the Continental Reformation during a period of almost seven years did much to relieve the cultural insularity of the realm and to place it in the forefront of European interest. We should not forget that during the reign of Edward VI England was the only powerful national monarchy unequivocally to have embraced Protestantism and that for a brief season it seemed almost predictable that Edward VI, youthful, full of enthusiasm, and indubitably Protestant, might become its political champion and that the intellectual and theological leadership of Protestantism might also become rooted in his realm. Hence English affairs and the rapid spread of the English Reformation were watched with a consuming interest during these hopeful years. We find in consequence in the many hundreds of letters passing between the refugees, English and Continental, a great store of sources for the English Reformation and the testimony of a momentary catholicity of Protestant thought and aspiration.

We have seen in the many letters already cited that it was principally Cranmer who gave direction and encouragement to these developments and it was he who was responsible for the numerous invitations, often supported by the King, to induce Continental reformers either to visit or to settle in England. For many years he retained an especially warm interest in German ecclesiastical affairs, dating back in fact to his own diplomatic mission to Germany and his marriage with Osiander's niece. His relations with the great Archbishop Hermann von Wied of Cologne were especially intimate, while with the tempestuous Luther and the somewhat diffident Melanchthon he sought as well to find a common spiritual standing-ground. But,

---

[1] S.P. Dom., Edw. VI, XIV, 2, 3i, 13; *ibid.* XV, 55; *A.P.C.*, III, 509–510: Mar. 22, 1552; *ibid.* IV, 180: Nov. 29, 1552.

[2] Green, in *Som. Archaeol. and Nat. Hist. Soc. Proc.*, XXVI, ii, 22; Cowell, in *Huguenot Soc. Proc.*, XIII, 495.

Cranmer's intellectual and spiritual ties with Germany notwithstanding, the predominant influence and the effective vigour among the scholars and preachers who found their way to England, or who lent the full weight of their support to the Reformation proceeding there, was at first Zwinglian and then Calvinistic. We have dealt with the principal of these reformers, but there were a great many others, on the whole of the second rank of eminence, who gave serious consideration to invitations to attend in England or who were seeking such appointments.

Thus Bullinger's correspondence makes it clear that in 1549 Augustine Mainardo, the leading minister in Italian Rhaetia, was attracted by a call to remove to England to gain surcease from his battles with local heresies.[1] So too Vergerio, who had until his renunciation in 1549 been Bishop of Capodistria and a valued diplomatist for the Holy See, now also embroiled in Rhaetia, repeatedly enjoined Bullinger to gain an invitation for him from England, dedicating two of his treatises to Edward VI. Vergerio's interest in England was sustained, and Morison, who met him in Augsburg, was persuaded that the Italian reformer would add substantial strength to evangelical Protestantism.[2] The delicately developed negotiations continued until 1552 when, after Musculus had declined the invitation to succeed Bucer at Cambridge, Lasky and other of his English friends urged the Italian divine to come in the hope of securing the appointment. But Vergerio, with real modesty, indicated that he could not so over-estimate himself and would prefer, if called, to serve as preacher to the Italian congregation in London.[3] Vergerio was to accompany Morison when he returned to England, but there were further delays until the plan was abandoned on the death of the King.

How these invitations were arranged and carried forward is well documented in Lasky's correspondence with Bullinger when the difficult appointment of Bucer's successor was under consideration. Lasky tells us that Cranmer had consulted him—as we know he had others—on invitations which he hoped to extend to several learned men. In addition to Vergerio and Musculus, whom Cranmer had

[1] *Bullingers Korrespondenz mit den Graubündnern*, ed. by Traugott Schiess (3 vols., *Quellen zur Schweizer Geschichte*, XXIII–XXV, Basel, 1904–1906), I, 145–146, 147, 148–149.

[2] Weller, E., 'Uebersicht der litterarischen Thätigkeit des Pietro Paolo Vergerio, Bischofs von Capodistria', *Serapeum*, XIX (Leipzig, 1858), 65–77, 81–91, 97–101; Hubert, Friedrich, *Vergerios publizistische Tätigkeit, etc.* (Breslau, 1893), 108–112; *Bullingers Korrespondenz*, I, 184, 190, 191, 196, 203, 212, 231, 246.

[3] *Ibid.* 256: July 10, 1552; Hubert, *Vergerios publizistische Tätigkeit*, 113–114.

repeatedly invited some years earlier,[1] Lasky had also proposed
Theodore Bibliander and, almost incredibly, Sebastian Castellio.
Cranmer on his part mentioned Brenz, brushing aside Lasky's
protest of his unorthodoxy on the doctrine of the eucharist, with the
comment that this he already knew. Cranmer further revealed that
John Hales had been commissioned to arrange for the removal to
England of both Musculus and Bibliander if they could be per-
suaded to cast their lot with the reformed Church of England. Two
months later Lasky once more wrote to Bullinger to say that neither
Musculus nor Bibliander could gain permission to leave their
posts, and now urged on the Swiss divine the qualifications of
Castellio and Coelius Curio, the latter being a close friend of
Hooper's and since 1547 a professor at Basel.[2]

Tender, brooding, and sustained as was Bullinger's concern for
the fledgling Church of England, it remains true that as the reign
progressed his influence was gradually being replaced by the
immensely powerful and vigorous thought of John Calvin, whose
writings were rapidly being made available in English and who did
not hesitate to lend harshly honest, if arrogantly phrased, advice to
the Lord Protector and to the King himself. In all, six of Calvin's
works were translated and published in English during the course
of the reign; one, which we shall notice, was published in French,
and still another in Latin.

Of great influence, too, in securing the spread of Calvinistic
teachings was a work entitled *The forme of common prayers used in the
churches of Geneva*, a powerful piece of propaganda, all the more
effective because the translator, William Huycke, gave it no special
commendation. The work described in detail the order of service
and set out at length the Calvinistic mode of celebrating the Lord's
Supper with a full rendering of the prayers employed in the service.
After a long exhortation to the communicants the minister concluded, 'So then this shall be sufficient to satisfy and content us: to
take the bread and wine as sure signs and witnesses of God's
promises adjoined unto them: and therewithal to search spiritually
the effect and substance of the same, where God's Word doth say
we shall find it.'[3] Then the minister closed with a short and clearly
expressed statement of the differences between the godly service of
the true Church and the error-ridden service of the mass. This
quite perfectly timed publication pointed the way in which England

[1] Robinson, *Original letters*, I, 334–337; *ibid.* II, 680.
[2] Gerdes, *Serinium antiquarium*, IV, i, 470–472, cited in Gorham, *Gleanings*, 245–248,
264, 266.   [3] *The forme of common prayers, etc.* ([L., 1550]), Fiiᵛ–Fiii.

was to go as the great work of preparing the second *Book of Common Prayer* was begun.

We have observed that Calvin's first direct intervention in English affairs was a sternly admonitory letter to Somerset in October, 1548 in which he urged an immediate furthering of the Reformation in England, the firm repression of the risings which had so weakened the realm, and the weeding out of all remaining popish survivals.[1] A year later Calvin expressed to Bucer his continuing concern for England, urging him to attempt to persuade the Protector, as he had himself sought to do, of the importance of abolishing all ceremonies reminiscent of popery. This he particularly hoped Bucer, who had so long, though falsely, been accused of seeking compromises on important matters of faith, would do. He added the hope that the reformed churches might end their divisive disagreements and bury them in oblivion.[2] Much the same advice was given by the Genevan in a letter sent directly to the King, reminding him in cool and forthright terms that though it was true that certain indifferent matters might be borne with, this must not lead to confusion of purpose in the work of reformation. In England, he was persuaded, the over-riding problem was the weakness of the clergy, which still reflected the ignorance and barbarism which popery had fostered. He accordingly advised Edward to make certain that all popery be extirpated from the universities, so that godly clergy might be bred, while urging that the refugee clergy who had come to England be accorded full Christian liberty.[3] These views were further elaborated in a letter to his colleague Farel in which Calvin despaired of the clergy of England. In all probability no real progress could be gained until the King began personally to govern. He was persuaded that 'the revenues of the church were gorged by the nobles', while 'in the meantime they hire men of no repute at a paltry salary, who discharge the duties, or at least occupy the place of pastors'. But even though there was no immediate prospect for improvement, 'I will not cease to give them all a sharp rebuke' and will continue to write frequently to the King.[4]

John Calvin was as persistent as he was blunt in hammering on what he regarded as the principal weaknesses of the Church of England. In a short letter to Somerset, dated July 25, 1551, he

---

[1] Jordan, *Edward VI*, 126.
[2] Calvin to Bucer, *c*. Oct. 1549, most easily available in Gorham, *Gleanings*, 115–117.
[3] Robinson, *Original letters*, II, 709–710: [Jan. 1, 1551].
[4] Calvin, *Opera*, ed. 1667, IX, 240.

again insisted that the great want in England was an able clergy. This was occasioned, in part at least, because popery had not been wholly driven from the universities and because clerical incomes were so very low. It must be said that the condition of the clergy engenders nothing but contempt for them, which, he concluded, must be apparent even to those in England who were 'deriving profit from the property of the Church'.[1]

But Calvin lent no direct aid, just as he politely evaded Cranmer's urging that he lend his name to a great Protestant assembly which should meet in England. He could offer no more than the hope that Cranmer would persevere in his irenic intentions.[2] When Cranmer pressed hard to secure the conference, which he hoped would bring Calvin, Melanchthon, and Bullinger to England, he found himself frustrated by Melanchthon's weary diffidence and Calvin's icy aloofness in the Church which God had planted in Geneva. Then, this noble and hopeful undertaking having failed, Calvin urged that even though no consensus had been possible, Cranmer should proceed to the planned amendment of the Book of Common Prayer. Others would help, but the principal responsibility would necessarily rest with Cranmer. Speed, he declared, was of the essence, for he feared that 'so many autumns should be spent in delay, that at length the cold of an eternal winter should succeed'.[3] He reminded the primate that the remaining popish corruptions in the present Book were so many as almost to overwhelm the pure worship of God. To this great and necessary task Cranmer should now set himself, with the aid of Peter Martyr.[4] But his great hope, so he wrote to Cheke, lay in the young King. There was, for Calvin, rare courtesy as there was deep conviction, when he declared it had been due to Cheke's tuition that 'England possesses a king, not only of the noblest disposition, but moulded by your labours to mature excellence beyond his age, who may stretch forth his hand to the distressed or rather afflicted Church in these miserable times'.[5] The hope that Calvin held for the future leadership of a truly reformed Protestantism was wholly in vain. With Edward's death a few months later there passed the last lingering hope for a Protestant consensus. With that death, too, 'the cold of . . . winter' did succeed in England.

---

[1] Sloane MS. 4277, #24.
[2] Robinson, *Original letters*, II, 713–714: Calvin to Cranmer, [Apr. 1], 1552.
[3] *Ibid.* I, 23, 24–25, 26.
[4] Calvin, *Opera*, ed. 1667, IX, 61, cited in Gorham, *Gleanings*, 277–280:[June], 1552.
[5] *Ibid.* 288–290, citing Calvin, *Opera*, ed. 1667, IX, 68: Feb. 13, 1553.

10. THE PROBLEM OF RADICAL SECTARIANISM (1549–1553)

We have already commented on the horror evoked amongst normally tolerant churchmen when it became evident that radical sectarianism was finding root in England, even in the extreme form of Anabaptism.[1] The responsible reformers, and especially those charged with the administration of the Church, were frightened and appalled when they observed the centripetal thrust inherent in Protestantism and were unsure regarding methods for the control of bizarre heretical beliefs, some of which seem certainly to betray madness rather than illumination. They were especially concerned by evidences that Anabaptism, fragmented but spreading after the fall of Münster, was seeping into England and was planting itself in areas connected with the cloth trade and in regions where earlier Lollardy survived. We have seen, too, that severe measures were employed in the late Henrician period to stamp out the Anabaptist heresies, at least twenty-one persons—English, Flemish, French, and Dutch in national origin—being burned because of what were thought to be their Anabaptist persuasions. For a brief season these heretics were driven under ground, but during Somerset's tenure of power the almost complete freedom of religion which appertained, the generous and uninhibited welcome extended to religious refugees, and the exempt spiritual authority vested in the Strangers' Church fostered the further infiltration of radical sectaries and the tendency for such heretics to gather in aggregates for worship.

An examination of the heresies charged against persons arraigned on suspicion of heresy in the late Henrician and Edwardian periods suggests that their doctrinal views were not clearly held or stated, were actually highly individualistic, and were frequently so bemused and incoherent as to suggest madness. Almost all of them did violently deny the validity of infant baptism, some of them denied the Incarnation, and most of them held opinions which might with reasonable accuracy be described as Socinian, Pelagian, Millenarian, or mystical. Some of these accused heretics also held vaguely formulated communistic views, and among almost all of them there were strongly held tenets of faith which can be described with reasonable accuracy as spiritual and political anarchism. Hence it is no wonder that the responsible authorities in church and state began to move with some vigour against sectarian radicalism

[1] Jordan, *Edward VI*, 225–229.

as part of the whole reflex action of repression which was the immediate consequence of the great risings of 1549.

The abhorrence of Anabaptist views was especially marked amongst the evangelical clergy of the Church of England, men who had held so strongly, if naively, the conviction that freedom to read and ponder the Bible and attendance on the free preaching of the Gospel must of necessity bring the nation to the establishment and full support of the true Church. Hence Latimer was particularly sensitive to these heresies, in his sermon preached before the King on March 29, 1549, denouncing the Anabaptists for their anarchical teachings and stating, surely with heroic exaggeration, that by credible testimony there were as many as five hundred of the sect in one unnamed town.[1] So too, the less excitable Hooper in June, 1549 wrote to Bullinger that the Anabaptists were trooping to his famous London lectures and were giving him great trouble because of their contentious and decidedly heretical interruptions.[2] To combat them frontally Hooper later in the same year wrote his *Lesson of the Incarnation of Christ*, which he hoped might quiet them by the solid refutation of their central position,[3] while in a further effort to destroy their intellectual and theological credibility treatises against the Anabaptists by Bullinger and Calvin were hastily translated and published.

The gathering evidence of radical heresy, particularly in the London area, gravely alarmed the Council, especially when it became known that the Anabaptist heresies were spreading into Essex, Kent, and Sussex. Hence, as we have seen, a powerful commission was established in April, 1549, composed of Cranmer and six other bishops, Petre and Smith from the Privy Council, and others, and was instructed to search out all heretics, to excommunicate and imprison them, or to hand them over to the civil power for further action as circumstances might determine. The commission immediately set about its work, with the result that in May several Londoners were examined and persuaded to abjure a mixture of Anabaptist and Socinian opinions, all yielding save for Joan Bocher and George van Parris, whose tragic fate now concerns us.[4]

Joan Bocher, possibly the wife of a London butcher named Thombe, who was one of those who had recanted, troubled Cranmer and his colleagues particularly because she had been in serious

---

[1] Latimer, *The fourth sermon*, in *Works*, I, 151–152.
[2] Robinson, *Original letters*, I, 65–66.
[3] Hooper, *Later writings*, 1–18.
[4] Jordan, *Edward VI*, 228–229.

difficulties at an earlier date. She took pride in the fact that she had been one of those who had first distributed Tyndale's New Testament and there is evidence that she had known Anne Askewe well in her days of adversity. She had earlier (1542) been before Cranmer on heresy charges, but he had dealt lightly with her in the hope of reformation. She had undoubtedly been spreading her views more recently in both London and Kent, having been reported to the Privy Council by Kentish magistrates as a confirmed Anabaptist. Now before the Edwardian commission she partially at least abjured her Socinian views, but could not be shaken from her amazing conviction that Christ took no flesh from the Virgin, but passed through her miraculously, as through a glass. This view she also expressed by the contention that the Word was made flesh in the Virgin by consent of her 'inward man', and hence that Christ took no flesh from her. There were other, though related, heresies which she professed, but she would yield on no point, declaring that she was sustained by the example of Anne Askewe: 'It is a godly matter', she contended,

'to consider your ignorance. Not long since you burned Anne Askewe for a piece of bread, and yet came yourselves to believe and propose the same doctrine for which you burned her, and now, forsooth, you will needs burn me for a piece of flesh, and in the end you will come to believe this also, when you have read the Scriptures and understood them'.

From these positions she could not be moved and the commission for the time being took no action beyond formal excommunication and imprisonment. Doubt was expressed, indeed, whether the death sentence could be imposed, since Somerset had swept away the infamous heresy act, until Rich pointed out that the King might at will order her execution within the frame of the common law. This Somerset was unprepared to countenance, and the grisly conclusion was not undertaken until well after he had fallen from power.[1]

During the course of a full year repeated efforts were made by the most persuasive of the reformers to gain a recantation from Joan Bocher. Among those who reasoned and prayed with her were bishops Ridley and Goodrich, and the two famous preachers Lever

---

[1] Latimer, *Works*, II, 114; Stow, *Annales*, 596; Strype, *Memorials*, II, i, 335; Burnet, *Reformation*, V, 246–249; Wilkins, *Concilia*, IV, 39–44; Wriothesley, *Chronicle*, II, 10–11; *Grey Friars Chronicle*, 58–59.

and Hutchinson, but no one could move her from what Hutchinson declared to be her central error; that the Virgin had both a corporal and a spiritual seed, and that Christ, though born of her, sprang from the spiritual seed alone.[1] The final decision to burn Joan was taken in early April, 1550 shortly after Ridley was translated to London and, significantly, just as Somerset, now with no real power, resumed his seat in the Council. For a week, we are told, Ridley and Goodrich made a last and unsuccessful effort to reclaim her from her errors, the Council on April 27th forwarding a warrant to the Lord Chancellor to prepare a writ to the sheriff of London to proceed with execution by burning as an heretic.[2] The terrible sentence was carried out on May 2nd. Scory preached before her at the place of execution, the evidently fearless, and probably mad, woman saying to him only that 'he lied like a knave'.[3] The King, as always without a trace of emotion, recorded on that day simply that

'Joan Bocher, otherwise called Joan of Kent, was burned for holding that Christ was not incarnate of the Virgin Mary, being condemned the year before but kept in hope of conversion; and . . . the Bishop of London and the Bishop of Ely were to persuade her. But she withstood them and reviled the preacher that preached at her death.'[4]

We simply do not know where the onus for this barbarous act lies. The Council itself bears the central responsibility, and there is of course the almost certain fact that it was resolved to act before Somerset regained any power or influence in that body. There is more than a suggestion that Ridley, determined to wipe out Anabaptism in his diocese, lent strong support to the final decision. Foxe and Hayward recited the legend that it was Cranmer who persuaded the reluctant King to sign the warrant, whereas in fact it was signed by the Council. None the less Foxe was probably correct in maintaining that Cranmer bore a direct moral responsibility, and certain it is that he did nothing to oppose the dreadful action.[5] It seems probable, indeed, that it was Foxe himself who through 'a certain friend' interceded vainly for Joan's life, with the subtle and

---

[1] *The works of Roger Hutchinson, etc.*, ed. by John Bruce (Parker Soc., Cambridge, 1842), 145–146.   [2] *A.P.C.*, III, 19.

[3] *Grey Friars Chronicle*, 66; *A breviat chronicle, etc.* (Canterbury, 1552; STC #9170), Nii.

[4] Edward VI, *Chronicle*, 28; *vide* also the comments of Stow, *Annales*, 604; *Two London chronicles*, 21.

[5] Egerton MS. 2877, ff. 14b–15; Ridley, *Cranmer*, 292–293; Hayward, *Edward VI*, 272 [mispaged]; Foxe, *Acts and monuments*, V, 699.

persuasive argument that 'even though she might infect a few by living, she would confirm more if she were punished with death'.

There was, unhappily, still another execution for heresy, evidently quite unconnected with the Bocher case. A new commission charged with ferreting out heresies had been appointed on January 18, 1551, which investigated the case of a Dutch (or Flemish) surgeon, a refugee who had fled from the Low Countries first to Paris and then to England. George van Parris, as he was known, had aroused controversy in the German church in London and was denounced by the congregation to the heresy commission as an Anabaptist. One can with all charity say that Parris seems to have been a fanatic, eating only once every two days and prostrating himself for long periods before each meal. He seems, however, to have been mild in temper, was not argumentative—perhaps because he knew no English—and was quietly unmoved by all the efforts to reason with him. Cranmer, Ridley, Coverdale, and the others on the commission in early April found him to be an Arian who completely and stubbornly denied the divinity of Christ. Coverdale, acting as interpreter, established that Parris believed that 'God the Father is only God; and that Christ is none very god', which was heresy to believe. Parris was found guilty of heresy on April 7th and, refusing to recant, was burned at the stake at Smithfield on April 24, 1551.[1]

We may be laying a quite undue emphasis on these two executions for heresy which so indelibly mar the tolerance and relative religious freedom of this reign. Insignificant they certainly were when set in an historical background which includes Henry VIII's sporadic but brutal burning of Protestants and butchery of Catholic conservatives or Queen Mary's systematic effort to extirpate a faith which had already captured the imagination and devotion of a considerable and high-minded proportion of the realm. These two terrible incidents, like all persecution, sprang from fear: in one instance fear of a probably mad woman's cloudy, but obdurately held, errors respecting a central doctrine of the Christian Church, and in the other to give warning that heresies would not be freely tolerated amongst the refugees who had for months been streaming into England. These acts of persecution also sprang from that moment of terrible fear in 1549 when it had seemed that the English society might be ruptured by anarchical insurrections, which had

---

[1] Edward VI, *Chronicle*, 58; Wilkins, *Concilia*, IV, 44–45; Burnet, *Reformation*, V, 249; Stow, *Annales*, 604; Wriothesley, *Chronicle*, II, 47; Rymer, *Foedera*, XV, 250; *Breviat chronicle*, Nii.

shaken the responsible, the propertied, and the godly. They proceeded, too, from the inevitably defensive position in which Protestantism stood, for they gave substance to the Roman Catholic contention that from Protestantism there would spread red ruin and anarchy. Cranmer himself sought to explain to his secretary's (Morice's) brother, why he dealt so severely with the wilder of the Protestant heretics and so mildly with Romanist conservatism. The Catholics, he maintained, should not by harshness be prevented from embracing a truth which they had never known. But those who have known and accepted the Gospel must set a good example, and from them we must require a higher standard of faith and conduct.[1] Here we doubtless have the principal explanation of how such gentle and civilized men as Cranmer, Ridley, Latimer, and even Coverdale could take on their consciences the burning of Bocher and Parris.

These apprehensions, these yearnings for Protestant doctrinal responsibility and discipline, were supported by most of the reformed clergy of the period, usually in language of denunciation which was shriller than it need have been. Perhaps two brief annotations will suffice. Becke, writing in 1550, warned in a crude rhyme of the Anabaptist heresy respecting the incarnation which, he correctly said, had in one form or another plagued the Church from the earliest times. He then concluded:

> Let us pray unto God long to maintain and defend
> The state of this realm and God's true religion.
> Let us also give thanks to God which hath send [sic]
> Us a king to all princes a president and patron
> A Council most catholic for a Christian congregation
> To surcease all sedition to punish false teachers
> And to stablish true doctrine God send us good preachers.[2]

So too the staunchly Protestant, but cantankerous John Philpot denounced in the harshest terms the Arianism which he thought was already fragmenting the Church in England, for it is to a degree concealed by the constant and unscrupulous citing of Scriptures by men who have no other intention than to bring God's Church to ruin. Such heresies simply must be extirpated.[3] But, be it said, even amongst the most orthodox of Protestant

---

[1] Nichols, *Narratives of the Reformation* (Camden Soc. LXXVII), 246–247.

[2] Becke, Edmund, *A brefe confutacion, etc.* ([L.], 1550), no pagin.

[3] Philpot, John, *An apologie, etc.*, in *The examinations and writings of John Philpot, etc.*, ed. by Robert Eden (Parker Soc., Cambridge, 1842), 302–303. Philpot, who was burned by Mary, even while in prison awaiting trial violently attacked certain of his fellow prisoners who, he said, held Pelagian views.

divines there could also be great charity and a clearer understanding of the nature of religious thought. William Turner, who at various times in his amazing life was physician, traveller, botanist, humanist, and divine,[1] pointed out that Christ's Church had always been troubled with spawning heresies. In the twenty years that had elasped since he knew Latimer at Cambridge, he had himself first struggled with popish errors and now he was assailed by new and dangerous heresies, the worst of which was Pelagianism. Recently in a lecture at Islesworth (Middlesex) he had spoken at length against the view that since children have no original sin they should not be baptized. Now he sought to establish beyond peradventure the orthodox doctrine in order to help in halting the spread of Anabaptism. But Turner made it crystal clear that in his view heresy simply could not be overcome by persecutions and burnings. Heresies are not material things; they cannot be destroyed by fire, but rather by the spiritual weapons of refutation and God's Word. England, confused as she is by sectarian heresies, must find her best—her only—defence in the founding of more schools, the spread of literacy, and the support of young scholars, so that the spiritual war which must be waged against heresy will be well sustained. Here we find the voice of sanity and reason which, as we have seen, was heard and accepted by many sensitive and powerful men, especially amongst the laity of England—men who must have been horrified, as Turner most certainly was, by the burnings which had marred the temple of the reformed faith.

The heresy commissions and the Council seem to have been vigilant in the search for heresies, especially in the period when Bocher and Parris were being investigated and tried. In early February a Scot, William Lermouth, was examined for seditious preaching against the nobles, bishops, and magistrates as well as the Book of Common Prayer, and released under bond of 1000 marks. Lermouth may, indeed, have been connected with three other suspects from Kent and Sussex who were examined in connection with religious meetings of a sectarian sort which had recently been held in Suffolk on weekdays.[2] So too, the day after Joan Bocher's condemnation an Anabaptist named Putto, a Colchester tanner, was brought by Cranmer before the heresy commission, but on recanting was released subject to bearing his faggot at Paul's Cross and later at Colchester.[3]

---

[1] We shall later comment more fully on Turner's thought (*post*, 369–370), though we may say here that a full-length study of this extraordinary man would be most useful.
[2] *A.P.C.*, II, 379, 380–381: Feb. 2 and 3, 1550.   [3] Strype, *Memorials*, II, i, 336.

Far more dangerous, in the Council's view, were groups of suspected men who were holding meetings in and near Bocking in Essex and in several places in Kent, though evidently centring on Faversham. In late January, 1551 one Upcharde of Bocking was interrogated concerning meetings, attended also by Kentish men, at which about forty persons had discussed such topics as whether it was necessary to kneel at prayer. On the following day an even larger group, of about sixty persons, met at his house to discuss scriptural matters, most of the beliefs expounded appearing to be more nearly Zwinglian than Anabaptist. The consensus was that whether to kneel or stand, to be covered or uncovered at prayer, were really immaterial, since it was the heart before God that was important. Upcharde and an associate named Simpson were committed to jail for a season, while the Council turned to its examination of the connected Kentish group as well as of several additional Essex suspects. Only seven of these can be identified as to status: one a schoolmaster at Maidstone, four clothiers, one a cowherd, and another a labourer. After a fairly rigorous examination of twelve of the group, nothing could be ascertained save that they confessed that they had assembled for scriptural discussion, that they shared doubts regarding the doctrine of predestination, that they had withdrawn from the communion of their parish churches, and held 'divers other evil opinions'. Five of the men, including Cole, the schoolmaster, were committed to prison for a season, while the others were released under bond, provided they met with their ordinary for the resolution of any doubt in religion.[1] We have all too little information regarding this group, so evidently instilled with missionary vigour, but enough surely to say that it was not Anabaptist in its teachings or interests. It may rather be regarded as an important, and a very early, evidence of indigenous and radical sectarianism.

Though the leaders at least of the sectarian party in Kent and Essex, dealt with so carefully by the Council itself, were certainly not Anabaptists, some members of this loosely organized association were probably involved in still another appearance of heresy in Kent in the following year. They may have been influenced by one Robert Cooke who, though almost certainly an Anabaptist, somehow found it possible to carry on his teachings for a season without molestation. Cooke seems in point of fact to have debated with William Turner[2] on the doctrine of original sin and infant baptism

---

[1] *A.P.C.*, III, 53, 198–199, 206–207; Strype, *Memorials*, II, i, 385; Harl. MS. 421, ff. 133–134; Lansdowne MS. 980, #82, f. 95.   [2] *Vide ante*, 332.

and at an uncertain date to have written a tract entitled *The Confutation of the Errors of the Careless by Necessity*.[1] But the Council was more disturbed by the appearance in Kent of a new sect of Antinomian persuasion, later to flourish as the Family of Love, which it ordered Cranmer to investigate after he had considered an heretical treatise in their hands and had examined a man and woman who had been sent to him.[2] In preparation for the journey which Cranmer was making into Kent, in part to probe the new appearance of heresy there, the Council was arranging for a new commission and wished the Archbishop to delay his departure until they could confer with him.[3] We have found no further reference to this intended investigation and have, indeed, the sense that radical sectarianism had by the autumn of 1552 been brought under effective control by a government which had been badly shaken by the Bocher and Parris episodes. It seemed that the centrist religious position, so perfectly exemplified by the thought and policies of Cranmer and Ridley, had triumphed and that the fractionating tendencies so inherent in Protestantism had been stayed.

[1] Williams, G. H., *The radical Reformation* (Philadelphia, 1962), 781.
[2] *A.P.C.*, IV, 131: Sept. 26, 1552.
[3] *Ibid.* 138: Oct. 8, 1552.

IX

THE TRIUMPH OF PROTESTANTISM
(1551–1553)

1. PARLIAMENT IN SESSION (FIRST PARLIAMENT, FOURTH SESSION: JANUARY 23, 1552–APRIL 15, 1552)

A. *The secular measures*

After repeated postponements occasioned by political crisis and malaise Parliament was convened for its fourth session on January 23, 1552, almost two years after the close of the last meeting. Northumberland had seen to it that Somerset's execution was carried out the day before the session assembled, since he was fearful of the considerable support for the Duke amongst members in both Houses and quite as importantly because the mood of the City of London was so volatile and decidedly ominous. Friendly though distant peers were summoned to attend,[1] while feuding peers like Wharton and Dacre were dragooned into composing their difficulties, at least while Parliament was sitting. The young King had personally assumed a share in discussions in the Council regarding the agenda for the session, though the 'aid or subsidy ... to be required of the subjects at this Parliament' was never to be provided, despite the financial straits of the government. Moreover, stubborn opposition speedily exhibited itself in the House of Commons to a number of secular measures which the Council wished enacted into law.

Though the agenda for this rather short session was heavy, it is interesting to observe that the Commons was more than usually concerned with procedural questions and relatively minor matters of privilege. Thus on February 9th the burgesses from Sandwich were ordered to stand aside until 'the perfect return be known' of their election.[2] Servants of two members were granted

[1] S.P. Dom., Edw. VI, XIV, 1: Jan. 8, 1552; *A.P.C.*, III, 499–500.
[2] *C.J.*, I, 17; unfortunately, no return of members from Kent to this Parliament has been found (*Members of Parliament*, pt. I: *Parliaments of England, 1213–1702*, in *Parliamentary Papers*, 1878, LXII, 375); Lansdowne MS. 94, #8, f. 17.

protection against arrest from London creditors,[1] while a great deal of time was devoted to a thornier matter of privilege when a French complainant petitioned that protection be revoked for still another servant, Hugh Flood. Flood was in fact stripped of his privilege and was ordered to be conveyed by the Sergeant-at-Arms to the custody of the Sheriff of London. On the way Flood, after assaulting a London sergeant, made his escape, only to be recaptured and, by the authority of the House, sent to the Compter, there to remain under the custody of the Commons or the Privy Council. But so intent was the House on retaining control of the case that it seems to have devoted the whole of the last day of the session to deciding that Flood must remain in the Compter until he had given satisfaction to the complainant and then was to be delivered to the Sergeant of the House of Commons for his discharge.[2]

Of the several important secular measures which the government wished to be enacted into law, one was a bill substantially altering the traditional law of treason. The draft, introduced in the Lords on February 16th, gained approval there four days later, with only Lord Wentworth voting against it, but it immediately met strenuous opposition when it was introduced in the Commons on February 20th. Some weeks later after 'certain notes drawn out of the bill' were brought in by Sergeant Morgan and others, a new bill was drafted and, after further alterations, was passed by the Commons on April 13th and by the Lords on the following day. It declared that the intention was to strike down 'shameful slanders' describing the King as 'an heretic, schismatic, tyrant, infidel, or usurper'. Offenders who made such statements by 'writing, printing, painting, carving, or graving' should be guilty of high treason in the first instance, as were persons holding any fortress or ship of the King who on notice refused to surrender the same within six days. It was further enacted that any such treason committed outside the realm might be tried *in absentia* in any shire of the realm, provided, however, that offenders might surrender to the Chief Justice within one year to contest the indictment. The moderating effect of the highly articulate opposition of many in the Commons to the measure was reflected principally in two provisions: that offences under the act by 'open preaching or words' must be prosecuted within a period of three months, and that no person should be indicted or convicted of treason unless formally accused by two lawful accusers who, if living, must give evidence at the trial.[3]

---

[1] *C.J.*, I, 18.   [2] *Ibid.* 21, 23.   [3] See footnote on p. 337.

Serious and revealing difficulties were also experienced by the government in driving through a private bill, to which the royal assent had been gained in advance, to repeal the entail of 32 Henry VIII against the Duke of Somerset's first marriage, procured, it was stated, 'by the power of his second wife over him'. The bill was first challenged by the Lords, who feared that such a measure might unsettle all land tenures, and was then re-drafted by the Commons who also declined to pass a supplementary bill confirming *ex post facto* the attainder of the Duke. Still another amendment dissolving the contract for the marriage of Somerset's son to the daughter of the Earl of Oxford was lost by a vote of 69 to 68, while the bill for striking down the entail remained belaboured until the very end of the session when it was passed, carrying with it the forfeiture of much of the Duke's estate to the crown.[1]

The most important of the statutes passed in this session were concerned with cautious social and economic reforms, the pre-occupation of Parliament with the subject being suggested by the fact that seventeen of the twenty-six public laws enacted dealt with such matters. Great care was taken in 5 and 6 Edward VI, c. 2, 'for the provision and relief of the poor', which sought to differentiate between 'valiant beggars, idle, and loitering persons' and the worthy poor. Each parish was required to maintain a list of the truly poor and to elect two responsible persons who should 'gently ask and demand of every man and woman' a weekly pledge and contribution to funds for the parochial care of such poor persons. Any

---

[3] *Statutes of the realm*, IV, i, 144–146: 5 and 6 Edward VI, c. 11. It was held in the early seventeenth century that the provision requiring two accusers had been repealed by 1–2 Philip and Mary, c. 10, but Coke maintained that it had not. The doubt was relieved by statute in 1696 (Holdsworth, W. S., *A history of English law*, IV (L., [1924]), 499).

[1] The bill had been carefully prepared in advance and seems to have been introduced on the first day of the session. The Henrician parliamentary action in settling the inheritance on the children of Somerset's second marriage was declared repealed and John Seymour, the eldest surviving son of the first marriage, was restored in blood and inheritance. The earlier act was declared to have been procured by 'corrupt and sinister labour', and, contrary to the usage of private bills, neither the King's signature nor stamp having been added. Such property as Somerset had before the passage of the act of 32 Henry VIII was to pass to John Seymour or his heirs; all acquired since was to pass to the King as a consequence of the Duke's treason, subject to the payment of his debts, the support of the children of the second marriage, and compensation for those cheated by Somerset.

The bill, as originally drafted, likewise confirmed the attainders of Somerset, Arundell, Stanhope, Vane, and Partridge, the estates and titles to be forfeited to the King. The bill, as amended, was passed by Parliament on April 13. (S.P. Dom., Edw. VI, XIV, 20 (a long document covering 32 sides); *C.J.*, I, 19, 20, 23; Burnet, *Reformation*, II, 328; Jordan, *Edward VI*, 46.)

person financially able to make such a contribution who refused to do so, or who dissuaded others from doing so, was first to be remonstrated with by his clergyman and that failing was to be reported to the bishop who should persuade or reform the recalcitrant. This measure not only represents a remarkable softening of the extremely severe statute passed in the early months of the reign but may be said to fall just short of the great Elizabethan legislation in that it failed to invoke the taxing power where private charity was unable to meet the need.[1]

The continuing concern with enclosures was reflected in an act 'for the maintenance and increase of tillage and corn' (5 and 6 Edward VI, c. 5) which, while intending to tax lands that had been withdrawn fron tillage since 1509, was so hazily drawn and so weak in the mechanism provided for enforcement as to be without consequence. The singular want of clarity in the measure doubtless arose from the fact that the bill was re-drafted by both the Lords and the Commons in the course of consideration, emerging into law as nothing more than a pious gesture.[2] Far better drawn were measures designed to secure a reformation in the standards of the cloth trade, inspired by the serious falling-off in the European demand for English woollens which had set in during the course of 1551. We may say that 5 and 6 Edward VI, c. 6, was a serious and certainly an ambitious effort to lay down much higher and more strictly enforced standards of cloth-making, the bill having been re-drafted and tightened after what amounted to a parliamentary enquiry in which numerous clothiers were examined. The measure was national in its scope, precise specifications being laid down for twenty-two varieties of cloth, most of which were given geographical appellations.[3] Closely related to this important enactment was 5 and 6 Edward VI, c. 7, which carefully restricted the storage, buying, and selling of wools and limited the trade to manufacturers of cloth or to Merchants of the Staple in order to prevent speculative transactions and hoarding.[4] And, finally, in this cluster of statutes, 5 and 6 Edward VI, c. 8, sought to enforce higher standards of quality by strictly forbidding the weaving of broadcloths by anyone who had not served a seven-year term in the art of 'broad woollen cloth making', the measure being passed after a joint committee of the two Houses had sharpened the phrasing of the bill.[5]

Less important, but displaying a lively and a fairly sophisticated

---

[1] *Statutes of the realm*, IV, i, 131–132; Jordan, *Philanthropy in England*, 86.
[2] *Statutes of the realm*, IV, i, 134–136.   [3] *Ibid.* 136–141.
[4] *Ibid.* 141–142.   [5] *Ibid.* 142.

concern with the economy of the realm, were several other measures designed to strengthen and reform it. Thus 5 and 6 Edward
VI, c. 14, sought to give sharper definition to old offences of forestalling, regrating, and engrossing, which were now more clearly
defined and forbidden, though here Parliament was seeking to
legislate in an area of impossible economic complexity.[1] An act laid
against the regrating of tanned leather (5 and 6 Edward VI, c. 15)
seems loosely framed and unenforceable,[2] while still another (5 and
6 Edward VI, c. 18) repealed a statute of 4 Henry VII against
bringing in wine and woad in alien bottoms, thereby introducing a
substantial relaxation of commerce.[3] Three acts—for licensing tinkers
and pedlars, putting down gig mills, and regulating the making of
hats and dornicks in Norfolk—dealt with specific problems of
standards and competition, while an act to require the licensing and
bonding of ale-house-keepers was carefully drawn in order to bring
them under close supervision.[4] On balance it must be said that this
session of Parliament displayed an intelligent and certainly a continuous interest in the social and economic problems of the realm,
sharpened and inspired no doubt by the depression in the cloth
trade which had now set in as well as by the social turmoil which had
fed the great insurrections of the summer of 1549.

Impressive and forward-looking as were certain of these statutes,
it remains true to say that Parliament was essentially conservative
in its economic conceptions. The perfect testimony to its mood was
the act proscribing usury (5 and 6 Edward VI, c. 20) by the repeal
of 37 Henry VIII, c. 9, which had defined as usury any interest
taken above 10 per cent.[5] The preamble sets out eloquently an
economic and moral view very close indeed to that so vigorously
maintained by the Commonwealth Party, and more particularly
by Latimer and Lever. The statute declared that all usury was 'by
the Word of God utterly prohibited, as a vice most odious and
detestable', though so greedy were the covetous that even godly
teaching and threat of the vengeance of God could not restrain them
from 'such filthy gain and lucre' unless sharp temporal punishments
were provided. Hence the Henrician act was declared repealed and
'any manner of usury, increase, . . . gain, or interest to be had . . . or
hoped for over and above the sum or sums so lent' was flatly prohibited under pain of forfeiture of the amount and imprisonment at

[1] *Statutes of the realm*, IV, i, 148–150.   [2] *Ibid.* 150–151.
[3] *Ibid.* 154.
[4] *Ibid.* 155, 156, 157, 158.
[5] *Ibid.* 155.

the King's pleasure.[1] The bill seems to have encountered no considerable opposition in either House, though its intent ran counter to the
expanding commerce of the realm and to the interests of the classes
which dominated the House of Commons. Like so many of the
conservative Tudor statutes dealing with social and economic
abuses, it may well have been passed as a pious gesture with full
assurance that it would not and could not be stringently enforced.

These were the most important of the statutes passed by this
session of Parliament which sought to deal with the secular concerns
and needs of the realm. Almost more interesting were the many
bills, seventy-nine in all, which were introduced and discussed but
which failed of passage for one reason or another. It is noteworthy
that almost three-quarters of these measures dealt with aspects of
social or economic policy and that the thrust of these proposals undoubtedly betrays the articulate sympathy of a considerable number
of members who lent support to what may with fair accuracy be
described as the position of the Commonwealth Party.[2] Among these
'lost measures' was a bill dealing with vagabondage, which disappeared after one reading in the Commons; a bill for 'clothiers to
dwell in towns', which was abandoned after it was delivered to
Petre; and still another measure to secure the tilling of arable land,
which enjoyed only a single reading. One wishes more were known
of a bill against the 'plurality of farms and mansion houses' which
was carefully debated in the Commons, then re-drafted by lawyer
members and passed, only to be lost in the Lords. Proposed measures against 'casting of nuisances and carrion into brooks and rivers',
for further regulating journeymen and clothiers, against killing of
calves and weanlings, and for 'shipping of merchandise' all gained
no more than a first reading.

A bill was also brought in from the last session of Parliament which
made another attempt to require clothiers to live in towns and carry
on their business there, but it disappeared into committee, while an
interesting measure in effect prohibiting the leasing of lands for
pasture at rentals of £40 p.a. or more could not be carried beyond
its first reading. An important proposal prohibiting the severance of
land from houses and failure to leave at least thirty acres about a
house was carried in the space of ten days through all the stages in
the Commons to a *judicium* but could not be passed in the Lords.
A possibly very important bill which would have prohibited the
ownership of more than 2000 sheep was also passed by the Commons

---

[1] *Statutes of the realm*, IV, i, 155.
[2] These are taken principally from the *C.J.*, I, 16–23.

on March 3rd, but failed to gain more than a second reading in the Lords. This proposal reflected the strong sentiments of the reforming party in the Lower House which remained deeply concerned about tillage, enclosures, and sheep-grazing, and which maintained a steady pressure on the debate. Then on February 17th a bill for decayed houses of husbandry and tillage was introduced, but vanished after its second reading. A bill that required the tilling of one acre of land for every ten sheep kept survived a third reading, was debated once more on March 3rd, and then was lost in the Commons. Still another bill, about which we know very little, which sought the 'increase of tillage', was introduced in the Lords and was hurried through the Commons from the first reading to a favourable vote in three days, but for whatever reason failed to become law.

There were also as many as ten 'lost measures' that sought to regulate or to improve trade and urban life, most of which Parliament may have rejected because they were so narrowly specialized and detailed in their applicability. But there arose as well, and that quite suddenly and dramatically, a grave concern in this session because of the depletion of timber in south-eastern England as a consequence of the growth of the iron industry in Kent, Sussex, and Surrey. Parliament now sought to deal with the problem in a hurried and piece-meal fashion, thereby arousing most effective lobbying and resistance from the iron manufacturers of the region.

Rather early in the session (February 23, 1552) a bill was introduced in Commons to 'avoid iron mills near Horsham in Sussex'; it was committed three days later and brought to its third reading on March 16th despite the frantic representations of the iron masters thereby threatened. The opposition was so strong and articulate that the bill was defeated on a division in the House on April 5th. But the reforming, or perhaps more accurately the conservationist, party in the House was by no means finished with the issue, a bill, which disappeared in Commons after its first reading, being introduced to prohibit iron mills within twenty miles of London. So too failed alternative measures which would have prohibited the 'consuming of wood in iron mills' in the Thames valley and the engrossing of wood. The concern of a strong and pertinacious party in the Commons was now fastened on the problem, and attack after attack was made. A bill for the 'planting and setting of trees' was lost after a second reading, but the Commons passed a related bill for 'the increase and preservation of woods' (March 31st), as it did a measure prohibiting the export of wood, timber, and sea-coals, though neither measure became law. Bills of a very local character restricting the cutting of hedgerows in Middlesex and Hertfordshire and 'to preserve the woods near Guildford' also failed, as did bills to prohibit iron mills in the general region of Guildford and Farnham, and to protect the region near Reigate, all in Surrey.

The fourth, and final, session of Edward's first Parliament was, then, a lively, a troubled, and a 'searching' time. It is not too much to say that the very large number of bills failing of enactment displays more clearly than does the relatively modest body of statute law made, the apprehensions, the conscience, and the thrust of interest of reasonable and responsible men. It almost seems as though Somerset's ghost walked in this session of Parliament; nor is it too much to say that Northumberland and his supporters were well aware of the lingering influence of the Commonwealth Party. No subsidy had been gained by a desperately straitened government; several bills endorsed by the King and Council were either ignored or defeated in the House of Commons; and one has the sense that the legislative initiative had remained, so far as these secular matters were concerned, with the Commons. The King, now just emerging to a precocious maturity of concern, had wished for more from this Parliament to 'help to advance the profit of the Commonwealth'. As for the laws being made and enacted, he wished that those responsible, the nobility and the justices of the peace, would attend faithfully to their execution. Those among his servants who were themselves 'touched or blotted with those vices that be against these new laws to be established' should be replaced. Only then could the commonwealth which was England prosper.[1] Edward's concern was principally with the needs and the reforming of the civil state; but the most important legislation of this Parliament was the framing of a thoroughly Protestant establishment for the national church.

B. *The ecclesiastical measures: The adoption of the second 'Book of Common Prayer'*

The most important measure enacted into law by the last session of Edward's first Parliament was the act establishing the second *Book of Common Prayer* as the authorized and sole manual of worship for the Church of England. The task of preparing the draft had been almost entirely in Cranmer's hands. The great liturgical work which he now laid before Parliament reflected the increasingly

---

[1] Edward VI, *Chronicle*, 166–167.

evangelical sentiments of the Archbishop, who, even in the debates on the first Book, defended a position on the central question of the Lord's Supper which did not fully represent his own increasingly Protestant position.[1] Cranmer had, however, sensed the wisdom of proceeding slowly in the great task of settling the Church on firmly Protestant foundations and he had undoubtedly been deterred as well by Somerset's moderate Protestantism.

The first *Book of Common Prayer* had not in fact won the full approval of any party in English religious life. The determined Roman Catholic conservatives denounced it, or avoided it, because it was implicitly Protestant, while the evangelical party led by Hooper, and after Somerset's fall strongly supported by Northumberland and most of the Council, disliked it because the worship which it prescribed was too reminiscent of the Romish past and because of its ambiguity with respect to the doctrine of the mass. The pressure for revision was also heightened by the polite, but articulate, criticism of the principal refugee clergy in England, whose intellectual leaders, Martyr and Bucer, were themselves moving in their eucharistic thinking towards Zwinglian views and who were greatly affected by the consensus reached in May, 1549 by Calvin and Bullinger on the doctrine of the Lord's Supper.[2] Powerful intellectual support was also lent to the evangelical party in England by the blunt criticism of Calvin, who had analyzed the first Book in detail shortly after its adoption,[3] and who in 1551 brought direct irenic pressure to bear on Cranmer. Calvin reminded the Archbishop that

'the exalted position which you occupy fixes the eyes of all upon you. The people will follow your lead or remain inert under the cloak of your luke-warmness. Had you led the attack boldly three years ago, superstition would have been destroyed with less labour and conflict. Do not slumber at ease. Do not imagine you have reached the goal. . . . I fear that so many autumns wasted in procrastination may be followed by an eternal winter. I fear you may die with the knowledge that you have delayed too long and have left everything in confusion.'[4]

The whole weight of the evangelical criticism of the first *Book of Common Prayer* was concentrated in the detailed *Censura* prepared by Bucer on the request of Bishop Goodrich (Ely), with Cranmer's

[1] Jordan, *Edward VI*, 313–321.　　　[2] In the *Consensus Tigurinus*, so called.
[3] Robinson, *Original letters*, II, 707–709.　　[4] Calvin, *Opera*, XIII, 682–683.

full approval. There is evidence, too, that Peter Martyr, who had been given a Latin translation of the book by Cheke for study, 'by reason of my want of knowledge of the [English] language', had been invited to place his suggestions in Cranmer's hands.[1] Martyr further tells us that he had been assured by Cranmer that 'many things shall be changed' and that he had been informed by Cheke that if those revisions thought desirable encountered serious opposition in Parliament, the King himself would interpose his royal authority.[2] Martyr contented himself, however, with lending his own approval to the detailed criticisms so laboriously compiled by Bucer, save for one minor quibble respecting the service ordained for the communion of the sick.

Bucer tells us that his extensive criticisms of the first *Book of Common Prayer* were undertaken after a considered examination of the document had persuaded him that the whole of the work was 'very agreeable both with God's Word, and the observances of the ancient churches', though there remained many matters of detail which he proposed to bring under criticism.[3] What he sought was a purification of the service and the abolition of practices and statements which might easily be misunderstood. Thus he would wish the communion to be offered only in parish churches, since superstitious practices may be too easily concealed in private chapels. He stressed the need for frequent and stated communion services and would by specific prohibition abolish gestures and actions reminiscent of the mass. He emphasized, as well, the need for more and longer homilies, until 'the living word of the preacher' could be heard more widely in the realm. He took the view that though prayers for the spiritual repose of the dead were ancient, they should none the less be abolished because of their superstitious overtones. The universities must be fostered, plundering of parish resources prohibited, better order maintained in church services, and all possible means employed for strengthening the parochial clergy, for 'everywhere are parishes with mere readers instead of pastors: no many cannot so much as read'. Finally, Bucer eloquently maintained that a clear and concise statement of the doctrinal position of the Church of England must be promulgated, while pleading vainly that the Church clarify its position on the central teaching of the Holy Communion by the retention of the

---

[1] Parker MSS., Camb. C.C.C. MSS., CXIX, and printed in Strype, *Cranmer*, II, 898–901.

[2] Gorham, *Gleanings*, 229.

[3] Bucer, Martin, *Censura Martini Buceri*, etc., in *Scripta anglicana*, 456–503.

words, 'Humbly beseeching thee . . . that whosoever shall be par-
takers of this holy communion may worthily receive the most
precious body and blood of thy Son Jesus Christ'. And then he
closed with the solemn reminder that 'all men's eyes are today fixed
upon this realm, to which God has granted a king, bishops and
nobles, who will not permit any irreligious or excessive novelty'.[1]
The Church of England, these reforms being made, will then take
its place as the leader of a united Protestantism.

Valued as these recommendations certainly were, mounting as
criticism of the existing liturgy of the Church surely was, it remains
clear that the final statement of worship and belief enshrined in the
second *Book of Common Prayer* came from Cranmer. During the
last three years of the reign the Archbishop withdrew almost entirely
from the affairs of state to devote himself to doctrinal and liturgical
writing and to complete his own spiritual pilgrimage. Somewhat
before the end of July, 1550 his greatest controversial work, *A
Defence of the true and Catholic doctrine of the sacrament*, was
published, which explored boldly and with utter honesty the central
doctrinal question of Christian faith. Cranmer displayed great
learning and a marvellous command of scriptural and patristic
authority in this impressive and incredibly thorough denunciation
of the doctrine of transubstantiation, to which the work was principally dedicated. Threading through the argument, however, was
also an implicit rationalism from which proceeded his denunciation
of superstition, which at times may be said to presage Hooker's
greater work a half century later. But, while his complete denial of
transubstantiation stands crystal clear, it did not follow that his
embracing of outright Zwinglianism, towards which his mind
was propelled, was either clear or complete. There survives, as I
have read and re-read the *Defence*, an almost mystical residuum
which suggests a continued searching for the real presence, intellectually repudiated, perhaps, but still emotionally held.[2] Hence,
he concluded, all

'popish masses are to be clearly taken away . . . and the true use of
the Lord's Supper is to be restored again, wherein godly people

---

[1] Bucer, *Censura*, in *Scripta anglicana*, 463–476, 503. Valuable comments may be found
in Smyth, *Cranmer and the Reformation*, 237–243; Strype, *Cranmer*, I, 300–302; Hopf,
Constantin, *Martin Bucer and the English Reformation* (Oxford, 1946), 96–97, who,
however, may attribute to the *Censura* more influence than seems justified; and Messenger, *Reformation*, I, 510–516.

[2] Cranmer, Thomas, *A defence of the true and catholike doctrine of the Sacrament* (L.,
1550); in *The remains of Thomas Cranmer, etc.*, ed. by Henry Jenkyns (4 vols., Oxford,
1833), II, 275–463. For a different view, *vide* Ridley, *Cranmer*, 322.

assembled together may receive the sacrament every man for himself, to declare that he remembereth what benefit he hath received by the death of Christ, and to testify that he is a member of Christ's body, fed with his flesh, and drinking his blood spiritually.'[1]

These views, attained after long study and travail, Cranmer now sought to embody in the greatest of his works, the Second *Book of Common Prayer*.

We know little in detail regarding the preparation of the text of the *Prayer Book*, save that Cranmer had been lending personal attention to a further reform of the liturgy since April, 1549 and that his work proceeded in close association with Ridley. It was confidently expected, as Martyr wrote to Bucer as early as January, 1551, 'that many things shall be changed'.[2] Not long afterwards the text, now completed by Cranmer, was submitted to a number of the bishops, and probably to those who were at the time members of the commission engaged in the projected revision and codification of canon law.[3] We know as well that Cheke was at least informally present as a member of the Court, and it is probable that Cox was also consulted. Shortly afterwards, in early February, Martyr could report to Bucer that he had seen the new text, though he could give no judgement because of his ignorance of English. He could say as well that the bishops had agreed to many changes and reformations in the *Prayer Book*, though by no means all the suggestions made in the *Censura* had been accepted. This was true despite the fact that he had more than once urged Cranmer to move the whole way towards reformation, so 'there may be no further need for emendation: for, if frequent changes should take place in these matters, it might . . . easily come to pass that they would fall into general contempt'. He was persuaded that this was also Cranmer's private aspiration, but that he was restrained by episcopal colleagues 'who offer resolute opposition' and was fully supported only by Cheke, who 'earnestly favours simplicity'.[4]

Cranmer was, in point of fact, subject to heavy pressure not only from the conservatives in the bench of bishops but also from the evangelical Protestant party, whose principal spokesmen were Hooper and Knox and which enjoyed considerable, and now steady,

---

[1] Cranmer, *Defence*, in *Remains*, II, 455.
[2] Parker MSS., Camb. C.C.C. MSS., CXIX, as quoted in Gorham, *Gleanings*, 229.
[3] *Vide post*, 359ff.
[4] Camb. Univ. MSS., MM 4. 14, #6, as printed in Gorham, *Gleanings*, 232.

support from the Court and, somewhat erratically, from Northumberland. But the reins of control were firmly kept in Cranmer's hands in what may have been the final session for the consideration of the text by the commission of thirty-two charged with the revision of canon law. There seem to have been very few, if any, further changes made in the text.[1]

The first consideration lent by Parliament to the new manual of worship came on the first day of the session when the Council introduced in the Lords a measure 'requiring people to come to church'. This bill was read three times in the Lords, but only once in the Commons, before being withdrawn. Then a new measure to secure uniformity of worship was introduced in the Lords on March 9th, and on March 30th was in turn conjoined with still another bill for 'the due coming to common prayer'. The final draft, entitled *An act for the uniformity of common prayer and administration of the Sacraments*, was passed by the Lords on April 6th with three of the lay peers (Derby, Stourton, and Windsor) voting against the measure, as did two (Thirlby and Aldrich) of the twelve spiritual peers present on that day. The bill was laid before the Commons on the same day, passing through four readings before being enacted into law on April 14th.

The *Act of Uniformity* (5 and 6 Edward VI, c. 1) carefully avoided the repeal of the first statute (1549) establishing a uniform order of worship, being represented rather as an amendment and reformation of the earlier legislation. Thus it was stressed that there had been 'a very godly order set forth' earlier by Parliament for common prayer and worship in the mother tongue, which was declared to be agreeable to Scripture and the usage of the primitive church, though none the less 'a great number of people in divers parts of the realm have wilfully absented themselves' from the ordained worship. So too, it had been observed that 'divers doubts for the fashion and manner of administration of the authorized worship' had arisen, 'rather by the curiosity of the minister and mistakes than of any other worthy cause'. Hence, the King with Parliament had reviewed the *Book of Common Prayer* and had now revised and perfected it, under the authority of the earlier Act of Uniformity (2 and 3 Edward VI, c. 1). Then there were added punitive measures which formally brought to a close Somerset's remarkable, and on the whole amazingly successful, experiment in religious toleration as a policy of

---

[1] The not always reliable Ulmis is the only source for the suggestion that the text was laid before Convocation for debate there in January, 1552 (Robinson, *Original letters*, II, 444).

state. The laity were required to attend the prescribed service at the accustomed place and there to 'abide orderly and soberly' during the time of worship, under pain of censure by the church, while those attending any other form of service were subjected, upon conviction, to terms of imprisonment ranging from six months for the first offence to life for the third.[1]

It is also important to note that the statute enjoining the use of the new *Prayer Book* was not to take effect for a period of about seven months (November, 1552), in part to afford time for the completion of the projected Articles of Religion,[2] and even more importantly to permit Cranmer time to try once more to assemble a general council of Protestantism in the hope of finding a common meeting-ground of doctrine and worship based on the second *Book of Common Prayer*. Calvin's reply this time suggested that he, or his representative, might have come had there been further urging. Bullinger's reply has been lost, but his earlier interest in Cranmer's irenic dreams makes it probable that he or a deputy would have accepted, even though he disliked certain of the ceremonial survivals retained in the *Prayer Book*. But there was no reply at all from Melanchthon who, as before, was weary of conferences and in any event almost smugly content with the Lutheran formularies. Nor was this all, for the ruling junta was all too shortly to be preoccupied with problems of its own survival, as the health of the King grew steadily worse through the winter months of 1553.

The second *Book of Common Prayer* undoubtedly represents the furthermost limit of the movement of the Church of England towards evangelical Protestantism. Perhaps even more importantly, it ordained a liturgy—a service of worship—which broke radically with the remembered past and in consequence must have caused great spiritual and habitual dislocation in the parish churches across the realm. This Cranmer sought to explain and to justify in a remarkable preface to the *Book* when it was published in 1552. Ceremonies had gradually crept into the Church in the past which had obscured the glory of God and had blinded the people with superstitious usages. In these times the minds of men were diverse, some adhering to old and superstitious practices, while others would 'innovate all things, and so do despise the old, that nothing can like them but that is new'.[3] Further, the number and clutter of ceremonies had

---

[1] *Statutes of the realm*, IV, i, 130-131; *C.J.*, I, 16, 22, 23; *L.J.*, I, esp. 406, 417, 418, 421.   [2] *Vide post*, 354-357.

[3] *The booke of the common prayer*, etc. (L., 1549), in *The two liturgies*, etc., ed. by Joseph Ketley (Parker Soc., Cambridge, 1844), 197.

grown so great as to obscure the true nature and reality of worship. Hence the new order of worship had been placed squarely on the foundations of Scripture, while ceremonies had been adapted to the needs and traditions of England. In so doing,

'We condemn no other nations, nor prescribe anything, but to our own people only. For we think it convenient that every country should use such ceremonies, as they think best to the setting forth of God's honour or glory, and to the reducing of the people to a most perfect and godly living, without error or superstition.'[1]

The changes introduced were thorough and bold; they were all calculated to lend affirmation to the now completely Protestant structure of English worship and deliberately sought to re-state and reorganize the solemn ceremony of the mass, the very name of which was now changed to the Lord's Supper. In baptism, the exorcising, the blessing of the water, and the chrisom were all swept away; in confirmation the sign of the cross was abolished; all prayers for the dead, however decorously indirect, were forbidden and the burial rite was altered. But the great changes came in the structure and meaning of the communion service where the canon was divided into three separated fragments and the consecration of the elements was so ordered as to suggest a congregational communion. The medieval vestments were forbidden the priest and the surplice might not be used. Further, the altar was now legally replaced by a simple communion table, while the words of administration were carefully rendered in a form and with a meaning which were indubitably Protestant and which lay closer to the Zwinglian view of the Eucharist than to that of any other reformed church.[2]

[1] *The booke of the common prayer, etc.* (L., 1549), in *The two liturgies, etc.*, ed. by Joseph Ketley (Parker Soc., Cambridge, 1844), 199.

[2] A collation of the key phrases of the First (1549) and Second (1552) Books of Common Prayer may be helpful on this central matter.

1549

1. Then shall the priest first receive the communion in both kinds himself, and next deliver it to other ministers, if any be there present (that they may be ready to help the chief minister) and after to the people.

2. And when he delivereth the sacrament of the body of Christ, he shall say to everyone these words; 'the body of our Lord Jesus Christ which was given for thee, preserve thy body and soul unto everlasting life'.

1552

1. Then shall the minister receive the communion in both kinds himself, and next deliver it to other ministers, if any be there present (that they may help the chief minister) and after to the people in their hands kneeling.

2. And when he delivereth the bread, he shall say, 'Take and eat this in remembrance that Christ died for thee, and feed on him in thy heart by faith, with thanksgiving'.

The passage of the Act of Uniformity, imposing the second *Book of Common Prayer*, had been handled with considerable skill and the text seemed to have found a general acceptance. Martyr, after studying the work, thought the English worship was now free of all things 'which could nourish superstition'. He had the sense, too, that there remained within the Church little support for the doctrine of transubstantiation, the most dangerous point of controversy, though he was still troubled by the somewhat recondite question of whether grace was conferred by virtue of the sacraments and the related conviction that some merit was to be found in the doctrine of works.[1] But on the whole Martyr expressed himself as content with the doctrine and worship of the Church of England as now by law prescribed.

The not inconsiderable responsibility of printing and distributing the *Prayer Book* in the weeks remaining before it was ordered to be used was entrusted to Grafton, and a carefully composed scale of prices was set out. A little later Cranmer suggested to the Council that the 'commodity' which might result from the printing of the *Book* in French for the refugee congregations and the Channel Islands ought to be vested in Sir Hugh Paulet, who, under the supervision of the Lord Chancellor, had arranged a translation.[2]

All seemed ready for the ordained transition to the second *Book* when John Knox intervened with his immensely powerful rhetoric to support earlier protestations of Hooper and Lasky against the prescription of receiving the sacrament in a kneeling posture.[3] Knox had for some months been preaching at Berwick and Newcastle, inveighing against the mass and attracting the favourable attention of Northumberland, who in 1552 was often resident in Newcastle in his capacity as Warden General of the Northern Marches. While the work on printing the *Prayer Book* was being completed, Knox had been invited to preach in the London area and to conduct services before the King and Court. He chose this

---

1549

3. And the minister delivering the sacrament of the blood, and giving every one to drink once and no more, shall say; 'the blood of our Lord Jesus Christ which was shed for thee, preserve thy body and soul unto everlasting life'.

1552

3. And the minister that delivereth the cup shall say; 'Drink this in remembrance that Christ's blood was shed for thee, and be thankful'.

This material has been adapted from the useful formulation of F. E. Brightman, *The English rite, etc.* (2 vols., L., 1915), II, 700–701.

[1] Bradford, *Writings*, II, 400–403: Martyr to Bullinger, June 14, 1552.
[2] HMC, *Bath MSS. at Longleat*, II, 13: Aug. 26, 1552.
[3] Hooper, *Early writings*, 536.

critical moment to deliver a vehement attack on the idolatry implicit in kneeling at the reception of the communion, with so much effect that the Council nervously asked Cranmer, Ridley, and Martyr to consider the matter even though Parliament had already lent its full sanction to the *Prayer Book*.[1] Letters were at once dispatched to the printer commanding him to stay its printing and distribution 'until certain faults therein be corrected'.[2]

Cranmer was furious at this untimely and violent intervention, replying to the Council's nervous injunctions with an acerbity most unusual in him. 'I trust ye will not be moved by these glorious and unquiet spirits,' he wrote, 'which can like nothing but that is after their own fancy, and cease not to make trouble and disquietness when things be most quiet and in good order.' He pointed out that yearly revisions of the nation's worship would hardly be sufficient for such men as Knox. Such critics really held the view that all matters not specifically commanded by Scripture are 'unlawful and ungodly. But this saying is the chief foundation of the error of the Anabaptists and of divers other sects.'[3] To this contention Knox rejoined with an even more violent attack on the kneeling posture which, he asserted, was conjoined with a belief in transubstantiation and which made continued private idolatry possible. Hence we should 'without doubting or wavering', in the reception of the communion, pass 'to the table, not as slaves or servants, but as children of the King and the redeemed people . . . and therefore taught by Christ's example at this holy table, we sit as men placed in quietness and in full possession of our Kingdom'.[4]

This latest blast of Knox was undoubtedly before the Council on October 27th when it instructed the Lord Chancellor 'to cause to be joined unto the Book of Common Prayer lately set forth' a declaration signed by the King in explanation of the rubric touching kneeling.[5] Cranmer's views were then completely overridden by a proclamation explaining that the instruction for kneeling was no more than an humble acknowledgement of the benefits of Christ and was designed to secure an orderly service. But, to correct misapprehensions that had arisen, the proclamation declared that

---

[1] Robinson, *Original letters*, II, 591–592; Lorimer, Peter, *John Knox and the Church of England*, etc. (L., 1875), 102.

[2] *A.P.C.*, IV, 131: Sept. 27, 1552.

[3] S.P. Dom., Edw. VI, XV, 15: Oct. 7, 1552.

[4] Lorimer, *John Knox*, App., 267–274. This attack was addressed to articles 35 and 38 in the Articles of Religion then being considered. It may be dated between Oct. 20 and Oct. 27, 1552.

[5] *A.P.C.*, IV, 154.

'it is not meant thereby that any adoration is done or ought to be done either unto the sacramental bread or wine there being bodily received, or unto any real or essential presence there being of Christ's natural flesh and blood. For as concerning the sacramental bread and wine, they remain still in their very natural substances, and therefore may not be adored, for that were idolatry.'[1]

Thus was the famous *Black Rubric* inserted into the *Book of Common Prayer*, by the specific authority of the Privy Council, invoking the royal supremacy. The remarkable fact is that there is no mention whatsoever of the second *Book of Common Prayer* in Edward's *Chronicle*, for the King's mind and interests in these later days of his short reign had turned increasingly to secular concerns.

On November 1, 1552, the first service employing the new manual of worship was held at St Paul's in the forenoon when Ridley preached from the choir, 'in his rochet only, without cope or vestment'. The Bishop also took the afternoon service at Paul's Cross, the Lord Mayor, the aldermen, and the livery companies being present. In his sermon he set forth the new service at such length that the benediction was not pronounced until 5 p.m., the company returning home by torchlight.[2]

(1) *Lesser parliamentary measures and the 'Short Catechism'*

There were other ecclesiastical statutes enacted by this session of Parliament, though they seem minor indeed when set against the great act ordaining the second *Book of Common Prayer*. Thus, in order to lend secular support to spiritual sanctions, a severe law sought to restrain quarrelling and brawling on church premises, particularly if there was actual physical violence.[3] This measure seems to have been enacted without opposition, but not so 5 and 6 Edward VI, c. 12, which met strenuous opposition from the conservative peers and against which ten of their number cast their votes.[4] The resistance was petulant and symbolic, since the statute sought to do no more than declare the children of married priests to be legitimate and to relieve all doubts regarding such marriages, thereby protecting such children 'from the false and malicious statements of divers ill disposed persons'.[5] Still another minor enactment

---

[1] Hughes and Larkin, *Tudor proclamations*, I, 538–539: Oct. 27, 1552.
[2] Stow, *Annales*, 608.
[3] *Statutes of the realm*, IV, i, 133–134 (5 and 6 Edward VI, c. 4).
[4] They were: Shrewsbury, Derby, Rutland, Bath, Abergavenny, Stourton, Mounteagle, Sandys, Windsor, and Wharton. It is interesting that no spiritual peers voted in the negative.   [5] *Statutes of the realm*, IV, i, 146–147.

clarified and regularized the legal status of former religious persons, monks and chantry priests, who had withdrawn from the clergy and who were now declared to possess full rights in the inheritance and purchase of land.[1] More important by far was an act 'for the keeping of holy days and fasting days', which sought to give formal sanction and explanation to practices already on several occasions authorized by proclamations. The act, which evidently met no opposition, declared holy days and fasting days to be useful in reminding us of our duty and of God's mercies, though not for any saint's sake. Such days are appointed only for the worship of God. It was further provided that labourers, husbandmen, and fishermen were, when necessity should require, to stand exempt from the provisions of the statute which, be it noted, was armed with no more than ecclesiastical censures.[2]

The armour of the Protestant faith was further strengthened by the publication of *A short catechism* which, while not enjoying the sanction of an act of Parliament, lent full support to the second *Book of Common Prayer*, 'which of very late time was given to the Church of England by the King's authority and the Parliament'. Published in both English and Latin, this beautiful and persuasive work was especially adapted to the use of schoolmasters in the instruction of the young.[3] The dialogue, in which it is couched, between master and student is skilfully set out in easy, relaxed, and almost colloquial style. The book is above all else clear, natural, and deceptively simple in setting forward the elements of Christian faith. The tone of the work is sturdily and evangelically Protestant, though the condemnation of Roman practices remains muted and hence all the more effective. Thus the recently published *Prayer Book* was declared to be 'godly and in no point repugnant to the wholesome doctrine of the Gospel, but agreeable thereunto, furthering and beautifying the same not a little', and hence to be thankfully employed in God's worship. The Anabaptist and Millenarian heresies were rather gently condemned, the duty of Christian men to the poor was persuasively set forward, and a steady and confident statement of Protestant doctrine was most competently advanced. This quiet expression of Protestant faith seems to betoken the full coming of age of the reformed church in England.

[1] *Statutes of the realm*, IV, i, 147–148: 5 and 6 Edward VI, c. 13.
[2] *Ibid.* 132–133: 5 and 6 Edward VI, c. 3.
[3] We have used the Latin version (*Catechismus breuis, etc.*, L., 1553; STC #4811) and the English text (*A short catechisme*, L., 1553; STC #4812). There were several printings, there being only minor differences between STC ##4807 and 4812.

(2) The 'Articles of Faith' (1553)

The *Book of Common Prayer*, as has been suggested, did not set forward a clear and explicit doctrinal system, since it was designed as a manual of worship and, quite as importantly, because Cranmer for years hesitated to rivet on the Church an announced and inevitably controversial statement of belief so long as any prospect of Protestant union remained. He had, it is true, shared in framing the Henrician Articles of 1536 and the more ambitious thirteen Articles of 1538, but had moved cautiously in the Edwardian era, as he sought to keep the English doctrinal position moderate in temper, centrist in policy, and flexible in its relation to the other reformed creeds. Hence, though pressed by Bucer and Bullinger, bitterly criticized for his caution by Hooper, and now by Knox, he had been most reluctant to codify Anglican doctrine, until 'the order of bishops was brought to such a model, that the far greater part of them would agree to it'. The first great task, he believed, was to reform the worship of the church, which had now been done, but 'for speculative points there was not so pressing a necessity to have them all explained, since in these men might with less prejudice be left to a freedom in their opinions'.[1]

None the less, the preparation of the first *Book of Common Prayer* had inevitably required some measure of codification of doctrine, as did the examination of candidates for ordination and the questioning of the clergy during the visitations which the Archbishop and the more committedly Protestant of his bishops took very seriously indeed.[2] It is quite certain that by late 1549 Cranmer, with the discreet help of Ridley, was employing an unpublished and unauthorized doctrinal formulary for examining those seeking licences to preach.[3] Hooper, in Worcester, was also using this codification, with additions of his own, to set out a boldly Protestant doctrinal position in fifty articles, which, however, he had reduced to nineteen by 1552 when he undertook the visitation of the diocese of Gloucester. To this pressure was added Bucer's strong recommendation in his *Censura* that a public declaration of faith be set forth, while the Privy Council in 1551 required the Archbishop to proceed to the task.[4] Cranmer moved slowly and evidently somewhat reluctantly, but in 1551 completed a draft which was informally submitted to at

---

[1] Burnet, *Reformation*, II, 287. Burnet (*ibid.* V, 314–329) prints an admirable translation of the 42 Articles.

[2] Jordan, *Edward VI*, 313–326.

[3] Robinson, *Original letters*, I, 76: Hooper to Bullinger.

[4] Strype, *Cranmer*, I, 390–392.

least certain of the bishops. These articles of faith, forty-two in number, remained officially unauthorized and unannounced until in May, 1552 a brusque command was issued to the Archbishop by the Council to submit them for examination and to indicate whether they rested on the base of any public authority.[1]

The *Articles of Faith*, after a review by the Council, were then returned to Cranmer for revision, and in September, 1552, he forwarded them, now forty-five in number, to Cheke and Cecil, presumably for further consideration by the Council, from which the Archbishop had now effectively withdrawn. Cranmer must have been outraged indeed when the Council referred the *Articles* to the most evangelical clerical group in England, the royal chaplains, to whose number Knox was now added.[2] After at least one further revision in detail, Cranmer, weary of the whole matter, submitted the final document, in which the number of articles had been reduced to forty-two, with the request that they might now receive the royal authority and be required for the subscription of all the clergy. Then, Cranmer trusted, 'such a concord and quietness in religion shall shortly follow thereof, as else is not to be looked for [for] many years'.[3] Despite the querulous impatience of the Council there was a delay of more than a half year before the *Articles* were officially enjoined and printed by the direct commandment of the King, requiring the bishops to 'subscribe and observe' the *Articles of Faith* now newly set forth.[4] It seems probable that the intention had been to give them even more impressive sanction either by act of Parliament or by the formal approval of Convocation on the occasion of Edward's second Parliament summoned for March, 1553, but so short and troubled was the session that action was never taken. This may also explain why the quite false statement on the title page, *Articles agreed on by the Bishops, and other learned and godly men*, was left untouched. When Cranmer protested vehemently against the misrepresentation, the Council, deeply involved now with a domestic crisis, evasively replied that it was meant that the *Articles* 'should have been issued' in the time of Convocation.[5] The *Articles*, then, promulgated only a few weeks before the death of the King, had little effect on English religious thought or policy during

[1] *A.P.C.*, IV, 33: May 2, 1552.

[2] *Vide ante*, 274, for the appointment of this curious body; S.P. Dom., Edw. VI, XV, 28: Oct. 20, 1552; *A.P.C.*, IV, 148, 173.

[3] Cranmer, *Writings*, II, 441; HMC, *Bath MSS. at Longleat*, II, 14: Nov. 24, 1552.

[4] S.P. Dom., Edw. VI, XVIII, 25; copy in *ibid.* 26. The royal mandate appears in Ridley's Register under date of June 9, 1553 (cf. Strype, *Memorials*, II, ii, 105–107).

[5] Foxe, *Acts and monuments*, VI, 468.

this reign, their principal historical importance being the fact that the enduring Elizabethan statement of faith in the thirty-nine articles was drawn directly, with slight variations, from Cranmer's formulary.[1]

Study of the *Articles*, in their phrasing as well as their thrust of emphasis, suggests, in Dixon's words, that they were at once moderate and comprehensive since 'the broad soft touch of Cranmer lay upon them'.[2] There was little of vehemence of statement, and certain of the doctrinal issues most in dispute were gently and briefly discussed. Thus the doctrine of justification by faith was very succinctly and generally set out, while good works were simply left without consideration, save for a careful examination of the scholastic distinction between congruous merit and supererogation. The treatment of the doctrine of predestination was cautious and temperately phrased, but can only be regarded as Calvinistic in meaning and intent. Throughout the treatise there was a sustained but relatively moderate attack on Roman Catholicism and the papal pretensions, as well as a steady criticism of Roman practices long since regarded as superstitious by all the reformed faiths.[3]

But the important—the central—question was the doctrine of the Holy Eucharist, and here Cranmer was clear, forceful, and decidedly more Protestant than he had been in the statement on the matter even in the second *Book of Common Prayer*. The sacrament is not only a sign of love that Christians should bear for one another, but is also a sacrament 'of our redemption by Christ's death, insomuch that to such as rightly, worthily, and with faith receive the same, the bread which we break is a communion of the body of Christ'. But from the service of the Lord's Supper, and the content of the sacrament, the *Articles* clearly excise the doctrine of transubstantiation as not to be found in holy writ and, indeed, as 'repugnant to the plain words of Scripture'. The body of Christ cannot be present at one time in many and diverse places, and is and will continue to remain in heaven. Hence we may not believe 'the real, and bodily presence . . . of Christ's flesh and blood [to be] in the Sacrament of the Lord's Supper'.[4] This is in a full sense a Protestant teaching far closer to Zwingli than to Luther, though its roots lie deep in Cranmer's own

---

[1] The published version (STC #10034), which we follow, is extremely rare. One wonders whether this could mean that this was a preliminary draft which the Council intended to have approved officially by Parliament or Convocation, the plan collapsing because of the death of the King.   [2] Dixon, *Church of England*, III, 520.

[3] Dickens's comments (*English Reformation*, 251–253) on the doctrinal content of the *Articles* have been most helpful.

[4] *Articles agreed*, etc., art. 29.

spiritual progress. The *Articles*, taken as a whole, are, indeed, drawn from the English reformed experience and they retain a tentative and a moderate quality which was to contribute greatly to the enduring settlement of a generally accepted Anglican faith in the course of Queen Elizabeth's reign.

(3) *Proposals for the codification of ecclesiastical laws (1549–1553)*

We have seen that Cranmer had been brusquely and rather harshly handled in the matter of the *Articles* by Northumberland and the now dominant evangelical group possessed of ultimate power in the Council; he was to be humiliated and dragooned at about the same time in the equally important matter of the proposed reform of the ecclesiastical laws. This problem, like all of Edwardian religious policy, had Henrician roots. The whole structure of canon law may be said to have collapsed with the abolition of papal jurisdiction in the realm, while more specifically with the submission of the clergy (1532) Convocation had undertaken not to make law without the King's consent and to submit the whole *corpus* of existing canon law to his review.[1] This re-statement of the ecclesiastical law was regarded as of great importance, since the whole structure of moral and disciplinary order had been left in utter confusion, and most particularly the laws of marriage and divorce.[2] Parliament in 1533 had accordingly provided that such ecclesiastical laws as were not contrary to the 'laws, customs, and statutes' of the realm should remain in force, while indicating that the relation of the royal supremacy and the common law to the canon law must be examined and defined. Consequently, Parliament further provided that the King should appoint a commission of thirty-two members, half being clergy and half lawyers, which should effect a codification and clarification of canon law. This was, of course, an extremely difficult undertaking which was in fact never substantially advanced during Henry's lifetime, save as Cranmer, working with very little help from anyone, had by early 1544 compiled an ambitious codification of the canon law, which enjoyed no authority and which was never submitted to Convocation or to Parliament.[3]

These uncertainties, which the common lawyers were not inclined to remedy, were making it almost impossible to restore discipline in the church. The bishops were sorely troubled, early in the third

[1] Hughes, Philip, *The Reformation in England*. Vol. II: *Religio depopulata* (N.Y. 1954), 127–129.
[2] *Vide* Jordan, *Edward VI*, 365–367, for a notorious instance.
[3] Camb. C.C.C. MSS., CCCXI, and printed in Burnet, *Reformation*, IV, 520 ff.

session of Parliament (November 14, 1549) complaining that vice
and disorder were rampant which they possessed no clear power to
correct or examine. On November 18th a bill was accordingly drawn
for remedy, but, significantly, was rejected on its first reading on the
grounds that it gave the bishops too much power. An amended
bill was thereupon drafted and passed the Lords, with the full
support of the spiritual peers, but was rejected in the Commons on
its second reading on November 23rd, with the recommendation
that the earlier commission, which had in fact never functioned, be
revived.[1] A new bill was accordingly introduced in the Lords setting
the number of commissioners at sixteen, amended on January 31,
1550, to accommodate pressure from the House of Commons to
restore the number to thirty-two. This bill was finally passed on
February 1, 1550, over the opposition of ten of the bishops, of both
evangelical and conservative persuasion. Among these was Cranmer
who thought, surely with reason, that the bill was deliberately
designed to wrest the power of decision from the episcopacy.

The statute (3 and 4 Edward VI, c. 11) provided that the King
should be empowered at any time during the three years following
to name, with advice of the Council, sixteen clergy, four of them
bishops, and as many laymen, of whom four were to be learned in
the common law, to study the ecclesiastical laws 'of long time here
used' and to codify such laws as were convenient for the realm. The
laws so recommended and agreed on should be set forth by royal
proclamation, with the further provision that those executing such
laws should stand free of the penalties of *praemunire*. The statute
concluded with the carefully ordered statement that the Convocation should possess no power to establish any canon law 'repugnant
or contrary to any common law or statute in this realm'.[2]

The Council moved with glacial slowness in carrying out the
provisions of the statute, delaying a full six months before instructing the Chancellor to make out a commission to thirty-two named
persons,[3] and then a month later decided to constitute a working
committee of eight which was to 'rough hew' the codification before
presenting it to the full commission for its review.[4] Despite the
sentiments of Parliament and, for that matter, of Northumberland,
the working committee was heavily clerical in composition, there
being on the panel only two laymen, John Lucas, Master of Requests,

---

[1] Burnet, *Reformation*, II, 248.
[2] *Statutes of the realm*, IV, i, 111–112.
[3] *A.P.C.*, III, 382: Oct. 6, 1551.
[4] *Ibid.* 410: Nov. 9, 1551.

and Richard Goodrich.[1] There were, however, further delays and much indecision, the committee being revoked and the full panel of thirty-two considerably revised, with now an equal representation of lay and clerical members, and with Petre and Cecil providing a link with the Council. The King on February 10, 1552, authorized this ponderous body 'to examine, correct, and set forth' the ecclesiastical laws.[2]

The drafting of the *Reformatio Legum Ecclesiasticarum*, once begun, was completed with remarkable celerity under Cranmer's leadership by the adoption of most of the codification which, as we have noted, the Archbishop had been preparing for many years past. The capacity of the commission ran by statute for a limited time and hence it was of great importance that the completed text be submitted before Edward's second Parliament adjourned. But Northumberland's opposition to its ratification was at once bitter and implacable—a view shared more mildly by the strongly entrenched group of common lawyers in the Lower House. Cranmer submitted the text on behalf of the commission, but was overwhelmed by Northumberland's angry rejoinder 'openly and before all . . . that it should come to nothing, and warned him and his brother bishops to take good care what they were about', as Parliament had entrusted a charge to them which, he implied, they had illegally exceeded. He then launched into an ominous attack on the selfish opposition of certain bishops and clergy to the consideration being given to the goods and property of the Church, as well as the reorganization of the bishoprics which the King contemplated. This denunciation he closed by commanding the bishops henceforth to 'take care that the like should not occur again, and let them forbear calling into question in their sermons the acts of the prince and his ministers, else they should suffer with the evil preachers'.[3] The bottomless depths of Northumberland's secularism were fully revealed in this strange tirade; not only was the codification neither considered nor

[1] Those designated were, in addition, Cranmer, Goodrich (Ely), Richard Cox, Peter Martyr, Rowland Taylor of Hadleigh, May (Dean of St Paul's), Richard Goodrich, and Lucas.

[2] Edward VI, *Chronicle*, 110–111, for the full list and an analysis of the members. Cranmer, with his own private codification in hand, clearly dominated the work of the commission, though Rowland Taylor was credited by Strype as having made important contributions (Brown, W. J., 'Rowland Taylor, the Protestant martyr, 1509–1555', *Trans. Worcs., Arch. Soc.*, n.s. XXX (1954), 75). See also Martyr's comments to Bullinger, Mar. 8, 1552 (Robinson, *Original letters*, II, 503).

[3] *Cal. S.P. Span.*, XI, 33: Apr. 10, 1553; Gairdner, James, *Lollardy and the Reformation in England* (4 vols., L., 1908–1913), App. III, 400–401, following Rymer transcripts in PRO, vol. 146.

adopted, but the commission itself was permitted to lapse. The *Reformatio Legum Ecclesiasticarum* remained, in fact, an almost unknown manuscript until Foxe did homage to Cranmer by printing it in 1571.[1] Queen Elizabeth had no interest in grasping this nettle of dissension, and the ecclesiastical courts continued to carry on their functions without clear direction and often with methods and for purposes in sharp contrast to the increasing secularization of English life.

Though this impressive work was never to gain the force of law, it none the less deserves some comment for what it tells us of Cranmer's mind. It is probably well that the code was never adopted, since it would have perpetuated much that had become at once irrelevant and inimical in English life by the mid-sixteenth century. The work rests firmly on the postulate that the King is the supreme earthly head of the Church and that the faith propounded and defended by him must be accepted by all men of the realm. The code sought to bring even more fully under canon law such important matters as marriages, wills, legitimacy, adultery, blasphemy, sorcery, and fornication. In other words, in broad areas of human conduct and morals in which the temper of the age already called for secular jurisdiction, the proposed code would have riveted older and outworn views on the society.

But in this long work of fifty-two books (or titles) there was much that was also forward-looking and surely desirable. The bishops were to have a more direct concern for preaching, and an interesting plan for placing educated preachers of high ability in circuits within each diocese was set forward. Each bishop was likewise to be required to hold annually a synod of his clergy at which he would review the state of preaching and the quality of worship in his diocese. Excommunication was to be more frequently and widely employed for the imposition of spiritual discipline, and was to be lifted only after a formal and public act of penance and confession before the congregation and only by its express consent. Most important amongst its liberalizing virtues was a cool and sensible re-statement of the law of marriage. Twelve and fourteen years were declared to be the minimum age of marriage respectively for the girl and boy. Adultery was to be punished by imprisonment for life, while the property rights of wives, particularly those with jointures, were considerably improved. Most liberal of all was the provision that a divorce *a vinculo* could be granted by an ecclesiastical court

---

[1] *Reformatio legum ecclesiasticarum, etc.* (L., 1571; STC #6006). The work, strangely, is rather rare.

on grounds of adultery, desertion, or extreme and dangerous ill-treatment by either spouse, under which circumstances the innocent party, but not the guilty spouse, might re-marry.[1]

These were needed, and they would have been fruitful, reformations, but they were more than counter-balanced by fierce provisions which would have restored the trial and disposition of heresy to the ecclesiastical courts. It was flatly stated that any one who obdurately denied the essential doctrines of the Christian faith merited and should suffer punishment. Any person so accused must purge himself or stand condemned, though a series of appeals from the bishop, to the archbishop, to the King was outlined. Hardened heretics were to be burned, though if within sixteen days after conviction they renounced their beliefs and did public penance they were to be absolved. All other heretics, blasphemers, and witches were to be punished only by the spiritual censure of excommunication, including, interestingly, those who denied the validity of infant baptism. It must be added that the precise nature of the punishment of the intransigent heretic was left unclear. In the first title it is stated that those persons who obdurately denied the whole structure of the Christian faith should forfeit life and property, while in the third it is said that the unrepentant heretic must be accounted infamous and lose all legal rights. There was undoubtedly purposeful evasion on this all-important question, though Cranmer probably intended no extension of the laws already in hand for the punishment of extreme cases of heresy. But even as moderate and sensitive a prelate as Cranmer had in his career found it necessary to lend the august weight of his great office in the final decision to burn men and women. Such power was in itself a great and staining evil in England, even in the mid-sixteenth century.

[1] *Reformatio legum ecclesiasticarum*, esp. titles viii, ix, x, xvii, xx, xxx.

X

THE DEFINITION OF A PROTESTANT
POLITY (1551–1553)

1. THE GENERAL THRUST OF NORTHUMBERLAND'S POLICY

We have observed that the whole weight of conciliar policy under the dominance of the Duke of Northumberland had been steadily and increasingly towards an evangelical settlement of the Church of England. To put it perhaps more accurately, the thrust of Northumberland's policy had been in the direction of an evangelical Protestant party, whose great leader was Bishop Hooper, whose theological preferences were Zwinglian or Calvinistic, whose view of faith and worship displayed no nostalgia whatever for the ancient Church, and whose principal interest it was that all remaining Roman survivals be swept away and that a pure, an undefiled, Protestantism be vigorously preached and enforced throughout the realm.

This party had lent at least formal support to Northumberland's *coup d'état*, because they thought Somerset luke-warm in religion and Cranmer too moderate and too intricate in his theological and disciplinary leadership. These men—the precursors of the Elizabethan Puritans—also enjoyed the support of the King, who quite independently had by early 1551 adopted strongly Protestant views and who was thereafter on occasion to intervene directly with pressure which commanded both respect and obedience. It was to this party, then, that Northumberland lent his firm and unwavering support during his tenure of power. It is not too much to say that had he had another two years of hegemony in English policy, Northumberland might well have imposed an essentially Puritan complexion on the Church of England and on its bench of bishops.

These facts raise puzzling questions since Northumberland died in 1553 a professed and a communicating Roman Catholic, making the staggering statement that his sympathies had been secretly Catholic during the whole of the Edwardian era. It is at once pointless and hazardous for historians to probe into the faith of men long since dead, particularly when they reflect the pervading substance of a secularism which unfits them fully to comprehend the meaning of faith for men of an age still intensely spiritual in its ultimate concerns. But there are enough strands of evidence to permit at least a few questions and observations.

We must believe that Northumberland spoke truthfully within his lights and understanding just before his execution. He knew, just as certainly as had Somerset, that there was no recourse for him, that his life was required by sovereign power for too many reasons. All the evidence of his years in power suggest that Dudley was in the full sense of the term a politique and an adventurer whose essential concern was with power. He was not a pious man, he had no concern with theological questions, and his life may justly be said to have been irreligious. It had seemed to him, mistakenly in part, that the vitality, the spiritual power, and the religious future of England lay with the more evangelical party within the ambit of what could now be called Anglicanism. This party he accordingly embraced, just as when he was rallying the forces required to overthrow Somerset he seemed for a moment to have considered vital concessions to Catholicism. Northumberland was also undoubtedly moved by the reality of the King's own strong and expressed Protestantism, and Edward was a Tudor monarch disposed as early as 1551 to have his way in matters on which he had strong judgements. And, finally, it was clear to Northumberland that further spoils and power lay at hand if Protestant extremism were to triumph in England. This powerful motive, as we shall see, he was to exploit ruthlessly against the resources of the church during the last months of his tenure of power. Policy, discretion, and power, then, suggested this strange alliance with the evangelical Protestant faction. There would, and there did, still remain for him time to make his peace with God and the Church which he had so violently and steadily denied and opposed for many years past. In such matters, involving the tangled and often twisted spiritual concerns of all human beings, the ancient Church had always displayed an amazing and a complete spiritual tolerance. Indeed, it must. Its charity, then, was at the end quite capacious enough to embrace even the repentant Duke of Northumberland.

The gradual unfolding of Northumberland's ecclesiastical policy left many observers aghast. Thus as early as April, 1550 the Spanish ambassador could say with truth that all those immediately around the King were advanced Protestants and that the King personally took great delight in maintaining and arguing their doctrines.[1] And rather more than two years later, after watching English religious developments with a kind of fascinated horror, Scheyfve concluded that the introduction of the second *Book of Common Prayer* had removed 'all traces of the Roman Catholic ritual', save for the church ornaments which it was believed Northumberland meant to sweep into his tills, and that his power was now complete.[2] Only Cranmer and Ridley offered frontal resistance to the course of Northumberland's policy. But, as we have already observed, Cranmer was out of favour, much away from court, and on several occasions had been deeply humiliated by the Duke's deliberate insults. The break, as we shall note, became complete when the Archbishop courageously stood his ground in opposing the infamous effort to depose and ruin Bishop Tunstall of Durham. Ever after Cranmer bore Dudley's hatred. Ridley tells us in his *Piteous Lamentation* (1566) that he and Cranmer were 'both in high displeasure', Cranmer because of his steadfast support for Somerset, and both in the end for opposing the 'spoil of church goods, taken away only by commandment of the higher powers, without any law or order of justice'.

Northumberland was exploiting as well the increasingly fervent sympathy of the young King for the aims and aspirations of the evangelical party within the Church. Probably in April, 1551, Edward had sketched out in unfinished form a short essay on the needs of the Church which reveals the main heads of his concern.[3] The Word of God cannot be fruitfully set forth by preachers and teachers unless they prepare the minds of the people, as does a husbandman a seed-bed for his planting. England should be a nation at prayer, which cannot be achieved unless the people are 'continually . . . allured' to divine services. Further, an effective spiritual discipline must be sustained, whereby 'swearing, rioting, neglecting of God's Word, or suchlike vices, may be duly punished'. This goal for the religious community which is England cannot be reached unless the bishops firmly and steadily carry forward their proper functions, whereas in fact 'some for papistry, some for ignorance, some for age, some for their ill name, some for all these' lend little

---

[1] *Cal. S.P. Span.*, X, 70: Apr. 22, 1550.   [2] *Ibid.* 591–592: Nov. 20, 1552.

[3] The treatise, *Discourse on the reform of abuses in church and state*, is in Cotton MSS., Nero, C, x, ff. 113–117, and is printed in Edward VI, *Chronicle*, 159–167. It was probably inspired by Bucer's New Year's gift to the King in 1550–1551, *De regno Christi*. Bucer dealt in detail with the needs of the church, while Edward devoted no more than a short section of his essay to this subject before turning to a lengthy and remarkable discourse on the social and economic ills of the realm. *Vide post*, 411, for a further comment.

leadership in attaining the desired spiritual ends. The King reflected with satisfaction on the *Book of Common Prayer*, then under revision, but so weak was the episcopal bench that only those whose leadership may be trusted should be commissioned to impose a badly needed discipline on the realm.[1] Brief and staccato as these expressions of sentiment were, they reflected completely the judgement and disposition of the evangelical party within the Church to which Northumberland was now lending the full weight of his nearly sovereign powers.

The King's estimate of the religious situation was not greatly dissimilar from Bucer's considered judgement, as the strongly Protestant policy of Northumberland and the leaders of the Council began to be asserted. Bucer too found the bishops inadequate as a group, with the result that religion was in a 'very feeble state' for want of teachers and preachers.[2] But the remaining and persistent weakness he declared to be in the parochial clergy. Too many presentations were in lay, especially noble, hands, and appointments were made at the lowest possible stipend. Many parishes had not heard a sermon for years, while the former monastic clergy, often still popish in sympathy, were much employed 'merely for the sake of getting rid of the payment of their yearly pensions'.[3] Because of the conservatism of the fellows in the universities, the 'swarms of faithful ministers', so desperately needed, had simply not appeared. When the shocking state of the lower clergy was laid before the civil authority, the bishops were blamed, while they in turn pleaded that they could do nothing without further legislation. The inertia of most of the bishops, Bucer declared, was abetted by many of the nobility, recently enriched as they had been by the possessions of the Church. These men saw more gain for themselves in a weak and desolate Church, rather than in one dedicated to an evangelical reformation.[4] The thrust for reformation, he strongly suggested, was proceeding from the government itself by statutes, ordinances, and the forced removal of all superstitious objects. The great and ultimate hope was in the King, 'godly and learned to a miracle', who already 'is well acquainted with Latin . . . has a fair knowledge of Greek . . . and speaks Italian, and is learning French'. But the King was young and the pressures on the Church heavy and continuous.

[1] There are interesting similarities between this document and *Certain enormities in the Commonwealth to be reformed* (Oct. 1550) in Egerton MS. 2623, f. 9, an anonymous work in a hand which I cannot identify.

[2] Robinson, *Original letters*, II, 543: Bucer to Brenz.

[3] *Ibid.* 546: Bucer to Calvin.

[4] *Ibid.* 547.

Amongst the nobility there were very powerful persons who 'would reduce the . . . sacred ministry into a narrow compass', who held extreme views that would destroy the very meaning of the Lord's Supper, and who were disposed to force their intensely secular attitude towards the Church and its possessions.[1] The mainspring of this party, and now the principal ally of the evangelical Protestant party, was the Duke of Northumberland.

The evidences of official favour to evangelical Protestantism were numerous and they were persistent. Thus, to take a few examples, on Trinity Sunday, 1550, Thomas Kirkham was selected to preach at Paul's Cross where he vehemently denied that the Lord's Supper had any other meaning than as a memorial of Christ's all-sufficient sacrifice.[2] Some weeks later Corpus Christi was not observed as a holy day in London, while the Assumption of Our Lady was not kept in many London parishes. In late August another strongly evangelical clergyman, Stephen Caston, preaching at the Cross, vehemently denounced Mary Tudor as 'a great woman' in the realm who supported and maintained popery and superstition. Then, ominously, on March 22, 1551, several gentlemen, including Sir Anthony Browne, were clapped in the Fleet for having attended a celebration of the mass in Clerkenwell.[3]

The whole weight of policy and favour, then, was for months prior to the adoption of the second *Book of Common Prayer* lent to the evangelical party. In early 1552 there were significant changes and simplifications of the service in most London churches,[4] while in September the use of the organ in divine service was abandoned.[5] The clergy chosen to preach in the most influential pulpit in the realm, Paul's Cross, were usually advanced reformers, chosen with the consent and advice of the Council. So complete and detailed was the conciliar control of ecclesiastical policy that even Ridley felt it necessary to lay a request before Sir John Gates and William Cecil for permission to nominate a new precentor at St Paul's when Grindal should be translated to a bishopric.[6] It is clear that the famous and strongly evangelical preacher, Bernard Gilpin, owed his appointment as rector of Easington to the favour of the Council, though this fearless and sturdy man staggered the government by denouncing them, in a sermon before the King in late 1552, for what he described as the spoliation of the church.[7]

---

[1] Robinson, *Original letters*, II, 543–544.
[2] *Grey Friars Chronicle*, 67.
[3] *Ibid*. 67, 69.
[4] *Ibid*. 74.
[5] *Ibid*. 75.
[6] Lansdowne MS. 2, #104.
[7] *Ibid*. 3, #14: Dec. 20, 1552.

There can be no doubt that the King, already deeply interested in the details of policy, lent his full support to furthering the evangelical revolution now under way. One of the most interesting and important of his state papers (October 13, 1552), in form a memorandum prepared for a meeting of the Council, considered the thrust of policy in ecclesiastical matters. He wished all preachers in the realm to 'set their hands' to the support of the conformity of doctrine enjoined by the new *Prayer Book*. He desired authority for 'those bishops that be grave, learned, wise, sober, and of good religion' to bring the Church under a true spiritual discipline. He wished, too, that the Bishopric of Durham be divided, and carefully chosen bishops installed in both sees. He proposed that John Harley, one of his own chaplains and formerly chaplain to Northumberland, be appointed Bishop of Hereford, while he expressed, without elaboration, his sense of the need for more homilies and more injunctions to be laid by the bishops on the realm.[1] The mounting radicalism of ecclesiastical policy, prosecuted by the King for principally spiritual reasons, and by Northumberland for secular considerations, was also reflected in the quality and nature of appointments to high posts in the Church. A few of these should be examined in some detail.   *eg- Hooper, Ponet, Knox.*

Among those so preferred was John Bale, one of the greatest of English controversialists and scholars, who since Henrician times had been one of the most effective, as he was among the most radical, of the clergy. Despite his great gifts, both Somerset and Cranmer had withheld high preferment from Bale because of his violent anti-Catholicism and his complete independence from all authority. But Bale found a champion in Northumberland, to whom in 1551 he dedicated one of his numerous and always persuasive tracts.[2] Here he denounced the 'stout sturdy satellites of Antichrist' who brazenly opposed the Gospel in many parts of the realm, but especially in Hampshire, so long under Gardiner's sway. These enemies of the true faith, 'they brag, they boast, they dream, they dote', as they cling to the superstitious uses of the Romish past. They are moved by what is essentially a kind of rebellion, as they oppose the reforms of a monarch, to be compared only with Constantine. Bale called upon Northumberland to defend and nourish the reformation which the King sought to set forth. He knew there were those who spoke irreverently of the young King and his godly

---

[1] Edward VI, *Chronicle*, xxvii–xxviii, 179.
[2] Bale, John, *An expostulation or complaynte ag. the blasphemyes of a franticke papyst*, etc., ([L.], 1551]), no pagin.

proceedings; and there were those, equally dangerous, who alleged that the Council determined religious policy without the knowledge of the King. As recently as September 20, 1550, he had attended a service in Hampshire in which the priest spoke in Latin, turned his back to the congregation while administering the Sacrament, and 'turned and tossed . . . gaped and gaffed, kneeled and knocked, looked and licked, with both his thumbs at his ears, and other tricks more, that he made me xx times to remember Will Somer'.[1] Such spiritual leaders, still in covert opposition to the whole course of reform, must be ferreted out and their malicious influence destroyed. He would hope, indeed, that when the King 'cometh once of age, he will see another rule, and hang up an hundred of such heretic knaves'.[2]

This unquiet man, always magnificent under persecution, contentious when he had no adversary, was evidently troubling half of Hampshire from his parsonage at Bishopstoke. He tells us in his marvellous narrative style that in August, 1552 he went to Southampton to catch a glimpse of the King, then on progress.[3] While standing in the street to see the King, three of the Privy Chamber who knew Bale spoke with him, at which Edward marvelled because he had been told that Bale was dead. Edward immediately informed those of his Council present that Bale should be appointed to the Irish see of Ossory, which William Turner had just declined because of his ignorance of the language. Bale, shortly called before the Council, tells us that he pleaded age, poverty, and sickness, but could not baulk the will of the King that he should undertake once more a polemical crusade against popery in one of the most intransigently Catholic of all the Irish bishoprics.[4] Bale proceeded at the earliest possible moment to his see, where in the few months before Edward's death he preached constantly, stood embattled with his conservative cathedral chapter, and bewailed the dark popery of his uneducated parochial clergy.

When the news of Mary's accession reached Ireland, his spiritual flock 'rang all the bells in the cathedral minster and parish churches, they flung up their caps to the battlement of the great temple, with smilings and laughings most dissolutely'.[5] Nor was that all: a few days later (September 8th) a large band of armed thugs set upon and killed five of Bale's servants who were making hay in his field.

---

[1] Henry VIII's fool.
[2] Bale, *An expostulation*, B ii.　　　　[3] *Vide post*, 424–427.
[4] Bale, John, *The vocacyon of Johã Bale, etc.*, ([L.], 1553), fol. 17; Edward VI, *Chronicle*, 179.　　　　[5] Bale, *Vocacyon*, fol. 27.

That afternoon the civil authorities, four hundred in number, extricated Bale from imminent peril to Dublin where, with some justice but with customary imprudence, he denounced the Archbishop (Brown) as immoral, unreliable, and shifty in faith. A few days later he took ship for Flanders and exile, having in his flight lost the great library of books and manuscripts which were a portion of the collection he had retrieved for mankind after the spoliation of the monasteries.[1] This great but irascible man, zealously radical in his Protestantism, Puritan in his moral judgements, and one of the most famous of the preachers in England, was typical of the clergy which Northumberland and the monarch were advancing to posts of great power and responsibility.

Quite as vehemently Protestant, and in his way quite as learned, was William Turner, who had been educated at Cambridge where he proceeded M.A. in 1533. Appointed a fellow of Pembroke Hall in 1538, Turner published several scientific works, which with later contributions were to make him the most eminent of the early English botanists. He retired abroad in 1540 because of his radical Protestant views, having in his last year at Cambridge been intimately associated with both Latimer and Ridley. On the accession of Edward VI Turner returned to England where he was appointed both chaplain and physician to the Lord Protector. Turner's religious sentiments were, however, far more advanced than those of Somerset, and it was not until after the Duke's first fall from power that he gained preferment when in early 1551 he was appointed Dean of Wells to succeed the conservative John Goodman, who had been deprived by the joint efforts of Bishop Barlow and the Privy Council.[2]

Turner's religious thought grew increasingly radical as the reign advanced, tempered always, however, by his firmly held view that even the most serious of heresies could be put down only by the spiritual sword of God's Word.[3] As a physician and scientist, only extreme urgency, he said, compelled him to speak out against the survivals in English worship of the defiling and superstitious usages of the mass. These evil practices had for too long been sheltered by the contention that only those learned in theology should even discuss the doctrine. But men are not unlearned simply because they

---

[1] Bale, *Vocacyon*, fols. 29–41. This is a wonderful narrative, which should be reprinted.
[2] S.P. Dom., Edw. VI, X, 20; *ibid.* XIII, 1, 19; Jordan, *Edward VI*, 135, 332, 341, for references to Turner in other connections.
[3] Turner, William, *A preseruative . . . agaynst the poyson of Pelagius, etc.* ([L.], 1551), *Preface*.

are not priests.[1] England cannot hope for true and complete reformation until all men enjoy a perfect freedom in such great matters,
provided only that they support their views with Holy Scripture.
Nor was he in the least persuaded by the argument that to take
away all traces of the mass would unsettle the common people and
the ignorant. For one thing the King's subjects were 'more godly
and wiser' than was usually supposed, while in any event any
necessary risk must be taken to root out clearly idolatrous practices.[2] Even if there were in consequence political unrest for a
season, we are not bound to obey the command of the magistrate
in matters that are patently ungodly and unknown to Scripture.[3]
In his view, the Lord's Supper had none save a commemorative
meaning, and so the ruler and the Church must unequivocally
declare before the Reformation could be complete in England.
Turner wrote with great brilliance and with an absolute fearless-
ness, as he sketched out the design of the godly Christian community which he wanted England to be. One of the intellectual
leaders of the Protestant evangelical wing, he attracted the favourable attention of Northumberland and would almost certainly have
gained even higher preferment had not disaster overwhelmed a
Church which, in Turner's view, had not even in 1553 completely
cleansed itself.[4]

Northumberland, certainly with the direct approval of the King,
likewise showed great favour to John Ponet, who, though an early
convert at Cambridge, moved more gradually than most of his
evangelical colleagues towards the extreme Protestant position of
which Hooper was the moral and intellectual leader. Ponet had been
named a fellow of Queen's College, Cambridge, in 1532, where for
some years he taught and grounded himself in Greek, mathematics,

[1] Turner, William, A new dialogue, etc. (L., [1548?]), B iv–B v.
[2] Ibid., B v–B vi. The work was evidently written well before the adoption of the
second Prayer Book.
[3] Turner, A new dialogue, E iii.
[4] Turner again found refuge abroad during the Marian period. His two greatest works
(The huntyng of the Romyshe vuolfe ([Zurich, 1554]) and A new booke of spirituall physik,
etc. ([Basel?], 1555)) lie beyond our period. They appealed directly to the nobility and
gentry to stand fast in Protestantism and to bring down a tyrannous and idolatrous state.
His condemnation of Rome was bitter and sustained, being advanced by all sorts of
effective arguments. For example, he tells us that when recently a collection for the poor
was taken in all English parishes, those that were popish 'could not be brought to give
the fourth part . . . that the gospellers gave'. He argued as well that the great Catholic
bishops like Gardiner and Tunstall raised no voice in protest when Henry VIII despoiled
the property of the church by seizing the abbey lands, nor did they seriously oppose him
when he put away his wives at his own whim. (Turner, Huntyng of the Romyshe vuolfe,
D v[v].)

and astronomy. He was admitted to holy orders in 1536, though he remained at Cambridge as public lecturer on Greek and dean of his college until in 1543 he was appointed rector of a London parish to which two years later a living at Lavant, Sussex, was added. In 1546 he was created a chaplain to Cranmer, living for a season in the Archbishop's household and assisting him in his controversial works against both Smith and Gardiner. Ponet's first surviving work was the *Defence for mariage of priestes*, a careful and restrained attack on the teaching of clerical celibacy, which he declared to be unknown to Scripture, unnatural, and offensive to morals. Ponet also made an extensive study of patristic writings on the subject, which he successfully maintained had been perverted and twisted by popish writers who had been driven to the Fathers for their arguments.[1]

In 1550 Ponet and Hooper were jointly chosen to preach the Lenten sermons before the King and Court, on the occasion when Hooper outraged Cranmer by his fierce attack on the prescription of the new *Ordinal* with respect to the required vestments. Only one of several sermons preached by Ponet in this series survives, published in 1550 under the title, *A notable sermon concerninge the right use of the lordes supper*. It may be regarded as a pronouncement that he had embraced evangelical Protestantism, his position being clearly stated with great eloquence and learning. The fundamental fault of Rome had been that men and the law had been interposed between the Christian and God. Only slowly, even in England, had the purity and directness of the relation with Christ been affirmed. The greatest of all the interpolations had been the Roman practice of the mass which is at once superstitious and grossly deceptive. Ours must be a sacramental eating 'with our faith and inward belief, receiving a visible testimony of our inward belief in the face of the congregation'.[2] The long bondage to the priest and to the superstitions of the mass had resulted in a lay inertia in spiritual matters extremely difficult to correct and reform. Too many in England 'stand and remain still stiffly without searching any further',[3] while others simply take their beliefs as laid down by authority. The evangelical task, then, is to implant the understanding that it is 'necessary for every man to have eyes of his own, whereby

---

[1] Ponet, John, *A defence for mariage of priestes, by Scripture and aunciente writers, etc.* (L., [1549]), no pagin.

[2] Ponet, John, *A notable sermon concerninge the right use of the lordes supper, etc.* ([L.], 1550), C7–C7ᵛ, D iii.

[3] *Ibid.* F ii.

he may discern the true Church from the false, and the good doctrine from the bad, . . . Christian learning from papistry, and Christ from anti-Christ'.[1]

Ponet summoned England to undertake a thorough and an evangelical reformation. Who were those who opposed this necessary course? The analysis was an interesting one, and it foretold the heat of incipient Puritan zeal. They were the circuit judges whose principal interest had been in keeping the people quiet and submissive; they were the popish and the lazy priests, bishops, and schoolmasters. The principal assault must be on the ignorance and inertia of the youth of England, who 'shall live and enjoy the same land which we now possess and inhabit'. And, above all, some way must be found to carry the Gospel, the full glory of the Reformation, to the simple people, to make them more self-reliant and less credulous. The work of Reformation, as yet scarcely begun, is epitomized when the simple man in confession on his knees surrenders into the hands of the priest an imagined responsibility for his sins, but who in reality has surrendered the franchise of his Christian freedom.[2]

There was heat, but there was also great spiritual power, in Ponet's stalwart Protestantism. We do not know Cranmer's sentiments in the matter, but we do know that this was the evangelical Protestantism which Northumberland and his sovereign wished to advance. The King not long after the delivery of Ponet's sermon recorded with satisfaction his appointment to the see of Rochester.[3] A year later, following shortly on Gardiner's deprivation, Ponet was translated to the great see of Winchester, the *Acts of the Privy Council* recording that this was by the King's own designation.[4] It was ominous for the future security of the resources of the Church that Ponet, who thought bishops dangerously covetous, accepted 2000 marks a year for his maintenance, less than half the value of the temporalities of this, the richest see in the realm. Ponet was principally concerned during his brief episcopate with the preparation of a Latin catechism for use in schools.[5] He was immediately ejected on Queen Mary's accession, was then almost certainly implicated in Wyatt's rebellion, and then fled to Strassburg where he wrote his two greatest works, *An apologie fully aunswering by scriptures and*

---

[1] Ponet, John, *A notable sermon concerninge the right use of the lordes supper, etc.* ([L.], 1550), F vii[v].

[2] *Ibid.* G iv[v]–G iii.   [3] Edward VI, *Chronicle*, 38.

[4] *A.P.C.*, III, 231: Mar. 8, 1551; Edward VI, *Chronicle*, 58: Apr. 9, 1551; S.P. Dom., Edw. VI, XIII, 9: Mar. 23, 1551.

[5] *Ibid.* XV, 3: Sept. 7, 1552.

aunceant doctors, a blasphemose book (1556) and the famous *Shorte treatise of politike power* (1556), which exhibit with frightening candour the immense power and the danger to the state when religious truth, so clear to the embattled Calvinist, found itself under the lash of persecution.

Surely the most gifted—and by far the most disrupting—of all the evangelical Protestant leaders favoured by Northumberland was John Knox, who, as we have already observed, almost single-handedly forced Cranmer to accept the *Black Rubric* appended by the Council to the second *Book of Common Prayer*.[1] Northumberland completely misjudged Knox's temper of faith and mind, and was shortly to feel the sharp lash of the great Scot's tongue and pen. John Knox's fervour and absolute conviction were soon to teach England that Calvinism could singe the wings of sovereignty. This mistake of the Duke was one often made about Knox, who when 'truth' and the 'Lord's requirement' were not involved was at once gentle and mild in his relations. In fact, Knox was in a measure deceived about himself. For was he not to write in the *Faithful Admonition* that he was an over-gentle and fearful preacher: 'my wicked nature desired the favours, the estimation, and the praise of men . . . so privily and craftily did they enter into my breast that I could not perceive myself to be wounded till vainglory had almost gotten the upper hand'.[2] No more complete self-deception could be imagined. Northumberland had loosed in England the most formidable—as he was the most powerful and intellectually ruthless—of all the leaders of the Reformation in the British Isles; and we have never been disposed to underestimate Bishop Hooper.

On all other points, save the hated kneeling, Knox declared both the *Book of Common Prayer* and the *Articles* to be wholly consonant with the Word of God, and to them he lent his fervent and eloquent support.[3] Northumberland remained fully in support of Knox, in late October, 1552 writing to Cecil to lay before the King a recommendation for his appointment as Bishop of Rochester, which, he pointed out, would accomplish several useful purposes. Knox in his close proximity would not 'only be a whetstone, to quicken and sharp the Bishop of Canterbury, whereof he hath need,

[1] *Vide ante*, 350-352.
[2] Knox, John, *The works of John Knox*, ed. by David Laing (6 vols., Edinburgh, 1846-1864), III, 271.
[3] Lorimer, *John Knox*, 129; *Cal. S.P. Span.*, X, 593. Scheyfve wrote, 'The Duke of Northumberland has fetched hither a new Scots apostle from Newcastle, who has already begun to pick holes in the new and universal Reformation which they introduced last All Saints.'

but also he would be a great confounder of the Anabaptists lately sprung up in Kent'. Further, his removal from Newcastle would have the merit of dissolving the considerable number of Scots gathering there around this strong personality.[1]

Again, in late November, Northumberland prodded Cecil on the matter of the Scot's appointment to Rochester. But on December 7, 1552, Northumberland rather groggily reported that he had had a violent interview with Knox who, after a few months' residence in London and after coming to know Northumberland personally, now made it plain that he trusted neither the Duke nor the sincerity of his Protestantism. He was now persuaded that Dudley's interest lay in the spoliation of the Church and its resources, while Knox at bottom had no other purpose than the planting of God's true Church in England. Northumberland's letter to Cecil is a most remarkable document, for in it the Duke expresses an almost abject fear for himself and makes it plain that he had been roughly handled by the utterly fearless Scot. 'I do return him again, because I love not to have to do with men which be neither grateful nor pleaseable. I assure you I mind to have no more to do with him but to wish him pleaseable.' Knox had not only categorically declined Rochester, but had openly and abusively questioned his Protestantism, saying he 'cannot tell whether I am a dissembler in religion or not'. This, Northumberland continued, despite the fact that 'I have for twenty years [stood] to one kind of religion, in the same which I do now profess; and have, I thank the Lord, passed no small danger for it'. Hurt, frightened, and badly shaken by the wrath of Knox's denunciation, Northumberland spoke obscurely of evil reports being made of him to both King and Council, and protested his absolute loyalty to his sovereign. All that Knox had charged caused him to reflect on the fate of his own father, 'who after his master was gone, suffered death for doing his master's commandments . . . and yet could not his commandment be my father's charge after he was departed this life'.[2]

For the rest of his tenure of power Northumberland stood in terror of this evangel of the North, who spoke, as he often wrote, with the courage and assurance of an Old Testament prophet. In late December Knox returned to his pastorate at Newcastle, though the vicarage of All Hallows Breadstreet (London) was also shortly conferred on him.[3] But Northumberland, now prone to

---

[1] S.P. Dom., Edw. VI, XV, 35; printed in part in Tytler, *England*, II, 142–143.
[2] S.P. Dom., Edw. VI, XV, 66: Dec. 7, 1552; printed in Tytler, *England*, II, 148–150.
[3] *A.P.C.*, IV, 212: Feb. 2, 1553.

pour out his troubles to Cecil, remained shaken and profoundly discouraged. He felt it high time, so he wrote, to seek relief from his many burdens. He had sought to serve faithfully when his health permitted, but now in ill health, with few satisfactions save for the few children which God had allowed him, he had little cause to wish to live longer. 'I have', he confided to Cecil, 'entered into the bottom of my care[1].' But he could not shake free of the woes and fears engendered by John Knox. Almost immediately after his return to Newcastle Knox had been accused of nonconformity in complaints brought before the conservative Deputy Warden of the North, Lord Wharton. Wharton asked for guidance from Northumberland, who instructed him with bitter clarity that Knox was under no circumstance to be harassed, for the Scot stood high indeed in the favour of the King. The tone of Dudley's letter makes it certain that he did not dare permit any further molestation of Knox.[2] Power was now being gathered into the King's hands.

Criticism and mistrust of Northumberland, first so pointedly and courageously expressed by Knox, was now spreading amongst the leaders of the evangelical reformers whose cause, for devious reasons, he had done so much to encourage. In recent sermons Hooper, Lever, Grindal, and Bradford had severely criticized the religious policy of the Privy Council and had spoken out boldly against the Duke. And then in April, 1553 Knox was again called south to speak before the King. The text does not survive, but a year later, in his *Admonition*, Knox sketched out what he said. He had warned that godly kings were commonly served by dissemblers in religion, by men who cloaked their true sentiments in order to gain power of place. Such men were often blessed with worldly wisdom and experience, while concealing their true religious persuasion. And so, he reflected, a few months after Edward's death and in the cataclysm which had overtaken the Church of Christ, 'under that innocent king pestilent papists had [wielded] greatest authority'.[3]

2. THE ASSAULT ON THE CHURCH: THE BISHOPRICS

During the last three years of the reign an unsystematic but steadily increasing pressure was brought to bear on the remaining, and vital, financial resources of the Church of England. The principal attack was launched on the still large resources of the bishoprics

---

[1] S.P. Dom., Edw. VI, XVIII, 2: Jan. 3, 1553.   [2] *Ibid.*, 5: Jan. 9, 1553.
[3] Knox, *Works*, III, 282–283.

of the realm, with the consequence that when a bishop was appointed during this interval, the remaining resources of the see and its cathedral chapter stood in grave peril indeed. Ironically, this policy of gradual spoliation was made possible by the mildness of Somerset's general religious policy, for he had been quite unwilling to deprive even the most obdurately conservative of the bench of bishops which he inherited. The result was that when a considerable number of deprivations, deaths, and retirements occurred amongst the conservative bishops during the months of Northumberland's hegemony, the wealth of the see was invariably linked with the shortcomings of the Catholic prelate who was being replaced.

It must also be remembered that there were numerous causes for the unpopularity of the bishops, which when taken in combination made the temporalities of the prelates very vulnerable indeed. There was, for example, a growing and articulate body of influential lay sentiment, highly secular in temper, which agreed with Sir Philip Hoby, who, writing from Germany as early as 1548, suggested that the bishops should for both religious and political reasons be deprived of their 'princely and lordly estate'. Their incomes should be no more than was required for the true performing of their offices, from which 'vainglory' has long distracted them. And, as for the cathedral chapters, Hoby would suggest that all the prebends of the realm be at once expropriated and the incomes employed for the maintenance of poor and honest gentlemen who would defend the King and the realm.[1] Moderate and responsible religious leaders like Cranmer and Ridley were steadily disposed to protect and nourish the remaining wealth of the church, pointing out that the problem was to refurbish and reform the bench of bishops, which had been well begun by late 1550, in such wise that their spiritual functions and needs be adequately supported by their temporalities. Ominously for them, however, the leaders of the evangelical party, playing directly into Northumberland's hands in their distrust of the existing bench of bishops, were coming to question both the benefits and the necessity of episcopacy itself. Then there were the great preachers, men wielding considerable public influence, such as Latimer, Lever, Hooper, and Becon, who were full of wrath because the monastic and the chantry expropriations had not been employed for educational, social, and spiritual needs, and who would almost certainly have suggested further inroads into episcopal temporalities had they fully trusted Northumberland. And there was the Duke himself, skilfully exploiting evangelical

[1] Add. MS. 5828, f. 123b, based on two letters in Harl. MS. 523: Jan. 19, 1548.

sentiment, who looked upon the episcopal endowments as the last great treasure to be gained by the state for its secular uses and whose detestation of the bishops was so evident and so bitter that one is almost persuaded that he would, had he dared, have destroyed episcopacy itself.[1] But as the reign approached its end and as the full implications of Northumberland's policy became clearer, the evangelical party itself withdrew its support from the Duke because it had come to sense, with justice, if very late, dissembling and hypocrisy in his every religious action.

Northumberland may well have considered a broad attack on episcopal wealth and on the richer parochial livings of England and Wales during the fourth session of Parliament in early 1552, when he gathered elaborate data which could have had no other utility for him. An exhaustive collection was made of all the statutes and precedents which supported the supremacy of the King in all matters of ecclesiastical jurisdiction and which would necessarily form a legal base from which any attack on the episcopal temporalities would be launched.[2] Far more important and useful, to the Duke and to us, was a detailed listing of all the 'spiritual promotions' within the realm which possessed a value of £50 p.a. or more, providing an accurate and a tempting blueprint of the wealth of the church.[3]

The wealth of all the bishoprics of England and Wales was reckoned at £30,325 11s p.a., which if valued with a multiplier of 20 would suggest a total capital worth of £606,511. All other ecclesiastical offices in the realm worth £50 p.a. or more, and including cathedral offices, a number of collegiate appointments in the universities, a few hospital masterships, and sixty-four parochial livings, yields a total of £24,073 7s p.a., suggesting a capital worth of something like £481,467. In total, then, the really rich, and in most instances the vulnerable, ecclesiastical livings in England and Wales possessed a capital worth of almost £1,087,978. This was a very large treasure indeed, which, having survived many Henrician depredations, still totalled approximately half the whole value of the

---

[1] Christopher Morris (*The Tudors* (L., [1955]), 123) shares this view.

[2] S.P. Dom., Edw. VI, XVIII, 45. The document is undated, but internal evidence suggests early 1552 and also an organic connection with *ibid*. XV, 78, which may be dated 1552.

[3] *Ibid*. 78. This document, which extends to twenty-seven sides, first lists the temporalities of every bishopric in England and Wales, twenty-seven in all, and then by counties all the other spiritual emoluments with endowments yielding £50 p.a. or more. In reckoning the totals we have rounded off to the nearest shilling. In many instances, clearly, the valuations of the *Valor Ecclesiasticus* were those employed.

monastic expropriation, and very nearly as much as the worth of the remaining monastic wealth which had accrued to Edward on his accession.[1] This enormous resource also far exceeded the whole worth of the chantries of England. Moreover, it left unestimated the vast total of parochial wealth in the realm, which on a rough average hardly yielded £12 p.a., and suggests for all of England and Wales tithes and other endowments probably totalling something like £2,400,000 of capital value.[2] Both the remaining monastic wealth and the recently expropriated chantry resources were by 1552 sadly diminished, and a government which did not dare lay its financial needs before Parliament was doubtless sorely tempted once more to 'skim off the cream' of the great wealth which was the legacy of medieval piety. Whatever may have been Northumberland's purpose in preparing this careful and detailed study, the document reveals, for one thing, shocking differences in episcopal incomes which might well have been adjusted had the purpose been reformation rather than spoliation.[3]

Most of the dioceses of England did in fact suffer some encroachments on their endowments either in the later Henrician period or in the Edwardian era. Some detailed comment on at least a sampling of the bishoprics may be set out. Thus the considerable revenues of London were gravely weakened when in 1540 the new diocese of Westminster was carved out of its resources. In 1551, however, on the translation of Thirlby to Norwich, the sees were rejoined and the endowments presumably restored, though on the day of his consecration Ridley was obliged to exchange desirable properties in London and Middlesex, worth £526 19s 9d p.a., for less attractive parcels there and elsewhere. Then, documenting the secular rapacity of the ruling junta, a few days later the choicest of the former episcopal properties were granted in portions to Sir Thomas Darcy (Vice-Chamberlain), Lord Rich (Chancellor), and Lord Wentworth (Chamberlain).[4] Ridley was deeply shocked at this ruthless manipulation of the resources of the see, spilling out his rage to

---

[1] Jordan, *Philanthropy in England*, 59; Jordan, *Edward VI*, 111.

[2] If we reckon the number of parishes in England and Wales at about 10,000 (Jordan, *Philanthropy in England*, 27–28).

[3] The consideration of the problem was not new. As early as 1534 the Council had discussed endowing all bishoprics with a fixed (and on balance reduced) income of 1000 marks p.a., excepting for Canterbury which should have 2000 marks and York £1000. At the same time half of the income of collegiate churches and all endowments of archdeaconries were to be seized. (Scarisbrick, J. J., *Henry VIII* (Berkeley, 1968), 338, citing Cotton MSS., Cleopatra, E, iv, f. 174.)

[4] Rymer, *Foedera*, XV, 226; Newcourt, *Repertorium*, I, 617–618, 737; *ibid*. II, 87 159, 536; *Cal. Pat. Rolls, Edw. VI*, III, 404, 423–424.

Cecil who had asked for the favour of a few timber trees from one of the properties. He assured the Secretary of the gift, but concluded,

'If you knew the miserable spoil that was done in the vacation time [when the see was briefly vacant] by the King's officers upon my woods, whereby in times past so many good houses have been builded, and hereafter might have been . . . forsooth I do not doubt but you were able to move the whole country to lament and mourn the lamentable case of so pitiful a decay[1].'

The London temporalities were reckoned at no more than £1690 13s 6d p.a. in the survey of 1552, surely an inadequate income for the most populous and important see in the realm.[2]

Nor was Cranmer himself free of steady pressure from Northumberland during the last two years of the reign, even though, as we have seen, the Archbishop absented himself from Westminster whenever possible. But Northumberland's now vindictive dislike sought him out. Cecil, as usual, was the agent, but the Duke the inspirer of an ominous letter relating rumours of Cranmer's covetousness and of the great wealth which he and other bishops had amassed in the service of the crown. To this Cranmer replied in detail on July 21, 1552, indignantly denouncing the canard. His problem was in fact one of relative poverty, 'for I took not half so much care for my living, when I was a scholar of Cambridge, as I do at this present'. The income of the archdiocese had actually fallen by about £150 p.a. in the past ten years, Cranmer having by exchange paid heavy debts to Henry VIII, so that the total worth was set at £3223 18s 6d p.a. in the survey of 1552.[3] Humiliated though he was by Northumberland's attack, Cranmer stood his ground and his great see was not seriously molested or impaired. He rejoined that he was not personally rich, he was not covetous, and he knew no bishop, save possibly one, who could be described as rich, much less covetous.[4] This shocking and unmerited attack on Cranmer was all too typical of Northumberland's manner of proceeding: launch a violent and blanket attack on the position of an adversary, and then

[1] S.P. Dom., Edw. VI, XIII, 44: Sept. 16, 1551.

[2] *Ibid*. XV, 78 (I am including the Westminster temporalities, which were separately listed).

[3] *Ibid*. 78. The amount was not much less than the value of about £3466 set out by the *Valor Ecclesiasticus*, and slightly more than the £3164 10s 6d p.a. recorded in the survey of 1558 (du Boulay, F. R. H., 'Archbishop Cranmer and the Canterbury temporalities', *E.H.R.*, LXVII (1952), 34–36).

[4] Cranmer, *Works*, II, 437.

seek out for exploitation any cranny of weakness that might thus be revealed.

We have observed, too, that the great see of Winchester was gravely weakened in its resources—yielding £3885 3s 4d when Ponet, who was in truth quite indifferent to the temporalities, was translated to the bishopric. But he entered into an agreement, approved by the King, by which he received no more than 2000 marks p.a. for his maintenance. Most of the excess of income came into the hands of Paulet and others in or near the seats of power.[1]

In the once rich diocese of Exeter the looting was unrestrained, though Northumberland was here overmatched by the shrewd cupidity of Veysey, the ancient and intensely conservative prelate who was engaged in building a rich personal estate. Late in Henry VIII's reign the process of spoliation was well begun when long and favourable leases on prized portions were approved by the Crown, while in the Edwardian era the process of dismantling the temporalities was continued by grants to such favoured persons as Sir William Paget, Sir Thomas Darcy, Sir Thomas Speke, and Sir Andrew Dudley.[2] In his later years Veysey had begun the practice of taking annuities for outright grants, and when at last in August, 1551 he was forced to resign, Coverdale being appointed as his successor, he was given the rich annuity of £485 9s 3d for life, this being the net worth of his remaining temporalities and spiritualities. In this process of looting, the Crown and an unworthy bishop had permanently reduced the value of the temporalities of the great see by a full two thirds.[3]

And so the dreary and rapacious process continued, reaching a point of real and persistent plundering during the three years of Northumberland's tenure of power. Thus Sampson at Lichfield was obliged to alienate an estate with which to support a barony for Paget.[4] Holgate at York had on his installation in 1545 been compelled to surrender the remaining jurisdictional franchises of the see, but the diocese was not despoiled since he received in exchange substantial grants of tithes and patronage. But he too had gained Northumberland's animus and in the last year of the reign lay

[1] Cal. S.P. Span., X, 261: Apr. 9, 1551; A.P.C., III, 358–359; Strype, Memorials, II, ii, 264–265; Pollard, History of England, 52; S.P. Dom., Edw. VI, XV, 78; Edward VI, Chronicle, 58.

[2] S.P. Dom., Edw. VI, IV, 18: June 14, 1548; Rowse, A.L., Tudor Cornwall (L., 1941), 292–295.

[3] Rymer, Foedera, XV, 282, 286–289; Edward VI, Chronicle, 78; Rowse, Tudor Cornwall, 295; Dixon, Church of England, III, 275.

[4] Ibid. 275–276.

under heavy pressure. Dudley had purchased for himself the reversion of valuable monastic lands belonging to the diocese and demanded to see Holgate's deeds. Holgate stood his ground and it was not until 1553 that Dudley secured the leasehold and possession of the properties in question, in exchange for the return by the Crown of £600 of patronages which, it was agreed, had been unjustly taken from the see.[1] Kitchin, the conservative time-server at Llandaff, was under steady pressure and in the course of the reign alienated so much of the property under his control that his was left the poorest see in the realm.[2] Bush, of Bristol, was made of sterner stuff and would not yield even when haled before the Privy Council, refusing a governmental request that he grant 'upon reasonable recompense' a rich Somersetshire manor to Sir George Norton.[3] So too, Holbeach, who was appointed to Lincoln in August, 1547, was obliged before his enthronement on March 20, 1548, to grant to Somerset the great Oxfordshire manors of Thame, Dorchester, and Banbury, with other rich properties. The grants were in the form of an exchange, since the Crown yielded to the see thirty-six rectories formerly appropriated to monastic houses, as well as the site and remaining buildings of Thornton Abbey. But, as was usually the case in these formal exchanges, the bishopric could not bargain on level terms, with the consequence that its temporalities were considerably weakened.[4]

The most famous, as it was the most important, of Northumberland's interventions was the long and determined effort to unseat Bishop Tunstall of Durham. The case may, indeed, be regarded as of central significance because Cranmer lent the full weight of his support to his colleague, with whom he had long disagreed on theological matters, thereby pressing Dudley into ruthless pertinacity and at the same time incurring his deep enmity. Important as the incident is, the historical documentation is incomplete, particularly for the charges against Tunstall, and much of the affair remains shadowy. Tunstall, the perfect exemplar of the Henrician bishop, was seventy-six years of age when his troubles began, but had escaped the mental ossification of a Warham or a Veysey. A justly famous humanist, a skilled and effective diplomatist, Tunstall had done his duty under Edward VI and, however reluctantly, had

confirmed schism bhun. Cranmer + North.

[1] Dickens, A. G., *Robert Holgate, etc.* (L., 1955), 26–27.
[2] S.P. Dom., Edw. VI, XV, 78.
[3] *A.P.C.*, III, 210: Feb. 8, 1551.
[4] Cole, R. E. G., ed., *Chapter acts of the cathedral church of St. Mary of Lincoln, A.D. 1547–1559* (Lincoln Rec. Soc. Publ. XV, Horncastle, 1920), viii–ix; S.P. Dom., Edw. VI, XV, 78; Strype, *Memorials*, II, ii, 168.

imposed on his great diocese the statutes of reformation against which he had spoken and voted in the House of Lords. It may be further noted that he had taken no part whatsoever in the conspiracy resulting in Somerset's first fall, though after November 4, 1549, he was in London for the meeting of Parliament and was occasionally present at Council meetings. During the weeks of crisis Dudley was consistently friendly towards Tunstall, reappointing him to the Council of the North, arranging for a repayment in instalments of a loan from Henry VIII, and extending to the old bishop other modest favours.[1]

Moderate and long-suffering though he was in ecclesiastical matters, Tunstall was bedevilled and outraged by John Knox during his pastorate in Newcastle, finally citing the Scot in April, 1550 for having preached that the mass was completely idolatrous. Knox, already supported by Northumberland and the evangelicals in the Council, replied with a hot blast against his bishop, holding 'the mass to be, and at all times to have been, idolatry and [an] abomination before God', and for good measure adding that Tunstall was a murderer [of Christ in the mass], and a thief [pretending the forgiveness of sins].[2] None the less there was no indication of Dudley's ill-will until in December, 1551 one Ninian Menville formally accused the Bishop of misprision of treason with respect 'to a conspiracy in the North for the raising of a rebellion', presumably in support of Somerset. The Privy Council minute alleged that this knowledge of treason dated from 'about July 1550', and that a missing letter from Tunstall to Menville 'whereupon depended a great trial of the matter' had been found 'in a casket' of Somerset's at the time of his second arrest. Accordingly, it was ordered that Tunstall's goods and chattels in Durham and London should be taken into hand.[3] Northumberland, it appears, had some weeks earlier questioned the Bishop privately and rather obscurely, hinting that he 'marveled' that Tunstall had not revealed the incriminating letter. He had found Tunstall cold in his answers, yet full of perplexity and fear, and closed his report of the conversation with the ominous prophecy that Durham would yield to the King as much as Winchester 'if the cards be true'.[4]

No concrete proofs of the alleged conspiracy were ever produced, the 'plot', so called, having about it the air and odour of much of the

---

[1] Sturge, Charles, *Cuthbert Tunstal, etc.* (L., [1938]), 283–284. We shall depend heavily on this admirable account of Tunstall's troubles.

[2] Knox, *Works*, III, 32, 33–70.   [3] *A.P.C.*, III, 448–449: Dec. 20, 1551.

[4] S.P. Dom., Edw. VI, X, 31: Sept. 16, 1550.

evidence produced when Somerset's destruction was undertaken. The informant, Menville, a retainer of the Neville family, was a pardoned felon, an adventurer, and was prepared, it is quite clear, to bring forward just as much evidence as might be required. Paulet wrote rather obscurely to Cecil that the case was under consideration by him and Northumberland and indicated that he had informed the Lord Chancellor to be prepared to bring Tunstall to trial and to draft a proclamation which might be employed.[1] Tunstall, however, did not appear before the Council again until December, 1551, when, failing to give an explanation acceptable to his colleagues, he was committed to the Tower,[2] though the Council itself regarded the evidence of Menville as both suspect and inconclusive.[3]

Towards the end of the parliamentary session which had opened on January 23, 1552, Northumberland abandoned the strategy of bringing Tunstall to trial and instead took the extraordinary course of introducing a bill in the House of Lords (March 28, 1552) which would have declared him deprived by Act of Parliament. The measure was passed by the Lords despite the courageous and persistent opposition of Cranmer, who was joined only by Lord Stourton in the final vote on the measure. Meanwhile a second bill had been introduced in the Commons attainting Tunstall for misprision of treason, which encountered stalwart opposition and had to be abandoned when the government declined to meet the demand of the House that both Tunstall and his accusers be brought face to face before them.[4] This most embarrassing failure in Parliament was a serious blow both to Northumberland's pride and to his confidence, particularly since he had made it clear that on the deprivation of Tunstall he wished to secure for himself the palatine jurisdiction of Durham.[5]

Tunstall remained in the Tower, while Northumberland, not easily baulked, sought for other evidence to be employed in securing the Bishop's ruin. In the late summer, accordingly, a former servant in Somerset's household, Mrs Elizabeth Huggins, was closely questioned by Sir Robert Bowes and Sir Arthur Darcy in an effort to link her somewhat reckless sympathy for Somerset to the alleged conspiracy of the Bishop, but to no avail.[6] All other means having

[1] S.P. Dom., Edw. VI, XIII, 17: May 15, 1551.   [2] Edward VI, *Chronicle*, 101.
[3] It was hoped by the Council that Dean Robert Horne of Durham, a radical reformer, might be able to supply further proofs.
[4] Dixon, *Church of England*, III, 441–442; Strype, *Cranmer*, I, 415.
[5] S.P. Dom., Edw. VI, XIV, 18: Apr. 7, 1552.
[6] Harl. MS. 353, ff. 123–124b: Sept. 9, 1552; and cf. *ibid*. ff. 121, 121b–123.

failed, the Council a few days later ordered the Chief Justice of the
King's Bench (Cholmley) and six other lawyers, all of course laymen, to proceed as a commission for the examination of Tunstall,
granting it authority, if the findings so ordained, to deprive him of
his diocese. At the same time certain letters and 'other writings'
touching the case were delivered into the commission's hands.[1] The
commission met and carried forward its examination, the record of
which does not survive. As was predictable, it (on or about October
15th) declared Tunstall deprived.[2] The aged prelate was remanded
to the Tower, where he remained until the accession of Queen
Mary. Be it said his imprisonment was light, for after December he
was given 'liberty of the Tower' and such funds as were required
for his needs.[3]

The great see of Durham now lying vacant, Northumberland
moved at once towards his long-cherished plan for its reconstitu-
tion. Had the Duke been trustworthy and had his interest been
dedicated to the needs of the Church, there was, in fact, considerable merit in his plan to create two dioceses, the one at Durham
with 2000 marks p.a., and the other at Newcastle with 1000 marks.
There was merit too in the arguments that the diocese should be
cleanly separated from the historic palatine power of the Bishop, that
the see was too large for one bishop to serve, and that this was an
area of England which stood in grave need of enlightened leadership and vigorous preaching. Writing to Cecil only a few days after
Tunstall's deprivation, Northumberland stressed these points as
well as the over-riding one that such a settlement would leave at
least £2000 p.a. at the King's disposition, with 'all places better and
more godly furnished than ever it was from the beginning to this
day'.[4]

Northumberland pressed his proposal that Dean Horne, a vigorous critic of Tunstall on religious grounds and himself an evangelical reformer, be created Bishop of Durham, while Knox should
be named to Rochester where he would be 'a whetstone to quicken
and sharp the Bishop of Canterbury'. But, as we have earlier noted,
Knox not only refused the see but for good measure denounced

---

[1] *A.P.C.*, IV, 127: Sept. 21, 1552; Strype, *Cranmer*, I, 413–414. We have not been
able to find the materials thus submitted in evidence.

[2] Edward VI, *Chronicle*, 150: Oct. 15, 1552; Machyn, *Diary*, 26: Oct. 14, 1552.

[3] Strype, *Cranmer*, I, 414. Scheyfve's probably correct understanding was that the
commission found that Tunstall had come into the possession of seditious letters which
he had held for five days and had then forwarded directly to Somerset rather than to the
whole Council (*Cal. S.P. Span.*, X, 582: Oct. 29, 1552).

[4] S. P. Dom., Edw. VI, XV, 35: Oct. 28, 1552.

Northumberland to his face as a dissembler.[1] And Horne, on being apprised of the plan, refused in equally clear and insulting terms, adding that he too thought the King's principal minister to be a dissembler. Of Horne, Northumberland wished to hear no more. Suddenly, the Dean had become a peevish man, a greedy and malicious man, loose 'of his tongue and [one who] letteth not to talk upon his ale bench'. The Duke now wished for a 'soberer man' who did not stand on his own stubborn conceit, and who did not condemn 'every man's doing and conscience but his own'.[2] His enthusiasm for the evangelical reformers now completely quenched, Northumberland continued to press for the plan he had brought just short of fruition, for he now spoke in general and troubled terms respecting the appointments which he wished made, and that promptly, lest the region 'grow more and more barbarous'. He would rather have a 'stout honest man that knoweth his duty to God and to his sovereign lord, than one of these new obstinate doctors without humanity or honest conditions'. His repeated prescription, surely quite unwittingly, went far towards describing the very virtues for which Tunstall had for so long been noted. And as he reflected on the bench of bishops, indeed, they were 'so sotted of their wives and children that they forget both their poor neighbours and all other things which to their calling appertaineth'.[3]

As preparations were being made for the assembling of Edward's second Parliament, Northumberland, now somewhat chastened, wrote once more to Cecil requiring him 'to move my Lord to be [the] means to . . . place a grave and learned man in the see of Durham', and urging that great care be taken in the choice.[4] But the Duke had no more specific proposals to make; he seemed weary and distracted as he sought to suggest policy. The new Parliament did indeed pass the act dividing the see according to Dudley's scheme, but formal action on the appointments was not completed before the King's death. William Bill, a vigorous preacher and a moderate reformer, was to be appointed to Newcastle, while Ridley— so the plan ran—was to be translated from London to Durham. The County Palatine was in April, 1553 formally annexed to the crown.[5] But, as the King's illness was now evidently most serious and as

---

[1] Vide ante, 374.
[2] S. P. Dom., Edw. VI, XV, 62: Dec. 3, 1552.
[3] Ibid. XVIII, 1 and 3: Jan. 2 and 6, 1553.
[4] Ibid. 8: Jan. 19, 1553. The manuscript is badly torn and the full sense cannot be gained.
[5] The registers of Cuthbert Tunstall, etc., ed. by Gladys Hinde (Surtees Soc. Publ. CLXI, L., 1952), xi, xii; VCH, Durham, II, 33–34; ibid. III, 28–29.

political considerations became of absorbing gravity, these intended measures were never carried out. One of Queen Mary's first actions was to reconstitute the bishopric of Durham and to restore Tunstall.

In all the later phases of the effort to partition the bishopric of Durham, it is evident that Northumberland had lost control of policy and that his prestige had been severely impaired. So too, as we reflect on his steady spoliation of the bishoprics of the realm, one can only conclude that he gained relatively little treasure for himself, more for his supporters in the Council, and still more for the state, but at a very high price. By the close of 1552 his policy was in fact in ruins, and he had gained the bitter and disillusioned hatred of the evangelical reformers, who had now taken a correct, if belated, measure of the man and his religious aspirations. From the outset, the great centrist party in the Church of England, led by Cranmer and Ridley, had suspected him and were now in implacable opposition, while the Romanists regarded him as at once dangerous and completely secular. It seems probable that his nerve was gone and his confidence utterly shaken after the terrible indictments which Knox and Horne, and—one should add—Latimer and Hooper, had laid against his character and his faith. Decisions in ecclesiastical matters were being taken firmly into the hands of the King, just as his fatal illness overtook him. As we have had occasion to stress, Edward VI was also almost completely secular in his ecclesiastical concerns, but he was at the same time in his faith a deeply pious Protestant, disposed towards warm support of the evangelical—the reforming—party in the Church of England. But he was scarcely able to do more than mark out the lines of his policy as Supreme Head of the Church of England before all lay in ruins with his death.

3. THE ASSAULT ON THE CHURCH: CHURCH GOODS

The policy of the government with respect to the temporalities of the great bishops aroused some measure of concern and doubtless considerable resentment, but it scarcely touched the wealth and the furniture of religion to be found in the thousands of parishes across the length and breadth of the realm. But when the pressure of the state began to be applied towards the expropriation of a large proportion of the moveable wealth of each parish church, the sacred vessels of the sacraments, the ornaments of worship, the vestments of the priest, and all plate—regarded both as a local dedication to faith and as a common treasure store to be employed for local secular needs in dire times—men were deeply concerned and could only conclude that the whole structure of worship in their community stood in danger. This policy of expropriation had, it so happens, many justifications and perhaps much of spiritual merit, within the requirements of reformation, but it was generally viewed as still another evidence of Northumberland's rapacity. Moreover, the whole confused policy which the government gradually evolved towards church goods was complicated and misunderstood in its relation to other and earlier expropriations which were in fact still under way, or at the least still subject to the slow accounting of the revenue courts. There were still stores of abbey plate and other moveables which remained undelivered, as witness an order from the Council to Holgate at York to surrender immediately to the York Mint 'seventeen score and four ounces of silver', as well as 'a shrine of silver and gilt and some gold' which were held at York Minster in the custody of the prebendaries.[1] Even more confusing was the fact that under the act expropriating the chantries, moveables, often physically used and displayed in parish churches, had been confiscated but were being assembled and paid in, subject to interminable delays and not a little of concealment. The total reported worth of £8087 10s for these moveables, as indicated by the commissioners, was, as we have seen, not much more than a nominal appraisal because of the widespread concealments and embezzlements which had taken place.[2]

It was the passage of the second Act of Uniformity (April 14, 1552), authorizing as it did the new Prayer Book, which supplied both the legal and the doctrinal basis for the general expropriation so long feared. Almost the whole of the plate, the vestments of the priest, and the instrumentalities of worship organically connected with the sacrifice of the mass, were now by law forbidden. There were, therefore, in the closing months of the reign most compelling reasons why a systematic expropriation of the 'vessels of superstition' should and must proceed; England could scarcely become a Protestant realm unless precisely this were done. And the fruits of expropriation belonged to the Crown. It is ironic that Northumberland should, quite unjustly in this one instance, have borne the blame of historical judgement for an action which both logic and religious policy dictated.

[1] Pocock, Nicholas, 'Papers of Archbishop Holgate', in *E.H.R.*, IX (July, 1894), 545.
[2] *Vide ante*, 192.

Long before the final decision was taken, however, there was a lively concern in the Council because of information and rumours that churchwardens and parishes were secreting, selling, or embezzling plate because of the general apprehension that an expropriation was intended. Accordingly, in December, 1547 the bishops were instructed to prepare an inventory of church plate in their several dioceses and to 'see the same preserved entirely to the churches, without embezzling or private sales'. Few of the episcopal certificates for this survey are extant, but there is abundant evidence that its consequences was the further stimulation of the very sales that the Council had hoped to halt.[1] This the Council fully understood when it warned Holgate at York that 'sundry persons upon some vague bruits or rather their own rashness' were selling plate, jewels, and even bells from churches on their own authority, and enjoined him to search the churches of his province to ascertain the facts and to list the names of such persons and the value of the church goods thus illegally sold.[2]

With some prodding, the inventory returns did drift in, the punctilious Bird of Chester being one of the first to reply.[3] A much more ambitious and detailed return was made by the Bishop of London, which suggests that shrewd and knowledgeable churchwardens in the City were already disposing of church plate and applying the proceeds to worthy, if unauthorized causes.[4] From Canterbury, where the cathedral chapter was never fully controlled by Cranmer, came the ominous intelligence that certain of the chapter had set aside gold, silver, and bejewelled objects to be sold for the benefit of the cathedral fabric.[5] The Council not only forbade the action, but a few weeks later required the delivery to the Mint of all the 'jewels and plate of gold and silver' which by Henry VIII's permission they had retained.[6]

The episcopal inventories having proved neither complete nor carefully gathered, the Council, very properly alarmed by widespread conversions of church plate, on February 15, 1549, ordered an elaborate inventory to be made in every shire in the realm. The Council explained that there had already been much illegal selling of church goods, a great deal of concealment and embezzlement, and no little of contention and disagreement within parishes. Hence the

---

[1] *A.P.C.*, II, App., 535–536; *The inventories of church goods, etc.*, ed. by William Page (Surtees Soc. Publ., CXVII, Durham, 1897), xi–xii.
[2] Pocock, in *E.H.R.*, IX, 546, with Holgate's reply (*ibid.* 547).
[3] S. P. Dom., Edw. VI, III, 4: Jan. 12, 1548.
[4] *Ibid.* V, 19: undated.   [5] *A.P.C.*, II, 139–140: Oct. 23, 1547.
[6] *Ibid.* App., 542: Jan. 29, 1548.

sheriffs and justices of the peace of each county were appointed commissioners of survey, were to divide each county, to visit each
church personally, and then to meet with the clergyman, the churchwardens, and three or four in addition of 'the discreetest and most
substantial men' in every parish in order to compile a true and complete inventory of church moveables. It was further stipulated that
all alienations made in the year past were null and void and must
promptly be restored, unless 'made by the common consent of the
parish and the money thereof applied to any common good use',
while henceforth no alienation should be made, under pain, without
the express approval of the Privy Council.[1]

One wishes more were known regarding an order of the Council
on March 3, 1551, which states that in view of the King's need for a
'mass of money', commissioners should be appointed in all the
shires to take into the King's hands all remaining church plate.[2]
Though this was a period of severe fiscal crisis, which was to continue for many months, there was no special emergency which
could explain this extraordinary resolution, while the adoption of
the second *Book of Common Prayer* lay well in the future. The tone
and purport of the document suggests that a surely tempting decision had been made, animated by secular interests and intentions,
which, after reflection, was not then implemented. In any event
nothing more was heard of what was surely a rash resolution.

There followed a delay of more than ten months during which
there is a curious silence in the official records regarding the whole
matter and during which a great deal of the church plate of England
was either sold, embezzled, or secreted. There is evidence, too, that
the inventories, demanded first in 1547 and then more vigorously in
1549, remained incomplete as governmental pressure was relaxed.
But a decision was taken just two days before the final session of
Edward's first Parliament to press immediately for the completion
of the census of church goods,[3] since the Council intended to make
the passage of the Act of Uniformity, ordering the use of the second
Prayer Book, the first order of business. The Council was informed
that many articles not required for public worship had quite
illegally fallen into private hands, so that 'men's halls were hung with

---

[1] S.P. Dom., Edw. VI, VI, 25: Feb. 15, 1549. Such permissions were fairly freely
granted, as for example to Sandwich where plate was to be used to finance harbour
repairs (*A.P.C.*, III, 104: Aug. 14, 1550); to Cheddar, Somerset, where church goods to
the value of £40 might be used for scouring the river there (*ibid.* 154: Nov. 7, 1550); and
to Fobbing, Essex, to the limit of £30 for church repairs (*ibid.* 335: Aug. 18, 1551).

[2] *A.P.C.*, III, 228.

[3] Edward VI, *Chronicle*, 119: Jan. 21.

altar-cloths, that tables and beds [were] covered with copes instead of carpets and coverlets', that 'many drank at their daily needs in chalices; and no wonder if in proportion it came to the share of their horses to be watered on rich coffins of marble'. Accordingly, new instructions were issued on January 29, 1552, to the commissions appointed three years earlier, requiring them to complete their inventories of church goods with all due speed, to account for all goods now in private hands, and by indentures to list and reserve for the King's use all such property save for 'one, two, or more chalices or cups, according to the multitude of the people . . . and also such other ornaments as by their discretion shall seem requisite for the divine service in each such place'.[1]

Again, there was a delay before the planned expropriation was finally ordered. In part, this was occasioned by the necessity for giving the commissioners time to complete what was intended to be a thorough and detailed survey, somewhat complicated by the decision in December, 1552 to add an inventory of plate, jewels, lead, and bell-metal from monasteries and chantries which was not yet in the King's hands.[2] The Council must also have been concerned with the legal basis of this intended action, to which there was already some learned opposition,[3] since it had regarded it as unwise to lay before Parliament an enabling act which, as had been the case with the chantry wealth, would have given a firm statutory basis for the intended action. The Council, already extremely nervous as it planned to introduce the *Prayer Book*, had no wish further to exacerbate public sentiment and hence in the end proceeded by the prescriptive powers of the King, by inference depending on the two great acts of Supremacy and Uniformity. Most importantly, the final order for seizure could hardly be put into effect until the service as prescribed by the new *Book of Common Prayer* went into effect in November, 1552 with its clear and severely chaste administration of the Lord's Supper.

It was not until early 1553, in point of fact, that the expropriation was at last ordered, the Council requesting the Lord Chancellor to draft the necessary warrants for the commissioners, whose ranks were now augmented to fill vacancies in the several shires.[4] There

---

[1] *A.P.C.*, III, 467: Jan. 29, 1552; *Instructions given by the King's Majesty . . . for the survey of church goods* (1552), in Cardwell, *Documentary annals*, I, 110 ff.; Fuller, *Church history*, IV, 98–102. These instructions were supplemented on Apr. 12th, just two days before the formal passage of the Act of Uniformity.

[2] S.P. Dom., Edw. VI, XV, 76.

[3] As an example, *vide ibid.* 77: Dec. ?, 1552, for an argument that it was unlawful thus to transfer church property to secular uses.   [4] *A.P.C.*, IV, 219: Feb. 16, 1553.

were troubles and uncertainties in almost every county, creating what must have been deep concern for the Duke and his followers. A few examples will suffice. In Herefordshire the commissioners found that plate had been stolen and they were seeking to recover it. An inventory which had been sent in from Derby had apparently been lost and a copy was hence being forwarded to the government. Lord de la Warr was finding much less plate in Sussex than he had expected, many of the parishes being very poor. In the West Riding the commissioners, who had hoped to complete their task by the end of May, as ordered by the Council, could only say that they would do their work as rapidly as possible. The Devonshire commissioners were forwarding their report on June 16th, but warned that there might well be inaccuracies because of the ignorance of the people who had certified mistakenly that objects were of gold when examination proved that they were not. Still, they could at least say that 'in the execution of this commission we have found the people very quiet and conformable', and 'joyful' to increase the King's treasure.[1] Perhaps a more accurate and just appraisal was that of a Protestant clergyman of Wickersley (Yorks): 'Thus betwixt making and marring during King Edward's time, they took the spoil of that, which King Henry could not take, for shortness of life.'[2]

Ironically enough, there had not been time to complete the expropriation, much less to sell or melt down all of the plate, before the death of the King overwhelmed Northumberland and his policy. Thus in Kent the commissioners were unable to deliver the expropriated plate even from the Canterbury churches until June 1st, from the Weald churches not until June 16th. There was simply not sufficient time for accounting, for delivery, and assembly of the hundreds of articles involved in most counties, and surely not in Kent where most of the plate fell into the hands of Mary's government and was applied for principally secular purposes by this most Catholic of sovereigns.[3] So large an undertaking, under way across the whole realm, could not be halted once well under way.[4] Mary

---

[1] Stowe MS. 141, ff. 59–69. These reports, unhappily lacking in much detail, extend from May 19 to June 16, 1553.

[2] Dickens, A. G., ed., *Tudor treatises* (Yorks. Arch. Soc., Record Ser. CXXV, 1959), 140.

[3] Robertson, Scott, 'Queen Mary's responsibility for parish church goods seized by King Edward's commissioners', in *Archaeologia Cantiana*, XIV (1882), 314–315; VCH, *Kent*, II, 78.

[4] The Marian Council did when possible seek to stay the course of expropriation (*A.P.C.*, IV, 327, 329, 338, 348, 360).

did launch an enquiry (1556) into the accounts handed in by the
commissioners and may well have been solaced by their report that
they had been as generous as possible in what they had left in the
churches. In any event, much of the wealth had already been sold
before their arrival and the gains disposed principally for the repair
of churches.[1]

By far the most revealing estimate of the effect of the simpli-
fication and reform of the ritual, in part to be achieved by the
seizure of superfluous plate, is to be found in the relatively few surviving churchwardens' accounts for this early period.[2] Here we discover and can almost measure the slow and cautious progress of the
Reformation until the cataclysm of change imposed by the second
Prayer Book broke over usually conservative village and rural
churches, or was anticipated and more in those parishes, most often
in towns and cities, which under evangelical leadership had already
become thoroughly Protestant in the ministrations of divine services. Thus in St Martin's, Leicester, as early as 1545–1546 the
wardens entered receipts of £24-odd for the sale of plate, the proceeds probably being used for the repair of the fabric. Then in 1547
there were numerous records of sales of such items as cloths,
tabernacles, iron, brass, and a disused organ, yielding £13 2s 2d, a
portion of which was disbursed to the poor of the city.[3] This process
was also under way in other churches of the city, always after
parish decision, most sales being of old and long since disused
ecclesiastical lumber.[4] Then in 1553, *after* the visitation of the commissioners, still more sales were made, the proceeds probably being
used, in part at least, for the rather tardy purchase of Erasmus'
Paraphrases for 7s, for the new *Book of Common Prayer*, and 4d 'for
a book concerning the rebels which was read in the church'.[5]

Similarly, in the rural parish of Bethersden, Kent, the accounts
for the parish church show a remarkable sensitivity to the religious
changes ordered by law and injunction. The records for 1545–1546
display an interesting complexion of life in the community just
before the Edwardian changes began. The parish had received,
doubtless by bequests, tiny plots of land, several sheep, and two
houses, all producing an annual income of £2 15s 10d, which was

---

[1] Robertson, in *Arch. Cant.*, XIV (1882), 322.

[2] Most of those thus far found have been published, and all these, we believe, have
been examined.

[3] North, Thomas, ed., *The accounts of the churchwardens of S. Martin's, Leicester,
1489–1844* (Leicester, 1884), 11, 27–29.

[4] Thompson, James, *The history of Leicester, etc.* (Leicester, 1849), 237–238.

[5] North, *Accounts of S. Martin's*, 61.

typically employed for lights and tapers, minor repairs, and a small stipend to the parish clerk. The tide of change began to sweep over this parish when during 1546–1548 payments were made for the 'blotting out of St Christopher', while the wardens anticipated the future by the sale of a cope and other 'church goods' for a total of £1 2s 11d, which was probably reflected in the £1 17s 4d paid out for poor relief. In 1549 the command to prepare an inventory of church goods for the commissioners was heeded, requiring a visit to Canterbury (1s), to London (5s 4d), and two trips to Ashford (5s), as well as 1s 8d for making the two inventories and 4d to the vicar for copying it. In 1549, too, 2d was paid out for the *Book of Articles*, and 10s for 'the book of Erasmus', while a little later the *Book of Common Prayer* was bought at the fixed price of 4s and the *Paraphrases* for 1s. In 1551 an extra copy of the *Paraphrases* was sold at a profit, while the now disused altar brought £1. Then in 1552–1553 there is an entry of 1s paid out for the preparation of the second inventory of church goods, while three 'new books' (of *Common Prayer*) were purchased. The annal of change was concluded by an outlay in 1553 of 8d for the dinner and 9d for the expenses of the wardens when they delivered the church goods of the parish to the King's commissioners waiting at Ashford.[1]

We find in the surviving churchwardens' accounts, too, a most interesting, and probably typical, annal of the efforts of most parish officials to save the resources of their churches by the sale, on parish vote, of church goods and the immediate outlay of the proceeds for what were generally regarded as acceptable charitable uses. One must remember, in this connection, that these modest stores of silver, fine fabrics, and even base metals had long been regarded as emergency reserves of wealth to be drawn on in times of great local crisis and then gradually to be replaced as more normal times returned. Men of the age viewed these supposedly sacred objects in a much more robust and secular fashion than have many historians in commenting on this expropriation. The Lord, it was often reflected, was quite as well served from a chalice of pewter as from one of the purest silver. Hence the churchwardens, tough-minded and practical men as they tended to be, were quite prepared to move quickly, and they hoped within the law, at the first sniff of the possibility of royal seizure.

In Devonshire, as yet by no means recovered from the ravages of 1549, the parish authorities acted decisively in anticipation of royal

[1] Mercer, F. R., *Churchwardens' accounts at Betrysden 1515–1573* (*Kent Records* V, Ashford, 1928), 83–84, 85–86, 88–89, 90–91, 93, 97–98, 99–100.

policy. At Exeter, then much in royal favour, eight of the city parishes raised £228 12s 4d from the sale of church goods towards building the canal which its burgher leadership had so long desired. The royal commissioners did bind the city to repay this large sum on demand, but after skilful and protracted negotiations even this bond was cancelled.[1] So too, in East Devonshire numerous parishes joined together in the sale of church plate, employing the proceeds towards making an harbour at Ottermouth.[2] At Bix Brand and Bix Gibwen in Oxfordshire, the wardens had hastily sold silver ornaments and vestments, employing the money for the purchase of a Bible (13s 4d), the *Paraphrases*, and the *Book of Common Prayer* (15s), and the balance on church repairs.[3] In Cornwall, too, there had been sales of plate by the churchwardens, a particularly large sum of £20 having been used to build a market-house for Gluvias (Penryn), while in a number of parishes in the Hundred of West plate had been sold or pledged to help defray local costs sustained in 1548 when levies were sent to Helston to aid in putting down the stir connected with the murder of William Body.[4]

The inventory made in 1552 for Cambridgeshire disclosed that in at least eleven parishes sales had been made by the wardens with parish approval. Much of the money thus gained had been expended for church repairs, but the widespread pattern of laying out such moneys for municipal betterment may also be observed here. In these parishes the receipts were employed for building banks and sluices in the fen region, while in one (Downham) the funds were used to 'make a common way into our fens'. In the rich and populous town of Wisbech an unusually large amount, £45 2s 4d, had been laid out, with additional sums from other sources, to pay men sent in 1549 against the Norfolk rebels, for work on sluices, and paving the market-place.[5] The churchwardens of Peterborough (Northants), with the consent of 'the whole town', certified that they had sold a large silver cross in anticipation of expropriation, devoting most of the unstated sum derived for badly needed repairs on a

---

[1] Cresswell, B. F., *The Edwardian inventories for . . . Exeter, etc.* (Alcuin Club Coll. XX, L., 1916), xiv. Coverdale, the then mayor of Exeter, Sir Peter Carew, Sir Thomas Denys, and two aldermen were members of the commission.

[2] Cresswell, B. F., *The church goods commission in Devon (1549–1552)*, in *Devonshire Assoc. Report and Transactions*, XLIII (1911), 252–253.

[3] Graham, Rose, *The Edwardian inventories of church goods* (Oxfordshire Rec. Soc. I, Oxford, 1919), xxvi.

[4] Snell, L. S., *The Edwardian inventories of church goods for Cornwall, etc.* (Exeter, [1955]), xix; Jordan, *Edward VI*, 439–440.

[5] VCH, *Cambs*, II, 173.

bridge.[1] The churchwardens of Suffolk were also at once well informed and fore-handed, for the inventories disclose that a great deal of plate had been sold prior to 1553 and the receipts applied principally to municipal uses. Among other parishes so reporting, Aldeburgh had sold plate to the value of £40 for the setting forth of soldiers, while Ashfield had employed £2 for the same purpose. Rich Beccles had gained £59 which had been used towards the building of the church steeple, while £40 additional had been dedicated to the repair of a bridge and of the church fabric.[2] The returns for the North Riding reveal the same pattern of action in parishes led by aggressive and informed churchwardens.[3] At Hornsea (in Holderness) ornaments were sold by 'consent of all the inhabitants', and receipts totalling £22 6s 8d were dedicated to the repair and improvement of the local pier, while at Hunmanby a small sum thus gained was used for needed church repairs. At Cottingham a bell had been sold for £23 and the amount employed for church uses, and at Lund on the Wolds (East Riding) £3 6s 8d had been received, of which £2 was for the setting forth of soldiers and the balance for church repair.[4]

In a large proportion of parishes in which Protestant sentiment was strong or in which the churchwardens were reasonably well informed of the drift of governmental policy, it is evident that through the whole of the Edwardian period an anticipatory sale of church moveables was under way, normally with the formal consent of the parishioners, and that these receipts were in almost all cases being dedicated to municipal uses of many sorts, or to general charitable uses. This stubborn concern with the liquid resources of the parish was particularly strong in Essex, close to London, well-informed, and a centre of Protestant strength. Indeed, as early as 1547 a great deal of plate had been sold in four of the deaneries which may accurately be described as the region of old Lollard strength in the county. A possibly inexact sampling of nineteen parishes suggests that the considerable sum of £277 had been gained by these sales, mostly to London dealers, all with parish consent, and the funds assigned to church repairs, municipal uses of various sorts, the care of the poor, and the pay of soldiers.[5] At St Thomas

---

[1] Stowe MS. 141, f. 70: c. June, 1553.
[2] VCH, *Suffolk*, II, 33–34.
[3] The reports for the West and East Ridings are scrappy and incomplete.
[4] *Inventories of church goods* (Surtees Soc. XCVII), 49–50, 58, 71, 84.
[5] VCH, *Essex*, II, 26; Dickin, E. P., 'The embezzled church goods of Essex', in *Essex Archaeol. Soc. Trans.*, XIII (1915), 157–171; Oxley, James E., *The Reformation in Essex to the death of Mary* (Manchester, [1965]), 169–176.

Church in Oxford, silver to the value of £7 16s had been sold and the funds invested for poor relief.[1] In Surrey, the principal parishioners of St Nicholas in Guildford informed the commissioners that they had sold all plate and ornaments not now required for worship, partly because they feared it might be stolen and also in order better to furnish and arrange their building for the Protestant service, it being 'framed and fashioned . . . like a papistical cell of Rome'.[2] The churchwardens' accounts for the rural parish of Bletchingley, also in Surrey, listed receipts from the sale of a wide range of moveables of £31 11s 4d, which had been used for repair and decoration, the removal of the rood loft and other such outlays.[3] The inventory prepared in 1551 for the rich church of Bermondsey (Surrey), including some goods from the former monastery, indicated that much was left, though plate to the value of £21 17s had been sold and the proceeds dedicated to the arrangement of the church for the new ritual of worship and for minor changes and repairs.[4] In Warwickshire, too, gains from the sale of plate were dedicated to such uses as poor relief, bridge repairs, town and market pavements, the support of schools, and the construction of a town toilet.[5] To conclude our sampling of community sales of plate in anticipation of expropriation, we may mention considerable amounts in various towns in Lincolnshire where resources were assigned to such uses as church repairs, paving, ditching, the support of education, securing municipal incorporation, wharf repairs, and payment of expenses incurred in providing troops against the Norfolk rebels.[6]

But not in all the parishes of England, we may be sure, did the churchwardens proceed with the probity and the marked concern for local needs found in the sampling which we have just completed. From 1547 onwards to the expropriation at the close of the reign, the government professed, among other reasons for its commissions to secure inventories and its ultimate action of seizure, that it was moved by known instances of theft and embezzlement of the moveable properties of the church. This view Edward himself certainly held, when he recorded that the captain of the Isle of

[1] VCH, *Oxon*, II, 35.
[2] HMC, *7th rpt.*, App., 609: *Molyneux MSS*.
[3] *Loseley MSS.*, ed. Kempe, 163–165.
[4] *Ibid.* 169–170.
[5] VCH, *Warwickshire*, II, 32. Among the communities were Grendon, Corley, Ansley, Stratford-on-Avon, Mancetter, Nuneaton, and Hampton-on-Avon.
[6] Walker, R. B., 'Reformation and reaction in the county of Lincoln, *etc.*' in *Lincs Archit. and Archaeol. Soc., Reports and Papers*, n.s. IX, i (1961), 55.

Guernsey was warned to 'take heed to the church plate that it be not stolen away but kept safe till further order be taken'.[1] The evidence of the inventories and of the commissioners' reports would suggest that there was relatively little embezzlement or private seizure, though a few such instances were indeed spectacular. More serious, one may be certain, was the often precipitate and ill-informed sale of moveables at a fraction of their true value, or the stripping of tombs and gravestones of their brass in clear violation of the terms and intent of the law.[2]

But there were instances of outright theft and private spoliation. We are told that in Yorkshire a gentleman 'stole the great bell forth of the steeple of St John's [Laughton-en-le-Morthen] and carried it away in the night'.[3] In the City of York in 1551 it was reported that parishioners were removing the leaden roofs of their churches for sale and re-roofing them with tiles.[4] The Privy Council, outraged by reports that the parishioners of East Dereham, Norfolk, had stripped their church of plate, bells, and jewels, commanded the justices of the peace to investigate and enforce restitution if the rumours were true.[5] The aldermen of Stamford advised Cecil that a commission should in all conscience be appointed to require two citizens there, both presumably churchwardens, to give an accounting for the sale of church property on their own authority.[6] Even more serious were the allegations of certain parishioners of Thame (Oxon), who maintained that in 1547 church moveables had been placed in the custody of 'divers honest men of the town', two being churchwardens and one a chantry priest. These trustees had, it was said, sold off the property in stages, without any accounting to the parish.[7] Even uglier are the implications in an extraordinary letter of Francis Ayscough, written in early 1553 to Cecil. Ayscough had found that St Mary's Church in Grimsby, now almost disused because of the decay of the town, bore a great deal of lead and might legally be united to the parish of St James, if the consent of the

---

[1] Edward VI, *Chronicle*, 136.
[2] Dickens, *Tudor treatises*, 138-139.
[3] *Ibid.*, 139.
[4] VCH, *City of York*, 118, from *York Civic Records*, V (Yorks. Archaeol. Soc., Record Series CX), 53-54.
[5] *A.P.C.*, III, 148: Oct. 26, 1550.
[6] S.P. Dom., Edw. VI, XV, 23: Oct. 14, 1552.
[7] VCH, *Oxon*, II, 34; *ibid*. VII, 210; Graham, *Edwardian inventories*, xxv. The allegation is on the face of it improbable. Only a few of the great and very rich London churches had goods even approaching the alleged value. One suspects that certain of the churchwardens were in fact trying to convert concealed abbey or chantry plate and ornaments to parish uses.

King and of Sir Thomas Heneage, the patrons, were gained. His proposal was that Cecil should have the lead, worth £400, and he the stones and timbers 'at a reasonable price' if the Secretary would secure the legal dissolution of the parish. There is no evidence that Cecil, who could be devious and self-serving in financial matters, undertook what would have been a most reprehensible, and dangerous, action. But the very suggestion bespeaks the somewhat opaque moral standards of the age.[1] The Council, of which Cecil was now a member, was in fact being as vigilant as it could as it sought by commissions and by direct interventions to stay the depletion of the goods of the church. Thus it moved at once on information that the clergyman at Radnage (Bucks) had persuaded his parishioners to secrete a large portion of the church goods, promising them that the time would soon come when the old ceremonies would be restored and the treasured plate required.[2] Of embezzlement and private looting of church goods there was, then, relatively little; of pious and risky concealment there was much more. One bears a certain sympathy for the courageous convictions of the vicar of Radnage.

What the commissioners discovered in most rural counties was that a considerable proportion of the parishes were ill supplied with the instrumentalities of worship in terms of the requirements of the ancient faith and even, in not a few instances, of the reformed worship ordered by the second *Book of Common Prayer*. In typical rural counties not much more than half the churches and chapels were reported on at all by the commissioners, the clear inference being that they possessed little that was of monetary worth to the state. In most of the ill-furnished parishes the reasons were evidently the intransigent poverty or backwardness of the community; in others much had already been sold; and in still others, though not a great number, there was concealment or embezzlement. A few instances from the county returns will suggest the details.

In Dorset, where there were returns from 265 churches and chapels, 8 parishes reported they had no chalice, only 41 had more than one, while the remaining 216 owned one—these last, of course, not being subject to confiscation.[3] The commissioners' report for Huntingdonshire (1552) was particularly full for the 39 of 90 parish churches which reported at all. Of these, 5 seemed to have had no chalice, 15 the exempt one, and the rest two or more. In this

---

[1] HMC, *Salisbury MSS.*, I, 109: Feb. 20, 1553.
[2] *A.P.C.*, IV, 252, 254: Apr. 10 and 14, 1553.
[3] VCH, *Dorset*, II, 28.

county, as in most, almost all churches had two candlesticks for the altar, there being evidence that many had already been sold or concealed.[1] In neighbouring Bedfordshire, where the inventory prepared in 1549 will be cited, only 14 of the 145 parish churches were reported. All evidently possessed a chalice, though the holdings were in general pitifully meagre. Thus only 5 of the reporting churches seem to have had candlesticks, there were censers in fewer than half, and pixes were listed for only 3 churches, though they had been required for the ancient ritual.[2] So too, in Leicestershire, where the holdings of 45 parish churches were reported on July 29, 1552, it is quite clear that they were now, and had long been, poor indeed. Only one (Melton Mowbray) of all those listing their assets could be described as handsomely furnished. Here, all churches reported only the exempt chalice, save for one which had two and another which had none. In only about half the churches of this county were candlesticks listed, and most of these were of small value.[3]

By far the most detailed, and valuable, of the records relating to church moveables are those for the rich London parishes, where the churchwardens had for some years been following a policy of converting church goods to other and unthreatened parochial purposes. There were in the London of this decade 106 parish churches, for 89 of which surviving churchwardens' accounts provide most adequate documentation.[4] It is our reckoning that the total worth of goods already sold by the churchwardens, and accounted for to the commissioners, was £9876 17s 1d for these 89 parishes, and one would suppose not far from £11,000 were our data complete. This is a very large amount indeed and it means that in average terms the wardens of a typical London parish had, with its consent, sold goods to the value of about £111 before the government issued the order

[1] Lomas, S. C., ed., *The Edwardian inventories for Huntingdonshire* (Alcuin Club Coll. VII, L., 1906), xvi, 1–55.

[2] Eeles, F. C., ed., *The Edwardian inventories for Bedfordshire* (Alcuin Club Coll., VI, L., 1905), xiii–xiv.

[3] Day, E. H., 'The Edwardian inventories for Leicestershire', in *Assoc. Archit. Soc., Reports and Papers* XXXI, ii (1912), 441–470.

[4] They are in PRO, Exchequer K.R., Church Goods, E 117. We have used H. B. Walters (*London churches at the Reformation, etc.*, L., 1939), who has presented the accounts fully and with accuracy. Further page references need not be given. Walters stated that the inventories were complete for 95 parishes, though our count is 93, four of which are either incomplete or incomprehensible. It may also be observed that the 17 missing or incomplete inventory returns were from parishes which almost certainly possessed a slightly greater than average wealth of goods, 5 being large and very rich churches—among them St Helen's Bishopsgate, St Bartholomew the Great, and St James Garlickhithe.

for the long expected expropriation. Inevitably, the value of the goods sold varied greatly, from more than £200 in receipts in 11 parishes to amounts of less than £40 in 15 poorer, or less fore-handed, parishes.[1] These receipts had been expended or invested with great shrewdness in outlays which were easily defended, un-recoverable, and consonant with the religious policy of the crown. Thus, in all, £6792 11s had been spent, in order of decreasing amounts, for the following uses: repair of the church fabric; church renovations; adapting the internal structure to the requirements of the new communion service; the purchase of new and often ex-tremely expensive communion cups; the removal of altars, rood lofts, and images, and the repairs necessary after such Protestant adaptations. Hence a great deal was laid out on churches which were declared at least to be nearly ruinous; one is persuaded that the church fabric of the City gained a most salutary refurbishment during these years. In at least twelve instances—and the wardens could have made a persuasive argument in eight more—it seems clear that the parishes had deliberately spent more for these pious uses than the total of the receipts from sales, thus making their position quite impregnable.

The churchwardens, then, had laid out almost 70 per cent of the total receipts from the sales of plate and other moveable property on church repairs and renovations, though the cold fact is that in this decade of great charitable giving by London merchants only a tiny sum, less than 1 per cent, was given by them for these pur-poses.[2] The churchwardens were simply employing great skill and prudence by making irrevocable investments of parish wealth for purposes in which they had no great personal interest but which were none the less unimpeachable. Somewhat riskier, though the outlays were in fact not seriously challenged, was a total of £1268 18s which had been invested for the general uses and support of the parish churches or for the relief of poor parishioners, most of it in the purchase or building of houses near the church benefiting from these now charitable endowments. A relatively minor total of £84 7s of the receipts was given for the outright needs of the poor, despite the growing preoccupation of the City merchants and tradesmen with this critical social need. There remained a much larger sum (£1731 1s) which was reported as unspent by divers churchwardens, representing balances from sales, a fair fraction of

---

[1] In several cases it seems certain that sales had been deterred because of the opposition of the incumbent.

[2] Jordan, *Charities of London*, 292-294.

which was solemnly declared to be committed to church necessities or to repairs already under way.

A by no means exhaustive study of the churchwardens who had accomplished this remarkable feat of conversion of assets suggests that they were overwhelmingly of middling rank in the merchant and tradesman classes, something like a third of their number being members of the great Livery Companies. These men, charged with the administration of a great deal of wealth, had been delicately sensitive to the changes under way and the threat of confiscation by the state. They had sold the church goods steadily, systematically, and skilfully from the first regnal year to the day of their sovereign's death. In all but five instances it is made clear that these sales had been concluded with the full consent of all the wardens and of the whole parish. The situation in London differed dramatically from that of the rural churches of the realm. These churches were relatively immensely rich as compared with country churches, yet a far greater proportion of the moveable wealth was diverted in London than in any other county of England. It is important, too, to reflect that these sales were made from parishes which were mostly stoutly Protestant or, at the least, intensely secular in their aspirations. Hence there was in London almost nothing of the foot-dragging, the thefts, or the desperate concealments so common in the realm at large. By the close of the reign, it seems safe to conclude, more than two-thirds of the church goods had already been sold—and thus lay safe even from the Crown and the all-consuming grasp of the Duke of Northumberland. The expropriation of the plate and the sacramental ornaments of the ancient church was necessary because England wished now to become in a full sense the Protestant community which law, governmental policy, and the warm zeal of very powerful and dedicated groups of men declared it to be. But it is pleasant to reflect that a large proportion of this visible and to many men sacred wealth had in fact been transmuted into social ends and uses which made of England a more fitting dwelling place for Christian men.[1]

---

[1] One is saddened, however, by the monotonous entry of sales of Latin books, or simply old books, all too often to bookbinders, of which we cite as examples the sale by St Mary-le-Bow of twenty-one books to a London stationer for 50s; certain 'books of parchment' by St Mary Colechurch for 19s; Latin books for 39s, and 'old books' for 6s 8d by St Mary Magdalene, Old Fish Street; 8s for old books sold to a bookbinder, whose name could not be remembered, by St Michael Bassishaw; certain 'defaced books' sold by St Nicholas Cole Abbey for 13s 4d; and the forty-one books sold by the wardens of St Thomas Apostle, to an unknown buyer, for £1. But there were some compensations, for in almost all parishes at least a modest portion of the receipts were used for the purchase of English Bibles, the *Paraphrases*, and, of course, the new service books.

XI

THE COMPLETION OF THE KING'S EDUCATION AND THE BEGINNING OF MATURE CONCERNS (1550–1553)

1. THE YOUNG KING (1550–1552)

We have already suggested that the dominance of Edward's tutors in his personal and intellectual life and development was beginning to draw to a close in the course of 1550 and that they, and certainly he, regarded his formal education as completed by the spring of the next year, when he was not yet quite fourteen years of age.[1] He was an amazingly precocious boy, who took delight in the process as well as in the fruits of learning. He must have been a joy to teach, despite the occasional evidences of intellectual arrogance and a rapidly growing sense of what can only be described as royal self-confidence. It should also be observed that his reading and, above all, his writing were carried forward in an impressive fashion during the remaining months of his life, for his was a mind that was animated by a deep intellectual curiosity.

Despite his undoubted intellectual interests and attainments, care had been taken to ground him in other concerns and graces, which old-fashioned men of the court still thought more becoming, or at least more usual, for a reigning monarch. Soranzo reported that Somerset had wished the King's formal education stressed, while Northumberland, always a professional soldier in his tastes and attitudes, had somewhat altered the young monarch's activities in order to ensure that he could ride, handle weapons properly, and engage in carefully restricted martial exercises. The consequence was that Edward 'soon commenced arming and tilting, managing horses, and delighting in every sort of exercise, drawing the bow, playing rackets, hunting, and so forth, indefatigably, though he

[1] *Vide ante*, 22 ff.

never neglected his studies' as set by his tutors.[1] Indeed, so enthralled was the King with these vigorous pursuits that Lever, in preaching before him, warned that there would be those who would seek to divert him from the problems of the state and the society by such pastimes. But his concern must be with his people and the building of the Church of God.[2] It was Northumberland, as well, Soranzo accurately sensed, who diverted the King with lavish entertainments and more pocket money, while at the same time preparing him for the exercise of power by acquainting him in detail with the public business, the routines of the Council, and his position in the realm at large. The result was, the admiring Venetian concluded, 'that there is perhaps no instance on record of any other King of that age being more beloved, or who gave greater promise'.[3]

The young King also was indulged in the excitement—and danger—of hunting, it being reverently noted by the priest of Barkham (Berks) parish in 1552 that he had 'hunted in the bear wood in the forest of Windsor and there did his grace kill a great buck'.[4] But the martial and field excitements never came, as Lever feared they might, to dominate the interests of the King, who remained in truth an intellectual with steadily growing aesthetic tastes. We have seen that he found great pleasure in masques and plays, while his already well-formed musical taste found expression in his playing on the lute and probably on the virginal. He likewise found pleasure in listening to music, maintaining a considerable orchestra, composed mostly of Italians and Flemings, which included 18 trumpeters, 7 viall players, 4 sackbuts, a harpist, a bagpiper, a drummer, a rebeck player, and 8 minstrels.[5]

Like all his family, too, the King loved pageantry and elaborate displays at court. Probably the longest, and certainly the most excited, entry in his *Chronicle* was a detailed account of a mock naval battle staged on the Thames at Deptford for him and the French diplomatists then in London, enlivened by 'clods, squibs, canes of fire, darts . . . and bombards'. So realistic was the display, in fact, that one of the engaging pinnaces was accidentally sunk and

---

[1] *Cal. S.P. Ven.*, V, 535; Edward VI, *Chronicle*, 57, 62, 97, 104–105, 106, for instances; *Loseley MSS.*, ed. Kempe, 55.   [2] Strype, *Memorials*, II, i, 427.

[3] *Cal. S.P. Ven.*, V, 536.

[4] Oddly enough, so jotted down by John Langridge, the parish priest, on a page of his copy of *The mirror of the blessed life of Christ* (Camb. Trinity Coll. MSS., B 15, 16, f. 134).

[5] Trevelyan MSS., as cited in Nichols, *Remains*, I, ccxxi–ccxxii; Add. MSS., 5755, f. 266; Edward VI, *Chronicle*, 73; *vide ante*, 20.

more than twenty of the crew had to swim for shore.[1] Edward was quite as enthralled by the elaborate hospitality arranged for St André when he brought the Order of St Michael and won the King's heart—and a portrait—by possessing precisely the right touch in dealing with a monarch who was still a boy.[2] So too, the wardrobe accounts are replete with charges for rich stuffs, liveries, and trappings for gifts and for court functions, as well as a somewhat pathetic entry for the delivery of one yard of crimson taffeta 'to be employed to our use upon the furnishing of our little bed for our own lying'.[3]

In many respects the most revealing documents bearing on the personal development of the young King are the nine letters written by him to his childhood friend and henchman, Barnaby Fitzpatrick. Fitzpatrick was on August 15, 1551, together with Robert Dudley, sworn as a gentleman of the Privy Chamber and then shortly was sent to France for travel and to complete his education as a gentleman of the chamber in the court of Henry II.[4] The King's letters to his absent friend, written between November, 1551 and November, 1552, are a strange mixture of boyish enthusiasm and spontaneity, giving way suddenly and always unpredictably to the 'royal manner' of a sovereign who was after all a Tudor. The King arranged for Barnaby to cross with Clinton, going over on a diplomatic mission, with an adequate allowance and with four body servants. He was to accept any service offered, to study French diligently, and to fit himself into the routines of French court life. He should take every opportunity to travel in France, though more in the company of gentlemen than any 'pressing into the company of ladies there'.[5]

Edward expressed concern when Barnaby reported that his attendance on the French king made it extremely difficult to avoid participating in religious services and the mass. Edward's advice was that he should feign business if possible, but if courtesy re-

---

[1] Edward VI, *Chronicle*, 36–37.

[2] *Vide ante*, 132–134; Edward VI, *Chronicle*, 69–73 *passim*.

[3] *Catalogi codicum manuscriptorum bibliothecae Bodleianae*, ed. by H. O. Coxe, pt. i (Oxford, 1858), no. CCCXXVIII, ff. 1–35; Harl. MS. 284, #74, f. 120.

[4] Barnaby, whose mother was a daughter of the Earl of Ormonde, was the son of an Irish chieftain who after the rebellion of 1537 made his subscription to the English authorities. In reward he was created Baron of Upper Ossory (1541) and was knighted in 1543. The son was sent to the English court, really as an hostage, for his education, being one of the group of boys for a time educated with Edward. He was in France for about a year.

[5] We follow the excellently edited texts of Nichols for these letters (in *Remains*, I, 63–89).

quired him to attend he was not to look on the mass, 'but in the mean season [to] read the Scripture, or some good book, and give no reverence to the mass at all'. Again, he warned Barnaby to avoid the company of women, though he might dance at court if 'measure be your mean'. More stalwart pursuits like riding, shooting, and tennis should occupy his leisure, not, however, to the exclusion of reading.[1] As summer approached, Edward expressed great satisfaction that Barnaby was to see active service against the Emperor, enjoining him to acquire skill in military matters, to write fully, and to describe what he saw.[2] Perhaps the most informal and lively of the King's letters was written from Hampshire, during the royal progress there in August, 1552.

'For whereas you all have been occupied in killing of your enemies, in long marchings, in pained journeys, in extreme heat, in sore skirmishings, and divers assaults, we have been occupied in killing of wild beasts, in pleasant journeys, in good fare, in viewing of fair countries, and rather have sought how to fortify our own than to spoil another man's.'[3]

A few weeks later, when Barnaby had been away for almost a year, Edward ordered him to arrange for his withdrawal from Henry's service as soon as the armies went into winter quarters. The King evidently missed the buoyant company of his friend, though he had added somewhat delphically that there were other reasons which he would explain when he saw him. Barnaby left the French court on December 9th, bearing with him warm testimonials from the King of France himself, to arrive at a court already troubled by the first shadowy evidences of Edward's fatal illness.[4]

We have observed that, though the young King's formal education was well advanced as early as 1549, it was carried forward with undiminished vigour until the close of 1552, one must assume principally because of the deep love of learning, the intellectual curiosity, which animated the boy. Even as early as 1548 and 1549 he was reading Isocrates, the *De officiis* and the *Tusculan questions* of Cicero, on all of which he was taking elaborate notes for the digests which he loved to make.[5] These readings were evidently followed by

---

[1] Nichols, *Remains*, I, 69–72. The same letter (Dec. 20, 1551) comments coldly on Somerset's arraignment for 'felonious treason'.   [2] *Ibid.* 79–80: May 3, 1552.
[3] *Ibid.* 80–82: Aug. 22, 1552.   [4] *Ibid.* 86–89.
[5] Arundel MS. (BM), 510, as cited by Baldwin, T. W., *William Shakspere's small Latine & lesse Greeke* (2 vols., Urbana, 1944), I, 225–230.

some work in Pliny Secundus before he turned in January, 1549 to Cicero's *Orations against Cataline*, which was completed in late April and from which he gleaned a particularly large body of notes. The carefully mustered notes make it clear that Cheke's reading with him was analytic, precepts being drawn from the text of both a rhetorical and logical nature.[1]

It was at about this point in the King's education that Cheke retired to the university for a brief season, possibly because of his slight connection with the machinations which entrapped Thomas Seymour in the toils of treason.[2] From Cambridge he wrote to Somerset to review his progress with the King. Edward, he submitted, was already learned, though his knowledge, like 'all learning, be it never so great, except it be sifted with much use and experience . . . can be no wisdom, but only a void and a waste knowledge'. His learning, then, must now be refined and matured by those who counselled him. He must be taught caution and to avoid false pride. 'I have no cause to mistrust, but love is full of fear when there is no cause; and my duty ready to admonish aforehand, for fear of a cause.'[3] Cheke was happily back at his task in a few months, but it is possible that during his absence Sir Anthony Cooke was appointed to carry forward the task of education, continuing on at least an informal basis, particularly since Cox retired from his post in February, 1550.[4]

We are fortunate in that at about this time the Princess Elizabeth's famous tutor, Roger Ascham, visited Cheke in London, being on his way to assist Morison in his diplomatic mission to the Emperor. Not many weeks later, in a letter to Sturmius, he des-

---

[1] Arundel MS. (BM), 510, as cited by Baldwin, T. W., *William Shakspere's small Latine & lesse Greeke* (2 vols., Urbana, 1944), I, 231–233. To this work we express a general debt beyond this and the following paragraph.

[2] *Vide* Jordan, *Edward VI*, 375, 376.

[3] Harington, Henry, *Nugae antiquae*, I, 43–46; printed in Nichols, *Remains*, I, ccxlv–ccxlvii.

[4] There has been a persistent report that Cooke did serve as one of the King's tutors, with, however, no solid documentary evidence. Edward makes no reference to him in this role in the *Chronicle*, though Cooke was in 1550, and perhaps earlier, a gentleman of the Privy Chamber (PRO, E 315/221/131). The principal authority for the story is a letter from Hooper (Robinson, *Original letters*, I, 81) who in March 1550 states unequivocally that Cooke was a royal tutor, while in May of the same year Cooke was certainly granted an annuity of £100 for life for having provided 'training in good letters and manners' to the King (PRO, E 315/221/131). Cooke was at court through the whole of the reign and his services were much valued. Finally, Bale in his *Index britanniae scriptorum* (ed. by R. L. Poole and Mary Bateson, Oxford, 1902, p. 32) says that Cooke was one of the royal preceptors. This note rests heavily on the researches of my student, Mrs Marjorie McIntosh, whose valuable dissertation, *The Cooke family of Gidea Hall, Essex, 1460–1661*, it is hoped, will in due time be published.

ribed with great enthusiasm the intellectual progress of the King.[1] Edward needed no spur for his learning, but in Cheke he had the ideal teacher. Already the King has mastered Latin: 'he understands with accuracy, speaks with propriety, writes with facility, combined with judgment'. In Greek, Cheke had moved his pupil into Aristotle, without the usual preparation in Xenophon, so that he would from the outset master abstruse materials rather than being bemused by history. He had studied the *Dialectic* and was now reading the *Ethics* with his tutor, after which Cheke proposed to move to the *Rhetoric*. And his grasp of both languages was so sure that he could turn Cicero from the Latin into Greek.[2]

During the course of 1551 Edward's tuition was further concentrated on the Greek language and authors, considerable time having been devoted to Plato, until in August Cheke and his royal pupil began the reading of Demosthenes.[3] The Greek authors were all studied analytically, with elaborate notes, word lists, and related set exercises, most of which have been preserved, the last one dated June 4, 1552, when the King's formal education was probably ended. In this last year, too, the study of history received considerable emphasis. Much earlier (1547) the King had read something of Justin, and at appropriate points in the curriculum had been introduced to Livy and Sallust. But after 1550 Cheke, as a rather daring pedagogical innovation, had begun the reading of contemporary treatises on Roman antiquity, including the recently published (1534) work of Huttichius, entitled *Imperatorum et Caesarum vitae*. At the same time, far more consistent emphasis was lent to the study of the modern languages, especially French, in which the King became remarkably proficient.[4]

Cheke had also taken great pains throughout the curriculum to stress the moral training which he believed was best induced by drawing out from the classical texts moral observations to be set in rather extended compositions, or declamations, which, as we have already noted, Edward produced in considerable number.[5] Cheke's achievements and interests were, in fact, quite perfectly set out in what may be described as a farewell letter to his royal student, written in the interval May–August, 1552, when Cheke was desperately ill.[6] The King had been well grounded in virtue and

---

[1] Ascham, Roger, *The whole works, etc.*, ed. by Rev. Dr Giles (3 vols. in 4, L., 1864–1865), I, i, lxvii.   [2] *Ibid.* I, ii, 226–228; Strype, *Memorials*, II, i, 426–427.
[3] Baldwin, *William Shakspere's small Latine*, 243.
[4] *A.P.C.*, III, 89: July 31, 1550, noting a payment of £50 to Belmain; Royal MSS., 16.E.xxxvii, for Peter du Ploiche's dedication of French manuscript works to Edward.
[5] *Vide ante*, 22.   [6] Probably with pneumonia.

good learning, and was now ready to undertake the governance of
his realm, to which he trusted those who served him would 'faithfully, truly, and plainly give you counsel'. Kings lie under a much
heavier responsibility than do other men, and must learn to take
both advice and censure from those who serve them closely and
honestly. But Edward must beware of those who 'of all things make
fair weather, and, whatsoever they shall see to the contrary, shall
tell you all is well'. Such men serve themselves, not the King.
Cheke reminded Edward that he had read well and broadly in both
history and philosophy, but crowning all was his careful study of
Aristotle and his *Politics*. In spiritual matters he would beg him to
continue with the study of the Bible, and especially with the New
Testament, the Book of Wisdom, and the Proverbs.[1]

This poignant valedictory may be said, then, to mark the end of
the King's formal education, but there are many indications that
this bookish and intellectually curious boy continued his reading and
study with an ever-broadening range of interest and attention. An
anonymous, but evidently well-informed, writer, shortly after the
King's death, spoke of him as well learned in Latin, Greek, French,
Spanish, and Italian. The range of his intellectual interests included as well logic, natural philosophy, and astronomy.[2] His
knowledge was in fact encyclopedic, for he could name the ports,
the havens, and the creeks of England, Scotland, and France, and
knew their trade, the tides, and what burthen of vessel might use
them. Nor was that all, for we are told that he was well informed
regarding the gentry of his realm, their names, their hospitality, and
their religion.[3] The breadth of his learning may be well illustrated by
an examination of the 72 books which in all probability belonged to
the King and which are still preserved in the Royal Library of the
British Museum. They comprise works in six languages, of which
27 are classical texts or otherwise concerned with antiquity; 10
possess a medieval interest; 2 are legal in subject matter, while 33

---

[1] Harington, *Nugae antiquae*, I, 8, 20–21. Cheke asked the King to grant lands for the
bringing up of his young son, and implored as well that charity and liberty be extended
to the deprived Bishop Day, 'my bringer up', for 'at his hands I got an entry to some
skill in learning'. On May 29th Ridley informed Cecil that Cheke was improved in health
(Lansdowne MS. 3, f. 28), while Ulmis reported on August 9th that the great humanist
had recovered (Robinson, *Original letters*, II, 456).

[2] In 1551 the King composed a treatise in defence of astronomy, and in the same year
a quadrant (still preserved) was made for his use. Nicholas Kratzer, a Bavarian who had
emigrated to England in 1517 and who had lectured at Oxford on astronomy, was named
the royal astronomer with a grant of £5 a quarter (Nichols, *Remains*, I, ccxvii).

[3] Egerton MS. 2877, ff. 14b–15 (1553?); Foxe (*Acts and monuments*, V, 700) evidently
used this source.

were works of modern authors or modern texts, with a heavy emphasis on the reformed religion.[1]

Undoubtedly the most objective contemporary estimate of the King and his intellectual abilities was that set down by Hieronymus Cardano in October, 1552.[2] Cardano, at once an Italian physician of some eminence and an astrologer, had at least one audience with the King, who greatly impressed him by his mastery of languages and his liveliness of mind. The King 'spoke Latin as politely and fluently as I did', while their conversation persuaded the physician that the King was well versed in logic, natural philosophy, and music. Edward himself spoke of Cardano's work, *De varietate rerum*, and they dwelt at length on the causes and nature of comets, the King's questions being sharp as well as apposite. It was the Italian's conclusion that Edward 'began to love the liberal arts before he knew them; and to know them before he could use them'. Cardano also noted that 'when the gravity of a king was needful, he carried himself like an old man; and yet he was always affable and gentle, as became his age'.[3]

This estimate, set down shortly after the audience, may well be close to the mark, for Cardano, a skilled and experienced observer, eschewed the adulation which characterized the contemporary English comments on the young King. He found Edward to be slightly below the average in stature, gray in eyes, of fair complexion, and of a becoming carriage. He thought one of his shoulder blades to be slightly high, and there is the suggestion that he thought him nearsighted and possibly slightly deaf.[4] None the less, he predicted a

---

[1] Nichols, *Remains*, I, cccxxv–cccxlii. There are also 8 manuscript volumes in the collection, including a sermon by Latimer, Belmain's French version of the second *Book of Common Prayer*, and a translation by William Thomas of 'The narration of Josaphat Barbaro, citizen of Venice'.

[2] Cardano was passing through England on his way to Edinburgh where he had been summoned to treat John Hamilton, Archbishop of St Andrews. Cardano tells us that while in London he lodged with Cheke, whose horoscope he also calculated. The observations on Edward were recorded in a series of twelve 'Nativities' (or horoscopes) in a volume entitled *Geniturarum exempla* (L., 1555), of which that of Edward was done in detail. (Nichols, *Remains*, I, ccviii–ccxii.)

[3] Cardano, *Opera* (L., 1663), V, 503–508; quoted in part in Burnet, *Reformation*, V, 125–126.

[4] In addition to Cardano's careful description, we can gain from the numerous life portraits a probably accurate conception of the King's appearance. In the discussion following we owe much to the as yet unpublished *Portraits of Edward VI*, under preparation over many years by the late Mr Launcelot Surry and his son, Mr Nigel Surry, M.A.(Oxon.), of Portsmouth, who has kindly lent me the typescript of this excellently done catalogue.

There is ample documentary evidence that Edward was painted during his lifetime by both Holbein and William Scrots [Stretes], and that it is at least possible that he was

long life for the King, though warning that at the ages of 32, 34, and 55 he would be subject to various ailments. This 'nativity', it must be remembered, was not published until well after Edward's death, and the impressive objectivity of the work is all the more convincing because Cardano did not revise his conclusions.[1]

An equally objective estimate of Edward's abilities and rapidly increasing maturity may be gained from an examination of the political papers and memoranda prepared by the King in his own hand, and for his private use, between April, 1551 and January, 1553. These were in the main 'position papers' in which the King

painted as well by Levina Teerlinc, John Shute, and Hans Eworth. The justly famous Holbein set the pattern, but from 1550 onwards, Holbein having died in 1543, Scrots established a kind of artistic monopoly in turning out portraits of the King, including at least three that were used as gifts in the Anglo-French marriage treaty negotiations. Interestingly, most of the total of 99 surviving portraits were Elizabethan copies derived principally from Holbein and Scrots, the avid interest not ending until 1607 when a portrait was commissioned by Christ's Hospital, Abingdon (Surry #58) and 1608 when James I ordered a copy made of a portrait 'now remaining at Whitehall'. Thereafter, though not catalogued by Surry, the copies continued to be turned out in considerable number throughout the seventeenth century, particularly for gentle families and for the charitable foundations bearing the King's name.

The amazing stability of the English society over the past four centuries is suggested by the fact that even today 66 of the total of 99 portraits and 8 drawings catalogued remain in private or in institutional hands in England, while another 16, including several of the greatest, are quite as firmly in crown possession or in the national galleries. Seven, including perhaps the greatest of the Holbeins, have found their way to the United States (4 being in New York, 1 in Washington, 1 in Chicago, and 1 in Los Angeles), while there are 3 in France, 1 in Basel, 1 in Leningrad, and 1, improbably, in Morocco. The remaining 12 are held by unknown persons, probably mostly in England.

The wanderings and histories of a few of the more famous of the portraits may be of interest. The great Holbein representation of Edward as a baby of fourteen months was given to Henry VIII by the artist as a New Year's gift in 1539. It was listed in the royal inventory of 1547, but in 1655 was in the possession of the Earl of Arundel. At an uncertain date it was acquired by the Dukes of Brunswick/Lüneburg, but was in time acquired by the Welfen Museum in Hanover. In 1925 it was purchased by Andrew W. Mellon, being now part of the collection in the National Gallery in Washington. Surry #13, once wrongly attributed to Holbein—a wonderful representation of the Prince at the age of seven—was sold by a Hampstead dealer to Viscount Lee of Fareham for £300 in 1922, being then sold by Duveen to Mr Jules Bache of New York in 1928 for £15,000 and then in 1943 passing to the Metropolitan Museum as part of the Bache Collection. Historically, Surry #48 is one of the most interesting. Painted by Scrots, it was almost certainly the portrait given by Edward to St André (Jacques d'Albon), who made such a favourable impression on the King during his special embassy to London in 1551. It long hung in St André's favourite residence, the Chateau de St André Apchon, until 1789 when it was confiscated and sold by the revolutionary government. It was recovered from an unknown owner in the mid-nineteenth century by Dr Frederic Noelas, a resident of St André, who bequeathed it to his daughter, Mme Victor Mollein, who in 1943 presented it to the Joseph Dechelette Museum at Roanne.

[1] He explained the appalling error in his astrological calculations by pointing out a miscalculation which he had made and by the fact that he was unable to observe the sun and moon while in audience with the King.

was seeking to lay down the lines of policy for his reign, quite independently and often in decided contrast to that of the Duke of Northumberland and the majority of the Privy Council. The earliest of these, which internal evidence suggests was prepared in about April, 1551, was entitled, *Discourse on the reform of abuses in church and state*.[1] The memorandum, rather roughly drawn and evidently unfinished, may have been begun in response to Martin Bucer's *De Regno Christi*, presented to the King as a New Year's gift in 1551, but the treatment of ecclesiastical matters was at once brief and rather perfunctory.[2] Edward then turned to a fairly lengthy consideration of the social and economic ills of his realm, reflecting surely the broad outlines of policy which had so recently occasioned the ruin of the Duke of Somerset. With great vigour and clarity of style the King depicted an ideal commonwealth in which 'no person . . . shall have more than the proportion of the country will bear. For as it is convenient to enrich the country, so it is hurtful immoderately to enrich any one part[3].' This view of the society was broadly hierarchical, but the King was toying with the very radical thought that upper limits might be set on the income of each class. The whole structure of the society had been strained by undue grazing, the decline in the quality of essential products, and the vaulting ambitions of too many men. Landowners were now 'not content with 2,000 sheep, but they must have 20,000 or else they think themselves not well [off]; they must [have] twenty mile square [of] their own land . . . and four or five crafts to live by is too little, such hell-hounds be they[4]'. All this simply must be reformed by law and policy, the chief instruments being better education, the just enforcement of laws, the example of the rulers, and the punishment of vagabonds and idle persons. He had already indicated, possibly to the Council, what new laws he thought desirable, as well as his wish that superfluous 'statutes were brought into one sum together and made more plain and short[5]'. The views here expressed clearly owe much to both Somerset's policy and Latimer's moving eloquence, but there is in the exposition the persuasive certainty that they were also the King's own. This is far more than formal rhetoric; there was here as well a deep conviction regarding the reform of the state, which Edward knew full well ran counter to the stubbornly held views of the dominant classes of the realm.[6]

Edward's mind was decidedly practical and administrative in its

---

[1] Cotton MSS., Nero, C, x, ff. 113–117; edited and presented in full in Edward VI, *Chronicle*, 159–167.   [2] *Ibid.* xxiv.   [3] *Ibid.* 161.
[4] *Ibid.* 164.   [5] *Ibid.* 166.   [6] *Ibid.* xxv.

nature, notwithstanding this one lengthy attempt to deal rather abstrusely with the problems of the society over which God had placed him. He loved ordered memoranda, dockets of things to be done, and the formal assembling of arguments *pro* and *contra* on all major questions of policy. The quite perfect exemplar of this turn of mind was his elaborate memorandum prepared for the consideration of the Council on March 9, 1552, laying out a blueprint for erecting in England a market designed to replace Antwerp as the *entrepôt* for European trade.[1] It was his expressed hope that English commerce and finance might thereby be strengthened and to a degree freed of the commercial disruptions occasioned by the chronic Habsburg-Valois wars, which swept back and forth across the traditional and vital north-south lines of European commerce.[2] The plan was set forward with great care and fullness, with an effort to assess its weaknesses as well as its strengths. European trade practices and trade routes were examined in some detail and the impressive merits of Southampton as the site were thoughtfully analysed. What was lacking was an understanding that neither English commerce nor finance was yet strong or mature enough to provide the necessary base of skills, capital, and traditions to make the plan feasible. Though the slow decline of Antwerp was now under way, the centre of gravity of European trade and finance was to shift to Amsterdam, not, as yet, towards England. None the less these proposals were in no sense naive in conception or in presentation. 'The document displays . . . the intelligent and sustained interest of the young King in economic affairs and exhibits a certain boldness of vision and spirit which was by this date beginning to characterize his approach to most matters of state.'[3]

Considerable light is thrown on the King's interests and preoccupations by several other documents in his own hand, all probably composed between the summer of 1552 and early 1553 when ill health overwhelmed him. There are brief but trenchant observations on the financial position of the government in mid-1552 which prepared the way for a thorough consideration of the whole range of fiscal policy to be undertaken by the Council in the autumn. Edward's chief concern was with the remaining external debt, held principally in Antwerp, which he hoped could be liquidated by applying all internal debts owed to him, by a subsidy (£80,000), and by the export of the whole of the church plate shortly to be con-

---

[1] Cotton MSS., Nero, C, x, ff. 85 ff.; full text in Edward VI, *Chronicle*, 168–173.
[2] *Ibid*. xxv–xxvi.
[3] *Ibid*. xxvi.

fiscated. These foreign debts were, in fact, to be approximately half paid down before the close of the reign, while the restoration of the purity of the coinage and Gresham's manipulative abilities were to secure the restoration of English credit.[1]

The greater difficulty, however, was the fact that the whole governmental budget was badly unbalanced and that neither Somerset nor Northumberland ever felt sufficiently strong to call upon Parliament for really effective relief by the taxing power. These, and other problems, were carefully set down by the King in a remarkable document which centres on the fiscal crisis and then ranges out widely to a searching set of proposals involving financial, economic, religious, and military reforms. This memorandum, according to Cecil's endorsement, was meant for full discussion at a meeting of the Council held on October 13, 1552.[2] The King's chief preoccupation was financial, for he wished to secure 'a mass of money', totalling £300,000, which would extinguish his internal as well as the external debts. Towards this end, he was contemplating additional savings in the household, a considerable reduction of the military establishment at home and abroad, a further sale of lands and church goods, and greater efficiency and savings by merging the Court of Augmentations with certain other revenue courts into a single department.[3] The King was resolved as well to further the advancement of evangelical Protestantism by placing greater disciplinary power in the hands of 'learned, wise, sober' bishops who were 'of good religion', by prodding the lower clergy 'to be more diligent in their office', and to secure more sound preaching.[4] He was still resolved to found a great mart of trade in England, though he was now giving consideration to two sites, the one at Southampton and the other at Hull. Though he intended to reduce the military establishment sharply, he none the less wished additional and more modern fortifications at key points like Portsmouth, Berwick, Dover, Calais, and Guînes, while he regarded harbour and pier improvements at a number of ports as badly

---

[1] Edward VI, *Chronicle*, xxvii, 174–175 (from Lansdowne MS. 1236, f. 21); *A.P.C.*, III, 223; *ibid.* IV, 219, 265, 270.

[2] Edward VI, *Chronicle*, 176–180. Unfortunately, the record of the Council meeting for this date is even sparser than is usual for this period. The memorandum, which may be found in Lansdowne MS. 1236 ff. 19–20, bears no formal title, but is headed: *A summary of matters to be concluded.* Cecil's own endorsement was entitled [*The*] *Kynges Mat. Memoryall 13: Octob., 1552.*

[3] Edward VI, *Chronicle*, 177. The recommendations respecting the revenue courts anticipated the report of a commission appointed to consider the matter. For a fuller discussion, *vide post*, 444–447.

[4] Edward VI, *Chronicle*, 179.

needed.[1] This most interesting document outlines the King's aspirations for the realm. He must have known that there were not in hand the resources for carrying out the whole of his great design for years to come. Many of the points here set out he had stated before, for there was in Edward a stubborn tenacity of purpose in securing ends to which he was emotionally or intellectually committed. His temperament was not a little like that of his royal grandfather.

The most important of the young King's papers regarding governmental policy and organization may more appropriately be reserved for later discussion.[2] But there remains a remarkable treatise, probably principally compiled in late 1552, which we have entitled *Notes on the English occupation of France in the reign of Henry VI*. The treatise is in form a set of research notes, never organized and not completed, which deal with the history of a late phase (1427–1434) of the Hundred Years' War. There was little concern with the military annal of these years, but there was a detailed consideration of the manner in which taxes and other funds were raised in France for financing the impressive operations undertaken in these years, together with a full analysis of the military resources required. The King used a fairly wide range of sources for his study, which concentrated on the period of Bedford's regency in France.[3] What remains uncertain and most puzzling is the reason for the young sovereign's interest in this rather dull and somewhat inglorious period of the war. There is the possibility that the similarity of the young Henry VI under the protector-uncle Bedford with his own recent experience in the days of Somerset may have been his concern. But the focus of the work is rather on Fastolf and the blunt, honest, and informed advice which he had given to an earlier Somerset. Fastolf remains the hero of the piece. Certainly no mad design for an invasion of France was in Edward's mind or was ever contemplated by either of his chief ministers. Probably, then, the study was academic and sentimental, for Edward loved the lore of the past when captains were giants who walked the earth. But his own policy and actions were in fact cautious, pragmatic, and well considered. The dreams were there, but they too aspired to a restoration of English strength, both at home and abroad, to a building of a state and of a church in which his subjects might find more of peace, of well-being, and of dignity. The stuff of possible greatness was in Edward VI.

[1] Edward VI, *Chronicle*, 180.   [2] *Vide post*, 451 ff.
[3] Edward VI, *Chronicle*, xxxi–xxxii, for a discussion of his sources; *ibid*. 185–190, for the document.

2. THE THOUGHT AND INFLUENCE OF WILLIAM THOMAS

We have dealt at some length with the various influences which had helped in moulding the mind and interests of the King. Cheke and Cox, surely, amongst his teachers had had the predominant role in shaping a precocious and an innately stubborn mind, though we believe as well that John Belmain had not been without effect in establishing the firm Calvinism which in the end may be said most closely to have expressed the King's theological position. Sudeley had for a season insinuated himself into the confidence of the boy, but Edward withdrew from the association directly he understood that these blandishments were designed to advance his uncle's own mad plottings. Somerset had, of course, the principal share in bringing up the young King, and though Edward also turned away from him, in a cold and merciless rejection, it remains evident that the Protector's moral and social aspirations for the building of a reformed society in England had to a degree permeated his nephew's social and political thinking. Then, too, the warm zeal and the immensely powerful preaching of the leaders of the evangelical party in the Church of England—men like Latimer, Lever, and Hooper—had deeply influenced the boy and had helped to dispose him to a considerable sympathy with the ideals of the Commonwealth Men. Ridley, a great and in many ways an underestimated bishop, was much respected by the King and at critical points had used his influence towards persuading Edward to acts and policies of notable magnanimity. Northumberland was close to the young King in the two periods of great crisis when Somerset's authority and then his life were destroyed. But during the term of his own dominance in the Council the Duke seems not to have sought to bring undue personal influence to bear; instead, he undoubtedly encouraged the King to begin the assumption of royal power and seems to have treated Edward with full deference and more than formal respect.

There is also evidence that the young King was to some degree influenced during the last two years of his life by a relatively minor governmental official, William Thomas, a man of considerable attainments and abilities, though there always remained about him a kind of roguish quality, a kind of conspiratorial air. Thomas was of respectable Welsh extraction and was educated at Oxford, where he was probably graduated in 1529. His career remains obscure until 1540 when he gained minor preferment in connection with the administration of monastic pensions. We know, too, that he left

England in 1545, probably in part because of his advanced Protestant views, though he was also under suspicion of having defrauded his patron, Sir Anthony Browne. He was abroad, mostly in Italy, for four years, travelling widely and establishing himself as a popular writer on Italian history and culture. His legal difficulties in England pursued him and he was jailed for a short season in Venice, when his bills of exchange were stopped on representations from home. But he never lost a warm and intense loyalty to his native country. On receiving news of Henry VIII's death, Thomas at once composed a panegyric on his life and virtues, written with great verve and shrewd insights, which remained in its original Italian form until it was published as *The Pilgrim* in 1552. He also compiled, while still in Italy, a solid and useful work on Italian grammar, which he supplemented by an Italian-English dictionary of about 9000 words, which was not published until 1550, after Thomas had returned home. Even better known, and very popular indeed, was his *History of Italy*, probably written in April, 1548 and published, with a dedication to John Dudley, in September, 1549.[1]

Thomas ventured his return to England in late 1548 or early 1549. Sir Anthony Browne was now dead, and Cecil now lent him protection, while Sir Walter Mildmay, whose sister he was later to marry, made the arrangements for the publication of his Italian grammar. Thomas was evidently an attractive man, persuasive in his contacts with others, though his published works at least are all marked by conventional superficiality and a certain glibness of presentation.[2] Thomas evidently had attracted the favourable attention of the numerous intellectuals who dominated the junior range of the governmental structure and he rose rapidly in rank and notice after being appointed a clerk to the Council in April, 1550, the *Registers* from that date until September, 1551 being principally in his hand.[3] In this period he was buying modest parcels of monastic and chantry lands, while his services to the Council were rewarded in January, 1551 by a gift of £248.[4] Thomas went abroad in May, 1551 as secretary to Northampton's mission to France to negotiate the marriage treaty for Edward with the Princess Elizabeth. It was

---

[1] Edward VI, *Chronicle*, xx–xxi; Adair, E. R., 'William Thomas, *etc.*', in Seton-Watson, *Tudor studies*, 133–138; Thomas, William, *The history of Italy*, ed. by George B. Parks (Ithaca, N.Y., 1963), ix–xi.

[2] Professor Hanna H. Gray, who has assisted me greatly by her comments, has for some years past been engaged on what will surely be the definitive treatment of this interesting man.

[3] Adair, in Seton-Watson, *Tudor studies*, 140; *A.P.C.*, III, 3–4: Apr. 19, 1550.

[4] *Ibid.* 186.

shortly after his return, and probably in September, 1551, that
he gained indirect access to Edward himself through the good
offices of Sir Nicholas Throckmorton, then a knight of the Privy
Chamber, and set before the King eighty-five topics, any one of
which he undertook to expound fully on the request of his royal
master.[1]

From the numerous documents which Thomas prepared for the
King, a strong inference may be drawn that there was little or no
direct contact between them, though Edward was attracted by the
harmless conspiratorial arrangements suggested by Thomas himself.
Thomas undertook to send him a *Topic* each week when his duties in
the Council permitted, and assured him 'that no creature living is or
shall be privy either to this or to any of the rest through me, which I
do keep so secret to this end, that your majesty may utter these
matters as of your own study; whereby it shall have the greater
credit with your Council'.[2] Thomas could be most ingratiating
indeed. Thus in forwarding the topics, Thomas pointed out that
he had been emboldened to offer to prepare discourses on any of
them by the fact that thus far the King's education had been principally in language and scripture, rather than in matters of policy and
history. These topics, only one of which dealt with religion, were
matters for debate and discourse, which 'your highness may either
for pastime, or in Council, propose to the wisest man'.

The first of the six *Discourses*, prepared almost certainly in
September, 1551, was also the most important and is in fact the one
which was surely used by Edward and which possibly influenced his
thinking on the whole delicate matter of restoring the purity of the
coinage. The King seems secretly to have asked for this 'position
paper' through the good offices of Throckmorton. When it was
ready for presentation, Thomas was away from court and it was
handed to Edward by a 'Mr Fitzwilliam'.[3] Thomas's memorandum,
though briefly and rather conventionally stated, urged a restoration of
the purity of the coinage and a carefully undertaken devaluation in
order to assist the economy. The whole question was under consideration in the Council from September 6th to October 13th and
the expertise and general point of view expressed by the King in his
private journal suggest that he had lent careful and sympathetic

[1] Einstein, Lewis, *Tudor ideals* (N.Y., 1951), 78, for Thomas's abilities.
[2] Cotton MSS., Vespasian, D, xviii, ff. 2–45, where the six *Discourses* actually prepared by Thomas may be found. The long list of proposed *Topics* may be seen in Cotton
MSS., Titus, B, ii, ff. 85–90; printed in Strype, *Memorials*, II, i, 157–161.
[3] *Ibid.* II, ii, 389. This was John Fitzwilliam, a friend of Thomas who was later
singled out as a possible assassin of Mary Tudor.

attention to the *Discourse* which he had in hand.[1] In this paper
Thomas argued that all men were moved by the desire for gain,
which they measure in terms of gold and silver. But the English
coinage does not possess the firm value of bullion, and the people
'esteem it so little, that they will employ it to great disadvantage
rather than keep it'. The velocity of the exchange of coinage is
inspired by the wish to secure bullion or earlier coins of assured
fineness, which has greatly raised prices by a 'multitude of bar-
gains' and has so weakened the esteem for the coinage that it must
be quickly and fully restored in bullion value. Already, he submitted, debasements of the coinage have cost the people of the realm
eight shillings in the pound, and 'not one of a thousand' was content
with the fiscal policy that had been followed. In the great re-coinage
which should be undertaken, the King should content himself with
a modest profit of 5 per cent, which should immediately be invested
in land unless royal resources were further to be weakened.[2] All this,
though briefly stated and certainly roughly hewn, was, of course,
excellent economic advice and presented a conception of policy not
far off from that which the King himself undoubtedly favoured.

Of the remaining *Discourses* only one escapes the easy superficiality
to which Thomas was naturally inclined. This paper dealt with the
necessities of English foreign policy, for he was frank to say that
there had been a lamentable decline in English power and prestige.
Henry VIII was powerful and feared, whereas 'we are both hated
and contemned of them all'. The possibility of gaining strength by a
firm alliance with a major European power must be forgone because
there was no other strong Protestant state with which to treat.
Hence diplomacy and policy must be addressed to gaining time for
an England 'in manner environed of enemies'. The best recourse
was to ameliorate the Emperor and to seek a closer understanding
with him, even though this might mean some negotiation and compromise in religion. Such dissembling might, in fact, regain the
loyalty of the intransigent Catholics, though nothing will be lost if a
steady course be set towards an ultimate and a thorough reformation.
Such Protestant powers as Denmark and the German princedoms
Thomas regarded as at once too weak and unreliable to serve
England's diplomatic needs. France should be dealt with most carefully, but the key to successful policy with her is to arouse false fears
of a complete capitulation to the Emperor.[3] This recommendation

---

[1] Edward VI, *Chronicle*, 80–86, for the relevant entries.
[2] Cotton MSS., Vespasian, D, xviii, ff. 28–31; Strype, *Memorials*, II, ii, 389–391.
[3] *Ibid.* 34–45; Strype, *Memorials*, II, ii, 382–389.

was, of course, not far off from Northumberland's supine and paralysed diplomacy, but it does possess a certain toughness and sense of direction missing in English foreign relations since the fall of Somerset.

The remaining four *Discourses* were thin, conventional, and in structure little more than self-evident jottings from which helpful determinations of policy could scarcely be found. As an example, the essay on *Whether it be expedient to vary with time* began with quotations from the Bible and Petrarch, was heavily larded with not very apposite historical examples from antiquity, and managed to work in one quotation from Machiavelli, arguing little save that a prince should always seem to maintain a free hand in his policy. Thomas was not a considerable thinker, though he may for a short season have influenced the King at a moment when important decisions were in process of being made. The most important fact is, of course, that here we do have evidence that Edward was seeking independent advice; that he had already learned that he must arrive at his own judgements if he were to govern well and strongly. This capacity he was fully to demonstrate before his short reign was ended.[1]

3. THE BEGINNINGS OF THE ASSUMPTION OF POWER (1551–1552)

We have observed that there are abundant evidences that Edward VI had attained a considerable measure of maturity by mid-1551 and that he was beginning to concern himself with a broad range of governmental and administrative problems. His studies were never abandoned, for as late as the spring of 1552 he was spending his evenings having a recent book of Bullinger's read to him and then subjecting it to careful analysis.[2] The extraordinary Court of the young King was described at some length by Petruccio Ubaldini, the famous humanist and illustrator, who had come to England in 1545 on the invitation of Henry VIII and who was also employed

[1] A few remarks on Thomas's later career might be made. In 1552, when Sir Thomas Chaloner resigned, he was appointed a senior clerk of the Council, at a salary of £40 p.a. But he was constitutionally restless, seeking Cecil's aid in securing a diplomatic post in Venice, where he would like to stay for a year or two (S.P. Dom., Edw. VI, XIV, 59). This suit was unsuccessful, but in March, 1553 he was serving in the English embassy in Flanders. Though obviously in danger, on the accession of Queen Mary he returned to England, where he sought out Sir Peter Carew and became involved in a bizarre plot to assassinate the Queen. He was arrested on charges of high treason, failed in an attempted suicide, and on May 18, 1554, was executed.

[2] Robinson, *Original letters*, I, 315: John Willock to Bullinger, May 12, 1552.

by Edward until 1552 when he returned to Italy.[1] He pictures the Court as bound by rigid formalities and by a contrived adulation for the King. Even his sisters, when they attend him at Court, may not sit under the royal canopy or take a comfortable chair. When the King dined, even more elaborate formalities were observed, for on one occasion he had seen Elizabeth kneel five times before her brother, while taking her place. The King was given to rich and striking clothing, his livery being green and white, but his personal preference running to red, white, and violet, the last colour being so prized by him that no one else dared wear a hat of this shade. All his clothes were heavily embroidered in gold, silver, and pearls. The young King was of regal carriage and mien, graceful and poised in his dealings with others, and pleasant and generous in his feelings for his people.[2]

Northumberland had from early 1551 been fully aware of the King's growing interest in the process of governance and had encouraged his occasional attendance at Council. He was also now to a degree constrained by the fact that the monarch chose to see much of the flow of governmental memoranda as well as the diplomatic correspondence, with which the Council was chiefly concerned. The King was likewise intervening in matters which interested him and was, as a boy with considerable administrative ability, especially persistent in seeing, and on occasion altering, the agenda dockets which he wished prepared and circulated before conciliar discussions or decisions were undertaken.[3] And the King would on occasion make alterations or amendments, as for example when he struck out one name from the commission being appointed to carry forward deprivation proceedings against Heath and Day, adding two names of his own selection.[4] That the King had now to be reckoned with in both political and religious matters of policy and detail was soon generally understood. The imperial ambassador in March, 1552 noted that he was by that date normally attending Council meetings when state business was scheduled and was lending his personal authority to the conclusions there reached.[5] Later in the same year

---

[1] Only to return to England in 1562, where he resided until 1586.

[2] This manuscript work had considerable circulation in several copies. There are texts in the Imperial Library at Vienna (Foscarini MSS., cod. 184, #6626, ff. 336-466), in the Royal Archives of Denmark, in the Bibliothèque Nationale (#15888), in Add. MSS., 10169, ff. 1-125; and a printed summary, which we have employed, in Raumer, *Briefe aus Paris*, pt. ii, 66 ff.

[3] S. P. Dom., Edw. VI, XIII, 10, 11, 12, for an example of the procedure on which he was coming to insist.

[4] *Ibid.* 50: Sept., 1551.

[5] *Cal. S.P. Span.*, X, 493: Mar. 30, 1552.

the diplomatist reported that the King was daily blending his studies with exercises in riding and fencing, while not neglecting attendance on Council meetings. Further, Edward on his own authority was settling matters that interested him, though the ambassador still remained suspicious of the motives and plans of the Duke of Northumberland.[1]

Even clearer evidences of the King's personal intervention in the affairs of state may be found in the preparations, under his direction, for the session of Parliament which was to be re-convened on January 23, 1552.[2] Less than a week earlier Edward had set down in his own hand certain matters which he wished the Council to conclude and then, a few days later, his wishes with respect to the legislation to be enacted by the Parliament. He wanted earnest attention paid to the final clearing of his debts, not later than 'February next coming'. He wished as well a decision on bishops who should be nominated and he wanted assurances that funds were in hand for the payment of his ambassadors. He required the Council to take action for the strict control of prices in the City of London, so that members attending Parliament should 'not be wholly discouraged, impoverished, or worried' during their stay in the capital. The problem of foreign exchange was to be considered again, the charges against Tunstall resolved legally, and, grimly enough, Somerset and his confederates punished according to law 'as appertaineth to our surety and [the] quietness of our realm'.[3]

The King's memorandum for the new legislation which he wanted included two measures dealing with the estate of the church, to ensure to each incumbent that the full value of his living should be paid by the patron and that no spiritual person might conclude a lease on church lands for a term longer than twenty-one years. He likewise wished a sterner law against re-grating, a stronger prohibition against severing houses from lands which had appertained to them, and that it be declared a felony to export bullion illegally. The King was also concerned with the depletion of timber resources by the iron mills in southern England, the proposed legislation evoking, as we have seen, lively debate, the pleading of special interests, and a variety of measures, none of which passed into law, for the curing of the evil.[4] Finally, the King drew up in his own hand a curious sumptuary bill which sought to control excessive

---

[1] *Cal. S.P. Span.*, X, 592: Nov. 20, 1552.   [2] *Vide ante*, 335 ff.
[3] Cotton MSS., Vespasian, F, xiii, 171; in Nichols, *Remains*, II, 489–490.
[4] S.P. Dom., Edw. VI, XIV, 4; printed in Nichols, *Remains*, II, 491–495; *vide ante*, 341–342, for the debates on the iron mills and their depredations.

outlays on apparel by assigning clothing in terms of gradations of social classes. Thus no one beneath the rank of baron should be permitted cloth of silver or gold, while for the lower orders no husbandman was to wear any dyed cloth or leather tanned or dressed outside the realm.[1] These thwarted proposals tell us a great deal about the slope and thrust of the King's interests and concerns, though no one of them attained the dignity of statute law in the final session of Edward's first Parliament. The overriding interests of the King were economic and there was in certain of his proposals a view of the English society which must have recalled to the members the Commonwealth Party in its season of influence. It seems quite sure that few outside the Council sensed that these abortive, but still interesting and important, measures emanated from the King himself, who was clearly now beginning to rule.

There was also about the *corpus* of the King's legislative proposals a more than faint suggestion of pedantry and perhaps even of a too great fondness for the details of administration. Certain it is that these traits do characterize his continued and personal concern with the re-casting of the statutes of the Order of the Garter from 1548 until he gave effect to the new statutes, of his own drafting, on April 24, 1552.[2] The King's interest, which was as sustained as it was intense, was in the complete revision of the ritual of the Order so that all traces of Roman Catholicism should be eliminated and that its surplus funds be devoted to scholars in the universities, the care of roads, and charitable uses. In all, the King prepared three drafts, one in Latin and two in English, which in the end Cecil brought to a final and authoritative draft.[3] Even Northumberland, who loathed clerkly duties of any sort, had to express a judgement on the three drafts which the King had produced. Somewhat shame-facedly he confessed to Darcy, 'for so much as it is all in Latin, I can but give a guess at it, yet nevertheless I am so bold to express my understanding in some part of it'.[4] The Duke had no suggestions beyond a clearer statement of the royal control over the Order, but declared his willingness to discuss that point with Cecil [Chancellor

---

[1] Petyt MSS., Inner Temple, 538, vol. 47, f. 318; printed in Nichols, *Remains*, II, 495–498. The bill was read once and then languished. A similar bill was passed in Mary's first Parliament. *Vide* also *C.J.*, I, 20; Hooper, Wilfrid, 'The Tudor sumptuary laws', in *E.H.R.*, XXX (1915), 436.

[2] Edward VI, *Chronicle*, 120. In the earlier revisions (1548) the Council had ordered minor changes in the ritual and the elimination of the requiem mass.

[3] Cotton MSS., Nero, C, x, 13, ff. 93–101, 102–106; S.P. Dom., Edw. VI, XVII: 1552; Harl. MS. 394, with the King's amendments.

[4] S.P. Dom., Edw. VI, XVIII, 4.

of the Order] and others, if that should be the King's wish. It is clear that the King found great pleasure and satisfaction in the task which he had completed alone; the pageantry of the Order appealed to a king who was still a boy; Rome had been routed; and there stood in final form a task which he had set for himself and which he had brought to a happy end.

4. ROYAL ILLNESS AND ROYAL PLEASURE (1552)

The King's health had from the moment of his birth been a matter of deep concern to the Council, and, for that matter, to the realm at large. During his infancy Henry VIII had been almost obsessively nervous about his health, imposing something very close to quarantine on the Prince's household and surrounding him with a staff of physicians responsible for his welfare.[1] The King's health, his attainment of maturity and his ultimate marriage, and the male heir to the throne which might in time be the issue of such a union, were desperately important if the Tudor dynasty were to be preserved and if England were to be spared the grim risks of internal disturbance. One of the most damaging of the charges against Somerset was that, during Warwick's conspiracy against him, when he carried the King by night from Hampton Court to Windsor, with a resulting cold for Edward, he had been playing fast and loose with the almost sacred person of the King.[2]

The fact seems to be that Edward enjoyed normal health throughout his childhood and boyhood, save for a slight disposition towards upper respiratory infections. Then, quite suddenly, on April 2, 1552, he fell seriously ill with what the King himself tells us was diagnosed as measles and smallpox. Present medical judgement would suggest that this could hardly have been the case, for the two diseases in combination would almost certainly have killed the patient.[3] This may to a degree be confirmed by the King's report to his friend Barnaby Fitzpatrick, in which he says, 'we have a little been troubled with the small pox, which hath letted us to write hitherto; but now we have shaken that quite away'.[4] Whichever disease it may have been, the King made a rapid recovery, though on April 15th he notes that he was not well enough to attend in person

[1] Jordan, *Edward VI*, 36–39.
[2] *Ibid.* 510.
[3] Edward VI, *Chronicle*, 117. I am grateful to Dr. Sven Gundersen, Dr Victor Balboni, and to Dr David Ruml, for their expert judgement in the matter.
[4] Nichols, *Remains*, II, 79–80.

on the dissolution of Parliament, though 'I signed a bill containing the names of the acts which I would have pass, which bill was read in the House'.[1] A week later he was attending to the entries in his *Chronicle* in normal fashion. On the 23rd he was present in the Abbey at a special service, and not quite a week thereafter when the Spanish ambassador saw him the King seemed well recovered.[2] Quite certainly his doctors thought him beyond any danger of relapse by May 12th when he rode through Greenwich Park to Blackheath with his body-guard and ran at the rings with lords and knights who were in his company.[3]

At about this date, too, the Council turned, with the King, to a discussion of Edward's first royal progress. Though he had acquired from his books and charts a formidable knowledge of the geography of the realm, the King had not in fact been more than thirty miles from London since his accession, his movements having been confined to the numerous royal castles which lay in an arc about London. Edward himself participated with great enthusiasm in planning the elaborate progress, the first of what was expected to be a series of great royal journeys throughout the realm.[4] He was to be attended by fifteen of the Privy Council, to whom at the outset were appointed the incredible total of 345 'bands of men of arms [to] go with me [on] this progress'.[5] All the great officers of state, then, were to accompany him, save for Northumberland who left in mid-June for the Scottish Border to reorganize the defences there, not to return until the end of August. This imposing company of lords and gentlemen was, of course, only the beginning, for there were as well many hundreds from the royal household, servants for all, grooms, and the inevitable hangers-on. This vast concourse, which the King tells us numbered nearly 4000 (?) persons on horse, set out bravely enough, but at Petworth, the second point of stay, it was determined that the number must be sharply reduced, for the company were so numerous as 'to eat up the country; for there was little meadow nor hay all the way as I went'.[6] Accordingly, the Privy Council decreed that the number of Councillors on progress be reduced to nine and the body-guard bands to 135 in all in order to

---

[1] Edward VI, *Chronicle*, 119.

[2] *Cal. S.P. Span.*, X, 507–508.

[3] Machyn, *Diary*, 18. His sister, Elizabeth, was either unduly conservative or slightly negligent, waiting until September 20 to forward a warm note of congratulation on Edward's recovery (Lansdowne MS. 94, #11).

[4] Edward VI, *Chronicle*, 123: May 17, 1552.

[5] *Ibid.* 124.

[6] *Ibid.* 137: July 24, 1552.

lessen the burdens of forage and provender on the countryside through which the progress passed and tarried.[1]

The first stop, as well as the assembling-point, of the progress was Guildford, which the King reached on July 15th, then on the 21st to Petworth where the great house had been in crown hands since 1536.[2] Thence the company moved on to Cowdray, Sir Anthony Browne's house, which Edward in a letter to Barnaby described as 'a goodly house . . . where we were marvelously, yea, rather excessively, banqueted'.[3] On July 27th the progress reached Halnaker, another great house, built about forty years earlier by Thomas, Lord de la Warr, which the King described only as 'a pretty house'.[4] Edward reached Warblington, hard by Havant (Hampshire), on the 2nd of August, 'a fair great old house' which had recently been conveyed by the crown to Sir Richard Cotton, and then, after a very short stay, moved on to Bishop's Waltham where the company paused for several days[5] and where the King found good hunting and good cheer. The King's party reached Portsmouth on August 8th, and on the next day Edward devoted himself to an inspection of the defences there, which he found most inadequate and which he resolved to strengthen by the building of two forts to be so designed as to control the entrance to the harbour, where the royal fleet was often berthed.[6] On the following day he seems to have participated in the decision to send Henry Dudley and '140 good soldiers' to Guînes to counter the aggressive weight of the French on its frontier, and then proceeded to Titchfield, about two miles to the west of Fareham (Hants), where Wriothesley had recently built his great country seat and where he was buried. Thence the King removed for a short stay in Southampton where, as we have seen, he met the famous John Bale, who had come in from the country for a glimpse of the King and who returned home that day a designated Irish bishop.[7] From Southampton the great concourse

---

[1] *A.P.C.*, IV, 100–101. Seven of the Council were in company for the whole progress. They were Winchester, Bedford, Suffolk, Northampton, Darcy, Gates, and Cecil. Clinton, Huntingdon, and Sir John Mason joined the party at Salisbury, Petre at Basing, Northumberland at Mottisfont.

[2] Edward VI, *Chronicle*, 137. It was returned to the Percy family in 1557.

[3] Nichols, *Remains*, I, 80; VCH, *Sussex*, I, 515–516. The great pile had been built about 20 years earlier by Sir Anthony's half-brother, Sir William Fitz-William.

[4] Edward VI, *Chronicle*, 137; Nichols, *Remains*, I, 81.

[5] The property had long been the country seat of the Bishops of Winchester, but had recently been surrendered by Ponet to the crown on his elevation, and then in turn granted to the Marquis of Winchester (Edward VI, *Chronicle*, 138).

[6] Edward VI, *Chronicle*, 138–139 and footnotes there.

[7] *Ibid.* 139; Nichols, *Remains*, I, 81; *vide ante*, 368.

continued on to Beaulieu,[1] and then on August 19th arrived in Christchurch, where the King wrote his most informal letter to Barnaby and where a meeting of record of the Privy Council was held.[2]

Then, moving somewhat more rapidly, the royal party lodged at Woodlands, Sir Edward Willoughby's estate in the parish of Horton (Dorset), and thence on August 24th reached Salisbury.[3] The earlier plan to visit Poole was cancelled because of rumours of the sweating sickness there, though the King expressed to Barnaby the private conviction that this was not the case.[4] At Salisbury several important administrative decisions were taken before the King moved on to Wilton, conveyed by the crown to Sir William Herbert in 1544 and recently converted by the Earl of Pembroke, as he now was, from the old conventual buildings into a magnificent residence.[5] Here Edward was entertained with sumptuous splendour, the King being served from plates of pure gold and the court officials from silver gilt, and then at the moment of his departure the whole of the plate was presented to the King.[6]

The royal party reached Mottisfont (Hampshire) on September 2nd, being lavishly entertained by Thomas, Lord Sandys of the Vyne, whose father had converted this former priory into a great and comfortable country house. Here, it seems fairly certain, Northumberland, having returned from the North, joined the progress and applauded the decision already taken to shorten the itinerary because of the rumours of plague and sweat in southern England.[7] Then, moving more rapidly, the royal progress pressed on to Winchester, where the King was lodged in the Bishop's Palace, and from thence on September 7th to Basing, where Paulet had rebuilt the old castle on a vast and sumptuous scale.[8] Moving on now without lengthy visits, the royal concourse reached Donnington Castle, the seat of the Duke of Suffolk, on September 10th. Here the King paused for two days, while a meeting of the Council was held at the great house, which lay 'beside the town of Newbury [Berks]'.[9] Continuing towards Windsor, the King and his company

---

[1] Edward VI, *Chronicle*, 139.

[2] VCH, *Hants*, V, 88; *A.P.C.*, IV, 114–115; Edward VI, *Chronicle*, 140; Nichols, *Remains*, I, 80–82.

[3] Edward VI, *Chronicle*, 140–141.

[4] Nichols, *Remains*, I, 87: Sept. 24, 1552.   [5] Edward VI, *Chronicle*, 142.

[6] *Cal. S.P. Span.*, X, 566: Scheyfve to Queen Regent, Sept. 23, 1552.

[7] S.P. Dom., Edw. VI, XV, 1: Northumberland to Cecil, Sept. 3, 1552; Edward VI, *Chronicle*, 142; *Cal. S.P. Span.*, X, 561–562: Scheyfve to Queen Regent, Sept. 10, 1552.

[8] Edward VI, *Chronicle*, 142.

[9] VCH, *Berks*, IV, 92–93; Edward VI, *Chronicle*, 142.

reached Reading on September 13th, where the civic greeting given Edward was doubtless typical of those which took place in the numerous country and market-towns through which the progress had passed. As the company entered the outskirts, the mayor, 'with the substance of the inhabitants . . . in their best apparels', met the royal party at Colley Cross, and then, kneeling before the King, kissed his mace and handed it to Edward, 'who most gently stayed his horse and received it', and at once returned it to the mayor. Then the procession rode into the town where the King lodged in an expropriated monastery, retained by Henry VIII as a royal palace. In expression of the town's loyalty, the mayor made a free gift of two yoke of oxen to the King, 'which cost xv *li.*, the charges whereof was borne by the inhabitants of the said town'.[1]

This first and only progress of King Edward ended on September 15th when he returned to Windsor Castle, where during his absence work was well begun on a new and adequate water supply for that vast pile.[2] It is evident that the long journey had given much pleasure to the King, even during the later stages when the Council was beginning to tire and when it became increasingly worried because of rumours of the sweat in southern England. Edward had conducted himself with great dignity, had visited some of his most powerful subjects, and had shown himself in five of the counties of England in which as recently as 1549 there had been overt manifestations of malaise and disaffection. His feet had been on the soil of England, he had seen much and his perceptive and encyclopedic mind had stored much away. He returned to Windsor Castle, for which he had never cared, in a true sense the King of England. He was in fact almost ready to rule the nation and he was already reaching out for the substance of the power that was his. But it was not to be, for within a matter of months the wasting disease which was to kill him had taken him within its grip.

5. THE PENALTIES OF FEAR: THE PROBLEM OF PUBLIC ORDER (OCTOBER, 1551–1553)

It should again be noted that the King was not accompanied on the whole of his somewhat idyllic progress by his chief minister, the Duke of Northumberland. The Duke had so arranged his affairs

---

[1] Edward VI, *Chronicle*, 143; *Reading records. Diary of the Corporation*, I (ed. by J. M. Guilding, L., 1892), 228–229; HMC, *11th rpt.*, App. VII, 182; Nichols, *Remains*, II, 454.

[2] Edward VI, *Chronicle*, 143; VCH, *Berks*, III, 33.

that he was absent on his great Border command, which he had in fact sorely neglected, during most of the progress, though there was in truth no crisis in the North that required his presence.[1] He had expressed doubt in any case regarding the wisdom of the royal journey and he had advised in mid-course that the itinerary should be considerably curtailed. Northumberland had no taste for public and uncontrolled confrontation with what may be described as 'a random sampling' of the population of England, for he knew, and was deeply embittered by the fact, that he was at once feared and disliked by the generality of the King's subjects.

We have already observed that following on the overthrow of Somerset in 1549 and the necessarily brutal repression of serious insurrection, Northumberland, and his Council, had ruled subject to the mitigation of a kind of obsessive fright.[2] Each spring these fears mounted to a climax as the dread summer season came on. The government used all powers of intelligence, commissions, direct administration, and the judicial competence vested in the Council to hold the country steady until each summer was past. These fears were greatly enhanced and deepened after the violent shock to the realm occasioned by the trial and execution of the former Lord Protector. The government, in point of fact, was much stronger and more effective than Northumberland believed it to be, in large part certainly because men knew or sensed that the King's coming of royal age was near at hand. But a heavy price was paid for this near hysteria in Northumberland's troubled and jumbled mind: a complete paralysis of foreign policy; expensive and dubious military dispositions; a pandering to black reaction in the social and economic policies demanded by Parliament after the revolts were over; and an embracing of the evangelical faction in the Church of England. We should now sketch at least lightly a sampling—and it is only that—of the neurotic concern of the Privy Council with threats to political stability, threats both real and imaginary.

Minor instances of riotous conduct or trouble-making were, it was assumed, ferreted out and punished by the local authorities by the exercise of their own substantial administrative and police power. But in the period under review the ruling junta in the Privy Council supplemented this normal authority by a constant and fearful

---

[1] The decision for Northumberland to go to the Border was formally taken by the Council on May 22. He was to repair to the North, settle the region in good order, and then return as soon as possible (*A.P.C.*, IV, 55). His departure was somewhat delayed because of illness in his own household (*ibid.* 66).

[2] *Vide ante*, 56–59, for the years 1549–1551.

activity of its own, reaching out from London to investigate, interrogate, and usually to punish suspicious persons and activities, sometimes of the most trivial sort. The Council's concern was particularly concentrated in the Home Counties, in all of which two or more such incidents occurred, save in Sussex, with a fringe area of unquiet in the Midland Counties of Warwickshire and Oxfordshire. It is worth noting that, so far as our evidence goes, Wiltshire, Somerset, Cornwall, and Norfolk, all deeply involved in the great insurrection of 1549, remained relatively quiet during the remainder of the reign.

Quite typical of the way the Privy Council proceeded was the case of Isaac Herne, a shoemaker of Wokingham (Berks), who was alleged to have procured five other malcontents to 'rise and make a rebellious assembly', employing these words: 'If you will you may now assemble a good company together' and 'then we will have the rents of farms and prices of victuals to be brought lower again as they were in King Richard's time.'[1] In general, the country had lain quiet and inert during the summer of 1551 as the terrible epidemic of sweating sickness swept across much of the realm,[2] but there was of course mounting concern as preparations were being made by Northumberland for the arrest and trial of Somerset. The imperial ambassador reported in September that there were stirs in Reading and in Wales, which had, however, been quickly quieted.[3] The Council, sitting at Oatlands in late September, ordered an obscure Londoner to be pilloried for seditious utterances,[4] while at about the same time seven persons, mostly servants, in three, possibly four, counties were ordered arrested and interrogated because of suspicious conduct.[5] Letters were also dispatched to the sheriff of Suffolk to apprehend one Francis Clopton, who was later examined by the Council and released under bond of £40, for having spread the rumour that Rich, the Lord Chancellor, 'should leave the seal'.[6]

Somerset's arrest in mid-October and the preparation for his trial naturally enough caused Northumberland and his supporters in the Council to take every possible precaution, even against persons in no way involved in the 'conspiracy' of the former Lord Protector. Two sailors in Essex were proceeded against for treasonable

---

[1] Edward VI, *Chronicle*, 78; *Cal. Pat. Rolls, Edw. VI*, IV, 343 (Herne was here pardoned for his offences).

[2] *Vide post*, 466–471. [3] *Cal. S.P. Span.*, X, 368: Sept. 14, 1551.

[4] S.P. Dom., Edw. VI, XIII, 48: Sept. 25, 1551.

[5] *A.P.C.*, III, 372–373. I have found no record of the examination or imprisonment of these persons.

[6] *Ibid.* 372, 398: Sept. 30 and Oct. 26, 1551.

gossip, while a month later the Council ordered the justices of that county to deliver up such persons as were involved in an attempted stir. After examination, two men, sent back to Essex from the Fleet for pillorying, were ordered held in gaol until further notice.[1] At about the same time the Council issued instructions for a discreet investigation of security measures in the Fleet, in part at least because one Flint, of Sussex, ordered held in close confinement because of his undoubted share in a serious conspiracy to raise Hampshire and Sussex in 1549,[2] was in fact permitted to converse with persons outside the gate.[3]

Far more ominous was the spread of rumours that Dudley was about to seize personal power—a bruit never fully quieted during the remainder of the reign. Quite typical was the offence of one Anthony Gyllot of Coventry, who had said that Northumberland had set up a mint at Dudley Castle and that he had himself seen a coin bearing the ragged staff on one side and the bear on the other. Gyllot was committed to the Marshalsea,[4] a few weeks later being freed and returned to Coventry with orders to the authorities there to keep him under surveillance. A day or so later three yeomen of the guard were in difficulties with the Council for having circulated the same story in London.[5] Rumours were also abroad that Northumberland intended to usurp the throne, typical of which was the story spread about in London that one of the King's physicians,[6] one Korvar,[7] and an unnamed groom were planning to destroy the King. The disjointed notes regarding the case suggest a serious search for the rumour-monger, who, however, could not be tracked down.[8] Malicious attacks on Northumberland were particularly rife, and increasingly vicious, in London in the weeks just before Somerset's execution and were, of course, almost impossible to dispel. On All Hallows Day, 1551, a fray almost broke out in St Paul's when several of Northumberland's swordsmen attempted to pull the chain of office from the neck of the Sheriff of London. When the service ended and the procession withdrew there was further violence, broken up when the Lord Mayor sent several who were involved to the Compter.[9] Stories were also abroad in London

---

[1] A.P.C., III, 410, 420: Nov. 10 and 19, 1551.
[2] Jordan, Edward VI, 450–451.
[3] A.P.C., III, 384: Oct. 10, 1551.
[4] Ibid. 375, 469–470.   [5] Ibid. 377, 391, 417.
[6] Dr Huicke (spelled in sources in a variety of ways).
[7] Clearly so spelled in the document. I have been unable to identify the person.
[8] S.P. Dom., Edw. VI, XIII, 78: Dec. 1551.
[9] Grey Friars Chronicle, 71–72.

regarding the new coinage being issued under the authority of a proclamation made in late October,[1] which many maligned as carrying the ragged staff and symbolizing Northumberland's accession to power.[2] More serious by far were reports from paid informers that plans were being made for a rising in and near Abingdon, which were investigated, without yielding solid information, by a special commission of oyer and terminer appointed by the Council.[3]

We have seen that Northumberland and his followers were in fact able to maintain order after the execution of the former Lord Protector. For some months, indeed, English sentiment and normal gossiping seem to have been paralysed by a kind of terror and certainly by a confused comprehension of what had happened. One thing England did come quickly to understand: that it was ruled by a ruthless soldier who would countenance no overt disaffection. But as the spring months approached the nervous Council began again to be deeply disturbed by evidences of agitation. In late March the justices of the peace in Hampshire were ordered to punish one Harry Brabon, who did not deny that he had called the King a 'poor child'.[4] The Council took seriously indeed the 'lewd prophecies and other slanderous matters' touching the King and Council uttered by one Hartlepoole and a former secretary of the Duke of Norfolk, named Clarke. The two men were held in prison while Hartlepoole's wife and the Countess of Sussex were briefly jailed to teach them 'a lesson to beware of sorcery'.[5]

In May the Council was evidently greatly exercised by discontent, which it thought approached a stir, in the chronically disaffected county of Hampshire. A commission was appointed to search out possible conspiracy in the shire on the basis of writings in the possession of the Council.[6] At about the same date Thomas Fawding, a fellow of Eton College, was straitly examined by the Council for 'certain lewd words' which he had heard regarding the succession to the crown, and was committed to the Fleet when he pleaded that he could not remember who had spoken the words.[7] The irrepressible vigour of London sentiment also occasioned apprehension in the Council, even a 'goodly May-pole' celebration at Fenchurch

---

[1] Hughes and Larkin, *Tudor proclamations*, I, 535–536.
[2] *Grey Friars Chronicle*, 73.
[3] *A.P.C.*, III, 421, 423: Nov. 21, 1551.
[4] *Ibid.* IV, 4: Mar. 26, 1552.
[5] *Ibid.* 12: Apr. 4, 1552; *ibid.* 131: Sept. 27, 1552.
[6] *Ibid.* 45: May 12, 1552.
[7] *Ibid.* 46–47: May 14, 1552.

being broken up,[1] while at about the same time Lord Northampton led a muster of the royal troops before the King in bristling array.[2] In May, too, the obsessive fears of the government were evident in the special appointments of Lords Lieutenants 'for this summer', members of the Council being vested with great military powers in nineteen English counties. In areas of special concern there were multiple appointments, four Lieutenants being named for Norfolk and Essex, and three each for Middlesex and Suffolk.[3] Meanwhile in London suspects were being haled before the Council, as for example John Wilding who was committed to the Marshalsea on suspicion of seditious sentiments,[4] and John Lawton who was to be pilloried for a seditious ballad and then whipped out of the City, as well as William Martin, his printer, who was bound in £100 and required to report to the Council at weekly intervals.[5]

Then, interestingly and somewhat inexplicably, the concern of the Privy Council with these cases almost entirely ceased during the dreaded summer months. In part this may be due to the vigilance of the Council and to the elaborate precautions which had been taken. But possibly even more important was the stubborn insistence of the King on making his progress through the most chronically disaffected areas, Essex aside, of his realm. The presence of the King among his people, the absence of the Duke of Northumberland, and the impression gained that the young monarch was soon to begin to govern in person, all must have had a quieting effect on the whole of the realm.

But with the end of this idyllic summer, the flow to the Privy Council of such cases, now considerably more ominous than those noted in the earlier months of Northumberland's dominance, was resumed. Viewed with very serious concern was the case of Elizabeth Huggins, formerly a servant in the household of the Duchess of Somerset, who was more recently employed by Sir William Stafford of Essex. The information was supplied by Stafford who swore that this talkative woman had horrified him by maintaining that Somerset had been innocent of the charges against him, could have broken from custody had he tried, and that it was Northumberland who had been responsible for Somerset's death. The King, she declared, was an 'unnatural nephew' and she wished she had the 'jerking of him'. Mrs Huggins, examined in the Tower by Sir Robert Bowes and

---

[1] Machyn, *Diary*, 19–20: May 26, 1552.
[2] Edward VI, *Chronicle*, 123; Machyn, *Diary*, 18–19.
[3] *A.P.C.*, IV, 49–50: May 16, 1552.
[4] *Ibid*. 81.   [5] *Ibid*. 69, 70: June 7, 1552.

Sir Arthur Darcy, denied the precise charges made against her, but admitted that she had said that those responsible for Somerset's death would answer for his blood, just as 'the ld. admiral's blood' was on Somerset's hands. At a later stage of the examination she admitted having said that the world condemned Northumberland for Somerset's blood, and when pressed she explained that by 'the world' she meant the mass of the people. In spite of her evasive skills, Mrs Huggins was held in the Tower until June 16, 1553.[1] In this rambling, hazy, and inconclusive examination is to be found much of the essence of the many seditious libels being laid against Northumberland, libels from which he was never able to clear himself. The Duke's power and will were in the end severely depleted by the knowledge that he was hated by most of the people of England.

The Council employed every possible device to ferret out the source of rumours and libels, particularly when they were laid against the character and policy of the Duke. Informers were used, the nobility and gentry were encouraged to forward information, however insubstantial, and the Lieutenants and county nobility were constantly adjured to do their duty. Thus Westmorland, from distant Yorkshire, acknowledging the Council's instructions regarding 'false slanders and rumours spoken of the Duke', wrote that he had sent up to them one John Burghe who denied having accused Northumberland of thefts of the King's goods in London.[2] The Council thanked the Earl for 'boulting out' such lewd reports and committed Burghe to the Tower. At the same session, John Kyrton was committed to the Fleet for having said that Northumberland should be commanded to absent himself from court, while the investigation of the slanderous remarks of one Thomas Wayneman was further advanced, leading ultimately to his outlawry.[3]

This sort of detailed and direct examination, needless to say, took endless time, and one is compelled to believe that from September, 1552 to the end of the reign the Council must have spent a heavy proportion of its time in the pursuit of phantoms which could never quite be brought to earth. Thus in October they ordered an investigation of a 'fond sermon' preached by James Bilney at Chigwell (Essex), seeking to make certain that rumours and reports arising

[1] Harl. MS. 353, ff. 121, 121b–123.
[2] S.P. Dom., Edw. VI, XV, 7: Westmorland to Cecil, Richmond, Sept. 17, 1552. The letter also suggests that Westmorland felt under pressure from Cecil with respect to a land transaction between them. See *ibid.* 50, for the disposition of the case.
[3] *A.P.C.*, IV, 129, 130, 141, 175, 208, 243.

from it were stayed.[1] There were ugly overtones in Northumberland's personal intervention with Cecil in the case of one Hawkins, a schoolmaster who had earlier been in difficulty with the Council. Now it appeared that under examination by Darcy, Lieutenant of the Tower, he had confessed to distributing libellous bills with an intent to foment rebellion. He would name no accomplices and Northumberland's clear instruction was that he be further examined, 'either by fair means or foul to cause him to declare his counsellors or comforters'. In other words, torture was to be used and this was to be 'kept very close and secret'.[2] It was, then, a nervous and a frightened Northumberland who was directing what was close to a reign of terror, and so it was to continue to the end.[3]

These were actions of a badly frightened and an insecure government which knew full well that there remained a deep-rooted admiration for Somerset which had now taken the form of a festering hatred—and fear—of the Duke of Northumberland. During the last six months of the reign these instances of disaffection—they were never much more than that—increased in number and geographical spread, as it became widely rumoured that the sands of the King's life were now running out. Yet it should be observed that there was during the whole of Northumberland's tenure of power no considerable commotion, much less a stir, for the apparatus of authority and order were too alert and too ruthless to make concerted opposition possible. Indeed, as these isolated acts of disaffection mounted in number and intensity during the last months of the reign, it can be fairly said that the Privy Council devoted its consecutive attention to little else. But our sampling of the nature and quality of this restless and brooding malaise has doubtless been sufficient.

6. THE WEAKENING OF THE MILITARY RESOURCES OF THE STATE (1550–1553)

One of the charges laid against Somerset, and with some justice, was that he had maintained a military establishment well beyond the limits of the straitened financial resources of the Crown and had engaged England in almost constant war with Scotland and with

---

[1] *A.P.C.*, IV, 136: Oct. 5, 1552.

[2] S.P. Dom., Edw. VI, XV, 34: Oct. 27, 1552. The prisoner was probably John Hawkins who in November, 1551 had been bound in the sum of £40 for future good conduct (*A.P.C.*, III, 412–413).

[3] Many more instances might be cited from October, 1552 forward, especially in S.P. Dom., Edw. VI and *A.P.C.*, IV, *passim*.

France. Further, the searing insurrection of 1549 had been quieted only after heavy outlays, particularly since it was regarded as far too dangerous to rely on the usual county levies, with the consequence that very large sums were expended for the mercenary troops, which, with the addition of forces gathered by the gentry, may be said to have restored order. Northumberland, as we have seen, completely reversed Somerset's foreign policy, concluding with France and with Scotland a peace which reduced England to the role of a second-rate power but which at least did permit a sharp contraction of the huge military establishment, at home and abroad, which Somerset had maintained at costs threatening the financial solvency of the government. Furthermore, Northumberland was most reluctant to place confidence in the normal conscript levies, since he was deeply conscious of the insecurity of his own position. He experimented instead with the creation of a small standing army, stiffened with mercenary companies, which would be augmented by approximately 1000 heavy cavalry, to be at the disposal of members of the ruling junta at the cost of the state. The measures taken, as we shall note, had the effect of creating what has with justice been called 'a menacing revival of aristocratic military power'.[1]

The first step in this direction was taken in late 1550 when, as the King noted, a 'band of horsemen' numbering 700 men was to be created and disposed under the insignia and command of thirteen nobles, though two, Sadler and Darcy, were in fact not of that rank.[2] Some weeks later when this highly dubious policy was further discussed in the Council, it was determined after some disagreement that a standing army should be raised for the security of the King's person and for 'the stay of the unquiet subjects', those appointed to the command of 100 of the horse to have allowances of £500 each.[3] Various dates were set for the first muster of the new force, but it was not until December, in part to intimidate London before Somerset was brought to trial, that 'the new band of men of arms, the pensioners, and the old men of arms' all paraded past the King on the grounds of St James's Palace, the whole muster numbering about 1000 men.[4]

Northumberland, at about the time of Somerset's execution, gave over to his eldest son, the Earl of Warwick, 50 of the company

---

[1] Stone, Lawrence, *The crisis of the aristocracy, 1558–1641* (Oxford, 1965), 207.
[2] Edward VI, *Chronicle*, 50.   [3] *A.P.C.*, III, 225: Feb. 26, 1551.
[4] Edward VI, *Chronicle*, 100; *A.P.C.*, III, 399, ordering the muster; the pay of each horseman was stated as £20 p.a. (*Two London chronicles* (Camden Misc. XII), 25).

of 100 cavalry and 100 light horse which had served under his command at the expense of the state,[1] while a few weeks later Sir Ralph Sadler was appointed commander of a troop of 50 men-at-arms.[2] The somewhat casual and experimental arrangements thus far prevailing were to a degree regularized when, in April, 1552, warrants were issued for the payment of the bands of favoured nobles at the rate, in most cases, of £10 a year for each man serving.[3] In May a general muster of the whole force was held at Greenwich, only 100 not being present, together with the pensioners and the other household troops in what was evidently a lavish and colourful display of martial elegance, if not of might.[4] But the heavy costs, exceeding £20,000 p.a. for the cavalry bands, were found to be insupportable and it was prophetic when on June 23rd four of the bands were stricken from the rolls,[5] while in the general, and strait, retrenchments in household outlays ordered in September, 1552 letters were dispatched for the discharge of all the men-at-arms, effective at Michaelmas next following.[6] Hence it was that Northumberland was left without formidable military resources when the crisis precipitated by the King's death overwhelmed him. It had been an interesting, and a very expensive, experiment in the creation of a kind of standing feudal array. England was as well rid of it as it was to be rid of the Duke of Northumberland.

During this same interval the military establishment generally was being rapidly reduced both in number and in effectiveness. The process began shortly after the conclusion of the treaty of peace with France and the cession of Boulogne in late March, 1550. In July the famous garrison troops of Boulogne were formally mustered out and the first half of the indemnity paid by Henry II was principally applied to the arrears of wages for troops in France, Ireland, and along the Scottish Border.[7] Already, too, arrangements had been made for the payment and discharge of 600–700 of the mercenary forces and passports had been issued for their return home.[8] These were in large part the hated mercenaries who had borne the brunt of the suppression of the insurrection of 1549, their place

---

[1] Edward VI, *Chronicle*, 107.
[2] *Ibid*. 109.
[3] In all, warrants were ordered for the muster of 1100 such troops, almost wholly under the command of nobles who were members of the Privy Council (*A.P.C.*, IV, 15: Apr. 8, 1552; *et vide* S.P. Dom., Edw. VI, XIV, 21).
[4] Egerton MS. 2877, f. 182b; Edward VI, *Chronicle*, 123, 132.
[5] *Ibid*. 132.
[6] *Ibid*. 145.
[7] *Ibid*. 41.
[8] *A.P.C.*, III, 54: June 24, 1550.

being taken by discharged Boulognese. At the same time, however, mercenary forces to the number of 800 were retained and assigned to garrison duty in the six counties where there was chronic disaffection.[1] Furthermore, the heavy costs of maintaining a large corps of mounted artillery were sharply curtailed, again with the exception of units scattered through the disaffected counties.[2]

At the same time, naval outlays were even more drastically reduced, the great force, so brilliantly commanded by Clinton and Wyndham, simply being swept from the seas and the short period of English naval dominance in the Channel and in the North Sea being renounced. The decisive order came when in June, 1550 the Council issued instructions that the whole of the fleet was to be laid up and the crews discharged, save, of course, for skeleton crews and for a relatively strong squadron to be based on Portsmouth.[3] The fleet simply mouldered and rotted away during the next two years, and then, it seems probable, in October, 1552 even normal and badly needed munitions were further reduced by the Council.[4] This was done, despite the fact that in August, 1552 twenty-one of the royal ships were noted as in ill repair; by mid-1555 only four of those named were still carried in the naval lists. Doubtless profoundly discouraged, the most capable of the professional naval commanders, Thomas Wyndham and William Winter, left the Admiralty towards the close of the reign to embark on trading ventures. In any effective sense, it is almost accurate to say, there was no royal navy left in 1553. The great store of vessels, of experience, and of command bequeathed by Henry VIII had in a very short period been wholly dissipated.[5]

So too, the complex and modern system of coastal fortifications on which Henry in his last years had spent so much of his substance and to which he had lent his steady personal concern, was at first weakened by periodic reductions in garrison strength and then towards the close of the reign in large part simply abandoned. The one exception in Northumberland's policy of jettisoning the vast capital outlay which Henry VIII had made in England's fixed defences was Calais, where even after 1550 the never-ceasing and expensive tasks of repairs, replacement of out-moded ordnance, and

---

[1] *A.P.C.*, III, 81: July 17, 1550; Strype, *Memorials*, II, i, 459–461. They were disposed: Essex and Sussex, 200 each; 100 each in Dorset, Hampshire, Kent, and Suffolk.
[2] *Cal. S.P. Span.*, X, 592: Nov. 20, 1552.
[3] *A.P.C.*, III, 43: June 8, 1550.
[4] Edward VI, *Chronicle*, 176: Oct. 11, 1552.
[5] Much of this paragraph rests on the researches of Mr Tom Glasgow, Jr., of Charlotte, N.C., who has kindly placed his notes at my disposal,

extending the fortifications was never abandoned. At the same time, however, the great garrison, severely drawn down during the insurrection of 1549, was not restored to full strength, and was then further reduced in September, 1550 on the grounds that its presence simply induced the French to match it.[1] Then, a few months later, a sharp further reduction of 600 more veteran troops was ordered at Calais, despite the vehement representations of the English commanders.[2]

This process of demobilization, spurred always by financial need, was continued to the close of the reign. The policy was all the more incomprehensible since Northumberland was a highly gifted professional soldier who must have pursued this course with some measure of trepidation mixed with embarrassment. Central to his policy, however, was the hope of building up a small but an élite standing army whose principal function would be the quick striking down of rebellion in any quarter of the realm. This objective he simply could not attain without a substantial reduction in the military and naval establishments and the abandonment of the Henrician system of coastal defences mounted against France. The whole direction and intent of his foreign policy was, therefore, the preservation of peace with France at almost any price, including the complete abandonment of the English position in Scotland. Northumberland's room for manoeuvre was strait because the base of his own power was infirm and because he did not dare lay the full financial needs of the state before Parliament. He and his supporters had drawn down the wealth of the crown too rapidly, too avariciously, and too recklessly.

Meanwhile, to the end of the reign the steady process of demobilization—of military contraction—was continued. In May, 1552 further reductions were made in the garrisons of key fortified points in Cornwall and Dorset, while a survey was ordered to determine whether more blockhouses in Kent might be abandoned.[3] Sir Philip Hoby in August of the same year protested that the Ordnance Office was paralysed for want of appropriations, and that one of his gunpowder makers was in the Compter because his rent was in default, even though it was in fact chargeable to the King as part of his compensation.[4] The search for further economies went on, none

---

[1] *A.P.C.*, III, 123: Sept. 12, 1550.
[2] *Ibid.* 206: Feb. 3, 1551. At the same time 12 artillerymen were ordered returned to England for assignment there (*ibid.* 207).
[3] *Ibid.* IV, 34: May 4, 1552.
[4] S.P. Dom., Edw. VI, XIV, 56: Aug. 3, 1552.

the less, the soldiers manning the bulwarks in Essex being discharged in order to effect a saving estimated at £700,[1] while the
standing force of 2000 troops holding Ireland had earlier been
reduced by one-fourth.[2] Even the working force and the garrison at
Calais were once more, and dangerously, reduced as the reign
came towards its end, there being a note of desperation in the instructions forwarded to the Lord Deputy that 'if any of the soldiers that
are to be discharged shall seem desirous to serve the Emperor or
French King, in that case they shall not seem directly to licence
them so to do, but rather to permit them as it were by stealth to
depart, and to wink at it'.[3] And, fittingly enough, the final entry in
this sad and surely inglorious annal was the warrant issued only
days before the King's death for the costs of conveying ordnance
from certain of the coastal fortifications to the Tower of London.[4]
The dissolution of the great military and naval establishment which
Henry VIII had nurtured with so much of the wealth of the realm
and which the Duke of Somerset had maintained and employed with
such quixotic energy now stood complete. Edward VI had come to
the throne of a first-rate European power; he died the sovereign of a
second-rate power wobbling erratically as a satellite of France.

[1] Edward VI, *Chronicle*, 147.
[2] *Ibid.* 123: May 18, 1552.
[3] *A.P.C.*, IV, 260: Apr. 22, 1553.
[4] *Ibid.* 286: June 11, 1553.

XII

THE APPRENTICESHIP OF POWER

I. CONCERN WITH THE REFORM OF ADMINISTRATION

It is remarkable that the relative weakness of the central government which characterized most of the Edwardian era seems in no important way to have impaired the functioning of local administration in the realm, save in those areas torn briefly, though violently, by the dangerous risings of 1549. The peace, the sense of order, and the relatively sophisticated governance of the first two Tudors may be said, in a true sense, to have found its vindication in the fact that administration of local affairs continued to function almost automatically and with reasonable efficiency. In part, too, the reactionary domestic policy of Northumberland, born of his fear of Somerset's magical hold on the commons of the realm, gained the warm approval of most of the nobility and gentry of England, who had been very frightened indeed by the events of the summer of 1549. It may be said, then, that a complex and relatively well-developed network of administrative and legal relationships bound the society together and proved itself effective and vigorous even during the dislocations of the Edwardian era.[1]

Edward, as he began to reach out towards power, was not inclined to touch, even experimentally, the structure of local administration or the sinews which bound it to the central government. His interest—and it was considerable—was rather with the administrative structure of his central government, and to this he was to lend thoughtful and constructive attention. The Privy Council, the revenue courts, and the senior civil service, if the term may be used, were to be his primary concerns. The King's interest in the efficiency and competence of his government was apparent from a very early age. One may believe, indeed, that it sprang at once from the orderly and somewhat 'clerkly' manner in which his own mind

---

[1] We hope, in another connection, to deal at some length with the functioning of local administration during the Edwardian and Marian 'interlude'.

worked and from his growing determination to enforce standards of administration which would assure him of governmental honesty, as well as all the revenues which he could properly garner. As early as August, 1550 he had asked a committee, of which the Master of Requests was chairman, to draw up an abbreviated table of the laws and statutes 'that were not wholly unprofitable' to be laid before his Council, for the King was persuaded that there was a superfluity of laws in his realm.[1] A few days later he spoke approvingly of a self-denying ordinance invoked by the Council by which all members agreed not to 'speak in any man's behalf' for lands, reversions of offices, leases of manors, or unusual concessions, because of the financial crisis which by this date had almost overwhelmed the government.[2]

A year later the King's hand may almost certainly be seen in a resolution of the Council to desist from laying unconsidered documents before him for signature, it being ordered that henceforward such papers must be submitted by one of the clerks of the signet, and hence be in final form.[3] At about this date we also see a relatively early example of the memoranda which Edward loved to have drawn up for his study or to prepare himself for the consideration of the Council. He wished a thorough examination of all the funds due to him, 'for therein is thought to be much deceit', and he was anxious that the commission lately appointed to consider the reorganization of the revenue courts be carried forward promptly.[4] Not long afterwards we observe another of the memoranda which at the King's urging now began to be prepared as dockets for Council meetings.[5] These were usually in Cecil's hand, perhaps in part because the King and the Secretary were both inclined towards a thorough and ordered documentation of any business. An example may be observed in one of Cecil's small notebooks, with almost shorthand notations on Council business, which dates from early 1552.[6] These memoranda—one could say agenda—became so frequent as to be routine from this date forward until the final illness of the King resulted in a relapse to the disorganized habits of mind of the Duke of Northumberland.

---

[1] Edward VI, *Chronicle*, 43–44. [2] *Ibid.* 44–45: Aug. 17, 1550.

[3] *A.P.C.*, III, 366: Sept. 27, 1551.

[4] S.P. Dom., Edw. VI, V, 25. The calendar date (1548?) for the document is incorrect; it may be dated by internal evidence (Herbert's creation as an Earl) as October, 1551, or later. The memorandum bears a close relation to *ibid.* II, 30 and 31.

[5] *Ibid*, XIII, 79: Dec. ?, 1549.

[6] *Ibid.* V, 24. Again, internal evidence suggests a much later dating (c. Feb. 1552) than that affixed by the Calendar.

Notwithstanding the greater interest and vigilance of the King and the increased care given to auditing of accounts since the shocking malfeasance of Sharington in the Bristol mint,[1] the slightly increased efficiency of the central administration was not proof against either negligence or criminal rapacity. Thus in January, 1551 Sir Martin Bowes, a London merchant and sub-treasurer of the mint, was found to be approximately £10,000 in arrears in his accounts and the bulk of his debt had to be funded over a term of years.[2]

Far worse and more revealing of the incredible weaknesses, or laxity, in the revenue courts, and in the central administration generally, were the malfeasances and the criminal actions of John Beaumont, who evidently corrupted all that he touched. Born of a Leicestershire gentle family, and after 1550 Recorder of Leicester,[3] Beaumont had turned to the law and to administration after his training at the Inner Temple. Late in the reign of Henry VIII he had challenged the territorial interests of Henry Grey in Leicestershire, incurring Dorset's enmity and also a rebuke for his arrogance from the Privy Council. Beaumont from early 1545 until December, 1550 held the lucrative post of Receiver-General of the Court of Wards and Liveries, combining those duties with a career as a judge in Chancery. Then in late 1550 he resigned the receivership, on being appointed Master of the Rolls, but was forced to surrender that high office in June, 1552 when he was finally brought to heel.

The Court of Wards and Liveries, in which most of Beaumont's defalcations took place, had been created late in Henry VIII's reign.[4] The first master was Paulet, Master of Wards since 1526, who served continuously until 1554, but who, incredibly, seems to have been completely unaware of Beaumont's criminal activities. The Court was yielding a net revenue to the Crown of rather less than £10,000 p.a. during Beaumont's connection with it, though the accounts remain muddled because of his skilful financial manipulations.[5] When Paulet, now Lord Treasurer, under instruction began to make a careful survey of the whole of the King's revenue, Beaumont's peculations were revealed and he was committed to the Fleet on February 11, 1552, still on no more than vague suspicions of

[1] Jordan, *Edward VI*, 382–385.
[2] *A.P.C.*, III, 188: Jan. 10, 1551.
[3] VCH, *Leics*, IV, 71.
[4] By 32 Henry VIII, c. 46, and 33 Henry VIII, c. 22.
[5] Bell, H. E., *An introduction to the history and records of the Court of Wards & Liveries* (Cambridge, 1953), App., Table A; Hurstfield, Joel, 'Corruption and reform under Edward VI and Mary: the example of wardship', in *E.H.R.*, LXVIII (1953), 25–27.

misconduct.[1] The investigation was pressed by Northumberland, working principally through Cecil and Lord Darcy, who wished the articles of the charge to be carefully drawn by legal counsel.[2] The investigation disclosed crimes of two quite different sorts. As a judge and Master of the Rolls, Beaumont had forged the name of Charles Brandon, Duke of Suffolk, to a deed drawn in favour of Lady Powis, the Duke's elder daughter, having persuaded Lady Powis, then suing in his court, to convey the lands thus fraudulently gained to him for an arranged sum of money. Lady Powis's suit had been against Beaumont's old enemy, Dorset, now Duke of Suffolk. Thus, in the King's words, he had induced a jury to perjury and for good measure had concealed a felony of one of his own servants.[3]

The investigation and a careful audit disclosed as well that Beaumont had consistently neglected to pay in moneys due to the King from the Court of Wards, though he could plead with some justice that the amounts were in fact carried as debits in his accounts. But he had also been guilty of theft of sums totalling £11,823 from the revenues paid in by guardians of wards of the court. There was in addition £9765 which he had used for his own speculations, though this sum was in fact carried as arrearages in his books, out of which no one save the former Receiver could make much sense. Beaumont confessed to his crimes and acknowledged a debt totalling £20,871 18s 8d. On May 28th he conveyed to the King 'all my manors, lands, and tenements . . . and also my goods and chattels, moveable and unmoveable, whatsoever they be'.[4] Then, with the indecent haste of official looting which characterized the ruling junta, Northumberland almost immediately ordered that of Beaumont's surrendered lands, the Earl of Huntingdon should have Gracedieu, the parsonage of Donnington, and the manors of Throughstone and Swannington, with the further notation that when Paget surrendered his lands towards payment of his fine, Huntingdon and the Lord Chamberlain were not to be forgotten.[5]

The shock of the Beaumont case added impetus to the plans already under discussion for the reform of administrative practices,

---

[1] A.P.C., III, 478: Feb. 11, 1552; Edward VI dates the arrest as Feb. 9, 1552 (Chronicle, 109).

[2] S.P. Dom., Edw. VI, XIV, 34.

[3] Edward VI, Chronicle, 109 n. 30, 128–129.

[4] Nichols, Remains, II, 427; Lodge, Illustrations, I, 175; Hurstfield, in E.H.R., LXVIII (1953), 23–28. We should express, as well, a more precise debt to this brilliant essay of Professor Hurstfield, on which we have drawn heavily.

[5] Strype, Memorials, II, ii, 499–500. It may be noted that Beaumont's predecessor in the Court, Philip Parris, surrendered his office owing arrears of £2000.

especially in the revenue courts. The pressure for this overhauling of an antiquated and exceedingly cumbersome process of administration came in part certainly from Edward VI, who devoted considerable, and evidently outraged, attention to the Beaumont affair in his *Chronicle* and who from this time forward had under constant advisement the reform of the administrative apparatus, including the Privy Council itself.

2. THE QUEST FOR SOLUTIONS (1551–1553)

The ultimate sanction compelling the government to reorganize and reform itself, was, however, not so much the scandal raised by the looting of servants like Sharington and Beaumont, as the cold fact that it was under the lash of chronically insufficient income in a period of spiralling inflation. Nor, it was clear from the outset, were the household or the essential governmental services and outlays greatly padded or exorbitant. The expenditures for the household proper ran to approximately £55,475 p.a., or a little less than those of Henry VIII, and in a time when the purchasing power of money had fallen by nearly half. Token retrenchments were, however, undertaken in 1552 when various dining allowances were withdrawn,[1] while we have seen that during these months there was a steady and severe reduction in the outlays for the military establishment. Another source would suggest that about £13,831 was expended for the maintenance of the various revenue courts, and here there was undoubtedly scandalous bureaucratic padding as well as a costly inefficiency. The several state and judicial departments, including the palatine jurisdictions, cost no more than about £7405, while the reduced costs for manning and maintaining 'towns and castles of war, bulwarks', and fortifications were now a little more than £18,000.[2] Only in these great heads of outlay did there seem to be much hope of retrenchment.

The King was early persuaded that the principal area for reform and the promise of greater royal income lay in the five separate

---

[1] Edward VI, *Chronicle*, 145.
[2] These data are drawn from the undated table (*c.* 1552) in S.P. Dom., Edw. VI, Addenda, IV, 27. This source would place the total outlay, the fixed armament costs included, at about £72,260. An evidently related, and also undated, document (Harl. MS. 240) sets the total at £63,518 17s 4d, there being, however, numerous exclusions. Internal evidence would date the second source as 1551. Dietz (*English government finance, 1485–1558* (Urbana, Ill., 1920), 190), drawing from the declared accounts, sets an *average* figure of slightly more than £49,250 p.a. for the household for the six full regnal years.

revenue courts: Exchequer, Augmentations, Duchy of Lancaster, First Fruits, and Wards, where notoriously there was over-staffing of offices, overlapping of functions, lack of proper administrative and auditing controls, and an absence of contact between the courts.[1] There were in the Court of Augmentations two civil servants of great ability and probity, both restive and both certainly recommending needed reforms and economies. Sir Walter Mildmay, the most gifted of all the revenue officials, and surely the most trusted, wished an accounting to be made in all the courts and, probably on his representations, a commission was designated on December 30, 1551, 'for calling in my debts', in the King's phrase.[2] The commission thus named was instructed to collect or to re-arrange all debts and arrearages due to the Crown and to secure a strict audit of accounts. So effective was the work of the commission that by the close of the fiscal year 1552 a total of £16,667 of delinquent moneys had been paid in. The other gifted and restive official in Augmentations was Sir Richard Sackville, appointed Chancellor of the Court in August, 1548 when Sir Edward North was eased out.[3] In February, 1550 substantial powers in the Court were granted to Sackville, authorizing actions normally reserved to the King or the Privy Council.[4]

The advice of Sackville and Mildmay was doubtless to a degree reflected in the decision of the King in March, 1552 to appoint a commission of nine members charged with the task of reviewing the functions of all the revenue courts, of which number Mildmay was one.[5] The commission was vested with wide powers of investigation and recommendation, the results of its labours over a period of eight months being a thorough and carefully documented analysis of the whole financial structure of the government. The report, handed in on December 10, 1552, set the income of the Crown at £271,912, paid in through the five revenue courts, but proportionately with a very heavy flow to Augmentations. At the same time, the outlay for the last fiscal year (1551) was estimated to be £235,398, leaving on paper a healthy surplus, which was, however, completely illusory since the analysis did not comprehend the whole of

---

[1] Elton, G. R., *The Tudor revolution in government* (Cambridge, 1953), 230.
[2] Edward VI, *Chronicle*, 102.   [3] Richardson, *Court of Augmentations*, 189–190.
[4] *Cal. Pat. Rolls, Edw. VI*, III, 214–216.
[5] The other members were Darcy, Thirlby, Gates, Petre, Bowes, Cotton, Gosnold, and Wroth. Several of them had recently served on a commission to review and settle accounts, particularly with towns and victuallers, from the recent war with Scotland and France. The document (S.P. Dom., Edw. VI, II, 31, misdated 1547(?)), internal evidence suggests, may be dated early 1552.

the military establishment and its outlays, save for the modest sum of £9733 for garrisoning the remaining fortresses and fortified points within the realm.[1] By far the largest single head was £63,285 p.a. hypothecated for pensions and annuities, including, be it observed, continuing clerical pensions, amounting to a considerable proportion of the whole outlay, which could not, in the nature of things, be reduced substantially for some years to come.[2]

The commission closed its report with carefully considered recommendations for reform and greater efficiency of administration. Their principal proposal was for a fusing of the five revenue courts into a single court, which, it was reckoned, would result in a saving of perhaps £18,526 p.a. on official salaries, and, as importantly, a great gain in efficiency of operation. Much stricter accounting and procedural methods were likewise recommended in order to be rid of the persistent arrearages which tempted officials to corruption and made the control of receipts almost impossible. As the signal example the commission pointed to Wards and Liveries, some of whose accounts remained imperfectly audited as far back as 1545, thereby creating 'great unsurety for the King'.[3] And, finally, the commission urged the setting aside—surely very belatedly—of a sacrosanct reserve of crown lands which would at the least ensure the ultimate strengthening of the Crown.

The Council, spurred by the King's determined interest in all matters connected with administrative reform, moved quickly to lend its approval to the commission's report by framing the initial legislation which must be the foundation of the intended overhaul. Thus in March, 1553 the statutes 7 Edward VI c. 1 and c. 2 enacted that the revenue officers should be placed under sufficient bonds, provided for more reliable and prompt audits, and vested in the King power to merge all the revenue courts by letters patent and to dissolve those then existing. But the time remaining was too short; the King's illness now paralysed the springs of action; and the whole thrust for reform was for the moment dissipated. Nothing more could be done under Edward, but the momentum carried

---

[1] Elton, G. R., *The Tudor constitution. Documents and commentary* (Cambridge, 1960), 44–46, following Harl. MS. 7383, #1; Add. MS. 30,198, ff. 5–52, provides another draft, which we have followed in some particulars. Our treatment owes much to Elton's analysis in *Tudor revolution*, 230–238; to W. C. Richardson, *Tudor chamber administration, etc.* (Baton Rouge, 1952), 393 ff.; and to his surely definitive account of the work of the Royal Commission of 1552, shortly to be published. Professor Richardson's elaborate notes on pensioners and other annuitants are also of great value.

[2] *Vide ante*, 196–200, for remarks on the failure to fund the chantry pensions.

[3] Add. MS. 30,198, f. 51.

forward into the reign of Queen Mary whose first Parliament in effect re-enacted the Edwardian statutes, the Queen then by letters patent dissolving the Courts of Augmentation and of First Fruits by joining them with the Exchequer, but leaving untouched the Duchy of Lancaster and Wards and Liveries.[1] These changes, then, were planned under Edward VI, 'and it was only the accident of death that made them "Marian" reforms'.[2]

During the months when the commission on the revenue courts was proceeding with its important task, there was also abundant evidence that on the insistence of the King the Council itself was carrying forward its work with greater attention to detail and a more intelligent planning of its dockets. There were, as we have seen, earlier evidences of this more systematic procedure,[3] while after about February, 1552 it was becoming habitual, save for the occasional direct interventions by Northumberland, who had little taste for this sort of clerkly concern. A sampling of the records over a fairly wide spectrum of business and time may be helpful in assessing the background of this important reform in the work and structure of the Council.

Thus in February, 1552 an extensive draft was completed of matters to be taken up in full Council, which included the consideration of military affairs in Calais, Ireland, and Scotland, reports on negotiations with the Hanse, the proposed union of certain bishoprics, the work of the commission on the canon law, the state of the fortifications, and the breaking up of Somerset's household.[4] It seems quite certain that the King was directly responsible for the principal business laid out in the docket of the session of March 4 (1552) which was to find money wherewith to send certain naval vessels out to sea, to instruct a commission headed by Westmorland for the final settlement of the frontier with Scotland, and to reach decisions respecting the Irish currency and the operation of the mines there.[5] A procedural reformation was ordered by the Council shortly afterwards when it was stipulated that no document should be laid before the King for signature until it had first been

---

[1] Cotton MSS., Titus, B, iv, 9, ff. 60–65 (now ff. 62–67) sets out the full particulars for the Marian action. It is a legal brief elucidating the Queen's authority to act by letters patent, while in thirty-six articles and ordinances which were appended, the administrative and financial details ordering the fusion of the courts were elucidated.

[2] Elton, *Tudor revolution*, 239.

[3] *Vide ante*, 441 ff.

[4] S.P. Dom., Edw. VI, XIV, 8, which seems to be a final draft of similar memoranda to be found in *ibid.* 7 and 9.

[5] *Ibid.* 15; Edward VI, *Chronicle*, 114 (of even date).

approved in draft either by one of the principal secretaries or by one of the clerks of the Council.[1] The King was also personally involved in a review made by the Council of bills then before Parliament, to determine which were 'thought meet to pass and to be read; other[s], for avoiding tediousness, to be omitted and no more bills to be taken.'[2] as he was with a commission appointed for the execution of penal laws and proclamations and the oversight of the courts.[3]

A heavy docket of 'matters to be remembered in the Council' also reflects certain of the King's preoccupations, including a commission for the further sale of chantry lands, a review of forts still being manned, a discussion of a map of the Scottish frontier, the laying up of the *Saker* and the *Falcon*, minor diplomatic problems, and 'ten thousand pounds' weight in the Tower to be coined in Ireland at 6 oz. the shilling'.[4] Rather routine matters were to be considered by the Council in mid-May, though the King's steady preoccupation with the defences of Portsmouth and the Isle of Wight may be noted, as well as his concern that the charges against Beaumont be carefully sifted and the disposition of the case against Lord Paget be concluded.[5] So too, the docket of 'matters unperfected' at the end of May dealt principally with warrants for relatively small payments for divers purposes, save that a proclamation was to be considered 'forbidding resort of suitors' to the King during the royal progress then being planned.[6] A careful review and determination of various minor grants, leases, and presentations was made in early June, ranging downwards from a lease to Cecil for twenty-one years of Combe Park [Combe Nevil], Surrey, from Somerset's lands, to payments to the King's laundress, one of his players of interludes, and to a groom of the chamber.[7] This having been done, 'it was agreed that none of my Council should move me in any suit of lands—for forfeits above £20, for reversions of leases, or any other extraordinary suits—till the state of my revenues were further known'.[8] With this, significantly, these jottings of memoranda now regularly laid before the Council cease entirely until the King had returned from the progress which so enthralled him.

---

[1] *A.P.C.*, III, 500: Mar. 9, 1552; and see *ibid.* 366: Sept. 27, 1551, for an earlier intimation of this reform.   [2] Edward VI, *Chronicle*, 115.
[3] S.P. Dom., Edw. VI, XIV, 16, 17; Edward VI, *Chronicle*, 115.
[4] S.P. Dom., Edw. VI, XIV, 22: April ?, 1552.
[5] *Ibid.* 26: probably May 14, 1552; Edward VI, *Chronicle*, 124.
[6] S.P. Dom., Edw. VI, XIV, 36. One of the items here jotted down is in Cecil's hand.
[7] *Ibid.* 40: Docquet Items (June 7–June 10, 1552).
[8] Edward VI, *Chronicle*, 132.

Edward reached Windsor, and the end of his long journey, on September 15 (1552), then removed in about a fortnight to Hampton Court for a longer stay there.[1] It is significant that the flow of these memoranda on public business began again immediately, reaching its peak in the weeks remaining before November 30th when they suddenly slacken off, when the King also abruptly ended his attention to his *Chronicle*, and when, very possibly, the onset of his fatal disease may have begun. In this brief interval we have noted no less than six of these 'position papers' in whose preparation the King undoubtedly had a part. The first, probably prepared at Windsor, dealt with accumulated diplomatic matters and with relations to Scotland and Ireland, as well as firmly setting down for consideration 'the appointing of the mart, and order thereof', a matter in which the King was deeply interested and regarding which he had composed an impressive memorandum a few months earlier.[2] Again, towards the end of September, the further consideration of the proposed mart was set down to be discussed 'now in the opportunity of the time'. The items listed also reflected the King's almost fanatical resolution to complete the discharge of his internal and external debts, the determination to press forward with the reform of the revenue courts, and the further savings that might be gained by decommissioning even more of the blockhouses. At the same time the state of the King's ships, now almost all berthed in the Medway, was to be examined and the work on the great fortifications at Calais pressed forward.[3]

In a different hand and differently organized was a memorandum of October 4, 1552, almost surely emanating from Northumberland, which recommended new commands in the Tower, in Berwick, and at Guînes and Calais, the latter two matters being resolved not wholly to his satisfaction by the appointment of Lord Willliam Howard as Deputy of Calais, and of Lord Grey, recently under suspicion as a friend of Somerset, as commander at Guînes.[4] The details of these appointments were still under consideration when the next memorandum was prepared, though the principal concern was with another governmental intervention designed to secure control over the export of cloths as part of Gresham's highly successful effort to manipulate the exchange and retain some measure

---

[1] Edward VI, *Chronicle*, 143, 145.
[2] S.P. Dom., Edw. VI, XV, 4; Edward VI, *Chronicle*, 168–171; *vide ante*, 413–414.
[3] S.P. Dom., Edw. VI, XV, 10: Sept. 29, 1552; Edward VI, *Chronicle*, 144–147, for more intimate comment on some of these matters.
[4] S.P. Dom., Edw. VI, XV, 14; Edward VI, *Chronicle*, 147.

of jurisdiction over cloth prices.[1] The next, dated October 20th, confirmed the appointments at Calais and Guînes as well as the plan to stay the cloth fleet, approved a further reduction in coastal defences in Kent, prepared the way for the final order for the seizure of surplus church goods, and proposed for consideration a number of other administrative and ecclesiastical problems.[2] The last of these memoranda, seeking as they all did to order the agenda of the Council to the King's requirements, was in Cecil's hand and dealt principally with military and diplomatic appointments which should be made, and the consideration of a packet of documents betraying the diplomatic perfidy of France and Scotland which the Regent of the Netherlands had covertly placed in Gresham's hands.[3]

There were, then, clear indications of Edward's gradual assumption of power and of the administrative control of his government for a period of more than a year, with an abrupt relaxing of that power and concern during the last months of his short life. The King's interests, as we have seen, ranged over the whole broad spectrum of government, while he was learning to use the Privy Council, the central agency of administration, as the testing place for his ideas and aspirations. But he was not fully content even with

[1] S.P. Dom., Edw. VI, XV, 40; vide post, 464–466.
[2] This memorandum (S.P. Dom., Edw. VI, XV, 27), partly in Cecil's hand, may be presented in full as typical of the documents which we have had under consideration.

20th October 1552.

[No heading.]

Lord William deputy of Calais.
Sir Andrew Dudley to be called home.
My L. Grey captain of Guînes.
The merchant adventurers' suits.
A general levy of cloths at Antwerp.
Merchants of the staple.
Piracy at Rye and Dover.
The prest to the L. Grey and Sir Anthony Aucher to be repaid to Mr. Peckham.
The discharge of blockhouses in Kent, etc.
Commissioners for the seizure of church goods.
A brief of the dispute at Windsor for the King.

[Miscellaneous notes in Cecil's hand:]
Dyrrick and bills / Tower / Mr. Knoks / B. of Caterb. / The book in the B. of Durh. / Mr. Petr. letter [etc.]

[Scribbled notes, on dorse, also by Cecil:]
Commendations.
Judgements given by due process in the law, as by the commissioners was showed and proved. Yet the French King remembr. the gr. freds. would in some part gratify the King. With Mr. Syd. and Mr. Wytrs ships. And the order taken for the cost.
[3] S.P. Dom., Edw. VI, XV, 51: Nov. 24, 1552; Edward VI, *Chronicle*, 155–156, the King's comments being the last entry save one in his Journal. The Regent's revelation related to the George Paris affair (*vide ante*, 171).

it and its methods of dispatching business, perhaps his most important administrative action being an elaborate plan for its reorganization and reformation. To this last mature concern of the young sovereign we should now turn.

Some thought had been given to the procedures of the Council as early as March, 1550(?) in a most interesting document which almost certainly emanated from Paget, then seeking restoration to favour.[1] The memorandum reflects at once existing procedures in the functioning of the Council and insinuates suggestions for the improvement of its work. The members were piously enjoined 'to love one another as brethren, or dear friends' and to bring before the whole body those who libelled any member. Six of the Council at the least should be in continual attendance at court, of whom the Chancellor, Treasurer, Lord Great Master, Lord Privy Seal, Lord Great Chamberlain, or Lord Chamberlain, must be two and a Secretary the third. The Council should meet on at least three days in each week for the conduct of its business, in sessions extending from 8 a.m. until dinner and then from 2 p.m. to 4 p.m., with a special session on Sunday afternoon for the hearing of private suits. All correspondence should be laid before the body by the Secretary at the usual hour, save that in critical matters he should consult the senior Councillors present, who might wish to convene a special session. All supplications to the King were to be delivered to the Master of Requests, while all offices and benefices within the King's grant should be recommended to him by the majority vote of those present, as determined by secret balloting with black and white balls. The clerks of the Council should keep the records of its deliberations, prepare all money warrants, and digest the substance of correspondence for presentation by the Secretary at the next meeting. The first order of business at a Council meeting should be to sign the minutes, leaving spaces for absent members to sign at a later date. The Secretary's duties were defined as the keeping of letters, minutes of letters to and from the King or Council, and such other 'writings as shall be treated upon by the Council'. And, finally, no Councillor should speak or write for his friends in any matter of justice, 'nor in any other matter above one time, for that the request of a Councillor is in a manner a commandment'.[2]

---

[1] Egerton MS. 2603, ff. 33–34. The document is not in Paget's hand. On the back, in a different and unknown hand, it is endorsed 'The remembrance given to my master by my Lord Paget'. Still another hand has endorsed it: 'Advice to the King's Council.'

[2] *Ibid*. ff. 33–34.

Whether Paget's memorandum was ever seen by Edward is uncertain, but it is unlikely. It was about a year later that the King began to display a lively personal interest in the procedure of the Council, which he thought already overburdened, particularly by matters of finance. This problem the King and his advisers sought to solve by the appointment of commissions, principally from the ranks of the Council itself, but including as well persons with expert knowledge who were drawn from outside. The most important of these, as we have seen, was appointed in March, 1552, to examine the functioning of the revenue courts.[1] Even earlier, on December 30, 1551, a joint commission had been charged with determining and calling in the debts due to the King,[2] while on March 3, 1552, a joint commission had been charged with the execution of the penal laws and the general oversight of the courts.[3] In still another memorandum the King listed thirty-one Councillors and nine others, who were 'now called into commission' to deal with the range of immediate problems just described, while twenty-one named Councillors, senior in prestige and experience, thereby to some degree relieved, were to meet regularly 'to attend to the matters of state' and to consult weekly with the King.[4]

In a related document dated March 9, 1552, we are told that the King regarded the Council as greatly overworked and that the plan for the use of commissions was designed to free the members from the burden of detail. Hence the commissioners were to hear all suits coming to Requests from the King or Council, save for those that should be kept secret. All other suits were to be assigned to the proper court. The ordering of debts owed by the crown was to be allowed by the commissioners, while all complaints arising from violations of the penal laws should be referred by them to the proper court.[5] These arrangements may, then, be said to represent the first stage of Edward's reorganization of the work and structure of the Council.[6]

---

[1] *Vide ante*, 444–447.
[2] Edward VI, *Chronicle*, 102.
[3] *Ibid.* 115.
[4] Cotton MSS., Nero, C, x, f. 79.
[5] Add. MS. 11,406 (Caesar papers), ff. 236–238, 239–240: Mar. 9, 1552.
[6] Abortive scheme for reorganizing Privy Council. The Privy Council consists of the following:

1. Canterbury (Cranmer)	6. Duke of Suffolk
2. Ely (Lord Chancellor) Goodrich	7. Northampton
3. Lord Treasurer (Marquis of Winchester)	8. Shrewsbury
4. Northumberland	9. Earl of Westmorland
5. Lord Privy Seal	10. Earl of Huntingdon

After a period of experimentation extending over some months the King drafted a detailed and certainly impressive paper on the reorganization of the Council which was docketed for consideration on January 15, 1553. Edward's memorandum was entitled, *Certain articles devised and delivered by the King's Majesty for the quicker, better, and more orderly dispatch of causes by His Majesty's Privy Council.*[1] There is preserved an accurate abstract of the document in Sir William Petre's hand, presumably prepared by the Secretary for his own use and consideration.[2]

The scheme of reorganization was designed to limit the functions of the Privy Council to really essential matters of policy, to assign designated days for the consideration of various classes of business,

11. Earl of Pembroke
12. Viscount Hereford
13. Lord Admiral (Clinton)
14. Lord Chamberlain (Lord Darcy)
15. Lord Cobham
16. Lord Rich
17. Comptroller (Sir Richard Cotton)
18. Treasurer (Sir Thomas Cheyney)
19. Vice-chamberlain (Sir John Gates)
20. Secretary Petre
21. Secretary Cecil
22. Sir Philip Hoby
23. Sir Robert Bowes
24. Sir John Gage
25. Sir John Mason
26. Ralph Sadler
27. Sir John Baker

28. Judge Bromley
29. Judge Montague
30. Mr. Wotton
31. Mr. North
Now to be commissioned
32. London (Ridley)
33. Norwich (Thirlby)
34. Sir Thomas Wroth
35. Sir Richard Cotton [see #17]
36. Sir Walter Mildmay
37. Mr. Solicitor [now #38; may refer to recent Sol. Gen., Edw. Griffith]
38. Mr. Gosnold
39. Mr. Cooke
40. Mr. Lucas

These Councillors were to be divided into several committees with various responsibilities:

(1) For suits which were formerly brought to full council: these to be determined, denied, or sent to common law courts by 5, 14, 15, 22, 25, 26, 30, 32, 39, 40 (39–40 being masters of requests)

(2) To punish offences at law, violators of proclamations, to watch over disorders in the shires: 5, 11, 14, 20, 22, 23, 27, 30, 34, 37, 38

(3) Affairs of state, at which the King means to sit once a week: 1, 2, 3, 4, 5, 6, 7, 8, 9, 11, 12, 13, 14, 17, 18, 19, 20, 21, 22, 23, 30

(4) Financial affairs. To look to all the courts, and especially Augmentations, First Fruits, Wards, to see that all revenues due are accounted for each half year, and to consider superfluous charges; general oversight: 14, 23, 33, 34, 35, 36, 38

(5) For the bulwarks, to be in commission in their several jurisdictions: 14, 17, 18

As for the rest in the Council, some return to their homes after parliament rises, others are sick. But all shall be admitted to the Council when they are at hand. These committees to sit separately. [Document breaks off.]

(The lists may be found in Cotton MSS., Nero, C, x, f. 79. Printed texts are in Elton, *Tudor constitution*, 96–97; Nichols, *Remains*, II, 498–502; and Burnet, *Reformation*, v, 117–120. We believe the document may be dated Mar., 1552.)

[1] Edward VI, *Chronicle*, 181–183, following Cotton MSS., Nero, C, x, ff. 86–89.
[2] S.P. Dom., Edw. VI, I, 15. The calendar mistakenly dates this 1547.

to regularize the procedures, and to ensure that matters of high importance could be immediately brought to their attention.[1] Thus all suits and petitions—routine business—were to be considered by the Council on Monday mornings and resolved on Saturday afternoons, 'those day[s], and none others, [to] be assigned to that purpose'. Care was to be taken that such cases should whenever possible be assigned to other courts for trial. It was the King's pleasure and command that on Sundays ('provided that on Sundays they be present at common prayer *added in margin*') the Council attend strictly to the public affairs of the realm and conclude the settlement of matters considered the week before.[2] Reflecting the practice of having the King set the agenda in its principal items, which, as we have seen, had been in practical effect for months, this procedure was systematized by the provision that the King and a Secretary would order the agenda for the coming week on Sunday nights, while on Saturday a list of matters concluded would be submitted to the King for his final approval.[3]

The *Articles* also provided that no Councillor should absent himself from Court for more than two days unless at least eight of the Council were left, and then only with the King's consent. Six members should constitute a quorum for the determination of causes, though if as many as four were present they might 'reason and debate things', postponing the decision until a quorum was present.[4] If weighty matters were docketed for consideration, when 'it shall please the King's Majesty himself to be at the debating of, then warning shall be given, whereby the more may be at the debating of it'. Important and lengthy questions once taken up should if possible be concluded on the same day, and, if that proved impossible, at the least a summary should be prepared of the arguments in order to expedite a later consideration. When 'long, tedious, and busy' problems were under discussion, the King wished such matters to be delegated to a sub-committee, which would in due time bring in a recommendation, with reasons, to the full Council. Finally, the King made it clear that it was his intent that matters of great importance and urgency should be discussed immediately, and that the whole design was to recover an elasticity

---

[1] Emmison, F. G., 'A plan of Edward VI and Secretary Petre for reorganizing the Privy Council's work, *etc.*', in *Bull. Inst. Hist. Research*, XXXI, no. 84 (L., 1958), 205–206. This admirable study has settled numerous questions respecting this important undertaking; on it we have drawn heavily in this analysis.

[2] Edward VI, *Chronicle*, 181.

[3] *Ibid.* 182.

[4] *Ibid.* 182–183.

of action which had been to a degree lost in the mass of detail now considered by his Councillors.[1]

The King's carefully ordered *Articles* were brought in to the Council on the stated date (January 15, 1553), but unfortunately the minutes for this session carry no record of what could not have been in the event more than a preliminary discussion of a matter of the first importance. The Council minutes are inadequate for the whole of the last year of the reign, and for the last six months are irregular, defective, and uninformative. Moreover, as the King's fatal illness set in, a serious deterioration in the normal functioning of the Council inevitably occurred, for the ruling junta was now preoccupied with the problem of the succession. There is accordingly no evidence that the King's plan of reorganization of the work of his Council was ever carefully considered, much less that it was ever brought fully into effect. It remains, therefore, a kind of pathetic monument to a young King of unusual ability and breadth of interest who left this plan of what he wished to accomplish when power came fully into his hands. But this was not to be; during the last weeks of his life, Edward too was almost completely preoccupied with the problem of the succession.

[1] Edward VI, *Chronicle*, 183; S.P. Dom., Edw. VI, I, 15.

XIII

CRISIS IN THE SOCIETY (1550–1553)

1. NORTHUMBERLAND'S FISCAL ADMINISTRATION

We have seen in the earlier volume of this work that Northumberland inherited from the Lord Protector a budget badly out of balance, a shockingly debased coinage, a rapidly mounting inflation, and a considerable and vexing royal debt both at home and abroad.[1] The principal cause for the financial straits in which England found herself was the fact that Henry VIII in the last years of his life had expended upwards of £2,100,000 on his wars with France and Scotland, imposing a heavy strain on resources, which Somerset promptly compounded by his feckless wars with the same powers which consumed something like £1,356,000 in addition to the normally rather heavy outlay for the defence establishment.[2] Only a small proportion of these huge expenditures, in their very nature inflationary, was met by parliamentary grants of taxes, the great bulk of this charge on the economy being met by the sale of monastic lands by Henry VIII and of monastic and chantry lands by Edward VI. During the reign of Edward VI, as we have observed, the Crown sold to meet a portion of its needs crown lands with a capital value of £424,109 15s and then further, and seriously, weakened the resources of the state by free gifts of land to the capital worth of £408,489, a shocking proportion of which was conveyed to the ruling junta or to its supporters amongst the nobility and the upper gentry.[3] The financial difficulties thereby created were all the worse because an essentially weak government never dared fully to lay the King's needs before Parliament, with the result that no more than £299,000 of Edward's total revenues were to be derived from taxation, thereby lending further force to an inflation with which the state was trying to deal principally by fiat.

---

[1] Jordan, *Edward VI*, 397–402.

[2] HMC, *Salisbury MSS.*, I, 99–124: Sept. 29, 1552, for a detailed analysis, including the cost of suppressing the insurrections of 1549.   [3] Jordan, *Edward VI*, 103–124.

The outstanding debt in 1551, when we find a most helpful 'Brief of all the King's Majesty's debts', was actually not overwhelming in amount, but it was vexatious, unmanageable, and largely unfunded because the Crown budget was itself so badly out of balance. The external debt, held mostly by the Fuggers and the Antwerp firm of Schetz, at this time totalled £132,372 10s, all in short-term obligations extending from November 1, 1552, to September 1, 1553. This debt carried an embarrassingly high interest rate, could not be successfully funded, and was the more difficult to discharge because the balance of trade, after the cloth depression beginning in 1551, ran heavily against England. There was also at this date an internal debt in the amount of £108,807 4s 10d, much of which represented arrearages due to various governmental accounts. In total, then, the royal debt in late 1551 amounted to £241,179 14s 10d, or something like 1·5 times the normal revenues of the Crown from all non-parliamentary sources.[1]

We have noted that, as the King came into his early maturity, he was deeply preoccupied with the whole financial policy of the Crown, was seeking to effect savings as well as greater efficiency in the central administrative apparatus of his government and to find resources wherewith his debts, and especially those outstanding in Antwerp, might be paid.[2] At least slight progress was made over a period of about a year when Cecil in October, 1552 drew up still another schedule for his sovereign. The external debts had by this date been somewhat reduced to £110,860 and with a slightly better staggering of the due dates. At the same time, the internal debt stood practically unchanged at £108,826 19s 10d, a heavy proportion of which was accounted for by large debits in the Household and Chamber accounts. Cecil's own recommendation was that the foreign debt be further drawn down by the sale of chantry lands to the value of £12,000, by exploiting the monopoly on the export of lead, and by the sale of superfluous church plate. He likewise toyed at least with the imposition of an export tax on cloth to yield perhaps £40,000, and offered the interesting suggestion that a number of leading London merchants be called before the Council, presumably for their advice.[3] The King had been searching as well for means of freeing himself from the pressures of the Antwerp bankers,

---

[1] Lansdowne MS. 2, #55, f. 122; *A.P.C.*, III, 33: May 18, 1550, for a partial refunding at a slightly earlier date; Edward VI, *Chronicle*, 60, for an extension of a portion of the floating external debt on most embarrassing terms.

[2] *Vide ante*, 421, 444–447.

[3] HMC, *Salisbury MSS.*, I, 99: Oct. 2, 1552; printed in Haynes, *State papers*, I, 126–128.

hoping to gain his discharge by the application of debts due to him (£100,000), by the use of a possible subsidy (£80,000), and by the immediate confiscation and sale of church plate.[1]

It may well be that these careful and wholly orthodox reviews were induced by the costly failure of a bizarre scheme for paying the royal debts, presumably advanced by Sir John York, a friend to Northumberland, a leading London merchant, and the master of the Southwark mint. Most of the payments received from France for the cession of Boulogne had been immediately applied to arrears in the military establishments at Calais, in the North, and in Ireland. But of the second instalment £8000 seems to have been withheld for speculation on the Antwerp exchange under a wild assurance from York that the money could be doubled in value each month.[2] In early October, 1550 York committed himself to this hazardous undertaking, for which he now required £15,000 for the further minting of debased coinage and more especially 'to abase the exchange' in Antwerp.[3] Further light is thrown on this ill-starred venture by a warrant issued to Sir Edmund Peckham to deliver to York 'for the furtherance of certain necessary services . . . in our affairs' all the coin minted from such bullion as York should bring to the mint, presumably for the hazardous venture which he now undertook.[4] The payments were made to York in December, 1550, shortly before he passed overseas to begin his speculations, possibly with the knowledge of the Fuggers who much desired the closing of their English accounts.[5]

What happened in Antwerp remains obscure, but the King plaintively recorded in his *Chronicle* on March 8, 1551, that Sir John York had had a loss of £2000 of silver bullion, as had his associates, Sir Andrew Judd and Sir John Gresham, both London merchants of known probity.[6] Edward declared the loss was due to the treason of certain Englishmen. What happened, it is clear, was that these speculators for the government's account were betrayed to the Flemish authorities when on the point of smuggling out £4000 in bullion, quite illegally. The imperial ambassador reported on April 9 that 'for the last few days no one has talked about anything [else] here . . . and the Council have been much exercised about it'.[7] Since the property seized belonged in fact to the King, diplomatic representations were at first considered, but it was

---

[1] Edward VI, *Chronicle*, 174–175; endorsed by Cecil.
[2] *Ibid.* 48–49.   [3] *Ibid.* 49.
[4] S.P. Dom., Edw. VI, X, 45: Oct. 8, 1550.
[5] HMC, *Salisbury MSS.*, I, 81; *A.P.C.*, III, 219: Feb. 19, 1551.
[6] Edward VI, *Chronicle*, 54.   [7] *Cal. S.P. Span.*, X, 264.

doubtless concluded that the loss should be taken in view of the embarrassing circumstances.[1] A further measure of the financial incompetence of Sir John York is afforded by the fact that about a year later an audit of his mint accounts disclosed heavy arrearages and inaccuracies which were not pardoned until he had paid the large sum of £9532 6s 2d to amend his records.[2]

Meanwhile, the government pursued a fiscal policy quite as irresponsible as the speculative undertaking which it covertly sanctioned for Sir John York. In July, 1549 the mints had resumed coinage on a fairly large scale, employing bullion in hand from the chantry expropriations, a small amount from remaining monastic plate, and small stores of bullion purchased abroad. A heavier teston was now coined, but the silver content remained unchanged. Then on May 11, 1551, the silver content was lowered by half, resulting in a large gain for the mint and making it profitable to re-mint all of the Henrician currency still in circulation. This move was accompanied by an infamous decision ordering a devaluation of the coinage from 12d to 9d, to be effective on July 8, 1551, which had the effect of engendering a panic and, in London particularly, a flight from money into commodities.[3] To the consternation of the Council prices rose abruptly, with especially serious consequences since the harvest of 1551 was scant. In an effort to curb the panic, the government ordered the devaluation to take effect immediately and then a month later devalued the teston still further to 6d. So nervous was the whole economy that the immediate effect was once more inflationary, though in the autumn of 1551 a severe deflation did set in, prices of commodities not in short physical supply dropping abruptly. The next move of a now nervous and 'lunging' government was to announce a wholly new coinage on October 30th, with a shilling 80 grains fine in exchange for two of the base testons, but this proposal had to be withdrawn when a frightened and now completely confused population simply held on to such coins as they had. By December, 1551, so undermined was public confidence that gold coins had literally disappeared into private hands or had been melted down and, most illegally, smuggled out to Continental markets.[4]

---

[1] Edward VI, *Chronicle*, 54. [2] *Cal. Pat. Rolls, Edw. VI*, IV, 301.
[3] S.P. Dom., Edw. VI, XIII, 29. The proclamation, dated June without a day specified, was sent to the sheriffs on July 1st, with the warning that the seal should not be broken until the morning of July 8th.
[4] For the official actions taken, *vide* Hughes and Larkin, *Tudor proclamations*, I, 518–519 (Apr. 30, 1551), 520–522 (May 11, 1551), and the condensed version in HMC, *Salisbury MSS.*, I, 86; S.P. Dom., Edw. VI, XIII, 47, with the clear indication

These manipulations were all the more irresponsible since the King and Council had determined as early as April, 1551 that the coinage must be restored to a purer and more stable standard. The temptation of debasement had, however, been too strong, the King himself noting that it was agreed by the Council 'to make twenty thousand pound weight for necessity somewhat baser, [in order] to get gains [of] £160,000 clear, by which the debt of the realm might be paid, the country defended from any sudden attempt, and the coin amended'.[1] The profits taken were in fact somewhat smaller (£114,500) before the complete collapse of confidence occurred and a monetary crisis triggered by the Council's utterly irresponsible policy. In the course of a long and dreary interval of fiscal madness, the total profits of the Crown had been of the order of £1,270,000, this being in effect a tax laid indirectly on the wealth and substance of the realm by deliberate and continued debasements.[2] The Council had sought to set aside £30,000 as a last reserve for the King from the final debasement, as well as £80,000 held in the Tower, but the profits in the main seeped out to Calais, the Border, and to Ireland, leaving the still substantial foreign debt in a most hazardous position.[3] The desperate English financial plight, by no means unique in the Europe of this generation, was followed with morbid fascination by the diplomatists accredited to London. Thus Scheyfve

---

of Edward's insistence that the coinage be restored and his detailed views on the patterns for the new coinage (Sept. 25, 1551); HMC, *Salisbury MSS.*, I, 88, and Hughes and Larkin, *Tudor proclamations*, I, 525, for the advancement of the date of devaluation; *ibid.* 529–530, and S.P. Dom., Edw. VI, XIII, 33, 34, for the further devaluations; Hughes and Larkin, *Tudor proclamations*, I, 535–536, for the announcement of the new coinage (Oct. 30, 1551); Harl. MS. 7614, f. 263, for an unissued proclamation (Dec. 21, 1551) curbing speculation on the new coinage.

These moves were followed by the King in detail and with a growing conviction that a sound coinage must be restored at any bearable cost to the government. *Vide* Edward VI, *Chronicle*, 58, 63–64, 66, 70, 71, 77, 80, 82 (for experiments in various finenesses at the mint), 83, 84, 86; Ashmole MS. 862, #62, ff. 399–408 (Council's order for minting new coinage, Oct. 5, 1551). The London panic and the flight from coins to goods is attested by a London *Chronicle* (*Two London chronicles* (Camden Misc. XII)), 23; *Grey Friars Chronicle*, 70: Aug. 17, 1551; Stow, *Annales*, 606; *Cal. S.P. Span.*, X, 300 (June ?, 1551), 322–323 (July 6, 1551); Robinson, *Original letters*, II, 727; *A.P.C.*, III, 272: May 10, 1551. As early as Oct. 21, 1550, Mason was reporting to the Council from France that English gold coins had found their way in quantity to that realm (*Cal. S.P. For.*, *Edw. VI*, #248).

The most useful secondary authorities for these developments are Dietz, *English government finance*, 196–197; Feavearyear, Albert, *The pound sterling* (Oxford, 1931; 2nd ed., 1963), 62–71; de Roover, Raymond, *Gresham on foreign exchange, etc.* (Cambridge, Mass., 1949), 56–59.   [1] Edward VI, *Chronicle*, 58.

[2] Challis, C. E., 'The debasement of the coinage, 1542–1551', in *Econ. Hist. Rev.*, ser. 2, XX (1967), 454. The period extends from May, 1544 to July, 1551.

[3] *A.P.C.*, III, 305: June 15, 1551.

reported in late December that the currency had lost half of its former value and spoke of the rumours that the new coinage would bear Northumberland's insignia—rumours which could never be quite dispelled.[1] The more sophisticated Barbaro correctly concluded that Edward's fiscal crisis stemmed from Henry VIII's vast military outlays and from the warlike policy of the early years of Edward's own reign. Further, the King was ill-advised by those who urged that the increasingly debased coinage would remain in England and that he could maintain the monetary relation of his coinage to gold by royal fiat. This policy had occasioned great loss to the entire nation, for the 'standard becomes more and more debased daily, and they have well nigh come to coin false money, plating copper with silver which is soon consumed; so this infamous money has fallen into such disrepute that those who make purchases with it pay fourfold, and thus with good reason the ruin of the country is anticipated'.[2]

The government now at last understood that immediate and drastic action must be taken to restore the coinage—and its exchange value. On March 15, 1552, a payment was made to the Fuggers to prevent a default in Flanders.[3] At the same time severe, but temporary, restrictions were laid on the shipment or exchange of English coins and bullion abroad,[4] while the establishment of a new, and restored, coinage was announced, setting the bullion value of silver coin at approximately the fineness of the coinage prior to 1527 and minting new gold coinage which bore a reasonable and defensible relation of 11·05 to 1 for silver. Drastic economies were ordered by the Council in the military outlays, the household expense was sharply reduced, debts were called in, and Gresham was authorized to launch his successful scheme for the restoration of the exchange. The effect of these measures was sharply deflationary, especially since the amount of coinage in circulation had been greatly reduced, though Northumberland did not dare call in the stores of debased coinage still circulating in the realm; this severe, but ultimately necessary, step awaited the accession of Queen Elizabeth.[5] The Council had sufficient confidence in the announced

---

[1] Cal. S.P. Span., X, 424–425: Dec. 27, 1551.
[2] Cal. S.P. Ven., V, 359; vide also ibid. 551.
[3] A.P.C., III, 505: Mar. 15, 1552.
[4] Schanz, Georg, Englische Handelspolitik gegen Ende des Mittelalters, etc. (2 vols., Leipzig, 1881), II, 647.
[5] The discussion in this paragraph owes much to Oman, C. W. C., 'The Tudors and the currency, 1526–1560', in Trans. Royal Hist. Soc., n.xs.IX (1895), 183–184, and to de Roover, Gresham, 59–60.

policy, put immediately into effect, to free the economy somewhat from the strict exchange regulations which had prevailed for some months past. It now declared that 'the exchange and rechange of money shall be at liberty', subject only to the laws long in effect relating to the export of coin and bullion.[1]

But this moment of confidence passed swiftly, for the monetary crisis came some months after the reforms and retrenchments were introduced and before their bite became fully effective. By May, 1552 the government was having grave difficulties in meeting even its day-to-day obligations. At that time, for example, the Council ordered the payment of £600 due to Morison, on a diplomatic appointment abroad, with the note that if the Treasurer 'have not so much in his hands', it should be advanced by Augmentations. It is clear that the amount could not be raised in either court, and four days later outstanding reliefs were ordered paid to the crown immediately.[2] Again, in July, an obligation of £300 due to the Lieutenant of the Tower embarrassed the government, which was searching for pockets where this relatively small sum might be found.[3] The climax, however, surely came in August, 1552 when payments on warrants were actually suspended on the frail excuse that 'his Highness is presently in progress and [is] resolved not to be troubled with payments until his return'.[4]

It seems evident that in the early spring of 1552, perhaps when the heroic step of restoring the coinage was taken, the Duke of Northumberland, who confessed he had no head for figures, entrusted the management of the financial affairs of the realm principally to Cecil and to Winchester, with expert advice being given by Mildmay and Gresham.[5] Under their leadership the Council at last moved with considerable vigour to restore internal solvency and confidence. The City of London endorsed renewal notes for the debts in Flanders, while the Merchants of the Staple and the Merchant Adventurers advanced funds directly to the government in order to pay debts as they fell due.[6] Earlier proclamations against

---

[1] Harl. MS. 7614, f. 218. The document was not, I think, issued, as intended, as a proclamation.

[2] *A.P.C.*, IV, 41, 46: May 10 and 14, 1552.

[3] *Ibid.* 97–98: July 20, 1552.

[4] *Ibid.* 109: Aug. 8, 1552.

[5] On June 16, 1551, when the coinage of £160,000 was undertaken, the Duke in a long and tangled letter to the Council reveals a complete misunderstanding of the whole fiscal situation. He pleaded 'small experience' in such matters, wherein he 'has found so little pleasure that he would rather be dead then live such a life as this two or three years they have been in' (HMC, *Salisbury MSS.*, I, 86–87).

[6] S.P. Dom., Edw. VI, XV, 13: Oct. 3, 1552; *A.P.C.*, IV, 217: Feb. 12, 1553.

excessive prices for victuals and other necessaries were rigorously enforced and a fairly successful effort was made to quiet rumours regarding further manipulation of the coinage.[1] The Council, fifteen strong, in early June met in the Guildhall with the Lord Mayor, the aldermen, and the Wardens of the Livery Companies, where the Lord Chancellor denounced the high prices prevailing in London, whereas in the remainder of the realm such prices had already fallen by 'half in half'. London's very liberties, he warned, would be in danger unless immediate and strong action were taken, while just a few days later the pillorying of a merchant and a baker for overcharging gave weight to the pressure now being applied by the Council to secure a fall in prices.[2]

These measures were to a degree effective in restoring the economy, but they were not of themselves sufficient. The royal coffers were augmented principally by the sale of crown lands beginning in late 1552 and reaching a peak in the first six months of 1553. In the slightly more than six remaining months of Edward's life the enormous total of £144,259 8s of crown lands was sold, in part to replenish the treasury and in part to strengthen Northumberland's power.[3] And, finally, as Edward had indicated must be done, the reluctant decision was taken to convene the King's second Parliament and to lay the crown's financial requirements before it. After the 'murmuring or grudging' which Northumberland predicted, a single subsidy and two-tenths and fifteenths were voted, whereupon Parliament was almost immediately dissolved. The tax was from the outset very unpopular and thought to be unnecessary. It was in fact never collected, being remitted by one of the first of Queen Mary's official actions.

The reformation of the currency and the enhancement of the liquid royal resources were also, as we have observed, organically related to the external debt and the financing and security of the English cloth trade, which were all intimately inter-connected with the great market and banking centre at Antwerp.[4] Henry VIII had found it necessary to send a royal agent to Antwerp to represent him, his debts, and his interests. Stephen Vaughan served for some time in this capacity, being succeeded by William Dansell, who was somewhat unfairly condemned by the Council as being at once dilatory and indiscreet. He was dismissed from the post in April,

---

[1] For instances, vide A.P.C., III, 483 and 495: Feb. 22 and 28, 1552.
[2] Wriothesley, Chronicle, II, 71.   [3] Jordan, Edward VI, 106, 118.
[4] Vide Jordan, Edward VI, 408-409, for a brief comment on the economic hegemony of Antwerp in this period.

1551.[1] Several London merchants were then consulted, including Sir Thomas Gresham, an eminently successful mercer and the son of still another famous merchant, Sir Richard Gresham. In Gresham's words,

'I was sent for unto the Council, and brought by them before the King's Majesty, to know my opinion . . . what way with least charge his Majesty might grow out of debt. And after my device was declared, the King's Highness and the Council required me to take the room in hand, without my suit or labour for the same'.[2]

Gresham crossed almost at once to Antwerp, where he already knew personally most of the banking firms and where he lodged with Schetz, one of England's creditors. He was unbelievably active during the remainder of the reign, crossing back and forth to England, we are told, at least forty times in these months.[3] His principal concern was in seeing that all royal debts were met by payment or renewal, and, as English credit was gradually restored, to insist that the due dates on obligations might be more evenly staggered and extended. The most difficult period was March 1 to July 27, 1552, when he was obliged to meet due dates for more than £106,000, all of which were met by re-fundings, save for £14,000 (Fl.) which he was able to pay from credit balances accumulated in Flanders.[4] Confronted again with large re-fundings in August, 1552 the Council confessed that it could advance no payments to the Fuggers or to Schetz, 'weighty considerations' having obliged it to use funds accumulated for other necessary purposes, and Gresham was again compelled to negotiate with very little in hand.[5] His success in this extremely difficult task was so brilliant that he now was emboldened to intimate that he must have a free hand in his negotiations and manipulations, with understandable pride pointing out that he had been re-funding at 12 per cent whereas the Emperor could not borrow in Antwerp at 16 per cent.[6] He then outlined a plan whereby, if the Council would secretly advance to him £1200 weekly, he would be able so to manipulate the exchange as to steady and then to improve the worth of sterling, in two years securing the payments of the King's debts abroad, which he stated at £108,000.[7] These requirements the Council accepted with

---

[1] *A.P.C.*, IV, 9, 40: Mar. 31 and May 9, 1552.   [2] Cotton MSS., Otho, E, x, f. 43.
[3] Burgon, J. W., *The life and times of Sir Thomas Gresham, etc.* (2 vols., L., 1839), I, 80.
[4] *A.P.C..*, IV, 27: Apr. 26, 1552.
[5] Cotton MSS., Galba, B, xii, 54, ff. 205-206 (part of the document is charred and unreadable).   [6] Burgon, *Gresham*, I, 92.
[7] Cotton MSS., Galba, B, xii, 54, f. 209: Aug. 21, 1552.

unaccustomed dispatch (September 8th), ordering Peckham to forward the required sum weekly from the sale of crown lands.[1] At about the same date, we would suppose, lists of credits in Antwerp, held by London merchants and totalling £13,236 14s 2d, were being accumulated for Gresham's exchange transactions.[2]

These operations suggest, in fact, the clue to Gresham's amazing success in manipulating the Antwerp exchange rate in such wise as to restore sterling. It was his steady aim to gain and retain ultimate control of the exchange rate by maintaining a shortage of bills on London in the Antwerp market and to exercise a substantial control over cloth shipments from which English credits there were principally derived. His operations were conducted with great discretion, straws being commonly used to mask his forays, particularly when he was remitting to Antwerp.[3] With the payments being forwarded to him by the Council, Gresham usually fed sterling into the market in sums of not more than £200–£300 daily, well below the amounts that would depress the market, in exchange for Flemish pounds wherewith credits for payments on his sovereign's external debts could be gathered. Then in the autumn of 1552, when the cloth fleet was laden, he in effect gained complete control over the shipment, in order to secure strong bargaining powers in the sale of England's principal export, whose value ran from £100,000 to £150,000 p.a. When this fleet, consisting of sixty vessels escorted by two warships and two pinnaces, was about to sail, the exchange was at 16s and Gresham persuaded the Council to permit the accumulation of a credit of £60,000 in Antwerp at 15s, payable in London at a slightly later date.[4] This bold device placed in Gresham's hands a large credit which he then employed to settle the exchange at about 19s, which in April, 1553, aided by the deflationary measures in effect at home, he employed again to drive up, and then to hold, the exchange rate from par to 23s 4d. In May, 1553 Gresham was in a sufficiently strong position, using credits 'warily and circumspectly' accumulated, together with a large cloth credit advanced by the Staple and the Merchant Adventurers, to pay off on the due dates a total of £36,371 on the royal debts.[5]

[1] A.P.C., IV, 123.

[2] Cotton MSS., Galba, B, xii, 46, ff. 186–187. The document bears no date and is in part illegible because of faulty binding.

[3] Buckley, H., 'Sir Thomas Gresham and the foreign exchanges', in Econ. Journal, XXXIV (1924), 595–596.

[4] A.P.C., IV, 145: Oct. 18, 1552; Cal. S.P. Span., X, 569, 581: Oct. 10 and 29, 1552; Stow (Annales, 608) states the amount as about £48,000; Edward VI, Chronicle, 116.

[5] A.P.C., IV, 183,199: Dec. 2 and 31, 1552; ibid. 267: May 5, 1553; HMC, Salisbury MSS., I, 117: Apr. 12, 1553.

It is pleasant to record that by the time of Edward's death the external debt was being liquidated, sterling commanded a substantial premium in the Antwerp market, and the balance of payments had been completely restored with a reverse flow of bullion of more than £100,000 to England. Much of the credit for this amazing achievement remains due to Gresham, who with great skill, steady pertinacity, and a clearly formulated policy had disciplined the entire economy to secure a restitution of English credit and trade. His policy had been hard on the merchant fraternity, including his own uncle, Sir John, who 'doth storm at the matter', having held £4000–£5000 in wools, over the sale of which he had lost control. In a larger, and truer, sense Gresham's great exploit was, of course, made possible by the savage devaluation under way in England during the last two years of the reign. It is also true that Gresham was too enamoured of the formal rate of exchange, not fully realizing that 'movements in the rate of exchange are ultimately the effects rather than the cause of changes in price levels'.[1] But it had been a brilliant and impressive achievement, laying the foundations for the great contribution which he was to make to Elizabethan trade and fiscal policy.

2. THE SWEATING SICKNESS (1551)

The year 1551 might with some justification be called 'the year of disaster' for Edwardian England. The full implication of Northumberland's foreign policy, with its surrender of a strong military position in Scotland and its supine cession of diplomatic hegemony to France, had now become all too clear and was generally disliked. These were the months, too, when the final ruin—the destruction—of Somerset was undertaken by Northumberland, which was severely to weaken Dudley's credit and finally his strength in many segments of national life, for it created a government by faction. This was the year, too, when fiscal policy was at its weakest, when there was a severe loss of confidence not only in the coin of the realm but in the fidelity of those who exercised power in the King's name. So too, in 1551 the government was fearful and nervous as it assessed its position in the realm and as the Privy Council lent an almost obsessive attention to the maintenance of public order. This was the year, as well, when the market for English woollens began suddenly and sharply to contract, with the consequence that the spectre of

---

[1] Buckley, in *Econ. Jour.*, XXXIV (1924), 601; and see de Roover's comments (*Gresham*, 220–223).

urban—of industrial—unemployment first began to rise in England. Even more immediately serious was the fact that the harvest of 1551 was dangerously scant, creating serious problems of actual physical scarcity in many parts of the realm, as well as a vicious rise in prices which the government could not fully control. As if these critical difficulties were not enough, this was the year as well when much of England was swept with a virulent epidemic of that dread and mysterious disease, the sweating sickness.

The realm had thus far during the reign been tolerably free of all epidemics, and especially from the dreaded bubonic-pneumonic plague, which, however, seems to have remained endemic in England during much of the Tudor period.[1] There had been one outbreak of the plague, extending from November, 1547, when it first made its appearance in London, until late 1548 when it subsided abruptly. This epidemic claimed its greatest toll in London, as usual, but seems to have been of at least moderate severity in such places as Cambridge, Wansted, Haddington, and in rural Devonshire, where in one parish the number of deaths in 1546-7 rose to about six times the normal total.[2]

Less well known in England, but quite as feared because of its incredibly high incidence of death, was the sweating sickness which broke out without warning in April, 1551. This disease appears first to have been epidemic in England in 1485, when it may have been spread in London by Henry VII's troops and when it raged with a very high mortality rate for about two months in the late summer and early autumn. There was another much less virulent outbreak in 1507-8, which again began in London and spread out at least as far as Oxford and Chester, followed in a decade (1517) by still another epidemic, centring once more in London. The curious periodicity of the disease continued, when it appeared once more, again in London, in 1528 and seems then to have swept over much of the realm as well as to North Germany, Denmark, the Rhine cities, and Switzerland.[3] Then, after an intermission of almost a

---

[1] Mullett, C. F., *The bubonic plague and England* (Lexington, Ky., 1956), 4–9, 48, points out that 'plague' had become a generic term covering diseases like typhus which contemporaries could not distinguish. The pneumonic plague spread directly from man to man, whereas the bubonic was spread only by the bite of the rat flea.

[2] Creighton, Charles, *A history of epidemics in Britain from A.D. 664, etc.* (2 vols., Cambridge, 1891–1894), I, 303–305; Mullett, *Bubonic plague*, 48; Wriothesley, *Chronicle*, II, 5; *York civic records*, V (Yorks Archaeol. Soc., Records ser. CX), 29–41, where the epidemic broke out in June 1550 and persisted for a year; Stow, *Annales*, 605; Hoskins, W. G., 'Epidemics in English history', in *The Listener*, LXXII (1964), 1044–1046.

[3] Creighton, *Epidemics*, I, 239–243, 251–257; Cox, J. C., *The parish registers of England* (L., 1910), 142–144; Hecker, J. F. C., *The epidemics of the Middle Ages* (L., 1844), 182, 184.

quarter of a century, the epidemic—the Great Sweat—appeared once more in its most destructive and widespread visitation which, strangely enough, seems to mark the disappearance of the disease in epidemic form in England and probably in Europe generally.

The course of the disease in 1551 was carefully and lengthily described by Dr John Caius, in his *A Boke or Counseill*, which, while marred by vanity and a strangely garrulous quality, none the less gives us an accurate clinical description of the course of the disease in patients.[1] Caius, and other writers on the disease, tell us that its onset came usually without warning at night. The first stages were marked by chills and tremors, followed by a very high fever, great weakness, a severe headache, often accompanied by heart pains, vomiting, and stupor. The heavy sweating appeared shortly after the onset and death came with frightening speed. A most eminent modern medical authority, in reviewing the symptoms, so often described by contemporaries, concluded that the disease was not typhus. The rapidity of the onset and the speed with which death came reminded him of infantile paralysis, meningitis, and influenza, though, as to the last, there remains no evidence of secondary pneumonia attacking those who survived. Dr Zinsser concluded that it must have been caused by an unknown filterable virus, which, long present on the Continent in a mild form, on passing into England in 1485 took on epidemic characteristics in a population which possessed no acquired immunity. It was his final judgement that the disease 'remains an entirely individual condition which could not—were it to reappear at present—be properly classified with any of the known infectious diseases'.[2]

It seems reasonably well established that the Great Sweat of 1551 broke out in Shrewsbury in late March,[3] had spread to London by

[1] John Caius (1510–1573), a native of Norwich, was educated at Gonville Hall, Cambridge. He repaired to Padua in 1539 where he took his degree in medicine in 1541. On his return to England in 1544 he gave lectures in anatomy in London and as a most successful practitioner rapidly gained a considerable fortune, which was ultimately to be employed for the re-founding of Gonville Hall.

Caius tells us, apologetically, that he has written this present work in English because of its topical importance for the nation, though he confessed his own preference for Latin and Greek. Caius traced the history as well as the symptoms of the disease, suggesting, wrongly, that it had now become endemic.

[2] Zinnser, Hans, *Rats, lice and history* (Boston, 1935), 99–100. Mullett (*Bubonic plague*, 56) comments on its resemblance to influenza, but agrees that it was probably not this disease. Creighton (*Epidemics*, I, 280) offers no final judgement, but came forward with a strange theory of 'soil poison'.

[3] Holinshed (*Chronicles*, III, 1031) says it began in April; Owen, Hugh, and J. B. Blakeway (*A history of Shrewsbury* (2 vols., L., 1825), I, 345) set the date as in the spring of 1551; Caius sets the date in April (*A boke, or counseill against the . . . sweatyng sickness* ([L.], 1552), f. 10ᵛ).

July 9th and to the North of England by September. The onset in London was very swift, with perhaps as many as one hundred reported deaths on July 10th, 120 on the next day, and reaching its 'most vehement' stage on July 12th. The number who died remains uncertain, but Stow does tell us that 960 died in London in the course of the first few days of the epidemic.[1] Caius confirmed the statement of Stow that people who were perfectly well one day were often dead the next day, while the heavy incidence of mortality was amongst men in the age bracket of thirty to forty years. We are told, as well, that 'sleeping in the beginning was present death, for if they were suffered to sleep but half a quarter of an hour, they never spake after, nor had any knowledge, but when they wakened fell into [the] pangs of death'.[2] The Court was quickly removed from Westminster to Hampton Court on July 10th, while the apprehension of the whole nation was revealed in a letter from the King and Council to the Bishops on July 18th instructing them to exhort all people to a 'diligent attendance at common prayer' to avert the displeasure of Almighty God who had visited the realm with this 'extreme plague of sudden death'.[3] Machyn observed that the disease in London seemed to strike merchants and the rich with particular severity,[4] while such prominent men, in and about the Court, as Lord Cromwell, Lord Powis, Sir John Luttrell, Sir Thomas Speke, and Sir John Wallop, that gifted soldier, all succumbed to it.[5] The fear and dread in London are perfectly documented by the letter of the merchant Otwell Johnson to his brother John, then in Bruges, saying there were already stricken houses in his parish of St Peter and Bartholomew. Then on July 10th Otwell himself died, his brother-in-law reporting that, coming home from business at seven, 'he went to his bed; and suddenly was in so extreme pain that within four or five hours we could get no word of him, and so continued in pain till three o'clock' when death took him.[6] The Venetian envoy, Soranzo, set the mortality in London at the certainly greatly exaggerated total of 5000, noting also the curious fact, confirmed from other sources, that children under the age of ten

---

[1] Stow, *Annales*, 605; Strype, *Memorials*, II, i, 491; Holinshed, *Chronicles*, III, 1031.
[2] *Ibid.* Holinshed, *Chronicles*, III, 1031; *Two London chronicles* (Camden Misc. XII), 24; Harl. MS. 353, f. 107, gives the death toll in London as 761 for July 9–16.
[3] S.P. Dom., Edw. VI, XIII, 30; Edward VI, *Chronicle*, 71. The King records on July 9th that the London sweat was 'more vehement than the old sweat' (of 1528). On July 11th he noted that he had gone to Hampton with very few of his household, one of his gentlemen and one of his grooms having contracted the disease at Westminster.
[4] Machyn, *Diary*, 7.   [5] Strype, *Memorials*, II, i, 493–494.
[6] As quoted in Winchester, *Tudor family*, 269–270.

seemed quite immune. There were, he added, twenty dreadful days while the epidemic raged, when all shops were closed, normal business simply stopped, and 'nothing [was] attended to, but the preservation of life'.[1]

The spread of the disease over much of England cannot be fully charted, but it does seem to have moved out fan-wise from Shrewsbury and then northwards up the east coast from London. It was certainly epidemic in Devonshire where in one parish (Uffculme) twenty-seven of the thirty-eight burials for the entire year were recorded during the first eleven days of August.[2] Cambridge was stricken by the epidemic as early as July 16th, while in Ulverston, Lancs, there were forty-two burials registered, whereas in normal circumstances only about one burial would have been recorded.[3] Cases were reported in Derbyshire,[4] while in August the sweat was certainly present in such scattered areas as Wales and the towns of Ludlow, Coventry, Oxford, and Loughborough. The last vicious flare of the disease was in York, where in October it reached epidemic proportions. Here strict quarantine regulations were at once imposed, begging prohibited, and ingress into the city carefully scrutinized.[5]

It would be quite bootless to undertake an estimate of the total number of lives claimed by this virulent and widespread epidemic; there were in 1551 too few parish records kept, and even those that were maintained, and which survive, often suggest that entries were forgotten or lumped together in the understandable hysteria of the moment. One may be permitted the fairly well supported guess that for London the death toll ran to not much under 2000, or perhaps 2·5 per cent of the total population of the City. But the epidemic was particularly severe in London and we know as well that there were large areas of the realm which seem to have remained almost wholly unaffected. The only contemporary estimate we have was that of the imperial ambassador who thought that as many as 50,000 had died in the whole realm, or something like 1·7 per cent of the entire population.[6] This figure may not be far from the mark. Scheyfve also correctly emphasized that the principal loss was in men in their prime of life, with the consequence that the qualitative loss may have affected the economy and society for some years to come.

[1] *Cal. S.P. Ven.*, V, 541–542.
[2] Lysons, Daniel and Samuel, *Magna Britannia, etc.*, VI, pt. ii (L., 1822), 539.
[3] Cox, *Parish registers*, 144.
[4] VCH, *Derbyshire*, II, 183 (I am assuming that the year given should be 1551 rather than 1550).   [5] *York civic records*, V (Yorks Archaeol. Soc., Records ser., CX), 68.
[6] *Cal. S.P. Span.*, X, 347: Aug. 25, 1551.

The qualitative loss to England was great indeed if one reflects on the deaths of the young Duke of Suffolk, Henry Brandon, and his brother Charles, who was just a year younger. These boys, very near the King in age and precocity, were the sons of Charles Brandon, who, following the death of Mary Tudor, his wife and the sister of Henry VIII, had married Katherine Willoughby, daughter of Lord Willoughby and Mary de Salinas, a lady-in-waiting to Katherine of Aragon. This remarkable woman, who has often found a place in our pages,[1] had seen to it that these handsome, vigorous, and brilliant boys enjoyed a thorough humanistic education under the tutelage of Thomas Wilson, an intellectual prodigy and a friend to both Cheke and Ascham. The elder son, who was for two intervals also a fellow student and companion to the King at Court, joined his brother as a student at Cambridge in the autumn of 1549. When cases of sweating sickness were observed in Cambridge, the anxious mother arranged for the removal of the boys to Buckden, the country seat of the Bishop of Lincoln, through the intervention of their then tutor, the famous Walter Haddon, Professor of Civil Law and University Orator. There the two boys died within a few hours of each other on July 14th, their mother arriving after the first son had died. Of them Wilson was to say in his *Art of Rhetoric*, 'Their towardness was such, and their gifts so great, that I know none which love learning, but hath sorrowed the lack of their being.'[2] Their normally buoyant mother withdrew completely for weeks, stricken with what seemed inconsolable grief, it being a full two months before she wrote even to her old and close friend, William Cecil), expressing her resignation at 'this most sharp and bitter' trial under which God had placed her.[3] But there was loss for England as well as for Katherine Willoughby, as witness the innumerable contemporary lamentations in the months to come. A great hope for the realm had been extinguished, something bright and clear and fine had been lost to England.

3. EFFORTS TO CONTROL AND ENHANCE THE ECONOMY

We sought in the first volume of this study to treat in some detail the related problems of the cloth trade, the great political and moral

---

[1] *Vide ante*, 72, 73, and Jordan, *Edward VI*, 130, 149, 370.

[2] Wilson, Sir Thomas, *The arte of rhetorique*, etc. (L., 1553), b iii[v].

[3] S.P. Dom., Edw. VI, XIII, 54; Goff, Lady Cecilie, *A woman of the Tudor age* (L., [1930]), 193–194, 201; Strype, *Memorials*, II, i, 491–492. It will be recalled that the Marquis of Dorset, who had married a half-sister of these boys, was after a short season created Duke of Suffolk (in the Grey line).

crisis which arose as a consequence of sheep-farming and enclosures, whether real or imagined, and the effect of inflation on the economy.[1] These were undoubtedly the principal, as they were the most controversial, of the economic problems of the age, and they were surely those which affected most directly the great majority of the King's subjects. We wish now to deal at some length with the efforts of the government to stabilize the economy by the control of prices and the distribution of necessaries, as it sought awkwardly but tenaciously to temper the consequences of inflation and of poor harvests. Then we shall turn to the considerable number of efforts being made to enlarge the economy by freeing the nation from its deeply rooted dependence upon wool and woollen cloth, an effort all the more important, as we now see, because of the long decline of the cloth trade which set in in 1551.

All Tudor governments intervened with as much regulatory power as they could muster when for whatever cause prices of the bread grains and other necessaries rose so far or so steeply as to condemn the mass of landless men, urban and rural, to privation if not to actual malnutrition. But no Tudor government was quite as sensitive to the dangers and hardships occasioned by spiralling victual prices as was the Edwardian. It was in the essentials a relatively unstable government, it had been obliged to repress two serious insurrections in 1549, and it was to a considerable degree culpable because of its own inflationary monetary policy. Then, to compound its difficulties, the government of the Duke of Northumberland had to reckon with serious and nationwide shortages of foodstuffs because the harvest of 1549 was at once light and over wide areas not fully gathered because of the risings, that of 1550 below average yield, and again in 1551 most inadequate—the effects in each case, of course, carrying over well into the spring of the following year. It was accordingly most sensitive to petitions, several of which bear clear traces of the thought of the Commonwealth Party, such as one in 1550 which purported to set out the 'lamentable complaint of the poor' in numerous counties, of the high prices of all necessaries, which was linked with the old complaints against rack-renting and sheep-farming.[2] The government was gravely concerned too by the overweening position of London in the economy and by the concentration of sophisticated wealth and economic power there. The corn

---

[1] Jordan, *Edward VI*, 398–438. I regret that *The agrarian history of England and Wales*, vol. IV: *1500–1640* (ed. by Joan Thirsk, Cambridge, 1967) was not available to me before my draft was completed. Though not altering substantially my own conclusions, the work rests on research at once deeper and more detailed than mine.

[2] HMC, *Salisbury MSS.*, I, 82.

trade had long been dominated by travelling 'badgers' who bought in the country and sold to London wholesalers, brewers, and bakers, who were bound to them by heavy credit advances. There was, in fact, some substance in the view of the Council that these men possessed the means for establishing control of supplies in London as well as in the grain-producing counties, and hence that they exerted considerable control over prices.[1] We shall present at least a modest sampling of the efforts, which were nearly continuous from 1550 onwards, of the Council to hold in check the sharp rise in prices induced by debasement, inflation, and poor harvests.[2]

As early as September 13, 1550, while the King was pausing at Nonsuch, the Council was carefully considering the text of a proclamation for 'bringing forth of grain', which it determined to send in partial draft to Northumberland for his review and approval.[3] Grains had long been exported by 'diverse evil natured people, neither minding the due observation of good laws, neither any preserving of [a] natural society, within their own country'. This document, composed with great care and published on September 24th, laid an absolute prohibition on the export of all grains, leather, salt, hides, and other necessaries so long as prices remained above stated levels, as for example 6s 8d per quarter for wheat and 5s for rye. In addition, all persons were flatly prohibited from buying or selling food grains and flour save for their household uses, with the exception of bakers and brewers who might carry in their inventory not more than 10 quarters of any listed grain. Heavy penalties were prescribed for violations, while exacting and thorough preparations were made for giving effect to the proclamation.[4] The justices of the peace were to divide each county into districts and to search out illegal stores of grain, to put 'to the verdict of honest men' claims regarding household requirements, and to seize and place on the legal market any surpluses found. To make enforcement all the tighter, similar instructions were sent to the Lords Lieutenant in the several counties, as well as to other 'special persons'.[5] These unusually elaborate administrative arrangements were then

[1] VCH, *Herts*, IV, 208, citing Lansdowne MS. 32, ff. 104, 107.
[2] If the average price of *All Arable Crops* be given an index value of 164 for 1548, the price index has been reckoned to be as follows for the remainder of the reign: 1549 = 236; 1550 = 329; 1551 = 293; 1552 = 285; 1553 = 234. The price index for *All Agricultural Products* seems to show much the same trend for these years. (*The agrarian history of England and Wales*, vol. IV: *1500–1640*, ed. by Joan Thirsk (Cambridge, 1967), 818, 848 (Tables I and VI).)
[3] *A.P.C.*, III, 125.
[4] Hughes and Larkin, *Tudor proclamations*, I, 499–503; Edward VI, *Chronicle*, 46–47.
[5] S.P. Dom., Edw. VI, X, 40, 41, 42, 43: Oct. 2, 1550.

supplemented by special instructions forwarded individually to the county notables and signed by the Council itself.[1] Care was taken as well to make certain that brewers were providing beer and ale at legal prices, rather than hoarding grain and malt. Thus even the Mayor of Winchester was deprived of his licence as a brewer for 'ungentle and unnatural behaviour' in refusing to brew, while the brewers of Southampton were warned that their licences would be revoked for similar offences.[2] The Council also lent its authority to informal commissions dispatched from London in search of stores of grain that might be forced onto the market, while the City government and the merchant leaders were bringing in heavy imports of foodstuffs from the Baltic region.[3]

So serious was the situation that less than a month later another proclamation was promulgated, setting out in detail the maximum allowable prices for all essential foodstuffs of a prescribed quality, with also a recital of the same powers, penalties, and means of enforcement laid down in the earlier document.[4] Further letters to all local authorities were also dispatched by the Council, requiring full and immediate obedience to the successive proclamations and pointing out that grain was in fact not moving into the markets of the realm.[5] Thus the Lords Lieutenant and the Presidents of the Council of the North and of Wales were again enjoined to lend full support to the proclamations in force governing the prices of victuals. They were to be assisted by 'certain special men' in the several counties.[6] These 'special men', who were directly addressed, were declared special commissioners to compel the delivery of grain and other foodstuffs for the market, for the King would no longer suffer the 'lewd behaviour' of those who violated his proclamations. Those holding illegal stores of foodstuffs, who refused to heed the King's command, should suffer expropriation and should be sent before the Council under charges of contempt, even if special force need be employed.[7] That the Council was applying all possible pressure is demonstrated in a letter to them from Lord de la Warr and Edward Shelley in Sussex, who pleaded inability to carry out their orders immediately in their country, where some justices of the peace were sick and some in London. They had, however, viewed the barns in the area of their jurisdiction, finding little surplus grain save for

---

[1] HMC, *Salisbury MSS.*, I, 81.   [2] VCH, *Hants*, V, 473–474.
[3] Wriothesley, *Chronicle*, II, 45.
[4] Edward VI, *Chronicle*, 49; Hughes and Larkin, *Tudor proclamations*, I, 504–509: Oct. 20, 1550.   [5] *Ibid.* 49–50.
[6] S.P. Dom., Edw. VI, XI, 6: Nov. 17, 1550.
[7] *Ibid.* 5: Nov. 17, 1550; the draft is heavily revised.

250 quarters of wheat which would be shipped immediately.[1] And from Boston (Lincs) came the report that a diligent search by the justices of Holland, next the town, disclosed no surplus of grain whatsoever. In consequence they had no other choice than to petition the Council for permission to buy desperately needed grain in other shires.[2]

Grains, the Council unhappily concluded, on the advice of responsible justices of the peace, were simply being withheld from the market, and this intelligence, joined with numerous complaints from leading persons in the market-towns, compelled the Council to rescind the order requiring the sale of grain at moderate prices as prescribed.[3] Prices immediately vaulted, so that in London by Easter, 1551 wheat was selling at 26s 8d the quarter, as compared with 13s 4d established in the proclamation of October 20, 1550. But at least grain was now flowing into the markets, and the crisis was passed when during Easter week a fleet of grain ships anchored, with wheat and rye from Holland and Brittany. The London authorities broke the inflationary spiral by setting the price of wheat at 22s the quarter.[4]

But, if the problem of the physical supply of the bread grains had been largely resolved, that of prices had most certainly not. The formidable John Hooper wrote to Cecil in April, 1551 demanding that action be taken to curb and then to lower prices. Sheep had replaced cattle, and now were held for wool and not as meat for hungry men. 'The prices of things be here [in Gloucestershire] as I tell you, the number of people be great; their little cottages and poor livings decay daily . . . [and] ye know what a grievous extreme, yea, in a manner unruly, evil hunger is.'[5] But matters were shortly to be worsened, rather than bettered, when in May the coinage was further debased, with an immediate and sharp rise in prices, especially in London.[6] The Council undertook the browbeating of the Mayor and his brethren; Northumberland threatened to hang butchers and spoke darkly of the foreigners in London; but prices could not be substantially reduced until the restoration of the coinage was accomplished.[7] The Council chose to blame regraters, engrossers, and speculators generally for the 'great and excessive prices' of foods and necessaries, prescribing by proclamation severe

[1] S.P. Dom., Edw. VI, XI. 10: Nov. 19, 1550.
[2] Ibid. 11: Nov. 19, 1550.
[3] Ibid. 15: Dec. 6, 1550; Edward VI, Chronicle, 50.
[4] Wriothesley, Chronicle, II, 47.   [5] Tytler, England, I, 364-367.
[6] Vide ante, 459.   [7] Wriothesley, Chronicle, II, 47-48.

penalties and adding livestock, butter, and cheese, to the list of commodities which might not be purchased for re-sale.[1] Then in September (1551), as ill news came in to the Council respecting the harvest, a proclamation was issued re-affixing the price scales already established for victuals, and rather lamely explaining that the King had sought with his new coinage to chasten 'the excessive prices of all things, [which] of good congruence should consequently fall and abate as by natural reason and equity necessarily it ought and should'. Once more evil men, speculators, and regraters were blamed, heavy penalties were invoked, and even justices of the peace were warned that their neglect would be ferreted out and punished by special commissions.[2] And a few months later pressure was once more applied to the government of the City, under threat to the liberties of London, requiring them to enforce rigidly the laws against excessive prices, which were declared now to be falling in the realm generally.[3]

The Council likewise acted with as much dispatch and energy as possible to control the supply of foodstuffs and to relieve pockets of local shortage when bread grains could be found. Thus in early February, 1550 instructions were issued to the sheriffs and justices in Bristol and Tewkesbury to lend their assistance in moving grain supplies to relieve the serious scarcity in the area.[4] Another proclamation was issued in May prohibiting the export of the bread grains and other listed foodstuffs,[5] strengthened in July by a harshly worded proclamation which stated that victuals were at once dear and in very scarce supply. Hence the export of all foodstuffs, as well as numerous other commodities, was absolutely prohibited under pain of loss of ship, loss of cargo, and fine and imprisonment.[6] The 'great scarcity of victuals and especially of flesh' was presented as the cause for a strict warning to abstain from the eating of all meat during Lent in 1551,[7] which was not only renewed in 1553, but was re-enforced by calling on the local authorities 'to devise some weekly search' for violations.[8] Encouragement, and permission, was given for the importation of still more grain, Thomas Watson, a victualler, being licensed in January, 1551 to bring in 12,000 quarters of rye

---

[1] Hughes and Larkin, *Tudor proclamations*, I, 526–527: July 24, 1551; Edward VI, *Chronicle*, 73.

[2] *Ibid.* 530–533; *A.P.C.*, III, 366; Edward VI, *Chronicle*, 81.

[3] *A.P.C.*, IV, 51 May 18, 1552.

[4] *Ibid.* II, 378: Feb. 2, 1550.

[5] Hughes and Larkin, *Tudor proclamations*, I, 490–491: May 7, 1550.

[6] *Ibid.* 495–496: July 3, 1550.   [7] *Ibid.* 510–512: Mar. 9, 1551.

[8] *Ibid.* 539–541: Feb. 14, 1553.

and 4000 of wheat from the Baltic to meet the needs of London and the South of England, which was probably included in the King's estimate that permission had been given for the purchase of 40,000 quarters from Denmark.[1] So too, the Council acted with a full sense of responsibility when it ordered 'sundry vessels' laden with herring and awaiting clearance at Rye, to proceed to London and there to discharge their whole cargo in order to meet the needs of the City.[2]

The chronic fiscal and economic problems which absorbed—and endangered—England during the second half of the reign evoked a considerable body of economic thought and discussion quite different in temper from the Commonwealth literature which had enlivened the thought of the Protectorship. One may say that the economic discussions of the first half of the reign were essentially moral and social,[3] those of the second half pragmatic and intensely secular in their concern. We should now turn to a brief analysis of contemporary thought in these later years, limiting ourselves to documents which we know found their way to the Council Board. The first two examples, both stemming directly from London merchant thought, are treatises which sought to grapple with the crisis in the coinage.

In early 1551 William Lane, a London merchant, wrote to Cecil because he thought, after conversations with 'Mr Yorke of the mint', that the new currency being coined was set at a rate much too dear for its intrinsic bullion worth. He submitted that the Council must face the harsh reality that it was the foreign exchange which determined the trading value of coinage, as exhibited by the fact that in the past few days the value of sterling had declined by about 7 per cent, even in anticipation of the new coinage. He recalled that on the occasion of the preceding debasement at least £100,000 in gold flowed out of England in a very short season. The Council was, then, continuing with a ruinous policy. He warned that further debasement, already under way, would lead to a still greater export of cloth, which in turn would evoke more cloth, from more wool, from more pastures, with a consequent calamitous decay of tillage and a 'scarcity of corn and the people unwrought'. He also warned that the inflation proceeding in England had led to a vast increase in imports, unsustained by a broad variety of exports, which had further drained out bullion. The debasement of the currency must, then, be halted, for it is nothing else than 'the private gain in

---

[1] *A.P.C.*, III, 202: Jan. 29, 1551; Edward VI, *Chronicle*, 52.
[2] *A.P.C.*, IV, 206–207, 217–218: Jan. 22 and Feb. 12, 1553.
[3] Jordan, *Edward VI*, 416–438.

coining to other men, supposed as to the King'. And, finally, and categorically, he demanded that base money be devalued to its true bullion value so confidence could be restored and an equilibrium of trade regained.[1]

A very different, indeed, an opposing, view was laid before the Council, probably in late 1551, by cloth merchants who had felt the sting of contemporary criticism and suspicion.[2] With somewhat muddy reasoning the petitioners argued that cloth merchants were being blamed for the fact that prices had not fallen after a measure of devaluation had been undertaken. They maintained that the economy rested ultimately on the price of raw wool, for when the clothier 'buys good cheap wool, he drapeth good cheap cloth to the merchant, who brings good cheap commodities into the realm'. The export difficulties have arisen from the fact that wool in the past six years has increased in price three times over, whereas in Flanders cloth sold at no more than it did twenty years previously. They blamed speculators and regraters who have driven up the price of wool, to the ruin of merchants who cannot control their selling prices abroad. Hence the solution urged was a tighter control over wool prices, the outlawing of false and imperfect cloth, and the recovery of a dominant position in a market in which English cloth was being driven out by a cheaper cloth made from Spanish wools. They pointed out as well that the cloth industry was the principal employer for the whole nation and its health vital to the security and prosperity of the state. They wished no restoration of the coinage in England, but did require that an artificial and harmful inflation in the price of wool be corrected by governmental action.

Similar lamentations were laid before the government by the Staplers, who in March, 1551 appealed for the restoration of their ancient liberty to ship wool abroad freely, but were informed that, as in the preceding year, the Staple would be controlled as an aspect of governmental policy.[3] The Staplers protested that there had been a ruinous decay in trade, mainly due 'to the great extremity that has of late been put on this fellowship'. Many of their fraternity were declared to be on the point of abandoning the trade in which there was simply no possibility of gain. The weakness in English exports of wool had created a kind of economic vacuum into which

---

[1] S.P. Dom., Edw. VI, XIII, 3: Jan. 18, 1551; reprinted in Tawney and Power, *Tudor economic documents*, II, 182–186.

[2] S.P. Dom., Edw. VI, XV, 4, #29; abstracted in *Cal. S.P. Dom.*, Edw. VI, VI, 420–421 (Addenda IV: 29). The document is undated, but internal evidence would place it between July, 1551 and Mar., 1552. One page is torn and the sense is not wholly clear.

[3] *A.P.C.*, III, 241: Mar. 25, 1551.

Spanish wools had moved. This competition, they urged, should be met by requiring all low-priced wools to be marketed by the Calais Staple, which could then compete successfully with the Spanish exports, particularly since 'the Spanish [wool] fleet will many times by long voyage and contrary winds disappoint the drapers'.[1]

Self-serving as these treatises were, they do exhibit a considerable vigour of thought and an amazing independence in the freedom with which they brought governmental policy under criticism. The thought of these men was often muddy, sometimes ill-argued, and certainly unsophisticated, but they were attempting to grapple with problems which were all but overwhelming the government itself. Far more cautious and decorous was a memorandum, evidently presenting the views of the Merchant Adventurers, which reveals that the King's stubborn, and precocious, wish to found a free mart in England, to rival if not to replace Antwerp,[2] had become rather widely known and was causing apprehension in affected quarters. The argument, cautiously advanced, was that whether the mart be established in London or in Calais, it would unsettle the entire mechanism of English trade. Among other ill effects, it was intimated, English shipping would suffer, the strict regulations on cloth quality would vanish, with a consequent weakening of English industry and the decay of all other ports aside from the favoured one. At the same time, if the plan should be carried forward, care must be taken to limit the privilege of trade to responsible merchants, lest 'every man of handicraft . . . should be a buyer and seller, [and] this thing should utterly decay and no merchants of substance would serve the King with their bodies and goods in time of need'. Hence the right to sell English wares to foreigners or to buy foreign goods in the proposed mart should be strictly limited to the Merchant Adventurers, whose freedom should be granted only to those who had served an apprenticeship of at least eight years. Then, as an important afterthought, the writer reminded the Council that the Antwerp market functioned only because great stores of credit financed its trade. This England too must provide, and foreigners must be 'trusted of great sums of money, and leave the realm with large quantities of our goods'.[3] This last was a chilling thought indeed. Though the Antwerp market was weakening and though the Emperor was laying heavy and unusual imposts on it, the fact was

---

[1] S.P. Dom., Edw. VI, XIII, 81; and cf. *ibid*. 82.

[2] *Vide ante*, 412. Edward, on balance, favoured Southampton for the mart.

[3] S.P. Dom., Edw. VI, XV, 4, #28 (*c*. 1552), and abstracted in *Cal. S.P. Dom.*, *Edw. VI*, VI, 420 (Addenda IV: 28).

that England could not as yet provide either the skills or the vast capital required for the financing of a considerable proportion of all international trade. Edward had raised no more than a vision of a future which still lay more than a century away.

The Merchant Adventurers also argued with considerable cogency that to funnel trade into one great port would further weaken shipping and commerce to the out-ports, already suffering from the over-arching commercial ascendancy of London and from the withering of the fisheries. Thus the inimitable Thomas Burnaby reminded Cecil that there were more sailors in one French town than there were in England from Land's End to the Mount.[1] Towns like Dover, Sandwich, Hythe, and Winchelsea have seen their shipping disappear, while he had himself seen thirty-seven timber ships sail from Rye with not an Englishman aboard. Much of this decay he blamed, not very persuasively, on the London Livery Companies, which spend their fortunes on 'great feasts' and ceremony. Every London company should maintain at least one ship for its trading. Even of London he says, 'I think there is never a city in Christendom, having the occupying that this city hath, that is so slenderly provided of ships'.[2]

The decline of the out-ports was real indeed, and it was a matter to which Cecil seems to have lent careful, if ineffective, attention. He endorsed a memorandum, at an uncertain date, which reckoned that as recently as 1529 at least 140 fishing boats were off Iceland, where now there were 43; 80 were off Scotland, where now there were but 10; and 220 in the North Sea where now only 80 fished. The causes were admittedly complex, but among them surely were the failure to observe the fish days, the competition of the Dutch, and the fact that many towns had priced fish too low.[3] Cecil himself seems to have begun a survey of the decayed port towns of the kingdom, though his detailed observations are limited largely to the Norfolk coast. To take but a few instances, King's Lynn, long maintained by Iceland and North Sea fishing, is now in decay: where once there were 300 mariners, there are now only twenty to thirty at the most. So too, from Burnham, where once '6 tall ships' fished to Iceland and there were 16 North Sea fishing craft, now 'no ships go to sea'. In two decades the fleet from Yarmouth had declined by two-thirds, and those left were unemployed. And so the dreary recital went on of a coast which for a variety of not fully understood

[1] Vide ante, 170.
[2] Lansdowne MS. 2, #85, ff. 187–191: Oct. 1, 1552.
[3] Cal. S.P. Dom., Edw. VI, VI, 426 (Addenda IV: 56).

reasons had lost its wealth and which no longer provided the King with ships and the men to sail them.[1]

The most impressive of the numerous memoranda seeking to explain and resolve the problems of the English society in the later years of Edward's reign was an anonymous treatise entitled, 'What is the chiefest cause that everything is now so dear within the realm and what the best remedy is therefor.'[2] The author boldly asserted that neither the alterations of the coinage nor its debasement explain the dearth of commodities in the realm, which is at bottom occasioned by the weakness of the economy. Money has value and meaning within the realm for which it is coined, and a sound economy is based on an exchange of ware for ware, not coins for ware. England's economic distress has arisen principally from its dependence upon wool and cloth exports which have been weak because they are commodities greatly overpriced. So too, the present dearth has been attributed to rack-renting, when actually there have never been as many freeholders as now, when the King has not raised the rents on crown lands, and when many of the old abbey leases have not been 'improved'.

The writer then advanced his own analysis of the causes of an inflation compounded by dearth. He was persuaded that the principal cause was to be found in the inordinate rise in the prices of commodities like wool, cloth, lead, and tin which have in effect forced England out of the European market for needed commodities and have obliged the merchants to flood the realm with relatively expensive luxuries. 'No doubt, if men were wise and abstained from superfluous things brought from overseas . . . their prices would soon fall.' This, the author contended, could actually be accomplished in respect to superfluous apparel if the King and Council 'would use our own commodities in their apparel', an example which would do' more good than twenty laws. England's

[1] S.P. Dom., Edw. VI, XV, 4, #28, f. 57.

[2] *Ibid.* f. 66. The manuscript may be dated as somewhat later than April 15, 1552, since it mentions bills considered in the final session of Edward's first Parliament, dissolved on that date. The hand is tantalizingly similar to that in Hales' known works and there are noticeable similarities to S.P. Dom., Edw. VI, V, 20 (1548), sometimes known as *The causes of the unreal dearth of provisions*, treated with the *corpus* of Hales's thought in the first volume of this study (pp. 395–397, 417–424, 431–432, 437–438). However, the structure of the argument and the thrust of the proposals are not always reminiscent of Hales. Moreover, that somewhat timorous man had been in some danger since the first fall of Somerset and would scarcely have risked this impressive critique which was certainly designed for the perusal of the Council. The thought of the piece may be characterized as that of a chastened Commonwealth Man, which, however, may be a fairly accurate description of Hales himself. Attempting no final attribution, we shall refer to the document as *The chiefest cause* and shall date it 1552(?). It deserves to be edited and printed.

essential commodities, then, should be exchanged either for essential imports or for bullion.

Nor should the problems and hardships occasioned by scarcity of victuals be tolerated. 'As this scarcity comes by man, so may it be redressed by man, showing the people how they should use their things and compelling them to do as they have been taught.' Thus the scarcity of food can quickly and completely be eased by the increase of tillage land, just as the excessive price for wool may be lowered by laws prohibiting regrating and speculative manipulation of the supply. The author would go well beyond the cautious intent of the recently passed statute (5 and 6 Edward VI, c. 14), obliging all landowners to raise cattle in graduated relation to the number of sheep pastured, by forcing men to 'till up' their pastures and to re-build decayed houses. He would also pass—and enforce—strict sumptuary laws against needless or marginal imports. At the same time, the whole weight of policy should be addressed to building new industries when competition with foreign sources of supply can be achieved. Hemp, linen fabric, canvas, leather points, paper, and fustians are but a few of the needed and useful products which could be made in England with English labour and materials.

The chiefest cause was, of course, relatively unsophisticated in its economic analysis and highly moralistic in its proposals for remedying the economic ills of the realm. The whole temper of the memorandum is clearly a subdued effort to revive the general social philosophy of the Commonwealth Party by a kind of insinuation of argument and proposals to meet, however inexpertly, the crisis raised in England by the twin evils of high prices and physical dearth. The principal causes, we now know, were the inability of a somewhat archaic and a tenaciously conservative agrarian economy to adapt itself quickly to the needs of a steadily increasing population, a sharply higher proportion of which was by 1553 urban in character. Then, too, there remained the fact that an undue proportion of English soil did lie under sheep pasture. Some years were to elapse—and some of them were hard years indeed—before the inexorable decline of the cloth trade brought the agrarian economy back to a more salutary equilibrium of land use.

4. DETERIORATION OF RELATIONS WITH THE HANSE (1547-1553)

The special privileges of North German merchants in England, long organized in the Hanse, stretched back for almost three centuries to the reign of Henry III when the merchants of Lübeck and Hamburg were given formal permission to establish their own 'hansas' in London under royal protection. Shortly afterwards, in 1282, the Guildhall of the Germans was established in London, while within a generation small trading communities had also been established in several East Coast towns such as King's Lynn, Boston, York, Hull, Ipswich, and Yarmouth. The London community, first formally called the Steelyard in a parliamentary petition of 1422, remained dominant in Hanse affairs and was supported by the Crown in its claims of jurisdiction over the other Counters.[1] The long-standing privileges of the Steelyard were confirmed by royal licence early in Edward's reign, and then were more formally granted on December 4, 1547.[2]

The Hanseatic merchants, well organized and disciplined, had exploited their commerce with great skill and in the course of the later Middle Ages had captured from England the rich trade to Danzig, while in the period of royal weakness in the fifteenth century they had all but gained a monopoly of the trade to Scandinavia. The commercial privileges initially granted by Edward VI, while duplicating those of his father, were in no sense reciprocal and were from the first to cause friction as a now bolder English commerce sought direct outlets to the Baltic. The Hanse had in fact passed the zenith of its amazing history, being now seriously weakened by the political fragmentation of Germany, the rise of ambitious Scandinavian monarchs, and by its defeat in 1536 in a costly war waged against Denmark.[3] The Hanse had, however, been to a degree protected and favoured by Henry VIII for diplomatic reasons, since he wished to ensure the maintenance of close relations with these now staunchly Lutheran cities and because it added something of strength in his dealings with the Emperor.

Waning though it was, the English trade carried on by the Steelyard was still very substantial at the beginning of Edward's reign.

[1] Harl. MS. 306, #16, f. 94b: Grants of privileges by the Kings of England to the Hanses or Steelyard, alias Guild-hall Teutonicorum, temp. Henry III–Edw. VI.

[2] *Inventare Hansischer Archive des sechzehnten Jahrhunderts*, vol. I: *Kölner Inventar*, ed. by Konstantin Höhlbaum (Leipzig, 1896), 30; vol. III: *Danziger Inventar, 1531–1591*, ed. by Paul Simson (Munich and Leipzig, 1913), 145, 148. When an ambitious plan was undertaken in the nineteenth century to publish inventories of the vast store of Hanseatic documents, the intention was to proceed first with the principal archives of Köln, Braunschweig, Danzig, and Lübeck, with shorter listings for other cities. The Köln-Archiv proved to be the central depository for documents, particularly in our period, in part because the Antwerp materials were transferred there late in the sixteenth century (*Kölner Inventar*, Intro., viii–xiv).

[3] Ramsay, *English overseas trade*, 104.

The principal export was cloth, mostly undyed, to the value of about £200,000 p.a., as well as considerable quantities of wool, lead, and tin.[1] Their imports into England were almost wholly in essential commodities—principally pitch, tar, wax, linen, and other Baltic wares—with some intermediate trade, which was particularly disliked, in salt, wine, and woad from southern France, and fish from Iceland and the Shetlands.[2] There is abundant evidence too that the Hanse was employing its monopoly position in a skilful effort to maintain an advantageous control over the prices of the essential Baltic commodities, such wares as wax, flax, iron, and copper being regulated with particular success.[3] It is also clear, from customs data for the period 1539–1546, that the Hanse was exporting a considerable proportion of all English goods directly from London, with strong positions in such commodities as cloth generally, undyed cloth, half-dyed cloth, and with a monopolistic hold on the now diminishing trade in wax.[4]

The Hanseatic trade was by the time of Edward's accession concentrated almost wholly in London, the Counters in the out-ports having largely been abandoned as their commerce was lost to the City. Thus in 1550 the once important factory at Boston was closed, while that at King's Lynn was weak and shortly to be abandoned.[5] The German community in the Steelyard was under tight and effective discipline, had long been trained in discretion, and was now, of course, a substantial element within the Strangers Church. Heavy fines were imposed for prosecuting anyone under English law without permission; no servant could be employed who was not Hanse-born; keeping of lewd women and whores was sternly forbidden; and any member leaving London with unpaid debts was to lose his privileges.[6] The most substantial of the merchants in this decorous and tightly knit society in our period was Paul Snepel whose firm was active in the Flemish and French trade as well as in Baltic commodities. In 1548–9 his exports from London

---

[1] Cotton MSS., Claudius, E, vii, f. 99: schedule of Steelyard shipments; printed in Lappenberg, J. M., *Urkundliche Geschichte des Hansischen Stahlhofes zu London* (Hamburg, 1851), pt. ii, 175–176.

[2] Ehrenberg, Richard, *Hamburg und England im Zeitalter der Königin Elisabeth* (Jena, 1896), 51–52, 327; Friedland, Klaus, 'Hamburger Englandfahrer, 1512–1557', in *Zeitschrift des Vereins für hamburgische Geschichte*, XLVI (1960), 23–24.

[3] See table in Schanz, *Englische Handelspolitik*, I, 223, citing Calthorpe MSS., XX, f. 123.

[4] Schanz, *Englische Handelspolitik*, II, 27, for the particulars.

[5] Lappenberg, *Geschichte des Stahlhofes*, pt. i, 164, 171.

[6] Höhlbaum, Konstantin, 'Auszug aus den Statuten und der Hausordnung des Stahlhofs', in *Hansische Geschichtsblätter*, XXVI (1898), 129–132.

totalled £4591 in worth, while about half of his imports were from the Netherlands in such wares as raisins, linen, carpets, oil, and copper vessels. He brought in as well hops and thread from Cologne, madder and woad from France. About a third of his imports were from the Baltic, such wares as linen, oakum, cod, flax, and meal predominating.[1]

The special privileges, and success, of the Hanse merchants, long resented by English merchants trading abroad, were to be violently attacked directly the weakening of the cloth trade in 1551 made competition increasingly bitter. As an example, the Hanse exported raw cloths for dyeing to Hamburg in a steadily rising curve from 1546–1547 to the abrogation in 1551–1552, at a time when, as we have seen, the cloth trade generally was in severe difficulties.[2] English mercantile resentment was also increased by an embargo laid by the Hanse in 1547 against the importation of English fine cloths, as well as by special concessions obtained by the Cologne merchants in the Antwerp market.[3] Relations were further worsened when, in July, 1547, a Hamburg vessel captured an English ship en route to the Baltic, which was taken into Danzig where a small riot occurred when Englishmen there protested the insults offered to an English flag aboard.[4] The Hanse office in London reported in October that the King and Council were outraged by penalties laid on the rioting English, recommending that Danzig speedily submit the facts.[5] The incident was reaching diplomatic proportions when in early 1548 the central Hanse authority in Lübeck insisted that apology be made to the English King and that English merchants be indemnified for their ill-treatment.[6] The Danzig fraternity did not yield easily, demanding a Hanse Parliament, but they were

[1] Friedland, in *Zeitschrift d. Vereins f. hamburgische Geschichte*, XLVI (1960), 27–29. The Snepel firm operated from France in a similar fashion. The house, weakened by the abrogation of the Hanse privileges, failed in 1566.

[2] The curve of exports to Hamburg in 'Stals' was as follows:

1546–1547	3274
1547–1548	3397
1548–1549	4590
1549–1550	5485
1550–1551	5620
1551–1552	5719

(Ehrenberg, *Hamburg und England*, 327; and see Cotton MSS., Claudius, E, vii, f. 99, for official figures on the whole of the cloths exported by the Hanse for these years, rising from 29,689 cloths for 1546–7 to 39,854 in 4 Edw. VI.)

[3] Weise, Erich, 'Die Hanse, England und die Merchants Adventurers, *etc.*', in *Jahrbuch des Kölnischen Geschichtsvereins*, 31–32 (1956–1957), 159.

[4] *Danziger Inventar*, 147–148.

[5] *Ibid*. 147.

[6] *Ibid*. 148: Jan. 17 and Feb. 20, 1548.

overborne when the London office warned of deep resentment in England and when the English government demanded protection for Englishmen in Danzig and the repeal of discriminatory duties.[1]

These frictions had been on the periphery of the Hanse interest, so to say, but more serious were the complaints lodged by Cologne with Lübeck in February, 1548 that all exports to Antwerp by members of the Köln Drittel had been prohibited, whereas impecunious young English traders were exporting commodities from England under false Hanse credentials. The Cologne fraternity in May protested directly to the English King, holding that the export restrictions then in force on English cloth violated privileges which had existed for centuries, while the Steelyard reported in June that restrictions had not been lifted and that, in an attempt to apply pressure, the Hanse would purchase no fine cloths at all in the London market.[2]

The vulnerable weakness of the whole Hanse position was deliberately probed by the English government when, in June, 1549, the King wrote to the Hanse cities in effect demanding that English merchants be granted reciprocal privileges and warning them, as well as Christian III of Denmark, to desist from giving further military aid to the Scots.[3] The English demands were debated in the Hanse parliament at Lübeck, which did undertake to prohibit military exports to Scotland, though it gave no more than an evasive acceptance to the other demands.[4] These rapidly deteriorating relations, furthered by constant complaints from the Merchant Adventurers, were exacerbated by a *cause célèbre* when a ship, with its cargo of fine cloths, belonging to an English merchant named Bannaster was seized at Danzig. The incident gained diplomatic proportions when on September 27, 1551, Edward demanded the release of Bannaster's goods, his protestation being fortified by a complaint to Christian III of Denmark, demanding also the release of the impounded vessel, being held on pretext of non-payment of Sound dues. The deeply disturbed London office wrote to Danzig that the Privy Council could not be placated by excuses or negotiations. Complaints by English merchants, it was stressed, had not been pressed too far because England was preoccupied with wars in Scotland and in France, but the English government now had a

---

[1] *Danziger Inventar*, 147–149.

[2] *Kölner Inventar*, 31–33.

[3] *Danziger Inventar*, 155; *45th rpt.*, Dep. Keeper of Public Records, App. II, 21: June 6, 1549, from Royal Copenhagen Archives, MS. I. c.

[4] *Kölner Inventar*, 340–341: July, 1549.

free hand and the tangled incident must be settled on terms agreeable to Bannaster. Danzig, however, remained obdurate, as usual, until a group of seventeen English merchants resident there appeared before the Council of the city to protest against the lack of reciprocity in trade relations as exemplified in the ill-treatment accorded Thomas Bannaster.[1]

The Bannaster case gave to the Merchant Adventurers precisely the justification and the leverage they required to launch a full-scale assault on the privileges of the Hanse. In early January, 1552 the London office reported that exports had been forbidden and strongly expressed the view that diplomatic negotiations in London were essential if grave consequences were to be avoided, which prompted the decision of Lübeck and Hamburg to send envoys to London immediately.[2] But there was in the English position no real hope of compromise, for almost at once the Merchant Adventurers filed a formal petition to the Council for the abrogation of all the commercial privileges of the Hanse.[3]

In what amounted to a judicial session the dispute between the Merchant Adventurers and the Hanse was heard by the Council on February 9, 1552, at which time the Steelyard exhibited a long series of documents establishing and confirming their liberties, 'which were not thought of such force as to overcome their faults'. At the same time, the London merchants submitted proofs that Hanse members in London had been guilty of exporting without duty goods belonging to persons not of the liberty, and of other frauds as well.[4] The judgement, delivered by the Council some days later, declared that the liberties of the Steelyard were void since it had 'no sufficient corporation to take the same'; that the alleged grants and privileges, from which English losses had amounted to £20,000 p.a., appertained to no certain towns; and that it was historically the intention that the Hanse transport English wares to their own cities and bring in no goods of their own. But now they took out English goods to many countries and imported goods from all countries to the injury of English commerce. Finally, a provision of their charter from Edward VI guaranteeing reciprocity had not been honoured by the Steelyard, with the result that the Baltic

[1] *Danziger Inventar*, 168–170; *A.P.C.*, III, 365; *Regesta diplomatica historiae Danicae*, etc., ser. 2, II (Copenhagen, 1907), 193, #2271.

[2] *Kölner Inventar*, 43–44: Jan. 8 and 11, 1552.

[3] S.P. Dom., Edw. VI, XIV, 10, 11; HMC, *Salisbury MSS.*, XIII (Addenda), 30; Friedland, in *Zeitschrift d. Vereins f. hamburgische Geschichte*, XLVI (1960), 39–40; Schanz, *Englische Handelspolitik*, I, 243–246, 348–349.

[4] *A.P.C.*, III, 475–476: Feb. 9, 1552; Rawl. MSS., C 394, #1, f. 107.

remained largely closed to English commerce. Hence all the privileges were declared abrogated, save that the Hanse remained free to trade in England on level terms with all other foreign merchants.[1]

The Hanse, neither unskilled in nor unaccustomed to diplomatic negotiations, determined at once to appeal the judgement, the first presentation being made directly to the King shortly after the findings.[2] While the appeal was pending, efforts were made to ensure that the alleged abuses of privileges would be corrected, though it is clear that neither Cologne nor Lübeck now entertained any considerable hope.[3] The reply from England, over the signature of the King, rejected entirely the Hanse petition and suggested that since a judicial verdict which found customs frauds had been rendered, any further negotiation was pointless.[4] The Hanse negotiators in London sought with considerable ingenuity to maintain diplomatic discussion on the whole of the issue, while at the same time warning the cities of the confederation to discontinue trade for a season.[5] But in late May a still more formal and complete rejection of the Hanse representations came when the Council recited once more the abuses of privilege by the 'majority of the Hanse', held any appeal against the judicial finding to be inadmissible, and complained of the intolerable burden still laid on English commerce by certain Hanse cities and most particularly by Danzig.[6] The pertinacious Hanse negotiators then laid before the Council a request that former privileges be continued until discussions were completed, at the least for cargoes lying in the Thames and wares already loaded for or from England. This petition was in effect granted, provided the clearance or unloading of cargoes be completed by reasonable and designated dates.[7] Though desultory discussions of both principle and detail were in fact continued, this in effect ended the matter until Mary in her first regnal year restored the Hanse privileges, which were then permanently to be abrogated by Queen Elizabeth.

---

[1] *A.P.C.*, III, 487–489: Feb. 24, 1552; *Cal. S.P. For.*, *Edw. VI*, #626; *Cal. S.P. Span.*, X, 425–426: Dec. 27, 1551; Edward VI, *Chronicle*, 107–108, 112–113, 121.

[2] *Kölner Inventar*, 45: Feb. 28, 1552; *Danziger Inventar*, 172 (warning that ships should not for the time being proceed to England).

[3] *Kölner Inventar*, 46; *Niederländische Akten*, I, 509.

[4] *Ibid.* 46: May 1, 1552; S.P. Dom., Edw. VI, XIV, 25.

[5] *Ibid.* 46, 47.

[6] *Ibid.* 47; *Danziger Inventar*, 173; Rawl. MSS., C 394, #7, ff. 121–146.

[7] Edward VI, *Chronicle*, 133; *A.P.C.*, IV, 92–93: July 8, 1552; *Kölner Inventar*, 47–48.

5. DISCOVERY AND EXPLORATION

It may be suggested that the revocation of the privileges of the Hanse was in a true sense a declaration of independence for English commerce and shipping which was even now beginning its long phase of development and restless growth. We may also say that English merchants during the course of the Edwardian period were chronically aggrieved because of onerous restrictions placed by the Emperor on the Antwerp mart, and most particularly by Charles V's decision to loose the Inquisition in the Low Countries. At the same time, the English cloth trade began visibly to weaken in 1551, suggesting to many, including the King, that new markets must be found for cloth and other English wares which might be sold competitively. The groundwork for English exploration and for opening up new markets had been laid, or at least signalized, when in 1547 the now aged but ebullient Sebastian Cabot was persuaded by a life pension of £166 p.a. 'to come out of Spain to serve and inhabit in England'.[1]

The first exploring and exploiting thrust was towards the South, beyond Spain, which at this time ranked second only to Flanders in the volume and tonnage of English trade. Throughout the reign English privateers had been harassing Spanish and Portuguese shipping, and such famous sailors as Hawkins, Reneger, and Wyndham had in these forays built up a considerable knowledge of the navigation of all the waters off the Iberian peninsula. Probably the first English voyage to Morocco was made in 1551, while in the next year three ships explored and traded along the Barbary Coast, employing Jewish middle-men who controlled the mechanism of trade. Arrangements were made for the export of cloth, timber, and fabricated iron from England, the vessels to bring back sugar and saltpetre. Despite angry Spanish protestations several ships, accompanied by two war vessels, ventured as far south as Guinea in 1553, though English trade on the Gold Coast was not of great significance until the traffic in slaves for the West Indies was opened.[2]

[1] Much to the Emperor's anger, it might be added. *A.P.C.*, II, 137: Oct. 9, 1547; *ibid*. III, 55: June 26, 1550.

[2] For this background we have drawn heavily on Wernham, *Before the Armada*, 204; Häpke, Rudolf, 'Die Handelspolitik der Tudors', in *Hansische Geschichtsblätter*, XX (1914), 397, 407–408; and Hadeler, Nicolaus, *Geschichte der holländischen Colonien auf der Goldküste, etc.* (Bonn, 1904), 36–37. It might here be remarked that Turkish control of the Mediterranean, as well as savage Venetian opposition, effectively barred English shipping from these waters until after the Battle of Lepanto (1571).

Important as these exploratory ventures were, they fell far short, in the English imagination, of the dream of opening up a new trade route to the fabled Indies. England possessed neither the ships nor the sailing knowledge to attempt the long Cape route, nor were her ships of sufficient burthen to fetch back a pay cargo.[1] Quite as importantly, it was assumed that the development of such a route would meet the same implacable resistance from Spain and Portugal as already barred English shipping to the New World in the West. Hence the possibility of opening up a new English route, anchored by naval superiority in the Channel and the North Sea, possessed great attraction indeed. Though Cabot was consulted, it seems certain that the principal inspirer of the undertaking to attempt a north-east passage was John Dee, an excellent geographer and cartographer, who, on his return from a long European stay, had been introduced by Cheke to William Cecil. Through Cecil he gained Northumberland's favour, was for a season tutor to his son, John Dudley, and was an intimate of Sidney, the Duke's son-in-law. Hence it was that in 1552–1553 a company was formed in which were enrolled not only City merchants but also such members of the Privy Council as Winchester, Bedford, Arundel, Pembroke, and Cecil. The company undertook to finance the preparation and out-fitting of the projected voyage, each member subscribing £25 to its stock, and a crown monopoly was granted on discovery and trade to the Indies, whether by a north-east or a north-west passage.[2]

The legal formalities were concluded when in mid-May, 1553 Lord Clinton, as Lord High Admiral, licensed Sir Hugh Willoughby to assume command of three ships of the Company of Merchant Adventurers on a voyage of discovery and vested in him full authority to take up or impress shipmasters, seamen, gunners, and ship-wrights and to impose discipline on his complement.[3] The three vessels being fitted and stocked were the *Bona Esperanza*, of 120 tons, carrying Willoughby as Captain General and William Jefferson as master; the *Edward Bonaventura*, of 160 tons, with the famed Richard Chancellor as Captain and Pilot Major of the fleet; and the *Bona Confidentia*, of 90 tons burthen, commanded by Cornelius Danforth.[4] The whole complement for the tiny fleet numbered 110,

---

[1] Wernham, *Before the Armada*, 205.

[2] The imperial ambassador reported in early March 1553 that three vessels were being fitted for the voyage, the keels being covered with lead sheets and each victualled for 18 months. He likewise reported in a later dispatch that £6000 was subscribed for the venture. (*Cal. S.P. Span.*, XI, 14; Hakluyt, *Voyages* (1905 ed.), III, 331.)

[3] Royal MSS., 13.B.i, f. 300.

[4] Sir Hugh Willoughby sprang from an old gentle family of Nottinghamshire. After

of whom 18 were merchants, 20 petty officers, 3 surgeons, and a minister, John Stafford, who was in the *Edward Bonaventura*.[1]

The ordinances governing the voyage and laying down the articles of discipline were, at least formally, drawn up by Sebastian Cabot. The course was to be set by a council of twelve, composed of the senior officers, of whom Willoughby was to have a double vote, three master mates, two merchants, and the chaplain. The merchants, and others skilled in writing, were to keep a complete log of the journey. Resolute prohibitions were laid against swearing, blasphemy, brawling, or gambling, while two services were to be conducted daily from the *Book of Common Prayer*. No trading was to be permitted without the express agreement of the Captain General, and a detailed record of all transactions with foreigners was to be brought back to London. In dealing with alien peoples the company was to avoid religious controversy, while, if possible, strangers were to be lured on board, it being remembered that 'if the person taken may be made drunk with beer, or wine, you shall know the secrets of his heart'. All of the company were enjoined to keep in mind that they represented the King, that the purpose of the voyage was to advance the good estate of the realm. Hence all should strive to 'satisfy the expectation of them, who at their great costs, charges, and expenses, have so furnished you in good sort, and plenty of all necessaries as the like was never in any realm seen, used, or known'.[2]

Meanwhile, formal letters missive in English, Latin, Greek, and other known tongues had been drawn up for Willoughby, investing him with power to discover strange countries in the name of the King.[3] He was also supplied with a letter commendatory 'towards the mighty empire of Cathay', in which Edward capaciously addressed 'all sovereigns of the Earth'. God, it was stated, had endowed all men with good affections towards those who venture into far parts of the earth. This humanity should encompass all men, but especially merchants, 'who wandering about the world, search both the land and the sea' to carry 'good and profitable things' and to bring home in exchange goods commodious to their own country.

military service with Somerset in Scotland, he remained in the North as Captain of Lowther Castle. Willoughby had had only slight sailing experience.

Chancellor was a more experienced seaman and certainly a far more competent navigator. After his visit to the Russian court in 1554, he made a second voyage to the White Sea in 1555, but was lost off the Aberdeenshire coast on the return voyage.

[1] Hakluyt, *Voyages*, II, 206, 212–214.
[2] Cabot, Sebastian, *Ordinances, instructions, etc.* (May 9, 1553), printed in *ibid.* 195 ff.
[3] Cotton MSS., Faustin, C, ii, 26, f. 110; Rawl. MSS., B 224, #6, ff. 38–40.

God has in His wisdom provided no one country with all things necessary to it, thereby promoting by means of trade the friendship of peoples one with another. It is for this reason that he has licensed Willoughby and his company to carry forward their voyage to countries as yet unknown to Englishmen. Hence he called upon all kings and princes to grant his servant free passage, full protection, and permission to trade, with the assurance that he would extend the same privileges to those who sought passage and trade into England.[1]

King Edward removed from Westminster to Greenwich, in what was fated to be his last move, on April 11th, proceeding by barge down the Thames. As he approached the Tower the great ordnance burst forth, echoed, as it were, by the salutes of all the ships berthed down to Radcliffe where the three vessels commanded by Willoughby lay for their heavy rigging and the taking on of the great stores of victuals and nautical necessaries.[2] Just a month later (May 10th) the 'three great ships . . . were set forth' on the adventure of 'the unknown voyage to Muscovy, and to unknown parts of the North Seas'.[3] Willoughby dropped down stream from Radcliffe to Deptford on the first day, and then on May 11th sailed, with gathering speed, past Greenwich where the gallant sight was watched from a window by the now fatally ill King, the ships 'shooting off our ordnance' in final salute as they passed.[4]

Willoughby's terse journal, found some time after his death from cold and starvation, records that the fleet dropped down the Thames in short hauls, not clearing until May 24th when it struck northward along the coast, spending most of the nights at anchor off coastal towns. They were off Yarmouth on May 30th, from whence the fleet put out to sea on a course which must on a very long leg have been nearly due north. Willoughby's sailing log is impossible to follow with certainty, but it seems sure that on July 14th they were in the Lofoten Islands, still well short of the North Cape. There they saw the islanders making hay and were welcomed by them during a stay of three days, the winds being contrary, while Willoughby took on stores. It was not until August 2nd that they had reached 70° latitude and, dangerously late, were bending around the North

[1] Hakluyt, *Voyages*, II, 209–211.
[2] Machyn, *Diary*, 33–34. Machyn was misguided in thinking they were preparing for a voyage to Newfoundland.
[3] Stow, *Annales*, 609. Stow misdates the beginning of the voyage as May 20th.
[4] Hakluyt, *Voyages*, II, 217. We shall follow Hakluyt's text, *Voyages*, II, 212–224 (which may also be found in Cotton MSS., Otho, E, viii, 10), of the *True copy of a note found written in one of the two ships . . . which wintered in Lappia, where Sir Hugh Willoughby and all his companions died*, etc.

Cape, where they were able to make contact with the shore and to gain the promise of a pilot who would come on board at Vardo. But Willoughby was unable to make port, a violent storm blowing them offshore and separating the three vessels. The *Esperanza* and the *Confidentia* made contact at sea after the storm had abated, but were never to see the *Edward Bonaventura*, Chancellor commanding, which appears to have literally been blown around the Cape and which in due course made port at Archangel in the White Sea.

It seems evident from the log that the two remaining vessels were completely lost. They were in very heavy weather for days and when on August 14th they made a landfall they were unable to put in because of raging seas and shore ice. For four days they sailed northwards, reaching—so Willoughby thought—72° latitude, comfortably north of the Cape, when leaks springing in the *Confidentia* compelled Willoughby to seek land by ordering a south-south-east course. The sailing log becomes completely obscure at this point, but it seems certain that they were dropping back to the west until September 14th when they were able to anchor off shores unknown to them and put in a boat. It seems probable that they had landed in an harbour later to be named Arzina [near Kegov], in Lapland, and very near to the then Norwegian-Russian border. Here they found abundant fish, saw game, and after staying a week and 'seeing the year far spent, and also very evil weather, at first snow, and hail, as though it had been the deep of winter, we thought it best to winter here'. Here, in fact, they were to die. Willoughby's *Journal* describes three scouting parties sent off in various directions, but no trace of a human being could be found. Here the *Journal* ends, it having been discovered in the summer of 1554 by Russian fishermen with the proofs of the death of a gallant expedition.[1]

In a true sense, however, the enterprise had not failed. Chancellor ultimately made his way to Moscow, where he was warmly received by Ivan IV, who was most anxious to secure cultural and economic ties with Western Europe. The basis was laid during this sojourn for the remarkably successful and lucrative trade of the Muscovy Company opened a few years later.[2] Perhaps even more importantly this expedition engaged the attention, as it stimulated the imagination, of England. It laid the basis for the age of exploration and discovery which lay just ahead.

---

[1] For indispensable help with the jumbled sailing directions we are greatly indebted to my yachting friend, Mr Sidney Gleason of Belmont, Mass.

[2] Ivan IV to Edward VI, Add. MSS., 6113, f. 176; Blümcke, Otto, 'Berichte und Akten, *etc.*', in *Hansische Geschichtsquellen*, VII (1894), vi.

XIV

THE ASSAULT ON THE SUCCESSION
(1553)

1. NORTHUMBERLAND'S DILEMMA: THE BITTER FRUITS OF POWER

The Duke of Northumberland had displayed effective and ruthless conspiratorial gifts in his destruction of Somerset; yet he had, as we have seen, sought to rule with the advice of the Council and with the approval of the politically and economically dominant social groups of the realm whom the Lord Protector had so badly frightened. We must bear constantly in mind that from the moment of his grasping of power in late 1549 until some not precisely certain date, very possibly February, 1553, he had anticipated that his trusteeship of power would be delivered intact to the King at a rapidly approaching date. He had been loyal to the King; he had encouraged as he had respected his rapidly widening interest in governmental affairs; and there is abundant evidence that in some respects at least he looked forward with personal satisfaction to his coming surrender of sovereign power. In 1553 Northumberland was just past fifty years of age. His health had begun to deteriorate during the period of his tenure of power. He had loudly protested his own impatience with the routine duties of governance, and he seems, as well, to have been unhappy and restive in the splendid isolation in which his rank and status had placed him. There was something poignant, as well as inexplicable, in his nature; but surely it may be said that there was in that nature nothing of treason against his master, the King. And then all this was abruptly and violently changed by the onset of Edward's fatal illness, by the almost hysterical pressure which the King himself deployed towards the end as he launched a desperate assault on the law of the succession.

Northumberland was also fully aware that powerful and articulate groups in the realm, as well as most of the commons, detested him, as they feared him, for the brutal destruction of Somerset on charges which one suspects all classes of men knew to be as false as they were defective. We have observed that Northumberland was fearful as he sensed in the realm a persistent and implacable restlessness. He was the object, too, of an irrepressible campaign of malicious libels attacking his regime and his intentions, which came to absorb a startling proportion of the business of the Privy Council.[1] In the Council itself he was uncertain of the true attitude of most of his colleagues towards him; he knew that of them at the least Cranmer, Rich, Bedford, and possibly Pembroke were in their hearts critical of him.[2] He knew, too, that most of the old nobility, ineffectual though many of them were, detested him as a *parvenu* and avoided London when they could. The Roman Catholics hated him for the ruthless betrayal of 1549–1550 and for his steady support of evangelical Protestantism, while the Protestant leaders had come to fear and distrust him as the bare bones of his complete secularism had become visible. These courageous and devoted men had attacked him frontally, while the most fanatically courageous of them, John Knox, had denounced him in withering terms to which the Duke did not dare make reply.[3] There was shrewd wisdom in an analysis of Northumberland's position made during these months by an anonymous observer. High and low alike, he concluded, feared and hated the Duke, but none quite dared to undertake anything against his will or to speak against his policy. Outwardly Northumberland remained mild, considerate, and pleasant, but this only masked an uncalm, proud, and vindictive man who at the bottom of his nature was a 'félon'. He appeared generous in his actions, but his gifts and grants were made to placate and bind those whom he feared, or to reward henchmen like Palmer and Gates who would undertake any violent action for him.[4]

A brief sampling of the steady and now violent libels against the Duke, with which the Council was so constantly preoccupied, will suggest the temper of the opposition to him and to his suspected policy in the last months of the reign. At the end of January the sheriff of Hampshire was required to punish one Allen Hudson for slanderous words regarding the Duke by cutting off one ear while he was pilloried in Southampton and the other in Winchester.[5] Not

[1] *Vide ante*, 428 ff.
[2] *Cal. S.P. Span.*, X, 565: Sept. 23, 1552; *ibid.* XI, 13: Feb. 21, 1553.
[3] *Vide ante*, 373–375.
[4] *Rélation de l'accusation et mort du Duc de Somerset* (Bibl. Nat. MS. 15888, ff. 205–210); summarized in Raumer, *Briefe aus Paris*, ii, 72 ff.
[5] *A.P.C.*, IV, 211: Jan. 30, 1553.

many days later the justices on assize in Devonshire were asked to examine and punish one Thomas Beer for 'lewd and seditious' words,[1] while in London in March Thomas Flood, a priest, was imprisoned briefly for slanderous utterances and two Irishmen were clapped in the Marshalsea for similar offences.[2] The Council was in April searching for a ship captain, Thomas Brown, who had voiced seditious sentiments.[3] Three persons were imprisoned and then pilloried in London for spreading false rumours concerning the King's health,[4] and a week later two Londoners were committed to prison for slanderous attacks on Northumberland.[5] These are but typical instances of disaffection, of uncertainty, of persistent rumours that Northumberland was poisoning the King, and of the dangerous charge that he was aiming at the throne.

If aiming at the throne ever so much as passed through Northumberland's mind, his actions and movements were as incomprehensible as they were inept. During the last year of Edward's life, a roughly compiled itinerary of the Duke's movements would suggest that he was away from Court on official duty or because of illness for approximately a third of the period, at the Court and attending Council for about the same length of time, and near London, usually at Chelsea, but not normally at Court for not quite the remaining third of his time.[6]

This is a period, too, in which Northumberland expressed to those he felt he could trust, and especially to Cecil, profound dissatisfaction with his career and a most persuasive suggestion that he would have welcomed relief from the responsibilities of power. This almost black mood of discouragement seems certainly to have set in at about the time of the death of his daughter-in-law, the wife of Lord Ambrose Dudley. The young woman, of whom he was very

---

[1] *A.P.C.*, IV, 220: Feb. 17, 1553.

[2] *Ibid.* 232, 234.

[3] *Ibid.* 257, 258–259.

[4] *Ibid.* 266–267.

[5] *Ibid.* 269.

[6] The Acts of the Privy Council have of course been used in this analysis, but, it may be suggested, are not in fact a reliable guide to actual attendance at meetings. Northumberland's longest consecutive absence in this period was in 1552 when on May 22nd it was agreed that he would go North to inspect the Border defences as General Warden, and with 'a pay of £10,000 to go before him' (Edward VI, *Chronicle*, 124). He was away from Court but did not leave for the North until mid-June, being delayed by illness in his family. His communications to the Council were few in number, though he did on July 25th ask his son-in-law, Sir Henry Sidney, to go to Court on his behalf (*Cal. S.P. Dom.*, *Edw. VI*, VI, 412–413 (Addenda IV: 8). He returned to southern England in late August. Then in late October one of his recurrent illnesses caused his absence from Court for some time.

fond, died of sweating sickness in Northumberland's household, just as he was about to set out for the North.[1] In a letter dated the day following, the Duke plaintively described the girl as 'merry and bright in the evening', and then dead within twenty-four hours after her seizure with 'a great sweat'.[2] Then for some time after his return from what must be called a perfunctory tour of the northern borders, Northumberland kept to his 'little house at Chelsea', where Scheyfve conjectured he was weighing radical changes in the bench of bishops and also in the peerage.[3] At about the same time, he wrote a discouraged and certainly ambiguous letter to Cecil and Petre, expressing himself as content with the King's appointment of persons to manage a 'weighty and secret affair',[4] while taking pains to exclude himself from responsibility as one 'who neither hath understanding nor wit meet for the association, nor body apt to render his duty, as the will and heart desireth'.[5]

This dark mood, almost of melancholy, did not pass, indeed it deepened profoundly with the new year. Again from his hide-a-way in Chelsea, beset by the stubborn resistance of Tunstall at Durham and denounced as a hypocrite by Knox and Latimer, Northumberland explained to Cecil why he did not return to Court and to the Council. He assured the Secretary that only ill health accounted for his absence. The time had come, he added, to seek relief from his burdens, to escape 'the multitude of cravers . . . that hangeth now daily at my gate for money' and favours. He plaintively asked what comfort remained at the end of his life after such long travail. He had served long and he had served faithfully, when health permitted, often going to his bed 'with a careful heart and a weary body', when others went to their pleasure. Now he found that little remained to cause him to wish to live much longer. Thus he had opened his heart to Cecil and to such others as he believed to be his friends: 'I have entered into the bottom of my care.'[6] Again from Chelsea, towards the end of January, Northumberland asked Cecil to intervene with the King on his behalf. The King had written regarding his special concern for the North of England, but he

---

[1] S.P. Dom., Edw. VI, XIV, 37: Northumberland to Sir John Gates, June 1, 1552.
[2] *Ibid.* 38: June 2, 1552, from Otford.
[3] *Cal. S.P. Span.*, X, 593: Nov. 20, 1552.
[4] The Duke probably referred to a commission appointed by the King to study the effects of the 'fall of money' under the terms of the last two proclamations (Edward VI, *Chronicle*, 155).
[5] HMC, *Salisbury MSS.*, I, 101–102: Nov. 23, 1552.
[6] S.P. Dom., Edw. VI, XVIII, 2: Jan. 3, 1553; rendered in part in Tytler, *England*, II, 154–156.

wished Edward to know with all assurances that his 'inward care' extended to the whole of the royal dominions, for 'if the North be well provided for, I must confess that the South shall be never a deal the worse'. He protested his absolute loyalty, and 'whatsoever shall be the King's pleasure, either in this or in all other, I trust I can confirm myself as humbly as any subject upon the earth'.[1]

These evidences which we have been following out convincingly suggest that at the close of January, 1553 Northumberland was sick, very tired, and almost completely disillusioned. There is no indication of further or thwarted ambition; there is strong evidence that he lent his whole approval to the rapid transfer of power to the King, which, in fact, he had done so much to institute and then to implement. There was no treason, no hint of overweening ambition, and no clinging to the structure of power in his actions or in his policy in these months as the seriousness of the King's illness became apparent. The imperious mood and language were gone. Northumberland, probably now fully sensing that he had ruled badly and was hated by most men of the realm, wished in his heart to lay down those sovereign tasks to which he had once aspired, but which were now his sore burdens.

During the last months of the reign, and more precisely after April, 1553, the lethargy, or illness, of Northumberland, combined with the increasingly grave illness of the King, spread by a kind of contagion to the Privy Council. What can only be described as a partial paralysis of government and a weakening of ordinary administration becomes all too apparent. We have seen that English diplomatists abroad were out of touch with the central government which neither transmitted instructions nor answered enquiries;[2] the records of the Privy Council become weak, irregular, and attenuated; the vein of correspondence and of official papers in the *State Papers Domestic* becomes thin and marginal in quality. One has the sense, as he peruses what does remain of record, of a slowing-down in the whole process of governance, of lassitude rather than of gathering conspiracy. This may perhaps be best illustrated by an examination of three of the memoranda that do exist of business brought before the sovereign authority—the Council—in the last weeks of the King's life. Petre's *Memorial* for the meeting set for April 29, 1553, dealt only with routine matters, save for merchants' complaints to be considered, further discussion with the Hanse, and a letter of instruction to be drafted for Sir Thomas Gresham.[3] A

---

[1] S.P. Dom., Edw. VI, XVIII, 9: Jan. 23, 1553.
[2] *Vide ante*, 158–159 et passim.   [3] HMC, *Salisbury MSS.*, I, 120.

similar document, dated June 3, 1553, presents what can only be described as a jumble of relatively minor administrative and military decisions which had evidently been accumulating for weeks.[1] The last significant memorial of Council business, dated June 11th, is at once better ordered and concerned with more important matters, though within a narrow range of consideration. Berwick, as always, was to be discussed, further reductions of coastal defences to be debated, and certain Irish questions to be resolved. That was all save, interestingly, a 'declaration of the King's pleasure in the new bishops', for it was proposed to appoint strongly evangelical clergy to four of the sees: Grindal to London, Bill to Newcastle, Merrick to Bangor, and Whitehead to Rochester—an intention, it may be observed, never carried out, for Edward's life was now to be measured in days.[2]

The paralysis of the Council, reflecting as it did Northumberland's own lethargy and uncertainties, was worsened because that body had earlier been purged of the adherents of Somerset, of those who possessed the courage and resolution to offer frontal opposition to Northumberland's naked power. Above all, Paget's credit had been utterly destroyed; Wriothesley was dead; and Arundel, whose abilities and integrity have been underrated, was without influence. So too, Rich, like so many of his former colleagues, had lived in fear of the brutality of reprisal which had always marked Northumberland's conception of policy and authority. He absented himself from Parliament in January, 1552, and it was to be almost a year before he was recorded as attending a meeting of the Council. He did attend Edward's last Parliament in March, 1553 and was present at a single meeting of the Council before immuring himself in his beloved house in Essex, from which he was ordered back to Court when it became clear that the King was dying.

There remained Cranmer who had on several occasions vigorously opposed Northumberland in Parliament on religious matters, but who since the fall of Somerset had sought to stand clear of political issues. His religious policy had, as we have seen, been seriously weakened by Dudley's complete Erastianism and secularism, and the Archbishop was evidently determined to avoid collision with the Duke in any save the most important ecclesiastical matters, the last of which had been his almost single-handed defence of Bishop Tunstall. In the summer of 1552, accordingly, he had removed to Croydon, in his own diocese. But even there Dudley's enmity had

[1] S.P. Dom., Edw. VI, XVIII, 27.
[2] Ibid. 28.

sought him out, through Cecil, in his false accusation that Cranmer had built up a personal fortune from the revenues of his see.[1] Appointed a member of the Kentish commission for the expropriation of church goods, the Archbishop, who was opposed to what he regarded as the rape of the Church, delayed action for months until Cecil, speaking once more for the Duke, warned him of the disfavour in which he was held.[2] So too, Cranmer moved slowly and laxly with the commission, which he necessarily headed, appointed to deal with the continued presence of Anabaptists in his diocese, provoking Northumberland to ominous threats and displeasure.[3] Cranmer had no wish to collide with the Duke, as he almost invariably did when they had met in these later years. Hence, after April, 1552 he disappeared from the records of the Council, save for one session of October 11th, until late February, 1553 when Parliament was about to be convened.[4]

The truth was that Northumberland had alienated the affection and trust of most of his older and highly placed colleagues in the Council and government, only certain minor figures like Gates and Palmer being bound to him by favours which flowed to them for their part in the destruction of Somerset. All men had come to fear him, few indeed now trusted him or wished to be his intimates. This Northumberland sensed, and the fact may well account in part for his discouragement and his withdrawal from the day-to-day control of public affairs over a long, and a most critical, period of time. The one important exception was Cecil, raised into public life and trusted by Somerset, whom he at the end not so much betrayed as repudiated in his quest for safety and security of position. It is a measure of Cecil's dexterity and instinct for survival that he quickly re-established his place in the government and had so far persuaded Northumberland of his loyalty and ability that he had by early 1552 been vested with considerable authority and administrative responsibilities. With Northumberland much away from Court and in a mood of black despair, Cecil became in fact the true administrator of governmental affairs. The dispatches from ambassadors were now almost invariably addressed to him and most of the instructions were from his hand, while all of the official business came quickly to pass before him. At the same time, instinctive memoranda-keeper though he was, very little survives that reflects

---

[1] *Vide ante*, 379; *et vide* HMC, *Bath MSS.*, at *Longleat*, II, 12–13: July 21, 1552.
[2] *Ibid.* 14.   [3] *Cal. S.P. Span.*, X, 591: Nov. 20, 1552; *vide ante*, 334.
[4] Baumgartner papers, Strype correspondence, vol. II, 34d division, #34 (*Cat. of MSS. in Univ. of Cambridge Library*, V, 37); Strype, *Cranmer*, I, 430–432.

his own thinking or views on the policy which he was administering.[1] Northumberland came to trust Cecil completely, unburdened himself to the Secretary with uncommon frankness, and sought the personal friendship of one a full two decades younger than himself. He could not know—for his judgement of men and motives was ever naive—that Cecil was through a long and distinguished life always to keep open one door of withdrawal from policy or personal commitment. Cecil had already morally betrayed his mentor Somerset; at the first certain smell of danger he stood ready to betray the confidence so pathetically vested in him by Northumberland.

Northumberland, as we have said, delegated much to Cecil and with an ever-increasing confidence and appearance of affection. In Janury, 1552 he assigned to him for settlement an acrimonious dispute between his own brother (Sir Andrew Dudley) and the Lord Deputy of Calais,[2] while a few days later he placed in his hands the arrangements for a meeting with the French ambassador.[3] In the spring, as he was preparing to proceed to the Northern Border, Northumberland assured Cecil that he would 'not omit to see' his friend's father 'as I go by him, though I do but drink a cup of wine with him at the door; for I will not trouble no friend's house of mine otherwise in this journey, my train is so great, and will be, whether I will it or not'.[4] Some days later Northumberland wrote again on matters of public business, but with an easy familiarity which one would suppose presumed personal friendship.[5] That much of the responsibility for administration was now imposed on Cecil is also amply demonstrated by a private notebook kept by him in July, 1552 which is concerned with the whole grist of public business which must be dispatched—memoranada for Council meetings, commitments made to individuals, suits to the King and Council, diplomatic reminders—and, somewhat incongruously, an itinerary of his own journey into Lincolnshire to visit his properties in that, his native, county.[6]

We have seen that Northumberland's dependence on Cecil and

---

[1] Professor Read suggested that Cecil as a discretionary measure may have destroyed such papers on Edward's death (*Cecil*, 76–77).

[2] S.P. Dom., Edw. VI, XIV, 1: Jan. 8, 1552.

[3] *Ibid*. 5: Jan. 27, 1552.

[4] *Ibid*. 34: May 31, 1552. Cecil's father, who was living in retirement, died shortly afterwards; *et* cf. *ibid*. 42.

[5] *Ibid*. 35, 40: May 31 and June 6, 1552.

[6] *Ibid*. 53: [July, 1552]. This interesting notebook of 16 pages deserves to be edited and printed.

the range and intimacy of his confidences to the Secretary became even greater as the reign wore on to its tumultuous close.[1] Then, at some uncertain date in April, when the King's early death was almost predictable, when Northumberland was bestirring himself to dangerous activity, and when the sense of impending crisis was in the air, Cecil withdrew himself from Court on the plea that he must attend to personal affairs occasioned by his father's recent death. In a most interesting, and surely delphic, letter from his colleague Petre, Cecil was advised to finish his affairs before his return, whatever the pressures might be. Then Petre concluded, 'I must confess to you of myself, that my old affection homewards is not less than it was wont, nor I think can be, having tasted of things here'.[2] At about this date Cecil in fact took to his bed at Wimbledon, one cannot refrain from suspecting because he feared Northumberland's recklessness and the tasks which he might now be called upon to undertake. This seems certainly to have been the conclusion of the Duke, who on May 7th wrote to Cecil in terms which scarcely concealed a dangerous and implicit anger. He had received a packet of Cecil's letters, but he would have wished that the Secretary could have delivered them in person. He must report that 'it was still said here, that you had but a grudging of an ague; but now we hear the contrary, and that you have been these three or four fits grievously handled'. The Duke continued with a condemnation of those of the Council whom he can 'scarcely awake . . . out of their wonted dreams'. Suffusing this letter too was an ill-concealed rage and more than the hint of his fear of betrayal from his own colleagues, softened towards its end by the news that the doctors now held hope for the King's recovery.[3]

It was at this time, too, that Sir John Cheke was appointed a third Secretary to the Council, for with Cecil stricken with an undiagnosable illness and the frightened Petre seeking to retire, the Privy Council was in effect deprived of those who had prepared its dockets and administered its affairs.[4] Lord John Audley wrote to Cecil on May 9th, commiserating with him and recommending what may be described as a 'broad spectrum of remedies', the chief of which was stewed 'sow pig' precisely 'nine days old'.[5] Pressure for his return was kept on Cecil, Petre on May 12th enquiring for Northumberland and the King 'whether you felt yourself so

[1] Vide ante, 496–498.   [2] HMC, Salisbury MSS., I, 120: Apr. 30, 1553.
[3] Strype, Memorials, II, ii, 505–506.
[4] Cal. S.P. Span., XI, 50.
[5] S.P. Dom., Edw. VI, XVIII, 21: May 9, 1553.

amended, as you thought you might be able without hurting your-self . . . [to] be at court', and enclosing for sealing letters which had been signed by the King.[1] Then three days later Petre cryptically mused, 'God deliver you from the physicians, and yet I fear me (as ill as I love it) I must shortly come to them'—probably Petre meant his friend to know that he was about to join him with a feigned illness of his own.[2]

Cecil, be it noted, did not return to Court until June 11th, on which date the judges were summoned before the Council to draw up in legal form Edward's plan for the alteration of the succession. In the end Cecil was compelled to sign the devise, but even as he did so he was preparing to betray Northumberland's trust. He was sketching out an *apologia* for his conduct, submitted to Queen Mary shortly after her accession—a brief of twenty-two heads in which he implored the Queen to understand that there 'is some difference from others that have more plainly offended'. His first inclination on hearing of the plot against her had been to flee the realm, but from this he was dissuaded by Cheke, 'who willed me for my satisfaction to read a dialogue of Plato, where Socrates, being in prison, was offered to escape and flee, and yet he would not. I read the Dialogue, whose reasons indeed did stay me.' He submitted that he had from the beginning misliked the conspiracy and had been moved to convey his lands, his leases, and part of his moveables. Those who really knew his mind—Anthony Cooke, Nicholas Bacon, Petre, Cheke, and members of his household—would testify that he was searching for ways to oppose the intended *coup d'état*. Thus he had refused to draw the proclamation, had 'dissembled the taking of my horse' to deal with the rising in Mary's favour in Lincolnshire and Northamptonshire, while in fact, with Winchester and Russell, he was seeking means to secure Windsor Castle and to raise the West in Mary's behalf. These plans he had also revealed to Arundel and Darcy, while, as always, with an alternative plan, he and Petre had resolved to join Mary if all else failed.[3] The instinct for sur-vival was strong indeed in Cecil. In the end, quite characteristically

---

[1] HMC, *Salisbury MSS.*, I, 121: May 12, 1553.

[2] *Ibid.* 121: May 15, 1553. One must conclude that Cecil's illness was feigned. Roger Alford, Cecil's servant and friend, twenty years later, and at Cecil's request, set out at length a private *apologia* for his master's conduct during these weeks. It is printed in full, and with fair accuracy, in Strype, *Annals of the Reformation*, IV, 485–489, from Cotton MSS., Titus, B, ii, F, ff. 374–378. I am grateful to my colleague, Professor Wallace MacCaffrey, for his help in locating the manuscript, Strype's reference being incomplete.

[3] Lansdowne MS. 104, #1, f. 1; printed in part in Tytler, *England*, II, 192–195; and see the possibly related Lansdowne MS. 104, #2, f. 3.

quoting Plato as he proceeded, he betrayed Northumberland far more effectively than he had his first master, Somerset. His abiding, and deep, loyalty, even in those days of his youth, was to the Princess who was destined to become England's greatest sovereign. But it is no wonder that Cecil in the famous days that lay ahead rarely spoke of his share in the government of Edward VI.

2. EDWARD'S SECOND PARLIAMENT (MARCH 1—MARCH 31, 1553)

Under pressure from the King and from the most powerful of his colleagues in the Council, Northumberland concluded in December, 1552 that a parliament must be convened. The precise date when this decision was made is not known, but it was some time before December 28th when Shrewsbury submitted a memorandum of important matters which should be dealt with in the now contemplated assembly.[1] It is important to observe that at this date the King's final illness had either not evidently begun or was at the most still regarded as a cold or a rheum, to which he had in earlier years been from time to time subject. It may even be that the decision to call Parliament had been under discussion since August, 1552 when, as we have seen, suspension of payments had for a brief time to be imposed.[2] Severe retrenchments had been ordered, the City Companies had made large advances, still more crown lands were ordered sold, the coinage had been reformed, and Gresham had begun his manipulations and re-fundings in Antwerp. But heroic, and ultimately successful, as these measures were, there still remained a fiscal gap which could not soon be closed without resort to Parliament for a subsidy. Northumberland somewhat grudgingly and certainly fearfully approved, being in the end persuaded that there was no other way left

'to bring his majesty out of the great debts wherein for one great part he was left by his . . . father . . . and augmented by the wilful government of the late Duke of Somerset who took upon him the Protectorship and government of his own authority. His highness, by the prudence of his father, left in peace with all princes, suddenly, by that man's unskilful protectorship, and less expert in government, was plunged into wars whereby His Majesty's charges were suddenly increased unto the point of six or seven score thousand pounds a year over and above the charges for the keeping of Boulogne'.

[1] S.P. Dom., Edw. VI, XV, 73.   [2] *Vide ante*, 456 ff. for the fiscal crisis of this period.

This dreadful load of debt had been handled by 'slender shifts', but now threatened to overwhelm the realm unless Parliament would lend its aid by the taxing power.[1]

Northumberland realized full well that there would be 'murmuring and grudging' in Parliament, and he was evidently shaken by a memorandum from Cecil who feared that the members might lay strictures against the vast stores of crown lands which had been so prodigally used to advance the estate of the new nobility in the Council. There is abundant evidence that Northumberland was fearful too, but in a letter to the Lord Chamberlain, dealing with various arrangements for the Parliament, he assumed a bold and defiant tone. He urged that the Crown's position and needs were clear to all members. The Council ought accordingly 'not to be so ceremonious as to imagine the objects [objections] of very forward persons, but rather to burden their minds and hearts with the King's Majesty's extreme debts and necessity as cannot be denied by no man'. Nor, in his view, should the Council deign to account to Parliament for the King's liberality 'in augmenting or advancing of his nobles, or of his benevolence showed to any his good servants', and thus 'give them occasion to take hold of your own arguments'. Then, returning to the business with which his letter was supposed to be concerned, the Duke reminded Darcy that the King must select the Speaker of the Commons and name a preacher for the opening of the session.[2] One additional matter of concern had arisen, for by mid-February, just as the returns of elections were coming in, it was apparent that the King's illness was serious and that he might not be sufficiently well to open or to dissolve the Parliament in person. Hence the Lord Chancellor, when consulted by Cecil, advised that there were precedents for the absence of the King, 'but they were ill taken afterwards', and he accordingly suggested that it would be best to have in hand a writ for the adjournment of Parliament which in its text would appoint the next meeting date.[3]

The decidedly insecure and apprehensive government likewise undertook by such means as it possessed to influence the choice of members for the House of Commons, often by explicitly suggesting those to represent the counties and by rather pious and general exhortations for most of the borough seats. As an example, the Council wrote to the Sheriff of Suffolk that, 'for the furtherance of

[1] S.P. Dom., Edw. VI, XV, 73: Dec. 28, 1552.
[2] Ibid. XVIII, 6: Chelsea, Jan. 14, 1553.
[3] HMC, Salisbury MSS., I, 108-109.

such causes as are to be propounded' to Parliament, there should be 'good regard had that the choice be made' of men of gravity and wisdom 'fit for their understanding and qualities to be in such a grave Council'. Two such gentlemen were accordingly recommended for return as knights of the shire: Sir William Drury and Sir Henry Bedingfield,[1] who were in fact so returned for the county. The Sheriff was further enjoined to inform such nominees that they were recommended by the Council, and on or before the election was to communicate to the electors of the county 'our consideration and care for the weal of . . . the same shire, and our good memory of these two persons who we have named'.[2] Similarly, Sir Richard Cotton, 'comptroller of our house', was successfully urged on the Hampshire electors as 'one whom we need not to commend, being for his place with us of no less knowledge than authority'.[3] Down the margin of the Suffolk letter was added a form, doubtless used in certain counties, enjoining care in the selection of borough members 'of knowledge and experience' for the Parliament to be chosen.

We know, too, that in at least one instance the King intimated his personal wish that a servant of the crown be returned as a member of the Parliament being convened.[4] So too in Stamford (Lincs), where he had great personal influence, Cecil had recommended the choice of his father-in-law, Sir Anthony Cooke, which the aldermen and his brothers had unanimously approved. But, so Cecil's close personal friend, Henry Lacy, reported, the electors preferred his own son, Robert Lacy of Lincoln's Inn, for the other seat, to the nominee suggested by the Lord Admiral.[5] At Grantham the electors informed Cecil that they could not return one of his nominees because of a previous commitment, and in at least one instance a nominee of the Duke of Northumberland failed to gain election. Professor Pollard counted fifteen persons who were specifically recommended for return by the Privy Council, of which number twelve were chosen, but this of itself scarcely suggests successful packing, since half of them had in fact sat in the last Parliament.[6]

---

[1] The latter name was inserted above an erasure of Sir William Waldegrave's.

[2] Lansdowne MS. 3, #19, f. 36.

[3] *Idem.*

[4] Harl. MS. 523, #21, f. 31: Council to Sir Philip Hoby.

[5] Lacy was in fact returned (HMC, *Salisbury MSS.*, I, 106; *Parl. Papers*, 1878, vol. 62: *Members of Parliament*, pt. I, p. 379).

[6] Pollard, *History of England*, 75; Professor Bindoff advances much the same reckoning: of 14 persons nominated, 11 were returned ('A kingdom at stake, 1553', in *History Today*, III (1953), 645).

In carrying forward these preparations Northumberland was also concerned with his strength in the House of Lords and with the fussy problem of how the peers should sit in Parliament. A list of the forty-nine lay peers to be summoned was jotted down, against which there are check-marks for thirteen who have only one possible common characteristic: a record of known support for the Duke.[1] Northumberland had likewise toyed with the suggestion that the eldest sons of the nobility might be brought by writ into Parliament in order to gain valuable training and experience for their future duties.[2] His thinking was further advanced in a long note on the subject addressed to Cecil in which he suggested that such fledgling peers, at least of the ultimate rank of earl or higher, might be summoned by writ not only to attend, but also 'to sit and have voice' in the Parliament.[3] This interesting scheme, which had much to commend it, quite beyond the fact that it would have given the Duke greater strength in the Lords, was not pursued further. Northumberland had enough problems to meet in Parliament without adding a constitutional innovation. Every effort, then, had been taken to secure a well-disposed Parliament, but there is really no persuasive evidence that the Parliament had been much altered in its composition by these rather heavy-handed interventions.[4] At the least we may conclude that it was not, as Froude seems to have thought it to be, an irregularly chosen Parliament of nominated notables.[5]

Edward's second Parliament was opened on March 1, 1553. 'Because the King was sickly', to use Stow's phrase, there were several variations in the usual procedure. For his greater convenience, the initial session was held in the royal palace of Whitehall, the members gathering in the chapel there, where Ridley preached and the King and several of the Lords took Holy Communion. The King and the peers then adjourned to the King's great chamber, 'the King sitting under his cloth of estate, and all the Lords in their

---

[1] Harl. MS. 158, f. 117 (should be numbered ff. 122–123).

[2] S.P. Dom., Edw. VI, XVIII, 6: Northumberland to Darcy, Jan. 14, 1553.

[3] *Ibid.* 8: Jan. 19, 1553. The document is badly torn and does not always make full sense.

[4] It should be said, however, that a comparison of the incomplete returns for the two Parliaments (*Members of Parliament*, pt. I, pp. 375–380) does suggest that not more than a quarter of the members returned in 1553 had also sat in Edward's first Parliament. Professor Neale suggests that about half would be the Elizabethan norm (*The Elizabethan House of Commons* (L., 1949), 309). Any detailed analysis of the two Edwardian Parliaments must await Professor Bindoff's forthcoming volume in the *History of Parliament* series.

[5] Froude, *History of England*, V, 463–464.

degrees'. To conserve the King's strength the Lord Chancellor
made 'a proposition' (i.e., the speech from the throne), whereupon
the session was adjourned until the following day when the Commons assembled at Westminster.[1]

As we have noted, Parliament had been convened for a single
purpose—to provide a desperately needed subsidy—with the result
that after the introduction of the subsidy bill on March 6th, the
measure was literally 'rammed' through in order to gain an early
dissolution, to remove the sick King from national attention, and to
avoid further and controversial bills which were being advanced in
the Commons. The result was the shortest session of Parliament, in
the Tudor period at least.[2] It is true that a list of eight desired laws
was in governmental hands at the opening,[3] but of these only the
subsidy bill and an act making the export of bullion a felony were
actually passed. Another measure ordering the affairs of the Merchant Adventurers was defeated, and still another for the preservation of timber had been introduced, but had not come to final action
before the dissolution was ordered. The four remaining governmental measures projected were, so far as the *Commons' Journal*
may be regarded as complete, never even brought to debate. This
short session was, then, harassed, nervous, and evidently regarded
by Northumberland and the reigning junta as an unwelcome
nuisance.

The subsidy bill, so central to the government's need and intentions, was introduced in the Commons on March 6th, and we are
told by the unfortunately laconic *Commons' Journal* that the next
day the 'King's Council and others [were] to meet in the Star
Chamber at 7 o'clock to consult' for the tax being demanded. The
bill passed readings on three successive days, being finally argued
and ordered engrossed on March 11th and then passed by the
Lower House on March 14th. There had been considerable difficulty in the Commons, the measure being in the end limited to a
subsidy and two tenths and fifteenths, the tax to be paid over a
term of two years, and carrying a rider setting out special auditing
provisions for the collectors and receivers. Then, being carried to
the Lords, it was rushed through in the space of four days, the final
vote being taken on March 18th.[4]

[1] Stow, *Annales*, 609; Nichols, *Remains*, I, clxxviii.

[2] Rivalled by the Elizabethan Parliament of 1576, which sat for four weeks and two
days.   [3] S.P. Dom., Edw. VI, XVIII, 13: Mar. 1(?), 1553.

[4] Our principal sources for the discussion of the legislative history of this Parliament
are the *C.J.*, the *L.J.*, and the *Statutes of the realm*. Hence we will eschew precise documentation, save for statute identifications.

One wonders—there is no documentary evidence—whether part of the difficulty experienced in the Commons was not occasioned by the largely false and wholly gratuitous attack on the character and policy of Somerset which the preamble to the act recites as the cause for the ills of the realm. The late Protector was blamed for the costly wars with France and Scotland, for ill-advised invasions, desperate enterprises, and 'sumptuous endless vain fortifications', bringing in costly mercenary troops, endangering England's credit overseas, and for the 'heap of calamities [which] fell upon all the realm immediately . . . [and] remaineth not wholly yet filled up'. Somerset was blamed too for the successive debasements of the coinage (including those of Henry VIII and Northumberland) which had shaken confidence and further weakened the King's estate. It was now declared to be the government's intention, with the aid of the subsidy, to unburden the King of 'his great intolerable weight and charges lying and growing in strangers' hands beyond the seas' and to restore the 'decayed house' of the commonwealth which was England.[1]

Short and hurried as the Parliament was, other important measures were passed, mostly of a constitutional or administrative nature. Thus 7 Edward VI, c. 1, opposed in its third reading by seven lay peers,[2] but unanimously passed in the Lords after changes in the draft, sought to tighten and speed the collection of royal revenues and reflected the King's growing concern with administrative laxity in financial matters. So too, as we have earlier noted,[3] legislative authority was lent to the recommendation of the royal commission which had proposed the merging of the several revenue courts.[4] Another act (7 Edward VI, c. 4) placed under bond those responsible for collecting tenths due from the bishops and set stated dates for the payment of such accounts to the Crown. And, finally, a statute of Edward IV conferring on the Crown augmented powers in prohibiting the export of bullion from the realm was revived, with the intention of tightening even further the control which the Council had now assumed over fiscal affairs.[5]

The economic and social legislation passed by this Parliament was perfunctory to say the least, largely we may suppose because Northumberland was determined on a short session and such measures always occasioned long debate and numerous re-draftings.

---

[1] 7 Edward VI, c. 12 (*Statutes of the realm*, IV, i, 176–189).
[2] They were Pembroke, Morley, Burgh, Bray, Wentworth, Bedford, and Rich.
[3] *Vide ante*, 446–447.   [4] 7 Edward VI, c. 2 (*Statutes of the realm*, IV, i, 164–165).
[5] *Ibid.* c. 6 (*Statutes of the realm*, IV, i, 170).

Hence only five of the fourteen statutes of a public nature passed by this Parliament relate to social and economic matters at all, and their unimportance may be guaged by the fact that the most significant was one 'to avoid the great price and excess of wines' (7 Edward VI, c. 5). The real purpose of this measure was to wipe out dubious taverns 'in back lanes, corners, and suspicious places', and rigorously to limit their number.

More numerous, and far more indicative of the mood and concern of the House of Commons, were twenty-two bills of a public character which were introduced in this Parliament but which failed to be enacted into law. Of these bills half dealt with economic policy, four with social problems, and one with the public weal generally. But Northumberland, having extracted from Parliament all he could of taxation, and with the necessary legislation required by the King in hand for the reform of the revenue courts, pressed with evident nervousness for a dissolution. Cranmer did once more urge the consideration of the codification of canon law, on which he had laboured for so long,[1] but was rudely rebuked by Northumberland, who warned him that the bishops must limit themselves to the spiritual functions with which they were charged: 'Let them forbear calling into question in their sermons the acts of the prince and his ministers, else they should suffer with the evil preachers.'[2] Northumberland wished no consideration of complex or controversial matters, principally certainly because it was now evident that the King's health was deteriorating. Parliament was accordingly dissolved on March 31st and on that same day Scheyfve reported that because of his health the King would spend Easter at Westminster rather than at Greenwich as was his wont, for 'he is not entirely recovered yet, and is still troubled by catarrh and a cough'.[3]

3. THE ILLNESS AND DEATH OF THE KING
(JANUARY–JULY 6, 1553)

We cannot date precisely the onset of the King's fatal illness which was a classical case of acute pulmonary tuberculosis, but which at the beginning was mistaken for one of the colds and 'catarrhal' conditions to which he was subject. We have noted abundant instances of his activity in the closing weeks of 1552, even though we remain puzzled by the abrupt and inexplicable

---

[1] *Vide ante*, 357–361.
[2] *Cal. S.P. Span.*, XI, 33: Apr. 10, 1553.
[3] *Ibid.* 22.

ending of his *Chronicle*, to which he was devoted by both temperament and habit, on November 30th. At the same time, as we have
seen, he remained directly concerned with the proposals for the reorganization of the Council, the final draft of which is in his hand
and which could not have been completed much before it was presented to the Council for preliminary discussion on January 15,
1553.[1] But so far as the now faulty and incomplete Council records
suggest, there was not to be any further consideration of these
ambitious proposals which, given the King's normal pertinacity, in
itself suggests that his illness may have gripped him in late January.
Illness notwithstanding, the King, as was his wont, had removed
from Westminster to Greenwich for an elaborate observance of the
holiday season.[2] At about that time, Stow tells us, Edward 'fell
sick of a cough . . . which grievously increased, and at last ended
in a consumption of the lights'.[3]

Northumberland's own indecision and concern are suggested by
the fact that both Mary and Elizabeth were kept informed of the
King's condition. It is not too much to say, indeed, that for the first
time in his tenure of power the Duke sought to deal with Mary with
respect and some measure of indulgence.[4] She was in fact called to
court to visit her brother, Lord Warwick (Northumberland's son)
and Lord William Howard meeting her on February 6th on the outskirts of London and conducting her with full honours through the
streets to her lodging. But on the evening of her arrival the King
was stricken with a chill and persistent fever, so that her audience
with him was postponed until the 10th, when she visited him in his
chamber. The King, so Scheyfve reported, spoke with Mary in
warm terms, but the conversation was confined to pleasant small-
talk, there being no mention of religion. Scheyfve, who was
securing information from the royal household, further reported
that the King suffered pain when in the grasp of fever, and that
inhalation was becoming more difficult. In fact, so the diplomatist
tells us, the Council had been warned by the attending physicians
that the illness was of the utmost gravity. But towards the close of
the month (February) the King seemed to mend, receiving Andrew

---

[1] Edward VI, *Chronicle*, xxviii–xxxi, 181–183; *vide ante*, 452–455.
[2] Machyn, *Diary*, 28–29; Stow, *Annales*, 609. We are told by Stow that the King took
great delight 'in his pastimes' of the full twelve-day holiday season. The 'pastimes' were
expensive, £705 6s having been laid out (*A.P.C.*, IV, 206).
[3] Stow, *Annales*, 609. Hayward, citing no contemporary authority, also puts the onset
of the illness in January, stating that there was from the beginning 'a tough, strong,
straining cough' (*Edward VI*, 323); and see Burnet, *Reformation*, II, 367.
[4] *Vide ante*, 256 ff.

Dudley, who had returned from Guînes, and his Council on the 24th, evoking from Winchester a fairly cheerful report of improvement just three days later.[1]

During March, as we have observed,[2] special and careful arrangements were made by the Council to protect the King during the session of Parliament which exactly filled that month. Scheyfve reported that Edward did not leave his room, that he was very weak and thin, and that the doctors warned that any change in his limited routine would place his life in great danger.[3] It was also Scheyfve's view that Northumberland was seeking to enhance his personal power and to provide for his own safety, though he had again written to the Princess Mary, keeping her fairly accurately informed respecting the King's illness. But there was some improvement in April, or perhaps the doctors were themselves beguiled by 'the present soft and bright weather', for the King was permitted to essay out into the small park at Westminster for short intervals, and then on April 11th made the easy, and final, journey by barge down to his favourite palace at Greenwich.[4] At the end of the month the new French ambassador, Antoine de Noailles, arrived in London, but because of the state of the King's health was unable to present his credentials. He was, however, invited to dine at Court, where he was entertained by Northumberland, the Privy Council, and a few other nobles who gave him the impression that no strong hope was entertained for the King's recovery.[5]

Tuberculosis is not only a terrible, it is a cruel, disease, since it is marked by a sanguine expectation and by periods of what can only be described as false hope on the part of the patient. And so it seems to have been with Edward during much of the month of May. On May 7th, Petre wrote to Cecil, who as we have seen was absenting himself from the Council in this dangerous period with a possibly imaginary ailment, to announce that the King was greatly improved, and that if he will remain 'close' for a few more days should be able to take the air at Greenwich 'in better case than he hath been a good while'.[6] On the same day Northumberland also wrote to Cecil, with what can only be regarded as excited happiness,

---

[1] *Cal. S.P. Span.*, XI, 9, 10, 13: Feb. 17 and 21, 1553; Machyn, *Diary*, 30–31; HMC, *Salisbury MSS.*, I, 111: Winchester to Cecil.

[2] *Vide ante*, 505.

[3] *Cal. S.P. Span.*, XI, 16–19: Mar. 17, 1553.

[4] *Ibid.* 32: Apr. 10, 1553; *vide ante*, 492; Froude, *History of England*, V, 481, 488.

[5] Noailles, Messieurs de, *Ambassades en Angleterre*, ed. by R. A. de Vertot and C. Villaret (5 vols., Leyden, 1763), II, 3–4; Nichols, *Remains*, I, clxxxvi.

[6] HMC, *Salisbury MSS.*, I, 121.

that he had for two or three days past been given 'joyful comfort' from the King's physicians. They now told him 'that our sovereign lord doth begin very joyfully to increase and amend, they having no doubt of the thorough recovery of his highness, the rather because his majesty is fully bent to follow their council and advice'.[1] This is not the language or the tone of a conspirator against the succession, but rather the instinctive response of one who hoped that a great burden might be lifted. On May 11th, as we have seen,[2] Hugh Willoughby and his little, but gallant, fleet let downstream past Greenwich, the King watching and listening from his window as the ordnance was fired in salute. A few days later the French ambassadors reported that they had been informed by the Council that the King had so improved that he could receive them in person. The brief audience was held on May 17th, at which time they thought Edward very weak and noted that he was racked by a steady cough.[3]

It was at this juncture that the complex and carefully arranged group of marriages connecting Northumberland at least vaguely with the royal line was consummated. These arrangements were actually begun a year earlier, suggesting again that Northumberland was disposing his affairs and gaining further alliances as well as a more elevated status for his line rather than that these efforts were in any direct sense an effort to gain control over the succession. Thus in 1552, long before there was any reason for doubting that the King would in due time marry and have heirs of his own, Northumberland was pressing for the marriage of his fourth, and only unmarried, son, Lord Guildford Dudley, with Margaret Clifford, who through her mother was of royal blood in the Brandon line.[4] The pressure was indeed heavy, Dudley having secured the intervention of both the King and Council in a bootless effort to persuade Cumberland, whose wife had died in 1547, to yield his consent.[5] Northumberland thus rebuffed turned to the Grey line,

[1] Lansdowne MS. 3, #23.   [2] *Vide ante*, 492.
[3] Noailles, *Ambassades*, II, 26–27.
[4] A rough outline of the relationships may be helpful:

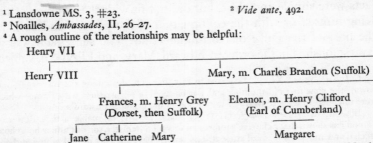

[5] Royal MSS., 18.C.xiv, f. 236. Margaret Clifford was briefly espoused to Northumberland's brother, Andrew, but the marriage was never concluded.

with which he already had close personal connections, the Duchess of Suffolk being still alive and the Duke, surely the most empty-headed peer of England, being his most fervent supporter in the Council. Arrangements were quickly made for the marriages of Guildford Dudley to Jane Grey, of Catherine Dudley to Lord Hastings, and of Catherine Grey to Pembroke's son, Lord Herbert. These nuptials were celebrated with great magnificence at North-umberland's London house on May 21st, with the King's full consent. With this inter-linking network of relationships the *arriviste* Northumberland had completed the high placing of his family; no more than that, we may with some confidence believe, was for the time being intended.[1]

But only a few days after the fateful marriage of Jane Grey to the shallow and vainglorious Guildford Dudley had taken place, Scheyfve was reliably informed that the King had suffered a relapse and that he was now very ill. It was now reported that he found sleep only under opiates. Even more alarming, 'the sputum which he brings up is livid, black, fetid, and full of carbon; it smells beyond measure'. The royal physicians now took the gloomy, and correct, view that the worsening symptoms portended death within three months and they had so informed the Duke of Northumber-land.[2] Sir John Cheke, writing to Bullinger on June 7th, spoke in discouraged terms of the chances for the King's survival,[3] while Scheyfve, writing on the 11th to the Emperor, reported that Edward's condition was very grave and expressed his conviction that North-umberland would move to seize the throne at the moment of his death.[4]

During these anxious weeks, before it could be assumed that the King's illness would in fact be fatal, the whole problem of the suc-cession must have been much in the minds of all the Councillors, as it surely was in the thinking of Charles V and Henry II. The legal facts were simple and clear, but did not fit with the thinking of the King himself or with the continuation of the power—and perhaps the life—of the Duke of Northumberland. The succession was in law established in the order of Edward, Mary, and Elizabeth, subject

---

[1] *Cal. S.P. Span.*, XI, 46. Scheyfve in this dispatch, describing the marriages, was now of the view that Northumberland was engaged in negotiations with France which were intended to deprive Mary of the throne in the event of Edward's death.

[2] Bindoff, in *History Today*, III (1953), 647. In this estimable article Professor Bindoff has shown that Scheyfve's informant was John Banister, son of a minor household official, and himself a medical student. His reports have the ring of undoubted authen-ticity.

[3] Robinson, *Original letters*, I, 141.   [4] *Cal. S.P. Span.*, XI, 50.

to such restrictions as Henry VIII might by will or letters patent place on it. Henry's will had confirmed this order and extended it, in what then seemed improbable eventualities, to the three Grey sisters by seniority and then to their cousin, Margaret Clifford.[1] Edward, with what advice remains uncertain—there may well have been none—was persuaded that the Henrician precedent permitted a reigning monarch to devise the Crown by will, quite ignoring the fact that Henry's own power was vested in him by an Act of Parliament, that he as a minor could not make a valid will, and that it was treason to attempt to change the succession so carefully laid down in his father's will.

The fundamental legal prohibitions notwithstanding, Edward had undertaken in his own hand to draft a *Devise* of the Crown, which had the effect of setting aside the claims of his two sisters and, following his father's will in this respect, of Mary Stuart.[2] The whole purpose of the *Devise* was to deny the throne to Mary Tudor because of her fanatical Catholicism. The exclusion of Elizabeth, which is puzzling, may have derived from the fact that she had once been bastardized by Parliament, that her claims were obviously junior to Mary's, and very probably because the King knew her well enough to be sure that she would not trifle with treasonable courses. The difficulty faced by Edward as he toyed with the problem of the succession was that of all the living descendants of Henry VII, the Scottish line being excluded, he was the only male. The original draft therefore ordered the succession in his own male heir and then in the non-existent heirs male of five collateral descendants of Henry VIII: Frances, Duchess of Suffolk; her three daughters, Jane, Catherine, and Mary; and Margaret Clifford, in that order.[3] Then when it became clear that his own death was not far off—that there were to be no Tudor heirs male—the succession was radically altered by a simple change of language: 'to the

---

[1] Bindoff, in *History Today*, III (1953), 643.

[2] This famous document, which was in form the rough draft of a will, cannot be precisely dated (Petyt MSS., Inner Temple, xlvii, f. 316). The bold, normal hand, almost as legible as typescript, could hardly have been written by Edward after the debilitating illness had become advanced. It would be my own conjecture that it was composed as early as January or February, when the King, probably without Northumberland's full knowledge, may have been considering taking the problem of the succession to Parliament. This view is strengthened by the fact that the original draft still contemplated the possibility of the King's own marriage and heirs of his own. Whenever it was drafted, it most certainly was brought out for revision near the date of Guildford Dudley's marriage to the Lady Jane Grey.

[3] *My devise for the succession*, Petyt MS. xlvii, f. 316. There is an excellently edited text of the document in Nichols, *Remains*, II, 571-572. See also the genealogical chart, *ante*, 513.

Lady Jane's heirs male' being revised to read, 'to the Lady Jane and her heirs male'. This one vastly important change having been made, and now certainly sensing that his end was near, Edward moved with the speed, the stubborn determination, and the fanatical resolution of which he had on numerous occasions shown he was capable. His resolve to bar Mary from the throne had now become something approaching a mania.

On June 12th, by the King's command, the chief justice and the law officers were summoned to his bedside and were ordered by Edward himself immediately to draw a formal will on the basis of the *Devise* which he handed to them. To this decision the Privy Council, including Cecil who had felt obliged to make a reluctant return to court on the preceding day and Petre who with much trepidation drew up the legal documents required, had been dragooned by the King's imperious insistence. Montague, the Lord Chief Justice, and his colleagues[1] met apart and after consideration thought that statutes regarding the succession so formidable that 'we refused to make the said books [the will], for the danger of treason'; whereupon, he was later to record, Northumberland 'fell into a great anger and rage, and called me traitor before all the Council, and said that in the quarrel of that matter he would fight in his shirt with any man living'.[2]

But it was the King, not Northumberland, who was in fact exerting continuous and irresistible pressure. On June 15th the judges were again called before him, and with 'sharp words and angry countenance' the King commanded Montague to obey on his allegiance, which several Lords standing by declared it manifest treason to refuse. In the sixteenth century a subject did not in England flatly disobey the direct command of his sovereign. Montague confessed that 'being in great fear as ever I was in my life before, seeing the King so earnest . . . and considering with myself the making of the book without the execution of it was no treason', resolved to do so but to have no part in the execution of the devise for the succession, though, he does not add, even with this view the Attorney General (Gosnold) did not agree. Hence, under intolerable pressure, he agreed to draft the letters patent according to the articles handed to him by the King. But the document as prepared, he warned the King and Council, did not void the Henrician statute which lay like a great barrier across the fixed but delirious resolution of the King.[3] Then a few days later (June 21st)

---

[1] Bromley, Baker, and Gosnold.   [2] HMC, *MSS. of Lord Montagu of Beaulieu*, 4.
[3] *Ibid.* 5.

Cranmer,[1] the Lord Chancellor, the Privy Councillors, twenty-two peers of the realm, judges, household officers, the Lord Mayor of London and the aldermen, the sheriffs of Middlesex, Surrey, and Kent, six Merchant Adventurers, and six members of the Staple—all the notables who could be found and bullied—endorsed the document, promising 'by our oaths and honours to observe, fully perform, and keep' the settling of the succession as commanded by the King.[2]

We can never know with certainty—events moved too swiftly and too much was unrecorded—but the evidence we do have is persuasive that the decision to alter the succession was the King's and that Northumberland found himself engulfed in a gigantic treason and facing almost immediate disaster when he undertook to carry out the King's resolution. We have seen that for many months the Duke had been ill, or absent, or melancholy. His thoughts were of retirement, not of great new adventures. He was without the burning religious conviction which was the mainspring of the King's decision and which explains his implacable resolution. He had kept Mary apprised of the King's illness and seems until very late indeed to have assumed that the succession would remain unaltered. He had organized no conspiracy until at the end he embraced Edward's own unconstitutional and grossly illegal undertaking. For once in his life, Northumberland seems to have been entrapped in a great conspiracy not of his own contriving. He knew that his closest colleagues feared him and that many of the Council and nobility hated him. As one of the foremost soldiers of his generation, he knew too that the dismantling of England's defences and armed forces had left him without the military resources required for such a gigantic overturn of an ordered state. Yet he was propelled to his doom by the ill-considered and fevered contriving of a desperate boy who knew that his own death was at hand. One need not be an admirer of the character of the Duke of Northumberland to feel a sense of pity at his inglorious end.

While these machinations were in progress, the King's health was declining steadily, and the imperial and French envoys were frantically seeking news—which proved to be amazingly accurate—from their sources at Court. In mid-June Scheyfve reported that the

---

[1] Cranmer, be it said, signed with great reluctance. He at first refused to sign, but after the King personally had told him that the judges had assured him that he might legally dispose the succession and after consulting the King's attorney, Edward Griffith, did lend his signature (Nichols, *Narratives of the Reformation* (Camden Soc. LXXVII), 225–226); Ridley, *Cranmer*, 345).

[2] Nichols, *Remains*, II, 572–573.

King was desperately ill, noting also that the great of the realm had been summoned to Court to lend their aid in a plot to deprive Mary of the succession.[1] The Princess Mary was at once bewildered and fearful, calling on the Emperor for his advice on the conduct of her affairs.[2] The French ambassador understood from one of the royal physicians on June 16th that all hope for the King had been abandoned and that the Lords of the Council were almost constantly concerned with the problem of the succession. Nor did he miss the obvious significance of the fact that the night watch of the City had been doubled and the armed forces in the Tower greatly strengthened.[3] Hoby, anxious for news in Brussels, wrote a few days later that rumours were rife there that Edward was in fact dead and that Mary had succeeded.[4] In London, public prayers for the King were instituted by the Earl of Bedford in the royal chapel, 'meet to be used of all the King's true subjects' and imploring God to look with pity upon Edward and the whole realm, since he had well begun 'the rooting out of error, idolatry, and superstition, and the planting of true religion, true worshipping and verity'.[5]

Meanwhile the Emperor, who had followed English developments closely but with a pessimistic view of Mary's peaceful succession, at last bestirred himself and on June 23rd informed the English government that he was sending immediately a special embassy composed of Courrières, Thoulouse, and the famous diplomatist, Renard.[6] They were instructed at Brussels to proceed at once and to seek by every possible means to secure a fuller and clearer understanding of what was occurring in England. It was the Emperor's conclusion that an attempt would be made to bar Mary from the throne on the grounds of her faith, and that this effort would probably be supported by France. If the ambassadors were permitted to talk with Mary, they were to advise great caution. If, as might well be the case, she was offered the throne by those now holding power on condition that she attempt no change in government or religion, she should accept these requirements, reserving, however, her own faith and worship.[7] One cannot help reflecting how different, and probably happier, the history of England might have been, had the government's policy—and the King's—been to secure precisely these conditions.

---

[1] *Cal. S.P. Span.*, XI, 54–55.   [2] *Ibid.* 57.
[3] Noailles, *Ambassades*, II, 40–41.
[4] HMC, *Salisbury MSS.*, I, 123: June 25, 1553.
[5] *A prayer sayd in the Kinges chappell in the tyme of hys Graces sicknes, etc.* ([L.], 1553).
[6] *Cal. S.P. Span.*, XI, 58–59.
[7] *Ibid.* 63–65: June 23, 1553.

The imperial ambassador, whose sources of information remained reliable, was towards the end forwarding almost daily bulletins to the Emperor. He wrote that the London populace sensed that the King's death was near when Bedford's prayer for his recovery was posted in the City.[1] In another dispatch on the same day Scheyfve related that the King 'had not the strength to stir, and can hardly breathe' and that normal bodily functions had halted. He now understood, though he cited no evidence, that there was strong opposition in the Council to Northumberland's plans, centring in Winchester, Bedford, and Cheyney.[2] Northumberland held a long meeting with de Noailles on the 26th, but was vague regarding the King's health and misleading with respect to the now heavy concentration of troops and naval vessels in the Thames, all of which was reported by Scheyfve to Charles V on the day following.[3]

During these tense and uncertain days Northumberland had continued his brief but friendly reports to the Princess Mary, accurately presenting the medical particulars and, of course, seeking to conceal as long as possible the facts regarding the King's devise for the succession. But we are told by Scheyfve categorically that the provisions of Edward's will were known in London and that Mary, having been summoned to the capital by the Privy Council, was warned by 'a friend' on July 3rd that she had best remove from her seat at Hunsdon (Herts) deeper into the country, whereupon, after spending the night of the 5th at Sawston Hall, she set out for Kenninghall (Norfolk), some sixty miles from London, conveniently near the coast if she must flee, and in a region where she enjoyed warm support amongst the gentry.[4] In London, meanwhile, there were endless rumours and a frightening tension respecting the condition of the King. There was a false report that he would show himself at Greenwich on Sunday, July 2nd, whereupon a great crowd gathered, only to be told that it would occur the next day, and then that the air was too chilly. The end came, mercifully, in the evening of July 6th, when, attended by his doctors, with his gentlemen friends Henry Sidney and Sir Thomas Wroth, and his favourite body-servant, Christopher Salmon, in attendance, and

[1] *Cal. S.P. Span.*, XI, 65: June 24, 1553.
[2] *Ibid.* 66–67.
[3] Noailles, *Ambassades*, II, 47–49; *Cal. S.P. Span.*, XI, 67: June 27, 1553.
[4] *Cal. S.P. Span.*, XI, 70: July 4, 1553; *Cal. S.P. Ven.*, V, 537; *The chronicle of Queen Jane, and of two years of Queen Mary, etc.*, ed. by J. G. Nichols (Camden Soc. XLVIII), 1–2. Mary was warned by both Sir Nicholas Throckmorton and Soranzo, the Venetian ambassador, and perhaps as well by others.

supported in Sidney's arms, he uttered his last words: 'I am faint; Lord have mercy upon me, and take my spirit.'[1]

4. THE SHATTERING OF THE CONSPIRACY

The King's death, which had been so often bruited about in London, was kept secret by the Council for two days so that its dispositions could be made and in the forlorn hope that Mary could be apprehended in her flight into Norfolk and Suffolk. Any further delay was, however, impossible, and on July 8th the Lord Mayor and five of the aldermen, together with representatives of the Staplers and the Merchant Adventurers, were summoned to Greenwich, where they were informed in confidence of Edward's death, were formally notified of his alterations in the succession and, under what pressure is not known, added their signatures to the document already subscribed by so many notables.[2] The news was abroad in London that evening, while a more formal announcement

---

[1] Foxe, *Acts and monuments*, VI, 352. There were always dark rumours of poisoning when a royal personage died in this period. But in the case of Edward they were particularly numerous and persistent. To take but a small sampling: the *Grey Friars Chronicle* (p. 78) noted at the time of death that 'some say he was poisoned'; Machyn tells us that everybody said the King died by poison (*Diary*, 35); Robert Parkyn, a clergyman in southern Yorkshire, was certain that death 'was through poisoning', as the common voice was spread amongst the people (*Narrative of the Reformation*, ed. by A. G. Dickens, in *E.H.R.*, LXII (1947), 77); Vincentius, in England with a Hanse delegation thought that the King had been poisoned (Hay, Denys, 'The "Narratio Historica" of P. Vincentius, 1553', in *E.H.R.*, LXIII (1948), 353-355), as did Burcher (Robinson, *Original letters*, II, 684-685). The same rumours were abroad in Germany (*Das Buch Weinsberg, etc.*, II, ed. by K. Höhlbaum (Publikationen der Gesellschaft für rheinische Geschichtskunde, IV, Leipzig, 1887), 32). It need scarcely be added that there is no evidence whatsoever to substantiate such a view. In all the accounts Northumberland was the villain of the piece, but, if his intentions were at once treasonable and nefarious, he needed above all else more time; if, as we believe, his was a most reluctant treason, imposed by Edward himself, what he would have wished was the survival and recovery of the King.

To complete these somewhat morbid particulars, Edward's funeral was delayed, because of the political uncertainties, until Aug. 8th. The officers of state and household were in attendance, but the twelve principal mourners failed to include most of the great Protestant Lords of the Council, who were, of course, in serious difficulties. Aside from Pembroke, most of the group were peers like Oxford, Worcester, Bath, Abergavenny, Windsor, Burgh, Berkeley, and Stourton, who had played no important role in Edwardian governmental affairs. The funeral at Westminster Abbey was sparsely attended, there being no lights burning, no Roman Catholic ceremonial, and no invitations to the foreign ambassadors. Edward was buried in Henry VII's chapel. No marker was ever raised to his memory. (Machyn, *Diary*, 39-40; Noailles, *Ambassades*, II, 108-109; Nichols, *Remains*, I, ccxlii.)

[2] Stow, *Annales*, 609-610; Wriothesley, *Chronicle*, 85; Froude, *History of England*, VI, 5. It should be here said that we shall depend heavily on Stow's masterly account of these tumultuous days. It is not only a prime source, but it happens also to be superb historical writing.

was made by the Council to the sheriffs and justices of nearby counties, stating that Mary was in flight towards Norfolk and the sea-coast, presumably either to pass overseas or to wait for military aid from abroad 'to the unquiet of the realm and the setting aside of the order of succession' as determined by the late King. To avoid these dangers and to 'preserve the realm from the tyranny of foreign wars', they were instructed to gather their forces and stand ready to 'repair unto us and to stand fast' in defence of Edward's ordinance for the governing of the succession, to maintain order in their counties, and to apprehend any who sought to make stirs.[1] Whatever remaining uncertainty there may have been in London regarding the essential facts was clarified by Bishop Ridley's intemperate and almost hysterical sermon on the next day (July 9th), when he bitterly denounced Mary for her fervent Catholicism and declared both Mary and Elizabeth to be bastards incapable of succeeding to the throne.

Lady Jane Grey, forced by her father into an unwanted marriage with Guildford Dudley, still a child, albeit a precocious and attractive one, and obviously as frightened as she was ill-informed of events, had pleaded her extreme youth in order to stay on with her mother. It seems probable, indeed, that she did not know the full facts regarding the *Devise* until Edward was on the point of death. Now she was taken, first to Northumberland's house in Chelsea, and then, almost against her will, to Syon House, where she was first informed of the King's death. Then on July 10th she was taken by river to the Tower where in the presence, among others, of Northumberland, Pembroke, Northampton, Huntingdon, and Arundel she was formally informed of the alteration in the succession and was at once proclaimed Queen. The household troops were immediately sworn to her, while Petre and Cheke were designated to wait upon the imperial ambassador to inform him of her succession.[2]

Either that evening or early the next morning messengers arrived at the Tower with news that Mary had safely reached East Anglia,

[1] HMC, *7th report*, App., 609: *Molyneux MSS*. This letter of advice was addressed to the Surrey authorities. It was signed by Cranmer, Goodrich, Winchester, Northumberland, Bedford, North, Arundel, Huntingdon, Pembroke, Richard Cotton, Darcy, and Cobham.

[2] Stow, *Annales*, 610; Robinson, *Original letters*, I, 274: Hilles to Bullinger; *Chronicle of Queen Jane* (Camden Soc. XLVIII), 2–3. We need not say more regarding this innocent girl than that, like most of her line, she displayed great intellectual capacities, was a devout Protestant, and was of a pleasing personality. For her tutors' comments on her and her family setting, see Robinson, *Original letters*, I, 278–279 (Aylmer to Bullinger), and 282, 290 (Haddon to Bullinger).

that she had already proclaimed herself Queen, had commanded the allegiance of the nobility, and had forwarded an appeal to the Emperor for his assistance. At about the same time her own messenger reached London with a letter to the Council in which she reminded them that her succession was ordered by Act of Parliament and by the will of her father, that she had proclaimed herself Queen of England, and that she required the loyalty of all her nobles. She was not, she concluded, unaware of the overt steps taken by the Council 'to undo the provisions made for our preferment'. Still, in order to avoid bloodshed, she stood ready to pardon their offences, on condition that they lend her allegiance by promulgating in London the proclamation of her accession.[1]

The Council replied to Mary on July 11th in stiff and ominous tones. Jane, they held, was Queen of England by the authority of letters patent properly executed by the late King and endorsed by most of the nobility of the realm. They reminded her that by an act of Parliament she stood illegitimate and unable to inherit and warned that she must at once forbear the creation of strife and submit. On the same day the Council explained events to the imperial authorities in Flanders, where Hoby was to announce the Lady Jane's accession to the throne. They had commanded the Lady Mary to conform herself, but she had failed to do so. Her support, it was explained, came from 'a few lewd, base people', whereas the gentry and nobility lent their loyalty to the new Queen. Lest the 'baser sort of people' grow unruly, Northumberland and Northampton would shortly proceed 'with a convenient force into the parts of Norfolk' to restore obedience.[2] London lay quiet on this day, but intelligence reaching Northumberland from his sons, Warwick and Sir Robert Dudley, who had tried vainly to intercept Mary on her way into Norfolk, was not hopeful. With no more than light scouting forces in their command, when they had moved in on Mary's gathering escort, they had suffered heavy desertions in their own ranks and had to withdraw. Robert Dudley then retired to Wisbech while trying unsuccessfully to win over King's Lynn for Queen Jane. But even Wisbech Castle was shortly to be taken over by neighbouring gentry in the name of Queen Mary.[3]

Meanwhile, in London the special mission from the Emperor, headed by Courrières and Renard, remained decidedly pessimistic

---

[1] *Chronicle of Queen Jane* (Camden Soc. XLVIII), 5; Holinshed, *Chronicles*, III, 1069–1070; Froude, *History of England*, VI, 13–15; Wriothesley, *Chronicle*, II, 87.

[2] Cotton MSS., Galba, B, xii, f. 250; Ellis, *Original letters*, ser. 3, III, 311–312.

[3] VCH, *Cambs*, IV, 252. Courrières and Renard thought Mary would almost surely be taken by Dudley, who had 300–400 horse (*Cal. S.P. Span.*, XI, 79–80: July 10, 1553).

regarding Mary's safety and not a little nonplussed by her willingness to incur such great risks. They had reached London on the day
of Edward's death. They feared that nothing could be done to
prevent Jane's succession, particularly because they were certain
that Northumberland had moved only after assurances of French
support. Hence they had sent agents to advise her not to proclaim
herself and to remain inert until support, if she was to gain any,
should manifest itself.[1] They were persuaded on the 10th, as Jane
entered the Tower and was proclaimed, that there was really no
hope left for Mary and hence had no intention of entering more than
formal protests because her rightful claim had been overridden.[2]
They were as discouraged on the day following, believing that Mary
could not possibly prevail unless a considerable number of the most
powerful nobles declared for her, and observing that there was no
evidence of any support for her in London.[3] Mary had, however,
disregarded their considered advice by proclaiming herself, and
now wished another messenger to come to her, which the ambassadors thought could not be arranged. On the next day Cobham and
Mason called formally on them in the name of the Council, setting
out the alterations made by Edward in the succession and informing
them that their mission must be regarded as ended. The Council had
expressly resolved that they might not see or communicate with
Mary, or, at their peril, attempt to lend her any aid. To this Courrières replied that if this were the case they must then ask for their
escort and prepare to leave the kingdom. This bold ploy was
successful, Mason and Cobham sitting 'staring at one another' and
begging them to make no move of departure until they had consulted with the Council.[4] The fact was that the ambassadors had
just received most encouraging news regarding the whole turbulent
and liquid situation.

The imperial envoys, and for that matter some of the Council,
were now receiving intelligence reports unquestionably suggesting
that all classes in the realm were beginning quite spontaneously to
rise to the support of Mary and what was generally regarded as her
undoubted claim to the throne. Scheyfve, as early as the 12th, was
reliably informed that Mary's position in Norfolk and Suffolk was
so strong that major forces would be required to overthrow her.
The Council, in an about-face, now wished Courrières and his

---

[1] *Cal. S.P. Span.*, XI, 73–74: July 7, 1553.
[2] *Ibid.* 77–80: July 10, 1553.
[3] *Ibid.* 81, 83: July 11, 1553.
[4] *Ibid.* 84–86: July 12, 1553.

colleagues to remain in England. On the next day they waited on the Council, warning them of French faithlessness, expressing the Emperor's hope that his cousin would marry an English subject, and assuring them of Charles's good intentions. The Council expressed the warm hope that the embassy would remain in London, though on the 14th the envoys were once more discouraged by the report of a messenger from Mary's camp who feared that 'destruction' was hanging over her unless more help came speedily to her support.[1]

The news reaching the Council on the 12th and 13th had been ominous indeed. On Mary's passage through Cambridge to Bury St Edmunds, and thence to Kenninghall and Framlingham, every family was obliged to make its decision, and such great gentle families as the Cornwallises, the Jernegans, the Bedingfields, and the Bacons cast their fortunes with the Princess.[2] Even more disturbing was the news that such peers and members of the upper gentry as the Earl of Bath, Sir Thomas Wharton (Lord Wharton's son), Sir John Mordaunt (son of Lord Mordaunt), Sir William Drury, Sir John Shelton, and the Earl of Sussex, with his son, had declared for Mary and were moving towards her with the not inconsiderable forces which they disposed.[3] There were credible reports, too, that the Earl of Derby was moving south from Cheshire with a large force pledged to Mary's cause, while even more immediately threatening was the news that Sir Edward Hastings (Huntingdon's brother) was raising Buckinghamshire for the Princess and that the formidable Sir Peter Carew had proclaimed her in Devonshire. Robert Dudley was now wandering in the fen country, quite unable to raise the gentry even in this Protestant stronghold.[4]

The most disturbing aspect of these spontaneous actions of a powerful segment of the ruling classes of the realm must have been that included amongst the nobles and great gentry were many known Protestants who were prepared, without any accurate knowledge of events, to risk their lives and fortunes for Mary. The decision being made now across the length and breadth of England was political—legitimist—in its nature. Expressing these sentiments quite perfectly was the Protestant Sir Nicholas Throckmorton, who claimed at least to have been the first to warn Mary of Edward's probable

---

[1] *Cal. S.P. Span.*, XI, 87, 88–89: July 12 and 14, 1553.
[2] Simpson, Alan, *The wealth of the gentry* (Chicago, 1961), 42.
[3] *Chronicle of Queen Jane* (Camden Soc. XLVIII), 4–5; Stow, *Annales*, 610; Wriothesley, *Chronicle*, II, 87.
[4] HMC, *3rd report*, App., 237: *MSS. of Sir Henry Bedingfield*.

death and the schemes being implemented to deprive her of the succession:

> Mourning, from Greenwich I did straight depart
> To London, to an house which bore our name.
> My brethren guessed by my heavy heart
> The King was dead, and I confessed the same:
> The hushing of his death I did unfold,
> Their meaning to proclaim Queen Jane I told.
>
> And, though I liked not the religion
> Which all her life Queen Mary had professed,
> Yet in my mind that wicked motion
> Right heirs for to displace I did detest.
> . . . .
> Wherefor from four of us the news was sent,
> How that her brother he was dead and gone;
> In post her goldsmith then from London went,
> By whom the message was dispatched anon.[1]

It was all too evident, then, despite the bold and elaborate plans laid for what amounted to a *coup d'état*, that any hope for the peaceful succession of Lady Jane Grey was gone. On July 13th, just a week after the King's death, Northumberland reckoned that he had under command in the London area sufficient armed force, constituted principally of the professional bands of the Conciliar nobility, to defeat the undisciplined and ill-armed power being gathered in defence of Mary and her claim to the throne. But he was afraid to leave London and the Privy Council, for he correctly detected that Arundel and Winchester were already disloyal and he suspected that others of the Council were at the least feeble in their support of the Edwardian *Devise* of the succession. He was shaken, too, when some units of the guard at first declined to move, but he immediately restored discipline and attracted re-enforcements by offering 10d a day for the service of those needed to fill the ranks. Force, he knew, must immediately be sent, lest the whole bizarre plan collapse of its own inherent weakness; but the insoluble problem was the command if he, as he should, remained personally in control in London. Suffolk was reliable, if slow and dull of mind, but the Lady Jane 'with weeping tears' insisted that her father remain with her. Northampton, too, was certainly loyal, but his one independent

---

[1] Throckmorton, Sir Nicholas, *Poetical autobiography*, in *Chronicle of Queen Jane* (Camden Soc. XLVIII), 2, from Cole MSS., xi, 272.

command in Norfolk in the black days of 1549 had been a disaster fed by his own blundering impatience. Grey was a fine and experienced professional soldier, but Northumberland dared never forget that he had been a loyal friend to Somerset. Northumberland's own sons were at once too young and inexperienced, while men like Palmer and Gates were more nearly henchmen than experienced field commanders. Both Bedford and Shrewsbury, though competent commanders, had at first disapproved of the alteration of the succession, while Pembroke, who disposed more power than any other noble in England, was subtle, unreliable, and of dubious loyalty.[1]

After the problem of the command had been thoroughly canvassed, the Council on July 12th prevailed upon Northumberland to take charge, it being urged 'that no man was so fit therefor, because he had achieved the victory in Norfolk once already and was therefore so feared that none durst once lift up their weapon against him; besides that he was the best man of war in the realm'. Once persuaded, the Duke moved with great dispatch. That night large stores of arms were moved into the Tower of London, where Suffolk was to have command, while on the morning of the 13th his retinue assembled in Durham Place and the waggons and stores were broken out. He designated Newmarket as the place of assembly, arranged that the power coming up to his colleagues of the Council should be dispatched to him, and then just before noon on the 13th assembled the Council for a final meeting before he set out on his dark adventure.[2]

Northumberland's speech to the Council was grim, full of foreboding, and tinctured with an obvious distrust of his colleagues. He went as commander quite as much for them as for the Queen, and he left his family and his fortune in their care. He trusted their honour, just as the Queen trusted them, 'who by your and our enticement, is rather of force placed therein, than by her own seeking and request'. He submitted that God's cause and 'fear of the papists' entrance' was the real issue, being the 'original ground' for the alteration of the succession. He concluded by averring that he had no distrust of them, 'but I have put you in remembrance thereof, what chance of variance soever might grow amongst you in my absence; and this I pray you, wish me no worse good speed in

---

[1] *Chronicle of Queen Jane* (Camden Soc. XLVIII), 5; Stow, *Annales*, 610; Froude, *History of England*, VI, 19–24.

[2] Stow, *Annales*, 610; Machyn, *Diary*, 36; *Chronicle of Queen Jane* (Camden Soc. XLVIII), 5–6.

this journey than you would have to yourselves'. The Lords, we are told, once more assured him of their fidelity, to which he replied, 'I pray God it be . . . let us go to dinner'.[1] That night the forces were mustered, and on the morning of the 14th the Duke left an ominously quiet London with about 600 men, followed in the afternoon by another contingent of 500 men under Gates's command, while the artillery and supply train set out a little later.[2] In all, it seems sure, Northumberland counted no more than 2000 troops, mostly of dubious loyalty, in this feckless venture into treason.

Northumberland had scarcely set out for East Anglia when still more, and now indubitably impressive, evidences indicated that an unled but powerfully spontaneous rising in support of Mary was under way. On the 15th news reached the Council that Mary had removed from Kenninghall, which she was advised was indefensible, to Norfolk's castle at Framlingham (Suffolk). Even more unsettling was the intelligence that in Buckinghamshire and Oxfordshire such powerful men as Lord Windsor, Sir Edward Hastings, Sir Edmund Peckham, and Sir John Williams had declared for Mary, and with a rapidly growing force had set out to hang on the rear of Northumberland's moving army.[3] Strongly Protestant Coventry had declared for Mary and the town was gathering aid for her.[4] In Gloucester the chamberlain's accounts record that on the command of the mayor and common council twenty-four soldiers and their captain were sent at a total cost of £21 2s 10d to give succour to the Queen against the machinations of the Duke of Northumberland.[5] Bishop Hooper, who had no trust in Northumberland, had sent men to Mary's aid, as had Judge Montague who, under intolerable pressure, had drafted the letters patent seeking to alter the succession. Mary had already been proclaimed at Norwich, which raised forces for her assistance, while the possibly decisive blow was the news that six warships, lying off Yarmouth to forestall a possible flight abroad by Mary, had in fact deserted to her cause.[6] So too, all over England men were soberly assuming what seemed grave risks by declining to set out in the musters which the Privy Council had ordered, as did Richard Troughton at Grantham (Lincs), who

---

[1] We combine two accounts: Stow, *Annales*, 611; *Chronicle of Queen Jane* (Camden Soc. XLVIII), 6–7.

[2] Stow, *Annales*, 611; *Chronicle of Queen Jane* (Camden Soc. XLVIII), 7–8; Machyn, *Diary*, 36.

[3] VCH, *Bucks*, IV, 527.

[4] HMC, *12th report*, App. pt. IX, 466: *Records of the Corporation of Gloucester.*

[5] VCH, *Warwicks*, II, 442.

[6] *Chronicle of Queen Jane* (Camden Soc. XLVIII), 8–9; Stow, *Annales*, 611.

ordered his servants to hide all his harness and gear, and who continuously 'stirred up men's hearts towards the name of Queen
Mary, as much as in me was, by song, advertisement, persuasion,
information, word and deed'.[1]

These events shook severely the resolution of the Council, almost
literally locked in the Tower by Suffolk, and from this moment
forward Pembroke, Cheyney, Cecil, and Winchester were fully
persuaded that the cause was lost. No re-enforcements whatever
were dispatched to Northumberland, who had reached Cambridge
with his tiny force on Sunday, July 16th, when he asked for the
prayers of the university. On the next day, with his forces beginning
to desert, he set out for Bury St Edmund's, but could go no further
when his troops refused to proceed, it being quite falsely rumoured
that there were in Mary's battle camp 30,000 men. Now, deserted by
his colleagues on the Council, with his own force melting away,
the Duke fell back on Cambridge and his ruin.[2]

Of all the Council in London, pledged as they were to complete
loyalty to Northumberland, only Suffolk, who had risked all on the
reckless gamble with his daughter's life and fortune, remained in
his confused fashion loyal to the alteration which the late King, and
now the Duke, sought to enforce on the Council and the realm. The
prime movers in the Council for the betrayal of Northumberland
were Pembroke, who, as we have seen, wielded great personal and
military power, and the Earl of Arundel, steadily misused and
badgered by the Duke,[3] who at the close of Edward's life had been
brought back to the centre of power. Both Arundel and Pembroke
had signed the alteration, but as soon as Northumberland had left
London the two earls began to contrive to free themselves from the
semi-confinement in the Tower imposed by Suffolk on all the
Councillors. Finally the two escaped and removed to Pembroke's
London house, Baynard's Castle, on pretence of a diplomatic conversation which they wished to have with the French ambassador.[4]
On July 19th the news was desperately bad: the Earl of Oxford with
his force had joined Mary. It was all too clear that Northumberland
had failed completely. The plain fact was that the Council disposed no military resources at all. Almost the whole of the Council

---

[1] This is a most interesting case. Troughton was in trouble in early 1555 because of an
apparently baseless charge that he had favoured Northumberland (Harl. MS. 6222; his
petition was printed in part by Frederic Madden in *Archaeologia*, XXIII (1831), 18–49).
[2] Stow, *Annales*, 611; Froude, *History of England*, VI, 28–31; *Cal. S.P. Span.*, XI,
91–92: July 16, 1553.   [3] *Vide ante*, 112–113.
[4] Godwin, Francis, *Rerum Anglicarum Henrico VIII, Edwardo VI, etc.* (L., 1616,
1628, *1653*), 366–368.

on this day made their way to Pembroke's house, where Arundel told the Lords that they had fallen into an error, some through affection and some through fear. He must now say that Northumberland was a thirster after blood, a man of 'very small or no conscience at all', and a tyrant. He pleaded that he was moved to denounce the Duke not for having kept him, most unjustly, a prisoner for almost a year, but rather by his concern for 'the safety of the commonwealth and [the] liberty of this kingdom'. Mary possessed the just and lawful claim to the throne; Northumberland had been moved by no other motive than a desire for power. They of the Council had been wrongly persuaded to an alteration of the succession, which it was now clear could lead only to a division of families, a rending of the realm, foreign intervention, and a terrible bloodbath. Hence one or the other faction must be repressed and the realm united around the lawful heir to the throne.[1] In this eloquent plea Arundel enjoyed the full support of Pembroke, as he did the relieved approval of such Councillors as Shrewsbury, Bedford, Cheyney, Paget, Mason, and Petre, and of the Lord Mayor and aldermen, who had been called to Baynard's Castle. A small band of 150 men was at once dispatched to the Tower, which Suffolk, without reliable force and without resolution of character, immediately yielded. There remained for him only the dolorous duty of informing his daughter that the Council had deserted her.[2]

These resolute and decisive measures having been taken, Pembroke, accompanied by the Lords of the Council and the senior officers of the City, went immediately to Cheapside where before an enormous and boisterous crowd Mary was proclaimed Queen. An eyewitness reported that there had never been such a scene in London:

'The number of caps that were thrown up . . . were not to be told. The Earl of Pembroke threw away his cap full of angelots. I saw myself money was thrown out at windows for joy. The bonfires were without number, and what with shouting and crying of the people, and ringing of bells, there could no one man hear what another said, besides banquetting and supping in the streets for joy'.[3]

[1] Nichols, J. Gough, 'The life of Henrye Fitzallen, *etc.*', in *Gent. Mag.*, CIII (1833), pt. ii, 119–120, from Royal MSS., 17.A.ix.

[2] Stow, *Annales*, 611–612; Nichols, in *Gent. Mag.*, CIII (1833), pt.ii, 120–121.

[3] Harl. MS. 353, #44, f. 139; there is another, and similar, account in Cotton MSS., Vitellius, F, V, f. 19 (printed in Machyn, *Diary*, 37), and still another in Royal MSS., 17.B.xxviii.

Sir John York, long a supporter of Northumberland, was nearly lynched in the streets when he made his appearance. Cries of 'Long live the Queen' resounded all night 'from such a concourse of people as never was seen, who came forth as if they had been waiting to hear that my Lady's right was restored to her'.[1]

At a late night session of the Council on this same tumultuous day orders to Northumberland were drafted and signed by the members (including Suffolk), requiring him to disband his forces, forbidding him to return to London without the Queen's express command, and promising that they would sue the Queen on his behalf, if he would 'show himself like a good quiet subject'.[2] At the same time, Arundel and Paget were dispatched with a letter to Queen Mary, announcing her proclamation, pledging their allegiance, and craving pardon. The Council further—and surely for most of them falsely—declared that their secret allegiance had been unshaken, but they had not until this time found means 'to utter our determination without great destruction and bloodshed, both of ourselves and others'. Northumberland, still in Cambridge, deserted by most of his force, and now utterly repudiated by his own colleagues, could do nothing else than wait until, on July 24th, the Earl of Arundel, who had suffered so much from the Duke, came from the Queen to arrest him. He could possibly have fled the realm during the two preceding days, but his spirit and his will were broken. He could only say to Arundel that he hoped for the mercy of the Queen. Arundel could merely reply: 'My Lord, you should have sought for mercy sooner; I must do according to my command-ment.' On the day following, this strange and complex man, who had fallen deep into treason by the counsel, if not the command, of his sovereign, disappeared into the Tower of London.

In a fortnight, then, the erosion of Northumberland's power had been completed. Though force had been raised and deployed by both the Council and the Queen, there had in fact been no blood shed. The matter of the succession had been resolved really by the will and resolute determination of the realm at large. What one observes during these amazing days was the triumph of the prin-ciple of legitimism, and an almost reverential trust in the decisions made by Henry VIII with respect to the succession. The greatness of Henry's power and his almost instinctive understanding of England's aspirations in a true sense arched over the inherent weak-nesses inevitable during the minority of his son and were strong

---

[1] *Cal. S.P. Span.*, XI, 94–96: July 19, 1553; Harl. MS. 353, #44, f. 139.
[2] Stow, *Annales*, 612.

enough to stand even against the stubborn determination of Edward VI to alter his father's judgement with respect to the succession. Mary, tragically enough, misunderstood completely the nature of her triumph; she thought it a personal vindication and an acquiescence by the nation in her resolution to restore the ancient faith by violent means. These extraordinary events were rather a vindication of her father's will and a magnificent testimony to his still overweening prestige. He had laid on England the cross of Mary's brief and tragic reign; but he had also ensured that the incomparable Elizabeth stood ready to succeed her. He had endowed England with nearly a half-century of continuing Tudor greatness.

The spontaneous gathering of national support to Mary's standard was also a remarkable demonstration of the structure of order and civil quiet which two generations of Tudor rule had bestowed on the English society. The strains and tensions of a regal minority, the reckless magnanimity and the heroic exploits of Somerset, and even the dour and frightened ruthlessness of Northumberland had not disordered the structure of regality—of sovereign power. During this fortnight, when England seemed poised for civil war, the good sense of the gentry and of the many towns which dispatched their forces towards Mary proved that the solid base of Tudor power and order remained unfractured.

We must, in concluding our discussion of Northumberland's attempted *coup d'état*, reflect once more on the tragedy of the Duke's career. He possessed great ability as a soldier and he was not without a certain grandeur of personality. His regime had from the outset been weak and fearful because he ruled under the shadow of Somerset's undoubted popularity and under the hatred of many Englishmen, of all classes, who regarded him as the judicial murderer of the Protector. For many months before Edward's death, Northumberland could trust no one fully; he was ill, tense, weary, and probably honestly musing on his retirement when Edward should assume the direction of policy. He had encouraged the young King to speak and to act with full authority, and one can say that for months before he was fatally stricken Edward was assuming more and more areas of decision. Northumberland was throughout his career loyal to the King and showed a far greater understanding of a sovereign, who was in part of his nature still a boy, than had the Duke of Somerset. Then at the end Edward himself—with an almost obsessive resolution—embraced a policy with respect to the succession to which he, not Northumberland, compelled the reluctant approval of the Council. Northumberland, when he set out for Norfolk, was attempting to execute a policy which his sovereign had really ordained. It was a wrong, a disastrous, policy and the evidence suggests that Northumberland himself half-understood as much when with feeble and morally uncommitted power he set out on his last adventure. The tragedy of the career was complete when, directly his overweening presence was removed, the Council—poor, feeble Suffolk aside—to a man betrayed his trust.

5. THE CHARACTER OF EDWARD VI

It must be remembered that Edward VI was not quite sixteen years of age at the time of his death. Even granting the extraordinary precocity and the consummate education of the King, the fact remains that he was still in many respects a boy when a wasting disease overtook him. But it is also true that the character, the interests, and the essential outlines of the King's policy and way of transacting the business of the state were already fairly clearly and maturely delineated well before his death. He possessed a sensitive and stubborn interest in administrative reforms; he was deeply and intelligently concerned with social and economic problems; he followed carefully the thrust of foreign affairs, though we find no evidence to suggest that he was as yet asserting a direct authority on its administration or direction. We have observed, too, that he was personally and continuously concerned with fiscal problems and had much to do with the restoration of the coinage and the stabilization of the exchange largely achieved before his death occurred. Nor can there be any doubt that the King was devoutly Protestant in his personal faith and that England had become, in the ultimate sense, a moderate, but none the less a dedicated, Protestant nation in the course of the reign. At the same time we have seen that Edward was no bigot; his interest in the Church was principally administrative; and a relatively slight proportion of his writings and of his personal interventions were concerned with religious matters.

In most of the areas of royal concern, then, Edward had very nearly completed his tuition and was already beginning to rule before his untimely death occurred. It would be quite true to say that Edward in his last year bore far more direct responsibility for royal decisions than had his father during his first regnal year, when his indolence and pleasure-seeking suggested a delayed adolescence. This precocity of the young King, recognized by the Council and by the realm at large, was well rooted in the really superb education which he had enjoyed and which he had in a formal sense largely completed during his fourteenth year. But his studies were never to be abandoned, for the King possessed an unfathomable intellectual curiosity and an absorbing love of learning. Yet from this aspect of his nature there sprang a weakness, which might in time have had serious consequences. The King had something of the clerk—the bureaucrat —in his nature; a persuasion that complex questions had been resolved and opposition quieted when he had settled a matter to his satisfaction in his *Chronicle* or in one of the many 'position papers' which he so evidently enjoyed composing. It is perhaps not too much to suggest that not only did Edward VI resemble Henry VII in appearance and sparseness of frame, but that his habits of mind, his love of tidiness, his concern regarding small outlays, his detestation of debt, and his clerkly satisfactions were startlingly similar to the nature of his paternal grandfather.

There are resemblances to Henry VII as well in deeper and also darker aspects of Edward's nature. For there was in Edward, as there most surely was in Henry, a certain coldness and an almost frightening hardness of character and temper. We have read his *Chronicle*, as we have his letters, many times and have brooded on the harshness of the personality. There is almost nothing that is warm, or joyful, or spontaneous in his nature, at least as revealed by his most intimate writings. The death of his maternal grandmother went unremarked. The execution of Somerset, his own uncle and his head of state, was dismissed with a cold and terse comment wholly devoid of sentiment. The destruction of his other uncle, deserved though it was, was noted only with a brutal comment. He found no joy or satisfaction in his sisters, both of whom were so evidently seeking his affection as well as his approval. Only in his letters to Fitzpatrick and in his really excited account of the visit of the Marshal St André to him was this posture of studied hardness for a fleeting moment relaxed. He had perhaps been too tightly disciplined and trained for the great office which he held. 'He had seen plots and counterplots around him, and he held neither Somerset nor Northumberland in full esteem or confidence. The young King was not fearful, but he was always alert, and he was almost invariably suspicious of men and their motives.'[1] He was not given to his father's choleric rages or to his thundering and savage acts of vengeance; rather he was cold, hard, and dour in his estimate of men. Yet we know enough of the young sovereign, of his capabilities, of his education, and of his first essays into the realities of

[1] Edward VI, *Chronicle*, xxiii.

power and its administration to be persuaded that potentially he may have been, after his great sister, the ablest of his incredibly gifted family. He understood England, he enjoyed an immense capacity for work as well as for learning, and his deep commitment to the social and economic needs of his people, his sense of their aspirations, might have made him a very great monarch indeed.

If we may draw cautious conclusions from the considerable body of contemporary evidence and, perhaps more importantly, from an amazing number of surviving portraits, Edward was in appearance of slender frame, of average height, of reddish hair, grey of eye, and marked, in all his portraits after babyhood, by a long, narrow face and a pale complexion. All the portraits, too, suggest a complex and diffident personality and what can only be described as a brooding loneliness. The amazing reputation and almost maudlin contemporary idealization of the young King is suggested by the fact that of all the Tudors he seems to be the most fully represented in drawings and pictures.[1]

Quite inevitably legends and lore began to cluster around the story of a king of great promise whose life had been snuffed out at so early an age, with the appalling historical consequence of the reign of his older sister. To all Protestants, in England and abroad, he had been, as they so often said, the Josiah of the true faith. Thus the never sentimental Calvin wrote when he heard of the death of Edward:

'At first, uncertain rumours flew about concerning the death of the King. . . . Afterwards more certain messengers than I could wish confirmed this intelligence . . . [that England had] been deprived of an incomparable treasure of which it was unworthy. Indeed, I consider that, by the death of one youth, the whole nation has been bereaved of the best of fathers'.[2]

This view was enshrined in the pages of that immensely skilful and dedicated apostle of Protestantism, John Foxe, and then was gradually absorbed into the folklore of the people. In fact, so lively was

---

[1] Thus, no adequate representation of Henry VIII is to be found before his thirty-fifth year, the earliest for Elizabeth dates from her ninth to her fourteenth year, while for Edward VI they may be dated in steady sequence from the time of his christening (1537) to the last certain life portrait executed in 1552. In all, and proceeding only as far as 1608, the amazing total of eight drawings and ninety-nine certainly identified portraits of the King, whether done in life or as copies, testify to the historical interest in this precocious but enigmatic boy who was a king. *Vide ante*, 409–410, for a full discussion of the portraits.

[2] Calvini *Opera* (1667), IX, 70, cited in Gorham, *Gleanings*, 300.

the truth and the legend that for a generation to come rumours persisted that Edward still lived and would return to solace his people.[1]
As late as 1587 one William Francis, a smith at Hatfield Broad Oak
(Essex), being asked what news was at London, replied that 'there
was one in the Tower which saith he is King Edward'. When a
neighbour protested that the King was dead, Francis answered, 'I
dare not say so', and maintained that he knew the 'man that carried
King Edward in a red mantle into Germany in a ship called the
"Harry" '. To this it was rejoined that all this was untrue, that
Edward lay where 'they use to bury kings'. But Francis could not
be persuaded, for he knew 'there was a piece of lead buried [there]
that was hollow, but there was nothing in it and that it was but a
monument'. Whereupon he was warned that his were 'naughty
words which ought not to be spoken'. In such wise are the myths
of the past formed, and even they add something to the texture and
meaning of history. Not yet sixteen when he died, Edward had won
his place not only in the history, but in the imagination and folklore
of his people.

[1] Cornford, M. E., 'A legend concerning Edward VI', in *E.H.R.*, XXIII (1908),
286–290; PRO Essex Ass. file 20/ 5A / 7; 21/7/19, 20 (1578); and file 35/29/H/33. (I
have Mr F. G. Emmison to thank for these documents.)

INDEX

Abell, John, 131

Abingdon (Berks), stir threatened in, 431

Albiac, Agnace d', 310

Aldeburgh (Suffolk), sale of church goods by parish, 395

Aldrich, Bishop Robert, 266, 347

Almshouses: growth of interest in, 235–239; decay of medieval foundations, 235–236; chantry almshouses preserved, 237; Edwardian foundations, 237–239

Altars: removal ordered (1550), 267–269; rapid compliance in London, 269

Ambleteuse, 168

Anabaptism (and Anabaptists): spread of to England, 326–327; fear of, 326; Henrician persecution of, 326; Latimer and Hooper denounce, 327; Commission to eradicate, 327; in south-eastern England (1549), 327; heresies of Bocher and Parris, 327–330; Becke on, 331; condemned, 353; see also 289, 295, 374, 500

Antinomianism, in Kent, 334

Antwerp: markets in, English complaints, 139–140, 479–480; threatened by the Inquisition, 141; decline of, 412; royal debts held in, 457–458, 463; Gresham's speculations in, 464–465; see also, 489

Appleyard: hanged for raising stir, 68–69

Ardres, 117, 161

Arran, James Hamilton, second Earl of: resents French hegemony in Scotland, 148–149;

directs boundary negotiations, 152

Articles of Faith: caution of Cranmer in preparing, 354; completion of (1552), 355; issued by King, 355; doctrinal quality of, 356–357

Arundel, Earl of, *see* Fitzalan, Henry

Arundell, Sir John, 28, 76

Arundell, Sir Thomas: execution of, 110–111; *see also* 28, 76, 83, 94

Ascham, Roger: Praise for Edward's attainments, 406

Ashfield (Suffolk): sale of church goods in, 395

Atwood, Lawrence, 59

Aubespine, Claude de, 173

Augmentations, Court of, 187, 200, 444–445

Aumale, Claude, Duke d': commands English mercenary troops, 156–157

Austin Friars, London: given by King as refugee church, 313–315

Ayscough, Francis: proposal of, 397

Bacon, Sir Nicholas, 503

Bale, John: violent anti-Catholicism of, 367–368; King appoints as Bishop of Ossory, 368; flight of from Ireland, 368–369; *see also* 277, 425

Banbury (Oxon): disorder in, 63

Bannaster, Thomas: ship seized by Danzig Hanse, 486–487; English demands regarding, 487

Barbaro, Daniel, Venetian ambassador: assessment of political situation, 80–81; on strength of evangelical Anglicanism, 276; on English fiscal crisis (1551), 461

Barkham (Berks), 403

Barlow, Bishop William, 18, 278, 320, 369

Basing (Hants): Edward VI visits, 426

Basingstoke (Hants), 369

Bath: disorders in, 105

Beaulieu (Hants): Edward VI visits, 426

Beaumont, John: career of, 442; malfeasances of, 442–444, 448

Becke, Edmund: on Anabaptism, 331

Beckwith, Sir Leonard, 152

Becon, Thomas: career of, 281–282; preaching of, 282–283; see also, 18, 277

Bedford, Earl of, see Russell, John

Bedfordshire: schools in (1553), poor in church goods, 399

Bedingfield, Sir Henry: Council recommends for Parliament, 506

Beer, Thomas: 'lewd words' against Northumberland, 496

Belmain, John, 17, 19, 21, 22, 415

Bentley, Dr, 19

Berkshire: disorders in, 65, 67, 429, 431; chantry returns from, 189; schools in (1553), 233

Bermondsey (Surrey): sale of church goods in, 396

Bernher, Augustine: on Latimer, 279

Berwick, 147, 150, 166, 350, 413, 449, 499

Bethersden (Kent): sale of church goods by, 392–393

Bethlehem Hospital (London): refounding and endowing of, 217–218

Bieston, Roger: preaches charitable responsibility, 214

Bill, Dr Thomas, 19

Bill, William, 274, 385, 499

Bilney, James: seditious sermon of, 433–434

Bilney, Thomas, 278

Bird, Bishop John: returns inventory of church goods, 388

Bishops (and Bishoprics): unpopularity of, 376; spoliation of, 378–386

Bishop's Waltham (Hants): Edward VI visits, 425

Blackness (France), 117

Blackwell Hall (London), 219

Blaurer, Albert, 310

Blaurer, Ambrose, 310

Bletchingley (Surrey): sale of church goods in, 396

Bocher, Joan: heresis of, 327–329; execution of, 329–330

Bocking (Essex) heresy in, 333

Boisdauphin, René de Laval, Seigneur de, 132, 134

Bolemberg (France), 117

Bona Confidentia, the, 490

Bona Esperanza, the, 490

Bonner, Bishop Edmund: deprivation of, 246; see also 29, 54, 158, 241, 249, 271

Book of Common Prayer, the first: Northumberland's support of, 29–30, 265; Somerset, and, 109; criticism of by conservatives and by evangelicals, by Calvin, 342–343; Bucer's Censura and, 343–345; see also, 251, 268, 272, 307

Book of Common Prayer, the second: Cranmer's drafting of, 346–347; Act of Uniformity passed, 347 ff.; delay in imposition of, 348; analysis of, 348–350; on the Communion, 349; printing of, 350; French translation of, 350; Knox attacks kneeling posture,

Book of Common Prayer—contd.
350–352; supported by *A Short Catechism*, 353; makes most church goods superfluous, 387–388; *and see* 324, 365, 366, 373

Book of Homilies, 273

Boston (Lincs): grain shortage in, 475; Hanse community in, 483

Boulogne: strengthening of (1550), 35; French resolve to take, 117–118; attack on, 118–119; cession of, 120–122; *see also*, 46, 60, 119, 123, 132, 134, 136, 144, 148, 168, 169

Bourton-on-the-Hill (Glos), 253

Bowes, Sir Robert: retains Border command, 149; recommendations on Scottish frontier, 151–152; questions Tunstall, 383, and Mrs Huggins, 432–433; *see also* 50, 81, 152

Brabon, Henry: disaffection of, 431

Bradford, John, 274, 275, 276

Brandon, Charles, first Duke of Suffolk, 443

Brandon, Charles and Henry (2nd Duke of Suffolk): die of sweating sickness, 471

Brassey, Robert: conservative ministry of, 269

Brende, John, 89, 112

Bridewell (London): founding and endowing of, 221–223

Bristol: chantry returns, 189; chantry priest's income in, 194; schools in (1553), 233; food scarcity in, 476

Bromley, Sir Thomas (Judge), 93

Brooke, George, ninth Baron Cobham, 49, 72, 119, 122, 132, 523

Broughty Castle, 147

Browne, Sir Anthony, 102, 253, 416, 425

Brown, Thomas: seditious words of, 496

Bruen, Captain van, 20

Brussels, 159, 171, 175, 178, 518

Bubonic plague, 467

Bucer, Martin: weaknesses of the Church of England, 273–274, 365–366; declines to support Hooper, 296; career of, at Cambridge, 307–308; relations of with Edward VI, 308; death of, 308; his *Censura* of *First Book of Common Prayer*, 343–345; *see also*, 29, 49, 307, 346, 354, 411

Buckinghamshire: disorders in, 62, 64; schools in (1553), 233; rises for Mary, 527

Bullinger, Henry, 29, 61, 267, 322, 327, 348, 354, 419, 514

Burgh, John: libels Northumberland, 433

Burgoyne, Francis, 104

Burnaby, Thomas: anti-French tract by, 170; criticism of economic policy (1552) 480; deplores decline of shipping, 480

Burnet, Bishop Gilbert, 23, 250

Bury St Edmunds, 528

Bush, Bishop Paul, 381

Cabot, Sebastian, 136, 489, 490, 491

Caius, Dr John: on the sweating sickness, 468

Calais: great strength of, 123–125; boundary dispute in, 124; Petitt inspects, 124–125; Willoughby commands, 125; English believe threatened, 145; reduction in garrison of, 437–438; *see also* 35, 112, 116, 117, 119, 120, 122, 132, 161, 167, 168, 170, 413, 447, 449, 450, 479

Calvin, John: influence on and interest in, Church of England,

Calvin—*contd.*
323–325; letter to Somerset, and King, 324–325; declines English visit, 325; on Edward VI, 534; *see also* 21, 104, 317, 348

Cambridgeshire: chantry return missing, 189; schools in (1553), 233; sale of church goods in, 394

Cambridge: bubonic plague in, 467; Northumberland at, 528

Cambridge, University of: Bucer at, 307–308; *see also* 21, 73, 185, 369, 370

Camden, William: on number of chantries, 191

Canterbury (Kent): King's School, 231; religious refugees in, 318; church goods at, 388; *see also* 391

Cardano, Hieronymus: estimate of Edward VI, 409–410

Cardmaker, John, 274

Carew, Sir Peter, 524

Carlisle, 150, 252

Castellio, Sebastian, 323

Caston, Stephen: evangelical preaching of, 366

Cavendish, Sir William, 19

Cawarden, Sir Thomas, 98

Cecil, Sir William (Privy Councillor): appointment of, to Council, 50–51; knighted, 53; support to Somerset, 72; withdrawal from Somerset, 82, 84; denounces Somerset to Scheyfve, 85–86; increasing diplomatic responsibility of, 158–159; and Glastonbury experiment, 319; friend to William Thomas, 416; study of royal debts (1552), 457–458; concern for decline of fishing, 480–481; Northumberland's confidences, to, 496–497; rapid rise (1552–1553) in power, 500–503; withdraws from Court

in crisis (1553), 502–503; signs *Devise*, 503, 516; his later *apologia*, 503–504; effort to influence parliamentary elections, 506; deserts Northumberland, 528; *see also* 25, 34, 36, 48, 58, 68, 75, 100, 103, 131, 153, 158, 171, 172, 180, 219, 223, 248, 262, 299, 306, 366, 373, 374, 375, 379, 383, 384, 397–398, 422, 441, 448, 462, 475, 490, 500, 505, 512

Chaloner, Sir Thomas, 152, 154, 178

Chamberlain, Edward, 35

Chamberlain, Sir Thomas: raises problem of diplomatic immunity, 142; urges amity with Netherlands, 174; *see also* 139, 158, 171, 175, 178

Chancellor, Richard: pilot major Willoughby's fleet, 490; arrives in Moscow, 493

chantries: late rise of, 181–182; defined, 181–182; Protestant denunciation of, 182, 186; monastic, gifts to (1480–1540), 182–183; Henrician legislation on, 183; Edwardian statute expropriates, 183–185; bill opposed by Cranmer, 184; analysis of chantries act, 184–187; ambiguity of act, 186; administration of the act, 187–188; analysis of chantry returns, 188–194; number of, 191–192; wealth of, estimated, 192–194; chantry priests (number, income, and pensions), 194–196; wealth of, dedicated to social uses, at expropriation, 196–198; wealth of, dedicated to social uses by government, 198–199; sale of expropriated properties, 199–203; probity of administration of sales, 200–201; moral wrath at disposal of wealth of, 201–203;

chantries—*contd.*
expropriation and charitable giving, 208–209; charitable funding in London, 211–212; education undamaged by seizure, 229–230; almshouses unharmed by seizure, 237
charitable giving: 1480–1600, 204–205; *temp.* Edward VI, 205–206; secular nature of, 207–208; reasons for secularization of charity, 208–214; failure to employ chantry wealth triggers, 208–209; problem of poverty, and, 209–211; Somerset and, 210–211; Edward VI and, 211; London merchant wealth and, 211–212; evangelical Protestantism, and, 213–214; founding and endowing of London hospitals, 216–223; founding and endowing of schools, 223–235; secular school foundations *temp.* Edward VI, 231–235; decay of medieval almshouses, 235–236; Edwardian almshouse foundations, 236–239
Charles V, Holy Roman Emperor: refuses aid to Boulogne, 118–119, 135, 145; outline of Imperial policy, 135; overweening strength of (1549–1550), 135–136; Maurice attacks, 136; seeks English neutrality, 136, 140; protests English separate peace with Scotland, 136–137; the problem of Mary Tudor's conscience, 137–138; admits the Inquisition to Netherlands, 141; the problem of diplomatic immunity, 141–144; angered by Morison, 142–143; Wotton conciliates, 143–144; the grievance of Mary Tudor, 143; on the English reformation, 144; concerned by Anglo-French en-

tente, 145; English policy disturbs, 159; defeat of (1552), 163–164; invokes treaty for English aid, 164–165; beginnings of shift to entente with England, 168–174; special envoys to, 169, 174–180; Dudley's overtures to, 175; Emperor's diplomatic scepticism, 175; English overtures rejected, 177; seeks guarantees for Mary's conscience, 256–257, 259; threatens war, 260; further protests regarding Mary, 263; sends special envoys to protect Mary (1553), 518–519; *see also* 92, 104, 113, 127, 166, 179, 489, 514
Cheke, Sir John: knighted, 53; interest in religious refugees, 313; his education of Edward VI, 406–408; 'farewell' letter to Edward VI, 407–408; appointed secretary to Council, 502; *see also* 17, 21, 308, 325, 344, 346, 415, 490, 503, 514, 521
Chelmsford (Essex): disorders in, 63, 66; chantries in, 188; *see also sub* Mildmay, Sir Walter
The *Chiefest Cause* (1552): reminiscent of Hales's works, 481; plea for restoration of balance of trade, 481–482; for a balance of tillage, 482; urges sumptuary laws, 482.
Chigwell (Essex), 433
Cholmley, Sir Roger, 384
Christchurch (Hants): Edward VI visits, 426
Church of England: Northumberland supports, 265; act against images, 265–266; new *Ordinal* for, 266–267; removal of altars in, 268–269; Ridley's leadership in, 270–274; want of preaching in, 273–274; strength of evangelical party in, 275–292,

Church of England—*contd.*
307; thought of evangelical group, 285–292; evangelicals in motion towards Puritanism, 292; indigenous quality of, 307; Calvin's interest in and influence on, 323–325; Protestantism of, complete with *Articles of Faith*, 356–357; Northumberland's support of evangelicals in, 362–363; King's support of evangelical Anglicanism, 364–365, 367–369; evangelical party assails Northumberland (1552–1553), 375; evangelical distrust of episcopacy, 376; survey of episcopal wealth in, 377–378

church goods: religious reasons for confiscation of, 386–387; second *Prayer Book* makes superfluous, 387–388; national inventory of ordered (Dec., 1547), 388; second inventory of, ordered (1549), 388–389; abortive order for seizure (1551), 389; sale and embezzlement of, 388–389; detailed inventory ordered (Jan. 1552), 390–391; order for expropriation (Jan., 1552), 390–391; difficulties in collection, 391; seizure completed by Queen Mary, 391–392; view of, by sixteenth-century men, 393; government's fear of theft and concealment, 396–397; most parishes ill-furnished with, 398–399; of London, 399–401

church goods, sales of in anticipation of expropriation: Leicester, 392; Kent, 392–393; Devonshire, 394; Oxfordshire, 394; Cornwall, 394; Cambridge-shire, 394; Peterborough, 394–395; Suffolk, 395; Yorkshire (N.R.), 395; Essex, 395; Surrey, 396; Warwickshire, 396; Lincoln, 396

Cirencester (Glos): Catholicism in, 300

Coke, John: praise for evangelical preachers, 276

de Coligny, Odet, Cardinal of Châtillon, 129

Cox, Richard, 17, 21, 102, 277, 406

Châtillon, Gaspard de Coligny, Seigneur de, in command before Boulogne, 117; attack of, on Boulogne, 118; Boulogne surrendered to, 121–122; diplomatic visit to England, 122

Chedsey, William: Roman Catholic activity of, 250

Chemault, Jean Pot de Rhodes, Seigneur de, 134

Cherbourg, 170

Cheshire: Chantry returns defective, 189; schools in (1553), 233

Chester, 467

Cheyney, Sir Thomas, 65, 119, 529

Chichester, 247, 248

Christian III, King of Denmark, 486

Christ's Hospital (London): founding and endowment of, 218, 219–220

Chronicle, The, of Edward VI, 23–27; as an historical source, 24–25

Cleves, Anne of, 104

Clifford, Henry, second Earl of Cumberland: refuses Guildford Dudley for Margaret Clifford, 513

Clinton, Lord, *see* Fiennes, Edward

Clopton, Francis: a rumour monger, 429

cloth merchants (tract of 1551): inflation blamed on poor quality of cloth, 478

Cobham, Baron, *see* Brooke, George

coinage, debasement of, *see* fiscal crisis

Coke, Sir Edward, 91

Colas, Jeromo, 310

Colchester: disorders in, 63; religious refugees in, 318; heresy in, 332

Cologne (Hanse): Hanseatic trade to, 485, 486; Hanse complaints on restrictions, 486

Colthurst, Matthew, 105

Commonwealth Party (or Men) (Often rendered 'Commonwealth's Men' by contemporaries): concern for poverty, 210–211; see also, 26, 37, 43–44, 108–109, 201, 202, 227, 280, 290, 300, 339, 340, 482

Cooke, Sir Anthony, 406, 503, 506

Cooke, Robert: alleged heretic, 333

Cornish: administrator of Glastonbury experiment, 319–320

Cornwall: schools in (1553), 233; sale of church goods in, 394; see also 57, 438

Corpus Christi College (Oxford), 249

Cottingham (Yorks): sale of church goods by parish, 395

Cotton, Sir Richard: recommended to Hants electors, 506; see also 49, 425

Council, see Privy Council

Council of Trent, 135, 136

Courrières, Jean de Montmorency, Seigneur de: seeks better relations for Flanders, 162–163

Coventry and Lichfield, Bishopric of, see Lichfield

Coventry: opposition to chantries act, 184; disaffection in, 430; sweating sickness in, 470; declares for Mary, 527

Coverdale, Miles, 274, 278, 330, 380

Cowdray (Sussex): Edward VI visits, 425

Crane, William: confessions of,

against Somerset: 89; see also 91, 94, 97, 112

Cranmer, Thomas, Archbishop of Canterbury: opposes chantries act, 183, 186, 187; attitude towards Roman Catholicism, 250; and new Ordinal, 266–267; close bonds to Ridley, 270–271; submission of Hooper to, 297–298; irenic interests of, 307–308, 321–322, 325, 348; interest of, in religious refugees, 313, 321–322; and Joan Bocher, 328, 329, 331; consideration of successor to Bucer, 322–323; view of heresy, 331; Defence marks his Protestantism, 345–346; drafting of Second Book of Common Prayer, 346–347; assistance received, 346; delays enforcement, 348; final position on the Eucharist, 349; angered by Knox's intervention, but overridden, 351–352; issues Short Catechism, 353; doctrinal caution of, 354; informal codification of doctrine (1549), 354; completes Forty-two Articles, 355; completes his spiritual pilgrimage, 356–357; codification of ecclesiastical laws, 357–359; Northumberland's attack on, 359–360; growing fear of Northumberland's policy, 364; Dudley accuses of covetousness, 379–380; support of Tunstall by, 381, 383; enduring enmity of Northumberland to, 499–500; withdraws from Court, 499–500; see also 21, 22, 29, 32, 63, 70, 104, 248, 260, 268, 278, 293, 297, 309, 310, 314, 327, 330, 350, 367, 371, 373, 376, 495, 510, 516–517

Croft, Sir James, 35

Cromwell, Gregory, second Baron Cromwell, 469

Culpepper, Alexander, 132
Cumberland, county of: schools in (1553), 233
Cumberland, Earl of, see Clifford, Henry
Curio, Coelius, 323

Dacre, William, fourth Baron Dacre of the North: restrains Scottish Border raids, 150; see also 81, 335
Damvillers, 163
Danforth, Cornelius, 490
Dansell, William: agent at Antwerp, 463
Danzig (Hanse): captures English ship (1547), 485; English protest regarding, 485; seize Bannaster's ship and cargo, 486; see also 488
Darcy, Sir Arthur, 383, 432–433, 434, 435
Darcy, Sir Thomas, first Baron Darcy of Chiche: episcopal lands to, 378, 380; see also 20, 422, 443, 503, 505
Day, Bishop George: refusal to remove altars, 247–248; deprived, 248; see also 54, 266, 269, 420
Dee, John, 490
de la Warr, Baron, see West, Thomas
Deleen (Delvin), Walter: appointed to clergy, Stranger's Church, 314; minister to new French-Walloon Church, 316–317
Derby, Earl of, see Stanley, Edward
Derbyshire: schools in (1553), 233; church goods in, 391
Dereham (Norfolk), 63
Devereux, Walter, third Baron Ferrers, Viscount Hereford (cr. 1550), 49
Devonshire: chantry returns 189; schools in (1553), 233; church

goods, and sales of, 391, 394; bubonic plague in, 467; sweating sickness in, 470; Northumberland libelled in, 496
Discovery and Exploration: by Hawkins, Wyndham and Reneger, 489; to Morocco, Barbary coast, and Guinea, 489; dream of a northern passage, 490; Willoughby appointed to command, 490; ordinances for voyages and letters commendatory, 491–492; the voyage and disaster, 492–493; Chancellor reaches Moscow, 493
Dixon, R. W., 284
Dobbs, Sir Richard, 219
Donnington Castle: Edward VI visits, 426
Dorset: chantry returns defective, 189; schools in (1553), 233; poor in church goods, 398; see also 60, 438
Dorset, Marquis of, see Grey, Henry
Dover, 118, 413, 480
Drury, Sir William, 506, 524
Dryander, Francis, 29
Dubois, Jehan, 257–258
Dudley, Sir Andrew: special envoy to Emperor, 174–175; audiences with Regent and Charles V, 175; gains church lands, 380; see also 20, 501, 511–512
Dudley, Henry: commands Thames fleet, 162; appointed to Guînes, 425
Dudley, John (Lord Lisle and Earl of Warwick), 264, 435–436, 523
Dudley, John, Viscount Lisle (cr. 1542), Earl of Warwick (cr. 1547), Duke of Northumberland (cr. 1551): Household changes by, 20–21; brief favour to Catholicism, 28–29, 241;

Dudley—*contd.*

support of *Prayer Book* by, 29–30; Princess Mary's judgement on, 31; religious policy of, 30–32; secures dominance in Council, 32–36; fear of Parliament, 44–48; illness and absence (1550), 48; 'General Warden of the North', 49; followers raised to Council, 49–53; created Duke of Northumberland, 53; attack of, on Rich, 54–56; fear of public disorder, 56–69; altercation with Vane, 64–65; seeks conciliation with Somerset, 72–73, 106; policy opposed by Somerset, 73–75; warns Whalley respecting Somerset, 75–76; knitting of conspiracy against Somerset, 81–82; denounces Somerset to King, 83–84; Somerset's intention toward, 90; clash of, with Arundel, 90–91; presses early trial of Somerset, 92–93; withdraws treason charges, 96–97; distractions for the King, 98–99; his dislike of Somerset, 106; humiliation of Paget, 113–115; and war with France (1549), 116–117; sues for peace, 119–120; cession by, of Boulogne, 120–122; weakness of foreign policy of, 123, 131; entertains French envoys, 134; foreign policy unsettling to Emperor, 135; weakness of in Scotland, 147–149; inspects northern borders (1552), 155; increasing neglect of diplomacy by, 157–159; Charles V invokes treaty for aid, 164–165; doubts Stuckley's 'revelation', 167; shift towards imperial entente, 168–174; policy of, weakened by war costs, 169; effort of to mediate Habsburg-Valois war, 174–180;

incomprehensibility of policy, 177; support of evangelical Protestants, by, 265, 362–363; favour of, to Hooper, 293, 294; wishes further reform in *Prayer Book*, 343; supports Knox on kneeling, 350; attacks Cranmer, 359; true religious sentiments of, 362–363; Scheyfve on religious policy, of, 363–364; enmity to Cranmer and Ridley, 364, 379–380; extends favour to Bale, 367, Turner, 370, Ponet, 370–373, and to Knox, 373; Knox denounces as a dissembler, 374–375; secularism of, 376–377; assault by, on the bishops, 377 ff.; survey of episcopal revenues, 377–378; seeks lands from York, 380–381; attack of on Tunstall and Durham, 381–386; enthusiasm for evangelicals withers, 386; his ecclesiastical policy in ruins, 386; unjustly blamed for seizure of church goods, 387; relaxes King's education, 402–403; encourages King to attend Council, 420–421; in north during King's progress, 424, 426; his power greater than he thinks, 427–428; rumours regarding, 430–431, 432–433; seeks a small standing army, 435–436; financial crisis compels military reduction, 434–439; establishes a conciliar striking force, 435–436; overawes London, 435; erosion of military power, 437–438; French alliance essential to, 438–439; fiscal ignorance of, 462; his situation, 494; his enemies, real and imaginary, 495; slanderous libels against, 495–496; illness and melancholy, 496–498; reassures King of full loyalty, 498; 'the bottom of my

Dudley—*contd.*
care' (Jan. 1553), 497–498; weakening of central administration, 498–500; deep enmity of to Cranmer, 499–500; growing dependence of, on Cecil, 500–504; efforts to influence parliamentary elections, 505–506; plan of, for House of Lords, 507; reports Edward improving, 512–513; arranges the 'Dudley' marriages, 513–514; the King's illness and the succession, 514–515; the King's pressure for acceptance of his *Devise*, 515–517; finds self entrapped in treason, 517; undertakes command against Mary, 525–526; betrayed by Council, 528–529; arrested at Cambridge, 530; reflections on his character, 531–532; *see also* 20, 27, 28, 35, 37, 44, 50, 51, 54, 62, 63, 83, 86, 87, 91, 94, 96, 97, 100, 103, 135, 153, 171, 241, 249, 251, 296, 335, 366, 367, 422, 441, 447, 458, 461, 472–473, 521, 522

Dudley, Robert, 404, 522, 524

Dunglass, 147, 148

Durham: schools in (1553), 233

Durham, Bishopric of: plan for division of, 384–386; *see also sub* Tunstall

East Dereham (Norfolk): theft of church goods in, 397

East Malling (Kent), 59

Economic controls, by government: concern regarding prices and food supply, 472; proclamation for 'bringing forth of grain', 473; rigour of the controls, 474–475; import of grain authorized, 475; proclamation (1550) on food-stuffs, 474; special commissions to enforce grain de-

livery, 474; price restraints relaxed, 475; Council denounces London prices, 475–476; further food imports, 476–477; remedies urged by economic tracts, 477–482

Education: spreading interest in, 223–228; humanism and, 225; undamaged by chantry expropriation, 227–229; secular educational giving, 231–235

Edward Bonaventura, The, 490

Edward I, 181

Edward VI: education of, 17–27; household of, 18–20; *Chronicle* of, 23–27; rebukes Lord Rich, 55; coldness of, 77, 103; hostility of, to Somerset, 82; distractions arranged for, 98–99; and Somerset's execution, 100; Order of St Michael for, 128, 133; marriage treaty of, with Elizabeth of France, 127–134, 159–160; captivated by St André; 133–134; entertains Mary of Lorraine, 153–154; Charles V invokes treaty for aid, 164–165; increasing participation in diplomacy, 165–166; beginnings of shift towards imperial entente, 168–174; concern of, for social needs, 211; interest in, and aid to, founding London royal hospitals, 218–223; presses proceedings against Bishop Heath, 247; efforts of, to force Mary's conscience, 258–259, 260; last visit of Mary to, 264; appoints royal chaplains, 274; preaching before, 277; support of Hooper, by, 294; relations of with Bucer, 308; founds London refugee church, 313, 315; Calvin's letter to, 324; desires revision first *Prayer Book*, 344; issues the *Articles of Faith*, 355; supports

Edward VI—*contd.*
    evangelical group in Church,
    362, 364–365, 368; further re-
    forms desired (1552), 367; en-
    largement of interests by North-
    umberland, 402–404; correspon-
    dence with Fitzpatrick, 404–405;
    completion of formal education,
    405–408; Cheke's 'farewell letter'
    to, 407–408; intellectual attain-
    ments of, 408–409; Cardano's
    estimate of, 409–410; portraits
    of, 409–410; his conception of
    the Commonwealth, 411–412;
    administrative grasp of, 412;
    interest in fiscal reforms, and
    work of Council, 412–413; his-
    torical interests of, 414; in-
    fluence of William Thomas on,
    415–419; the Court of, 419–
    420; attendance at Council,
    420–421; memoranda on Coun-
    cil business, 420, 421, 422; legis-
    lation wished in second Parlia-
    ment, 421–422; economic in-
    terests of, 422; ordinances by,
    for Order of the Garter, 422–
    423; severe illness of, 423–424;
    royal progress of, 424–427; mil-
    itary interest of, 425; his pro-
    gress quiets realm, 432; approves
    a conciliar striking force, 435–
    436; growing interest of in
    central administration, 440–441;
    stream of memoranda begins,
    441; concern of, for fiscal crisis,
    444–445; the Commission on
    the revenue courts, 444–447;
    further memoranda for the Coun-
    cil, 447–451; studies reform of
    Council procedure, 451–454;
    reckless gifts and sales of crown
    lands, under, 456, 463; debts of
    (external and internal), 457–
    458; comments on York's spec-
    ulative losses, 458–459; restora-

tion of the coinage, 461–463;
    demands reciprocal treatment
    by Hanse, 486; and Willoughby's
    voyage, 491–492; the King's
    illness and concern of Council,
    505; opens second Parliament
    (1553), 507–508; and the prob-
    lem of the succession, 514–515;
    his *Devise*, 515–516; pressure
    by, for acceptance of, 516–517;
    the course of his illness, 494,
    504, 507, 510, 511, 513, 517–
    520; death of, 519–520; reflec-
    tions on his character, 532–535;
    see also 131, 178, 202, 310,
    427
Ehrenberg Castle, 163
Eleanor (of Castile), 181
Elizabeth, the Princess, 22, 515
Elizabeth (of France): negotiations
    for marriage treaty with, 128–
    134, 160
Emperor, *see* Charles V
Englefield, Sir Francis, 263
Erasmus, Desiderius, 21, 314
Erskine, Thomas, 148
Essex, County of: disorders in,
    58, 59, 60, 61, 62–63, 429–430,
    433–434; concern of Council
    for, 66; schools in (1553), 233;
    Protestant extremism in, 271;
    heresy in, 332–334; sale of
    church goods in, 395; fear of
    rising in (1552), 432; *see also*
    51, 58, 188, 231, 274, 439
Essex, Earl of, *see* Parr, William
Eton College, 21, 185, 231, 431
Evangelical party: *see* Church of
    England
Exchequer, Court of, 445
Exeter, bishopric of: looted by
    Veysey, 380
Exploration: *see* Discovery and
    Exploration
Eyemouth, 147
Eyre, John, 18

Falmouth, 167

Farnham (Surrey): iron-making near, 342

Fastolf, Sir John, 414

Fawdling, Thomas: disaffection of, 431

Ferrar, Bishop Robert, 274, 278

Ferrers, George, 98–99

Fiennes, Edward, ninth Lord Clinton, 49, 67–68, 82, 110, 121, 132, 140, 160, 169, 404, 437, 490

Fiscal crisis (1550–1553): financial irresponsibility of Henry VIII and Somerset, 456–457; reckless dispersion of crown lands, 456; external and internal debts of crown, 457–458; costly speculations of Sir John York, 458–459; debasement and devaluations, 459; economic disturbances resulting, 459–461; restoration of the coinage (1552), 461–463; payments suspended, 461–462; City lends relief, 462; crown sustained by further land sales, 463; Gresham's successful operations in Antwerp, 464–466

Fisher, Henry, 47

Fisher, Thomas, 112

Fitzalan, Henry, twelfth Earl of Arundel: loss of favour, by, 30–31; arrest of, 85; interrogation of, 89, 97; ruin of, 112–113; deserts Northumberland, and denounces, 528–529; arrests Northumberland, 530; see also 20, 28–29, 91, 490, 503, 521, 525

Fitzpatrick, Barnaby: French stay of, 160; ordered home, 167; King's correspondence with, 404–405; see also 22, 27

Flanders, see Netherlands

Fleet, the royal, 437

Flint: restraints on tightened, 430

Flood, Hugh, 336

Flood, Thomas, 496

Florio, Michael Angelo, 317

Ford, Edmund, trouble-maker, 63

Foreign policy (English): France declares war (1549), 116–117; Charles declines aid, 118–119; Northumberland sues for peace, 119; peace concluded, 120–122; weakness of English position, 123; strengthening of Calais, 123–125; France wishes English neutrality, 126–127; marriage negotiations with France, 127–134; criticism of French policy, 131; outline of Imperial policy, 135; problem of Mary Tudor, 137–138; commercial frictions with Flanders, 139–140; Charles wishes English neutrality, 140; problem of diplomatic immunity, 141–144; continued concern Emperor with Anglo-French entente, 145; weakening English influence in Scotland, 146–155; negotiations for Scottish frontier, 151–155; withdrawal from European affairs, 155–174; decline of English diplomacy, 157–159; marriage treaty concluded, 159–160; France seeks English entrance to war, 160–161; commercial difficulties with Netherlands, 161–163; emperor invokes treaty, 164–165; King's consideration of diplomatic policy, 166; beginnings of entente with Emperor, 168–174; anti-French sentiment in England, 169–171; French alliance essential to Dudley, 438–439

Foxe, John, 277, 329, 360

Framlingham (Suffolk), 527

France: foreign policy of: declares war on England, 116–117; attack

France—*contd.*

on Boulogne, 118–119; Northumberland sues for peace, and cedes Boulogne, 119–122; pressure on Calais, 123–125; importance of English neutrality to, 126–127; marriage negotiations with England, 127–134; fear of imperial power, by, 136–137; attack of, on Charles V, 136–137; overweening strength of, in Scotland, 146–154; cherish English neutrality, 156–157; English mercenaries enrolled, 157; marriage treaty concluded, 159–160; erosion of entente with England, 168–174; seeks to cure English grievances, 172–174; rebuffs English diplomacy, 178; religious refugees from, in England, 310, 311, 317–318

Francis, William: contributes to myth, 535

French (and Walloon) church, London, 316–317

Froude, James Anthony, 507

Fuller, Thomas, 201

Füss, John, 157

Gardiner, Bishop Stephen: Somerset's friendship to, 74, 76; on chantries act, 186; imprisonment of, 241; religious position of, 241–242; Somerset seeks his release, 242–243; refuses subscription, 243–244; deprived, 244–245; *see also* 29, 48, 54, 74, 241, 249, 283, 309, 372

Gates, Sir Henry, 110

Gates, Sir John: appointment of to Council, 51–52; represses disorder in Essex, 59, 63; *see also* 49, 110, 114, 366, 495, 500, 526, 527

Gawdy, Thomas, 184

German Church: *see* Stranger's Church

Germany: religious refugees from, 310–311, 312

Gerrard, Philip, 213

Gilpin, Bernard: ministry of in Northumberland, 276; favour of Council towards, 366; denounces Northumberland's ecclesiastical policy, 366

Glastonbury: refugee settlement founded in by Somerset, 318–321

Gloucester, Diocese of: poor state of, temporal and spiritual, 298–299; Hooper's administration of, 301–306; disciplining of clergy in, 300–303; visitation of, by Hooper, 301–304; ignorance and inertness of clergy in, 303–304; conservatism of cathedral clergy of, 305

Gloucestershire: discontent in, 67; schools in (1553), 233

Goodman, John, 369

Goodrich, Richard, 359

Goodrich, Bishop Thomas, 49, 56, 127, 131, 142, 244, 268, 328–329, 343

Gosnold, John, 516

Grammar Schools: *see* schools

Grantham (Lincs), 506, 527

Gravesend (Kent), 59, 132

Gray, William, 70

Greames, George, 252

Greenway, 64

Greenwich, 99, 511, 519

Gresham, Sir John: losses of, 458, 466

Gresham, Sir Thomas: diplomatic conversations, with Scheyfve, 168; made English agent in Antwerp, 464; success in refundings, 464; controlled speculation on Exchange; control of cloth exports fortifies policy, 465; *see also* 171, 449, 462, 498, 504

Grey, Henry, third Marquis of Dorset, Duke of Suffolk (cr.

Grey—*contd.*

1551): created Duke of Suffolk, 53; made Warden Northern Marches, 151; entertains King, 426; trouble of, with Beaumont, 442–443; daughter's marriage arranged, 514; deserted by Council colleagues, 528–529; *see also* 36, 49, 525

Grey, Lady Jane: marriage of, to Lord Guildford Dudley, 514; proclaimed Queen, 521; melting of support for, 525–527

Grey, William, thirteenth Baron Grey de Wilton, 61, 83, 85, 90, 91, 106, 112, 149, 168, 449, 526

Griffin, Sir Edward (Solicitor General): hangs prisoner in Leicester, 68–69

Grindal, Edmund, 274, 499

Guidotti, Anthony: peace overtures to France, 119

Guildford (Surrey): iron-making near, 342; sale of church goods in, 396; Edward VI visits, 425

Guînes, 112, 124, 165, 170, 413, 425, 449, 450, 512

Gyllot (also Gyller, Gylles, Giles), Anthony: malicious rumours of, 430

Haberdasher's Company (London): funding of chantry wealth by, 212

Haddington, 147

Haddon, Walter, 471

Hales, Sir James, 184, 244

Hales, John, 26

Halnaker (Surrey), 165, 425

Hamburg, 485, 487

Hammond, Lawrence, 83, 85, 94

Hampshire: disorder in, 62, 431, 495; chantry return from, 189–190; schools in (1553), 233; Bale's unquiet ministry in, 367; Council seeks to influence election in (1553), 506; *see also* 60, 430

Hampton Court, 18, 82, 133, 153, 423, 449, 469

Hancock, Thomas, 84

Hanseatic League (Hanse cities): medieval privileges of, in England, 482–483; weakened in sixteenth century, 483; value and nature of trade with England *temp.* Edward VI, 484; the Danzig incident, 485–486; English pressure on, 486–487; concern of, regarding English status, 487; special privileges abrogated, 487–488

Harley, Bishop John, 274, 367

Harrington, Sir John, 67

Harrison, William: on dispersion of schools *c.* 1577, 228

Hartford, Captain Henry, 20

Hartgill, William, 61

Hastings, Sir Edward, 35, 524

Hastings, Francis, second Earl of Huntingdon, 35, 49, 65, 82, 443, 521

Hatfield Broad Oak, Essex, 535

Hawkins, (John?), tortured on Northumberland's order, 434

Hawkins, John (seaman), 489

Hayes, Thomas, 47

Heath, Bishop Nicholas: refusal of, to accept new *Ordinal*, 246; deprived, 247; *see also* 54, 266, 281, 420

Heathfield (Kent), 60

Heneage, Sir Thomas, 398

Henry II, King of France: importance of English neutrality to, 126–127; Garter for, 127–129; gifts of, to English envoys, 131; terms of peace, 176–178; *see also* 34, 83, 88, 116, 119, 122, 125, 128, 129, 130, 131, 138, 156, 160, 163–164, 167, 169, 173, 177, 404, 436

Henry VI (King of England), 414

Henry VII (King of England), 218, 515

Henry VIII (King of England): chantry legislation of, 183; and the Anabaptists, 326; financial imprudence of, 456; his will and the succession, 514-515, 530-531; see also 21, 27, 47, 52, 57, 114, 152, 196, 200, 214, 217, 240, 243, 244, 249, 256, 259, 266, 298, 330, 379, 380, 388, 416, 419, 423, 437, 439, 483, 509

Herbert, William, first Earl of Pembroke: created Earl, 53; ordered to West, 60; entertains king at Wilton, 426; deserts Northumberland, 528; see also 83, 91, 92, 94, 96, 106, 130, 153, 164, 491, 521, 526

Hereford, 67

Herefordshire: schools in (1553), 233; church goods in, 391

Herne, Isaac, 429

Hertfordshire: parliamentary election in, 47; chantry returns of, 190; schools in (1553), 233

Hilles, Richard, 294

Hoby, Sir Philip: seeks trade betterment in Netherlands, 162; wishes chastening of bishops, 376; announced Lady Jane's accession, 522; see also 49, 119, 127, 131, 138, 144, 145, 161, 163, 172, 257, 438, 518

Holbeach, Bishop Henry, 18, 244, 381

Holcroft, Sir Thomas, 93, 112

Holgate, Robert (Archbishop of York): resists Dudley, 380-381; see also 387, 388

Holinshed, Raphael: on Somerset, 109-110; see also 98

Holland: religious refugees from, 311, 312; grain from, 475, and see Netherlands

Holland, Thomas, 105

Holy Roman Emperor, see Charles V

Home Castle, 147

Hooper, Bishop John: fears of, 29, 241; ferrets out Romanist priests, 253; power of, as preacher, 283-285; Zwinglian leanings of, 283; learning of, 284; uncompromising nature of, 293; proposed as Bishop of Gloucester, 293-294; bitter controversy regarding Ordinal and prescribed vestments, 294-298; Foxe on, as bishop, 299; career of, as Bishop of Gloucester, 299-306; ignorance and inertness of his clergy, 303-305; greatness of, as Bishop, 305-306; interest in religious refugees, 313; denounces Anabaptists, 327; social concern of, 299-300, 475; sends aid to Mary, 527; see also 19, 48, 201, 213, 227, 273, 274, 277, 307, 314, 346, 350, 354, 362, 371, 415

Horne, Robert (Dean of Durham), 274, 384-385

Hornsea (Yorks): sale of church goods in, 395

Hospitals: founding and endowing of London Royal Hospitals, 216-223, and see charitable giving

Houghton (Northumberland): Gilpin's ministry in, 276-277

Howard, Thomas, third Duke of Norfolk, 33

Howard, William, Baron Howard of Effingham, 449, 511

Hudson, Allen: slanders Northumberland, 495

Huggins, Elizabeth: questioned regarding Tunstall, 383; disaffection of, 432-433

Huicke, Dr, 19

Hull, 413, 483

Hunmanby (Yorks): sale of church goods in, 395

Hunsdon (Herts), 519

Huntingdon, Earl of, see Hastings, Francis

Huntingdonshire: chantry return from, 190; schools in (1553), 233; poor in church goods, 398–399

Huycke, William: Calvinism of, 323–324

Hyde Park, 134

Iceland: decline of fishing off, 480

images, removal of, 265–266

Innsbruck, 103, 163

Interim, the, 135, 293, 306

Ipswich (Suffolk): disaffection in, 67; Hanse community in, 483

Isle of Ely, 43

Isley, Sir Henry, 64

Ivan IV (of Russia), 493

Jefferson, William, 490

Jersey, Isle of, 117

Johnson, John, aspirant for chantry lands, 201

Johnson, Otwell, 202, 469

Judd, Sir Andrew (Lord Mayor London): improves lot of orphans, 215; speculative losses of, 458

Julien, Jerome, 310

Kenninghall (Norfolk), 519, 524

Keilway [Kellaway], Robert, 187

Kent: disorders in, 58, 59, 60, 61, 64; schools in (1553), 233; heresy in, 332–334; see also 58, 132, 391, 450

Kingston, Sir Anthony: Hooper disciplines for immorality, 301; see also 304

King's College (Cambridge), 269

King's Lynn: opposition in, to chantries act, 184; decline of

fishing from, 480; see also 483, 522

Kirkham, Thomas: evangelical preaching of, 366

Kitchin, Bishop Anthony, 381

Knox, John: attacks kneeling at communion, 350; Cranmer's reply to, 351; gains the Black Rubric, 352; Northumberland proposes for bishopric, 373; assails Northumberland as a dissembler, 374–375; attacks Tunstall for popery, 382; offered see of Rochester, 384–385; see also 274, 277, 346, 354, 495, 497

Lacy, Robert: preferred for Parliament in Stamford, 506

Lancashire: schools in (1553), 233; Bradford's ministry in, 276; see also 57, 231

Lancaster, Duchy of, 445

Lane, William: economic thought of, 477–478

Lansac, Louis de Saint-Gelais, Seigneur de, 152

Lasco, John à, see Lasky

Lasky, John: career of, 313–314; appointed superintendent of Stranger's Church, 314; see also 283, 296, 307, 315, 317, 322, 350

Latimer, Hugh: support of education, by, 224, 227; career of, 278; greatness as preacher, 279–281; Bernher on, 279; denounces Anabaptists, 327; see also 18–19, 26, 182, 201, 213, 274, 293, 298, 339, 411, 415, 497

Lauder, 147, 148

Lavant (Sussex), 371

Lawton, John: seditious ballad writer, 432

Lee, Sir Richard, 149

Leek, Sir Francis, 80

Leicester: sale of church plate in, 392

Leicestershire: disaffection in, 67, 68–69; chantry return of, 190; schools in (1553), 233; poor in church goods, 399

Leland, John, 188

Lermouth, William: a seditious sectary, 332

Lever, Thomas: denounces sale of chantry lands, 201, 202–203; support of education, by, 224, 227; preaching of, 281; see also 213, 274, 277, 339, 415

Lichfield and Coventry, diocese of: episcopal lands ceded, 380

Lincoln, diocese of: lands of ceded, 381

Lincolnshire: chantry returns of, 190; schools in (1553), 233; sale of church goods in, 396; effort to influence parliamentary election in, 506

Linton (Kent), 59

Llandaff, Bishopric of: wealth of ceded, 381

Lofoten Islands, 492

London: disorders in, 58, 59–60, 61, 62, 429, 430–431, 432, 496; government concern for order in, 66; Council solidifies control of, 87; sympathy of, for Somerset, 91, 96; Council overawes, 97–98; control of, during Somerset's execution, 100–101; experiments in, with care of poor, 210, 215–216; merchant wealth in, and charitable giving, 211–212; chantry wealth socially funded in, 212; founding of Royal Hospitals in, 216–223; widespread founding of schools by, 223–224; Roman Catholicism in, 252; Romanist libels in, 254–255; removal of altars in, 269; Ridley's visitation of diocese of, 271–274; most religious refugees settle in, 310–311; iron-making near, 341; strength of evangelical Protestantism in, 366; seizure church goods anticipated in, 399–401; fear of rising in (1552), 432; relief to crown in fiscal crisis, 462; bubonic plague (1548) in, 467; sweating sickness in, 467; the 'Great Sweat' (1551) in, 468–469; mortality in, 469–470; overweening economic power of, 472–473; alleged decline in shipping of, 480; the Hanse in, 486; celebrates proclamation of Mary Tudor, 529–530; see also 26, 475, 477

London, diocese of: spoliation of resources of, 378–379

Longin, Laurens (treasurer to Emperor in Flanders), 171

Lovett, Thomas, 60

Low Countries, see Netherlands, Holland, and Flanders

Lübeck (Hanse), 483, 485, 486, 487, 488

Lucas, John, 358

Ludlow (Salop): sweating sickness in, 470

Lund on the Wolds (Yorks): sale of church goods in, 395

Luttrell, Sir John: dies of sweating sickness, 469

Luxemburg, 163

MacCaffrey, Professor Wallace T., 503

Machyn, Henry: on the 'Great Sweat' in London, 469

Magdalen College (Oxford), 250

Mainardo, Augustine, 322

Maldon (Essex), 257

Maler, Josua: on order of worship in Stranger's Church, 316

Manners, Henry, second Earl of Rutland: support for Somerset sought, 80; directs withdrawal

Manners—*contd.*
from Scotland, 147–148; in-
adequacy of, 148
Manners, Sir Richard, 60
Marcott (Rutland): disturbance in,
68
Marillac, Charles de (French ambassador to Emperor), 126–127
Martin, William: a seditious
printer, 432
Martyr, Peter: on want of preachers, 273–274; declines support
to Hooper, 296–297; on Hooper
as a bishop, 301; career of, at
Oxford, 308–309; criticism of
first *Prayer Book*, by, 343–344;
praise of, for second *Prayer
Book*, 350; *see also* 285, 307,
325, 346
Mary, Queen Dowager of Hun-
gary, Regent of the Netherlands: criticism of Scheyfve,
137; recommends invasion of
England, 138, 140, 156; seeks
English neutrality (1550), 140,
141; expects English intervention, 156; trade difficulties with
England, 161–162; de Courrières seeks assistance, 162;
Dudley's meeting with, 175;
rebuffs English diplomatic intervention, 179; *see also* 135, 139,
140, 145, 164, 168
Mary Stuart (Queen of Scots), 127,
128–129, 148, 150
Mary of Lorraine (Guise Queen
Mother): journey of, to France,
150, 153; passage through England, 153–154
Mary, the Princess: judgement of,
on Northumberland, 31; plan
to flee the realm, 137–138, 257–
258; resists pressure on conscience, 137–138; Charles V
presents her case, 143; better
treatment of, 177; kindness of

Somerset to, 256; Charles V
seeks guarantees for, 257, 263;
King's insistence on obedience
to law, 258–259, 260; defies
King and Council, 259; masses
for household forbidden, 260–
263; hysterical assault on Council, 262; tacit understanding on
private masses, 263–264; better
treatment of, 263–264; last visit
of to Edward, 264, 511; informed on King's health, 512,
517; Edward's *Devise*, 515–516;
Scheyfve senses plot against,
518; Charles V sends embassy
for her protection, 518; warned,
sets out for Kenninghall, 519,
521; demands allegiance of Council and proclaimed Queen in
Norfolk, 522; spontaneous rising
in support of, 524–525; re-
moves to Framlingham (Suffolk),
527; Council proclaims in London, 529; beneficiary of legitimism in nation, 530–531; *see
also* 54, 74, 76, 113, 139, 140,
145, 159, 177, 253, 289, 366, 503
Mason, Sir John (ambassador), 49,
120, 125, 126, 127, 130, 132, 145,
150, 161, 523, 529
Maurice, Duke of Saxony: defection of, 135; attack on Charles
V, 136, 146; brilliant campaign
of, 163; death of, 178; *see also*
157, 160
Maxwell, Sir John: raids English
frontier, 150
May, William, 269
Mecklenburg, Duke of, 157
Melanchthon, 321, 325, 348
Menville, Ninian: accusations of,
against Tunstall, 382–383
mercenary troops: favoured by
Northumberland, 435; in disaffected counties, 436–437; *see
also* 20

Merchant Adventurers: economic thought of, 479–480; oppose free mart in England, 479; protest Hanse privileges, 486–487; petition Council for abrogation, 487

Meutas, Sir Peter, 132

Micronius, Martin (Martin Flandrus): preaches to Flemish refugees, 313, and to Stranger's Church, 314

Middlesex, County of: disorder in, 60; chantry return of, 190

Mildmay, Thomas, 63

Mildmay, Sir Walter: on commission for the chantry act, 187, 188, 201; friend of William Thomas, 416; on commission for the revenue courts, 445–447

Mont, Christopher, 178–179

Montague, Sir Edward: forced to accept the *Devise*, 516; declares for Mary, 527

Montmèdy, 163

Montmorency, Constable Anne de: conversations with, 125–126; sends mission to England, 128 ff; diplomatic satisfaction for, 134; *see also*, 88, 163, 170

Moore, Henry, 252

Mordaunt, Sir John, 524

Morgan, Sir Richard, 253

Morison, Sir Richard: criticism of Somerset, by 82, 103–104; theological wrangling with Charles V, 142–143; decision to recall, 143; delicate mission of, to Emperor, 169; *see also* 104, 145, 158, 175, 178, 180, 260, 322, 406, 462

Morton (Berks): disorder in, 64

Mottisfont (Hants): Edward VI visits, 426

Mühlberg, Battle of, 135

Muscovy Company, 493

Musculus, Wolfgang, 312, 322

Netherlands, the: commercial frictions with, 139–140, 159; English trade with hampered by war, 161; emigration from, to England, 310, 311, 312; *see also* 25, 485, and *see* Holland, Flanders

Neville, Sir Henry, 20, 53

Neville, Henry, fifth Earl of Westmorland, 49, 154, 447

Newcastle, 350, 374, 384

Newdigate, Francis, 85, 93, 94

Newnhambridge (Neuillet), 123

Nichols, J. G., 22n., 23n.

Noailles, Antoine de: mission of to England, 512; reports on King's illness, 512, 513; reports Council disturbed at succession, 518; meets with Northumberland, 519

Norfolk: disorder in reported, 62–63; chantry return missing, 190; estimate of chantry wealth in, 193; schools in (1553), 233; theft of church goods in, 397; fear of risings in (1552), 432; *see also* 57, 339

Norfolk, Duke of, *see* Howard, Thomas

Norham Castle, 151, 152, 154

North Cape, 492, 493

North Sea: decline of fishing in, 480

Northampton, Marquis of, *see* Parr, William

Northamptonshire: disaffection in, 67, 69, 105; schools in (1553) 233; *see also* 201, 503

Northumberland, Duke of, *see* Dudley, John

Northumberland: disorder in, 151, 433; schools in (1553), 233; Gilpin's ministry in, 276–277

Norton, Sir George: seeks episcopal lands, 381

Norwich, 318, 527

Nottinghamshire: disorder in, 60; chantry return from, 190; schools in (1553), 233

Oatlands, 18, 429
Ochino, Bernardino, 29, 285, 307, 312
Oglethorpe, Owen, 250
Oliver, John, 127
Ordinal (1550): Heath refuses to endorse, 246–247; Protestant nature of, 266–267; Hooper's attack on, 267; divisive controversy on, 294–298
Ossory, Bishopric of: John Bale as bishop, 368–369
Overend, William, 184
Oxford, Earl of, *see* Vere, John de
Oxford, City of, 396
Oxford University, 29, 185, 309
Oxfordshire: disorders in, 60, 63, 67; schools in (1553), 233; sale of church goods in, 394; theft of church goods in, 397; sweating sickness in, 470; rises for Mary, 527

Paget, Sir William, first Baron Paget of Beaudesert: restoration of (1550), 34; fails to gain favour, 51; arrest of, 84; imprisonment of, 93; Northumberland's humiliation of, 113–115; ruin of, 114–115; negotiations of, with France, 121–122; assurances of, to Emperor, 137; lands gained from Exeter, 380— from Lichfield, 380; suggestions for Council reorganization (1550?), 451–452; deserts Northumberland, 529; *see also* 36, 41, 70, 88, 90, 97, 104, 118, 120, 158, 259, 499
Palmer, Sir Thomas: favour of Northumberland to, 52–53; 'con-

fession' of, 83; arrest of, 85; enlarged confession of, 87–88; *see also* 91, 94, 95, 97, 103, 149, 154, 495, 500, 526
Paris, George, 171
Parker, Sir Henry, 47
Parker, Matthew, 274, 277, 278
Parliament: Northumberland's fear of, 45–48; government's effort to pack (1551), 47; wishes canon law codified, 357
Parliament, first, the first session (1547): chantries act passed by, 183–185
Parliament, first, third session (1549–1550): course of, 36–44; reactionary mood of, 37; bills failing in, 43–44; requests commission for reform of ecclesiastical law, 349
Parliament, first, fourth session (1552): case of privilege, 335–336; Commons force modification of new treason law, 336; on Somerset's marriage and estates, 337; and economic problems 337–340; bills for regulation of iron-making, 341–342; passage of Act of Uniformity, 347
Parliament, second (1553): King's wishes for legislation, by, 421–422; Dudley reluctant to convene, 504; financial need impels, 504–505; criticism to be ignored, 505; efforts to influence elections to, 505–506; Northumberland's scheme for strengthening House of Lords, 507; opened by King, 507–508; subsidy bill hurried through, 508; legislation of, 509; *and see* statutes
Parr, Catherine, Queen of England, 22
Parr, William, Earl of Essex (cr. 1543), Marquis of Northampton (cr. 1547): heads English

Parr—*contd.*

embassy to France, 127–131; entertainment of, 128–129; negotiation of dowry, 130; overawes London, 432; loyal to Northumberland, 525; *see also* 20, 65, 91, 92, 96, 104, 106, 128, 129, 130, 131, 243, 521

Parris, George van: execution of for heresy, 330

Partridge, Sir Miles, 85, 91, 93, 97, 110–111

Paston, Sir Thomas, 19

Paulet, William, first Baron St John of Basing (cr. 1539), Earl of Wiltshire (cr. 1550), Marquis of Winchester (cr. 1551): created Marquis of Winchester, 53; gains land, 380; entertains Edward VI, 426; and Court of Wards, 442; on King's health, 512; *see also* 20, 34, 93, 104, 242, 258, 315, 383, 462, 490, 503, 519, 525, 528

Paulet, Sir Hugh, 350

Paul's Cross (London): powerful evangelical preaching at, 277–278, 366

Peckham, Sir Edmund, 458, 527

Pembroke, Earl of, *see* Herbert William

Penn, Bartholomew, 19

Penne, Thomas: disciplined for heresy, 300–301

Perne, Andrew, 274

Peterborough: sale of church goods in, 394–395

Petitt, Thomas: strengthens Calais defences, 124–125

Petre, Sir William, Privy Councillor: memorandum on Council, 453; reports King improved, 512; deserts Northumberland, 529; *see also* 25, 50, 58, 120, 142, 171, 172, 219, 243, 262, 327, 498, 502, 521

Petworth (Sussex): Edward VI visits, 424, 425

Phelps, William, 300

Philanthropy, *see* charitable giving

Philpot, John: on heresy, 331

Pickering, Sir William, 88, 127, 145, 158, 160, 167

Ploiche, Pierre du, 310

Pollard, Professor A. F., 506

Ponet, Bishop John: anti-Romanism of, 371; evangelical preaching of, 371–372; cedes lands from Winchester, 380 *see also* 22, 260, 277

Poole (Dorset), 84, 87, 426

poor, *see* charitable giving

Porter, Henry, 184

Portman, William, 93

Portsmouth: Edward VI visits, 425; *see also* 35, 413, 448

Posterne Park (Kent): altercation at, 64

Poulain, Valérand: administers Glastonbury experiment, 318–321

poverty: problem of, and charitable giving, 209–211; London's experiments with care of, 210, 215–216; *see also* charitable giving

Powis, Lady, suit of, 443

prayers for dead: *see* chantries

preaching: want of, 273–274; great power of evangelical leaders, 275–292; Coke's praise of, 276; before King, 277; at Paul's Cross, 277–278; of Latimer, 279–281; of Lever, 281; of Becon, 281–282; of Hooper, 283–285; of evangelicals as a group, 285–292; Bucer on, 365–366; of Kirkham, 366; of Caston, 366; of Bale, 367–369, of Turner, 369–370; of Ponet, 371–373; of Knox, 373–375

Prescot (Lancs): slow progress Reformation in, 269

Privy Council: Warwick dominates, 32–36; new commission for, 33–34; and parliamentary elections, 47; membership of, Nov. 1551, 50; in March, 1552, 452–453; concern of, for public order, 56–59, 60–68; proclamation for 'perfect quiteness' (1551), 65–66; success of policy (1551), 67; Somerset re-admitted to, 72–73; hostility to Somerset, 77; malaise in, 78–79; Somerset denounced by, 86; anxiety of concerning London, 87; Palmer's accusation against Somerset, 87–88; interrogation of Somerset's followers, 88–90; fear of London sentiment, 97–98; orders Somerset's execution, 100; policy towards Mary angers Charles V, 137–138; commercial frictions with Flanders, 139–140; troubled by Inquisition in Netherlands, 141; problem of diplomatic immunity, 141–144; reversal of Scottish policy, 146–147; negotiations for Scottish frontier, 151–155; decline in diplomatic competence of, 157–159; Emperor invokes treaty for aid, 164–165; increasing participation of King in meetings, 165–166; Stuckley's 'revelations' to, 167–168; review of English war costs, 169; French seek to cure frictions, 171–173; claims on France, 172–174; confused in policy, 178–179; clarifies intent of Chantry Act, 186; examination and trial of Gardiner, 242–245; deprives Heath, and Day, 246–248; mildness of towards Roman Catholicism, 249–255; pressure on Princess Mary, 257–259; disturbed by the Emperor's threats, 260–261; prohibits masses for Mary's household, 260–263; tacit understanding regarding Mary's worship, 262–263; dislikes Hooper's attack on *Ordinal*, 267, 294; orders removal of altars, 268–269; appoint Hooper Bishop of Gloucester, 293–294; Council's controversy with Hooper, 294–298; favour of, to Stranger's Church, 315; continues Glastonbury experiment, 320–321; commission to eradicate Anabaptism, 327; orders burning of Joan Bocher, 329; supports Knox on kneeling posture, 350–352; urges completion *Articles of Faith*, 354–355; appoints commission for reform of ecclesiastical laws, 358–359; support of evangelical party by, 366; orders inventory of church goods (1547), 388; second inventory ordered, 388–389; abortive order for expropriation (1551), 389; King begins attendance of (1551), 420; King's memoranda for, 420, 421, 422; preoccupation of, with disaffection, 427–434; reduction of military establishment, 437–438; King's suggestions to, 441; Beaumont case and, 442–444; and the mounting fiscal crisis (1551), 444–445; and the commission on revenue courts, 444–447; King's memoranda for, 447–451; study of reform of procedures of, 451–455; King's plan of reorganization, 453–455; sparseness of minutes of (1553), 455; orders debasement and devaluation (1551), 459; efforts of to order economy, 472–477; concern regarding prices, 472–473; proclamation for 'bringing forth of

Privy Council—*contd.*

grain', 473; rigorous economic administration, 474–475; further efforts at price control, 474, 476; special commission for delivery of grain, 474; relaxes price restraints, 475, and denounces London prices, 475–476; arranges for importation of foodstuffs, 474, 476–477; economic tracts addressed to, 477–482; negotiations of with Hanse, 484–487; abrogates Hanse privileges, 487–488; Northumberland's weakening control of, 495; weakening of central administration, 498–499; decay of (1552–1553), 499–500; rise of Cecil to power in, 500–503; Cheke appointed secretary to, 502; convenes second parliament (1553), 505; efforts to influence elections to, 505–506; pressure on to accept Edward's *Devise*, 516–517; orders public prayers for King, 518; announces death of King, 520; proclaims Lady Jane as Queen, 521; Mary commands the allegiance of, 522; Dudley's speech to, 526–527; betrays Northumberland, 528–529; proclaims Mary in London, 529

Protestantism: and the charitable impulse, 208–209, 213–214; evangelical and, 213–214; and the founding of schools, 224; Warwick lends support to, 265; advanced by evangelical preaching, 275–292; evangelical thought, and, 285–292; evangelical party in motion towards Puritanism, 292

public order: *see* Dudley, John, Privy Council

Putto: an Anabaptist, 332

Queen's College (Cambridge), 370

Radcliffe, Henry, second Earl of Sussex, 524

Radnage (Bucks): concealments in, 398

Reading: entertains Edward VI, 427; disaffection in, 429; *see also*, 47, 62

Redman, John, 18

Reformatio legum ecclesiasticarum: analysis of, 360–361; *see also* Cranmer, Dudley

refugees, religious: from France and Netherlands, 310; nationality of uncertain, 310–311; estimates of number, 311–312; social and economic background of, 312; Vauville preaches to French, 312; Stranger's Church established for, 313–317; in Norwich, Colchester, Southampton and Canterbury, 318; Zwinglian and Calvinistic temper of, 322

Renard, Simon (Imperial ambassador to France): heads mission to England, 518; *see also*, 92, 118, 127, 129, 132, 137, 141

revenue courts, commission on, 444–447

Rich, Richard, first Baron Rich of Leeze: early career of, 54; fall of, 55–56; gains episcopal lands, 378; *see also* 58, 104, 262, 315, 328, 429, 495, 499

Ridley, Bishop Nicholas: leadership in founding London Hospitals, 219–220, 222; and new *Ordinal*, 266–267; spiritual development of, 270–271; dislike for Protestant extremism, 271; Bishop of Rochester (1547) and of London (1550), 271; visitation of London diocese, 271–274; stimulation of preaching by, 273–274; controversy of, with

Ridley—*contd.*
Hooper, 294–295; doubts of, on Stranger's Church, 315; first employs second *Book of Common Prayer*, 352; fears Northumberland's religious policy, 364; protests spoliation of diocese, 378–379; *see also* 18, 58, 244, 246, 260, 268, 278, 293, 294, 330, 354, 366, 507

Rivière, François de la, 314

Rochester, Sir Robert, 258, 262, 263

Rogers, Sir Edward, 20

Roman Catholicism: Northumberland's momentary favour to, 28–29; mildness of treatment of, 249, 250–251; in London, 252; libels advancing, 253–255

Rowe, George, before Council, 250–251

Roxburgh, 147

Rugg, Bishop William: resigns see, 248

Rumford (Essex): disorder in, 61

Russell, Lord John, first Baron Russell of Cheneys, first Earl of Bedford (cr. 1550): ordered to the West, 60, 62; Lord Lieutenant in the West, 65; *see also* 20, 34, 82, 106, 120, 490, 495, 503, 518, 519, 526

Ruthven, Master of, 152

Rutland, county of: disaffection in, 67–68; schools in (1553), 233

Rutland, Earl of, *see* Manners, Henry

Rye (Sussex), 132, 477, 480

Sackville, Sir Richard, 445

Sadler, Sir Ralph, 47, 435, 436

St André, Jacques d'Albon: heads mission to England (1551), 128, 131–134; charms Edward VI, 133–134, 404; *see also* 27, 134

St Bartholomew's Hospital (London): refounding and endowing of, 216–217

St Mauris, John de, 141

St Michael, Order of: for Edward VI, 128, 133

St Paul's Cathedral (London), 352

St Thomas's Hospital (London): founding and endowing of, 218–219, 220, 222

Salisbury: Edward VI visits, 426

Salmon, Christopher, 519

Sampson, Bishop Richard: cedes episcopal lands, 380; *see also* 266

Sandwich (Kent): parliamentary election questioned, 334; *see also* 480

Sandys of the Vyne, Thomas, second Lord, 426

Saunders, Sir Thomas, 47

Savoy Hospital (London), 218, 222

Scepperus, Corneille: surveys Netherlands' naval problems, 161–162

Scheyfve, Jean (Imperial ambassador to England): reports disaffection, 61, 80; Council denounces Somerset to, 85–86; analysis of charges against Somerset, 87; believes Somerset not guilty, 104; appointed to England, 137, 139; urges settlement Flemish frictions, 139–140; conversation with Northumberland, 168; conversation with Gresham, 168; Andrew Dudley meets with, 175; on Northumberland's religious policy, 363–364; reports Edward attending Council, 420–421; comment on fiscal crisis (1551), 460–461; on King's illness, 510, 512, 514, 517–518; pessimistic estimate of Mary's position (July 10, 1553), 522–523; *see also* 98–99, 141, 142, 143, 145, 159, 163, 164–165, 260, 264, 424, 511

Schmalkaldic League: defeat of by Emperor, 135
schools, founding of: reasons for interest in, 224–228; support of evangelical Protestantism for, 224; humanism and, 225; assault on poverty and, 225; local pride and, 226; disappointment at chantry wealth use, and, 226–227; bill for 'making schools', 227; favour of chantry commissioners to, 227–228; Harrison on the achievement, 228; founding and endowment of (1480–1540), 228; founding and support of in Edwardian era, 228–229; preservation and strengthening of chantry schools, 229–230; secular foundations, Edwardian era, 231–235; strength of secular foundations, 234
Schmutz, Alexander, 310
Scilly Isles, 35
Scotland: lessening of English power in, 146–155; French hegemony in, 148; piracy off English coasts, 149; border raids from, 150; see also 88, 120–121, 152, 153, 155
Sedgwick, Thomas, 308
Selve, Odet de, 117
Seth, William: examined for Roman Catholic activity, 249
Seymour, Alexander, 83
Seymour, Anne, Duchess of Somerset: 31, 90, 107, 432
Seymour, Anne (dau. to Somerset), 73
Seymour, Edward, Duke of Somerset (cr. 1547): popularity of, 56; maintains the peace, 62, 67; charges against (1549) and conditional release, 71; re-admitted to Council, 72; opposition to Dudley's policy, 72–74; personal activities of (1550–

1551), 74–75; Whalley's activity for, 75–76; death of mother of, 77; seeks support in Council and Parliament, 78–79, 80–81; isolation of, 81–82; King's hostility to, 82; Palmer denounces, 83–84; first inklings of plot, 84–85; denounced by Council, 86; Palmer's enlarged accusations against, 87–88; discussions of with Arundel, 89–90; trial of, 92–98; execution of, 98–105; devotions of, 100; speech at execution, 101–102; disorder at execution, 101–102; character of, 105–110; political weakness of, 107–108; concern of, for social betterment, 210–211; employment of intellectuals by, 224; trial of toleration by, 109–110, 240–241, 251; protection of Gardiner by, 242, 245–246; kindness of, to Princess Mary, 256; urges concessions to Hooper, 294; interest of in Glastonbury experiment, 318–321; declines to burn Joan Bocher, 328; marriage and estate overturned by Parliament, 337; and William Turner, 369; surviving influence on the King, 411; heavy costs of his policy, 434–435, 456–457; see also 17–18, 26, 29–30, 31, 32, 33–34, 36, 39, 40, 51, 53, 133, 135, 146, 251, 362, 367, 415, 423, 428, 439, 499, 504, 509
Seymour, Sir John, 47, 85, 94
Seymour, Thomas, Baron Seymour of Sudeley, 18, 27, 211
Sharington, Sir William, 442
Sheen, 73, 134
Shelley, Edward, 475
A Short Catechism (1553), 353
Shrewsbury: the 'Great Sweat' breaks out in, 468

Shrewsbury, Earl of, *see* Talbot, Francis
Shropshire: chantry returns from, 190; chantry priests income in, 194; schools in (1553), 233
Sidney, Sir Henry: knighted, 53; special envoy to Emperor, 174–175; *see also* 20, 519
Sidney, Sir William, 110
Sittingbourne (Kent): disorder in, 61
Six Articles Act, 278
Smith, Sir Clement, 253
Smith, Dr Richard, 249
Smith, Sir Thomas, 32, 58, 70, 127, 172, 327
Snepel, Paul (Hanse merchant), 485
Somerset, county of: schools in (1553), 233
Somerset, Duke of, *see* Seymour, Edward
Sopley (Hants), 251
Soranzo, Giacomo: believes Protestantism prevailed in England (1554), 276; on Edward's education, 402–403; on terror of sweating sickness, 469–470
Southampton: disorder in, 62, 495; religious refugees in, 318; King wishes free mart in, 412, 413; Edward VI visits, 425
Southampton, Earl of, *see* Wriothesley, Thomas
Southwark, 62, 212
Southwell, Sir Richard, 28, 31
Southwell, Sir Robert, 28
Speke, Sir Thomas, 380, 469
Stafford, Sir Robert: protests Appleyard hanging, 68–69
Stafford, Sir William, 432
Staffordshire, 115, 233
Stamford (Lincs): effort to influence electors in, 506
Stanhope, Sir Michael: execution of, 110; *see also* 32, 91, 93, 97

Stanley, Edward, third Earl of Derby: difficulties of with Northumberland, 78–79; *see also* 266, 269, 347, 524
Staplers: tract of (1551); proposes free market for wool, 478–479
Statutes, parliamentary:
37 Henry VIII, c. 4: for reformation of chantries
1 Edward VI, c. 14 (1549) expropriating chantries (183–185)
3 & 4 Edward VI, c. 10 (265–266)
3 & 4 Edward VI, c. 12: *Ordinal* authorized (266–267)
3 & 4 Edward VI, c. 3: enclosure of commons and waste (40–41)
3 & 4 Edward VI, c. 5: for punishment unlawful assemblies (37–38)
3 & 4 Edward VI, c. 15: prohibiting prophecy (39)
3 & 4 Edward VI, c. 16: control of vagabondage (41–42)
3 & 4 Edward VI: various religious measures (342–361)
3 & 4 Edward VI, c. 11: for reform of ecclesiastical laws (358)
5 & 6 Edward VI, c. 1: Act of Uniformity (347 ff.)
5 & 6 Edward VI, c. 11: act of treasons (336)
5 & 6 Edward VI, c. 2: for relief of the poor (337–338)
5 & 6 Edward VI, c. 5: for increase of tillage and corn (338)
5 & 6 Edward VI, c. 6: standards of clothmaking (338)
5 & 6 Edward VI, c. 7: buying and selling of wools (338)
5 & 6 Edward VI, c. 8: apprenticeships in clothmaking (338)
5 & 6 Edward VI, c. 20: proscription of usury (339–340)

Statutes—*contd.*

5 & 6 Edward VI, c. 12: legitimizing of clerical children (352)

5 & 6 Edward VI, c. 3: defining fasting (353)

7 Edward VI, c. 1: for collection of King's revenues (509)

7 Edward VI, c. 2: for merging revenue courts (509)

7 Edward VI, c. 6: prohibiting export of bullion (509)

7 Edward VI, c. 5: price and excise of wine (510)

Stepney: Roman Catholicism in, 252

Stipendiary priests, *see* Chantries

Stourton, William, seventh Baron Stourton, 61, 266, 347, 383

Stow, John: account of Somerset's execution, 101–102; on sweat in London, 469; *see also* 94, 507, 511

Strange, Lord, 89, 95

Stranger's Church (London): given Austin Friars, 313; founding of, 313–316; Lasky named superindent, 313–314; assistant clergy for, 314–315; order of worship in, 316; French (and Walloon) church separates, 316–317; Italian church separates, 317; *see also* 283, 330; *London and refugees*

Sturgeon, John, 47

succession (to throne): as ordained by Henry VIII's will, 514–515; the *Devise* of Edward VI, 515–516; pressure by Edward VI to alter, 516–517; *see also* Edward VI, Dudley, John

Suffolk: disorders in, 58, 61, 67, 429; schools in (1553), 233; sale of church goods in, 395; fear of rising in (1552), 432; Council's effort to influence electors in, 505–506

Suffolk, Duchess of, *see* Willoughby, Katherine

Suffolk, first Duke of, *see* Brandon, Charles

Suffolk, second Duke of, *see* Brandon, Henry

Suffolk, Duke of (cr. 1551), *see* Grey, Henry

Surrey, county of: parliamentary election in, 47; schools in (1553), 233; sale of church goods in, 396

Surrey, Earl of, *see* Howard, Henry

Sussex, county of: disorders in, 58, 60, 61, 63, 430; schools in (1553), 233; church goods scanty, 391; grain short in, 475

Sussex, Earl of, *see* Radcliffe, Henry

sweating sickness, epidemic of: first appearance in England (1485), 467; periodic epidemics of, 467; Dr John Caius on, 468; Dr Hans Zinnser on, 468; breaks out in Shrewsbury (1551), 468; high mortality from, 469–470; Machyn and Stow on, 469; death of Charles and Henry Brandon from, 477

Syon House, 521

Talbot, Francis, fifth Earl of Shrewsbury: difficulties of, with Northumberland, 78–79; *see also* 201, 504, 526

Tathwell (Lincs): Romanism at, 252

Taylor, Bishop John, 18, 277

Teerlinc, Levina, 19

Tewkesbury, 476

Thame (Oxon): theft of church goods in, 397

Thirlby, Bishop Thomas, 152, 158, 164, 179, 266, 347, 378

Thomas, William: on Northampton's mission, 130, 416;

Thomas—*contd.*
writings of, 416–417; Clerk of Privy Council, 416; prepares 'position papers' for King, 417–419

Throckmorton, Sir Nicholas, 82, 104, 417, 524

Thynne, Sir John, 32, 112

Titchfield (Hants), 30, 425

Tittenhanger Park (Herts), 40

Todenham (Glos): Romanist vicar at, 253

toleration, religious: trial of, under Somerset, 109–110, 240–241, 251

Tomson, William, 105

Toto, Anthony, 19

Townshend, Sir Roger, 59

Traheron, Bartholomew, 61

Tresham, Sir Thomas: moves on stir, 68

Troughton, Richard: declares for Mary, 527

Tunstall, Bishop Cuthbert: career of, 381; friend to Somerset, 382; attacked for popery by Knox, 382; Menville accuses of treason, 382–383; imprisoned, 383; trial of in Parliament fails, 383; deprived by commission, 384; *see also* 76, 248, 266, 421, 497, 499

Turner, William: on refutation of heresy, 332, 333–334; evangelical preaching of, 368–370

Ubaldini, Petruccio: description of the Court, 419–420

Ulmis, John ab, 36, 294, 310

Ulmis, Walter, 310

Upcharde: alleged heresy of, 333

Uppingham (Rutland): disorder in, 68

Utenhove, John: role in founding Stranger's Church, 315; *see also* 283, 318

Van der Delft, François (imperial ambassador): recalled (1550), 137; fears for Princess Mary, 257; *see also* 17, 30, 31, 35, 48, 110, 136

Vane, Sir Ralph: altercation, of, with Northumberland, 64, 80; arrest of, 85; Palmer's testimony against, 87–88; execution of, 110; *see also* 53, 83, 91, 94, 97

Vannes, Peter, 158

Vaughan, Stephen, 19, 463

Vauville, Richard: preacher to French refugees, 312; among clergy in Stranger's Church, 314

Vere, John de, sixteenth Earl of Oxford: declares for Mary, 528

Vergerio, Bishop Peter Paul: interest of in England, 322

vestiarian controversy: *see* Hooper, John

Veysey, Bishop John: forced resignation of, 248; loots his diocese, 380

Vicary, Thomas, 217

Villach, 163

Villandry, Claude de Breton, Seigneur de: proposals for settlement English commercial claims, 172–173

Wade [Waad], Armigil: to Calais, 124; interest of, in religious refugees, 313

Wakeman, Bishop John: administration of Gloucester, 298–299

Waldegrave, Sir Edward, 263

Wales: chantry returns from, 190; schools in (1553), 233; disorders reported in, 429

Wallop, Sir John, 469

Warblington (Hants): Edward VI visits, 425

war costs: English outlays (1542–1552), 169

Wards, Court of: malfeasance in, 442–443; study of, 445–446

Warenne, Christopher, 184

Warwickshire: chantry returns from, 190; schools in (1553), 233; sale of church goods in, 396; disaffection in, 430

Warwick, Earl of, see Dudley, John

Watson, Thomas: imports large cargoes food grains, 476–477

Wayneman, Thomas: outlawed for sedition, 433

Wells, Thomas, a troublemaker, 62

Wentworth, Thomas, first Baron Wentworth, 20, 34, 77–78

Wentworth, Thomas, second Baron Wentworth, 336, 378

West, Thomas, ninth Baron de la Warr, 391, 425, 475

Western Rising (1549), 33, 251

Westminster, bishopric of, 378

Westminster, 85, 99, 511

Westminster Abbey, 181

Westmorland, county of: schools in (1553), 233

Westmorland, Earl of, see Neville, Henry

Whalley, Richard: career of, 75; Northumberland warns, 75; seeks support for Somerset, 79–80; imprisoned, 80; ruin of, 111

Wharton, Thomas, first Baron Wharton: named Northumberland's deputy in north, 149; see also 106, 149, 154, 266, 335, 375

Wharton, Sir Thomas, 524

White, John, 252

Whitered, William, 59

Wied, Archbishop Hermann von, 321

Wilding, John, 432

Williams, John (Chancellor of Gloucester), 305

Willoughby, Sir Edward, 426

Willoughby, Sir Hugh: commands voyage for northeast passage, 490–493

Willoughby, Katherine (widow of Charles Brandon, first Duke of Suffolk): her assistance to Somerset, 72–73; withdraws from Somerset, 82; death of sons of, 471

Willoughby, William, first Baron Willoughby of Parham, 125

Wilson, Sir Thomas, 471

Wilton (Wilts): Edward VI visits, 426

Wiltshire: schools in (1553), 233

Winchester College, 185, 231, 252

Winchester, Bishopric of; Ponet consecrated, 372; spoliation of wealth of, 380

Winchester (Hants): Edward VI visits, 426; see also 475, 495

Winchester, Marquis of, see Paulet, William

Windsor, William, second Baron Windsor, 266, 347

Windsor Castle, 18, 82, 85, 427, 449

Wingfield, Sir Anthony, 34, 262

Winter, William (and George): claims of on France, 172; see also 437, 489

Wisbech (Cambs.), 63, 522

Wokingham (Berks): stir in, 67; disorder in, 429

Woodcock, Mrs: warning of, to Somerset, 84

Woodlands (Dorset): Edward VI visits, 426

Woodstock (Oxon) disturbance at, 67

Woolwich, 122

Worcestershire: disaffection in, 67; schools in (1553), 233

Wotton, Dr Nicholas: distrusts France, 126; assurances to Emperor, 137; sent to Emperor,

Wotton—*contd.*
143; assures Emperor regarding Mary Tudor's private mass, 261; *see also* 131, 145, 164, 172, 177, 263
Wriothesley, Thomas, first Earl of Southampton (cr. 1547), 28–29, 30, 425, 499
Wroth, Sir Thomas, 20, 519
Wyatt, Sir Thomas, 125
Wyndham, Thomas, 437, 489

Yarmouth: decline of fishing from, 480; fleet at, declares for Mary, 527

York, Archbishopric of: Holgate defends wealth of, 380–381
York, city of, 470, 483
Yorkshire: chantry returns of, 190; schools in (1553), 233; church goods in, 391, 395; theft of church goods in, 397
York, Sir John: losses by international speculations, 458–459; *see also* 71, 477, 530
Young, John: Romanist at Cambridge, 308

Zifridus, Dr Cornelius, 19

GEORGE ALLEN & UNWIN LTD

Head Office
40 Museum Street, London, W.C.1
Telephone: 01-405 8577

Sales, Distribution and Accounts Departments
Park Lane, Hemel Hempstead, Herts.
Telephone: 0442 3244

Athens: 7 Stadiou Street, Athens 125
Auckland: P.O. Box 36013, Northcote, Auckland, 9
Barbados: P.O. Box 222, Bridgetown
Beirut: Deeb Building, Jeanne d'Arc Street
Bombay: P.O. Box 21, 103-105 Fort Street, Bombay 1
Calcutta: 285J Bepin Behari Ganguli Street, Calcutta 12
Decca: Alico Building, 18 Motijheel, Dacca 2
Delhi: 1/18B Asaf Ali Road, New Delhi 1
Hong Kong: 105 Wing on Mansion, 26 Hankow Road, Kowloon
Ibadan: P.O. Box 62
Johannesburg: P.O. Box 23134, Joubert Park
Karachi: Karachi Chambers, McLeod Road, Karachi 2
Lahore: 22 Falettis' Hotel, Egerton Road
Madras: 2/18 Mount Road, Madras 2
Manila: P.O. Box 157, Quezon City D-502
Mexico: Serapio Rendon 125 Mexico 4 D.F.
Nairobi: P.O. Box 30583
Rio de Janeiro: Caixa Postal 2537-Zc-00
Singapore: 36c Prinsep Street, Singapore 7
Sydney, N.S.W.: Bradley House, 55 York Street, Sydney,
N.S.W. 2000
Tokyo: C.P.O. Box 1728, Tokyo 100-91
Toronto: 145 Adelaide Street West, Toronto 1

W. K. JORDAN

Edward VI: The Young King

Edward VI: The Young King deals with the full range of Edwardian history, with special attention to the political, diplomatic, religious, and social history of the reign. The years with which the present volume is concerned were those in which Somerset enjoyed his supremacy, and to his character, achievements, and weaknesses a full and somewhat poignant attention is lent. In describing the general structure of the study, the author has written: 'The work has . . . a probably old-fashioned quality, of which, however, we are so far unashamed that we have indulged ourselves even with battles, broils, and death-bed or . . . scaffold scenes.' But the work is far more than that; it deals generously with one of the most interesting and decisive periods in English history.

'This book rests on prodigious learning. It is written with warmth and urbanity.' *Daily Telegraph*
'His unrivalled knowledge and subtle, compassionate understanding as one of the leading American historians of Tudor England.' *Spectator*
'Truly a history of the country as a whole and not of just the microcosm in the vicinity of the capital.' *Times Educational Supplement*
'Professor Jordan's book undoubtedly makes a valuable contribution to our knowledge of an important and perplexing period of history.'
Contemporary Review

NORMAN F. CANTOR

The English

The English is a major interpretation of English history.
    Norman F. Cantor has set out to re-examine the events, the men, the laws and institutions, without the prejudices of earlier historians and in the light of all that modern psychology, sociology and literature have taught us about man and society. His aim has been to write a history that will enable the contemporary reader to understand the significance of the English experience.
    The result, in this first of two volumes, is a work of extraordinary insight and illumination, taking the reader from the England of the Anglo-Saxon invasion to the dawn of the industrial and democratic era.

'Professor Cantor has undoubtedly written a most informed and well-balanced book on historiographical constitutional and legal matters. The style is so buoyant and energetic that the study of historiography, law and politics becomes a pleasure, almost an adventure, never a bore.'
Contemporary Review